THIRD EDITION

Approaches to Psychology

THIRD
EDITION

Approaches to Psychology

WILLIAM E. GLASSMAN

Open University Press
Buckingham · Philadelphia

Open University Press
Celtic Court
22 Ballmoor
Buckingham
MK18 1XW

e-mail: enquiries@openup.co.uk
world wide web: http://www.openup.co.uk

and
325 Chestnut Street
Philadelphia, PA 19106, USA

First edition published 1979
Reprinted 1984, 1986, 1988, 1989, 1991

Second edition published 1995
Reprinted 1997

First published in this third edition 2000

A catalogue record of this book is available from the British Library

ISBN 0 335 20545 3 (pbk)

Library of Congress Cataloging-in-Publication Data

Glassman, William E., 1947–
    Approaches to psychology / William E. Glassman.—3rd ed.
        p.   cm.
    Includes bibliographical references and index.
    ISBN 0–335–20545–3 (pbk.)
    1. Psychology.   I. Title.
    BF121.G56   2000
    150—dc21   99–056326

Typeset by Graphicraft Limited, Hong Kong
Printed in Great Britain by Butler & Tanner Ltd, Frome and London

Never did any science originate,
but by a poetic perception.
Ralph Waldo Emerson

Contents

List of Figures   xiv
Preface   xvi

I Behaviour and Psychology   I

The Magic of Behaviour   1
Introduction   2
The Challenge of Psychology   3
Why Different Approaches?   4
Perception and Theorizing   5
The Origins of Psychology   11
Methods of Studying Behaviour   15
The Role of the Scientific Method in Psychology   15
Introspectionism and Public Observation   16
Measures of Behaviour, Research Settings and Research Methods   18
Interviews and Surveys as Self-report Procedures   20
  Surveys and Sampling Procedures   21
  Limitations of Self-reports   22
Naturalistic Observation and Unobtrusive Measures   23
Case Studies   24
Correlational Research   26
Experiments   28
Quasi-experiments   33
Ethics in Psychological Research   35
Conclusion   38
Chapter Summary   39
Key Terms and Concepts   40
Suggestions for Further Reading   40

2 The Biological Approach   42

Looking for the Mind   42
Introduction   43
The Nature of the Physiological System   46
Mind, Brain and the CNS   46
  Neurons and the Nervous System   47
  The Brain   50

Studying the Brain   54
   Electrical Recording and Stimulation   55
   Computerized Imaging Techniques   58
Chemical Processes in Behaviour   59
   Neurotransmitters   59
   Hormones   61
Interactions of Mind and Body in Behaviour   62
The Effects of Body on Mind   63
   The Study of Drug Effects   63
   Types of Psychoactive Drugs   66
   The Split Brain and the Whole Mind   69
   The Split Brain and the Normal Brain   73
The Effects of Mind on Body   75
   Stress   76
   Medicine and the Mind   80
The Hereditary Basis of Behaviour   83
Basic Mechanisms of Heredity   84
Nature and Nurture in Behaviour   88
Evolution and Behaviour   90
Conclusion   93
Chapter Summary   94
Key Terms and Concepts   95
Suggestions for Further Reading   95

3   The Behaviourist Approach   **97**

Mind Doesn't Matter   97
Introduction   98
Basic Assumptions of Behaviourism   99
The Pioneers of Behaviourism   100
Stimuli and Responses   103
Classical Conditioning   104
Classical Conditioning Phenomena   107
   Stimulus Generalization and Discrimination   107
   Extinction and Spontaneous Recovery   111
   Higher-Order Conditioning   112
Applications of Classical Conditioning   114
   Conditioned Emotional Responses   114
   Conditioned Drug and Immune Responses   116
Operant Conditioning   118
Skinner and Operant Conditioning   119
Reinforcers and Reinforcement   121
   Contingencies of Reinforcement   123
Operant Conditioning Phenomena   126
   Shaping and the Learning Process   126
   Extinction   127
   Schedules of Reinforcement   128
   Discriminative Stimuli   133
   Non-contingent Reinforcement   134

Applications and Implications of Conditioning 135
Negative Reinforcers and the Aversive Control of Operant Behaviour 135
Interrelationships of Classical and Operant Conditioning 137
Autonomic Conditioning and Biofeedback 139
Biological Constraints on Learning 141
Conclusion 145
Chapter Summary 146
Key Terms and Concepts 147
Suggestions for Further Reading 147

4 The Cognitive Approach 149

Thought and Action 149
Introduction 150
Perception and Cognition 154
Learning and Memory 155
Learning as Information Gathering 155
Memory as the Retention of Learning 156
A Basic Model of Memory 157
Encoding and Storage in Memory 159
Forgetting 163
Forgetting in STM 163
Forgetting in LTM 165
Memory as Reconstruction 169
Eyewitness Testimony 170
Improving Memory 172
Problem Solving 176
Defining Problems 176
Stages of Problem Solving 176
Types of Problems 177
Models of Problem Solving 178
Gestalt Theory 178
Problem Solving as Information Processing 180
Algorithms 181
Heuristics 182
Creativity in Problem Solving 183
The Formation of Problem Solving Skills 184
Language 185
Language Learning 186
Of Apes and Language 188
Language and Thinking 189
The Cognitive Viewpoint in Other Areas 191
Attitudes and Cognitive Dissonance 191
Attribution Theory 193
Cognition and Emotions 195
Conclusion 197
Chapter Summary 199
Key Terms and Concepts 200
Suggestions for Further Reading 200

5   The Psychodynamic Approach   201

Motivation and the Mind	201
Introduction	202
Freud and Psychoanalysis	203
Freud's Assumptions about Behaviour	204
Exploring the Workings of the Mind	205
Freud's Theory of Consciousness	206
Dreams and Symbolic Expression	208
Drives and the Psychodynamics of Behaviour	209
Freud's Psychodynamic Model of Personality	211
Psychosexual Stages of Development	214
Oral Stage	214
Anal Stage	215
Phallic Stage	216
Latency Stage	219
Genital Stage	220
Fixation and Regression During Development	220
Anxiety and Defence Mechanisms	222
Observing the Unconscious in Behaviour	228
Assessing Freud's Work	232
Neo-Freudian and Non-Freudian Psychodynamic Theories	236
Carl Jung and the Collective Unconscious	237
Alfred Adler and Individual Psychology	241
Other Psychodynamic Theorists	243
Conclusion	245
Chapter Summary	247
Key Terms and Concepts	248
Suggestions for Further Reading	248

6   The Humanistic Approach   249

Keeping the Person in 'Personality'	249
Introduction	250
Carl Rogers's Theory	253
Self Theory and Personality	255
The Organism and the Actualizing Tendency	255
The Phenomenal Field and the Self	256
The Ideal Self, Congruence and Incongruence	257
Personality Development and Conditions for Growth	258
Conditions of Worth and the Would–Should Dilemma	259
Conditional and Unconditional Positive Regard	260
Congruence and Conditions for Growth	261
Human Potential and the Fully Functioning Person	264
Abraham Maslow's Theory	268
Motivation and the Hierarchy of Needs	269
Needs and Self-development	272
Self-actualization and Peak Experiences	274

Maslow's Concept of Healthy Growth   276
Extending the Humanistic Approach   279
Existential Psychology   279
Frankl's Logotherapy   280
Conclusion   284
Chapter Summary   286
Key Terms and Concepts   287
Suggestions for Further Reading   287

7   Perspectives on Development   **288**

Observing the Journey of Life   288
Introduction   289
Methods of Studying Development   290
Issues in Interpreting Development   294
   Continuity versus Discontinuity   294
   Generality versus Specificity of Models   295
   Heredity and Environment   296
Personality and Sex Role Development   300
Personality and Its Origins   300
Perspectives on Personality   301
   The Biological Approach   301
   The Behaviourist Approach   302
   The Cognitive Approach   303
   The Psychodynamic Approach   306
   The Humanistic Approach   306
The Development of Sex Roles   308
   The Biological Approach   308
   The Behaviourist Approach   310
   The Cognitive Approach   311
   The Psychodynamic Approach   312
   The Humanistic Approach   313
Conclusion   315
Chapter Summary   316
Key Terms and Concepts   317
Suggestions for Further Reading   317

8   Perspectives on Social Behaviour   **318**

The Individual and Society   318
Introduction   319
Methods of Studying Social Behaviour   320
Perspectives on Aggression   322
Defining Aggression   323
Methods of Studying Aggression   324
Theories of Aggression   325
   The Biological Approach   325
   The Behaviourist Approach   328

The Cognitive Approach   331
The Psychodynamic Approach   334
The Humanistic Approach   336
Comparing the Approaches   338
Aggression and the Media   340
Perspectives on Pro-social Behaviour   344
Defining Pro-social Behaviour   344
Theories of Altruism   345
The Biological Approach   345
The Behaviourist Approach   346
The Cognitive Approach   347
The Psychodynamic Approach   348
The Humanistic Approach   348
Altruism and Bystander Behaviour   350
Conclusion   352
Chapter Summary   353
Key Terms and Concepts   355
Suggestions for Further Reading   355

9   Perspectives on Abnormal Behaviour   **356**

Who and What Is Normal?   356
Introduction   358
Abnormality in Historical Context   358
Classifying Abnormal Behaviour   359
Perspectives on Aetiology and Treatment   363
The Biological Approach   364
The Behaviourist Approach   365
The Cognitive Approach   368
The Psychodynamic Approach   371
The Humanistic Approach   374
Evaluating Therapeutic Techniques   376
Understanding Schizophrenia   380
The Medical Model and Schizophrenia   382
Alternatives to the Medical Model of Schizophrenia   385
The Behaviourist Approach   385
The Cognitive Approach   387
The Psychodynamic Approach   389
The Humanistic Approach   390
Evaluating Our Understanding of Schizophrenia   392
Conclusion   393
Chapter Summary   395
Key Terms and Concepts   396
Suggestions for Further Reading   397

10   Psychology in Perspective   **398**

Searching for Answers   398
Introduction   399

Reconsidering the Origins of the Approaches   399
Perception and Theory Formation   400
Objective Evidence versus Shifting Paradigms   402
Paradigms in Psychology   403
Psychology and Science   405
Limitations of the Scientific Method for Psychology   405
The Search for a New Methodology   407
Psychology and Culture   409
The Many and the One   411
Seeking Convergence   412
Embracing Pluralism   413
Conclusion   415
Chapter Summary   416
Key Terms and Concepts   417
Suggestions for Further Reading   417

Appendix: Research Methods and Statistics   419

Making Sense of the Evidence   419
Introduction   420
The Logic of Research   420
Making Observations: Measurement and Sampling   420
Designing Research   423
Pitfalls in Experimental Research   423
    Confounds   424
    Bias   424
Going from Observation to Interpretation   427
Statistics – Making Sense of the Data   428
Descriptive Statistics – Describing the Data   428
    Frequency Distributions   430
    Measures of Central Tendency   431
    Measures of Variability   433
    Properties of Normal Distributions 436
    Correlations   437
Inferential Statistics   439
    Sampling and Variability   439
    Drawing Inferences from a Normal Distribution 439
    Inferences about the Significance of Results 440
    Decision Errors in Interpreting Data 441
Conclusion   443
Chapter Summary   444
Key Terms and Concepts   445
Suggestions for Further Reading   445

Glossary   446
References   467
Index   493

List of Figures

1.1	Ambiguous figures	6
1.2	Ambiguous figures	6
1.3	Ambiguous figures	6
1.4	The Gestalt concept of closure	7
1.5	The Gestalt concept of similarity	7
1.6	The Gestalt concept of proximity	8
1.7	The interaction of induction and deduction in research	17
1.8	Correlation of academic grades	27
1.9	Latané and Darley's field experiment	32
1.10	Basic types of research methods in psychology	34
2.1	The central and peripheral nervous systems	48
2.2	Neurons and neural transmission	49
2.3	Exterior view of the cortex	51
2.4	Tactile and motor representation in the cortex	52
2.5	Internal view of the brain	53
2.6	Major neurotransmitters and their functions	60
2.7	The endocrine system and hormonal functions	61
2.8	Hemispheric specialization	72
2.9	A schematic diagram of the body's response to stress	77
2.10	The Holmes–Rahe life-change scale	79
2.11	Unigenic inheritance	86
2.12	Certainty of genetic relatedness and emotional closeness	92
3.1	The basic classical conditioning procedure	106
3.2	Stimulus generalization	108
3.3	Pure generalization	109
3.4	Stimulus discrimination	110
3.5	Higher-order conditioning	113
3.6	Contingencies of reinforcement	125
3.7	Schedules of reinforcement	129
3.8	Biofeedback	140
3.9	Seligman's preparedness continuum	143
4.1	A general model of memory	158
4.2	A test of short-term memory	164
4.3	Retroactive and proactive interference	166
4.4	A walk down memory lane	173
4.5	Maximizing use of memory	175
4.6	Persistence of set in problem solving	179

4.7	Stages of language development	187
5.1	Graphic representations of Freud's theory	213
5.2	Repression and recovered memories of abuse	224
5.3	Studying verbal slips	229
5.4	Ambiguous stimuli and projective tests	230
5.5	Symbolism in psychoanalytic theories	240
5.6	Erikson's and Freud's models of development	244
6.1	Values in the mature person	266
6.2	Maslow's hierarchy of needs	271
6.3	Characteristics of self-actualized individuals	277
7.1	Research designs in developmental research	293
7.2	Piaget's theory of cognitive development	296
7.3	Heredity and environment in studies of twins	298
7.4	Parents, peers and personality	305
7.5	Stereotypes of male and female gender roles	311
8.1	Perspectives on aggression	338
8.2	Effects of the introduction of television	342
8.3	Categories of pro-social behaviour	345
8.4	Determining response to an emergency	351
9.1	Classifying mental disorders	361
9.2	Incidence rates for mental disorders	362
9.3	The basic procedure for systematic desensitization	367
9.4	Comparing the efficacy of behaviour modification and psychoanalysis	373
9.5	A meta-analysis of treatment results	378
9.6	Major sub-types of schizophrenia	381
A.1	Subject bias in experiments	425
A.2	Analysing the frequency distribution for a set of data	429
A.3	A frequency distribution graph	430
A.4	A frequency distribution for salaries in company 'X'	432
A.5	A skewed frequency distribution	432
A.6	A normal distribution	434
A.7	Comparing groups	434
A.8	Correlational patterns	438
A.9	Errors in evaluating hypotheses	442

Preface to the Third Edition

At the university where I teach, and most others, introductory psychology is one of the most popular courses. This reflects the interest which most people have in understanding human behaviour – both their own, and that of others. While an introductory course should acknowledge this interest, it must also be an introduction to psychology as a discipline. In meeting these goals, the choice of a textbook is often crucial.

There are many possibilities in selecting course materials for introductory psychology. My own experience as a student involved a course which had no text; instead it used a set of readings which included several short books and a number of articles. While this gave the impression of encountering psychologists 'in their own words', it represented a very heavy burden of reading, and little coherence. Indeed, it was several courses later before I began really to grasp the outlines of the discipline, and what made it distinct from other fields of study. Hence, that first course failed one of the important requirements for an introductory course – providing a coherent understanding of the nature of psychology.

While using a textbook might seem to present a simple solution, there are literally dozens of introductory texts in print, and most seem to follow a formula which is less than satisfactory. Over more than twenty years, I have encountered many texts, and used more than a dozen in my classes. From my experiences as a teacher, and the feedback from several thousand students, I have come to recognize certain factors which seem important in a textbook.

Most textbooks today tend to be rather large volumes which provide an impressive amount of factual knowledge. Unfortunately, as teaching tools, these texts tend to have several limitations. First, they are both too large and too expensive. No student can really hope to assimilate all the detail which is provided, and often they find the mass of information overwhelming. So, they end up paying for content that isn't needed. Second, most students come to psychology with an interest in *human* behaviour, yet find that a large proportion of their text is devoted to research on other species. While such research clearly is part of psychology, it is often not handled in ways that help students to understand its relevance to understanding human behaviour. Third, by presenting a survey of various sub-areas such as 'perception', 'development' and 'motivation', texts fail to provide a coherent framework for the discipline as a whole. In the end, it becomes as disjointed for students as my own text-less experience was.

Out of these concerns emerged this book, which is designed to offer a relatively brief, coherent introduction to psychology which emphasizes the understanding of *human* behaviour. The emphasis on human behaviour was the easiest goal to meet, since much of psychological research is focused on people; animal research is included only where it clearly relates to our understanding of human behaviour. The goal of brevity was met by making a conscious decision to be selective rather than encyclopaedic. In order to define criteria for such selection, it was necessary to choose some organizing principles – which in fact related to the third goal, coherence.

The organizing structure of the book is based on the historical reality that psychology has been based on several different conceptual frameworks, each with its own assumptions, methods and theories. Thus, the examination of five frameworks (or approaches, as they are called in this text) forms the central focus of the book. Underlying this structure is a concern with the process of *how* we arrive at knowledge of behaviour – not just that different approaches exist, but how and why they arose. A central theme of the book is that the processes of perception can be used to explain both human behaviour and the nature of the discipline of psychology. That organizing structure has proven remarkably popular with students and instructors in previous editions. This edition remains faithful to the basic concepts and goals of the earlier editions.

The changes in this edition involve three goals: to clarify and update the material of the previous edition where necessary; to provide coverage of new topics where appropriate; and to provide more structural aids to readers. With regard to the first goal, this book represents a line-by-line rewrite of the previous edition, while maintaining a similar overall structure. Readers will find discussion of new developments and new material in every chapter, and many new references for both research and further reading. The purpose of such changes has not been to be current for currency's sake, but to select material which contributes to the original goals of the text. Hence, the changes are meant to enhance the original conception, not to alter it. Overall, the book is modestly larger than the previous edition, but still provides a brief introduction to psychology – and one which provides a coherent understanding of the origins and nature of the discipline.

In terms of providing guidance to readers, it was felt important to retain and, where appropriate, build on existing features intended to make it more helpful. In addition to an extensive end glossary, important terms are also highlighted and defined in context where they first occur, with formal definitions being provided in the margin. In this edition, the number of terms defined has been increased by approximately 10 per cent. In the interests of both clarity and reader appeal, the number of illustrations has been increased as well; as in the previous edition, the choice of illustrations is intended to provide relevant information, not simply graphic fillers. Each chapter continues to begin with an overall outline to help readers grasp the structure of what lies ahead, and concludes with a point-form summary and list of key terms and concepts. It is hoped that these features will aid students in the process of studying and reviewing, without distracting from the flow of the text itself.

In addition, the number of discussion questions, which are dispersed throughout the book with the label 'For further consideration', has been significantly increased, with questions now appearing after each sub-section. These questions are meant to encourage readers to apply the ideas within the text as a means of enhancing understanding. In general, they go beyond simple rote review, but are not intended to be completely open-ended. Some ask students to reflect on their own experiences; others may prove amenable to group discussions. While 'critical thinking' has become a much-abused buzzword in the past few years, these questions are intended to provoke involvement and reflection.

In writing this book, I have been clearly aware of my own limitations, and of my debts to others. The first edition of this book was a collaborative effort of six people, including myself. Since the second edition, I have been the sole author, but I still wish to acknowledge my colleagues who collaborated on the first edition. Whatever the evolution of this book has been, they were all part of its origin, and part of a productive collaborative experience: Gordon R. Emslie, Paul H. Hirschorn, Judith Kelly Waalen, John Medcof and John Roth. To all of them, I give my thanks.

A further debt must be accorded to those readers and reviewers who provided comments on the previous edition, and thereby contributed to making this book better. Most of them must go unnamed, but I do want to acknowledge the assistance of several colleagues at Ryerson Polytechnic University who read the draft versions of various portions of this edition: Kent Campbell, David Day, Mary Easton, Gordon Emslie, Marcia Moshe, Brian Rabinowicz, Craig Ramsey, John Turtle and Judy Waalen. All provided thoughtful comments and valuable criticism, and I feel strongly that the book is better for their efforts.

I also wish to thank my family, who sacrificed in many ways during the time that this project consumed. My sons, Dave and Danny, aged ten and five respectively, have been understanding of the many nights and week-ends which this project took up. Their interruptions have been a frequent relief when the task has grown heavy, and their curiosity and enthusiasm is a constant reminder of just how remarkable our existence is. My wife, Lies Weijs, has been invaluable, emotionally, intellectually and logistically. She has provided encouragement when I needed it, and bore the burdens of family demands when I could not fulfil them. Further, as a reader who is a non-expert in psychology, she provided insightful and intelligent feedback on clarity and readability. Family life and career often seem at odds in our society; in this case, my family has my gratitude and love for all that they have given to this project, and to my life.

At Open University Press, I wish to thank Justin Vaughan, publisher for psychology, for being what a good publisher should be: a source of encouragement, an information resource and a gentle taskmaster when necessary. Thanks are also due to Viv Cracknell of the editorial staff for her efforts in seeing the manuscript through the complexities of publication. Everyone at Open University Press who has been involved in this project, from the time I first undertook to write the previous edition, has been both professional and supportive, for which I am very appreciative.

William E. Glassman
Toronto, June 1999

Behaviour and Psychology

The Magic of Behaviour
Introduction
The Challenge of Psychology
Why Different Approaches?
Perception and Theorizing
The Origins of Psychology
Methods of Studying Behaviour
The Role of the Scientific Method in Psychology
Introspectionism and Public Observation
Measures of Behaviour, Research Settings and
  Research Methods
Interviews and Surveys as Self-report Procedures

Surveys and Sampling Procedures
  Limitations of Self-reports
Naturalistic Observation and Unobtrusive Measures
Case Studies
Correlational Research
Experiments
Quasi-experiments
Ethics in Psychological Research
Conclusion
Chapter Summary
Key Terms and Concepts
Suggestions for Further Reading

The Magic of Behaviour

When I was a child, my father sometimes took me to see magic shows. To a boy of ten, this was a wondrous and exciting event. The tricks performed were usually pretty standard – producing objects from hats or boxes, making things disappear and so on. I knew even then that these feats were not supernatural, but based on some sort of deception or gimmickry – in a word, 'tricks'. Nonetheless, they held me spellbound, wondering how it was all accomplished.

I was reminded of this recently, while teaching a course in problem solving. One day after class, a student in his thirties told me of having recently seen a magic show. After describing some of the tricks, he had the inevitable question: 'How is it done?'

As children or adults, we are curious about the world, and when faced with the unexpected or unexplained, we are driven to increase our understanding. Magic shows represent a special kind of mystery, because what we *think* we see is somehow different from the underlying reality. Indeed, one of the most basic tools in a magician's repertoire is *misdirection* – getting the audience to focus on an irrelevant detail, while ignoring a crucial manoeuvre by the magician. By manipulating our attention and expectations, magicians draw us into a world which entertains us precisely because it is hard to understand.

Studying psychology in some ways is like viewing a magic show, in that the study of behaviour evokes the desire to understand, and often challenges our expectations. In trying to make sense of behaviour, psychologists encounter both the wondrous and the baffling. Consider the case of a horse called 'clever Hans'. Hans had been 'educated' by his owner for four years, and subsequently seemed capable of answering questions in history, geography, mathematics and more. People came from near and far to see clever Hans, and most went away convinced that he really *was* educated. Ultimately, it was a psychologist named Oskar Pfungst who figured out the true explanation. (Of course, Hans really didn't understand history and so on; later in this chapter, we will discuss what was really happening.) Although an 'educated' horse is unusual, it is not really surprising that a psychologist was involved in understanding it. Understanding behaviour in all its forms is, after all, the primary goal of psychology.

Introduction

Throughout human history, people have sought ways to make sense of the world, and there have been many attempts to formalize the understanding of behaviour. Astrology, for example, arose out of the belief that human actions were influenced by the stars. Often, theories of behaviour have been stimulated by developments in other fields. For instance, in the eighteenth century, anatomists studying the brain proposed that there was a relationship between brain size and mental abilities. This led to the development of **phrenology**, which asserted that one could assess ability by examining the shape of the skull. While phrenology and astrology have been largely discredited, their goal of understanding and explaining the way people act seems similar to that of psychology. So what makes psychology different?

The simple answer is that psychology differs in the method it uses in the search for understanding. Unlike astrology, phrenology or even 'common sense', psychology utilizes a form of systematic observation and analysis that is often called 'the scientific method'. In fact, **psychology** is often defined as 'the scientific study of behaviour'. Definitions, of course, have limitations, and this one does, too. For example, some psychologists would interpret 'behaviour' to mean both overt responses and conscious experience, while others would be more restrictive. Similarly, some psychologists include the behaviour of other species, while some are concerned only with human behaviour. Despite such variations in the focus of interests, the

phrenology a now-discredited eighteenth-century theory which asserted that one could assess ability by examining the shape of the skull

psychology the scientific study of behaviour and experience *methods* used in psychology are *scientific*. That is, the methods are primarily based on a tradition which originated with the natural sciences of physics, chemistry and biology.

The Challenge of Psychology

All scientists emphasize certain common principles, like the importance of careful observation, minimizing sources of error and testing alternative explanations. At the same time, the methods of psychologists differ from those of physicists or chemists, because what psychologists study is different: the actions (and interactions) of living creatures. This means that psychological researchers face challenges which are unique to their discipline.

One challenge is related to *complexity*. Physicists studying atomic particles typically deal with only a limited number of particles at once – a hundred particles interacting would be a very complex system. By contrast, a physiological psychologist studying the human brain is dealing with a structure composed of several *billion* interconnected cells – the most complex structure in the known universe! Even for non-physiological researchers, there is tremendous diversity to consider – for example, studying language is complicated by the several thousand languages and dialects known, each with its own vocabulary and grammar. Given the richness of human behaviour, psychologists must contend with a vast range of possibilities, and a correspondingly large variety of data (observations). By comparison, the possible interactions between two chemical elements, or the dynamics of a moving object, are relatively simple.

A second challenge faced by psychologists is sometimes referred to as the problem of **self-awareness** (Hofstadter 1979). While physicists studying atoms are themselves composed of atoms, most researchers would say that this has no impact on the problems they study. By contrast, psychologists studying human behaviour are simultaneously *producing* human behaviour. At first glance, this may not seem like a problem – it might even be seen as a convenience. In fact, historically, a number of noted psychologists studied their own behaviour as part of their broader studies: Sigmund Freud, the founder of psychoanalysis, studied his own dreams as well as those of his patients (Freud 1900). William James, a pioneering American psychologist, favoured introspectionism – studying the contents of one's conscious awareness – over laboratory research. In doing so, he popularized the phrases 'stream of consciousness' and 'armchair psychology' (James 1890). Eventually, however, it was recognized that self-observation is prone to many sources of error, not the least of which is bias – researchers may falsely interpret their own behaviour as consistent with their theoretical ideas.

A related concern arises when observing the behaviour of others. While measurement can be demanding even in simple physical systems, psychological observation is complicated by the fact that one is dealing with independent, living organisms, not inanimate particles. In particular, observing human behaviour can lead to **reactivity**, the tendency for people to alter their behaviour when they are being observed. (As a simple case, consider how many people who sing to themselves stop if they realize someone is

self-awareness the capacity for individuals or other living organisms consciously to observe their own behaviour

reactivity the tendency for people to alter their behaviour when they are being observed

listening.) In order to deal with reactivity, psychologists often resort to complicated research designs, sometimes including deliberate deception. (The methods used will be discussed in more detail later in this chapter.) In the end, observing human behaviour proves more difficult than observing simple physical systems.

Another challenge arises in terms of identifying the causes of behaviour. Traditionally, science has valued the identification of causes as an important part of 'understanding', and psychology has tended to accept this goal. However, the reality is that many different factors can influence behaviour in a given situation. Consider an example: the child welfare authorities are called in when someone is reported to have hit their child. It turns out the father was drinking, had just lost his job and was himself abused as a child. Is the cause of his abusive behaviour the alcohol, the job loss, his early upbringing, a combination of these or some factor not identified? In any situation, there are many factors which influence behaviour: some are internal, some are part of the immediate situation and some are part of past experience. Each of these represents a type of cause, but developing a complete description of such causes in a given situation is a difficult (if not impossible) task.

Why Different Approaches?

It is not surprising, given the richness and complexity of behaviour, that psychologists have evolved different approaches to understanding it. Ideally, we would have one simple set of principles which would explain every aspect of human experience. At present, no such theory has been developed which has met with broad acceptance. Instead, there are a range of approaches which differ in terms of their basic assumptions, their methods and their theoretical structures. In effect, each approach represents a distinct framework for the study of behaviour. While most psychology books emphasize the research findings in psychology, organized according to traditional topic areas like learning and perception, this book focuses instead on the frameworks which have been developed in psychology, as defined by the major approaches. By understanding how these frameworks arose, and how they differ, one can better evaluate the significance of each approach, as well as make sense of the field as a whole.

The traditional model of science says that scientists formulate theories based on the information they have gathered from research. Hence, one might imagine that each approach arose as an attempt to improve on existing theories. This viewpoint, while a bit simplistic, is partially valid. In some cases, theorists *do* react against what they see as limitations or errors in the work of others. For example, Carl Jung split from his mentor, Sigmund Freud, partly because of disagreements about the meaning of sexuality. At the same time, other factors also come into play. Thomas Kuhn (1970), a specialist in the philosophy of science, has argued that the acceptance or rejection of particular frameworks or approaches (which he calls 'paradigms') depends on human preferences as well as the available evidence. (See Chapter 10 for more on Kuhn's ideas.) That is, the development and evaluation of a theory depends not simply on the available data, but also on social and personal factors, including the experiences of the researcher and the prevailing culture. To understand this, we need to examine how we actually perceive the world.

Perception and Theorizing

Most individuals tend to assume that what we experience depends on what is 'out there' – that is, that our senses simply convey information about the physical stimuli which we encounter. This implies a direct record of the external world, similar to the way a video camera records a scene. However, the process of perceiving is actually much more complex. **Perception** is an *active* process involving selection, organization and interpretation, *not* a passive mirroring of the external world.

perception the process of selection, organization and interpretation of information about the world conveyed by the senses

Let us consider first the process of *selection*. At every moment, we encounter a tremendous variety of stimuli – sights, sounds, smells etc. Unfortunately, the human brain has a limited capacity to deal with incoming information. (Imagine going to a television store and trying to watch several channels on different televisions simultaneously – parts of one or more programmes are inevitably missed.) In order to cope with the sensory barrage, our perceptual system focuses on some aspects of the situation, while ignoring others. This process of choosing stimuli is called **selective attention**. One example is the way we focus on one conversation, while filtering out other voices and sounds, at a party or other crowded location. (The nature of attention, and its limits, will be discussed further in Chapter 4.)

selective attention the perceptual process of selectively focusing on particular stimulus elements

Perception, then, is partly determined by the external stimuli that we encounter, as filtered by selective attention. (This stimulus-based process is sometimes called 'bottom-up' processing.) At the same time, perceptual experience is also influenced by various internal factors, such as our prior experience and expectations. These factors (referred to as 'top-down' processing) influence both the way that we interpret selected stimuli and what we select. Consider two examples: in Figure 1.1, what do you see? (Look *now*!) While the figure *could* be interpreted as either a duck or a rabbit, most native English speakers see the rabbit first, because they have learned to scan images in a left-to-right sequence. In this case, past experience influences the processing order. (Individuals brought up to read in a different sequence, like the right-to-left sequence of Hebrew, would often perceive it differently. To explore this issue further, try making a copy of the image reversed, and show it to a friend to see what happens.)

A different source of influence is illustrated in the next two figures. In Figure 1.2, what are the letters? Now, compare this with Figure 1.3. What are the elements in the centre – numbers, or the letter B? In this situation, the presence of other letters or numbers – what we might call the *context* of the stimuli – leads us to interpret the same elements differently.

So-called **ambiguous figures**, which can be interpreted in different ways, have long been of interest to psychologists studying perception. Such figures

ambiguous figure any stimulus which can be perceived in more than one way

Figure 1.1   Ambiguous figures Is this a rabbit or a duck? What we see can change, even when the stimulus stays the same.

Figure 1.2   Ambiguous figures What do you see between the A and the C? Compare this to Figure 1.3.

Figure 1.3   Ambiguous figures What do you see between the 12 and the 14? Compare this to Figure 1.2; note how context alters our expectations, and thereby what we perceive.

Gestalt theory a theory of behaviour pioneered in the early part of the twentieth century by Kohler, Wertheimer and others, which emphasized the active, creative nature of perception and learning (*Gestalt* is German, and means roughly 'organized whole')

illustrate that what we perceive is not based simply on what is 'out there', but is also influenced by internal processes. On first encounter, it may seem that ambiguous figures have little to do with everyday experience – but they actually underscore the processes which are part of *all* perception. In trying to make sense of the world, we look for familiar patterns, and we interpret what we encounter based on our prior experiences. When faced with a situation where there is incomplete information, we fill in the gaps according to what seems probable. (For example, in a noisy environment, we fill in small gaps in what someone says based on the words we *do* hear.) This view of perception as an active, creative process was pioneered in the early part of the twentieth century by **Gestalt theory** (the word *Gestalt* is German, and means roughly 'organized whole'). Gestalt psychologists argued that perceptual experience is the result of active synthesis, based on a number of basic principles. Among the most important of these was the concept of

Figure 1.4 The Gestalt concept of closure What do you see in these two figures? Note that both are easily recognizable, even though both are based on incomplete outlines.

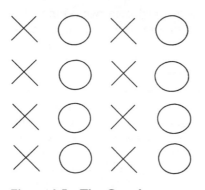

Figure 1.5 The Gestalt concept of similarity Note how we tend to see the figure as columns rather than rows, because of grouping the similar shapes.

closure in perception, the tendency to fill in incomplete patterns to produce a coherent whole

similarity a Gestalt principle of perceptual organization, based on grouping together similar elements (e.g. shape or size)

proximity a Gestalt principle which states that elements which are close together tend to be perceived as a group

schema (plural 'schemata') a mental framework which organizes knowledge, beliefs and expectations, and is used to guide behaviour

closure, which is the tendency to fill in incomplete patterns to produce a coherent whole (see Figure 1.4). Closure helps to explain why tasks like proofreading can be difficult: we tend to see what we expect to see (a correct word), instead of an error. Other Gestalt organizational principles include **similarity** (grouping similar items together) and **proximity** (elements which are close together tend to form a group) (see Figures 1.5 and 1.6).

The interpretations we make when perceiving are seldom random; instead, they reflect the way we have structured our previous knowledge and experience. From early infancy, we analyse and interpret our experiences, seeking patterns to help us make sense of the world. Some of these patterns are fairly simple concepts, like 'food' or 'chair'. As we develop, we form more complex structures called **schemata**. Some schemata are scripts to guide our actions in particular situations. For example, when dining out, a 'restaurant' script tells us that in a restaurant we order from a menu, are served by someone and are expected to pay for what we order. Schemata can also be used to organize our knowledge of objects and people. For

Figure 1.6   The Gestalt concept of proximity Note how we tend to see the figure as rows rather than columns, because of grouping those which are closer together.

example, a schema for 'bedroom' would include knowledge of the various objects found in a bedroom, as well as their functions. Our attitudes towards people, such as stereotypes, can also be considered schemata (Baldwin 1992).

Whether simple or complex, schemata influence the way we perceive the world around us. Depending on the schema one has, the same situation may be interpreted differently: an old chair at a flea market may be perceived as junk by one person; another person, more knowledgeable about furniture, may recognize it as a Georgian antique. A Brazilian settler may see a rainforest as something to be cleared in order to create a farm; an environmental activist may see the same forest as a priceless ecosystem.

In many cases, it is impossible to label a particular interpretation as correct or incorrect. Thus, in each of the above examples, both points of view have meaning. At the same time, it should be obvious that the use of schemata also creates the risk of distortions in the way we see the world. Sometimes the distortions may be relatively benign, but in other cases, the errors may be more serious – especially when our schemata involve faulty or inaccurate assumptions. Consider social stereotypes: Often stereotypes are formed initially from some specific experience or an observation of one or more individuals. The **stereotype** is created when this information is then generalized to apply to *all* members of a group, regardless of circumstances. This creates difficulties when circumstances change, but the stereotype doesn't, or when a stereotype is used as a substitute for gathering accurate information about a person. For example, a friend once reported an experience that his six-year-old son had at school. The teacher had asked the children to 'draw a picture of your father relaxing'. When the teacher saw the boy drawing a picture of a man chopping wood, she said, 'No, I said draw him *relaxing.*' Bursting into tears, the six-year-old exclaimed (correctly), 'But my Daddy *does* chop wood to relax!' (By contrast, his father's 'work' involved sitting at a desk all day.) The teacher's stereotype, not the boy's drawing, was the problem. Stereotypes, as mental schemata, can lead us to prejudge others – and *all* schemata carry this risk of distorting reality.

stereotype an oversimplified and often inaccurate perception of an individual based on generalizing from schemata related to the individual's group membership

Even when we are not consciously aware of using schemata, they are part of our perceptual process. Our perceptions of friends and family members are based on many, many experiences. Over time, the schemata we form from these experiences can have more influence on our perceptions than the present reality. Consider the following examples: As parents, we tend to overlook the changes in our maturing children, and fail to recognize that they are no longer as dependent as they were as toddlers. As adults, we can be shocked to realize that our elderly parents now need to be cared for as if *we* were the parents. Friends may change both physically and emotionally, and we still perceive them as they *used* to be. In each case, the mental schema is inconsistent with the person before us. Typically we are unaware of these distortions; somewhat ironically, we tend to believe that family and friends are the people we know best, because we have such elaborate schemata to deal with them.

confirmation bias a form of cognitive error based on the tendency to seek out information which supports one's beliefs, and to ignore contradictory information

The likelihood that we will recognize such distortions is reduced by a phenomenon called **confirmation bias**. Generally, we tend to focus on information that confirms our beliefs, and ignore potentially contradictory information. Ironically, the more confident we are in our beliefs, the more likely is the danger of distortion, because we are less likely to look for information that might reveal our error. Thus, a doctor with thirty years of experience is less likely to recognize when he has made a diagnostic error than a newly graduated intern – precisely because greater experience instils greater confidence (Halpern 1989).

This is not to say that schemata are undesirable – most of the time, they aid us in efficiently and accurately processing the vast amount of sensory information that we encounter. Rather, it is to emphasize that perception is an imperfect process, even as it is a crucial one in our dealings with the world. Schemata help us to make sense of the wealth of sensory information around us. On balance, the risk of errors is largely offset by the benefits gained from organizing our experiences. In addition, by *understanding* the perceptual process, we are more likely to avoid the kinds of errors we have discussed.

We began this discussion of perceptual processes in response to the question, 'Why different approaches?' By now it should be obvious that researchers depend on the same perceptual processes as other people, with the same limitations. Still, it may not be apparent how these perceptual limitations have led to divergent approaches within psychology. To understand this, recall what was said earlier about the challenges involved in studying behaviour. In particular, we noted that human behaviour is almost infinitely complex and variable. Faced with this complexity and variability, how is a researcher to proceed?

Since 'studying everything' is impossible, some degree of selection is inevitable in research. Researchers make choices, focusing on one aspect or type of behaviour (e.g. physiological processes, or a problem like aggression), or sometimes one species (humans, chimpanzees, bees etc.). The choices made may reflect the researcher's interests, theoretical assumptions or other aspects of the individual's schemata. In other words, the process of deciding what to study, and how to study it, is influenced by the processes of perception which we have been discussing.

Thus, the process of doing research involves selection in the same sense that perception in general does. Faced with a range of choices, many individuals interested in behaviour decide to follow a research path already defined by others. In some cases, however, circumstances and schemata combine in a way that leads certain individuals to break new ground. In effect, they make choices of what to study, and how, that come to define a new framework or approach to the study of behaviour. In the long run, the development of any approach involves the contributions of many people, but in the beginning there is usually a key figure, whose personal choices serve to define the nature of the approach.

Psychology as a discipline is characterized by not one, but several, different approaches. The longest part of this book will be devoted to exploring five major ones: the biological, behaviourist, cognitive, psychodynamic and humanistic approaches. In each case, we will explore the origins of the approach, the individuals involved in its development and the assumptions and methods which characterize it. Inevitably, you will find points of disagreement between the approaches, as well as apparent limitations of each. Faced with this situation, you may well wonder which approach is the 'real' psychology. While such a query is natural, it may not be the most productive way to view the situation.

It is frequently noted in introductory texts that psychology is a relatively young field, tracing its origins back only about a hundred years or so. This is just as frequently followed by statements about how one cannot expect much coherence from a young field, as if apologizing for a toddler who is a messy eater – that is, one shouldn't expect much more. This sentiment not only downplays the accomplishments of psychology, but is also probably erroneous, because it assumes that coherence is *necessary* to a mature field. (Modern physics, by comparison, still grapples with differing models of basic forces, without having a unified theory.)

This general issue deserves more detailed exploration, but the purpose here is to suggest that disagreement is not always a weakness. (See Chapter 10 for a further discussion.) Physics, a much older discipline than psychology, has long recognized the concept of **complementarity** – different frameworks may be separately valid, without being reducible one into the other (Blackburn 1971). For example, light can be described as a wave or a particle, depending on the circumstances. Each representation has value, without implying that one is right and one is wrong in an absolute sense. In the same way, the differing approaches to behaviour which we will consider may also reflect complementarity. Seen in this way, the basic concern becomes how *useful* an approach is, not which is completely correct.

If the preceding example seems too abstract, consider the following story. A group of blind men were making a pilgrimage together in India, when they met a man leading an elephant. None of the blind men had ever encountered an elephant before, and they proceeded to touch it. One man, grasping the trunk, exclaimed, 'Oh! An elephant is like a snake!' Another, wrapping his arms around one of the elephant's legs, said, 'No! An elephant is like a tree, with rough bark!' A third, grasping the end of the elephant's tail, countered, 'You're both wrong! An elephant is hairy, like a camel!' They proceeded to argue vehemently, never realizing that they were each partly right, but

complementarity a concept developed by physicists to deal with the existence of two models which are both useful, but not directly reconcilable

that none was completely right. Their disagreements stemmed from making different observations, and making different interpretations based on those observations. In a similar way, each approach to psychology may be only a partial view of the whole subject. And, like the interpretations of the blind men, each approach may have something to offer in our attempt to understand behaviour, even if no one approach can answer all questions.

In considering the five approaches, the process of perception can help us to understand how the origin of each approach is related to the experiences and schemata of the individuals who pioneered it. In addition, we will need to consider the intellectual and social context in which the approaches were developed, because people do not live (or work) in a vacuum; each of us is influenced by the ideas and attitudes of the society we live in. (Consider, for example, changes in social attitudes from the 'hippie' 1960s to the 'end of millennium' 1990s.) In this sense, the lives of the pioneers of psychology, and the cultural contexts in which they lived, are not simply historical details, but important clues to understanding each approach. (The impact of culture is a broad issue, and while it is not possible to consider all alternatives here, it should be evident that people in all cultures have strived to understand human behaviour, and have sometimes developed frameworks very different from those we will discuss. For further discussion of this issue, see Chapter 10.) Psychology is a human endeavour, and throughout the book, we will try to convey an understanding of the people who have influenced its development. For the moment, let us consider the general context in which psychology as a discipline emerged.

| For further consideration | In what ways do you think your own perceptions of the world may be influenced by your previous experiences? Have you ever misjudged someone on first encounter? |

The Origins of Psychology

Psychology did not exist as a specific discipline until the end of the nineteenth century. Formally, its inception is usually traced to the creation of Wilhelm Wundt's laboratory of experimental psychology, established in Leipzig in 1875. While it is convenient to point to a specific date, psychology is not a baby with a specific 'birth date'; its genesis really involved a number of elements, from the creation of laboratories, to the formation of university psychology departments, to the growth of public recognition of the discipline. In this sense, its 'birth' really extends over roughly the last three decades of the nineteenth century.

In a broader sense, it can be argued that the origins of psychology go back even further. What has been called the first 'psychology experiment' was performed in ancient Egypt, in about 700 BC (Hunt 1993). In order to explore the origins of language, the king of Egypt arranged for a child to be reared by a shepherd, who was ordered never to speak to the boy. When the grown child was later presented to the king, supposedly the first sounds he made sounded like the Egyptian word for 'bread'. The king concluded that the Egyptian language must be innate, thus demonstrating the inherent superiority of Egyptian culture!

In general terms, psychology emerged out of two traditions: philosophy and natural science. Philosophers have always been concerned with understanding the meaning of human experience, and many basic concepts in psychology trace their origin back to philosophy. For example, John Locke was deliberating the role of learning in behaviour in his *Essay Concerning Human Understanding*, published in 1690. In addition, philosophy, like the humanities more generally, has posed questions about awareness, motivation and values that have also been of concern to psychologists. Along with philosophy's interest in human experience, psychology has been influenced by the study of the natural world. Physics and the other natural sciences have been important to psychology both conceptually and in terms of methods of study. In particular, the success of the physical sciences in using experiments to develop explanations based on causation led to psychology seeking to do the same. Later, as the biological sciences began to develop, they too became sources of influence in the development of psychology. An oft-cited example is the impact of Darwin's work on evolution, with its emphasis on the innate origins of behaviour.

Hence, both philosophy and science have been influential in shaping the nature of psychology. The continuity of these influences is indicated in a 1970 review of research on memory by Tulving and Madigan. Looking at the then-current findings, they began by suggesting, only partly in jest, that there was very little that would have surprised Aristotle (perhaps the greatest of the early Greek philosopher-scientists)! To see more clearly how psychology developed from these sources, we will consider two of the great pioneers: Wilhelm Wundt and William James. Taken together, their contributions laid the foundation for most of modern psychology, while reflecting the impact of philosophy and natural science.

Wilhelm Wundt was born in Germany in 1832, and received a medical degree at the University of Heidelberg, graduating at the top of his class in 1855. Shortly after, he went to Berlin, to study for a short time under Johannes Müller, who had earlier established the first laboratory of experimental physiology. Wundt's contact with Müller, while brief, had a significant influence on him, inspiring him to give up medicine to pursue research in physiological processes. Wundt's training led him to study behaviour by examining elementary sensory processes. His background in medicine made it natural to emphasize physiological aspects of behaviour, though he also hoped that eventually psychology could analyse higher mental processes. By today's standards, his equipment and techniques were primitive, but the impact of his work was far-reaching.

At this time, psychology did not exist as a distinct discipline; as a result, Wundt's appointment at the University of Leipzig was as a professor of 'scientific philosophy' (as opposed to classical philosophy). Thus, a man whose training was in medicine and physiology became a founder of psychology, while teaching as a philosopher! Out of these unusual circumstances emerged the new discipline, and Wundt played a significant role, through both his own work and his impact on his students: while Wundt himself was designated

---

Wilhelm Wundt

Wilhelm Wundt (1832–1920) was born in Baden, Germany, the son of a Lutheran pastor. He received a degree in medicine from the University of Heidelberg in 1855, graduating at the top of his class. Over time, his interests turned towards research in physiology, particularly sensory processes. This led him to an interest in psychology, and in 1875 he founded what is regarded as the first laboratory of experimental psychology, at the University of Leipzig. Wundt hoped that eventually the study of sensory processes would lead to an understanding of higher mental processes, and he wrote papers on all aspects of psychology, from physiological processes to social behaviour. A prolific writer as well as researcher, he published almost 500 articles and books, totalling almost 60,000 printed pages. As a teacher and researcher, he influenced many early psychologists, but the approach he took to the study of behaviour, called *structuralism*, has been supplanted by other approaches within psychology. Despite this, Wundt is often regarded as the founder of modern psychology.

---

a 'philosopher', he advocated the creation of a new field of experimental psychology. By the end of the century, psychology departments were created at several universities, and some of the founders of these programmes (e.g. E. B. Titchner and J. M. Cattell) studied under Wundt. As a result, Wundt's conception of an experimental psychology – physiologically oriented, emphasizing basic sensory processes – was an important influence in the early development of psychology.

Interestingly, one of the other early giants of psychology, William James, also began as a medical student. James, the elder brother of the novelist Henry James, was born to a wealthy family in Boston, Massachusetts, in 1842. Unlike Wundt, James was an indifferent student, and tried several fields before finally receiving a medical degree from Harvard when he was almost thirty. At this point (1872), he was asked to teach half of a course in physiology at Harvard; within three years the course had evolved into a study of 'the relations between physiology and psychology'. Three years after that, he dropped the physiological component, and began teaching a course which was explicitly psychological.

It was at this time that James was asked by publisher Henry Holt to prepare a textbook on psychology. He accepted, thinking it would be a straightforward task. After all, he was fluent in German and French as well as English, and knew most of the existing literature (including Wundt's work). Writing the book turned into a mammoth enterprise, consuming almost twelve years, and resulting in two massive volumes totalling approximately one thousand pages. James himself was ultimately dissatisfied with his efforts, telling Holt, '*1st*, that there is no such thing as a *science* of psychology, and *2nd*, that W. J. is an incapable' (quoted by Fancher 1979: 160). In fact, by the time of the publication of *Principles of Psychology* in 1890, James's interests had turned towards philosophy, and with the exception of *Varieties of Religious Experience* (1902), his significant later work was all philosophical, not psychological. In his later years, his appointment at Harvard was in philosophy.

William James

William James (1842–1910) was one of the most influential and articulate of the early American psychologists. Indeed, his writing is so clear and engaging that it has been said that he wrote like a novelist. (Interestingly, his younger brother Henry is often regarded as the creator of the psychological novel.) He came from a wealthy family, and travelled extensively during his career, from the salons of Europe to the jungles of Brazil. His academic career was spent at Harvard University, first as a student, then as a professor. His student career was undistinguished: he started in chemistry, switched to medicine, took a foray into biology and eventually, after several interruptions, finished his medical degree when he was almost 30. He began his teaching career as an instructor in physiology at Harvard, but gradually incorporated more psychological content, so that by 1878 the course was purely psychological in focus. At this time, he was approached to write a psychology textbook; the task took more than a decade to complete, but his *Principles of Psychology* became one of the most influential texts in the history of the discipline, and is still in print. Over time, however, his interests shifted towards philosophy, and he finished his career in the philosophy department at Harvard. Within psychology, he is perhaps best known for coining the phrase 'the stream of consciousness'; the approach he founded, called *functionalism*, has remained influential, particularly among cognitive psychologists.

functionalism an approach to the study of behaviour pioneered by William James, which emphasizes the analysis of the processes by which the mind works, as opposed to the study of the mind's contents advocated by structuralism

structuralism an approach to psychology pioneered by Wundt which attempted to analyse the contents of the mind, using the introspectionist method

From this brief biography, and James's own comment, one might conclude that his efforts in psychology had little impact on the developing field. In fact, nothing could be further from the truth. Like his brother Henry, William James was a gifted writer, and his *Principles of Psychology* was both influential and widely read – it is probably the best-selling textbook in the history of psychology. (It is still in print.) More importantly, he was an incisive thinker, and his analysis of basic problems set the framework for later research in many areas, from emotion to consciousness. An indifferent experimentalist (although he *did* set up a laboratory for teaching purposes in 1875, the same year as Wundt), he favoured analysing how the mind functioned rather than observing its basic parts. Consequently, he expressed little interest in Wundt's approach, which he once compared to trying to understand a house by studying each of its bricks (James 1884). In turn, Wundt was less than impressed with James, saying of *Principles of Psychology*, 'It is literature, it is beautiful, but it is not psychology' (quoted by Fancher 1979: 128).

Wundt and James each played a major role in shaping the direction of psychology as a discipline. Contemporaries, they each began as a medical student and ended as a professor of philosophy (at least in title, if not content). In this sense, they highlight the double heritage of psychology – the natural sciences and philosophy. At the same time, they differed significantly in their approach to the study of behaviour and the mind. James's approach, with its emphasis on how the mind works, came to be known as **functionalism**, while Wundt's study of basic mental processes became known as **structuralism**. Wundt was a precise and prolific experimenter, while James cared little for the laboratory. Yet, taken together, they point towards two crucial aspects of modern psychology: the importance of making careful observations, and the importance of asking the proper questions. While neither man's views are accepted completely today, their efforts and insights provided much of the foundation for the new discipline. If psychologists today seem to see further than they did, it is partly because (as Isaac Newton once said of his own accomplishments) they are standing on the shoulders of giants.

Psychology, then, traces its origins to rather divergent roots. This diversity is still evident in the current form of the discipline, which extends in many directions. Today, there are individuals involved in psychology who look at everything from intracellular chemistry to the causes of forgetting to the nature of romantic love. In some cases, they may feel more comfortable talking with colleagues in other disciplines than with other types of psychologists. Some would see this as a failing, and it is *possible* that time will support that view. At present, though, one can view this diversity as simply a reflection of the complexity of both psychology's origins and its subject matter. One might draw an analogy to the medieval world view, which saw man as the measure of all things, and therefore placed humanity at the centre of the universe: psychology is clearly not the measure of all things, but it is perhaps fitting that the study of human behaviour should have links extending into all the domains of human knowledge, from natural sciences to humanities.

| **For further consideration** | William James emphasized asking good questions over gathering data; Wilhelm Wundt was concerned with gathering data. Which aspect appeals to you? If you could go back in time, which one would you rather talk to, and why? |

Methods of Studying Behaviour

The Role of the Scientific Method in Psychology

Given the complexity and diversity of human behaviour, how does one go about studying it? While the five approaches differ in the methods they emphasize, all psychologists share a belief in the observational methods of science as the foundation of psychological research. We noted earlier that psychology is distinguished from pursuits like astrology or phrenology, or even common sense wisdom like proverbs, by being a science. But what exactly does that mean?

empirical based on making observations, as in an *empirical* theory

First and foremost, psychology is **empirical** – that is, it is based on making observations. Precisely what observations researchers are interested in varies according to the approach, but there is a common emphasis on *objective* observation; normally, this means that observations can be verified by different observers. In this sense, psychology is a public endeavour, which cannot depend on secret knowledge or mystic inspiration. (More will be said about this in conjunction with introspectionism.)

The emphasis on empiricism is important, but what determines what is to be observed, and how? A friend of mine likes to 'people watch' by sitting in a pavement cafe; if I join him, does that make our observations scientific?

theory a structured set of principles intended to explain a set of phenomena

induction a process of reasoning based on forming general principles from specific observations
deduction the process of drawing specific conclusions from a set of general principles
hypothesis a statement describing a proposed relationship between two types of variables; a conclusion derived from a theory which can be evaluated by making further observations

To decide, one has to remember that the goal of psychology is to understand behaviour – and understanding requires more than a random cataloguing of observations. By itself, counting how many people go by a pavement cafe has no scientific value. At the very least, one must *classify* those observations in some way, which may lead to relating them to something else (perhaps the weather, or time of day, or some other factor). That is, science depends on organized observation, in the belief that classification of observations will ultimately lead to explaining those observations (Robinson 1985). Understanding and explanation require formulating general principles; at the highest level, a structured set of principles is called a **theory**. A theory provides a coherent structure for relating various observations, and often permits prediction of future observations. Traditionally, theories in science have explained observed events by identifying their causes; at the very least, a theory provides a way of generalizing across specific observations. Hence, observations and theories are complementary to each other.

Essentially, observations and theory are connected by two basic cognitive processes: inductive and deductive reasoning. **Induction** involves forming general principles from specific observations. The story of Isaac Newton discovering gravity by being hit by a falling apple is doubtless folklore. What is *not* folklore is that Newton saw a connection between falling apples and orbiting planets – that is, gravity was a general principle that could be used to link these observations. **Deduction**, by contrast, involves drawing specific conclusions from a set of general principles. For example, Freud believed that aggression is an innate drive which can be expressed in destructive behaviour. From this, it follows that if someone commits murder, it is because of this innate drive. Most commonly in science, deduction is used to derive a **hypothesis** – a specific conclusion from a theory which can be evaluated by making further observations.

Which comes first, you may ask, inductively forming principles from observations, or deductively deriving hypotheses to be tested by observing? In reality, this is much like the old chestnut about whether the chicken or the egg comes first: there is no clear answer. In practice, researchers use both processes, in a more or less continuous interaction (see Figure 1.7). Sometimes, past experience will lead to an interest in particular phenomena, and then observations will lead to a theoretical insight. Alternatively, thinking about a theory may lead to discovering a new implication, which then must be tested for accuracy by making appropriate observations. As we will see in the following chapters, both types of process have played important roles in the development of the five approaches. As supporters of the scientific method, all approaches share common concerns: to make careful, consistent observations, to avoid errors and to develop clear theories. Despite the general agreement on these principles, there is still room for a range of particular techniques when gathering information.

Introspectionism and Public Observation

At first glance, it might seem that the best way to learn about behaviour would be to analyse carefully your own behaviour. After all, whom do you

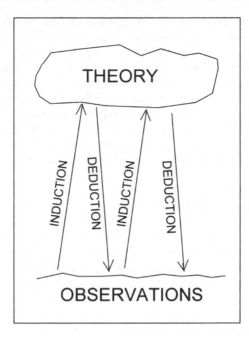

Figure 1.7   The interaction of induction and deduction in research Research involves an interaction between generalizations derived from observations (induction) and the formulation of predictions about reality derived from theory (deduction). Most researchers use both, and trying to say which comes first is rather like the question about the chicken and the egg.

introspectionism a method of gathering data in which the individual attempts to analyse the content of their conscious mind; associated with the structuralist approach

know more intimately than yourself? This approach, called **introspectionism**, was in fact used in various forms by a number of early psychologists, including Wundt and James. Despite its early popularity, introspectionism (literally, 'looking within') proved to be a questionable technique. Even when it involved carefully structured forms of self-analysis, as in Wundt's case, the method ultimately failed. In part, this was due to the limitations inherent in the perceptual process, as we have discussed. But a second weakness stems from its inherently private nature. Suppose two people, trained in Wundtian introspection, view two colour samples. One person says one is red, and one is pink – that is, they differ in one sensory characteristic, defined by colour. The other says that they are both the same colour, but that they differ in saturation (purity of the colour), with the 'pink' one being a mixture of red and white. In essence, they disagree as to whether their experience of the stimuli reflects one quality, or two. How can we resolve this dispute? One may be wrong, or each may be correct about their own experience, but since we have no way to determine, we are no closer to a general understanding of what is involved in perceiving a colour sample.

To avoid these dilemmas, psychology, like other forms of science, has come to emphasize *public* techniques of observation, which make it possible for observers to agree on what has occurred. Even so, this principle takes many forms, since researchers sometimes disagree as to what is 'public'. In general, any aspect of behaviour which can be observed consistently (that is, produces agreement among observers) is considered open for possible study. For example, an arm movement is public. Many physiological responses can also be considered 'public', in that the technologies used for measuring them produce results which observers can agree on. When one refers to mental states, it becomes more ambiguous: some psychologists believe that reports of mental states are inherently unreliable, and cannot be considered public. Others argue that as long as the *results* of such reports are consistent, then it is possible to devise public measures of mental events. For example, studies of memory depend on what people are able to report remembering, and those reports are considered a public measure of memory.

operational definition a term whose meaning is derived from the processes or observable events used to measure it

Some researchers also extend the requirement for public observation to the way terms are defined. So-called **operational definitions** must be based on observable events. For example, to define *love* as 'a feeling in the heart' is not acceptable as an operational definition, because it is not based on an observable event. However, defining it as 'giving a dozen roses to someone' is operational. The difficulty with such definitions, as this example suggests, is that sometimes an operational definition seems unrelated to the concept which it supposedly defines. Consequently, while all researchers accept the importance of using public processes to confirm observations, not all psychologists see value in operational definitions.

For further consideration

If you feel hungry, can this feeling be publicly observed? Can you think of a way to measure hunger that could qualify as a public observation?

Measures of Behaviour, Research Settings and Research Methods

In research on behaviour, there are a number of ways of gathering information. As a result, a researcher must make choices in terms of how to measure behaviour, what sort of setting to use and what type of research method to employ. In the remainder of this chapter, we will be looking at the various possibilities in some detail. However, before we do so, it is useful to describe briefly the kinds of options that exist.

self-report a method of gathering data which involves asking individuals to describe their behaviour or mental state in some way, such as an interview, survey or psychological inventory
think-aloud protocol a transcript of the comments made when individuals are asked to describe their thoughts and behaviour while working on a task such as problem solving
direct observation any observational technique which depends on direct measurement of behaviour by the researcher, rather than asking individuals to report their behaviour

Generally speaking, observation can be based on two different ways of measuring behaviour: *self-report* and *direct observation*. **Self-report** involves asking the person to indicate his or her behaviour or mental state in some way. Self-report procedures are used in many situations, but most commonly in interviews, surveys and psychological testing. For example, a survey might ask individuals how often they consume alcohol. Self-report has the attraction of seeming very direct, and in some cases it allows researchers to access information which is otherwise unobtainable. For example, in cognitive research, experimenters may ask people to think aloud while trying to solve a problem. The comments are transcribed as **think-aloud protocols**, which may reveal information about the participants' thought processes.

The alternative to self-report procedures is for researchers to use **direct observation** of the behaviour of interest; in this case, the researcher observes behaviour in some way that does not depend on what the individual says. Direct observation by an independent person tends to be more neutral or objective than self-report, and is more easily verified by having multiple observers. Overall, observation is used most frequently in experiments, although observational methods take many forms, as we will see. The choice to use self-report or direct observation as a method of measuring behaviour represents one of the basic decisions a researcher must make when beginning the study of a particular issue. In addition, there are decisions about what type of setting to use, and the type of research method.

The choice of **research setting** concerns whether to observe behaviour in a *laboratory setting*, which involves having participants come to a special location (the laboratory), or in a *field setting*, which requires studying people in their natural environment. In a laboratory setting, it is possible to create particular conditions, in order to see how people behave in that situation. However, bringing individuals to a laboratory is also somewhat artificial, since participants will be very aware of being observed. By contrast, a field setting is more natural, but necessarily more difficult to control. For example, a researcher may be interested in how children interact while playing. Bringing them into a laboratory would make it possible to control what toys are available and other factors, but may also lead to non-spontaneous behaviour. By contrast, going to a playground to observe such interactions would be more natural, but would allow no control over what was played, by whom, or for how long, thus making comparisons more difficult. Hence, each type of setting has advantages and disadvantages.

The choice of setting is often closely linked to the **research method** chosen. An *experiment* is a procedure whereby a researcher systematically varies one or more factors in order to see what effect the changes have on behaviour. For example, in order to examine the effects of alcohol on coordination, a researcher might systematically vary the amount of alcohol which different subjects consume in the experiment. Experiments are normally conducted in a laboratory setting, since this normally makes it easier to control the factors one wishes to systematically vary. **Non-experimental methods**, sometimes called descriptive/correlational designs, do not involve direct control of any factor, in contrast to experiments. For example, testing individuals' coordination before and after they visit a bar would not provide any direct control over how much alcohol people drank. Consequently, such comparisons would not directly tell us anything about how *alcohol* affects coordination. Non-experimental methods include naturalistic observation, case studies and surveys, among others. *Quasi-experiments*, as the name suggests, are similar to experiments, but do not provide the same degree of control. Typically, quasi-experiments are used when studying characteristics which cannot be manipulated by the researcher (such as gender, age or medical condition), or in circumstances where manipulation would be unethical (e.g. getting people to smoke in order to see if smoking causes health problems).

The three characteristics of research – method, setting and measurement type – can be used to describe virtually all the techniques used in psychological research. As we consider some specific techniques, you should ask yourself where they fit in terms of these characteristics.

At this point, the description of research techniques may seem very abstract. Why, for example, would a researcher choose to use self-report in

research setting the context in which research is conducted, either a *laboratory setting* (which involves having participants come to a special location) or a *field setting* (which requires studying people in their natural environment)

research method a procedure for examining a problem and gathering observations; in broad terms, research methods are either experimental or non-experimental

non-experimental methods research methods which do not involve direct control of any factor, in contrast to experiments; sometimes called descriptive/correlational designs

a particular situation? To understand how psychologists make such decisions, let us consider a real-world problem: why do people help or not in an emergency? In recent years, there have been all-too-frequent reports in the news media of situations where someone is in trouble, and onlookers don't get involved. In one well-known case, a young woman named Kitty Genovese was on her way home from her job as a waitress in a New York restaurant. It was late, and the street was virtually deserted as she neared the building where she lived. Unfortunately, before she reached it, a man attacked her, stabbing her. She screamed, and her assailant ran off. Before she could reach home or other shelter, he returned. This time, a man leaned from his apartment window to yell at the attacker, who then retreated again. Kitty then tried to seek refuge in the lobby of an apartment building, only to be attacked again. Sadly, she died from the attack (Latané and Darley 1969).

As shocking as this story is, most people were more shocked to learn that despite her screams, *no one telephoned the police*, even though the whole sequence took nearly 40 minutes. At first glance, it appears to be a case of utter callousness: someone must have heard; why wouldn't they call? The police and reporters combed the area to seek witnesses, and found 38 people living close to the scene who acknowledged having been at home at the time. (One man said the sound of his window air conditioner blocked outside noise – on a night when it was nearly freezing!) Obviously, none of these people phoned the police. How can we understand this? Is it really the result of callousness and apathy? The tragic death of Kitty Genovese, and other similar incidents, led to the coining of a new term, **bystander apathy**, used to describe situations where people do not intervene in an emergency. For researchers, as for society in general, the challenge is to understand why such incidents happen; ideally, such understanding might lead to ways of increasing helping behaviour in the future. Faced with a problem like this, it is possible to proceed in many ways. Let us explore this situation further, seeing how psychologists might try to learn more about the underlying behaviour.

bystander apathy the failure of onlookers to intervene in an emergency; despite the label, the cause is often unrelated to apathy

For further consideration

Based on what has been said so far, do you think that self-reports or direct observation provide a more accurate means of determining how someone behaves; or how someone feels or thinks?

Interviews and Surveys as Self-report Procedures

interview a method of gathering data in which a researcher asks an individual questions; the format may be pre-planned and highly structured, or relatively free-flowing and unstructured

The police and reporters in the Kitty Genovese case used one possible method: **interviews**. In an interview, a researcher asks questions, which may be pre-planned and highly structured, or relatively free-flowing and unstructured. The responses from the person interviewed represent *self-report* data, since the person is describing his or her own behaviour. In the Genovese case, for example, a number of the people interviewed reported hearing the screams, or even watching the attack from their windows, and wondering why the police hadn't arrived. Rather than being apathetic, these people seemed very upset. When questioned as to why they hadn't phoned the police, these people typically stated that they *assumed* someone *else* had done so already. Of course, the reality was that no one had. Assuming the self-reports were accurate (as opposed to being a rationalization for not having helped), the interviews showed that these people had failed to phone because of a faulty assumption, *not* because they were apathetic. By suggesting an alternative to apathy as an explanation of the incident, the self-reports were very useful.

Another approach to the issue of bystander apathy would be to do a survey. A **survey** is a technique for determining the attitudes of a large number of people. Some surveys use predetermined response options; this is commonly called a *fixed-alternative* survey. For example, a researcher might ask, 'Would you be willing to aid a stranger in distress?', and allow the answers, 'Yes', 'No' or 'I'm not sure.' To provide a bit more choice, the researcher might give a rating scale, with several options, from very positive to very negative. The fixed-alternative technique has several advantages, including being easy to administer and easy to analyse. Its major limitation is that it allows little flexibility in answers, and thereby limits how much information can be obtained from respondents; in the worst case, the questions and response alternatives are seen as inappropriate by the person responding.

By contrast, *open-ended* surveys use skilled interviewers; they ask pre-arranged questions, but allow the respondent to give a spontaneous answer. At first glance, this may seem more useful than a survey with fixed alternatives, but it has several drawbacks. First, it requires a skilled interviewer to get clear responses without coaching or leading the person answering. (Coaching could of course lead to **bias**, a systematic distortion of results.) Second, it takes considerable effort to analyse the sometimes lengthy responses, and it becomes difficult to summarize responses from a large group of people. Even if one is willing to face these obstacles, responses may not always be very meaningful. In one survey which asked people 'What do you think is the most pressing problem facing the world today?', the majority of responses simply restated the day's newspaper headlines! Without adequate time to reflect on the questions, there is a danger of such superficial responses; the more complex the issue, the greater this problem is likely to be. In such cases, a series of carefully developed fixed-alternative questions may actually give more meaningful information about people's views than will open-ended questions.

Surveys, even when open-ended, are more structured than interviews, and are employed to gather information from a relatively large number of individuals. Today, surveys are used extensively by government, political parties, corporations, the news media and other groups. Sometimes it seems we are bombarded by reports of survey results, many of which are less than insightful. (Does it surprise you, for example, that immediately after the Berlin Wall went down, most Germans were optimistic about the future of their country, as one survey reported?)

Surveys and Sampling Procedures

Whether the issues are earthshaking or trivial, all surveys face a common problem: who to survey? At first glance, this may seem very straightforward

survey a technique for determining attitudes of many individuals by providing a pre-planned series of questions to which individuals respond

bias a source of error which results in a systematic distortion of results

population in statistics, the group whose characteristics one wishes to determine, and from which a sample is chosen

sample in statistics, a sub-group drawn from a population; in research, the group which one actually studies

representative sample in statistics, a sample whose composition matches the population from which it is drawn

– simply select a large number of people. Unfortunately, large numbers do not guarantee that a survey will provide meaningful results. To understand why, we need to consider two concepts: population and sample. A **population** is the group whose views one wishes to determine; a **sample** is the subgroup of the population which one actually studies. For example, if a political party wished to determine the attitudes of Canadian voters towards the Prime Minister, the population would be all Canadians eligible to vote. Since contacting some 15 million people would obviously be impossible, the researchers must use a smaller sample group. (In a case like this, they would probably contact between 200 and 1,000 people, depending on the number of sub-groups and desired variance.) In selecting a sample, the goal is to obtain a **representative sample** – that is, one which fairly represents the population of interest – and thereby reduce the likelihood of bias in the results. In the case of the election poll, suppose the researcher went to a large shopping centre in Toronto at lunch time, and stopped every third person that went by. This procedure would not result in a representative sample, since not all Canadian voters are likely to be found at that site. While various techniques exist for selecting a sample, they all share the goal of seeking a balanced representation of the population of interest. (For more information about sampling, see the Appendix.)

As you might expect, sampling procedures in surveys (and in other forms of research) always have some potential for error. In order to deal with this, proper surveys always calculate the probable margin of error, and report this with the results. If you don't see such figures indicated, be cautious – especially in comparing numbers which are close in size. For example, an election survey reported the percentage of people who favoured each political party in an upcoming election (Toulin 1993). In this survey, the margin of error was ±2 per cent, meaning that if a reported value was 12 per cent, the actual figure in the population was likely to be between 10 and 14 per cent. In this case, the margin of error meant that the difference between the third place party (12 per cent) and the fifth placed party (8 per cent) was more apparent than real.

Obviously, the process of obtaining a sample for a survey is not a simple matter, and one must be cautious in looking at survey results – especially when the numbers are taken out of context. Nonetheless, when properly conducted, surveys provide an excellent tool for determining the views of a large group of people.

Limitations of Self-reports

Self-report procedures like interviews and surveys are an important method of measuring behaviour; but their use also poses some problems. One basic concern is with accuracy – is self-report an accurate reflection of behaviour? After all, individuals may not always be clear about their own behaviour, because of lapses of attention, memory distortions or other factors. This problem was highlighted by a classic study of racial discrimination, which examined attitudes of restaurant and hotel owners to racial minorities (LaPiere 1934). (Because the study was done in the United States in the 1930s, human rights legislation was not a strong governing factor.) Travelling across the country with a young Chinese couple, LaPiere kept records of their experiences. Out of 251 establishments visited, only *one* refused to serve the couple (who typically went in first). Six months after their trip, a letter asking about policies was sent to the same establishments. The letter asked, 'Will you accept members of the Chinese race in your establishment?' Overall, 51 per cent replied to the letter, and of these, 92 per cent said they would *not* serve Chinese people. In this case, the owners *said* they were more discriminatory than they actually *behaved*! More commonly, a person may lie to a researcher in order to create a more favourable impression. For example, the man who said his air conditioner prevented him from hearing anything when Kitty Genovese was attacked was presumably lying, given the cold weather; in this case, the lie served to justify his failure to intervene. Because of such uncertainties, researchers using self-report procedures must always consider the possibility that what people report is not what they do (Wicker 1971).

Naturalistic Observation and Unobtrusive Measures

naturalistic observation
a research method which is based on observing behaviour in a natural setting, without interfering or attempting to control conditions

Since self-reports may be distorted in various ways, one might prefer to study behaviour through direct observation. One form of direct observation is **naturalistic observation**, which, as the name suggests, involves observing behaviour in a natural setting. Depending on the type of behaviour a researcher is interested in, this technique may be relatively simple or quite difficult. In the case of bystander apathy, a major hurdle is the unpredictability of emergencies, which makes it nearly impossible for a researcher to be present as events unfold. When the behaviour of interest is more frequent and/or more predictable, naturalistic observation has the advantage of presenting behaviour in a real-world context. Observing in a natural setting avoids the potential artificiality of the laboratory, and for many behaviours, such as social interactions, this can be a great benefit.

At the same time, naturalistic observation has some limitations. One obvious concern, referred to earlier, is *reactivity*: when people know they are being watched, they may act differently. In practice, this is often not a serious concern, since there are a number of ways to conceal the observation process. One technique, made famous by the television show *Candid Camera*, is to use a hidden camera. In other cases, researchers will be able to use a one-way mirror, or other form of blind, to make their presence less noticeable. (The day-care centre at my university has a one-way mirror, allowing students in the early learning programme to observe the children at play.) Sometimes, simply staying in a situation long enough to make one's presence familiar is sufficient to reduce reactivity. Alan King, a Canadian documentary filmmaker, is noted for spending weeks or months with the people he wishes to film. He has commented, 'I carry the camera from day one, but there's no film in it for the first week or so. After that, they're so used to it, they forget about my presence' (in one memorable film, *A Married Couple*, King ended up recording the break-up of a marriage) (King 1971).

participant observation
a non-experimental research method in which the researcher becomes part of a group he or she wishes to observe

Very close to King's approach is a variation of naturalistic observation called participant observation. In **participant observation**, the researcher becomes part of a group he or she wishes to observe. One example is described in *Among the Thugs*, in which author Bill Buford joined a group of English rowdies to learn more about fan violence (Buford 1991). His involvement became so intense that he was injured during a post-game riot! Apart from personal risk, participant observation also poses a risk of biasing the results, since the researcher's interaction with the group may alter what would otherwise occur. In addition, as involvement with the group increases, the researcher's objectivity is likely to be reduced.

unobtrusive measure an indirect measure of behaviour intended to avoid the reactivity which can occur with direct observation; such measures typically require making complex assumptions about the relationship of the measure to actual behaviour

In order to avoid the problem of reactivity, researchers will sometimes use **unobtrusive measures** as a means of recording behaviour. As the name implies, unobtrusive measures involve recording behaviour indirectly, rather than possibly disrupting it by direct observation. Examples include checking the frequency of borrowing of various library books as a means of determining which is most popular, or checking sales of travel insurance after an airline crash to measure changes in anxiety among travellers (Webb *et al.* 1972). Inventing unobtrusive ways to measure various behaviours can be a creative exercise, but such measures can also be very difficult to interpret. In one instance, an archaeologist attempted to determine whether men or women lived longer in ancient Rome by counting the number of tombstones for each sex. The assumption was that among married couples, the first to die would be more likely to receive a tombstone; thus, finding more tombstones for men meant women lived longer! Of course, this ignores a wide number of possible factors, from cultural norms about death to the impact of war on male mortality rates. Consequently, when using unobtrusive measures, there is always a need to make sure the characteristic observed is in fact measuring what one intends.

For further consideration

Imagine you want to measure soft drink preferences unobtrusively. What would you use as a measure? Could the results reflect something other than taste preferences?

Case Studies

case study a detailed description of a single individual, typically used to provide information on the person's history and to aid in interpreting the person's behaviour

One of the most fascinating aspects of psychology for many readers is the use of case studies. A **case study** is a detailed description of a single individual. Like a well-written biography, a good case study seems to capture the essence of a particular person's behaviour. While this sense of drama is certainly one of the attractions of case studies for general readers, the value of the case study method as a research tool stems from the contextual detail it provides on the behaviour of an individual. Case studies basically arose out of medical practice, where developing a clear picture of a patient's background and current symptoms formed an important diagnostic tool. Many basic advances in psychological understanding have come from case studies, particularly in the area of brain function. For example, the discovery of the speech area in the brain came about through the study of a patient who lost the ability to speak after a head injury. (See Chapter 2 for more detail.) Case studies are found in other areas as well. For example, Sigmund Freud (whose training was in medicine) emphasized case studies as a basic tool of psychoanalysis.

An effective case study can aid in treatment, and can also deepen our insight into behaviour in general. However, like other methods, case studies have their limitations. One important concern is representativeness: a case study is essentially a sample of one, and consequently, a researcher must be careful in generalizing to a larger population. For example, if a researcher studying Kitty Genovese's death focused on a single observer to the crime, the person might or might not reflect how other observers reacted. Fortunately, in many situations, the important aspects of a case may well be applicable to a broader group – for example, when studying basic neurological functions. (One of my early psychology mentors, whose specialization was the visual system, used to comment, 'In physiology, a sample of one is sufficient.') Unfortunately, one cannot always be certain whether a case is representative or not. In one well-known instance, Russian neurologist A. R. Luria reported on a man who had a remarkable memory – so remarkable, that he essentially never forgot *anything* (Luria 1968). In fact, the man (referred to as S) would write down things which he *wanted* to forget, in the hope that his mind would no longer be obliged to retain them! As Luria studied S, he discovered that he was also unusual in that his senses appeared 'cross-wired': sounds could create visual images, and had textures and colours as well. This sensory linkage, called *synaesthesia*, apparently was a factor in his unusual memory. Luria's account makes remarkable reading, but it is not clear how relevant the case is to our general understanding of either memory or sensory functioning. Such cases are extremely rare. Richard Cytowic, an American neurologist who has studied another individual with synesthesia, estimates that fewer than ten people in a million show any real indications of the phenomenon (Cytowic 1993). Consequently, such cases seem rather unrepresentative. As disappointing as this is, it does point out one of the ways that researchers evaluate representativeness – by looking for similar cases. If similar cases are found, this bolsters the representativeness of the behaviour.

A second limitation of most case studies is not so easily remedied. By their nature, clinical cases arise when someone seeks treatment; as a result, the doctor/researcher is presented with a situation whose causes are not directly known. (One of the purposes of developing a clinical history, of course, is to try to learn what preceded the current situation.) This frequently limits the ability to draw conclusions about causation, particularly for behaviour. For example, a doctor examines a teenage boy who has been in trouble with both school officials and the police. The case history reveals that the boy's delivery at birth was difficult, and may have resulted in minor brain damage. The boy's mother died when he was seven, and his father, who has remarried, is emotionally remote and physically abusive. Which of these factors, if any, account for the boy's current problems? In this type of situation, it is difficult to draw clear conclusions. In particular, there is a risk of confusing factors which may be significant with those which may be coincidental. Even in situations where some type of pre- and post-treatment comparisons might be possible, ethical standards require that concerns for the patient's well-being transcend any research goals. Consequently, case studies can be helpful in suggesting further directions for research, but are generally a poor tool for understanding the *causes* of behaviour.

In an unusual case study, a woman art teacher was reported to be able to memorize visual images in extraordinary detail, after only brief exposure. After extensive searching, no one else was found who could match her ability. Do you think this case should have been explored more extensively, or rejected as too unrepresentative? What if other individuals showed similar, but lesser, ability?

Correlational Research

Like surveys and naturalistic observation, most case studies represent non-experimental forms of research. Typically, the purpose of a case study is simply *descriptive*, to provide an accurate portrait of behaviour in a particular situation. While accurate descriptions of behaviour are an important starting point in research, description cannot conclusively tell us *why* behaviour occurs. Instead, a researcher may look for patterns which link different aspects of behaviour, such as age and willingness to help in an emergency. Any characteristic which can vary (like age) is called a **variable**; a pattern observed between two variables is called a **correlation**. Thus, if a person's willingness to help is related to their age, then this would represent a correlation. This correlational approach is commonly used in non-experimental studies, since finding patterns is one of the important ways of increasing our understanding of behaviour. Correlational methods are used to identify possible relationships between factors being studied (in the example above, age and probability of helping).

Correlations can enable researchers to make sense out of what might otherwise seem a jumble of data. For example, Figure 1.8 shows performance on a term examination compared to term paper grades for students in a course I recently taught. In this situation, I wanted to see how performance on the exam compared to that on the papers, since the scores reflect different types of assessment. By using a measurement called a **correlation coefficient**, it is possible to show that there is a moderately strong relationship between the two variables – that is, students tended to get similar grades on the two evaluations. Without the aid of correlational techniques, it would be difficult to know if there is a pattern or not. Thus, a researcher looking for links between measured variables can find correlations very helpful. (For a more detailed discussion of correlations and how they are measured, see the Appendix.)

The desire to find patterns in observational data is part of a larger goal, which is to understand how and why behaviour occurs. In fact, the desire to find correlations as a way of making sense of what we observe is not restricted to researchers. Studies have shown that the search for patterns is a natural human trait. Most of the time, finding patterns in our environment is adaptive – for instance, a young child quickly learns that brightly glowing objects, like stove burners and lights, are usually hot. Unfortunately, sometimes we see patterns where none actually exists; when this happens, it is called an **illusory correlation** (Halpern 1989). B. F. Skinner, the behaviourist, has suggested that many forms of superstitious behaviour arise when people falsely perceive connections between their behaviour and a desired

variable any measured characteristic which shows variation across cases or conditions

correlation a pattern or relationship observed between two variables

correlation coefficient a descriptive statistic measuring the degree of relationship between two variables. For positive correlations, it is a number which varies between 0.0 and +1.0, and for negative correlations between 0.0 and −1.0; in both cases, the closer the value is to 1, the stronger the relationship between the two variables

illusory correlation a cognitive error in which an individual perceives a relationship between variables where none actually exists

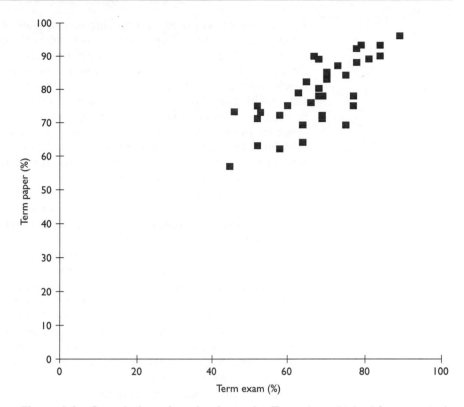

Figure 1.8 Correlation of academic grades These data, obtained from an actual class, show that there is a positive correlation (+0.75) between performance on term exams and on term papers.

or feared outcome (Skinner 1948a). In essence, such superstitions arise out of illusory correlations. (My favourite example from everyday life is what people do while waiting for elevator doors to close: often they tap the edge of the door, push the 'close' button repeatedly or engage in other actions which may actually do nothing to alter the programmed cycle of the elevator. Yet, because the action sometimes coincides with the doors closing, the person becomes convinced it worked!) Hence, while seeking patterns can be useful, in everyday life we should be wary of our tendency to see patterns even where none exist.

While finding patterns can help us to make sense of the world, correlations are limited in what they can tell us. The most important limitation concerns explaining *why* an observed pattern occurs. Ideally, we would like to be able to say something like 'A causes B' when we observe a correlation between variables A and B. Unfortunately, a correlation does *not* prove causation. In the above example, rather than exam performance directly causing term paper performance (or vice versa), it is likely that there are underlying factors (e.g. ability and hard work) that affect both types of grades.

It can be very tempting to draw conclusions about cause and effect when we see a pattern in events, but this is also a very error-prone process. For example, most people know that different species of birds have distinctly different songs – robins versus sparrows versus finches, for instance. That is, there is a relationship between song type and species. From this, one might conclude that each species sings its particular song *because* of its species (that is, that the song is genetically programmed). While this is consistent with everyday observations and plausible in terms of genetic theory, in fact it is wrong – birdsong requires *learning*, somewhat like human language does (Marler 1970). Or consider this example: a study done in Hamburg, Germany, found that over a period of years, there was a correlation between the number of storks nesting in the city and the number of human babies born. That is, more storks were found nesting in those years in which more human babies were born. Obviously, folk tales about storks bringing babies are not true, despite this observed pattern! (The reason for this pattern *may* be a series of underlying links in terms of storks choosing chimneys as nesting sites, and the number of chimneys increasing as human population grows – *or* it may be coincidence!)

In the end, finding a correlational pattern doesn't tell us *why* the pattern occurred; further research is required to find out its origin. Generally, one of three possible explanations applies: (a) one variable actually causes changes in the other; (b) there is a third factor linking the observed variables (for example, ability in the case of student grades); or (c) the observed pattern is really coincidental, and would not reoccur in a new set of similar observations. While one might gather further information by doing additional descriptive or correlational research, the best way to address questions of causation is by doing experiments.

For further consideration

The 'speak of the devil effect' refers to a phenomenon where you are talking about a friend, when suddenly they either appear or call on the telephone. Given the three possible explanations of correlations, how would you interpret this pattern?

Experiments

All the methods we have discussed thus far, from interviews to naturalistic observation, share the same limitation: they cannot answer questions about the causes of behaviour. In large part, this stems from the complexity of behaviour, and the many possible influences on it. For example, let us consider again the case of clever Hans, the 'educated' horse. As was described in the introduction to this chapter, Hans's owner spent several years trying to teach him mathematics, geography and other information, and seemed to have succeeded: Hans was able to answer questions correctly by tapping his foot to spell words, or shaking his head to answer yes or no. Finally, after Hans had become rather famous, a psychologist named Oskar Pfungst came to observe (Pfungst 1911).

Mr von Osten, the horse's owner, had already invited a number of psychologists and animal trainers to observe Hans, and all had come away convinced that the horse's ability was real. Pfungst was sceptical, however, and asked to be allowed to perform some simple experiments. One experiment showed that Hans could still perform if his owner was absent (thus ruling out fraud by the owner). A second test involved comparing how Hans performed with or without a blindfold. The results led to the conclusion that Hans used some sort of visual cues to determine his responses, since his performance was poor when wearing a blindfold. Eventually, by varying the conditions, Pfungst was able to identify the mechanism by which Hans figured out answers: members of the audience who knew the answer would unconsciously make minor head and facial movements in anticipation of Hans's response (e.g. slightly tilting the head down when expecting him to tap). While the cues varied from person to person, the general conclusion was supported by a further experiment, in which no one in the horse's view knew the answer; under these conditions, Hans could not answer correctly. Thus, rather than learning maths, history and geography, Hans had learned to read non-verbal cues in the onlookers, as a way of getting rewards of praise and carrots!

What is most striking in this story is how successful Hans was, and how long it took to discover the truth. Note that his owner was *not* engaged in deliberate fraud: he genuinely believed Hans was clever, and encouraged scientists and others to find an explanation. Only Pfungst was able to do so – by conducting a series of experiments. **Experiments**, unlike the most careful of descriptive and correlational methods, allow us to manipulate and control conditions in ways that make determining causation possible. In essence, these two factors – manipulation of a variable of interest, and control of factors that might confuse the situation – are what distinguish experimental methods from other forms of research. The experiments that Pfungst did all involved testing the same subject (Hans) under various conditions (e.g. with or without a blindfold). This is an example of a *within-subject design*, involving comparisons of the same individual (or group of individuals) under different conditions. As we will see, most experiments involve comparing different groups of individuals, a procedure called a *between-groups design*. Since Pfungst did his tests in Hans's ordinary environment, it represents an example of a **field experiment** (as compared to experiments done in a *laboratory setting*).

In any experiment, the researcher begins with a *hypothesis*, a statement describing a proposed relationship between two types of variables; the experiment is then designed as a way of testing the accuracy of this hypothesis. One type of variable, called an **independent variable**, is controlled by the researcher, in order to see what effect it has on behaviour. For example, Pfungst looked at the effect of Hans wearing a blindfold versus no blindfold. The other type of variable, called a **dependent variable**, is a measure of the behaviour under study. In Pfungst's experiments, the dependent variable was always whether Hans answered correctly or not. In the most simple form of experiment, there is a single independent and a single dependent variable, although, as we will see, more complex designs are frequently used.

In order to see how researchers use experiments to test hypotheses, let us return to the problem of bystander apathy. As you may recall, the results of interviews with nearby residents indicated that although no one intervened, those who observed the attack on Kitty Genovese were hardly apathetic about the experience. Faced with the phenomenon that people seemed concerned, but did not react, social psychologists Bibb Latané and John Darley

experiment a research design in which the experimenter uses a controlled situation and manipulates one or more factors (called *independent variables*) in order to determine their effect on one or more measures of behaviour (called *dependent variables*)

field experiment an experiment done in a natural setting, usually without the explicit awareness of participants; as contrasted to experiments done in a laboratory setting

independent variable a variable in an experiment which is systematically varied by the researcher, in order to see what effect it has on behaviour

dependent variable in an experiment, the behaviour measured in order to evaluate the effects of the independent variable

decided to explore the issue further (Latané and Darley 1969). As was noted previously, the interviews suggested that most people assumed *some-one else* had already telephoned the police. Given that several apartment buildings overlooked the location, it seemed reasonable for someone to imagine that other people were also aware of the attack, and therefore that others would have telephoned already. This meant that people had acted according to what they thought others were doing. Latané and Darley recognized that emergencies represent an unfamiliar and sometimes ambiguous situation, and that in such circumstances people often guide their behaviour by what others do. Consequently, the researchers decided to explore the effects of the presence of others on behaviour in an emergency. They did a series of experiments, of which we will discuss two.

The first experiment was done in a laboratory, and was dubbed 'A Lady in Distress'. Participants were recruited through ads asking for volunteers to take part in a consumer research study. (Latané and Darley recognized that telling people the true purpose of the study might distort their responses.) **Subjects** (the term refers to participants in research) either came alone or came with a friend; if alone, they found another volunteer, a confederate of the experimenters who was pretending to be a volunteer, or no one. These variations represented the levels of the independent variable – being alone, with a friend, with a stranger or with a stooge. Latané and Darley wanted to see what effect these variations had on the likelihood of someone intervening in a (staged) emergency: the measure of intervention became the dependent variable. In this experiment, the emergency involved an apparent injury to the woman conducting the consumer survey. When the subjects arrived, they were greeted by a woman wearing a white lab coat, who gave them a questionnaire, and then went into the next room. Through the partially opened door, subjects could hear the sounds of someone climbing on a chair, and then a crash, followed by a scream and sounds of evident distress. If you were sitting in the waiting room, would you go to help? Would it matter to you if a friend or stranger was present? What do you think Latané and Darley found?

The primary measure of helping behaviour was whether subjects did anything to intervene, ranging from going next door to simply calling out. (Latané and Darley also measured a second dependent variable, how long subjects waited before responding. While we will not discuss the results for this variable here, it is worth noting that experiments can have more than one dependent variable.) The main result was that individuals who were alone were the most likely to help: 70 per cent intervened. Groups consisting of two friends also showed a 70 per cent response rate, but since there were two people present, this is actually lower than would be expected if they acted independently. (Probability theory says the likelihood that at least one would respond, given the 70 per cent figure for a single person, is 91 per cent.) When two strangers witnessed the emergency, only 40 per cent of the time did one or both react (again, this is significantly less than the 91 per cent expected if they acted independently). When a stooge was present who deliberately ignored the emergency, the rate of intervention by subjects dropped to 7 per cent! Clearly, in this situation, the presence of another person reduced the rate of intervention.

subject in research, an individual who is the object of study or the participant in an experiment

Despite the relatively high level of response by individuals who were alone, Latané and Darley were concerned that the situation may have been too artificial. After all, the participants had come to a laboratory for a form of psychological research; maybe they were suspicious. While it would be difficult to conduct research on bystander apathy without some form of deception, Latané and Darley felt that the use of a laboratory design may have limited the usefulness of the research in terms of what is called external validity. **External validity** concerns the degree to which one can generalize the results beyond the specific situation. Obviously, if participants saw this situation as different from other types of emergencies, the experiment would have low external validity.

Faced with this concern, Latané and Darley decided to try a further experiment, which would be a *field experiment*. Like naturalistic observation, field experiments are done in a natural setting, without telling participants that their behaviour is being observed. Unlike naturalistic observation, field experiments involve the same elements of manipulation and control which are found in laboratory experiments. In this case, Latané and Darley decided to examine how people respond to a perceived theft in a store. Dubbed 'The Case of the Stolen Beer', the experiment involved repeatedly staging a 'theft' at a store selling beer in suburban New Jersey. (The store operator, of course, was a knowing participant, and the 'thieves' were actually confederates of the researchers.) As in the previous experiment, Latané and Darley were interested in the influence of another person's presence on response rates, but in this case, they also added a second independent variable: the number of robbers (one or two). As before, their hypothesis was that an individual would be more likely to intervene when alone than when others were present. The 'robbery' scenario was rehearsed to be consistent: while one or two customers (remember, the number of people present is an independent variable) were in the store, the robber (or robbers) would enter, ask the lone clerk for an item not on display, and while the clerk went to check the storeroom, the robbers would glance around, pick up a case of beer from a floor display, and walk out. When the clerk returned, he would ask the other customers if they'd seen what happened to the now-disappeared person(s). The customers, of course, did not know this was a staged event; from their point of view, the robbery was genuine. To measure rates of helping (the dependent variable), Latané and Darley defined helping as telling the clerk about the theft. (They felt it was unreasonable to insist on actively attempting to prevent the theft!)

One of the challenges of doing field experiments is the need to preserve consistency of conditions, while at the same time not revealing to participants that an experiment is in progress. (Note that, as in the previous study, this involved an element of deception.) In order to fulfil the conditions of the Latané and Darley experiment, it was necessary that the number of customers required (one or two) not change during the staging of the robbery; thus, if a customer entered or left the store *during* the scenario, the staging was aborted. While a number of aborted trials were necessary, eventually the researchers obtained results from 92 trials, half involving one customer, and half involving two. Since the customers did not know the robbery was staged, a secondary concern was to prevent harm to the confederates who

external validity an assessment of the degree to which one can generalize research results beyond the specific situation

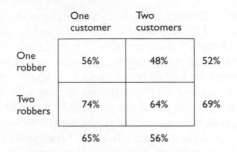

	One customer	Two customers	
One robber	56%	48%	52%
Two robbers	74%	64%	69%
	65%	56%	

Figure 1.9 Latané and Darley's field experiment This experiment actually used two independent variables: the number of customers present and the number of robbers involved. As the table shows, both variables had an influence, with people being most likely to report the theft when it was a single customer faced with two robbers. (Data from Latané and Darley 1969.)

were acting as robbers. Fortunately, no one attempted any heroic intervention that posed risk to those involved.

What would *you* do if you witnessed a theft like this? Would you attempt to stop the thieves, tell the clerk or pretend you didn't notice the theft? The results from The Stolen Beer experiment are shown in Figure 1.9. Note that the data are presented in a two-dimensional table, because there are two independent variables: the number of customers (subjects), and the number of robbers (confederates). Look carefully at the results: note that overall, people were more likely to respond when there were two robbers rather than one! Why do you think this was the case? (One possibility overlooked by Latané and Darley is that failure to intervene actively was *easier to justify* when there were two robbers because of the increased risks, so that customers were more willing to admit having seen the robbery in this circumstance.) Moreover, the pattern found in the previous study was supported: people are more likely to intervene when alone than when others are present.

The experiments by Latané and Darley thus support the hypothesis that the presence of others reduces helping behaviour in emergencies. This takes us a step further than the interview data or naturalistic observation, in suggesting that it is not apathy, but a social process of some sort, that inhibits helping behaviour. What exactly is the nature of that social process? Latané and Darley offered two possibilities: diffusion of responsibility, and social influence. **Diffusion of responsibility**, which can occur in any group situation, including committees, is the tendency to feel less personal responsibility when others are also perceived as responsible. (This is consistent with the reports in the Kitty Genovese case, when people assumed someone else must have called the police. While no real group existed, people apparently *perceived* themselves as part of a social unit defined by the locale.) **Social influence**, which is more subtle, reflects how others affect our behaviour – such as the tendency to look to others for guidance when facing an unfamiliar situation. For example, if you were at a formal banquet, and were uncertain which fork to use for the salad, you might try to see what fork other people were using. Unfortunately, the experiments described above cannot determine which of these two explanations is more important, though

diffusion of responsibility a lessening of an individual's feeling of responsibility in a situation which involves other people

social influence a general term for the various ways in which an individual's behaviour is affected by others, such as conformity pressures and social expectations and norms

social influence seems less likely than diffusion of responsibility as an explanation in this situation, since the people who saw the Genovese murder were isolated from each other. (Subsequent work has indicated that in fact *both* factors play a role in most emergency situations, as will be discussed in Chapter 8.) What the research *does* tell us is that 'bystander apathy' is a misnomer, since people who don't intervene behave that way for reasons very different from lack of concern.

<table>
<tr><td>

For further consideration

</td><td>

Do you think that the experiments by Latané and Darley are plausible as a means of studying bystander apathy? Would naturalistic observation during real emergencies be better in your view? Why or why not?

</td></tr>
</table>

Quasi-experiments

Although experiments provide a powerful tool for exploring the causes of behaviour, it is not always possible to do experiments, for practical or ethical reasons. For example, it is unethical to perform experiments which might violate individuals' basic human rights. (Note that the customers in the second Latané and Darley experiment were not asked if they wished to participate; by some standards, this creates a violation of their rights.) Apart from ethical concerns (which will be discussed below), it is not always possible to establish the control of a variable which is required for a true experiment. For example, experiments which compare different groups of subjects (called 'between-subjects designs') require that subjects be randomly assigned to the various groups (Jones 1995). Yet if a variable like age, sex or height is being studied, the researcher clearly cannot alter the characteristics of an individual in order to create random groups. To deal with these situations, researchers use a method called a **quasi-experiment** (Campbell and Stanley 1966). In a quasi-experiment, the subjects are assigned to groups according to the particular characteristic under study (for example, men versus women, or smokers versus non-smokers). In this type of situation, any observed differences in behaviour may be due to *either* the identified characteristic, *or* some other systematic difference between the groups. (For example, smokers may tend to exercise less than non-smokers.) Clearly, quasi-experiments do not provide as clear an outcome as do true experiments, but they offer a middle ground between experiments and correlational methods.

quasi-experiment a research design in which subjects are assigned to groups based on variables which cannot be manipulated by the researcher (e.g. age, sex)

To understand better how quasi-experiments work, let us consider an example related to sexual roles (this topic, and the study, will also be discussed in Chapter 8). People have long debated whether homosexuality is innate or learned. A study by LeVay attempted to address this by looking for structural differences in a part of the brain called the hypothalamus, which is believed to play a role in sexual behaviour (LeVay 1993). Because of the measurement techniques used, the study required using brains of individuals who had died. To determine sexual orientation (and thus determine which group each brain belonged to), LeVay used *case study* data indicating whether the individuals were known to have been homosexual, or presumed to have been heterosexual. As a control group, LeVay also examined the brains of women who were presumed to be heterosexual. Thus,

Method	Description	Uses and limitations
CORRELATIONAL	Observing without controlling variables	Useful where practical and/or ethical limitations prevent doing experiment, or for preliminary exploration of an issue
Survey	Verbal self-reports of behaviour	
Naturalistic observation	Observing in real-world setting	
Non-obtrusive measures	Indirect measures of behaviour	Not possible to interpret cause of observed behaviour
EXPERIMENT	Controlling situation and manipulating independent variable(s)	Only method to permit making interpretation of causation
Laboratory	Subjects come to experimental setting	Can be difficult to execute; sometimes not practical/ethical
Field	Done in real-world setting	
QUASI-EXPERIMENT	Controlling situation and selecting subjects according to characteristic of interest (e.g. age, gender)	Necessary for studying variables which cannot be controlled
Laboratory	Subjects come to experimental setting	Provides only limited information about possible causes
Field	Done in real-world setting	

Figure 1.10   Basic types of research methods in psychology Each method has its advantages and disadvantages, and researchers must consider the specifics of the research issue in order to determine which method is most appropriate for a particular situation.

the quasi-independent variable was sexual orientation, and the dependent variable was the size of the hypothalamus. The results indicated that the brains of the homosexual men were more like those of the women than those of the heterosexual men, implying that there is a biological link between brain structure and sexual orientation. Unfortunately, like all quasi-experiments, there are other possible interpretations of the results – for example, all of the homosexual group had died of AIDS, which might have resulted in changes in the brain. Alternatively, since brain structure can be influenced by experience, the structural differences might have been the *result* of sexual orientation rather than the *cause*. (While LeVay was very careful not to over-interpret his results, the popular press tended to be more hasty in their coverage of the study – an example of why one should be cautious when reading media coverage of research results!)

In the end, quasi-experiments have their place in the repertoire of research methods, just as the other methods we have discussed do (see Figure 1.10). Doing research requires making many choices, and good researchers always seek to balance a range of competing factors – not the least of which is a concern for ethical conduct.

For further consideration

Suppose you read that a research study demonstrated that twenty-year-olds liked different music from forty-year-olds. Would you conclude that musical tastes were a result of age? If not, what other variables might influence the results?

Ethics in Psychological Research

As we have seen, the desire to understand behaviour has led to the development of a variety of methods based on scientific principles. Over time, the application of these methods has significantly increased our understanding of human behaviour. While it would be comforting to portray psychology as simply the neutral and impartial pursuit of understanding, it is also true that research can be intrusive, and possibly even harmful. To say this is not to portray psychologists as evil, like some lab-coated villain in a low-budget movie, but to acknowledge that no human activity is value-free. The concern for values applies to all scientific endeavour, but the focus on living beings (animals as well as people) in psychology makes concerns about ethics more immediate than in the natural sciences. In part to foster high standards, the psychological associations in every major country publish codes of ethics for their members (e.g. Canadian Psychological Association 1991; American Psychological Association 1992; British Psychological Society 1993). Despite this attempt at uniformity, ethical standards in research, like all social standards, are shifting thresholds, which seldom produce universal agreement. Nonetheless, concern for ethics in the conduct of all research is an increasingly significant issue for both researchers and society, as Joseph Rotblat, a winner of the Nobel Peace Prize, has affirmed (Rotblat 1999).

The most basic ethical concern is the desire to avoid causing harm. While this seems very straightforward, in practice it can be more ambiguous. Consider this example from recent medical research: in the late 1980s, it was discovered that the drug AZT had some possible benefit in the treatment of AIDS. Since the drug was unapproved, doctors began a double-blind study to test its safety and effectiveness. However, because no other treatment existed for AIDS (a fatal disorder), trials were halted before the study was completed, in order to provide AZT to all participants. In this case, the concern was that it was unethical to withhold a promising drug from those in need (the placebo group). Unfortunately, cancelling of the study had the negative effect of slowing the process of evaluating AZT; consequently, it was not discovered until 1993 that AZT was not as appropriate for those who were HIV-positive but not yet showing symptoms of AIDS. Should the researchers have continued the original study, even if it meant denying some individuals with AIDS full dosages of AZT? Or did the immediate need outweigh the concern for future knowledge, and therefore the welfare of other individuals in the future? In circumstances like this, one sometimes finds conflicts between different ethical principles.

A case which directly involves psychological research relates to a famous study of **obedience to authority** (Milgram 1963). This study was concerned with how people respond to authority figures when instructed to do something they feel unwilling to do. (While often described as an 'experiment', Milgram's original study actually had no control group.) Subjects were recruited through a newspaper ad to participate in 'a study of learning and teaching methods'. When they arrived at the laboratory, a researcher in a white coat showed them an impressive-looking device which, it was explained, was used to punish wrong answers with a series of electric shocks. The volunteer was to be the 'teacher', while a 'learner' in the next room

obedience to authority the tendency to act in accordance with instructions from someone who is perceived as having social authority, even when it is counter to one's own inclinations

would receive the shocks. The teacher met the learner (actually a confederate of the experimenter) and watched while the electrodes were strapped to his wrists; the learner expressed some apprehension as to how the shocks might affect his heart condition. The researcher stated that, 'Although the shocks can be extremely painful, they cause no permanent tissue damage.' During the actual 'learning' session, the teacher and learner communicated from adjacent rooms, via an intercom. As the 'experiment' progressed, the researcher instructed the subject to increase the shock each time a wrong answer was given. (The shock apparatus had a series of switches in 15 volt increments, going from 15 to 450 volts – the latter was also labelled 'Danger XXX'.) Despite possible personal misgivings, protests from the learner and finally no sound at all from the learner, the subject acting as teacher was instructed by the researcher to go to the highest voltage level. It is hard, while sitting comfortably reading this account, to imagine how upsetting the participants found this situation. It may be even harder to understand why they continued – for in Milgram's original study, 65 per cent continued to the maximum shock level!

Milgram's study has subsequently become well known, both for its results and for the controversy over its methods. After participating in the study as described above, subjects discussed the experience with the researcher (a process called **debriefing**). At this time, subjects were told that the apparatus, as well as the entire situation, was simply a ruse; the 'learner' was never actually shocked, and his protests were carefully scripted acting. The *real* purpose of the study was to see how far people would go to obey an authority figure. The fact that most people went to the top of the scale, Milgram has argued, shows how important it is to understand the roots of obedience.

At the same time, many of Milgram's subjects found that complying was very upsetting, since they believed that the learner was actually suffering real shocks. For those who fully complied, this upset was perhaps compounded by the realization that, had the shocks been real, they might have killed someone. The debate then comes down to this: does the knowledge gained about obedience offset the emotional upset to the subjects? Milgram himself has gone to great lengths to justify the study, and has used follow-up studies of the original subjects to indicate that no enduring trauma ensued: after one year, 84 per cent were either glad or very glad to have taken part (Milgram 1964). However, this might be explained by the theory of cognitive dissonance, which says we tend to alter beliefs to fit with past actions (Festinger 1957); from this viewpoint, the subjects might have been trying to justify their original behaviour.

Critics have suggested Milgram was insensitive to the suffering of his subjects. For example, Baumrind criticized Milgram for statements like 'a mature and initially poised businessman . . . within 20 minutes . . . was reduced to a twitching, stuttering wreck' (Baumrind 1964). Brandt has offered a meta-analysis of the situation, suggesting that subjects' willingness to inflict suffering in the name of research was paralleled by Milgram's own willingness in the same cause. From this viewpoint, Brandt argues, the experiment was unnecessary, since Milgram's own attitude would tell him how others would respond (Brandt 1982). It seems clear that Milgram was not deliberately malevolent, and did in fact take considerable care to debrief

debriefing discussing the nature of a research study with participants at its conclusion, in order to explain the true nature and goals of the research and to answer any questions or concerns of participants

his subjects after their participation. At the same time, it seems probable that a less harmful technique could have been found to test the concept of obedience – although the results also would be likely to be perceived as less applicable to the real world. Ultimately, ethical standards *do* evolve, and it is probable that Milgram's research would *not* be approved if it were to be proposed today. (At my university, the rules of the ethical standards code state that the perceived benefits of research cannot be used to justify causing harm to research subjects.) In the end, Milgram's study highlights the difficulties of achieving consensus on ethical matters.

Milgram's study also points out the ethical conflicts raised by another issue: the use of deception in research. Technically, *deception* occurs whenever participants are not fully informed about their participation in research – although this is a rather stringent, and possibly unrealistic, standard. As has been noted already, the phenomenon of reactivity makes it impossible to provide full disclosure in all research situations. In naturalistic observation, for example, the researcher cannot typically seek the consent of those being observed before doing research, since that could lead to altered behaviour. In social psychology in general, whether observing in the field or doing experiments in the laboratory, research requirements often make it necessary to withhold information or even actively to deceive participants. Obviously, deception (and with it, the lack of opportunity for informed consent) is open to abuse, and must be used with caution. Most ethical codes, such as those of the American Psychological Association (APA) and the British Psychological Society (BPS), allow deception to be used, with certain restrictions (American Psychological Association 1992; British Psychological Society 1993). The guidelines require that the research cannot be done otherwise, that subjects are not coerced to participate, that subjects will be fully debriefed after participating – and that there be a justifiable value to the outcome of the research (normally, an increase in understanding of behaviour). Most researchers agree with this approach, and argue that under these conditions no real harm occurs to participants (Christensen 1988). Nonetheless, the issue is still contentious. Kelman has argued that the use of deception can undermine the relationship between researcher and participants, and suggests that deception should be used only when there is no alternative way to do the research (Kelman 1967). Warwick goes even further, suggesting that the willingness to use deception contributes to undermining public perceptions of the trustworthiness of public institutions (Warwick 1975). Brandt has argued that essentially the APA code amounts to saying the end justifies the means – it's all right to deceive subjects if society gets something out of it (Brandt 1982).

The concern about long-term effects of deception is illustrated by a follow-up to Milgram's study, which sought to demonstrate that the same effects could occur in the real world (Hofling *et al.* 1966). In this case, researchers set up a field experiment, in which nurses at a hospital received a telephone call from an unfamiliar staff doctor, instructing them to administer what appeared to be a toxic dose of medication to a patient. The doctor explained that he was on his way to the hospital and would sign the authorization when he arrived. (Of course, the situation was designed to ensure no actual harm came to patients.) True to expectation, 21 of 22 nurses tried to administer the toxic dosage! This study demonstrated the external validity of Milgram's results, and is cited approvingly by Zimbardo (1992) for this reason. What is *ignored* by both the original researchers and Zimbardo is the question of how this experience affected the nurses subsequently: did it make them more distrustful, and if so, is that ultimately good or bad? The consequences of such deception seem to extend well beyond the confines of the experiment itself.

In the end, this is an issue where it is impossible to find universal agreement. Having served on ethical review boards, I know that good researchers recognize that they bear a moral responsibility for their work, although cases do arise where researchers are not sufficiently sensitive to possible ethical conflicts. Ethical boards exist, in fact, to ensure that the proponent of a study is not the only one to evaluate its suitability. In my own research on cognitive processes, deception is not an issue, and the greatest risk to subjects is the possibility of boredom. However, some types of researchers have no such luxury, and must often balance the desire for knowledge against other kinds of values. At the very least, it is to the credit of the discipline that the debates about ethical issues are publicly argued. Psychology exists to enhance our understanding of ourselves, and as long as researchers remain sensitive to the ethical responsibility this entails, then psychology will represent *humane* behaviour as well as *human* behaviour.

| For further consideration | How would *you* feel if you were a subject in Milgram's study? Do you think it is an ethical study? Why or why not? |

Conclusion

In this chapter, we have looked at the history and basic characteristics of psychology as a discipline. In the process, two basic themes have emerged. The first is that the process of understanding behaviour is influenced by the perceptual processes we use in interpreting everything we experience. One aspect of this is the selective nature of perception. Given the complexity of behaviour, researchers are forced to be selective in what they study, and this is reflected in the nature of the different approaches to psychology which this book considers. Perception is also important in that we actively interpret the world, and the interpretations we make are based on the schemata we use to organize our thinking. Psychological theories are one example of the attempt to organize our understanding of the world. Hence, the existence of different approaches within psychology can be partly understood in terms of the processes of perception.

The second basic theme is that psychology faces particular challenges in the process of gathering information. Like the natural sciences, psychology is empirical, and emphasizes the importance of observations in developing an understanding of behaviour. However, physics or chemistry deal with inanimate matter, and the concepts can seem remote from personal experience. By contrast, psychology is concerned with the understanding of our own actions and experiences. Because people are self-aware, researchers must be careful that the process of observing does not alter the behaviour of interest. This concern underlies many of the research methods employed, from naturalistic observation to field experiments. In addition, because psychology deals with living creatures, ethical concerns exist which do not arise in the natural sciences. These two factors make psychology very different from the natural sciences.

At this stage, you may feel that the challenges are overwhelming, not only for psychologists as researchers, but also for you as a reader. If so, don't despair. This chapter has tried to outline some basic themes, but it cannot tell the whole story. Indeed, while much of the meaning lies in the themes, the excitement lies in the details – the specifics of how we act, and why. In the chapters ahead, you will encounter more of the specifics, and also develop a better understanding of the broader themes and issues. As you proceed, you will find that each chapter adds to your understanding of both behaviour and the way psychologists study it.

Each of us has wondered what we are, and why; psychologists have dedicated their lives to answering these questions. While no final answers can be offered, in the chapters ahead we will see that even partial answers can offer both excitement and insight.

Chapter Summary

- ◆ Psychology is defined as 'the scientific study of behaviour'. By *behaviour*, researchers variously mean observable responses, inner experience (thoughts, feelings etc.) or both – the variations are one of the factors that distinguish the different approaches within psychology. It is *scientific*, in that it is based on the methods of systematic observation and analysis which are part of all science.

- ◆ The task of understanding behaviour can be related to *perception*. Rather than being a passive representation of sensory input, perception is an active process of *selecting* and *interpreting* the information provided by our senses. Faced with the complexity and diversity of behaviour, psychologists make choices in terms of what aspects to study, the research methods to be used and other issues.

- ◆ These choices are reflected in the different *approaches* to the study of psychology, which differ in their basic assumptions about behaviour, as well as their methods and theories. In effect, each approach represents a distinct framework for the understanding of behaviour.

- ◆ Psychology developed from two different traditions, associated with philosophy and natural science. The influence of the natural sciences is seen in the work of Wilhelm Wundt, who founded the first major laboratory for psychology at Leipzig in 1879. The influence of philosophy is reflected in the ideas of William James, an American contemporary of Wundt's who wrote a highly influential text on psychology.

◆ Five major approaches have been influential within psychology: the *biological*, *behaviourist*, *cognitive*, *psychodynamic* and *humanistic*.

◆ In psychology there are many possible ways of collecting observations, which vary in terms of *measurement techniques* (*self-report* or *direct observation*), *setting* (in a *laboratory* or in the *field*) and *research method* (*experimental, non-experimental* and *quasi-experimental*).

◆ Non-experimental techniques include *interviews*, *surveys*, *case studies*, *naturalistic observation* and the use of *unobtrusive measures*. Non-experimental methods are *correlational* – that is, they assist us in finding patterns in behaviour, but do not directly identify the causes.

◆ Experimental methods always involve systematically varying one or more *independent variable* in order to see how the changes affect behaviour. This systematic manipulation, together with control of other factors in the situation, is intended to aid in understanding the *causes* of behaviour.

◆ Quasi-experimental methods are used to study variables that cannot be directly controlled, like age or gender, or in situations where manipulating a variable would be unethical. Quasi-experiments offer more insight into causation than do non-experimental methods, but can be more susceptible to interpretation problems than true experiments.

◆ One issue which is common to all psychological research is the importance of *ethics*. Among particular concerns are the possibility of causing harm, and the role of deception versus informed consent.

Key Terms and Concepts

case study	population
correlation	psychology
debriefing	quasi-experiment
dependent variable	representative sample
empirical	sample
experiment	schemata
hypothesis	self-report
independent variable	survey
interview	theory
naturalistic observation	unobtrusive measure

Suggestions for Further Reading

Fancher's *Pioneers of Psychology* provides a highly readable historical overview of psychology, focusing on the major figures who helped to shape the discipline.

Luria's *The Mind of a Mnemonist* is a short book which shows the value of case studies while providing a vivid account of a remarkable individual.

The Varieties of Religious Experience is a remarkable work, William James's last on psychology. It offers both an excellent introduction to James's thinking, and a still-relevant exploration of one of the most profound aspects of human experience.

If you are interested in learning more about research methods, you should read the Appendix in this book (It also includes suggestions for further reading.)

On Being a Scientist: Responsible Conduct in Research, published by the National Academy of Science, provides a thought-provoking discussion of ethical issues, including many specific examples. (It is available on the Web at http://www.nap.edu/readingroom/books/obas/contents/values.html)

Unobtrusive Measures: Non-reactive Research in the Social Sciences, by Webb *et al.*, is an interesting account of how to do research without intruding.

2

The Biological Approach

Looking for the Mind
Introduction
The Nature of the Physiological System
Mind, Brain, and the CNS
   Neurons and the Nervous System
   The Brain
Studying the Brain
   Electrical Recording and Stimulation
   Computerized Imaging Techniques
Chemical Processes in Behaviour
   Neurotransmitters
   Hormones
Interactions of Mind and Body in Behaviour
The Effects of Body on Mind
   The Study of Drug Effects

Types of Psychoactive Drugs
The Split Brain and the Whole Mind
The Split Brain and the Normal Brain
The Effects of Mind on Body
   Stress
   Medicine and the Mind
The Hereditary Basis of Behaviour
Basic Mechanisms of Heredity
Nature and Nurture in Behaviour
Evolution and Behaviour
Conclusion
Chapter Summary
Key Terms and Concepts
Suggestions for Further Reading

Looking for the Mind

Most people think of medicine as a profession that takes care of our bodies. Yet sometimes doctors are confronted with cases where the problem seems to go beyond the body. Instead, the focus becomes individuals' awareness of themselves and their surroundings – in short, the mind. Such cases can be extremely puzzling, but may also be useful in helping us to understand the mind. Let us briefly consider two such examples.

Oliver Sacks, a neurologist who is also a gifted writer, has described a remarkable case that he encountered (Sacks 1985). 'Dr P' was a music professor who was referred to Sacks because of a visual problem. He would confuse common objects, on one occasion mistaking his wife's head for his hat! Given a live rose to identify, he described it as 'a convoluted red form with a linear green attachment.' Shown photographs, he could identify only those with a distinguishing feature, such as Einstein's unruly hair. On the street, he sometimes patted a fire hydrant, thinking it was the head of a child. Indeed, he could only recognize people by voice, not by sight. Yet his eyes were fine – he could even spot a pin on the floor. In other respects, Dr P seemed normal; in fact, his musical gifts (with the exception of no longer being able to read music) were considerable. The only evident symptom, apart from his problems with visually recognizing faces and complex shapes, was a slight abnormality of reflexes on the left side. Here was a bizarre puzzle: how could someone find a pin, yet think that his wife's head was a hat? How is our awareness related to what our senses tell us?

If that seems puzzling, consider the phenomenon known as **phantom limb**. When individuals lose an arm or other limb, they will often continue to experience sensations which seem to come from the missing limb. Sometimes, the sensations are relatively benign – a feeling of cold, or an itching sensation (that sometimes can be relieved by scratching where the limb would be!), but often the sensation is one of intense pain in the missing limb. Since the pain is experienced in a non-existent limb, conventional pain remedies are typically of no value. Sometimes, the afflictions are even stranger than simple pain. Sacks has reported one case of a man who experienced his missing finger as extending straight out – accompanied by the fear that if his hand came near his face, the phantom finger would poke him in the eye! He *knew* the finger didn't exist, but could not escape the sensation, or the accompanying fear. Despite great efforts to understand and treat the problem, the full explanation of phantom limb remains a mystery.

Both these phenomena call into question the relationship between mind and body. Traditionally, **mind** is used to refer to our experience of awareness, or consciousness; it has no direct reference to physical form. The *body*, of course, refers to our physical being, and includes what many feel is the basis of mind – the brain. Are mind and body separate, and does their separateness account for cases like those above? Or are mind and body simply different aspects of an underlying unity? If they are a unity, then what accounts for the sometimes bizarre discrepancies between the two? William James, in his *Principles of Psychology*, stated that 'The explanation of consciousness [i.e. mind] is the ultimate question for psychology.' Although James made the statement over a hundred years ago, and much has been learned since, the answer to the question is still beyond our grasp. However, if we *do* find the answer, many believe it will come from research based on the biological approach.

phantom limb a mysterious phenomenon in which individuals who have lost a limb will often continue to experience sensations which seem to come from the missing limb

mind the inner subjective experience of conscious awareness; the term has no direct reference to physical form

Introduction

The biological approach to psychology, as its name implies, views the human being as a biological organism. What we do, and even what we think, is seen as having its basis in our physical structure. The approach has developed out of interest in two major concerns: the relationship between mind and body, and the influence of heredity on behaviour. Each is a reflection of our biological nature, and the study of them sometimes overlaps, but the two aspects have separate histories.

As one might guess, biological researchers tend to view behaviour as being purely physical. As a doctor commented while discussing possible physical causes of schizophrenia, 'Of *course* it has to be physical. There isn't anything else up there.' By 'up there', he was referring to the brain. Thus, his reasoning was based on the assumption that the brain determines behaviour. Although you may not find that very surprising, in earlier times it would have been seen as very radical. Even in the seventeenth century, most people believed the body was controlled by an intangible soul. Among those who believed in the soul was the French philosopher René Descartes (noted for his assertion, 'I think, therefore I am.'). A keen observer, but also deeply religious, Descartes tried to reconcile the apparent physical nature of the body with the intangible nature of the soul. The human body, he felt, was constructed like that of an animal – both were basically *machines*. However, he also believed that people (unlike animals) had a soul, which interacted with the physical body through a small gland in the brain called the pineal gland. Since in French the same word (*l'âme*) can be used for both 'mind' and 'soul', Descartes's idea became interpreted as referring to the relation between the mind and body; his view that mind and body are distinct, but can interact, became known as **dualism**. While Descartes saw the body's functioning in machine-like terms, his interactionist view (physical body interacting with intangible soul) was also a compromise. By separating the mind from the body, dualism created a split which has been the subject of much subsequent controversy (Damasio 1994). Rightly or wrongly, Descartes's concept became so well known that for the better part of two centuries, dualism was the dominant view in Western culture.

Despite its long history, dualism poses many contradictions. (For example, how can a non-physical mind control a physical body?) Today, researchers in the biological approach reject dualism in favor of *monism*, the belief that mind and body are a single entity. (In most respects this is equivalent to **materialism**, which assumes that all behaviour has a physical basis.) Materialism avoids many of the problems of Descartes's dualism, but that does not prove it is true. Like dualism, materialism is an *assumption*, and not every person (or every culture) accepts the same assumptions about the world. As recently as 1994, researcher Francis Crick (better known as the co-discoverer of the structure of DNA) felt justified in claiming that materialism was 'so alien to the ideas of most people alive today that it can truly be called astonishing' (Crick 1994: 3). Still, the materialist view which lies at the heart of the biological approach is increasingly influential in psychology today, and it is worth considering how this came about. Like many changes in our understanding, the shift from dualism to materialism occurred slowly, and was influenced by a series of discoveries.

Interestingly, one crucial insight came about almost by accident. In 1745 (about one hundred years after Descartes), a French priest-turned-physician named Julien de La Mettrie contracted a fever, and noticed that this physical condition affected his mental state as well as his physical state. Reflecting

dualism the view, first attributed to Descartes, that mind and body are distinct; Descartes believed the two could interact via the pineal gland in the brain

materialism the assumption that all behaviour has a physiological basis

on this after his recovery, he wrote a book called *L'histoire naturelle de l'âme* (*The Natural History of the Soul*). In the book, he argued that the body is but a machine, *and* that the soul is not different from the mind. Further, he said the mind was part of the body. This assertion, which clearly went beyond Descartes's position, caused a tremendous outcry, but La Mettrie held fast to his views. Ultimately, the opposition from religious and political authorities forced him to leave France for his personal safety.

By the time of the French Revolution (less than fifty years after La Mettrie), a physician named Cabanis was able to argue that guillotine victims were not conscious after beheading, because consciousness was the function of the brain, just as digestion was the function of the stomach. Still, no one had shown a specific connection between physiological structures and behaviour. Then, in 1861, a French doctor at the insane asylum at Bicêtre, Paul Broca, encountered a case in which a man lost the ability to speak coherently after a head injury. Later, Broca was able to demonstrate, by post-mortem autopsy, that the cause of the man's deficit lay in damage to a specific point in the brain. The proof of this **localization of function** (connecting a specific behaviour to a specific brain area) was the final step in the progression of ideas. The acceptance of this finding completed the gradual change in attitude, from seeing behaviour as governed by an intangible soul, to the modern view of behaviour as having a physiological basis. Of course, many others also contributed to our current knowledge and ideas. The brief history given here is simply meant to indicate how the basic assumptions about mind and body arose.

The other main aspect of the biological approach, the role of heredity in behaviour, also had a gradual development. (**Heredity** refers to the biological mechanism for transmitting characteristics across generations.) In the eighteenth century, people believed that each species of plant and animal had been independently created: as the Bible says, 'every living creature after his kind'. Still, there were indications that this might not be literally true. The great biologist Linnaeus had published a catalogue of over 4,000 plant and animal species in 1735, and his orderly categories suggested connections among species. Then, in 1809, a French naturalist named Lamarck presented the first widely known theory of species development, or evolution. Lamarck believed that variations developed through inheritance of acquired characteristics. For instance, giraffes acquired long necks because each generation strained a little further to get food, slightly stretching their necks, and passed this difference on to their offspring. Today, Lamarckian theory is generally discredited, but it was a significant step forward in suggesting that characteristics have a hereditary basis.

The real revolution in thought came with the work of Charles Darwin. Darwin's theory, published in *The Origin of Species* (1859), was that variations among individuals of a species would occur by chance, but could in turn be passed on. His doctrine of 'survival of the fittest' meant that only those variations which helped the individuals survive long enough to breed would be passed on. Through this process, which he called **natural selection,** Darwin was advocating not only the inheritance of characteristics, but also an evolutionary link between humans and all other species. In 1872 he

localization of function the assumption that specific functions are associated with specific areas of the brain

heredity the biological transmission of characteristics from one generation to another

natural selection the evolutionary process by which those random variations within a species which enhance reproductive success lead to perpetuation of new characteristics; in essence, individuals possessing traits which enhance survival and reproduction are likely to have more offspring

made this even clearer by writing *The Expression of the Emotions in Man and Animals*. (Actually, Darwin proposed the concept of inheritance, but specified no biological mechanism for its operation; it remained for the rediscovery of the work of an Austrian monk, Gregor Mendel, for a specific mechanism for heredity to be suggested.)

Like La Mettrie, Darwin came into conflict with religious doctrine, this time with the view that man was created 'in God's image'. In part, the controversy concerned how literally one should interpret the biblical concept. The controversy raged for many years, and is still not completely ended, but in time the evolutionary viewpoint expressed by Darwin became dominant. Despite not specifying precisely how heredity operated, Darwin's theory laid the basis for the study of hereditary influences on behaviour.

Today, these two concepts – *materialism* and *heredity* – are the foundation of the biological approach to psychology. The assumptions involved (that mind has a physiological basis, and that behaviour can be inherited) influence both the questions asked and the type of data collected. Compared to other approaches, the biological approach emphasizes 'getting inside the black box' – that is, looking at the internal structure of the organism. Broca showed that a specific defect in the brain could destroy speech in an otherwise normal person. Darwin showed that what we are is at least partly due to what our parents are. In this chapter, we will look at how these ideas have been applied to enhance our understanding of behaviour.

The Nature of the Physiological System

As previously noted, the biological approach emphasizes the physiological basis of behaviour. While the approach can be applied to any aspect of behaviour, the most challenging questions seem to be those relating to the interactions between mind and body. In everyday life, we encounter situations where the body affects the mind (as when coffee makes you tense), and also situations where the mind affects the body (as when executives get high blood pressure). What is the mechanism of such interactions? In this section, we will try to deal with this question in terms of what is currently known about the physiological basis of behaviour, and also consider some of the problems psychologists face in trying to develop answers.

Mind, Brain and the CNS

In trying to understand the interaction of mind and body, the first difficulty encountered is dealing with the terms involved. For instance, where is 'the mind'? Where is the 'self' that we experience? Terms like these, while seemingly clear in everyday usage, are not so clear when one tries to relate them to physiological structures.

Most people would equate 'mind' with 'brain', and this is partially correct. But in more precise terms, the word 'mind' refers to a psychological concept, not a physiological one. The *mind* is usually regarded as the seat of consciousness or awareness, not as a physiological structure. Current knowledge indicates that the brain is, indeed, involved in our experience of consciousness, but no one is currently certain just how, or whether consciousness involves only the brain. So, in discussing interactions of the physical (brain) and mental (mind), one is restricted to saying that somehow the two are connected, or even fundamentally the same, but the specifics are not clear. (As noted earlier, in part this is an *assumption* that researchers make. However, the alternative – that the mind is non-physical, perhaps a soul – would not only take us back before Descartes, but would also make scientific study irrelevant.) While no final answers can be given here, we will examine what is known about the structure of the physiological system and its influence on behaviour.

For further consideration

We all experience conscious awareness, but the connections between this awareness and behaviour are complex. For example, do you breathe in or out when you hit a ball (e.g. in tennis, golf or baseball)? If we are not aware, do you think that means that the mind is separate from the body? Why or why not?

Neurons and the Nervous System

neuron a cell of the nervous system (also called a nerve cell)
synapse the junction between two neurons, represented by a small physical gap which is bridged by the flow of neurotransmitter chemicals from the terminals of the 'sending' neuron
central nervous system (CNS) the brain, together with the nerve pathways of the spinal cord
peripheral nervous system (PNS) those nerve pathways which lie outside the central nervous system, involving sensation, motor control and regulation of internal organs
sensory neurons neurons in the PNS which carry information from the sense receptors to the CNS
motor neurons those neurons in the PNS which are responsible for initiating muscle activity
interneurons neurons which are part of the central nervous system

The human body is a remarkably complex system, comprised of trillions of individual living cells of many specialized types. Certain cells in the stomach lining, for example, do nothing but produce digestive secretions. Other cells fight disease, transport oxygen or store energy. Coordinating the activity of the many body systems requires communication, and this is one of the key functions of the nervous system. The specialized cells of the nervous system, called nerve cells or **neurons**, are like wires in that they carry an electro-chemical message from one point to another. Each time a neuron connects to another neuron, at a junction called a **synapse**, it is possible for a message to be switched to other areas. The brain, together with the nerve pathways of the spinal cord, forms the **central nervous system** (or **CNS**). Those nerve pathways outside the central nervous system form the **peripheral nervous system** (or **PNS**). **Sensory neurons** in the PNS carry messages from the outside world to the CNS via the sense receptors, such as those located in the eyes and ears, while **motor neurons** are responsible for initiating muscle activity, under the direction of the CNS. (The neurons which comprise the CNS are often called **interneurons**, because they are intermediate between sensory and motor neurons.) Although the brain is responsible for integrating incoming information and directing muscle activity, the spinal cord is a vital relay station. For instance, the first connection (or synapse) between your big toe and the brain is where the pathway enters your spinal cord. For protection, the spinal cord passes within the bones (vertebrae) of the spinal column, like wires in a flexible casing. Despite this protection, a back injury can result in disruption of the spinal cord, which can cause loss of all feeling (sensory input) and movement (motor control) below the point of injury (see Figure 2.1).

The basic unit of the nervous system is the neuron. In a sense, a neuron is like a wire through which an electrical signal passes. This signal, called a

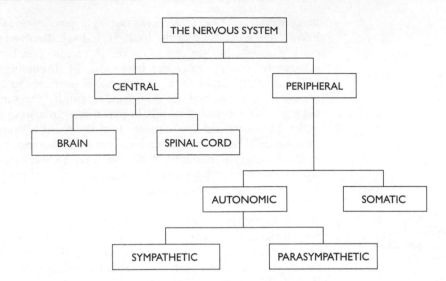

Figure 2.1 The central and peripheral nervous systems As the figure shows, the nervous system is subdivided into various subsystems, with the major distinction being between the CNS (brain and spinal cord) and the PNS (all those nerves not part of the CNS). The somatic system includes both sensory pathways (to the CNS) and motor pathways (from the CNS).

nerve impulse the electrical signal generated when a neuron is active, which normally passes from the dendrites, along the axon, to the terminals

axon the relatively elongated portion of a neuron between the cell body and the terminals which provides the signal pathway for a nerve impulse

myelin in a neuron, an insulating sheath around the axon, composed of the spirally wound membrane of Schwann cells, which serves to improve the efficiency of neural conduction

neurotransmitter a chemical released by the terminals of a neuron which plays a role in communication between neurons, across the synapse

nerve impulse, stays essentially the same (i.e. in amplitude) as it passes along the 'wire' or **axon**, and is also the same in every neuron (see Figure 2.2). While all neurons show the same basic structure and serve the same basic purpose, they show many differences in their details. One of the most striking variations is in length – the central wire or axon may range from less than 1 millimetre (for neurons in the brain) to about 1 metre (for peripheral neurons between the spinal chord and the toes)! Neurons also differ in terms of whether they are insulated or not: as with ordinary electrical wires, insulation improves efficiency by reducing signal losses. In neurons, the insulation consists of a fatty substance called **myelin**. (The myelin is actually composed of another specialized type of cell called a Schwann cell, which wraps itself around the axon to provide an insulating sheath.) Not all neurons in either the CNS or PNS are insulated ('myelinated'), although most of those in the brain of a healthy adult are. The process of forming myelin begins in the foetus, and the process is largely completed by about three years of age, though formation (and repair) continues throughout life. Across species, the degree of completion at birth is roughly paralleled by the degree of behavioural capacities; a new-born calf, for example, is both better myelinated and more capable at birth than a human infant. At the same time, destruction of the myelin sheath (in disorders like multiple sclerosis) can have disastrous effects on the nervous system and behaviour. When the electrical impulse reaches the terminals of the neuron, there is a small physical gap, called a *synapse*. Communication across the synapse occurs when the nerve impulse triggers the release of chemicals called **neurotransmitters**. As we will see in the next section, neurons can differ in terms of what neurotransmitter chemicals they use.

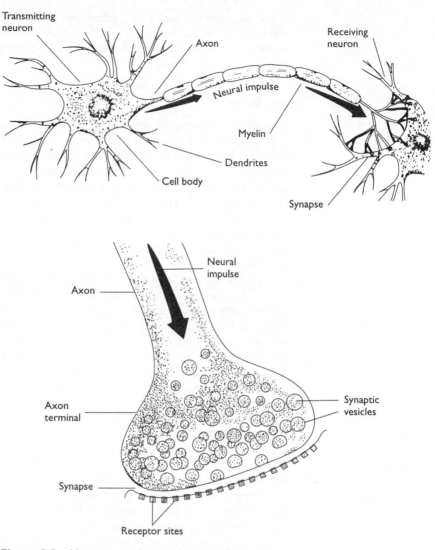

Figure 2.2 Neurons and neural transmission The structure of a neuron is illustrated in the upper figure, with the various parts. A neural impulse ('signal') travels from the dendrites, along the axon, to the terminals, where it must cross a physical gap, the synapse. Transmission across the synapse is by means of neurotransmitters, chemicals released by the synaptic vesicles, which then flow across the gap, to lock into receptor sites on the receiving neuron (see lower figure).

While the pathways of the peripheral nervous system are crucial in providing our links to the outer world for both sensation and movement, the central nervous system, with responsibility for integrating and controlling the whole system, is much more complex. As noted above, damage to the spinal cord can result in loss of feeling and paralysis; the brain itself is also vulnerable. (In the peripheral nervous system, severed nerves will often repair themselves; cases of a severed arm or leg being successfully reattached after an accident attest to this. Unfortunately, nerves in the central nervous system do not regenerate – hence damage to the spinal cord can result in permanent paraplegia.)

The Brain

brain the portion of the central nervous system which lies within the skull

Considered visually, the **brain** is not very impressive – a greyish lump weighing approximately three pounds, with an irregular surface of ridges and valleys. However, that superficial impression belies both its complexity and its capabilities. The brain consists of about 100 billion neurons (no one knows the exact number, since estimates are based on examining a small region, and extrapolating the number found to the whole structure). In turn, each neuron makes and receives connections with hundreds or possibly thousands of other neurons, resulting in a network of some one million billion connections in the cortex (the outer layer of the brain) alone (Edelman 1992; Damasio 1994).

Like the nervous system as a whole, the brain can be subdivided into many areas. Early anatomists looked for physical divisions (like the fissures on the cortex, or the almond shape of the amygdala in the limbic system), and then tried to deduce the functions. They *assumed* that specific functions are associated with specific areas, and this assumption, called *localization of function*, has led to many insights, as we will see. At the same time, the brain is a highly interconnected system, and it is worth keeping that in mind as we discuss what is known about the functions of different parts of the brain.

cortex the pink, somewhat wrinkled, outer layer of the brain which controls many of our higher functions, like speech and perception; from the Greek for 'bark' (as on a tree)

If you were to remove the top portion of a person's skull, you would see the pink, somewhat wrinkled outer layer of the brain, called the **cortex** (Greek for 'bark', as on a tree) (see Figure 2.3). Its wrinkled ('convoluted') appearance results from the cortex being folded on itself. Since maximum surface area seems important (simpler organisms have both smaller and less convoluted brains), this crumpling effect allows a large sheet to be compressed into the relatively small confines of the skull. (Imagine crumpling a large sheet of paper into a small wad.)

frontal lobe the area of the cortex in front of the central fissure, and above the lateral fissure; it is involved in the interpretation of emotion and experience

frontal lobotomy an operation, popular in the 1940s and 1950s, which involved sectioning or removing portions of the frontal lobes, in an attempt to treat cases of bipolar mood disorder or chronic pain; later shown to be largely ineffective as a therapeutic procedure

The cortex is made up of two distinct hemispheres, left and right, each of which basically controls the opposite side of the body (e.g. muscle movements in your right hand are initiated by your left hemisphere). In turn, the hemispheres can be broken down into smaller regions called *lobes*, which are identified by the valleys or 'fissures' on the surface. Surprisingly, there is considerable variation across individuals in the precise shape and location of the convolutions; despite this, the ridges and valleys make reliable landmarks for distinguishing major regions of the cortex. The two major landmarks are the central fissure, which divides each hemisphere roughly in half front-to-back, and the lateral fissure, which runs along the side of each hemisphere. The **frontal lobe** is the area in front of the central fissure, and above the lateral fissure; it is associated with subtle colourings of emotional response and experience. For this reason, an operation called a **frontal lobotomy**, which involved isolating or removing portions of the frontal lobes, was once used in an attempt to treat cases of bipolar mood disorder

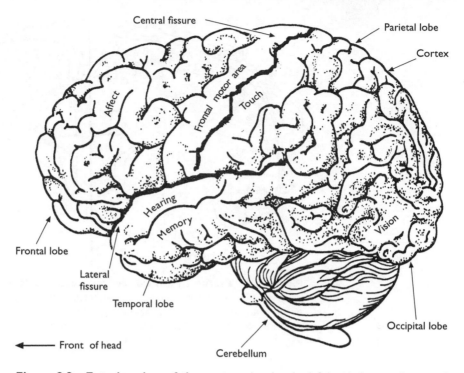

Figure 2.3 **Exterior view of the cortex**, showing the left hemisphere and areas of primary functions.

association areas areas of the cortex which have no primary function (such as receiving direct sensory data), but rather play a role in integrating activity from other brain areas

frontal motor area the area of the frontal lobes just before the central fissure which controls all voluntary movements of the muscles

parietal lobe the portion of the cortex just behind the central fissure and above the lateral fissure, whose primary function is the sense of touch

temporal lobe the region of the cortex below the lateral fissure; its primary functions are hearing and memory

occipital lobe the rearmost portion of the cortex, which is devoted solely to vision

or chronic pain. The procedure, popular in the 1940s and 1950s, was ultimately shown to be a poor treatment, and frontal lobotomies have been largely abandoned today (Goldstein 1950; Shorter 1997). Much of the frontal lobe seems to have no primary function (such as receiving direct sensory data), but rather plays a role in integrating activity from other brain areas; as a result, these parts are labelled **association areas**. By contrast, the area of the frontal lobes just before the central fissure is called the **frontal motor area**, because it controls all voluntary movements of the muscles. Interestingly, the body areas capable of very subtle motor control (e.g. hands, lips) show a greater representation in the frontal motor area than other body regions. In fact, researchers have created maps of the frontal motor area, detailing the body areas controlled. A similar mapping for the sense of touch exists for the portion of the **parietal lobe** just behind the central fissure (see Figure 2.4).

We also have some understanding of other portions of the cortex. The **temporal lobe**, located in the region below the lateral fissure, plays a role in hearing, language and memory for objects (Rodman 1997). In terms of language, a region of the left temporal lobe called Wernicke's area is crucial to make language meaningful. Patients with damage to this area typically have difficulty understanding words and sentences, and produce 'word salads' which are fluent, but make little sense. The **occipital lobe**, at the rear of the cortex, is devoted solely to vision. Given the large area devoted

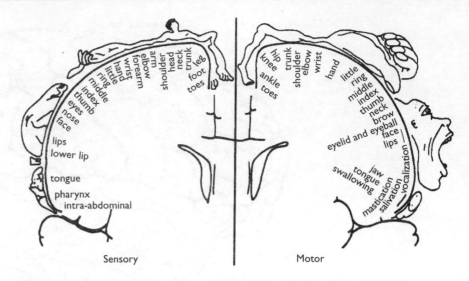

Figure 2.4   Tactile and motor representation in the cortex Penfield's research using electrical stimulation of the cortex has helped to clarify the localization of touch and motor control along the central fissure. (In the figure, the brain has been cut vertically along the fissure which divides the frontal motor area from the sensory region of the parietal lobe – compare Figure 2.3.) The relative size of the body parts shows the relative degree of cortical representation. (After Penfield and Rasmussen 1957.)

to it, one might speculate that vision is very complex, or very important, or both; the evidence suggests it is indeed both. The experience of seeing, like other senses, is dependent on brain activity as well as sensory activity. In the extreme case, a person with damage to the occipital lobe would be functionally blind, despite having perfectly functioning eyes. Recognition of this connection between brain function and sensory experience is another reason why researchers feel comfortable identifying the mind with the brain.

At the start of this chapter, we discussed the peculiar case of Dr P, who could see, but often failed to recognize what he saw, including faces. His problem is an example of **visual agnosia**, which refers to problems with visual recognition. Clearly, the primary visual areas of the brain were intact, since he could recognize simple forms like a pin, and had no difficulty avoiding obstacles in his path. Instead, his problem involved *integrating* the sensory information into a coherent whole, and relating it to other information, such as his memories of people. Disorders like this can be very perplexing, and indeed, in describing this case, Sacks (1985) does not specify the precise regions of the brain affected, or the cause of the damage. However, based on the symptoms, it is likely that it involves the role of the association areas for vision, which link visual sense data to functions in other parts of the brain. In particular, the pattern of problems (trouble in integrating complex patterns, along with abnormal motor reflexes on the left side of the body) suggests damage to the association areas of the right occipital

visual agnosia a general term for disorders which result in disruption of visual recognition

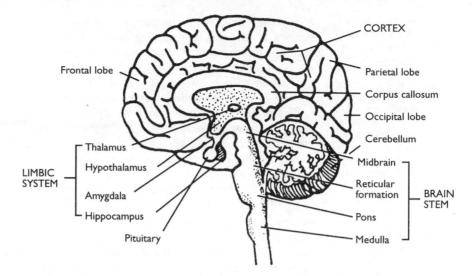

Figure 2.5   Internal view of the brain, showing the relatively 'old' parts of the brain, such as the limbic system, which are normally hidden by the surrounding cortex.

limbic system a series of sub-cortical structures which connect the cortex with other parts of the brain and which are important in many basic functions; among the main parts of the limbic system are the thalamus, hypothalamus, amygdala and hippocampus

hypothalamus one of the most important elements in the limbic system, the hypothalamus both regulates behaviours associated with hunger, thirst, sex and other basic drives, and plays a role in regulating hormonal functions

hippocampus a structure within the limbic system which is important to memory function

amygdala an almond-shaped structure in the limbic system which plays a role in basic emotions and possibly memory and stimulus evaluation

cerebellum ('little brain' in Latin) two small hemispheres located beneath the cortical hemispheres, at the back of the head; the cerebellum plays an important role in directing movement and balance

lobe. Despite the apparent localization of many cortical functions, we must always remember that the brain functions as a whole.

As noted, the cortex is like a crumpled sheet of paper; at the same time, it surrounds the other sections of the brain, much as the bark of a tree covers the interior. Below the cortex are subcortical networks which connect the cortex with other parts of the brain, notably the *limbic system* and the *brain stem* (see Figure 2.5). These regions are sometimes referred to as the 'primitive brain'. As the name implies, these structures control fundamental aspects of behaviour that we share with many lower organisms. The main parts of the **limbic system** are identified in Figure 2.5; among these, the most important is the **hypothalamus**, which both regulates behaviours associated with hunger, thirst, sex and other basic drives, and plays a role in regulating hormonal functions. The **hippocampus** is important to memory function; in a well-known case, a man who suffered damage to the hippocampus lost the ability to retain experiences which occurred subsequent to the surgery, but left prior memories intact (Milner 1965). (The damage disrupted transfer to long-term memory, as will be discussed in Chapter 4.) Next to the hippocampus is the **amygdala** (from Latin for 'almond', because of its shape), which plays a role in basic emotions like fear and rage. Emotions are a basic part of our behaviour, and recent research suggests the amygdala may also be involved in many functions, such as forming emotional memories (via its links to the hippocampus), and deciding what characteristics of stimuli are significant (LeDoux 1995).

Nestled beneath the large cortical hemispheres, at the back of the head, are two smaller hemispheres. These two hemispheres form the **cerebellum** (literally 'little brain' in Latin). The cerebellum plays an important role in directing movements and balance, particularly fine motor control activities

brain stem the region at the top of the spinal cord, composed of three primary structures: the medulla, the pons and the midbrain

medulla a small swelling at the top of the spinal cord composed of the cell bodies of neurons whose axons extend to the heart and other internal organs; its role is to regulate basic bodily processes

pons (Latin for 'bridge') a region in the brain stem above the medulla which provides connections between the cortex and cerebellum

reticular formation a diffuse network of nerve fibres which runs through the brain stem and limbic system, with connections both up to the cortex and down to the spinal cord; the reticular formation acts as a relay network controlling sensory inputs, and thereby plays a key role in regulating arousal level, alertness and sleep

like sewing or playing the piano, and also complex movements like gymnastics. It does this by receiving information from both the sensory nervous system and the cortex, with much of this information passing through an adjacent centre, the brain stem. In addition to guiding movements, the cerebellum also seems to play a role in sensory processing (distinguishing among stimuli), according to recent research (Gao *et al.* 1996).

The **brain stem** is the region at the top of the spinal cord, and is composed of three primary structures: the medulla, the pons, and part of the reticular formation. The **medulla**, a small swelling at the top of the spinal cord, has neurons whose axons extend to the heart and other internal organs; its role is thus to regulate basic bodily processes. Above it, the **pons** (Latin for 'bridge') provides connections between the cortex and cerebellum. A significant structure of the brain stem is the **reticular formation** (reticular means 'finely interwoven'), a diffuse network of nerve fibres which runs through the brain stem and limbic system, with connections both up to the cortex and down to the spinal cord. The reticular formation acts as a relay network, controlling sensory inputs; as such, it plays a key role in regulating our arousal level, controlling alertness and sleep.

Thus, the brain and nervous system are made up of a number of specific structures, which must function as an integrated system to regulate our behaviour. The description given here should not be taken as complete, but simply as an introduction to this incredible system. At the same time, this discussion has said little about *how* we know these things – for example, how do we know that motor functions are located in the frontal lobe?

For further consideration

Based on what we have discussed about the workings of the brain, consider the following science fiction scenario. A mad scientist kidnaps you, and renders you unconscious. Then he takes your brain, and places it in a bowl which provides nutrients, and is connected to a computer to provide 'sensations'. When you awake, would you be able to tell your brain was no longer in your body? Why or why not?

Studying the Brain

As with other approaches to psychology, our understanding of the brain has long been dependent on observation. At one time, researchers had to rely on clinical cases to study the workings of the brain. The use of clinical observation (*case studies*) has its drawbacks, particularly in terms of lack of control. For example, a person may receive a severe blow to the back of the head, and subsequently complain of numbness in one arm. Unfortunately, one cannot easily interpret the connection between the blow and the symptom, because the impact would have been transmitted throughout the skull. Thus, in this case, it does *not* mean that the occipital lobe (the area closest to the site of the blow) is involved in the sense of touch (the symptom). Occasionally, though, the clinical method can lead to important breakthroughs: Broca's discovery of the speech centre is one example. In this case, it was possible to study the patient in detail, since the problem existed for many years. In addition, after the patient's eventual death, an autopsy clearly showed a lesion (tissue injury) in the left frontal lobe, providing the basis for Broca's conclusion. Today, researchers have available a variety of techniques for identifying the function of various brain structures, beyond the use of clinical cases.

Electrical Recording and Stimulation

It has long been known that the brain somehow involves electrical activity. In ancient Rome, Pliny the Elder recommended the shock of an electric fish, applied to the forehead, to ease the pain of childbirth. Without knowing the mechanism, Pliny recognized that the shock stunned the patient, reducing conscious awareness (including pain). The electrical nature of nerve activity was first recognized by Luigi Galvani, an Italian anatomist, in 1791. Galvani observed that a frog's leg could be made to twitch at the touch of dissimilar metals. (Apparently he first noticed the effect when a butcher used metal tongs to reach for some frogs' legs hanging on a hook!) Galvani thought, wrongly, that the frog's leg generated the impulse, rather than being activated by the metal tool, which actually created a battery. While it was not long before the true nature of the process was recognized, the possible implications were ignored for nearly a century. It was only about seventy years ago that researchers began to study electrical activity in the brain in a systematic manner.

electroencephalograph (EEG – 'writing the electricity of the brain') a device for recording the electrical activity of the brain by means of electrodes placed on the scalp

In the 1920s, the first recordings of brainwave activity (as the electrical signals are called) were made using the **electroencephalograph** (EEG – 'writing the electricity of the brain'). The EEG allowed researchers to *record* activity, and is still an important tool today. Recently, EEGs were used to identify synchronized patterns of activity associated with perceptual recognition; researchers found that there was a burst of activity at the moment when an ambiguous visual stimulus was recognized as a face (Rodriguez *et al.* 1999). However, a limitation of the EEG is that it is essentially passive, allowing researchers to observe, but not intervene.

electrical stimulation of the brain (ESB) artificial stimulation of neurons by means of a current applied through an implanted electrode

In the 1950s, techniques developed that permitted more direct intervention, by means of **electrical stimulation** of nerve cells (sometimes called ESB, for 'electrical stimulation of the brain'). In this technique, small clusters of cells are activated by inserting a fine wire into the desired area, and then applying a small electric current. In 1954, researchers at Yale University (including W. W. Roberts) discovered that electrical stimulation of certain regions of the limbic system and midbrain in animals seemed to produce pain (Delgado *et al.* 1954). This was not too surprising: since an electrical shock to the fingertip can be painful, why not in the brain? However, in the same year, James Olds, working independently of Roberts, discovered that stimulation of certain areas of the limbic system could also produce *pleasure* (Olds and Milner 1954). Roberts and Olds were studying areas of the 'primitive brain' in animals, and the effects they discovered seemed to reflect primitive emotions and drives. These techniques, while striking in their findings, posed problems, because they involved looking at effects in animals

Wilder Penfield

Wilder Penfield (1891–1976) was born in Spokane, Washington. He was educated at Princeton University, and subsequently attended Oxford University as a Rhodes Scholar. It was at Oxford that the direction of his career took shape, as he met the distinguished neurologist Sir Charles Sherrington. After returning to the United States to obtain a medical degree at Johns Hopkins University, he returned to Oxford to study with Sherrington for two more years. Eventually, he established a practice in neurosurgery, first in the United States and then in Montreal, Canada. At Montreal, he became a professor at McGill University, and founded the Montreal Neurological Institute. This institute became one of the world's leading centres for neurology, and it was here that Penfield did his pioneering work on the mapping of cortical functions. In the course of doing surgery for epilepsy and other disorders, Penfield would identify the functions of various cortical regions by using electrical stimulation as the patient lay conscious on the operating table. This work has been widely hailed, and among other honours Penfield became a member of the Royal Society. He died in Montreal at the age of eighty-five.

and then trying to extrapolate the results to humans. However, at the same point in time Wilder Penfield, a neurosurgeon at the Montreal Neurological Institute, was working with individuals suffering from epilepsy. As part of the surgical procedure used to treat the disorder, he explored the effects of stimulation of the cortex in conscious individuals.

In many cases, epileptic seizures are triggered by random bursts of activity in a focal region, which then spread to other parts of the cortex. To treat individuals suffering from severe seizures of this type, Penfield would sometimes operate, destroying cells in the area where the seizure originated. In order to avoid damage to essential functions, Penfield needed to know what functions would be affected by the tissue he planned to remove. To find out, he would first stimulate various areas of the cortex, and observe the effects reported by the patient (who was conscious throughout the operation). From this, he would produce a 'map' of the cortex and its functions, making the surgery itself more accurate. In cases like this, both the search for knowledge and the alleviation of suffering can be served.

Electrical stimulation poses some basic questions about the brain and mind. One issue concerns the localization of functions. The materialist view argues that all functions of the mind are based on activity in the body. The simplest form of this view says that each aspect of behaviour is produced by a specific location in the brain – that is, that functions are localized. Broca offered support for this position when he pinpointed speech functions in the left cortical hemisphere. Similarly, Penfield's work indicated that specific regions of the cortex control particular movements, sensations and even memories (refer back to Figure 2.4 for his findings). Thus, it would seem that electrical stimulation may allow us to identify – and ultimately control – all aspects of behaviour.

This line of thought can give rise to all sorts of scenarios, ranging from people using ESB instead of drugs to control mood, to governments enforcing laws by means of computer-controlled systems implanted in each citizen's brain. These possibilities can seem frightening and Orwellian, and critics have been quick to raise questions. Typically, the questions focus on the moral aspect: who is to control the computers that control the ESB, and what sort of behaviours should be rewarded or punished? But before accepting this as a purely moral crisis, one should look more carefully at the scientific basis of the issue.

Problems *do* exist with ESB, and in some sense they are all connected with the issue of localization of function. If one accepts it in its simplest form, then there exists a specific centre responsible for any type of behaviour. At present, there is inadequate evidence to support this view. Lower animals show a great degree of physiological predetermination of their behaviour (often called 'instincts'). In humans, however, there appear to be relatively few such patterns, even for comparable behaviour. For example, while male stickleback fish show stereotyped courtship rituals, human males do so only to the extent that their culture dictates. If true localization of function does not exist, one must question whether complete control of every action would ever be possible. A second problem concerns variability across individuals. Gerald Edelman, a Nobel laureate in physiology, has noted that while the general patterns of brain structure are similar across individuals, the details of neural connections differ significantly. This implies that mapping of functions must still be done on a case-by-case basis, even if localization exists (Edelman 1992).

While electrical stimulation has greatly aided our understanding of the brain, it does have limitations as a research tool. First of all, ESB is an artificial process. Inserting an electrode destroys a few hundred cells in the immediate vicinity, and the effects of the stimulation itself are not the same as normal neural activity. Typically, the current applied is either some form of alternating current or a series of brief direct current pulses. The effect in either case is to stimulate artificially all the neurons in the immediate area, perhaps a few thousand cells. These cells then fire *in synchrony*, which is hardly typical of normal neural function over such a region. Thus, current techniques of ESB do initiate brain activity, but they do *not* duplicate the normal workings of the brain. Given the approximately ten *billion* neurons in the cortex alone, it is unlikely that ESB will ever mimic the brain's patterns over any significant area.

Electrical stimulation has been useful in increasing our understanding of the brain. In addition, clinical work like Penfield's has led to better, simpler methods of treating disorders like epilepsy. At the same time, it is inherently limited, in that it cannot tell us about how the brain functions as a whole. This means that larger scale functions, like consciousness, are unlikely to be revealed by ESB. For that, we must look to other approaches.

For further consideration

If technical and ethical constraints did not prevent it, would you be interested in having electrodes planted in a pleasure centre of your brain? What would be the advantages and disadvantages?

Computerized Imaging Techniques

More recently, a variety of techniques have been developed to study brain activity across large regions of the brain. These **computerized imaging** techniques, which use computers to assist in the analysis of information, are enabling researchers to gain new insights about brain function (Kevles 1996; Barinag 1997). While the details of each technique differ, they are similar in that the computer is used to convert a series of two-dimensional images into a three-dimensional model of the brain which can be viewed on a television monitor. The first technique, the *CAT scan*, was developed by British engineer Godfrey Hounsfield in 1971. It uses a series of X-ray images which are combined by a computer to create a 3-D picture of the brain. The limitation of the CAT scan, however, is that, like any X-ray, it shows physical structures, but reveals nothing about the *activity* within the brain.

Newer methods, notably PET (positron emission tomography) scans and magnetic resonance scans, have enabled doctors and researchers to study ongoing activity in the brain. In a *PET scan*, a short-lived radioactive substance is injected into the bloodstream along with glucose; when it reaches the brain, the active areas absorb more of the glucose, and with it, the radioactive tracer. Sensitive detectors then pinpoint the location of the tracer – and thereby tell researchers which parts of the brain are most active. *Magnetic resonance scans* (variously identified as either 'nuclear magnetic resonance scans' or 'magnetic resonance imaging' (MRI)) do not require injection of a radioactive tracer; instead, they utilize the response of electric charges within cells to large magnetic fields (called resonance) to identify areas of activity.

The new generation of scanning techniques enables researchers to examine aspects of brain function never before possible, without the need for invasive procedures like surgery. As such, scanning methods provide a new tool both for research into brain functions and to assist in the treatment of a range of disorders. For example, PET scans have identified markedly reduced activity in the cortex of depressed patients compared to normal individuals, and reduced frontal lobe activity in individuals with schizophrenia. MRI scans have proved equally useful. Using MRI to study cerebellar activity during sensory and motor tasks has led to recognition that the cerebellum does more than coordinate movement (Gao *et al.* 1996). More recently, MRIs have indicated that Penfield's classic mapping of the cortex (see Figure 2.4) may contain errors in the regions associated with the face; in particular, the parts associated with the forehead and chin should be reversed (Servos *et al.* 1999).

While very useful, computerized scanning techniques also have two major limitations: First, they are very expensive, and their use is unlikely to become routine for some time to come. Second, at present they are limited in their ability to pinpoint activity precisely – far less than electrical stimulation, for example. However, since PET scans and magnetic resonance are fairly recent, further improvements are likely to be seen in the years ahead.

In different ways, each of the above methods has contributed to our understanding of the brain. In many cases, the evidence seems to support the concept of localization of function. However, one must keep in mind that the brain is highly interconnected, and its activity is highly integrated (more of the brain is devoted to integration, via association areas, than to primary functions). Despite the existence of specialized functions, no one part can really be considered without the others. (An analogy might be a car: examining one part, such as the transmission, will not reveal the way the system as a whole functions.) As the example of Dr P (the music professor described by Oliver Sacks) shows, it is through the working of the whole that psychological processes are best seen.

<table>
<tr><td>

For further consideration

</td><td>

If you had access to scanning equipment, what aspect of behaviour would you like to study?

</td></tr>
</table>

Chemical Processes in Behaviour

As discussed in the preceding section, the CNS plays an essential role in coordinating behaviour. Neurons transmit sensory messages and allow motor responses to occur nearly instantaneously; the process of touching a hot stove and quickly removing one's hand is a good example. (This represents an example of a so-called *spinal reflex arc*, the simplest form of neural circuit; it involves only a sensory neuron and a motor neuron, which connect via a synapse in the spinal cord.) Despite the impression we may have from such experiences, nerve conduction is not truly instantaneous: the fastest speed for nerve impulses is about 150 metres per second in large myelinated sensory nerves, slowing to a mere tenth of a metre per second (point-to-point) in the brain stem. Our **reaction time** to respond to a stimulus is a reflection of the limits of this communication system. For example, in driving a car, it takes about three-quarters of a second to begin lifting your foot off the accelerator from the moment of seeing something you should stop for. At fifty m.p.h., you cover almost 17 metres in that time – and that doesn't count the time for the brakes to stop the car!

reaction time the time required to make a response to a stimulus, as measured by the interval between the stimulus and the response

Neurotransmitters

Despite being less than instantaneous, the nervous system is very effective in fulfilling its role as the body's communication network. Messages continually criss-cross, enabling us to perceive and respond to both our internal and external environments. In this system, the primary signals are the nerve impulses, racing along the axons. While the axon of a neuron may be compared to a wire which relays an electrical signal, a nerve impulse only travels within the neuron which generated it. At the junction between two neurons is a physical gap, the synapse. In order to bridge this gap, communication between neurons depends on an exchange of chemicals. These chemicals, called *neurotransmitters*, are released by the terminals of one neuron, and flow across the synaptic gap to the receptors of the next neuron. The first such substance identified was *acetylcholine*, which is released by motor neurons to activate muscle fibres; in the CNS, it has been implicated in learning and memory (Butt *et al.* 1997). Since acetylcholine was first identified in the 1930s, approximately 100 chemicals have been found which are involved in neural transmission (Cooper *et al.* 1991). Dopamine, for example, plays

Neurotransmitter	Where found in nervous system	Examples of functions
Acetylcholine	Throughout the brain Neuromuscular synapses	Learning and memory Control of muscles
Dopamine	Many locations, including Cerebellum, basal ganglia Limbic system	Motor activity, coordination Emotion and memory
Epinephrine	Many locations, including Sympathetic nervous system	Emotion, stress
GABA (gamma- aminobutyric acid)	Major inhibitory neurotransmitter found throughout brain	Anxiety, arousal, learning
Glutamate	Major excitatory neurotransmitter found throughout the nervous system	Anxiety, mood
Serotonin	Many locations, including Thalamus Brain stem	Sensory processing Sleep, arousal

Figure 2.6   Major neurotransmitters and their functions A range of
neurotransmitters exist in the nervous system, often serving different functions in
different parts of the brain.

a role in both motor control and sensory processing; low levels in motor
pathways produce Parkinson's disease, while high levels in sensory pathways
have been partially linked to schizophrenia. Recently, a study found that
playing battle-simulation video games raises dopamine levels, which may
account for their 'addictive' attraction to players (Koepp *et al.* 1998). While
it is not possible to review all the types of transmitters, it is worth noting
some basic concepts of neurotransmitter function. (See Figure 2.6 for an
overview of some of the major neurotransmitters and their functions.)

Neurotransmitter substances can function in various ways. Some neurotransmitters trigger activation of the neuron, called *excitation*; this is a bit
like stepping on the accelerator while driving a car. Others act to prevent
the neuron from firing, called *inhibition*; by reducing neural activity, this is
somewhat like stepping on the brakes while driving. Still other substances
act to block the excitatory or inhibitory chemicals, or to clear them away
after they have done their job. As we will see when we discuss drug effects,
this system provides the basis for a wide range of outcomes.

While well-adapted to providing quick responses, neuronal control has
its limitations. Neurons only communicate while they are active, and while
changes in activity can take place over fractions of a second, a neuron cannot
remain active indefinitely. Faced with constant stimulation, neurons begin
to reduce their response, a phenomenon called **habituation**. This means that
the nervous system is not well-suited to the regulation of slower-changing
processes like metabolism, growth and reproduction. To understand how
such processes are regulated, we must look at another type of chemical
process.

habituation a reduction in
neural response due to
continual stimulation

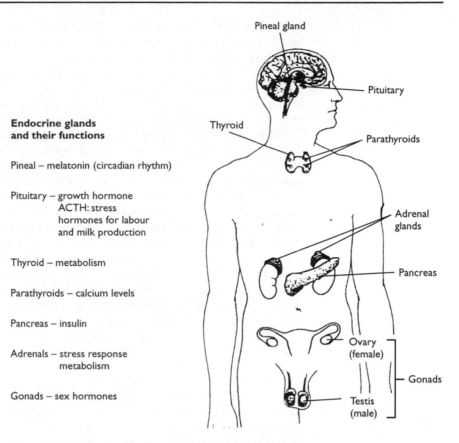

**Endocrine glands
and their functions**

Pineal – melatonin (circadian rhythm)

Pituitary – growth hormone
            ACTH: stress
            hormones for labour
            and milk production

Thyroid – metabolism

Parathyroids – calcium levels

Pancreas – insulin

Adrenals – stress response
            metabolism

Gonads – sex hormones

Figure 2.7   The endocrine system and hormonal functions The major hormone-secreting glands are illustrated, along with the functions of some of the major hormones produced.

Hormones

In contrast to the transient processes of nerve conduction, some bodily processes are based on another class of chemicals produced by glandular cells. These cells 'communicate' by means of chemical secretions. The most significant glands, from this standpoint, are the **endocrine glands**. These are a number of glands which secrete chemicals called **hormones** directly into the bloodstream, where they are carried to all parts of the body (see Figure 2.7). Given the time it takes for circulation through the body, the effect of these chemical messengers is not as swift as neural transmission – often it can be minutes, hours, weeks or longer before the response occurs. Not surprisingly, though, the effects are typically much longer lasting than those processes which are under direct neural control. In this sense, neural and hormonal processes are not competitive, but complementary.

At one time, the distinctions between neural and hormonal processes seemed both clear-cut and neat: the nervous system handled short-term functions with fast responses, and the endocrine system handled slower, long-term

endocrine glands ('ductless glands') glands which secrete chemicals called hormones directly into the bloodstream
hormone a chemical secreted by an endocrine gland; hormones are involved in many aspects of metabolism and long-term functioning of the body

functions. Instead, research in recent years has shown that the boundaries are not quite so distinct. One reason for this new view is the realization that the two systems directly interact. The *pituitary gland*, for example, which is sometimes called 'the master gland' because of its role in regulating other endocrine glands, also has direct linkages to the hypothalamus, whereby it can influence the nervous system. The hypothalamus, in turn, releases small amounts of hormones, which affect the endocrine system. While such interactions actually make sense – links between the systems presumably let the body function more effectively overall – they make separating their roles much harder. A couple of examples will indicate the concept. *Norepinephrine*, also called noradrenaline, is one example of such dual-purpose chemicals: it is one of the primary secretions of the adrenal glands, and also a neurotransmitter found in many parts of the nervous system (the neurons which use it as a neurotransmitter are called 'noradrenergic pathways'). *Vasopressin*, first identified as a hormone which influences blood pressure, is also used as a neurotransmitter by the hypothalamus, and has been shown to enhance memory and learning. While the method of delivery for neurotransmitters and hormones differs (i.e. release into the synapse or into the bloodstream), both processes involve receptors on the target (a neuron or a bodily organ), which are activated when the appropriate chemical binds to the receptor.

Similarly, it has been discovered that some chemicals influence neural transmission, while retaining roles as hormones. One example is the family of chemicals called *endorphins*, which can enhance our mood and reduce pain (Hoffman 1997). (The function of endorphins will be discussed further in relation to drug effects.) Variously called **neuropeptides** (a peptide is a short chain of amino acids) or neurohormones, they have further influenced our ideas about how the body functions, even as we try to puzzle out their role (Cooper *et al.* 1991). As time goes on, our understanding of the chemical processes which underlie behaviour will doubtless increase. At present, the new-found complexity is exciting, even as it cautions us never to assume we have the final picture.

neuropeptide a chemical, comprised of a short chain of amino acids, which can function both as a neurotransmitter and as a hormone; also called a neurohormone

For further consideration

Given that chemical processes are so important to the regulation of the nervous system, do you find it plausible that mental disorders could be caused by biochemical disturbances in the brain? What evidence would you look for?

Interactions of Mind and Body in Behaviour

Both neural and chemical processes are important to our understanding of the relationship between the brain and behaviour. In this chapter, we cannot cover all that is known about these processes. Rather, the intent is to give a basic description of how these physiological processes fit into the biological approach as a means of understanding behaviour. At the beginning of this chapter, we noted that the biological approach assumes that the mind is ultimately a product of the brain, with a physical basis.

This assumption is often referred to as *materialism*. At the same time, no one can presently explain precisely *how* mind and brain are connected, despite the progress made in understanding more basic functions. A person may be a type of 'machine' in the materialist sense, but it is an exceedingly complex machine. To help us understand this more clearly, we will examine some of the interactions between mind and body.

As already noted, it is impossible to identify the 'mind' with one particular brain structure, or portion of the body. Consciousness may depend on a normally functioning cortex, but other aspects of behaviour depend on other elements of the system. If we cannot localize the mind to a specific structure in the body, then how is it possible to study interactions of the two? It is precisely because they *are* separate conceptually, and require different types of description, that one can seek parallels. It is almost like trying to translate between two languages – words may not always be easy to match up, but in the end the ideas can be communicated. In this case, we are trying to translate between physiologically-based 'body' and psychologically-based 'mind'.

The Effects of Body on Mind

When we speak of effects of the body on the mind, we are referring to the effects of physically identifiable events (e.g. changes within the body) on psychological functioning and behaviour. Nearly all the identifiable events can be described in terms of neural and/or chemical processes. Obviously, this can include a wide range of effects, both transitory (e.g. a cup of coffee as a drug) and enduring (e.g. spinal injury or alcohol-induced memory deficits). In this section, we will focus on some problems which have significance because of what they tell us about the physical basis of behaviour. These include drugs, the electrical nature of brain activity and specialization in the brain.

The Study of Drug Effects

Technically, a drug is any substance which has an effect on living cells. Since this could include virtually any substance, including water, we will take a more restricted meaning of the term 'drug'. *Drugs* are chemical substances which are foreign to the body, either totally or in the form introduced. (For example, adrenaline is a hormone, but it may also be *injected* as a drug.) It is worth noting that not all drugs have discernible effects on *behaviour*. For example, penicillin reduces infections, but does not directly affect how we act. Nor need drugs always be medically prescribed: a morning cup of coffee is an example of drug use (or abuse), as is the illegal use of cocaine. The study of **psychoactive** (mind-affecting) **drugs** is a concern in both psychology and medicine, and has given rise to a hybrid field called *psychopharmacology*.

psychoactive drug a chemical agent which has a discernible effect on mental state or behaviour

The use of psychoactive drugs is probably as old as recorded history. Nearly every culture has used some type of fermented grain or vegetable to produce an alcoholic drink. Some South American tribes have long traditions of eating plants in order to produce hallucinations for religious rites. But it is only relatively recently that doctors have considered the use of drugs as a therapeutic tool, or that researchers have had effective methods to study drug effects.

Psychopharmacology today has become a complex field, but in the early days of drug research, research techniques were very pragmatic. Many psychoactive substances were first identified by studying plants which had already been used for folk remedies. For example, reserpine, one of the first tranquillizers, was originally isolated from Indian snakeroot; aspirin was isolated from willow bark. In other cases, researchers even experimented on themselves. Heinrich Kluver, a man noted for his contributions in other areas of physiological research, wrote a paper on his experience with mescaline, a hallucinogenic drug derived from a type of mushroom (Kluver 1966). Today, research techniques have become more formal and sophisticated.

The methods typically used today for research on psychoactive drugs are much like those for other types of drugs. Experimental animals are used to assess toxicity, strength and basis of effects. These assessments may involve intricate techniques and precision chemical analyses, such as injecting tiny amounts of the drug directly into specific regions of the brain, and then examining changes in neurotransmitter concentrations at nearby synapses. These methods often yield important information about the mechanism of drug actions, which is important to the preliminary screening of new drugs. Unfortunately, they do not provide sufficient information for a full understanding of drug effects.

Ultimately, psychoactive drugs must still be assessed by use on human subjects. There are several reasons for this. First, even the use of closely related species like chimpanzees does not always produce the same results as with people. Second, even if the effects are the same, assessing them in animals can be difficult. By definition, the key aspect of psychoactive drugs is their effect on behaviour, which can include changes in alertness, responsiveness, mood, memory and even perceptions. Obviously, it is difficult to assess these effects in animals. This leads to the most fundamental problem: how to categorize the effects of drugs.

By their nature, drugs operate on the physical system, yet the behavioural changes are primarily mental (perception, memory etc.). This leads back to the problem of linking mind and body. Consider some of the possible difficulties. (1) Some drugs will affect only certain clinical groups, and not other types of patients or normal individuals. (2) Some drugs affect sensory capacities in ways that are not directly expressed in behaviour. Consequently, even with verbal reports from subjects, it can be difficult to determine what is happening. (3) It is convenient to categorize drugs, but the categories may not always fit well with the subtleties of drug effects. For example, the label 'anti-depressant' focuses on one aspect of mood; however, drugs operate by affecting all neurons which have appropriate receptors, and this may involve much more than mood functions. The result can be a temptation to focus on an intended effect while overlooking various side-effects. For example, many drugs used to treat schizophrenia do so by affecting a neurotransmitter called *dopamine*. While such drugs can often reduce delusional thoughts and hallucinations, they also can affect motor responses, which also depend on dopamine. In the end, it can be very difficult to match behavioural descriptions, which are partly based on culture, to the physiological effects of a drug, which depend on complex sets of neural pathways (Snyder 1980). These problems are not insurmountable, as the increasing sophistication of psychopharmacology shows, but they do present continual challenges to researchers.

In addition to understanding in what ways a drug alters behaviour, we need to understand how it operates in the body. In this regard, there has been tremendous progress in recent years. Essentially, all psychoactive drugs operate by affecting communication between neurons. As was described earlier, communication across the synapse is dependent on neurotransmitters. These chemical messengers are released by the terminals at the end of the axon, and flow across the synaptic gap to the receptors on the next neuron (see Figure 2.2). The relationship of the receptor and the neurotransmitter may be compared to a lock and a key – only a particular shape of neurotransmitter molecule will fit in a given receptor. (There are also variations on this basic theme. Sometimes, a molecule will seem to fit, but not influence the neuron; this is something like a key which fits a lock, but won't turn. By blocking the receptor site, such a chemical may prevent the proper neurotransmitter from reaching its target receptor. In other cases, chemicals attack neurotransmitters in the synapse, destroying them before they can reach the receptors.) While this lock-and-key metaphor applies to all neurotransmitters and psychoactive drugs, it was the basis for one of the great discoveries of modern psychopharmacology: endorphins.

The story begins with interest in opiates – a family of drugs which includes morphine, heroin and opium, all derived from the opium poppy. Although opiates have been used for hundreds of years (notably through the smoking of opium), the basis for their euphoric effects was unknown. As psychopharmacology developed, it became clear that drugs which affect behaviour must do so by affecting neural activity. This suggested that there might be a type of neural receptor which opiates activate. Based on this reasoning, a young researcher named Candace Pert began looking for opiate receptors in the brain. After several failures, she succeeded – there were indeed opiate receptors in the human brain. What is more, comparative studies found that *many* species had such receptors – all the way down to the hagfish, which has existed essentially unchanged for 350 million years. This raised a new question: why should a 350 million-year-old fish have receptors for a chemical derived from a flower? The only reasonable answer seemed to be that there must be a similar chemical which occurs naturally in the brain. Given that the opiate receptor sites which Pert found were located in regions of the limbic system and brain stem that are associated with pain and emotion, it suggested that the body may produce its own natural painkillers. The race was on to find such chemicals, and within a year the search was successful. The first discovery was dubbed *enkephalin* (Greek for 'in the head'); shortly after, C. H. Li found what have become known as **endorphins** (for *end*ogenous – 'naturally occurring' – m*orphine*) (Villet 1978). It was quickly recognized that endorphins were not typical neurotransmitters, but were rather small molecules called peptides. This prompted increased interest in such neuropeptides – chemicals which function as both hormones and neurotransmitters (see 'Chemical processes in behaviour', above).

endorphin (*endogenous – 'naturally occurring' – morphine*) a neuropeptide which plays a significant role in pain and mood states

Subsequent research has found that, as Pert believed, endorphins play a role in pain relief, and may also mediate mood enhancement associated with exercise (so-called 'runner's high') (Hoffman 1997).

The discovery of endorphins is like a detective story: finding clues, making deductions about what they mean and testing hypotheses until the solution is found. It also provides a good model for how drugs are discovered and evaluated today: by examining the molecular shape, and matching it with receptor sites in the brain.

For further consideration

If you were a researcher for a drug company, what kinds of psychoactive drugs would you want to search for? Drugs to relieve pain? Depression or other disorders? Or would you focus on drugs to enhance intellectual performance and memory? Should drugs be used to treat problems, or to enhance life? Why?

Types of Psychoactive Drugs

Advances in psychopharmacology have led to an increasing diversity of psychoactive drugs, and also to more widespread usage. At the same time, the frequency of their use has led to a change in social attitudes, so that drugs are more widely accepted, and in fact may be actively sought. (Studies suggest that well over half the visits to doctors include writing a prescription – in part, because patients have come to see drugs as a panacea.) In addition to prescription drugs, there are a number of drugs which have behavioural effects, but these are often overlooked by consumers because of their non-prescription nature. For example, antihistamines, which are commonly used for the sinus problems of allergies, can also cause drowsiness – in fact, one common antihistamine, diphenhydramine, is marketed as an allergy medication, and separately as a non-prescription sleeping aid! Given their pervasive presence in our culture, it is worth examining some commonly encountered drugs and their effects.

Psychoactive drugs are commonly divided into various categories, according to the general nature of their effects on behaviour (although, as noted previously, such categories are often imprecise). One category often overlooked in daily experience is the **stimulants**. Stimulants act on both the CNS and the autonomic nervous system (a portion of the peripheral nervous system that controls such functions as heart rate and breathing, as well as general arousal level); in the CNS, they increase the activity in neurons which use *dopamine* as a neurotransmitter (Baldessarini and Tarzi 1996). (As noted earlier, dopamine affects a number of functions, including motor control and cognitive processes.) These drugs tend to decrease fatigue, increase physical activity and alertness, diminish hunger and produce a temporary elevation of mood. Both *caffeine* and *nicotine* are stimulants, although not as powerful as the prescription drugs known as *amphetamines*.

Because stimulants tend to diminish hunger, amphetamines are sometimes prescribed as 'diet pills'. Smokers often experience a related effect when they reduce their smoking: the reduced nicotine level leads to an increase in appetite. Amphetamines are also sometimes prescribed for treating hyperactive children, who show unusually high activity levels and an

stimulant a drug which increases activation of the CNS and the autonomic nervous system, typically by increasing levels of dopamine; these drugs tend to decrease fatigue, increase physical activity and alertness, diminish hunger and produce a temporary elevation of mood

inability to concentrate; for reasons which are not clear, amphetamines seem to calm them down. Beyond these uses, stimulants have very few legitimate applications. They do not really reduce depression, nor are they a proper substitute for sleep when fatigued. Yet their use (and misuse) is widespread – sometimes users are even unaware, since stimulants like caffeine can be found in many common foods.

Caffeine is found not only in coffee, but also in tea, cola and even chocolate bars. Children exposed to average amounts of cola and sweets may be accustomed to caffeine long before they ever taste coffee. Nicotine, found in cigarettes, is also a stimulant. Although stimulants like caffeine and nicotine are treated casually in our culture, they nonetheless can cause adverse effects. With prolonged use, the nervous system tends to adapt to the presence of the stimulants. This can result in the phenomenon of *tolerance*, whereby one needs higher and higher doses to maintain the effect. In extreme cases, misuse of drugs can lead to *addiction*, which is determined by the occurrence of symptoms of physical *withdrawal*: when a person is addicted, stopping usage of the drug provokes vomiting, muscle and heart tremors and seizures. (Note that addiction is *not* limited to stimulants – the pattern can arise with a variety of drugs.) While withdrawal symptoms to caffeine and nicotine are usually relatively mild, amphetamine abuse can be more serious. Chronic high doses of amphetamines can lead to marked side-effects, including hallucinations, delusions and even a psychosis very similar to paranoid schizophrenia. (This phenomenon is one reason why researchers believe schizophrenia may be caused by excessive dopamine levels, as will be discussed in Chapter 9.)

depressant a drug which reduces CNS activity, by enhancing the effects of the neurotransmitter GABA; in large doses, depressants can cause coma and even death

Curiously, individuals often confuse stimulants with **depressants**, which reduce CNS activity, and in large doses can cause coma and even death. Among the well-known depressants are alcohol and barbiturates. People often regard alcohol as a stimulant, because in small doses it reduces inhibitions and increases talkativeness. In reality, these effects are due to differential sensitivity to the depressant effects by different parts of the brain. The 'higher' functions of the cortex are the first to be affected, which can lead to less self-consciousness and a reduction in learned inhibitions. In large enough quantities, alcohol (like other depressants) is a general anaesthetic, producing loss of consciousness. Over time, large doses of alcohol can also cause severe physiological effects, including memory deficits and liver damage.

Alcohol and other depressants seem to enhance the effects of GABA, which is probably the most significant inhibitory neurotransmitter in the brain (see Figure 2.6). Not only do about a third of all neurons in the brain have GABA receptors, but GABA can also directly affect axons, changing the threshold for firing. Alcohol's GABA-enhancing effects are similar to those of tranquillizers like Valium (benzodiazepine). This mechanism not only accounts for the anti-anxiety effects of alcohol, but may also explain reported claims of tolerance and dependence for the benzodiazepines (Smith 1992).

Abuse of alcohol may well be endemic in our culture: it has been estimated that five per cent of the population in both the United States and Canada have a serious drinking problem, and alcoholism is a problem in virtually all countries (Helzer and Canino 1992). No one is certain whether alcoholism is based on a physiological malfunction or is based on learned drinking patterns. There is evidence that it runs in families, but this may mean either that there is a genetic cause or that the children learn patterns from their parents. In either case, most treatments show only limited rates of success. Alcohol may well be our largest drug problem.

While depressant drugs can alleviate anxiety, they differ significantly from anti-depressant drugs. **Anti-depressant** drugs are used to treat severe clinical depression, which is characterized by low mood state, fatigue and feelings of hopelessness. Early anti-depressant drugs, called *MAO inihibitors*, blocked the enzyme monoamine oxidase, which breaks down the neurotransmitters norepinephrine and serotonin. Unfortunately, this often created adverse side-effects, which is not surprising given the many ways these two neurotransmitters are used in the brain. More recently, a new class of anti-depressants has been developed, called *SSRIs* (selective serotonin reuptake inhibitors). As the name implies, they mainly affect neurons which use serotonin, and enhance the effects of serotonin by delaying its reuptake by the terminals of the neurons which released it. Not surprisingly, SSRIs (such as Prozac) tend to have fewer side-effects than the MAO inhibitors, since they do not affect the functioning of norepinephrine. The difference between the two classes of anti-depressants is a good example of how pharmacologists are seeking to develop drugs with more specific effects.

While by no means exhaustive, the preceding discussion should demonstrate that psychoactive drugs, both prescription and non-prescription, are extremely common. Their prevalence often lulls people into thinking they are harmless, yet chronic, casual use of drugs can be a danger in many ways. As noted, prolonged use can lead to tolerance and addiction. In other cases, side-effects may be infrequent but severe. (For example, Prozac can severely suppress appetite in some individuals; at one time, its manufacturer considered seeking certification for its use as a diet pill.) Another potential problem can arise due to the interaction of a drug with other drugs or even certain foods. For example, barbiturates (a depressant) can interact with alcohol (also a depressant) in a *synergistic* manner – that is, the effect of the two together is greater than for either alone. (Marilyn Monroe died from a combination of alcohol and barbiturates.) Some cheeses, such as Danish Blue or Roquefort, can also be dangerous or even lethal if consumed while taking certain drugs. (Not long ago, there was a public scare when it was discovered that some non-prescription hay fever remedies could interact with a common antibiotic, erythromycin, to produce potentially deadly heart irregularities.)

Our knowledge of synergistic effects is limited at present, and undiscovered combinations may exist. Unfortunately, casual attitudes towards drugs may lead to underestimating possible risks. For the present, the best approach seems to be caution: never take a drug without reason, and then only under a doctor's supervision. Always tell a doctor about medicines being taken which may have been prescribed by another doctor. If you take a drug, watch for drowsiness or other side-effects that may impair your ability to deal with your surroundings.

anti-depressant a drug which is used to treat clinical depression, primarily by enhancing the activity of the neurotransmitter serotonin

Mood-altering drugs are not new; nor are the circumstances that lead people to seek relief from anxiety. However, our understanding of the mechanism of such drugs is growing. The methods of research are becoming more sophisticated, and with them our ability to use drugs as a therapeutic tool. While no amount of research can ever determine social attitudes, ideally such attitudes are based on knowledge. To this end, the next few years offer hope of great strides in our ability to understand the role of drugs in mind–body interactions.

<table>
<tr><td>**For further consideration**</td><td>If you use caffeine (found in coffee, tea, colas and chocolate) or nicotine (found in tobacco), you might consider whether you notice any effects the next time you ingest the drug. If you don't notice any effects, could this mean you have developed a *tolerance* for the drug?</td></tr>
</table>

The Split Brain and the Whole Mind

According to the materialist view, consciousness *must* have a physical basis, most probably in the brain. The problem for researchers has been to find a way of identifying it. While research has produced support for the principle of localization of function, it still has not answered the question: where is the mind?

Normally, our experience of the world, our inner thoughts and feelings, seems unitary – that is, we have only a single consciousness. Yet the structure of the brain, especially the cortex, is basically two symmetrical halves. These halves, made up of the cortex and underlying structures, are called the **cerebral hemispheres**. Connecting the two hemispheres is a wide band of nerve fibres called the **corpus callosum**. Researchers have long known that each hemisphere is basically responsible for the opposite side of the body (e.g. your left hemisphere receives sensations from, and gives motor commands to, the right side of your body). Now, if consciousness is really associated with the cortex, then it implies that the unitary nature of our experience and awareness is based on the integration of the two hemispheres. This reasoning led pioneering psychologist Gustav Fechner to speculate, more than one hundred years ago, that if the two hemispheres were somehow separated, we would have *two* separate consciousnesses. Fechner never thought that this could be tested, but time has proven differently.

In the 1950s, psychologist Roger Sperry, working with monkeys, suggested that separating the two hemispheres by cutting the fibres of the corpus callosum had no grave effects on behaviour – certainly less than procedures like frontal lobotomy. Still, this gave no indication of what might happen in humans. One obvious difference between primates and people is that monkeys do not speak, and Broca had shown that speech was found in only one hemisphere. Consequently, no one was sure what would happen if the hemispheres were separated in a person.

The answer to the question came as a result of medical needs. In the 1960s, a Los Angeles surgeon named Philip Vogel was trying to treat patients with a long history of epilepsy. While in many cases epileptics could be treated with anti-seizure drugs (and more progress has been made since then), these

cerebral hemispheres two half spheres, made up of the cortex and underlying structures, which comprise the major portion of the brain
corpus callosum a wide band of nerve fibres which connect the two hemispheres

Roger W. Sperry

Roger Walcott Sperry (1913–) is an American neurological researcher who pioneered much of our understanding of hemispheric specialization. His career began relatively slowly, and he received his doctorate in zoology at the University of Chicago at the age of 28. While there, he worked with the biophysicist Paul Weiss, studying how the connections between neurons and muscles are formed. This led to further work on the regeneration of neural connections between the retina and brain in amphibians. While doing this work, he met biologist Norma Dupree, with whom he collaborated; they married in 1949. In 1952, he moved to the California Institute of Technology, where he remains a professor emeritus of psychobiology. In 1953, one of his graduate students, Ronald Myers, invented the split-brain procedure, the study of which later led to Sperry's most important discoveries; ironically, Myers's initial role is seldom cited in this regard. They first studied the effects of severing the corpus callosum in cats and primates; however, it was Sperry's later work on epileptic patients, in collaboration with neurosurgeon Joseph Bogen, that eventually led to Sperry sharing the 1981 Nobel Prize in Physiology or Medicine. Sperry's contributions continue to be carried further by his students, including Jerre Levy and Michael Gazzaniga.

patients did not respond to drug treatment; consequently, they had major seizures on average twice a week. In epilepsy, the random neural activity of a seizure usually starts at a point in one hemisphere and spreads, creating sensory distortions and convulsions. In cases of *grand mal* attacks, the seizure activity spreads from one hemisphere to the other across the bridge provided by the corpus callosum. In such cases, the recurring seizures can disrupt normal life, and even present a life-threatening situation. When all other treatments failed, Vogel tried a new and radical approach: by cutting the fibres of the corpus callosum, he hoped to restrict the seizure activity to one hemisphere, and thus prevent grand mal attacks. While he knew of Sperry's work, and there had been occasional clinical reports of damage to the corpus callosum, no one had ever purposely separated the hemispheres before. Vogel and his patients were venturing into new territory.

Medically, the treatment worked. Not only did it prevent further grand mal attacks, but (for reasons still unclear) it also reduced the frequency of more limited seizures. At the same time, it was desirable to know what negative effects, if any, the surgery had caused. Knowing of Sperry's research, Vogel asked him to collaborate on evaluating the patients. The results were a surprise to all concerned.

Initial observations suggested that the patients were remarkably normal. Everyday actions like walking and eating seemed to occur naturally. However, by a series of ingenious testing procedures, Sperry, Vogel and their associates discovered that, in fact, these individuals had an unusual mental syndrome. As Sperry reported, 'Instead of the normally unified single stream of consciousness, these patients behave in many ways as if they have two independent streams of conscious awareness, one in each hemisphere, each of which is cut off from and out of contact with the mental experience of the other' (Sperry 1968: 724). In other words, *two* minds, each functioning separately from the other – Fechner's prediction had been correct! (Ultimately, Sperry's research on the split brain led to his receiving the Nobel Prize in Physiology in 1981.)

To assess the effects of the surgery, the researchers had to use techniques whereby information was presented to only one hemisphere. The simplest case involved touch: if the split-brain person were given an object in their *left* hand while blindfolded, the left hand could later pick it out again, by touch, from a selection of several objects. However, if the *right* hand attempted to pick out the article previously held by the left hand, it did no better than chance. In the case of vision, the situation is a bit more complicated, because each eye is connected to *both* hemispheres. The division of visual processing is such that the visual world of each eye is divided in two, so that objects on the *left* side of the visual world (or *visual field*) are seen by the *right* hemisphere, while objects on the *right* side are seen by the *left* hemisphere, regardless of which eye is used (see Figure 2.8). Thus, if a person looks straight ahead and an image briefly appears to the left, only the right hemisphere receives the information. This led to an interesting discovery: because only the left hemisphere had language, a split-brain person presented with a word or picture on the left side (conveyed to the right hemisphere) could not say what they had seen! Only the left hemisphere seemed able to talk, while the right was silent. (Note, of course, that these effects only apply when the corpus callosum has been cut; in a normal individual, there is continual exchange of information between the two hemispheres.)

As it turns out, the differences are not quite what they first seemed. The right hemisphere, while usually unable to speak, is not completely ignorant of language. If presented with a word or picture, it can *point* to a corresponding picture or word. Thus, if the right hemisphere sees the word 'key', the left hand can correctly choose a key. At the same time, the right hemisphere has musical and spatial abilities which seem to be lacking in the left hemisphere. If given geometric figures to copy (such as a circle overlapping a square), the left hand (right hemisphere) does a better job of copying it than does the right hand (left hemisphere). This is particularly striking, since the patients Sperry tested were all right-handed, so in principle one might expect the right hand to be more skilled. For handwriting, the right hand *is* better; for drawing, it is not. (This raises a fascinating problem: since lettering is a type of artistic skill, why is it that the left hand, so superior for other drawing tasks, cannot reproduce letters and words? So far, this aspect of the split-brain phenomenon has not been fully explored.)

Despite the apparent handicap and dual-consciousness which they possess, split-brain individuals manage to cope very well in everyday life. Even tasks requiring motor coordination of the two hemispheres, such as riding a bicycle, can be mastered. Over time, it even seems that indirect methods of communicating between the two sides develop. For example, in one experiment, Sperry flashed either a red or green card to the left visual field (right hemisphere), and then asked the person to name (left hemisphere) the

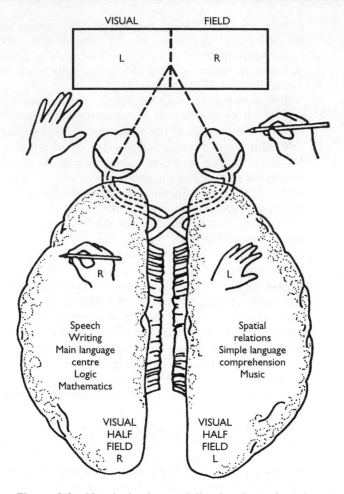

Figure 2.8 Hemispheric specialization Roger Sperry's work with split-brain individuals (note the cut fibres of the corpus callosum between the hemispheres) has helped to identify differences in the functions of the two sides of the brain. (After Sperry 1968.)

colour. As expected, the left hemisphere, not having seen the colour, did poorly. However, if allowed to reconsider, the person was always correct. What seemed to happen was that the right hemisphere, hearing the spoken response of the left hemisphere, would produce grimaces and other gestures if the answer was wrong. These cues let the left hemisphere know its error, which it then corrected!

Since Sperry's original research, a large number of studies have been done, even though the number of split-brain individuals is quite small (between 1962 and 1968, Vogel operated on a total of nine patients). Overall, the results have supported Sperry's original work, although it is now recognized that the differences between the hemispheres are not absolute (Trevarthen

1987). Still, the research does suggest several things: (a) if the corpus callosum is cut, the two hemispheres function independently; (b) each hemisphere seems to possess consciousness, but without awareness of the other (in one case, a patient, seeing her left hand make a response, exclaimed, 'I didn't do that!'); (c) the two hemispheres seem to show different types of specialized abilities, with the left hemisphere usually possessing language, logic and maths skills, and the right hemisphere spatial and musical skills.

The Split Brain and the Normal Brain

The striking nature of the split-brain findings makes it tempting to extend the conclusions to normal individuals. At the same time, it must be recognized that severing the corpus callosum is not a natural condition, and normally the two hemispheres freely communicate. Still, research seeking to test these findings in normal individuals does indicate that the two hemispheres tend to become specialized in ways similar to what has been observed in split-brain individuals. For example, clinical cases show that damage to the left hemisphere, whether by disease or trauma, can impair speech. (It should be noted that in a small percentage of people, primarily left-handers, the pattern of hemispheric specialization is modified or reversed.) Research has also suggested that there may be gender-related differences in organization and functioning. While at present the data are not conclusive, the indications are that language is less lateralized in women (i.e. that both hemispheres are involved), and that men are superior in spatial tasks (Shaywitz *et al.* 1995; Gazzaninga *et al.* 1998). (Interestingly, women seem to show variations in spatial performance related to oestrogen variations during the menstrual cycle, performing worse when oestrogen levels are high (Silverman and Phillips 1997).)

cerebral dominance the tendency for one hemisphere to be superior for particular functions, as expressed through behaviours like handedness

One issue that has arisen out of split-brain research is an increased interest in **cerebral dominance** – the tendency for one hemisphere to be superior for particular functions. In most individuals, one hand, foot, eye and ear are usually preferred for many actions – for instance, if standing, we begin walking with the dominant foot. Similarly, if using a camera or telescope, we usually focus with the dominant eye. Such preferences have been noted since ancient times, and the origin of cerebral dominance has caused much speculation among researchers. Evidence suggests that dominance, as seen in preferences for one side, is already developing at birth.

Handedness, which is the most visible indicator of dominance, has often been the focus of social prejudice. In many languages and cultures, being left-handed is viewed negatively. This can be seen in the way we use words: A 'left-handed compliment' is not really a compliment. To be 'right' is to be correct. A suspicious person is 'sinister' (Latin for left-handed), while a skilful person is 'dextrous' (Latin for right-handed). Similarly, a 'gauche' (French for left) remark is in bad taste. These usages reflect a form of cultural bias, and lead to questions about the origin of handedness, and dominance more generally.

Theories of the origin of handedness cover a broad range, including genetic factors, prenatal learning (position within the womb) and congenital brain damage (left-handedness being the result of such damage) (Previc 1991; Corballis 1997). At present, there is no conclusive evidence for any of these theories. While it is known that dominance is somehow related to hemispheric specialization (for example, stuttering in adults correlates highly with forcing right hand use for a left-handed child), no one is sure exactly what the connection is. Attempts to alter dominance *do* seem to have some impact on skills like language, but that does not prove that dominance is the source of specialization. In fact, the *pattern* of hemispheric specialization seems basically the same in both left- and right-dominant individuals (although left-handers are slightly more likely to show a reversed or mixed pattern of hemispheric specialization). In addition, there is no proven explanation as to why right-handedness (dominant left hemisphere) is the norm across races and cultures. Like many aspects of brain function, we still have many unanswered questions about handedness, dominance in general and hemispheric specialization. Even so, most researchers would agree that, despite social prejudices, one should not interfere if a child shows a preference for being left-handed.

The research on the split-brain and cerebral dominance brings us back to our initial questions: is localization of function correct, and does consciousness reside in the brain? The research on split-brain individuals seems to indicate that consciousness involves the cortex, for separating the cerebral hemispheres seems to split consciousness as well. However, since it involves such a large-scale division, it offers us very little information in terms of determining precisely *where* consciousness resides. After all, the hemispheres each involve cortex, underlying sub-cortical tissue, limbic system structures and so on, down into the brain stem, spinal cord and beyond. To say that the two sides of the body can each have their own consciousness does not tell us what sort of structure *produces* consciousness. A materialist view which assumes localization of function would argue that we should be able to find some particular neural circuit that represents conscious awareness. At present, no study has found such a circuit; current attempts to do so tend to limit themselves to particular aspects of consciousness, such as visual awareness or attention (Crick and Koch 1992; Newman 1995). The resulting ambiguity has led different researchers to take different points of view. In a book written shortly before his death, Penfield noted the absence of any evidence for the localization of consciousness. Consequently, he concluded that consciousness was not a function of the brain, and he essentially reverted to a form of dualism (Penfield 1975). Sperry, by contrast, simply rejects the idea that consciousness is localized, without abandoning materialism. He views consciousness as an *emergent property* of the brain (that is, a phenomenon which emerges from the system working as a whole), and suggests that no study of individual parts will enable us to pin it down (Sperry 1969). This view is supported by a recent French study, which found that the moment of visual recognition of an image was marked by synchronized activity across many areas of the brain (Rodriguez *et al.* 1999). Neurologist Antonio Damasio goes even further than Sperry, arguing that the mind is a product of the entire organism, operating as an ensemble (Damasio 1994). In his view, not only the brain must be considered, but also its links to the rest of the body; severing any of these links would also change the mind. (Thus, to go back to the 'brain in a vat' question raised earlier, Damasio would say a brain removed from the body could never function as a normal mind.) At present, all these views are ultimately speculative, but current data suggest both that there *is* localization of some functions, and that the nervous system works as a coherent unity. In this sense, it may well be that the mind *is* connected to the body – but the terms may remain forever separate in our descriptions.

For further consideration	Are you left- or right-handed? Consider the types of skills that are associated with each hemisphere. Do you see any relationship between your own dominant hemisphere and your relative abilities? (Remember, the preferred hand is associated with the *opposite* hemisphere.)

The Effects of Mind on Body

'Mind over matter'. The phrase has been used to describe many things, from accomplishing a difficult task to claims of levitation. The most common meaning is to describe how physical reactions are seemingly altered by mental processes. The view that this is paradoxical or impossible can be traced to Descartes's dualistic conception of mind and body, in which the mind has no physical basis. In this sort of framework, it becomes difficult to imagine how mental states could affect specific body functions. By contrast, in a materialist framework, where mind and body are linked, it becomes easier to conceive of such interactions. 'Mind' and 'brain' may represent different levels of description, but materialism assumes that they have a common physical foundation.

This unified view can help us to understand what would otherwise be inexplicable phenomena. A common example is the reaction to painful stimuli. Everyday observation demonstrates that different people react differently to similar physical traumas. To one person a trip to the dentist may be terrifying, whereas to another it is no more painful than scratching an itch. In our culture, childbirth is usually regarded as an intensely painful experience, yet members of some other cultures experience it differently (Melzack 1973). Thus, response to painful stimuli seems to show considerable variation. Pain researcher Ronald Melzack believes that such variations across individuals are owing to differing cognitive expectations and perceptions. Since cognitive processes (including perception and attitudes) are regarded as functions of the cortex, Melzack's theory says that the effects of expectations on pain response are mediated by cortical influences. Phantom limb phenomena, as mentioned in the introduction, may also be the product of the way the person interprets sensory inputs, rather than an automatic response (Melzack 1992). Such phenomena give new meaning to the phrase 'mind over matter', by suggesting that mental states can influence physical functioning and behaviour. In this section, we will consider some of the research that is helping to improve our understanding of the processes involved.

Stress

Like pain, stress is a common human experience. We are all familiar with stressful events: the boss wants to see you *now* about the last quarter's sales figures; or your heart races as you sit down to write a test; or you go to bed, only to hear the neighbour's stereo blaring away. The pulse-pounding, gut-wrenching sensations that result from such moments are common in modern life. When we recognize the feelings, we may experience the desire to run away to a desert island. Unfortunately, even this may not solve the problem of stress.

According to Hans Selye, the doctor who pioneered stress research, **stress** is the non-specific response of the body to any demand on it (Selye 1978). Simply being alive is 'stressful'; in this sense, there is no escape from stress. But not all stress situations are alike, nor are all reactions harmful. To understand this, first consider what happens when one experiences stress.

Biologically, stress reactions are an emergency response intended to prepare one for 'fight or flight'. A significant link in the body's chain of reactions to stressful situations is the release of hormones by the adrenal glands. The **adrenal glands**, located just above the kidneys, are made up of two portions, the *cortex* or outer covering, and the *medulla* or inner core. When stimulated, the adrenal medulla secretes *adrenaline* (also called epinephrine) and *noradrenaline* (norepinephrine). Each of these hormones plays a role in stress reactions. (As noted previously, the same chemicals also function as neurotransmitters.)

The release of adrenaline into the bloodstream triggers effects in both the brain and the peripheral nervous system. In the brain, it increases activity (particularly in the reticular formation, which controls overall arousal). In turn, the reticular formation sends signals to the autonomic branch of the peripheral nervous system, which shuts off digestion, increases heart rate and raises blood pressure, among other reactions (see Figure 2.9). Since among the organs affected by the autonomic nervous system are the adrenal glands, the sequence of responses is a so-called 'closed loop', which means that the stress reaction produced by adrenaline can be prolonged. Anyone who has been startled or has otherwise experienced sudden stress knows that the racing heartbeat and other signs can linger beyond the moment of stress.

Noradrenaline also plays a role in stress reactions, but more indirectly. Travelling through the bloodstream, it goes to the brain, where it activates another gland, the **pituitary**, which in turn releases another hormone, ACTH. ACTH in turn reaches the adrenals, causing the adrenal cortex to produce hormones called steroids. (Note that the adrenal *medulla*, not the *cortex*, produces noradrenaline and adrenaline.)

Steroids (sometimes called 'corticosteroids') play a role in a diverse range of body processes. They are involved in the normal regulation of water and sugar metabolism, including the quick release of sugar for energy under stress. They also affect the immune system, including inflammatory response. Synthetic forms of the steroids (e.g. cortisone) are also used in medicine for the treatment of allergic reactions, arthritis and shock. Steroids can also affect mood: one reaction to large doses of cortisone can be severe depression.

stress a term coined by Hans Selye to describe the non-specific response of the body to any demand on it

adrenal glands endocrine glands, located just above the kidneys, which play an important role in arousal and stress; the outer layer, the *cortex*, secretes corticosteroids, and the *medulla* (the inner core) secretes *adrenaline* (epinephrine) and *noradrenaline* (norepinephrine)

pituitary gland a small gland adjacent to the hypothalamus which regulates many endocrine functions, including growth, and also interacts with the nervous system via hypothalamic connections; in stress, it releases a hormone called ACTH, which triggers the release of steroids by the cortex of the adrenal glands; sometimes called 'the master gland' because of its many functions

steroids hormones produced by the cortex of the adrenal glands which are involved in the regulation of water and sugar metabolism, immune system function and other basic bodily processes; sometimes called 'corticosteroids'

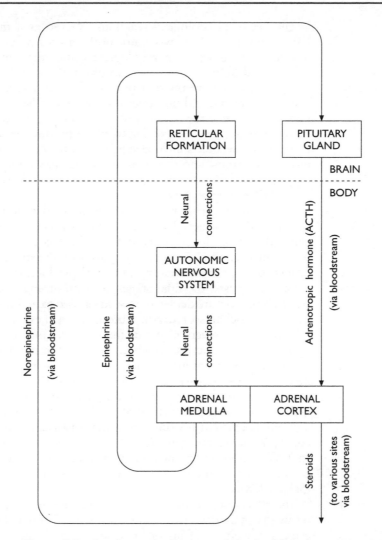

Figure 2.9   A schematic diagram of the body's response to stress Stress reactions involve a series of effects involving an interaction of the nervous system and the hormonal system. Note that the response involving epinephrine is a 'closed loop', which tends to be self-maintaining in the absence of offsetting interventions by the parasympathetic division of the autonomic nervous system.

While this description may seem to emphasize the role of the adrenal glands, the changes associated with stress are actually a complex sequence involving many parts of the body, as noted above. This sequence, sometimes called the 'fight or flight' response, has its origins far back in the evolution of the brain (similar patterns are found in all mammals, for example). The adrenals play a major role (e.g. injections of adrenaline can initiate many of the effects), but stress is an integrated response of the body to whatever is perceived as an emergency situation.

This set of physiological reactions evolved as a means of coping with danger, but it presents two major problems for modern humans. First, the 'danger' may often be psychological rather than physical (e.g. pressure to meet a deadline), and hence no physical response is either required or appropriate. This means that one is left with a surge of activity-oriented chemical changes, and no outlet for the energy. Second, the stress response may carry beyond the moment of crisis; under conditions of chronic stress, there can be severe effects owing to excess production of steroids and related changes. These effects include suppressing the body's immune system. Viral infections, asthma and rheumatoid arthritis are among the disorders which may be affected by stress responses (Selye 1976; Solomon 1990; Heninger 1995; O'Leary *et al.* 1997).

general adaptation syndrome a model of stages of stress identified by Hans Selye, ranging from acute stress (alarm) to outward coping (resistance) to finally depletion of bodily resources (exhaustion)

Selye identified what he called the **general adaptation syndrome** of stress, involving three stages. The initial, acute stress response identified above is called *alarm*. If the stress continues, there is a second stage, *resistance*, where the organism seems to be coping with the stress and *outward* signs of arousal disappear (internally, hormonal production, etc. continues). If the situation persists, the final stage, *exhaustion*, may be reached, where the body's resources are depleted; in studies with experimental animals, this has resulted in sickness or death. Autopsies on these animals reveal enlarged adrenal glands, severe ulcers of the stomach and shrinkage of the thymus gland and lymph nodes, which are involved in the body's immune system.

Interestingly, what first led Selye to the study of stress was an observation he made as a second-year medical student in 1926. As part of their clinical training, the students encountered patients suffering from a variety of disorders. Selye noted that 'they all looked sick'. His professors and fellow students laughed at his suggestion that disease, no matter what its nature, could produce certain consistent changes. Some ten years later, Selye returned to this question, and named the syndrome 'stress' (the term, borrowed from physics, was meant to refer to the effects of resisting an outside force) (Selye 1978).

The effects of chronic stress have been indirectly confirmed by research by two psychiatrists. In the late 1940s, Dr Thomas Holmes became interested in the effects of major life-changes on the health of his patients. For this purpose, he examined the case histories of more than 5,000 patients, and developed a 'stress barometer' of life changes (see Figure 2.10). Later, Dr Richard Rahe used Holmes's work as the basis for a study of 2,500 men in the US Navy. Using the stress scale as a predictor of illness over a twelve-month period, he found that those who underwent the highest number of life-changes suffered nearly twice as many ailments as those in the lowest category (Rahe 1972). While this research is correlational (as is much of the research on stress), the pattern has been supported in other studies (e.g. Brown and Harris 1989). For example, a study which followed laid-off Finnish workers over several months found high rates of depression and stress-related illnesses (Viinamaeki *et al.* 1996). Overall, the results tend to suggest that stress is a significant factor in determining health. (The possible mechanisms for this will be discussed below; see 'Medicine and the mind'.)

While it is clear that stress can have negative consequences, these consequences are not inevitable. Stress can be created by life situations, but the

A barometer of stress

Stressful experiences can have great impact on a person's ability to function. But what are stressful circumstances, and what types of experience typically cause the greatest stress? A long-term study by Rahe, referred to in the text, attempted to answer these questions by looking at the effects of various events on the probability of becoming ill. Generally, the effects were found to be additive – that is, people who went through more life changes were more likely to get sick. High stress levels seem to impair the body's ability to function.

A look at the table below will show you the estimated stress-value of various events. Rahe suggested that if your stress total went above 150 for any twelve-month period, you were in a high-risk group, and should heed the storm warnings of the stress barometer.

Rank	Life event	Stress score
1	Death of spouse	100
2	Divorce	75
3	Marital separation	65
4	Jail term	63
5	Death of close family member	63
6	Personal injury or illness	53
7	Marriage	50
8	Fired from job	47
9	Marital reconciliation	45
10	Retirement	45
18	Change to different line of work	36
25	Outstanding personal achievement	28
27	Begin or end school	26
32	Change residence	20
40	Change in eating habits	13
41	Vacation	13
43	Minor violations of the law	11

Adapted from Rahe (1972)

Figure 2.10   The Holmes–Rahe life-change scale

effects depend not only on the situation, but also on one's perception of the situation and one's mode of response (Endler 1997). Life-threatening situations by their nature create stress, but individuals will sometimes react to more minor situations (like a traffic jam) with the same fight-or-flight response. The individual's interpretation of the situation may in fact be the most important determinant of the effects of 'stressful' situations. As was discussed in Chapter 1, individuals perceive any situation in terms of their own cognitive schemata. Since materialists would argue that cognitive processes are embedded in the cortex, the link between perceptions and stress becomes potentially understandable as an interaction of the mind and body.

Psychologists David Glass and Jerome Singer have explored how our perceptions affect our response to stressful situations (Glass and Singer 1972). Their work, which concerns sources of urban stress, arose out of the observation that it is very hard to get agreement about what is a **stressor** (source of stress). For example, a person who has been thinking of making a career change may welcome an offer of early retirement, whereas a person content in their job may be very upset at a similar offer. Similarly, being pushed into cold water may sound stressful, yet every New Year's Day

stressor any factor which triggers a stress response in an individual

members of 'polar bear clubs' willingly jump into icy lakes or oceans. Thus, having control (or even feeling you have control) of the situation can reduce the effects of a stressor. This element of *perceived control* was also confirmed in a field experiment performed in a nursing home (Langer and Rodin 1976). Another factor influencing the impact of stressors is *predictability*. People who live near railway tracks often show no discomfort from the sounds, which tend to occur at fixed times. Visitors, however, may be greatly stressed by what they see as 'unpredictable' noise. Thus, the way we perceive the situation may be an important factor in reducing our susceptibility to stress.

Hans Selye has suggested that the way one *reacts* to a stressor is also an important factor. He distinguishes between those responses intended to *resist* the situation (*catatoxic* reactions) and those intended to help one *adapt* to the situation (*syntoxic* reactions). If someone cuts in front of you while driving, you may get angry and upset (an aggressive, catatoxic response), or you can laugh and dismiss the other driver's behaviour as foolish (an adaptive, syntoxic response). According to Selye, the syntoxic response is often the preferable one. However, sometimes people are caught in a double bind: when they are passive they wish they could be aggressive, and when they are aggressive they feel guilty. This self-conflict is itself stressful – and Selye concedes that we sometimes need catatoxic reactions of anger to act as a safety valve. Unfortunately, Selye offers very little in terms of defining which situations merit which response, causing critics to say his concept is either circular or meaningless. Certainly the criteria are imprecise, but, as Glass and Singer have noted, stressors are very difficult to define; it may be that defining an 'appropriate' response is also imprecise. Given the variations in the way individuals respond, Selye's message seems to come down to recognizing when you are stressed, and developing a range of possible coping responses. Perhaps the best illustration of positive adaptation was offered by Selye's own behaviour. At the time of writing his last book, he would normally get up at dawn to bicycle five miles to his office and then work until eight at night – and this from a 68-year-old man with two artificial hips!

For further consideration

What are the primary stressors in your life? Given the preceding discussion, can you envision steps you could take to reduce your level of stress?

Medicine and the Mind

One of the implications of research on stress is that our behaviour can affect our health. Since stressors are partly defined by our perceptions, and stress reactions affect the immune system, this points to a link between mental states and physical health. To many people, this is a surprising idea. After all, we have grown up accepting a model of health in which disease processes are due to pathological agents – either invading germs, or defective cell processes. Surely such events have nothing to do with laughter or loneliness?

In fact, research today seems to be pointing to a very different conception of health and healing. Consider some of the clues offered in the research considered already. While neural and hormonal pathways appear distinct, the two systems are also highly interrelated. Processes like chronic stress affect both systems – and also affect the immune system. Meditation in some ways appears to be the opposite of stress, with beneficial effects on body processes. At the same time, these effects are fairly diffuse, and certainly don't adequately explain how mental states could affect the course of disease.

Still, the possibility of mental states affecting the course of medical treatment has a long, if unconventional, history. Every doctor can tell stories about patients who have recovered despite an unfavourable prognosis, or, conversely, of patients who should have survived who died. Traditionally, if they spoke of such cases at all, doctors referred to 'the will to live' or similar phrases. One such case has become well known. In the 1970s, Norman Cousins, the long-time editor of *Saturday Review* magazine in the United States, was diagnosed with Hodgkin's disease, a form of cancer which attacks the immune system. His doctors were pessimistic about the outcome, but Cousins decided that giving up would only hasten his end. So, while treatment (chemotherapy etc.) was in progress, he embarked on a determined programme to bolster his spirits; perhaps the best-known aspect of his plan involved viewing classic comedy films in his hospital room. In the end, Cousins recovered. Although he was grateful to his doctors for their treatment, he also was convinced that, in the old phrase, laughter is truly the best medicine. As a result, he embarked on a quest both to document this belief and to understand the processes involved (Cousins 1989).

At the time of his recovery, Cousins's ideas were widely dismissed as delusional or, at best, a type of placebo effect. (**Placebo effect** refers to the phenomenon of inert substances labelled as drugs – e.g. a painkiller – producing effects similar to the real drug. Of course, how this occurs is in itself something of a medical puzzle!) Then, as new discoveries were made about the functioning of the immune system, new theories and data began to emerge. Today, the study of mental states and their effect on health is referred to as **psychoimmunology** (or sometimes psychoneuroimmunology) (Cohen and Herbert 1996). Just as research led to recognition of the interrelations between the nervous system and the endocrine system, so too is there a new awareness of the relationship of both of these to the functioning of the immune system.

Psychoimmunology is a fast-developing field, and it is impossible to summarize all the current research, but a few examples can help to clarify the direction in which the field is moving (for general reviews, see Ornstein and Swencionis 1990; Cohen and Herbert 1996). As noted in the discussion of stress, it has long been known that high stress levels increase the likelihood of disease (recall Holmes and Rahe's research). The more recent research suggests that a wide range of social-environmental factors may do so, and that the underlying linkage is suppression of immune functions. Generally, negative interpersonal events have been identified as measurably suppressing the immune system – for example, death of a loved one, or marital conflict (Maier and Laudenslager 1985; Solomon 1990; O'Leary *et al.* 1997). On the positive side, patients recovering from heart attacks progress faster if they have a pet for company (Cousins 1989). (Note that most studies are *quasi-experiments*, since researchers cannot control the life events. Nonetheless,

placebo effect a phenomenon whereby inert substances labelled as drugs (such as a painkiller) produce effects similar to the real drug

psychoimmunology the study of mental states and their effect on health, as expressed through the functions of the immune system; sometimes referred to as psychoneuroimmunology

the results suggest a pattern.) The question is, how do such circumstances get translated into immune responses?

While Hans Selye correctly noted that chronic stress resulted in deterioration of the immune system in experimental animals, he did not know the precise mechanism. Today, advances in biochemical techniques are helping to provide answers. One crucial clue seems to be the role of neuropeptides – particularly the 'natural opiates' called endorphins. As noted earlier, neuropeptides play a role both in the nervous system and as hormones. Endorphins serve as natural painkillers in the brain, and receptors for them have been identified at a number of sites, particularly in the brain stem. Interestingly, recent studies have shown that a number of types of immune cells, collectively called *monocytes*, also have receptors for endorphins – and that the endorphins play a role in regulating the activity of the immune cells (Maier and Laudenslager 1985; Pert 1990). At a higher level, there is evidence for interactions between the hypothalamus/pituitary/adrenal system of the fight-or-flight response and the immune system (Michelson *et al.* 1995). Interestingly, the first response to mild stress may actually be an increase in immune response, with adverse effects more likely with intense or prolonged stress. While many details remain to be clarified, the notion of mental states affecting health is no longer a delusion or fantasy.

At the same time, one must be cautious about drawing conclusions based on the available research. While mental states may play a role in health, none of the researchers involved is suggesting abandoning conventional medical treatment. If anything, the implication seems to be that doctor–patient relationships are more important than ever to effective health care. Thus, the traditional 'good bedside manner', downplayed in the rush of new medical technology, becomes once more an important adjunct to medical treatment. At the same time, an important concern has been raised by Marcia Angell, editor of the *New England Journal of Medicine*. Essentially, Angell argues that telling patients (particularly those with terminal illnesses) that their attitudes and behaviour produced their condition can add an unjustified burden of guilt to those already afflicted – especially in the absence of direct evidence (Angell 1985). Cancer, for example, may arise despite 'positive thinking', since other factors are clearly involved (including genetic factors and environmental hazards). Regardless of what future research on psychoimmunology reveals, the multi-faceted nature of health is unlikely to change. What *is* likely to change, however, is the concept that individuals must be passive in the face of illness.

From the point of view of psychology, the research on psychoimmunology adds a further dimension to our understanding of the relationship between mind and body. In some ways, it brings us full circle to where we started this chapter. We have seen how processes in the body affect our mental state, and in turn how mental processes can affect the body. Obviously, many questions remain, but the basic assumption of the materialists – that 'mind' and 'body' are different ways of talking about the same thing – seems relatively secure. While we may never be able to do away with one or the other term, research on mind/body issues has led to exciting discoveries about how we function. In the end, it is the advances in our understanding that justify the biological approach.

Still, there is one element of our biological nature that has not been discussed. The human brain is an incredibly complex structure, unparalleled (as far as we know) in the universe. The body, too, with its highly integrated systems, is a wondrous thing. How did it arise? How do nerve cells grow and develop into the specialized networks that make up the brain? What determines the variability found between individuals – not just in height or eye colour, but also in the brain (Edelman 1992)? To try to answer such questions, we must look at another aspect of the biological approach – the study of heredity.

For further consideration	An old saying suggests that 'laughter is the best medicine'. Discuss what this means in terms of the current research on psychoimmunology.

The Hereditary Basis of Behaviour

In the 1970s, a group of researchers announced that they had found a genetic pattern associated with criminal behaviour. They had discovered that certain men were born with an extra Y chromosome; individuals with the resulting XYY pattern, the researchers argued, tended to become criminals. This assertion led to great controversy, among both researchers and the general public. If someone could be identified at birth as a potential criminal, advocates argued, they could be closely watched, or even locked up before they could cause harm. Opponents questioned both the evidence and the moral principle of prejudging guilt. Soon, other researchers discovered that many XYY men existed who had no apparent history of criminal actions. Given this and other contrary evidence, the XYY-criminality theory was cast into doubt, and the controversy died (Gould 1981). Still, it is significant that, throughout the debate, *no one ever questioned the underlying assumption that behaviour could be inherited!*

The concept of inherited traits has become so widely known and accepted that it is difficult for us to recognize its impact on our thinking. Yet it is not much more than a hundred years since Charles Darwin suggested that variations could be passed on from one generation to another. 'Like father, like son', we say – but how *much* like, we barely realize. Even Darwin, although he believed in the phenomenon of inheritance, had no idea how heredity actually functioned.

evolution a theory to account for the development of species diversity by means of variations which are transmitted to offspring by inheritance; Darwin's theory of *natural selection* proposed that variations which enhance adaptability, and thereby enhance survival and reproduction rates, are the most likely to be transmitted

Darwin's ideas about inheritance between generations were closely linked to another concept: **evolution**. He recognized that variations existed within a species, and believed that such traits could be transmitted from parents to offspring. Traits which enhanced survival and reproduction rates were the most likely to be transmitted; thus, Darwin's principle of *natural selection* as the basis of evolution is sometimes referred to as 'survival of the fittest'. Darwin believed that the same process which produces variations within a species *also* produces the variations which are ultimately labelled as different species. Thus, all species are ultimately related through the mechanism of evolution. This concept of continuity between species was contentious in

Darwin's day (and sometimes still is), but it has significantly influenced the way we view behaviour. For example, one can compare human behaviour and physiology to that of other species as a tool for improving our understanding. (Chimpanzees, for example, are genetically very similar to humans.) This is not to say that chimpanzee studies, or those involving other species, are a substitute for research on humans. Rather, comparisons of similarities and differences can lead us to new questions, and new insights. In a similar vein, palaeoanthropologists and evolutionary psychologists study the ancestors of humanity to provide new insights into our own behaviour. Ultimately, the goal of such studies is not to diminish the wonder of human existence, but to understand better and appreciate who and what we are.

These concepts – *heredity* and *evolution* – have been significant in improving our knowledge of human behaviour. As we shall discuss, the pace of research in genetics in particular has been accelerating tremendously in the past few years, and no account can be fully current. However, an understanding of the foundations and assumptions underlying current research can help us to understand better the significance of what George Beadle, a Nobel laureate in genetics, has called 'the language of life' (Beadle and Beadle 1966).

Basic Mechanisms of Heredity

The word 'genetics' was coined by the English biologist William Bateson. In an article published in 1902, he urged his fellow researchers to look at the causes of inherited resemblances and differences, to understand 'the essential process by which the likeness of the parent is transmitted to the offspring'. At first, Bateson drew little response. For many years, the study of genetics was considered a bit eccentric, being based on taking inventories, raising generations of fruit flies, keeping animal pedigrees and talking about concepts like 'dominance', 'unit characters' and 'ratios'. At the same time, chemists were working on the chemical structures of enzymes and other organic chemicals. While it took many years before they realized it, both groups were working on the same problem. Ultimately, the result was the breaking of 'the code of life', embodied in chemical structure of genes. The **gene** came to be recognized as the basic unit of heredity, made up of strings of 'building blocks' called amino acids. Altogether, it is estimated that humans possess about 80,000 different genes, each regulating a different process. As recently as ten years ago, fewer than 1 per cent had been identified, but an international research effort called the Human Genome Project was organized to map the entire structure (Lee 1991). Originally, it was anticipated that it would take roughly fifteen years to identify the structure and function of each gene, but current estimates suggest a basic map will be completed in about the middle of the year 2000! Today, genetic research often takes place at the molecular level, but the beginnings were far less sophisticated.

What is perhaps most fascinating about the development of genetics is that the early population geneticists (like Bateson) came to a clear understanding of the basic properties of genetic inheritance *without* any knowledge of

gene the basic unit of heredity, made up of strings of 'building blocks' called amino acids; it is estimated that humans possess about 100,000 different genes, each regulating a different process

the underlying biochemistry. Consider this: the structure of DNA, which holds the basic structure of chromosomes of which genes are a part, was deciphered by James Watson and Francis Crick in 1953. However, it took roughly another *twenty* years before anyone isolated a single gene! Clearly, the key to heredity is the gene; clearly, too, the basic concepts of inheritance can be largely understood without any direct reference to the biochemical processes involved. In fact, the basic patterns of inheritance were actually worked out over a hundred years before the first gene was directly identified.

In the 1860s, Gregor Mendel was living as a monk in an Austrian monastery. The son of a farmer, he became interested in problems of plant hybridization (the crossing of different strains to produce new varieties). Working with garden peas, he set up an experimental plot to see if he could determine some orderly principles underlying the results of hybridization. As it turns out, he was wrong on many details, but correct in the general outline. Mendel discovered that an inherited characteristic passed from parent to offspring. (Mendel, of course, did not know that it was a *chemical* process, but he knew there must be a mechanism.) In any individual, this code is made up of two genes, forming a pair. When reproduction takes place, the gene pair is split, so that one parent contributes only one gene to the offspring; the other member of the offspring's gene pair comes from the other parent. Thus, the offspring carries genetic information from both parents.

As time went on, it was discovered that the mechanism of splitting and recombining depends on the chromosomes. Composed of double strands of DNA and proteins, **chromosomes** are the large-scale structures of heredity, containing the genes. In humans, there are twenty-three pairs of chromosomes, each holding thousands of genes, like pearls on a necklace. Because each of the twenty-three pairs of chromosomes splits and recombines independently of the others during reproduction, there are 2^{23} possible chromosome combinations from each parent, meaning that genetic recombination provides for almost limitless variety. (With over 8.4 million combinations from a single set of parents, the likelihood of even two siblings having identical sets of chromosomes is very small.) The result is that genetic mechanisms provide a basis for variability, as well as similarity, from parent to offspring.

The genetic code which an individual carries in the DNA of their cells is called the **genotype**. Genes function in pairs, and the gene-pair members for particular characteristics (e.g. blood type, eye colour) come in several variants, called *alleles*. Each allele represents the chemical code for a single variation. For example, basic blood types in people are based on three alleles, representing A, B and O. Normally, for a characteristic based on a single gene (i.e. one pair – called **unigenic** or Mendelian **inheritance**), one allele, called the *dominant* allele, will be expressed (that is, active) whenever it occurs in the gene pair. Other alleles will only be expressed (active, and therefore observable in the individual) if both members of the gene pair are the same. Because they are not as influential as the dominant form, these genes are called *recessive* alleles. For eye colour, brown is the dominant form, while blue is recessive (see Figure 2.11). Thus, the observed form

chromosomes thread-like genetic structures composed of double strands of DNA and proteins, containing the genes; in humans, there are 23 pairs of chromosomes

genotype the genetic code which an individual carries in the DNA of his or her cells

unigenic inheritance genetic transmission which is dependent on the action of a single pair of genes; also called Mendelian inheritance, in recognition of Gregor Mendel's pioneering work

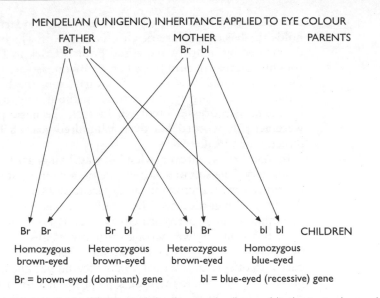

MENDELIAN (UNIGENIC) INHERITANCE APPLIED TO EYE COLOUR

FATHER   MOTHER   PARENTS

Br   bl   Br   bl

Br   Br   Br   bl   bl   Br   bl   bl   CHILDREN

Homozygous   Heterozygous   Heterozygous   Homozygous
brown-eyed   brown-eyed   brown-eyed   blue-eyed

Br = brown-eyed (dominant) gene   bl = blue-eyed (recessive) gene

Figure 2.11   Unigenic inheritance As discussed in the text, observed characteristics like eye colour depend on the individual's genetic make-up, inherited from the parents. If both parents are heterozygous brown-eyed, then the unigenic model says they have a 25 per cent chance of any child being homozygous blue-eyed, as the combinations suggest.

of the characteristic depends upon what pairing of dominant and/or recessive alleles of the gene is present. (Note: this description of eye colour is based on the classical model of unigenic inheritance; while it works very well for the vast majority of cases, research in recent years has indicated ways in which it oversimplifies, and hence occasionally leads to faulty predictions. For the purpose of understanding the basics of heredity, these subtleties are not critical.)

One must distinguish between the genotype, defined by the genes, and the *observed* characteristics of the individual, called the **phenotype**. One reason for this distinction has already been noted: a person may possess a recessive gene for blue eyes, but it will not be expressed if they also have a dominant gene for brown eyes. In terms of appearance, they would seem no different from a person with two brown genes. (Hence, one cannot always determine the genotype simply by observing the phenotypic appearance.)

More importantly, genes only determine a *potential* for a characteristic, which must then be realized through a long sequence of biochemical processes. Along the way, other factors, including environmental influences, may intervene. For example, an individual may be born with PKU (phenylketonuria), a metabolic disorder based on a recessive gene. If untreated, it can result in severe mental retardation. However, appropriate medical treatment and dietary restrictions can compensate if the disorder is detected early, and the individual need never suffer the effects. Depending on the particular characteristic, the amount of influence the environment has differs. The genetic code for most aspects of our physical structure is relatively rigid – for instance, dictating the location of the eyes. For traits related to behaviour,

phenotype the observed characteristics of the individual, based on the combination of genotype and environmental influences

such as intelligence, the reverse may be true – environment may play a decisive role. Consequently, one cannot easily generalize about genetic expression, except to note that the observed characteristics of an individual (the phenotype) are based on a combination of genotype and environmental influences. For psychologists, this is one of the most important aspects of heredity.

To summarize thus far, inheritance of characteristics is based on a chemical code carried by genes, which are themselves carried by the chromosomes. Genes function in pairs, and various forms (alleles) of the gene for a characteristic exist. The recombination of genes from parents to offspring provides a basis for genetic variability within families. Ultimately, though, the observed characteristics of an individual depend on the interaction of genetic and environmental factors. As we will discuss, determining the relative role of these factors in behaviour has been one of the major concerns of psychologists studying heredity.

One other issue needs to be considered in relation to genetic mechanisms: the origin of new traits. Although recombination provides for considerable variation, it does not provide for the creation of any *new* traits. Thus, if heredity functioned only in the way described above, there would be no possibility of evolution. Darwin recognized this, even without knowing anything about the basis of hereditary mechanisms. Along with the normal sequence of biochemical processes, it is possible for new gene forms, called **mutations**, to occur. Mutations are very rare, happening perhaps once in a million times. However, when they do occur, by whatever random process, a new trait may appear. Again, Darwin was alert to the significance of such events, which he expressed in the law of *natural selection*: any new trait which offers an advantage in terms of survival will tend to be passed on (because the individual is more likely to survive to reproduce). Conversely, any trait which weakens the ability to survive will normally disappear (if the individual dies before reproducing). Today, this is often referred to as 'survival of the fittest'. Recently, the possibility of a second mechanism for genetic variation has been identified: transfer of genes between different species (Amábile-Cuevas and Chicurel 1993). Whether by mutation or another mechanism, the emergence of new traits due to genetic variation is the basis of *evolution*, the development of species diversity. From a psychological point of view, this is significant, because it indicates that the development of human characteristics has a long history. The structure of our brain is linked to the structure of the brains of other species. In the same way, hands are related to flippers and wings. Darwin recognized these connections, but also knew that his contemporaries would not be likely to accept it. So, in his first book, *The Origin of Species*, he carefully avoided any mention of *human* evolution (Darwin 1859). Only in his later writings did he become more explicit.

Heredity, then, is an important key to understanding behaviour. To the extent that it provides the organizational code for the developing embryo, it underlies all that we have talked about in terms of physiological processes. Through evolution, humans have developed the characteristics and abilities that distinguish us from other species. The cortex of our brains, which in many respects seems more highly developed than in other species,

mutation a change in the genetic material of a cell; while rare, mutations can result in new characteristics which may be transmitted to descendants of the original cell

has played an important part in those gains. At the same time, the environment, through the effects of experience, has a significant impact on our cortex. What we are depends on both our genotype and our environment. For psychologists, the major challenge is to understand precisely how these two factors interact.

For further consideration

Our increasing understanding of genetics brings with it new dilemmas. For example, it is now possible to determine when an individual has the genes for a serious disorder, such as *Huntington's disease* (Huntington's disease is a fatal neurological disorder, which is due to a dominant gene, but is not expressed until the person is in their forties). If you had the gene for Huntington's disease, would you want to know? Do you think employers should have access to genetic information about their employees?

Nature and Nurture in Behaviour

Of all the disputes in psychology, perhaps the most contentious concerns the relative importance of heredity and experience. Long before Mendel formed his genetic theory, people had an intuitive belief that something like heredity existed. Plato, for example, talked about knowledge being inborn or 'native' to the person, rather than being acquired through experience. This led to the view of knowledge and behaviour called **nativism**, the belief that characteristics are innate (Weimer 1973).

nativism the philosophical view, held by Plato and others, that knowledge and behaviour are innate in origin

However, not everyone has taken this viewpoint. Other thinkers have maintained that all new-born babies are basically alike, and only develop unique characteristics as a result of differing experiences. John Locke, an English philosopher, expressed this view in 1690, saying the mind at birth is like a blank sheet of paper, on which experience is gradually written (Locke 1690). This view, which emphasizes the importance of environmental influences, is often called **empiricism**.

empiricism the philosophical position, first attributed to John Locke, that all knowledge is based on experience; hence, the basis of the view that behaviour is learned

The philosophical split between nativism and empiricism has led to arguments about the relative importance of heredity ('nature') and environmental factors ('nurture') in various aspects of human functioning. Advances in our knowledge of genetics have made it possible to identify specific genes related to a variety of disorders, such as Huntington's disease and Tay-Sachs disease (both are fatal disorders which affect the nervous system). With behaviour, the situation is more complex, in part because behavioural traits are likely to be influenced by a variety of genes, rather than a single gene as in the cases above. Intelligence, for example, is a characteristic for which the relative contributions of nature and nurture are still being assessed. Similarly, the role of heredity in mental disorders like schizophrenia is still not well understood. With such complex aspects of behaviour, the techniques involved in 'mapping' genes may prove of limited help for some time to come. Consequently, the study of genetic influences on behaviour typically involves methods familiar to traditional population genetics – tracing observed traits among related individuals.

Ideally, one would like to have total control of both genetic and environmental factors, so that they could be studied experimentally. Although this

concordance a technique for studying inheritance by examining characteristics of individuals whose genetic relationship is known

is impossible both technically and ethically, one can often approximate the ideal by doing concordance studies. **Concordance** (literally, 'agreement') studies examine characteristics of individuals whose genetic relationship is known. In these studies, *identical twins* are the preferred subjects, because they come from the same fertilized egg, and therefore have the same genetic make-up. (*Fraternal twins*, by contrast, are conceived at the same time, but because they come from separately fertilized eggs, they are genetically no more alike than any two siblings.) Because of the similar genetic make-up of identical twins, if a particular trait is controlled by the genes, then the twins should develop similarly, whether they are raised together or in different settings. Conversely, if environment plays the major role in a trait, then the degree of similarity between identical twins should depend on how they were raised: if raised in the same family, they should show some similarities, as do any siblings. If raised separately, however (e.g. in adoptive families), identical twins should be more like members of their adoptive families than like each other. Concordance studies also examine other genetic links, such as fraternal twins or other siblings, or parent–child comparisons. In each case, the goal is to measure behavioural similarities in accordance with what would be expected based on the degree of genetic similarity. (For example, on average, any child shares 50 per cent of their genes with each parent, as do siblings; a grandparent and grandchild share 25 per cent of their genes on average.)

Unfortunately, although the concept of concordance is fairly straightforward, the methodology is not as clear-cut as it may seem. Although identical twins are the preferred group, such twins are quite rare, and cases where they have been separated at an early age (due to parental death, family break-ups etc.) are rarer still. In addition, the fact of separation may make it difficult to locate both twins at a later time. (In some cases of separation in infancy followed by adoption, the children are not informed that they have a twin.) When separated twins *are* located, the degree of separation can be hard to assess. In one case, a researcher described twins as 'separated' who had been separated in name only – one of them was raised by the parents, and one by a maiden aunt who lived one hundred yards away (Shields 1962). Recently, by accessing adoption records, a group at the University of Minnesota has been able to identify a sizeable group of identical twins separated near birth (Bouchard *et al.* 1990). Determining early history is a crucial factor to the validity of concordance studies, because when twins actually have contact despite living under different roofs, it cannot be claimed that the environments are truly different. Even when twins are separated at birth and raised separately, they still share the same prenatal environment in the mother's womb. (For this reason, fraternal twins tend to be more alike than other siblings, since they are conceived and born at the same time – but this reflects an *environmental* influence, not heredity.) Consequently, it is a practical impossibility to find identical twins who have grown up in completely different environments, and assumptions about twins reared apart may overestimate the contribution of heredity to observed similarities.

At the other end of scale from looking at individuals with identical genotypes is the idea of studying two individuals (regardless of genotype) who have grown up in identical environments. Unfortunately, this is equally tricky. Twins raised in the same family appear, superficially, to meet this criterion because both prenatal and postnatal circumstances are shared. However, even when two children grow up in the same family, there is no guarantee that they will have identical experiences, or be treated in exactly the same way. This becomes especially clear when one considers fraternal twins of different sexes. Regardless of their shared prenatal environment, they are likely to encounter increasingly different circumstances as time goes on, due to social factors. (For a discussion of current research results, see Chapter 7.)

Despite the difficulties of conducting rigorous studies, concordance research has added to our knowledge of the role of nature and nurture in development. At one time, the tendency was to ask whether a characteristic was due to heredity *or* environment, implying that the answer must be one or the other. Today, we recognize that the picture is more complex, at least with regard to most forms of behaviour. Modern psychologists largely accept an interactionist view, which suggests that genetic and environmental influences are interwoven in determining behaviour. In this sense, the answer to the question, 'Is it nature or nurture?' is actually 'Both.'

For further consideration

Suppose that scientists created a clone (genetic duplicate) of you. Would you expect them to be identical to you when grown? What does your response tell you about your own view of the nature/nurture issue?

Evolution and Behaviour

While it can be difficult to determine precisely how much heredity influences behaviour, there is little doubt that it does play a significant role in what we are. However, the mechanism of heredity applies not just to transmission of characteristics from parents to children, but to the whole process of evolution described by Darwin. What we are as a species (and thereby as individuals) is influenced by our evolutionary history, and our heredity provides clear links to that history. For example, there is an approximately 98 per cent overlap in the genetic material of people and chimpanzees. The 2 per cent difference is obviously significant (for example, in the development of language areas in the cortex), but the implication is that we share a great deal of our nature with other species. This concept, which flows naturally from Darwin's theory as well as basic data about genetics, has led to the development of a new sub-area in psychology and biology, called **evolutionary psychology**.

evolutionary psychology
the application of evolutionary principles to the understanding of behaviour

Evolutionary psychology attempts to apply the principles of evolution in order to enhance our understanding of behaviour. In many ways, it traces its origin to the ideas of a Harvard University biologist, E. O. Wilson. Wilson, whose speciality is the study of ants, wrote a book advocating the application of evolutionary principles gleaned from the study of other species to human social behaviour (Wilson 1975). Wilson called this approach *sociobiology*, and wrote a text by the same name. Wilson's ideas were highly original, and also controversial, and that sense of controversy is still evident today in discussions of evolutionary psychology.

According to its advocates, both the body and the brain evolved in response to the pressures of natural selection; therefore, if a functional capacity exists in humans today, it must be because at some stage it conveyed a survival advantage (Tooby and Cosmides 1990; Buss 1995). They then attempt to analyse this sequence in reverse, by identifying a brain structure or behaviour, and then attempting to explain its development in a manner consistent with evolutionary principles. Sometimes, this process can be very useful, as when visual researcher Jerome Lettvin used ecologically relevant stimuli (bugs, stems etc.) to understand visual processing in the frog's eye (Lettvin *et al.* 1959). Lettvin reasoned that a frog's eye evolved to adapt to its environment, and that therefore such stimuli would be likely to provide a better understanding of functioning than would arbitrary stimuli like spots of light or simple lines. The resulting study, considered a classic, was both insightful and highly influential. In a similar vein, the idea that parts of the brain evolved at different rates, and in response to differing demands, is proving useful in our attempts to understand brain functions. For example, LeDoux has argued that because the brain structures involved in emotion evolved before the cortex, we should not assume that the cognitive (conscious) aspects of emotional experience provide a full picture of the role of emotions in our survival (LeDoux 1995).

Thus, evolutionary theory provides a useful point of reference as we strive to enhance our understanding of the brain. As Nobel laureate Gerald Edelman notes, we need to recognize that the nervous system has an evolutionary history which is relevant to its current structure and functioning (Edelman 1992). Yet there remains a significant gap between acknowledging that the brain has evolved, and determining the specific ways in which evolutionary theorizing can explain behaviour. For instance, Wilson has tried to argue that morality has an evolutionary basis, even though he admits that we lack the evidence to prove this assertion (Wilson 1998).

One area that has been hotly debated is the relevance of evolutionary interpretations of gender. It seems obvious that differences exist between men and women – for example, men are typically larger and stronger, and women tend to live longer. Does this mean there is an evolutionary reason for these differences, and therefore that gender differences can be understood by trying to interpret the survival value of these differences? Evolutionary psychologists say yes, and have used this notion to interpret many aspects of gender-related behaviour, particularly with regard to mate selection. For example, it is argued that men are by nature polygamous, because they are capable of impregnating multiple women over a short period of time, thereby increasing the likely survival rate for their genes. (Remember, natural selection says that traits evolve because they carry a survival advantage.) Women, it is argued, are by nature monogamous, because they must invest a great deal, both during pregnancy and after birth, to ensure that their child (and therefore their genes) survives. Whether one finds this reasoning plausible or not, the real question becomes: how can we evaluate it in a scientific way?

One basic problem is that the interpretations (like most ideas in evolutionary psychology) are essentially correlational and *post hoc* (that is, applied after the events they are trying to explain have already occurred). As such,

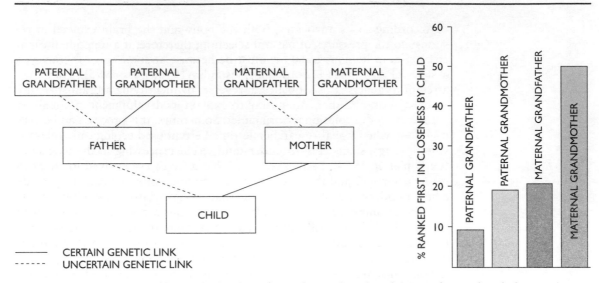

Figure 2.12 Certainty of genetic relatedness and emotional closeness
Retrospective ratings by adults of which grandparent was emotionally closest to them in childhood reveal a pattern consistent with a model based on certainty of genetic relatedness. (Data from Euler and Weitzel 1996.)

they don't easily allow for the predictive evaluations which most researchers favour. (Recall the discussions about experiments versus other research methods in Chapter 1.) This is a serious concern, and has led evolutionary psychologists to seek possible experimental tests. One example relates to the concept of *paternity uncertainty*. According to this theory, men are inherently less able to determine if a child carries their genes than women (since in a normal pregnancy the mother always knows that the egg has her genes, but the sperm may or may not be from the claimed father). Hence, evolutionary psychologists have argued that male forebears should be less willing to invest resources in children than are females. For example, a paternal grandfather cannot be certain that his son really is genetically related, and that man in turn cannot be certain his child is really his own. By contrast, a maternal grandmother is completely certain, because she knows her daughter carries her genes, and her daughter knows her own child carries her own genes (and therefore half of the grandmother's as well) (see Figure 2.12). Drawing on this reasoning, German researchers did a study in which they rated the emotional closeness between grandparents and their grandchildren; as seen in Figure 2.12, the predicted pattern emerged! (Euler and Weitzel 1996). This study is striking, both because it provides a clear pattern of results, and also because the outcome is one that most people would find very unexpected – but which is quite consistent with the evolutionary view. (It is worth noting that other factors, like where grandparents lived, their age, and the availability of other grandparents, did not show any patterns. Thus, alternative explanations are not obvious.)

At present, there is no clear consensus about the value of evolutionary psychology. Its advocates seem correct in suggesting that evolution has influenced what we are. The problem, though, is that making retrospective interpretations is fraught with many perils. As with any correlational research, alternative explanations are almost always possible. For example, recent studies have challenged many of the gender-related assertions mentioned above (Angier 1999). A further problem has been noted by Stephen Jay Gould, an American evolutionary theorist who has been a frequent critic of evolutionary psychology. Gould argues that as structures evolve, their function can also evolve – a process he calls *exaptation*. This type of change can then make it difficult to apply natural selection retrospectively as a means of explaining the current function. For example, Gould demonstrated that small wings would have had no value for flight, but would be very useful for regulating body temperature; only later, as they became larger, would their potential for flying emerge (Gould and Vrba 1981). Thus, one might propose that wings evolved to permit flying – but one would be wrong! Similarly, we cannot be certain that evolutionary explanations of behaviour are necessarily correct, even when they appear plausible. Ultimately, its value may lie in how it reshapes other types of research by suggesting new questions (as in the study of vision or emotion, as noted above), rather than in the specific explanations it provides. In the short run, it seems likely that the debates between the advocates and critics of evolutionary psychology will continue.

Conclusion

The biological approach is oriented towards understanding the physiological and genetic basis of our behaviour. Within psychology, it is the only approach which tries to explain behaviour in terms of the workings of the physical system. By contrast, consider psychoanalysis (see Chapter 5). Although Freud was trained in neurology, and believed that ultimately the system was biologically based, psychoanalysis uses concepts which are purely psychological, not physiological. Behaviourism (see Chapter 3) is even more extreme, regarding the body as a 'black box' whose workings are neither known nor relevant to explaining the relationships between stimuli and behaviour. Hence, the biological approach is alone in emphasizing the physical system.

The biological approach, by its nature, focuses on the internal processes associated with physiology and genetics. As important as these processes are in understanding behaviour, they are not the only source of influences. Each individual's behaviour represents a unique combination of genetic factors (*heredity*) and life experiences (*environment*). While the biological approach acknowledges the role of environmental factors such as stressors, it does not place primary emphasis on these factors, or the impact they can have on behaviour. Rather, the study of environmental influences is the focus of other approaches, such as behaviourism.

Over two hundred years ago, Julien de La Mettrie made the assumption that the mind has its physical basis in the brain. In the time since, this concept of *materialism* has gained increasing acceptance. Today, as our understanding of physiological processes increases, it seems more and more evident that mind and body *are* fundamentally linked. This is not to suggest that all the questions, such as the nature of consciousness, have been fully answered; in part, 'mind' and 'brain' may represent different levels of description, and hence the issue may never be completely reconciled. Still, our knowledge is increasing, and perhaps most significantly, the insights are being applied – in medicine, in business and in everyday activities. The concept of *stress* has become widely known, as have methods for coping with it. The use of *psychoactive drugs* has radically altered treatment of mental disorders, with the number of hospitalized patients in the United States being cut by more than half between 1955 and 1971. Advances in areas like *psychoimmunology* may have even greater impact in the future.

At the same time, problems remain. One of the greatest challenges concerns the complexity of the physiological system. There are approximately ten *billion* neurons in the cortex of the brain alone, which are interconnected in manifold ways. In addition, there are countless chemical interactions involving *neurotransmitters*, *hormones* and *neuropeptides* – plus environmental influences. This complexity makes achieving a complete understanding of the processes affecting behaviour a daunting goal. Even on a more limited scale, the ways in which factors interact make it difficult to make specific statements about one factor (e.g. stress as a cause of heart attacks) in the absence of knowledge about other factors (e.g. exercise and family history). Similarly, there is a growing awareness that what we are reflects in part our evolutionary history as a species, and this, too, is influencing the kinds of questions asked. All these factors point to the reality that the picture we have is not yet complete – but that is characteristic of science, and it is likely that the details yet to be discovered will be as interesting as those already known.

Chapter Summary

◆ The biological approach is based on the assumption of *materialism*, which asserts that all behaviour has a physiological basis.

◆ The two primary concerns of the biological approach are the workings of the nervous system, and the role of heredity in behaviour.

◆ The nervous system is composed of billions of individual nerve cells called *neurons*; the most significant component of the nervous system is the *brain*.

◆ Perhaps the most challenging question in the study of the brain is the understanding of the nature of consciousness, and the relationship between the *mind* and the brain.

◆ The effects of the body on the mind have been studied in various ways, including the effects of psychoactive *drugs*, the use of electrical stimulation of the brain (*ESB*) and the effects of severing the corpus callosum (*split brain*).

◆ The influence of mental processes on the body has been examined in terms of the effects of *stress*; more recently, researchers have begun to look at how mental states affect the immune system (*psychoimmunology*).

◆ The study of *heredity* involves the direct study of *genes* and how they function, and also looks at interactions between heredity and environment by the study of twins and other groups who have an identifiable genetic relationship (*concordance*).

◆ *Evolutionary psychology* applies the principles of evolution to gain insight into the way selection pressures have influenced behaviour.

Key Terms and Concepts

brain stem	hormone
central nervous system (CNS)	limbic system
cerebellum	materialism
cerebral dominance	nativism
chromosome	natural selection
concordance	nerve impulse
cortex	neuron
electrical stimulation of the brain (ESB)	neuropeptide
	neurotransmitters
empiricism	phenotype
endocrine glands	pituitary gland
evolutionary psychology	psychoactive drug
gene	psychoimmunology
genotype	stress
heredity	synapse

Suggestions for Further Reading

Colin Blakemore's *Mechanisms of the Mind* provides a very readable and entertaining history of research on the brain. For a more current overview, see Gazzaniga *et al.*'s *Cognitive Neuroscience: The Biology of the Mind*. To gain an appreciation of the complexities which doctors and researchers face, read *The Man Who Mistook His Wife for a Hat*, by Oliver Sacks, a neurologist who is both knowledgeable and wise.

Two interesting, if idiosyncratic, views of the relations between the brain and behaviour are *Descartes' Error*, by neurologist Antonio Damasio, and *Bright Air, Brilliant Fire*, by Nobel biologist Gerald Edelman. Damasio offers a new interpretation of emotions and cognition, while Edelman discusses how physiology and genetics are converging in their understanding of the nervous system.

For a fascinating account of the development of techniques for viewing the brain, from X-rays to the latest scanning devices, read Bettyann Kevles's *Naked to the Bone*.

The Stress of Life is probably the best of Selye's accounts of stress intended for the general reader. For a recent review of research on stress, consider Philip Rice's *Stress and Health*.

For readers interested in the fast-developing area of psychoimmunology, the most sophisticated overview is provided by Ornstein and Swencionis, in *The Healing Brain: A Scientific Reader*. Those seeking a simpler account may prefer Norman Cousins's *Head First: The Biology of Hope*, or Bill Moyers's *Healing and the Mind*, which was written to accompany a television series.

The awesome promise, and also potential problems, of our increasing knowledge of genetics is knowledgeably presented in Lee's *The Human Genome Project: Cracking the Genetic Code of Life*.

3

The Behaviourist Approach

Mind Doesn't Matter
Introduction
Basic Assumptions of Behaviourism
The Pioneers of Behaviourism
Stimuli and Responses
Classical Conditioning
Classical Conditioning Phenomena
  Stimulus Generalization and Discrimination
  Extinction and Spontaneous Recovery
  Higher-Order Conditioning
Applications of Classical Conditioning
  Conditioned Emotional Responses
  Conditioned Drug and Immune Responses
Operant Conditioning
Skinner and Operant Conditioning
Reinforcers and Reinforcement
  Contingencies of Reinforcement

Operant Conditioning Phenomena
  Shaping and the Learning Process
  Extinction
  Schedules of Reinforcement
  Discriminative Stimuli
  Non-contingent Reinforcement
Applications and Implications of Conditioning
Negative Reinforcers and the Aversive Control of
    Operant Behaviour
Interrelationships of Classical and Operant Conditioning
Autonomic Conditioning and Biofeedback
Biological Constraints on Learning
Conclusion
Chapter Summary
Key Terms and Concepts
Suggestions for Further Reading

Mind Doesn't Matter

One of the basic themes of this book is that behaviour can often be understood in different ways, represented by the five approaches. As we will see in this chapter, the behaviourists emphasize the relationships between the environment and behaviour. In doing so, they tend to ignore both physiological processes and mental events, even in circumstances that might invite such interpretations, as in an example reported by a psychologist named Israel Goldiamond (Goldiamond 1973).

As a result of a car accident, Goldiamond spent several months in hospital undergoing treatment for a spinal injury. During that period, he had the opportunity to observe his own behaviour, and that of other patients. At one point, he shared a room with a man who had suffered brain damage. This patient was often disoriented, urinating on walls and muttering about 'what the hell am I doing in Panama?' (He wasn't.)

Thus far, this story appears unremarkable – after all, we have spent Chapter 2 exploring how the brain controls behaviour. Yet, rather than focusing on the physiological processes that underlay the brain-damaged man's behaviour, Goldiamond examined the role of the environment. He noted, for example, that the man did not act oddly in the hospital cafeteria – a fact which the staff had overlooked. Goldiamond accounted for this by noting that the features of cafeterias are fairly universal, while those of a rehabilitation hospital are not familiar to most people. Hence, the man was only disoriented when he was in an unfamiliar setting. Furthermore, the hospital was located on a large lake, and the patient's room overlooked a naval pier – perhaps accounting for his questions about Panama. Goldiamond suggested that the man's urinating inappropriately could be dealt with by rewarding him with cigarettes for urinating properly – in effect, controlling the behaviour by means of an external incentive. As anticipated, the technique worked.

The point of this story is to show that looking at the brain is not always the best way to understand behaviour. Goldiamond, like other behaviourists, preferred to look at the role the environment plays in behaviour. There is no question that the man in the story had suffered brain damage. But it is equally clear that his behaviour could not be fully understood by looking *only* at the brain damage. In one sense, by placing such a heavy emphasis on *internal* events, the biological approach tends to give too little attention to the *external* context of behaviour – that is, the environment in which behaviour occurs. For example, using drugs to treat anxiety can lead to ignoring the circumstances which may be triggering the anxiety. In this chapter, we will turn to consideration of the external influences on behaviour, as seen from the behaviourist perspective.

Introduction

learning a change in behaviour which occurs as the result of experience

The *behaviourist approach* emphasizes the role of environmental stimuli in determining the way we act. In large measure, this means focusing on **learning**: changes in behaviour which occur as the result of experience. (By emphasizing experience, they exclude changes due to fatigue, injury or drug effects.) Behaviourists have added considerably to our understanding of learning through the study of what is called classical and operant conditioning, but before we examine what has been discovered, let us look at the basic assumptions and methods which distinguish behaviourism from the other approaches.

As with all approaches, the choice of focus is one of the factors which gives behaviourism its uniqueness. In this case, the behaviourist approach is commonly distinguished by its emphasis on the relationship between observable behaviour (*responses*) and environmental events (*stimuli*). Consider the simple interaction involved when a child reaches out towards a glowing fire, and then quickly draws back from the heat: first, the stimulus of the sparkling flame attracts their attention, so that they move their hand forward (stimulus of fire leads to response of reaching). Then, the heat of the fire leads to a reflexive withdrawal (stimulus of heat leads to withdrawal response). This, in turn, might lead the child to throw water on the fire, or take some other action. Thus, from the behaviourist perspective, human experience can be understood in terms of the interrelations between stimuli and responses.

Basic Assumptions of Behaviourism

While clearly differing from the biological approach in the kinds of data it emphasizes, the behavioural approach is also distinctive in terms of its basic assumptions, which are closely related to its historical origins. At the turn of the twentieth century, psychologists tended to emphasize either the experimental study of physiological processes or the introspective analysis of experience (see Chapter 1 for a review). Physiological research was hampered by the limited technology available (for example, not even X-rays or EEGs for studying the brain), and introspectionism was proving limited due to problems of subjectivity in describing sensory experience. Consequently, both had serious limitations. As an alternative, William James argued that psychologists should focus on how behaviour relates to its purpose (called *functionalism*), but he was often better at framing the issues than at doing research to solve them. Thus, none of the available methods was achieving unequivocal success. It was against this backdrop that behaviourism arose. (It should be noted that 'behaviourism', like other approaches, can refer to a number of theories, each with points of uniqueness. Nonetheless, it is possible to identify some common elements within the approach.)

While the temptation in discussing the behaviourist approach is to emphasize the type of data collected (the observable behaviours which give the approach its name), doing so ignores the broader assumptions which underlie the approach. The most fundamental of these is the scientific principle of parsimony. Sometimes called 'Occam's razor' after the English philosopher who first proposed it, **parsimony** emphasizes seeking the simplest possible explanation for any event. If, for example, one can explain a person's eating a pastry without referring to a non-observable concept like 'hunger' or 'oral personality', then parsimony says one should avoid using such concepts. Behaviourists reacted against introspectionism in part because it seemed to invoke too many vague concepts, and thereby lacked parsimony. Instead, behaviourism placed a heavy emphasis on the use of *operational definitions* (defining concepts in terms of observable events), and this led naturally to the focus on 'stimuli' and 'responses'. (For further discussion of operational definitions, refer back to Chapter 1.)

parsimony in the philosophy of science, the principle that states one should always seek the simplest possible explanation for any event

A second assumption of the behaviourist approach relates to the mechanism for behavioural change. Like functionalism, behaviourism emphasizes trying to understand the conditions under which behaviour occurs. When does a particular behaviour occur? What conditions lead to it? What changes in the environment result from it? Since relatively few behaviours in human beings are genetically programmed, this leads to a focus on the role of experience, which is expressed through learning. It is easy to say that the way we act depends on our past experiences, but just *how* does learning occur? Since the time of Aristotle, the basic explanation has been that we learn by *association* – that is, by forming connections between ideas and/or events. For example, if the sound of an electric tin opener leads a dog to run to the kitchen, we can speculate that the dog has formed an association between the sound of the tin opener and being fed (tinned food). This concept of **associationism**, which was also favoured by such English philosophers as David Hume and J. S. Mill, has had a fundamental influence on psychology, particularly for the behaviourists. As we shall see, behaviourist theories are essentially theories of how associations are formed.

Taken together, parsimony and associationism formed the foundation from which behaviourism arose. Exactly how, and what the result has been for our understanding of psychology, will form the substance of this chapter.

The Pioneers of Behaviourism

A hundred years ago, an American named Edwin L. Thorndike was studying for his PhD in the newly formed psychology department at Columbia University. (He started at Harvard, under William James, but transferred for financial reasons.) For his research, he studied problem solving in animals, using a series of puzzle-like tasks (e.g. confining a cat in a box, from which it could release itself by pressing against a lever). His dissertation, published in 1898, had the rather cognitive-sounding title of *Animal Intelligence* (Thorndike 1898).

Thorndike's work was influential in many ways, but he is today perhaps best known for what he called 'the law of effect'. In trying to analyse the conditions under which the animals he studied changed their behaviour – that is, learned – he focused on the relationship between a response and its consequences. Basically, the **law of effect** said that any response which leads to an outcome satisfying to the organism is likely to be repeated, and any response which leads to an unpleasant outcome is not likely to be repeated. This was a form of associationism, in that the organism (animal, person) was seen as making a connection between a response and its consequences. (This is technically called association by *contiguity*, in that it assumes the response and consequence must be closely linked in time and space.) While basically unoriginal – the idea that individuals respond to reward and punishment extends back to the Greeks – Thorndike's version could be said to differ in that *it was supported by experimental data* (Robinson 1979). By framing the issue in experimental (and therefore scientific) terms, Thorndike paved the way for the behaviouristic approach.

associationism the doctrine, supported by Aristotle, Hume and others, that mental processes, particularly learning, are based on forming connections between ideas and/or events

law of effect a principle of learning proposed by Thorndike, which stated that any response which leads to an outcome satisfying to the organism is likely to be repeated, and any response which leads to an unpleasant outcome is not likely to be repeated

Edwin Lynn Thorndike

Edwin L. Thorndike (1874–1949) was born in Williamsburg, a small town in western Massachusetts. After receiving his bachelor's degree from Wesleyan University, he went to Harvard University to study psychology under William James, but was forced to transfer to Columbia University because of financial difficulties. In the newly formed psychology department at Columbia, he studied under James McKeen Cattell, one of the most influential early American psychologists. For his research, he studied problem solving in animals, using a series of puzzle-like tasks (e.g. confining a cat in a box, from which it could release itself by pressing against a lever). His dissertation, published in 1898, had the rather cognitive-sounding title of *Animal Intelligence*. Thorndike is probably best known today for his 'law of effect', which foreshadowed Skinner's concept of reinforcement as a description of the role of consequences in learning. From 1899 he taught at Teachers College at Columbia, where he wrote prolifically on education as well as psychology. He died in New York at the age of seventy-five.

Thorndike's law of effect, while significant, was not without problems, in part because it was vague about what made something 'satisfying'. One way to resolve this was to seek physiologically-oriented mechanisms for 'satisfaction'. However, given turn of the century knowledge of physiology, this often required resorting to non-observable concepts which violated the principle of parsimony. A more radical approach, pioneered by John B. Watson, was to pare theorizing to the bone, restricting theoretical descriptions to factors which could be directly observed and measured.

John B. Watson was both gifted and provocative. As a student at the University of Chicago, he initially trained in introspectionism, but found its approach to psychology excessively vague, especially in its emphasis on mental processes. He began working with animals, and completed his PhD in three years – at that time he was the youngest such graduate from the university. After teaching for only four years at Chicago, he was offered a full professorship at Johns Hopkins University in Baltimore, and shortly after became chairman of the psychology department there – certainly remarkable career advancement.

Watson can only be described as zealous in promoting his ideas. Reading his major work, *Behaviorism* (1930) today, one is struck by the scorn he heaps on William James and others, and by his willingness to test his ideas whenever possible (even using his own children). Confident that he was correct, he was willing to extend his claims even when he lacked experimental support, as in his famous remark, 'Give me a dozen healthy infants, well-formed, and my own specified world to bring them up in and I'll guarantee to take any one at random and train him to become any type of specialist I might select – doctor, lawyer, artist, merchant-chief and yes, even beggar-man and thief, regardless of his talents, penchants, tendencies, abilities, vocations, and race of his ancestors.' What is often omitted in this quotation is the statement which follows it: '*I am going beyond my facts and I admit it, but so have the advocates of the contrary* and they have been doing it for thousands of years' (Watson 1930: 104; emphasis added). Clearly, Watson clearly did not shirk from confrontation in pursuing his ideas.

John B. Watson

John Broadus Watson (1878–1958) was the founder of behaviourism. Educated in a one-room schoolhouse in the American farm belt (like many of his era), he went on to complete his PhD at the University of Chicago. After a brief exploration of the introspectionist approach, he continued under John Dewey and James Angell, two of the pioneers of the functionalist approach. Watson was both gifted and outspoken – two characteristics which played a major role in his career. He completed his PhD in only three years and began teaching at the university; four years later, he was offered a full professorship in psychology at Johns Hopkins University, and shortly after became chairman of the department. In 1913 he began publishing the first of a series of publications which outlined his behaviourist approach, which quickly gained him both fame and notoriety – his statement about shaping a healthy infant in any way desired (quoted in the text) is characteristic of his assertive style. While at Johns Hopkins, he met graduate student Rosalie Rayner, who became his second wife. After collaborating with Rayner on the case of 'little Albert', Watson became interested in human sexual behaviour; his activities in this regard (including participant observation) did not sit well with the prevailing moral views, and he was finally dismissed. At this point, he took a job with the J. Walter Thompson advertising firm. Not surprisingly, he did well in his new role, embarking on studies of consumer behaviour, writing psychology articles for the general public and becoming a vice president of the advertising firm in less than four years. Thus, Watson not only founded an entire approach to psychology, but also was perhaps the first psychologist to apply psychological theory to advertising and marketing. He died in New York at the age of eighty.

Watson's writings and ideas were a lever that moved the world. In the following decades, until the mid-1950s, behaviourism became the dominant force in psychology, particularly in North America. The irony is that while the general approach became highly influential, most researchers never accepted Watson's extreme position, which is sometimes called *radical behaviourism*. (Even B. F. Skinner, the spiritual heir to Watson's work, has commented, 'A shortage of facts is always a problem in a new science, but in Watson's aggressive program in a field as vast as human behaviour it was especially damaging' (Skinner 1974: 6).) The greatest impact can be traced to three central elements: (a) the emphasis on observable responses and environmental stimuli; (b) the rejection of mentalistic concepts not grounded in direct observation; and (c) the focus on learning and experience as central to the understanding of human behaviour. Some seventy years of research, both basic and applied, has demonstrated that in many ways we are indeed what we learn.

Behaviourism, as already noted, has many variants; indeed, some would say it is more appropriate to speak of the behaviouris*tic* approach than the behaviourist approach. (Even E. C. Tolman, often regarded as one of the founders of the *cognitive* approach, considered himself a 'behaviourist' (Tolman 1932).) However, what all behaviourists share is an interest in how behaviour is learned, and an emphasis on explanations based on observable events. In this chapter, we will see how this approach has been applied to a variety of situations.

For further consideration

As noted, John B. Watson ended his career working in the field of marketing and advertising. As you consider the principles which follow, think about how they could be applied to encourage people to buy particular products.

Stimuli and Responses

Behaviourism, by focusing on *observable* events, sets its own limits on what can be studied. Thoughts, feelings and other inner mental states cannot be studied empirically, and so have no place in behaviourist theory. Genetic variation, while presumably contributing to differences among individuals, is also largely inaccessible. By contrast, environmental conditions are relatively easy to measure and study.

Taken as a whole, the environment involves colours, shapes, smells, sounds and many other characteristics. Obviously, it is impossible in an everyday setting to measure every element of a typical environment. However, in most cases, this would be unnecessary, because there are many environmental elements that typically do not seem to enter our awareness, and consequently have little impact. (Recall the discussion of perceptual processes in Chapter 1.) Nonetheless, behaviourists recognize that in order to study environmental influences on behaviour, one must be able to define rigorously the environmental characteristics involved in a situation. In practice, this means that research often involves limiting the complexity of the environment, particularly in laboratory studies. It *also* means that one must be able to define terms clearly. With regard to the environment, sights, sounds and smells are all considered examples of stimuli. A **stimulus** (often abbreviated as S) is any event, situation, object or factor that is measurable and may affect behaviour. Simple examples could include a red triangle, the ticking of a watch or a pinprick.

stimulus (often abbreviated as **S**) in general, any event, situation, object or factor that may affect behaviour; for the behaviourists, a measurable change in the environment

For a behaviourist, an important element in understanding a particular behaviour is to identify the stimulus (or stimuli) involved. From the examples above, this would seem to be a fairly straightforward task. In reality, however, it can sometimes be quite difficult to define which environmental elements are involved as stimuli in a particular situation. For example, a mother approaches her two-month-old infant, and the baby smiles. The mother seems to be the stimulus which elicits the baby's smiling. But is it the mother as a whole, or her face, or her expression, or her smell, or her touch, or some combination of these and other elements to which the baby is actually responding? In research, it would be necessary to identify the actual stimulus elements in order to understand the situation properly. (In this regard, the desire for *operational definitions* of terms, including stimuli, becomes understandable as a means of avoiding ambiguity.)

response in general, any reaction to a stimulus, whether overt or mental; in research, the behaviour which is measured

Similarly, it is necessary to describe clearly the behaviour being studied. Normally, the behaviour which is measured is called the **response** (often abbreviated as **R**). Again, this may seem very simple at first glance. For example, a person sitting at a table engages in eating. 'Eating' is obviously a response; however, a moment's thought will show that there can be tremendous variations in the behaviour described as eating. A finicky child may pick reluctantly at a disliked vegetable. A hungry person may ravenously devour a favourite dish. While both are 'eating', there is clearly a large difference in their behaviour. Consequently, researchers must be careful to describe a response in terms that are meaningful to the situation. Often this will require specifying the rate, intensity and/or other characteristics of the response.

One of the distinctions among responses that became evident to the early behaviourists was between reflexes and voluntary actions. **Reflexes** are unlearned responses that can be triggered by specific environmental stimuli. Examples of human reflexes include withdrawing the hand from a hot surface, or a baby's sucking on an object placed in the mouth. By contrast, **voluntary responses** are emitted – that is, they are not triggered by stimuli in the way reflexes are; typically, they involve more complex actions, which often require extensive practice. Thorndike, for example, in his studies of problem solving by animals, found that it took repeated trials for learning to occur. Voluntary behaviour can span a tremendous range, from simple actions like learning to use a fork, to complex behaviours like speaking a new language. Such differences led early behaviourists to the separate study of reflexes and voluntary responses. As we shall see, learning occurs in relation to both types of behaviour; as well, the differences between the two types may be less significant than they initially appear.

reflex an unlearned response that can be triggered by specific environmental stimuli, such as a baby's sucking on an object placed in the mouth
voluntary response a response which is controlled by the individual (i.e. emitted) rather than being triggered by specific stimuli as reflexes are

For further consideration

Pick an example of a simple everyday behaviour. Is it a reflex or voluntary? Can you identify the stimulus and the response?

Classical Conditioning

At the end of the nineteenth century, a Russian physiologist named Ivan Pavlov was engaged in a long-term project to understand the process of digestion. Beginning in 1879 and working primarily with dogs, his work earned him the Nobel Prize in 1904 (Windholz 1997). However, some time around 1902, he noticed a phenomenon which was to lead him in a new and unexpected direction. In order to study digestion, Pavlov measured a number of factors, including how much a dog salivated when it was given food. At some point, he noticed what he called 'psychic salivation' – a dog would salivate before it was actually given food. Since Pavlov believed that digestion involved a series of reflexes, he set out to determine what controlled this anticipatory response. What he discovered became the basis for what is now commonly called **classical conditioning** – the study of learning which involves reflex responses. Essentially, classical conditioning explores how a new stimulus can come to elicit an existing reflex response due to learning.

Pavlov's original studies have become so well known as to be the object of jokes (like the psychologist who salivates when he hears the name 'Pavlov'!). In simple outline, Pavlov found that by ringing a bell and then immediately giving the dog some food, the bell came to evoke the same response as the food itself – salivation. To understand why this is remarkable, we need to consider the elements of the situation more closely. As

classical conditioning the study of learning which involves reflex responses, in which a neutral stimulus comes to elicit an existing reflex response

Ivan Pavlov

Ivan Petrovich Pavlov (1849–1936) was a Russian physiologist who pioneered the study of classical conditioning. Born in Ryazan, Russia, he initially began seminary studies, but then changed to St Petersburg University, where he graduated in natural science, and subsequently received his doctorate in physiology from the Military Medical Academy in St Petersburg. After a few years spent in Germany, he went on to become a professor at the Military Medical Academy. His work on the physiology of digestion, begun in 1879, earned him the Nobel Prize in 1905. He first became aware of reflexes by reading Sechenov's work while still at seminary, but his own research on what became known as classical conditioning did not begin until about 1902. At this time, while still studying digestion in dogs, he noticed what he called 'psychic salivation' – a dog would salivate before it was actually given food. Since Pavlov believed that digestion involved a series of reflexes, he set out to determine what controlled this anticipatory response. Ultimately, his work on conditioning overshadowed the research which had earned him the Nobel Prize. He continued to be intellectually active, forming a genetics institute only a few years before his death at the age of eighty-seven.

unconditioned response a reflexive response produced by a specific stimulus, such as pupil contraction to bright light
unconditioned stimulus a stimulus which elicits a reflexive (unconditioned) response
neutral stimulus a stimulus which initially produces no specific response other than provoking attention; as conditioning proceeds, the neutral stimulus becomes a conditioned stimulus
conditioned stimulus a stimulus which by repeated pairings with an unconditioned stimulus comes to elicit a conditioned response
conditioned response a response to a previously neutral stimulus which has become a conditioned stimulus by repeated pairing with an unconditioned stimulus

Pavlov's lengthy studies of digestion showed, salivating at the presence of food is a basic neural reflex that requires no learning. For example, if you put a piece of chocolate in your mouth, you will salivate. A light shined in the eye will cause the pupil to contract. Reflex responses like these (and they exist in species from worms to humans) are referred to in classical conditioning as **unconditioned responses**. For any reflex, there is some stimulus which will *elicit* the response (e.g. food for salivating, light for pupil contraction); the stimulus which elicits an unconditioned response is called an **unconditioned stimulus**. Since 'conditioned' refers to *learned*, the term refers to the unlearned nature of reflexes. (Pavlov of course wrote in Russian, and actually used the term 'unconditional', but an early English translator erred, and the mistake has remained.)

If reflexes are unlearned, then what is the learning that occurs in classical conditioning? Pavlov noted that the learning is based on forming a connection between stimuli – in this case, the bell and the food. Ringing the bell initially had no effect on salivation – that is, with respect to the response of salivation, it was a **neutral stimulus**. (To be a stimulus, an environmental element must be something which the organism is aware of; normally this is demonstrated by the stimulus provoking attention, called an *orienting response*.) After repeated pairings with the food which was placed in its mouth, the sound of the bell came to elicit drooling. At this point, the sound has become a **conditioned stimulus**, and the salivating which results is called a **conditioned response** (to distinguish it from the response to food alone) (see Figure 3.1). In effect, the conditioned stimulus has become associated with the occurrence of food (Pavlov 1927).

In order to appreciate the significance of classical conditioning, we must examine its characteristics more closely. Since the response involved is essentially a pre-existing reflex, the learning actually consists of forming a

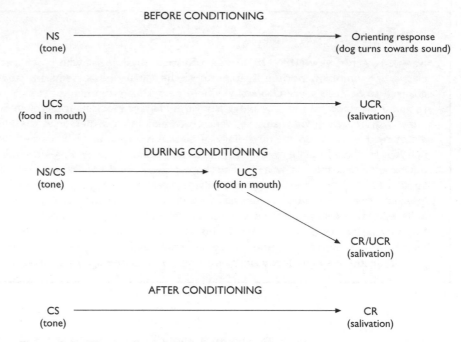

Figure 3.1   The basic classical conditioning procedure In classical conditioning, repeated pairing of a neutral stimulus (NS) with an unconditioned stimulus (UCS) results in conditioning, whereby the NS becomes conditioned (CS) to elicit the same type of response as the UCS did.

connection (association) between two stimuli (the CS and UCS). In order for optimal conditioning to occur, the conditioned stimulus (CS) must occur a second or so before the unconditioned stimulus (UCS). If the two occur simultaneously, conditioning may occur, but is typically weaker. If the CS is presented *after* the UCS (what is sometimes called *backward conditioning*), then *no* learning occurs. What this tells us is that conditioning is closely linked to the ability of the CS to serve as an advanced signal that the UCS is going to occur. This is further demonstrated by studies which show that conditioning is only likely when the CS *reliably* predicts the occurrence of the UCS. In some sense, what makes classical conditioning a valuable process for the organism is the fact that *it allows one to anticipate environmental events*. This notion that classical conditioning helps in adapting to the environment is supported by research on a phenomenon called *blocking*. If a new stimulus is presented simultaneously with an existing CS, conditioning to the new stimulus does not occur, because the original CS is already an adequate signal (Kamin 1969). Flashing a light to signal food is unnecessary, if a bell already serves that purpose. Conditioning, then, seems to occur because such learning is often adaptive.

Classical conditioning has been demonstrated in a wide variety of species, from worms to birds to primates. Thus, it appears to be a very fundamental form of learning. But given that much of human behaviour does not depend on reflex responses, it might seem that classical conditioning is of little significance in people. In fact, the reality seems to be just the opposite: examples of classical conditioning are pervasive in our lives. For example, we respond to stimuli associated with food – smells, pictures in advertisements, words like 'chocolate cake' – in much the way that Pavlov's dogs reacted: by increased digestive activity. In these cases, the food cues, having been associated with food itself (the UCS), are conditioned stimuli. Such food cues are among the most reliable of conditioned stimuli, because the sight and smell of food always precedes the actual eating of it. In films, directors will use sounds to enhance the emotional content of the story. For example, a particular theme may precede the repeated appearances of the villain in a horror film; viewers then come to associate the theme to the moments of mayhem that follow. (Of course, film images of violence are *themselves* conditioned stimuli, associated with past experiences of actual injury (UCS). This relates to the process of *higher-order conditioning*, which we will discuss later in the chapter.) Many people, when showering, develop a conditioned response of anxiety to the sound of a toilet flushing (CS), since it often results in a sudden increase in the temperature of the water (UCS)! Classical conditioning is thus a flexible process which allows us to anticipate biologically significant events (UCSs) by making an association to stimuli (CSs) which precede them.

For further consideration	Given the basic principles of classical conditioning, why do you think the advertising of products (from toothpaste to automobiles) typically involves the use of attractive models?

Classical Conditioning Phenomena

Stimulus Generalization and Discrimination

Having established the basic elements of classical conditioning, Pavlov (and later others) began to explore some variations of the original situation. One subject that interested him was the element of stimulus novelty: what would happen if a new stimulus was presented as a CS? Tests with unrelated stimuli quickly established that a neutral stimulus will not elicit a response which has been conditioned to a different stimulus (e.g. flashing a light will not elicit a CR if the previous CS was the sound of a bell). However, what would happen if a stimulus *similar to* the CS was used (e.g. a different bell)? Tests of this type revealed a new phenomenon, called **stimulus generalization**: stimuli similar to the original CS would tend to elicit the same CR. Research has shown that the degree of response is related to the degree of similarity between the new stimulus and the original CS (see Figure 3.2).

stimulus generalization in classical conditioning, the tendency to produce a CR to both the original CS and stimuli which are similar to it in some way

This may not seem like a very surprising result, but it is very profound in its implications. In everyday life, we seldom encounter the same precise situation twice. For example, the traffic pattern on a road is never identical on two occasions, requiring us to pay attention each time we drive the 'same' route. Even people change, as they wear different clothes, change their hair style etc. Given this reality, it is generally desirable to be able to ignore these minor variations – in other words, to generalize across basically similar stimuli. This is precisely what the studies of stimulus generalization

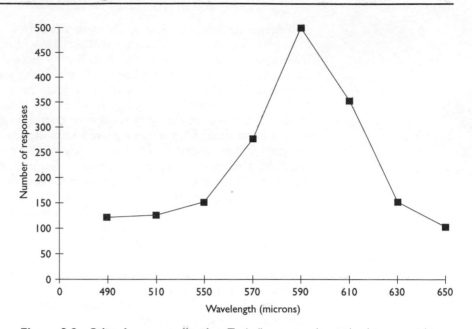

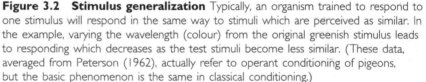

Figure 3.2 Stimulus generalization Typically, an organism trained to respond to one stimulus will respond in the same way to stimuli which are perceived as similar. In the example, varying the wavelength (colour) from the original greenish stimulus leads to responding which decreases as the test stimuli become less similar. (These data, averaged from Peterson (1962), actually refer to operant conditioning of pigeons, but the basic phenomenon is the same in classical conditioning.)

in classical conditioning demonstrate. In practical terms, stimulus generalization results in responding to *a whole class of related stimuli*, after initial learning with a single stimulus. A child who has learned to withdraw after touching a glowing burner on a gas stove will tend to generalize this withdrawal to other stimuli that are similarly bright and hot – electric burners, open fires, etc. In this sense, stimulus generalization generally enables organisms to adapt better to their environment.

How exactly can we define or measure 'similarity'? Ideally, we should have some general procedure, operationally defined, to measure similarity for any stimuli. Considerable attention has been given to this problem, but as yet there is no universal standard to determine similarity. Lacking a clear general definition, one must resort to defining similarity by observing the outcome of experimental tests. Thus, if two stimuli elicit essentially identical results, they are highly similar; if CS_1 produces a strong conditioned response, but CS_2 elicits only a weak response, then they are not very similar.

The fact that there is no reliable way to predefine similarity may seem a serious weakness, but in fact it may actually tell us something about the nature of stimulus generalization. The typical experiment produces results like those in Figure 3.2, where response intensity drops off as the stimulus difference increases. However, this is not the only possible outcome. Depending on experience during and prior to training, results can differ significantly.

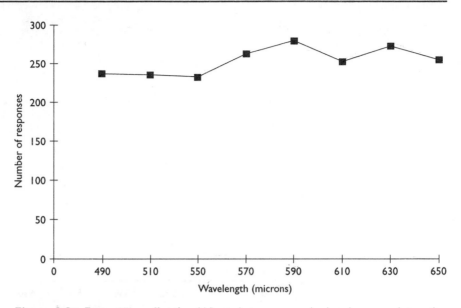

Figure 3.3 Pure generalization When pigeons were raised under monochromatic light, testing for stimulus generalization with other colours of light yielded essentially no differences in responding – in effect, the animals generalized to *any* colour of light. (Data averaged from Peterson 1962.)

For example, when two stimuli are randomly mixed as the CS during training, generalization is essentially equal to both (Grice and Hunter 1964). Even more interesting are the implications of experiments on stimulus generalization where the environment of the animals has been carefully controlled prior to conditioning. For example, if pigeons are reared from birth with only yellow light for illumination, and then a light is used as the CS, the pigeons will respond *equally* to *any* colour of light (Peterson 1962) (see Figure 3.3). In this situation, it seems that the absence of prior experience with colour as a stimulus characteristic leads to regarding all colours as similar. Babies show a somewhat comparable response, in that they initially smile at anyone who smiles at them, whether parent or stranger. Thus, it seems that the initial tendency of an organism is to generalize when encountering a new situation. (As a perceptual characteristic, this may also relate to such behaviours as stereotyping, which involve generalizing based on group membership.)

Why, then, do most experiments show the gradients seen in the first example? The answer seems to lie with another phenomenon which Pavlov studied. He noted that a dog conditioned to salivate to the presentation of a black square (CS) also salivated at the sight of a grey square – an example of stimulus generalization. Pavlov then ran a series of trials during which the black square was always followed by food (UCS), but the grey square was never followed by food. After a number of such trials, the dog reliably salivated to the black square, but no longer did when presented with the grey square. This was a demonstration of **stimulus discrimination**, whereby the organism is conditioned to *distinguish* between two stimuli (see Figure 3.4).

stimulus discrimination
selective responding to the CS, but not to stimuli which are similar in some way, as a result of training

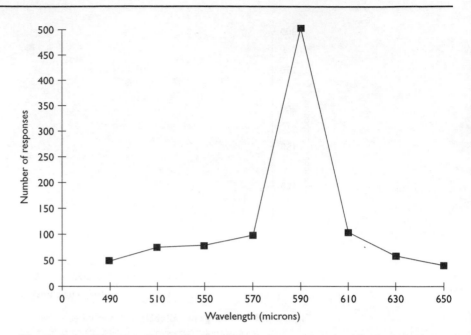

Figure 3.4 Stimulus discrimination When pigeons are trained in discrimination, the generalization gradient becomes much steeper (compare to Figure 3.2). Taken with the two previous graphs, this suggests that a 'typical' generalization response actually reflects a degree of discrimination, unlike the pure generalization produced when there has been no prior experience of stimulus variation (Figure 3.3).

Pavlov subsequently demonstrated that such discriminations can be remarkably precise, if training is continued with stimuli which become progressively more alike. What is notable is that *stimulus discrimination always requires training* – in the *absence* of such training, organisms tend to *generalize*.

If we then reconsider the puzzle of generalization gradients, what seems to emerge is the implication that 'typical' gradients reflect a *combination* of generalization and discrimination. In the everyday world, organisms learn that stimulus variations sometimes are significant, and sometimes are not. Pigeons, for example, may use their colour vision to determine when berries are ripe or not, but not to distinguish between berries and seeds. Typically, the smaller the colour difference, the less significant it would be. Only when they have *no prior experience* with colour variations (as in the unusual experiment described above) will they totally ignore colour differences. According to this analysis, trying to determine a universal standard of similarity is a hopeless task, since organisms will show varying response patterns depending on their past experience. In other words, learning based on classical conditioning is a cumulative process, with present behaviour being influenced by prior conditioning experiences.

While *what* we discriminate may depend on past experience, the *capacity* to discriminate can often be crucial to adaptation. For instance, detecting the difference between food which is safe or spoiled often depends on discriminating particular odour cues. Some occupations are closed to individuals with colour blindness, because job performance requires discrimination based on colour (e.g. certain types of electrical work, where wires are colour coded). Thus, in some circumstances, lacking the capacity to discriminate could seriously reduce our capacity to adapt, or even survive.

Extinction and Spontaneous Recovery

We have seen how classical conditioning, combined with stimulus generalization and discrimination, can lead to learning which is often highly adaptive. However, we have not said anything about how long the effects of conditioning last, or what happens if a conditioned response is *not* adaptive. A Russian researcher, W. H. Gantt, has commented on the possibility that conditioned responses, being persistent once formed, can turn an individual into 'a museum of antiquities' as time goes on. Many reactions would be based on particular past situations, and consequently might be either no longer useful, or even detrimental (Gantt 1966). For example, a person who broke an arm might continue to favour it (because of the pain associated with the original injury) long after healing had been completed. This would represent a form of persistent classical conditioning which, as Gantt suggested, would be maladaptive. Clearly, if *all* conditioning persists indefinitely, then the possibility of inappropriate responses becomes a serious possibility.

In part because of this possibility, Pavlov was also interested in the degree of permanence of classical conditioning. In order to test the limits, Pavlov and his colleagues first conditioned a dog to salivate at the sound of a bell. Once the response was well-established (by pairing the sound of the bell with a UCS of food placed in the dog's mouth), they continued to ring the bell, but no longer provided food. Under these conditions, the conditioned response (salivating) became weaker and weaker, and eventually ceased altogether. Pavlov referred to this cessation of responding when the CS is presented repeatedly *without* being paired with the UCS as **extinction**. Thus, extinction seems to suggest that what can be learned can be unlearned, and that conditioned responses are not necessarily permanent.

However, there are certain qualifiers that should be added to this conclusion. First, one should distinguish between active training in extinction, such as Pavlov used, and the persistence of conditioned responses in the absence of such training. Potentially, without active extinction, a conditioned response may simply remain dormant until the person encounters the CS again. For example, a fear response associated with the sound of a dentist's drill may persist despite lengthy intervals between visits, because no extinction training occurs. Another qualifier on the effectiveness of extinction concerns the *type* of conditioned response. Work by Gantt and others has indicated that internal responses like heart rate and blood pressure changes, which are frequently associated with stressful or emotional stimulus situations, are more persistent than simple muscle responses like withdrawing from a hot surface. This has implications for the conditioning of emotions, as we will see below.

Given that extinction occurs, one might ask what effect the passage of time will have on it. One might assume that the effects of extinction in 'erasing' the original conditioning would be as long-lasting as conditioning itself is in the absence of extinction. However, this is not really the case.

extinction in classical conditioning, the cessation of responding when the CS is presented repeatedly *without* being paired with the UCS

Pavlov found that if he waited several hours after extinguishing salivation to the bell, ringing the bell tended to elicit the conditioned response again. While the response was weaker than when originally learned, and could in turn be re-extinguished, the most striking point was that it reoccurred *at all*. Pavlov called this return of the conditioned response **spontaneous recovery**, which is defined as the restoration of the response when the CS is presented after some time has elapsed since extinction training. Spontaneous recovery of extinguished responses has been well-demonstrated in a variety of species, sometimes after long time periods. This implies that, in terms of conditioning, what we learn is never really forgotten, but at best is simply overlaid with different experience. Instances where old fears re-emerge long after we thought we had conquered them (e.g. fear of public speaking, fear of doctors) may reflect the enduring nature of conditioned behaviour. It seems that conditioned behaviour can be modified, but no conditioning is ever simply 'erased'.

spontaneous recovery
in classical conditioning, the reoccurrence of the CR when the CS is presented after some time has elapsed since extinction training

Higher-Order Conditioning

We have seen that the principles of classical conditioning provide a mechanism whereby new stimuli can come to elicit a reflex response. Typically, the conditioned stimulus serves as a signal allowing anticipation of the UCS, which can be helpful to the organism. Sometimes, the sequence involves stimuli like food or water, which are beneficial to the individual. In other cases, the CS may signal something harmful, like heat or electric shock. (For example, farm animals typically develop a fear of electric fences after a single experience of getting shocked.) However, sometimes we encounter situations where the conditioned stimulus seems to have no direct connection to an unconditioned stimulus. For example, a child hears the word 'cake' and begins to salivate. How can this arise from the processes we have discussed?

Pavlov proposed a possible mechanism for such remote associations in terms of what he called higher-order conditioning. In **higher-order conditioning**, a previously established conditioned stimulus is used as if it were an unconditioned stimulus to create conditioning to a new stimulus. While the description may seem complex, the process itself is easy to grasp. In Pavlov's original experiment, he first trained a dog to salivate to the sound of a buzzer (CS_1), using food as a UCS. Once conditioning was established, he introduced a new stimulus, a black square, which was repeatedly paired with the sound of the buzzer (but not food). After several such pairings, presenting the black square alone tended to elicit salivation (see Figure 3.5). Not surprisingly, the effect was rather weak, since each trial also functioned as extinction training for the original buzzer–food association. Pavlov called such conditioning *second-order* conditioning, and attempted to extend the sequence by using the black square as if it were a UCS, and attempting to link a new stimulus (*third-order* conditioning). Pavlov found this was not possible when food was the UCS; however, he *was* able to create third-order conditioning when conditioning leg withdrawal, with electric shock as the UCS. (This result may actually tell us more about the significance of stimuli like electric shock than it does about higher-order conditioning as

higher-order conditioning
a form of classical conditioning in which a previously established conditioned stimulus is used as if it were an unconditioned stimulus to create conditioning to a new stimulus

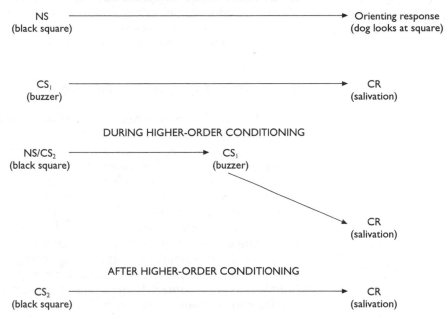

Figure 3.5 Higher-order conditioning Pavlov found that once a conditioned response had been established, the CS could be used as if it were a UCS in order to develop further conditioning; compare this to Figure 3.1, and note where the UCS would be.

such. As with extinction effects, the distinguishing element may be the use of stimuli associated with stress or emotions.)

Dogs, of course, are not exactly like people, and the everyday world is not exactly like the laboratory. Without the controlled conditions of a laboratory, it can be difficult to prove the existence of higher-order conditioning, but many researchers believe that analogues exist in human behaviour. For example, the child who salivates to the word 'cake' has probably previously developed a conditioned response of salivating to the sight of cake (the original CS). Then, in the process of learning to talk, the word 'cake' became associated to the sight of the object it described; by repeated pairing of 'cake' with the sight of cake, higher-order conditioning became established.

It is tempting, certainly, to speculate on how language learning may be closely linked to higher-order conditioning. Parents sometimes will verbalize (e.g. 'bad boy!') while physically punishing a child; it is easy to understand how 'bad boy!' would then come to evoke fear and withdrawal, almost like a physical blow. If later, receiving a poor grade on a school report card leads to 'bad boy!', a poor grade could itself become a conditioned stimulus for fear and withdrawal. Precisely how significant this process is in everyday life, no one really knows. At the very least, we know that words *do* elicit emotional reactions, and such reactions are consistent with higher-order conditioning. Rather than speculating further on this issue, let us examine some of the evidence for classical conditioning processes in everyday behaviour.

At around one year of age, babies begin to react negatively to strangers. What basic conditioning principle does this reflect? If you are introduced to someone by a close friend of yours, and you decide you like them immediately, what conditioning process might be involved?

Applications of Classical Conditioning

While deceptively simple at first glance, classical conditioning seems to be a potent process for learning in a wide variety of species. In humans, salivation to food cues, fear arousal in the shower when the sound of a toilet flushing occurs and a wide range of other instances show how a diverse range of stimuli can come to elicit reflex responses. Sometimes, time itself can be a conditioned stimulus. For example, most pet owners notice that their pets are sensitive to the timing of daily routines, ranging from meal times to the time a particular family member comes home. Since mammals (and a range of other species) have an internal biological clock, time of day can be an unseen stimulus for various responses, including hunger pangs. If you normally eat meals at a particular time of day, you have probably noticed that your stomach becomes active when that time approaches. This conditioned response enables your body to anticipate correctly the arrival of food (provided you don't skip a meal!). Still, the range of motor responses which are typically conditioned in people is limited in comparison to our overall behaviour. Let us look at some other areas where the role of classical conditioning has been explored.

Conditioned Emotional Responses

Pavlov's work on classical conditioning became known relatively quickly – perhaps because he was already famous for his work on digestion. (By contrast, an American named Louis Twitmeyer, who discovered the same phenomenon almost simultaneously with Pavlov, died essentially unrecognized.) Among those who saw the importance of this new paradigm was John B. Watson, who saw in Pavlov's work a model for the behaviourist methodology he was trying to foster. One area where he saw potential was in the study of emotions, which had previously been the domain of the introspectionists. The introspectionists studied emotions, like other aspects of experience, by trying to describe the mental states involved. Watson instead believed that emotions represented observable responses, and proceeded to study the issue by attempting to create emotional responses experimentally. While he used a number of subjects, including his own children, the best-known case was a study done with Rosalie Rayner, using a toddler identified as Albert (Watson and Rayner 1920).

Albert was an 11-month-old boy who had been admitted to hospital for reasons unrelated to Watson's research. Watson initially observed Albert at play, and tested his responses to various stimulus objects, including blocks, a ball of cotton, some furry material and a white rat. The boy, like most children of his age, seemed curious about these objects, examining and playing with them. Then, Watson and Rayner began systematically to associate the white rat with the noise of a loud metal gong. On the first conditioning trial, Albert approached the animal without fear. Suddenly, the sound of the gong arose behind him. The loud noise elicited a startle response (UCR), and also caused Albert to begin crying. Three times, the same sequence of events was repeated. Each time, Albert began crying at the sound of the gong. After a total of seven conditioning trials on two occasions, the white rat was presented alone – and Albert began crying. Thus, a fear reaction had been classically conditioned to the rat, which previously had been a neutral stimulus. Watson called this fear a **conditioned emotional response**.

About a week later, Watson and Rayner returned to test Albert again. This time, the experimenters showed Albert the objects from the original session. The toddler continued to show interest in the blocks and several masks. However, certain objects – balls of cotton, white fur and a Santa Claus mask with a white beard – elicited the same crying and withdrawal as the white rat. In terms of classical conditioning, Albert had *generalized* his response to any white, fluffy stimulus!

Having established that fear could be classically conditioned, Watson and Rayner then sought to eliminate the fear response. To accomplish this, they used Pavlov's extinction procedure – presenting the white rat without pairing it with the sound of the gong. They tried this several times over a three-week period, but found that, contrary to their expectations, the fear did not extinguish. Unfortunately, before they could pursue the matter further, Albert was discharged from the hospital, ending the test.

With hindsight, we can recognize two factors that contributed to the failure of extinction. One is the fact that fear responses, like various other responses of the autonomic nervous system, are hard to extinguish (Gantt 1966). (Recall Pavlov's experiences with higher-order conditioning – the conditioned fear produced by electric shock may account for his success in conditioning leg withdrawal to shock, but not salivation to food.) In addition, the occurrence of stimulus generalization (common for fear responses) tends to make extinction difficult, since a whole *range* of stimuli must be extinguished. Today, other techniques have been developed to deal with fear responses, since extinction training has such limited impact. (See Chapter 9 for a discussion of such techniques.)

Before we continue our discussion of conditioned emotional responses, it is appropriate to consider the ethics of the Watson and Rayner study. Not surprisingly, Watson and Rayner have been frequently criticized for the questionable ethics and potential harm of their test. Without attempting to second-guess past actions, it should be noted that the intent was not to harm Albert permanently; at the outset, Watson believed that both conditioning *and* extinction would be successful. At the same time, it is clear that the procedure involved suffering for Albert, and it is unlikely that such a test would pass current ethical standards (for a follow-up discussion of this study, see Harris 1979).

Watson and Rayner's demonstration, however questionable ethically, served to illustrate that emotional responses like fear could at least potentially arise from classical conditioning. In fact, most behaviourists would argue that phobias (a clinical category for irrational fears) can best be understood as conditioned emotional responses. Thus, anything from the

conditioned emotional response an emotional response such as fear which is established through classical conditioning

fear of water to the fear of dogs could result from a traumatic episode in which the stimulus (water, dogs etc.) was associated with a pain-evoking stimulus.

However, human emotions extend well beyond fear. Could other emotions also be classically conditioned? Behaviourists would assert not only that such conditioning can happen, but also that it is responsible for most of the emotional richness of our lives. A new-born infant may instinctively respond to contact with the mother's body, but later this pleasurable response becomes associated with the mother's face, and later still, objects in the home, and perhaps even the home itself. Individuals who experience pleasure at hearing a favourite old song are experiencing emotions which have become associated with the conditioned stimulus of the music. Even when we go to the cinema, conditioning is involved (probably through a higher-order process) in our responses to heroes, villains and a variety of plot situations.

Words may even be the most refined of stimuli in terms of emotional conditioning. Words have a literal meaning and an emotional meaning; what is curious is that the two often do not correspond. Terms of endearment may range from the silly to the meaningless, e.g. 'little cabbage' or 'snuggie-poo'. Even more interesting is the emotional response to profanity. For example, what are considered 'dirty words' vary from language to language: in English, most forbidden words relate to sexuality; in French, they usually relate to religion. Such differences relate not to the literal meaning of the words, but to the emotional significance of sexuality and religion in the respective cultures. When Shakespeare noted that 'a rose by any other name would smell as sweet', he recognized that the word is only a label – and labels depend on learning for their meaning. Without classical conditioning, it is likely that all language would be emotionally meaningless!

For further consideration

Most of us have various types of fears. Can you identify one fear which you feel affects you significantly? Can you recall a traumatic event that produced the fear (e.g. a fear of dogs resulting from having been bitten as a child)? If not, do you think this invalidates the idea that phobias are based on conditioning?

Conditioned Drug and Immune Responses

As discussed in relation to the biological approach to psychology, the human body is a highly integrated system, involving neural, hormonal and immuno-logical activity. Although we have not discussed the possible physiological mechanisms underlying classical conditioning, Pavlov believed that the mechanism was neural. Assuming this is true (and the available evidence supports this idea), one might still ask whether conditioning can influence other bodily processes, such as the response to drugs or disease. The exploration of such possibilities represents perhaps the most exciting area of conditioning research today.

Pavlov himself was interested in how drug reactions might be classically conditioned. In one study, the sound of a tone was repeatedly paired with a drug which induced vomiting (UCS); after several trials, the dog began to vomit to the sound of the tone alone. This suggests that stimuli present when a drug is administered may acquire the power to induce the drug's symptoms. For example, the smell of coffee may trigger the stimulating effect of caffeine.

Interestingly, more recent work has suggested that with some drugs the conditioned response is the *opposite* of the primary effect of the drug itself. For example, rats were conditioned by giving injections of morphine in a specific environment. While morphine normally reduces sensitivity to painful stimuli, the rats after conditioning showed *increased* sensitivity to pain when placed in the conditioning context (Siegel 1976). Similarly, diabetics taking insulin by injection sometimes show a decreased response to the insulin over time. It appears that the process of injection becomes a CS which counteracts the effects of the insulin.

Why would conditioning mimic the effects of some drugs, and counteract others? The explanation seems to relate to the type of drug, and the body's response to it. For some drugs, like the vomiting agent used by Pavlov, the body reacts by showing a strong reaction, which gradually diminishes as the drug dissipates. By contrast, certain drugs, such as morphine and insulin, interact with the body's natural mechanisms for maintaining equilibrium (called *homeostasis*). In these cases, there is an initial reaction triggered by the drug, which is then followed by an opposite reaction, triggered by the body's homeostatic mechanisms. As a result, the conditioned stimulus becomes associated with the second reaction – which is the opposite of that of the drug itself (Siegel *et al.* 1988).

While drugs, being artificially introduced, seem to interact with the body's own equilibrium processes, what about the immune system? Can classical conditioning affect the way our body reacts to disease? Recent research suggests this may be a real possibility. In one study, rats were given saccharine-sweetened water at the same time that they were injected with cyclosporine, a drug which inhibits immune system response. After several such pairings, tests showed that the taste of saccharine alone was able to suppress the immune system of the rats (Ader and Cohen 1975). Other studies have shown similar effects (see Ader and Cohen 1985). These studies imply that stimuli associated with low points of immune system functioning – e.g. gifts received during a major illness, or objects associated with the death of a loved one – may continue to impair immune response at later times. Conversely, researchers have also been able to use conditioning to *enhance* immune system response (Gorcynski *et al.* 1982; Alvarez-Borda *et al.* 1995). While the practical implications have yet to be adequately tested, it may well turn out that conditioning effects can influence our long-term health.

Research on conditioned emotional responses and drug/immune effects indicates that Pavlov's basic paradigm is still providing us with new insights into behaviour. The significance of classical conditioning is easily under-estimated, since involuntary responses are often overlooked in our daily experience; this is partly because they *are* involuntary, and operate with no conscious intervention. (Equally, conscious attempts at controlling reflexes have minimal success – as those who recognize that their fear responses are irrational can testify.) While we cannot say at present that all issues related to classical conditioning have been resolved, neither have we reached the limit in terms of finding new applications and insights.

For further consideration

In Chapter 2, we discussed how immune functions can be depressed by various adverse events in our lives. Given the evidence for conditioning of both emotions and the immune system, does this suggest why someone depressed by a friend's death would show lowered immune response?

Operant Conditioning

operant conditioning
in the behaviourist approach, the form of learning concerned with changes in emitted responses as a function of their consequences

As important as classical conditioning is, it must be recognized that it only deals with how new stimuli come to control existing involuntary responses. While reflexes and the 'gut-level' responses associated with emotions play a role in our everyday experience, most of our behaviour is self-generated, or *voluntary*. Behaviours like driving a car, working at a computer or calling a friend on the telephone are not elicited by conditioned stimuli. Instead, they are *emitted* – that is, generated by the individual as a way of influencing the surrounding environment. In order to understand the dynamics of such behaviour, we need to consider a different approach to learning. This approach, called **operant conditioning**, deals with how voluntary (emitted) responses change over time as a function of their consequences. For example, if Johnny climbs a tree (voluntary response) and gets hurt (consequence), he may not climb the tree thereafter.

To understand the origins of operant conditioning, we need to go back to the work of Edwin Thorndike. Although Thorndike was studying animal behaviour and learning at roughly the same time as Pavlov, his approach was very different. Whereas Pavlov began with an interest in digestion and then became interested in conditioning, Thorndike was initially interested in problem solving and intelligence. Consequently, instead of focusing on simple reflexes, Thorndike studied situations where an animal was actively interacting with its environment. In a typical experiment, a cat was confined in a 'puzzle box', a cage-like structure from which it could free itself by pressing a lever. As any cat owner can testify, cats generally dislike confinement; hence the cats were typically eager to escape. However, Thorndike increased the incentive by depriving the animals of food prior to testing, and then placing food outside the puzzle box, where it was visible to the cat. Not surprisingly, the cats learned to press the lever, thereby escaping and obtaining the food (Thorndike 1898).

Two primary conclusions emerged from Thorndike's work. The first was that if one measured *how long* it took a cat to escape, the time gradually declined with repeated trials. This improvement in performance represented a change in behaviour as a result of experience – in other words, *learning*. The other major conclusion concerned the relationship between the cat's behaviour and its consequences. Both escape and obtaining food appeared to be desirable outcomes for the cats, leading Thorndike to conclude that this satisfying outcome was what led to the behaviour being repeated. By contrast, flailing at the walls of the box, and other behaviours which did not lead to escape, declined. From observations like this, Thorndike formulated his *law of effect*: behaviour which leads to a satisfying outcome tends to be repeated, whereas behaviour that leads to an unsatisfactory outcome is unlikely to be repeated. Note that the law of effect makes no reference to reducing hunger, desire to escape or other mentalistic concepts. The observational nature of the principle was one of the factors which attracted the attention of Watson and later behaviourists.

Thorndike's research laid the foundation for the study of non-reflex behaviour. By emphasizing the connection between an action and its outcome, his law of effect provided a framework for studying such behaviour. In Thorndike's system, responses are initiated by the organism as part of dealing with its surroundings, not as a reflex triggered by an environmental stimulus. Depending on the consequences, a particular behaviour might or might not be repeated in the future. For example, a child who draws a picture and presents it to their mother may receive praise; this will encourage the child to draw more pictures in the future. On the other hand, if the child takes a biscuit without permission and is scolded, they are less likely to try this again. In its simplest form, the law of effect reaffirms what might be considered 'common sense'. At the same time, by suggesting an approach to the study of the broad range of non-reflex behaviours, it fits well with the developing behaviourist approach. Yet, while Thorndike's work was acknowledged by Watson, and stimulated a variety of subsequent research, it did not result in a coherent system comparable to Pavlov's paradigm until the work of B. F. Skinner in the 1930s.

For further consideration

In Thorndike's terms, what sort of things give you satisfaction? What things produce dissatisfaction? Why?

Skinner and Operant Conditioning

Within behaviourism, B. F. Skinner occupies a position of influence equal to, and in some ways greater than, that of John B. Watson. As the pioneer of operant conditioning, he almost single-handedly created a framework for the study of learned behaviour. Skinner's contributions are significant in terms of both research methods and conceptual analysis. To understand this, we need to consider the origins of his work.

While training as a graduate student at Harvard, Skinner was doing studies of animal behaviour somewhat similar to Thorndike's. Influenced by Watson, he found himself frustrated that so much of the vocabulary of psychology seemed clouded by the ambiguities of everyday language. In particular, he felt that terms referring to mental states were both vague and unnecessary to the understanding of behaviour. For Skinner, the inner workings of the mind (and the body) were a 'black box', inaccessible to direct observation. This point of view was shared by all behaviourists, but Skinner went further, arguing that even if thoughts and other mental states were open to study, they would have no real value in explaining behaviour. The environment in which a response occurs, the response itself and the response's consequence are all that are necessary to understand behaviour. By insisting that mental states are both inaccessible to study *and irrelevant to understanding behaviour*, Skinner was advocating a point of view which has come to be called **radical behaviourism**.

radical behaviourism a position adopted by Watson and Skinner which argues that mental states are both inaccessible to scientific study and irrelevant to understanding behaviour

B. F. Skinner

Burrhus Frederic Skinner (1904–90) is probably the best known American behaviourist, and the founder of operant conditioning. His early years were rather peripatetic – educated at Hamilton College and then Harvard (receiving his PhD in 1931), he taught at the University of Minnesota and Indiana University. During the Second World War, he did research with a military flavour, including a programme designed to teach pigeons to direct missiles to targets while flying in the nosecone; the technique was never implemented. In 1947 he returned to Harvard to deliver the annual William James Lectures; in 1948 he was appointed as a full professor at Harvard. Skinner's development of operant conditioning began while he was training as a graduate student at Harvard. Although his initial work on animal behaviour was somewhat similar to Thorndike's, he became influenced by Watson's ideas, and began a systematic attempt to purge psychology of mentalistic concepts and language. While his theories have remained controversial, the practical applications of operant conditioning have been widespead. Skinner died in Cambridge, Massachusetts, in 1990.

Given his concerns about amibiguities in language, one of Skinner's first goals was to develop new terms for describing and analysing behaviour. He began by coining the term *operant conditioning* to replace Thorndike's 'instrumental learning'; similarly, he renamed classical conditioning as 'respondent conditioning'. He referred to emitted behaviours as operant responses, arguing that 'voluntary behaviour' implies undesirable notions about free will. By developing this new vocabulary, he attempted to purge the study of behaviour of all excess conceptual baggage (Skinner 1987). (Skinner even went as far as to say that radical behaviourism is not a part of psychology, but an approach to understanding certain issues both inside and outside psychology.) Operant conditioning has in fact become established as a major form of behaviourism, as we shall see. While Skinner often argued that his approach is pragmatic, not theoretical (Skinner 1950), his critics have disagreed. In fact, Skinner's framework is generally regarded as a *meta-theory* – that is, a theory about what makes a good theory of behaviour. In this sense, the apparent simplicity of his ideas can sometimes be deceptive.

A second key aspect is the interaction between the *concepts* of operant conditioning and the *procedures* used. As a graduate student doing research with rats, Skinner found that the typical learning tasks, like mazes or Thorndike's puzzle boxes, required extensive labour. For each trial, the researcher had to put the animal in the box, record behaviour, retrieve the animal after the trial etc. In order to simplify this process, Skinner developed an apparatus which would allow the running of continuous trials, with behaviour automatically recorded. He called this apparatus an 'auto-environmental chamber', but since it resembled a small box with a lever within, it became known (to Skinner's lasting dismay) as a 'Skinner box'! While it accomplished Skinner's basic goal of automating Thorndike's approach, it also led to other consequences. The most notable of these concerns the measure of behaviour used. Since pressing the lever in the Skinner box could be considered analogous to the cat pressing the lever in Thorndike's puzzle box, counting the number of presses (that is, the frequency of response) became the standard measure of operant learning. In some respects, this is unfortunate, since despite Skinner's claims to not having a theory, operant conditioning has largely considered *only* the frequency of behaviour, ignoring such aspects as intensity, duration or quality of responses. (For example, there are many individual variations in a response like hitting a tennis ball – especially if one compares an amateur and a pro player!) While the focus on frequency was a practical consideration, it eventually became part of the overall conceptual framework as well – a case of research methods directing theory.

Although the analyses of behaviour which have resulted have often been highly effective, it should be noted that in everyday life frequency is not always the most meaningful aspect of behaviour. (For example, should we judge the quality of artists by *how many* works they create, or should we look at the *content* of their work?) Thus, operant conditioning, while claiming to be a pragmatic analysis unencumbered by theory, in fact has evolved out of a unique set of assumptions about both theory and methodology. As with other approaches to psychology, recognizing the foundations should help to make it easier to understand where it has led in the understanding of behaviour.

For further consideration

Are there situations where the frequency of response *is* a useful measure (e.g. the number of times an athlete scores)? How would you decide when it is useful or not?

Reinforcers and Reinforcement

One of the first issues which Skinner attempted to address was Thorndike's law of effect. While it is intuitively obvious that a response which leads to a satisfying consequence is likely to be repeated, Skinner was bothered by the vagueness of 'satisfying'. To avoid this, he coined a new term, 'reinforcer'. A **reinforcer** is a stimulus which, when it follows a response, results in an increase in the probability of the response recurring. Thus, unlike notions of 'satisfaction', a reinforcer becomes *an observable environmental event*. In everyday terms, a reinforcer is similar to what is often called a 'reward' – but, of course, Skinner would reject such words as being too imprecise for scientific purposes. **Reinforcement** is the process by which a reinforcer *increases* the probability of a response. (Note that in talking about probabilities, one is implicitly describing how *often* a response occurs, i.e. frequency.)

The most basic reinforcers are those which are necessary for survival – notably food and water. Such reinforcers are described as **primary reinforcers**, since they have an innate biological significance. For example, a baby cries because it is hungry. When it receives food, this serves as a reinforcer for the response of crying. As a result of this reinforcement process, the baby is more likely to cry the next time it is hungry. ('Hunger', of course, is a reference to an internal state which cannot be directly observed.

reinforcer a stimulus which, when it follows a response, results in an increase in the probability of the response recurring

reinforcement the process by which a reinforcer increases the probability of a response

primary reinforcer a stimulus whose capacity to act as a reinforcer is based on an innate biological significance, such as food or water

To avoid such terms, Skinner would talk about the length of time since the baby was last fed. Any parent who has monitored a baby's feeding schedule can testify that this is a reasonably accurate gauge of 'hunger'!) While food and water are the most common primary reinforcers, many other items (including clothing when it is cold, air to breathe and drugs such as nicotine or opiates) also seem to function as primary reinforcers. Interestingly, primary reinforcers also typically elicit some form of reflex response – that is, they are *also* unconditioned reinforcers, in terms of classical conditioning. Food, for example, is a primary reinforcer, but also elicits salivation. This dual nature underlines the fact that primary reinforcers seem to have direct biological significance.

conditioned reinforcer
stimuli which act as reinforcers but are not based on biological survival, such as attention, praise or money

By contrast, there are a large number of environmental events which seem to act as reinforcers, but are not based on biological survival. For example, attention, praise, money and trophies can all act as reinforcers. Reinforcing stimuli like these are described as **conditioned reinforcers**. As the name suggests, conditioned reinforcers are stimuli which assume reinforcing properties because they have been reliably associated with a primary reinforcer. (This is actually a form of classical conditioning, with the conditioned reinforcer and primary reinforcer related as CS and UCS, respectively.) For example, Skinner has argued that attention becomes a conditioned reinforcer in early infancy because it precedes (and is therefore associated with) receiving primary reinforcers: the baby cries, an adult comes to see what is wrong and then the adult provides a primary reinforcer like food or a dry nappy. A young child may receive praise for a particular action, and receive a biscuit; soon, praise itself becomes a reinforcer, because it is associated with the biscuit. Later, other conditioned reinforcers may develop as stimuli are paired with existing conditioned reinforcers. (Recall how higher-order conditioning allows new stimuli to become linked to existing conditioned stimuli.) Since conditioned reinforcers are based on learning, not innate factors, the potential range of such reinforcers is virtually unlimited. Perhaps the most powerful conditioned reinforcer in our society is money, which can be used to obtain a wide range of other reinforcers, both primary and conditioned.

Reinforcement, the process of increasing the frequency of a response by means of a reinforcer which follows the response, is at once both simple and subtle. One element which is important for proper reinforcement is contiguity – that is, the reinforcer should immediately follow the desired response. If a child does something desirable, then praise should be given *immediately*; if not, one runs the risk that the reinforcer will influence a subsequent response. For example, two-year-old Johnny goes to the potty instead of wetting his pants. Half an hour later, Johnny's mother realizes what has happened, and praises Johnny – who is now engaged in pulling books out of the bookcase. In this situation, the reinforcer is unlikely to be strongly associated to going to the potty, and may in fact reinforce the less desirable current behaviour! Parents sometimes misunderstand the significance of contiguity, but it is a powerful factor in operant conditioning. When the wrong response is reinforced, the tendency is to assume the principles don't work. But Skinner once commented that if an experiment doesn't turn out the way we expect, there is a temptation to tell the animal, 'Behave properly!' However, in such cases, the animal *always* behaves – the error is in our understanding (Skinner 1967).

Particularly when it comes to bad habits, people tend to invoke rationalizations for failing to change. A would-be dieter, or a heavy smoker, might say 'I lack willpower.' Skinner would argue that such phrases have no real explanatory value, and in fact obscure the actual dynamics of the situation. A smoker, for example, may worry that they will develop lung cancer some years hence, and thus wish to quit. When the attempt fails, the person concludes it is because of personal weakness. In fact, they are ignoring the actual reinforcers: the nicotine, the conditioned reinforcement of smoking being associated with enjoyable moments, possibly peer approval and so forth. Compared to these *immediate* reinforcers for the act of smoking, the perceived value of better health at some time *in the future* has much less effect on the response of quitting. Thus, both *what* the reinforcers are and *when* they are received are crucial to understanding the dynamics of behaviour.

One point which has been overlooked thus far is the question of negative consequences. Thorndike's law of effect stated that satisfying consequences increase a behaviour, but dissatisfying consequences make the behaviour less likely in the future. Skinner describes aversive consequences as examples of **negative reinforcers**. (The reinforcers we have been discussing thus far, which work to encourage responses, are normally called **positive reinforcers**.) Negative reinforcers can be either *primary* (such as a physical blow or electric shock) or *conditioned* (such as criticism, deliberate ignoring, fines). As Thorndike's work suggested, negative reinforcers do not affect a response in the same way that positive reinforcers do. In order to understand the differences, let us re-examine the nature of reinforcement.

negative reinforcer an aversive stimulus which when it follows a response serves to decrease the probability of the response in the future

positive reinforcer a stimulus which when it follows a response serves to increase the probability of the response in the future

Contingencies of Reinforcement

In general, operant responses are freely produced by the individual, but the likelihood of making a response is determined by its consequences on previous occasions. For example, if Tim is given a biscuit for having finished his peas at dinner, he is likely to eat his peas in the future. Thus, there is a relationship between the behaviour (the response of eating peas) and its consequence (the biscuit as positive reinforcer). In Skinner's terminology, the relationship between a response and a reinforcer is called the **contingency of reinforcement** (a 'contingency' describes how something depends on another event). As he realized, identifying the contingency is a powerful tool for understanding changes in behaviour.

contingency of reinforcement a description of the relationship between a response and a reinforcer

One type of contingency is *reinforcement*, as already mentioned. Reinforcement *always* results in an *increase* in the likelihood of a response. In the example above, it is easy to recognize that a biscuit is a positive reinforcer, and that the likelihood of eating peas will increase. Thus, when a response is followed immediately by a positive reinforcer, the response becomes more likely; Skinner called this process **positive reinforcement**, because it is reinforcement using a positive reinforcer.

positive reinforcement a process of increasing the probability of a response by immediately following the response with a desirable stimulus (a positive reinforcer)

A second possible contingency is when a response is immediately followed by a *negative* reinforcer. Since this represents an aversive consequence, do you think that it would make the response more likely in the future? Obviously, the answer is no – in fact, the response would become *less* likely. For example, 3-year-old Sally pokes a pin in an electric outlet, and receives a shock. In the future, Sally is not likely to repeat this action! Since the probability of the response does not increase, this cannot be termed a case of *reinforcement*. Instead, one would probably call it 'punishment' – and that is the term used in operant conditioning as well. (It is one of the rare cases where Skinner adopted a term with obvious everyday meaning.) **Punishment** is defined as a process whereby a response is followed by a *negative reinforcer*, which results in a decrease in the probability of the response.

punishment a process whereby a response is followed by a negative reinforcer, which results in a decrease in the probability of the response

The distinction between positive reinforcement and punishment gets at the heart of Skinner's approach. In order to understand the dynamics of learning, one must be able to identify the contingency which is involved. For example, parents and teachers often react to a child who is misbehaving by scolding the child. The intent, of course, is to decrease the undesirable behaviour – that is, to use *punishment*. What sometimes happens, however, is that the child continues to misbehave, and may even become more disruptive. The frustrated adult exclaims, 'I don't know what's wrong with that child! The more I punish him, the worse he behaves!' Skinner would respond by looking at the situation from the child's point of view (since the child is the one receiving a reinforcer). Given that the disruptive behaviour *increases*, Skinner would say that obviously the child is receiving reinforcement, and so the reinforcer (scolding) is actually a positive reinforcer for the child! At first glance, this may seem silly, but in fact, scolding requires paying attention to the child – and attention is a powerful positive reinforcer, especially for a child who feels neglected. What typically happens is that a busy adult ignores the child who plays quietly, but immediately responds to misbehaviour; so, in order to get attention, the child misbehaves more and more. The moral of this example is that the *organism* (i.e. the child) determines the significance of the reinforcer, *not* the environment which delivers the reinforcer (the adult, in this case).

Reinforcement and punishment represent the most common contingencies in operant conditioning – they are roughly equivalent to the old notion of 'the carrot and the stick' to train a mule. However, reinforcers can also be related to behaviour in other, more indirect, ways. For example, it is possible to produce an increase in behaviour by *terminating* or *withholding* a negative reinforcer (an aversive stimulus); this process is called **negative reinforcement**. For example, a teenager is nagged by a parent to clean up a messy bedroom. The nagging is, in this case, unpleasant – a negative reinforcer. When the teenager eventually (albeit reluctantly) cleans up the room, the parent stops nagging. If we look at this from the viewpoint of operant conditioning, the desired response is cleaning up the room. As long as the response is *not* made, a negative reinforcer is presented (the nagging). When the response is finally made, the negative reinforcer ceases!

negative reinforcement a process for increasing the probability of a response in which a response immediately leads to termination or withholding of an aversive stimulus (negative reinforcer); note that since the response increases in frequency, it is *not* equivalent to punishment

In the example just given, the teenager reacts to eliminate the nagging – that is, to *escape* from an existing negative reinforcer. In the future, they might respond at the first hint of parental displeasure, before the nagging actually begins. In this case, they would be responding before the reinforcer is given, in order to *avoid* it. (In this case, making the response leads to the

Desired change in behaviour

Type of reinforcer	Increase response	Decrease response
Positive reinforcer	POSITIVE REINFORCEMENT	OMISSION (withholding positive reinforcer)
Negative reinforcer	NEGATIVE REINFORCEMENT (escape, avoidance)	PUNISHMENT

Figure 3.6   Contingencies of reinforcement Skinner argues that in order to understand how operant responses change, one must look at both the type of reinforcer and its relationship to the response. (See text for definitions of forms of reinforcement.)

withholding of the negative reinforcer.) Thus, negative reinforcement actually has two variations, escape and avoidance. Normally, initial learning requires presenting the negative reinforcer until the response is made (i.e. escape); later, the individual anticipates the sequence, and responds before the negative reinforcer is presented (i.e. avoidance). Experiencing a 'sigh of relief' after getting out of an unpleasant situation (such as leaving the dentist's office) is characteristic of *escape*. Similarly, the anticipatory fear that you feel in some situations (e.g. if a large, unkempt stranger approaches on an isolated street) can trigger a response to *avoid* the situation (e.g. crossing to the other side of the street).

If you review the foregoing discussion of contingencies, it may occur to you that there is a fourth possibility, based on terminating or withholding a positive reinforcer. How would you react if your behaviour led to losing a positive reinforcer? For example, a teenager comes home very late, and loses driving privileges as a result. As you can imagine, when a response leads to terminating or withholding a positive reinforcer, the behaviour becomes less likely. (This contingency is sometimes called **omission**). Thus, the effects of omission, in terms of reducing the likelihood of a response, are similar to the effects of punishment. (See Figure 3.6 for a summary of the four contingencies.)

To recap what has been said about the process of reinforcement, one can understand the dynamics of behaviour by identifying the contingency of reinforcement involved. To do so, one must identify the response and the reinforcer, and how they are related. In doing so, one must remember that the value of the reinforcer is determined by the organism, not the environment. An example might help to clarify this. Imagine that you are offered a chocolate milkshake if you will sing a song. Assuming you like milkshakes, you will be likely to sing; thus, the milkshake is a positive reinforcer. Based on your rousing performance, you are offered a second shake if you sing another song. You do so, but drink the second shake more slowly. When you finish, you are offered a third shake for another song. At this point, the

omission a process whereby a response is followed by terminating or withholding a positive reinforcer, which results in a decrease in the probability of the response

prospect of consuming another milkshake is very unappealing, and you refuse to sing. Thus, what started out as a *positive* reinforcer has now become a *negative* reinforcer. The shakes haven't changed, but their value to the organism has – and that is the crucial point. Thus, one must look at how the behaviour changes in order to identify the contingency involved. As Skinner said, the organism always behaves, it is our understanding that is sometimes wrong.

For further consideration

As noted, there are two contingencies to increase behaviour, and two to decrease the likelihood of a response. Does it matter to you which is used? For instance, would you rather receive positive reinforcement or negative reinforcement? Why?

Operant Conditioning Phenomena

Shaping and the Learning Process

In all the examples we have discussed, the reinforcer was used to alter the likelihood of an existing response. While this shows the power of reinforcement, it also poses a problem. Since one cannot reinforce a response that doesn't occur at all, how do new behaviours arise? How can operant principles explain the development of complex behaviours? For example, how does a child learn to walk, or an adult learn to play the piano? One factor to recognize is that complex behaviours do not suddenly emerge fully formed. Instead, they tend to be formed out of a series of simpler behaviours, which can then be combined. A child learns to crawl, and to pull itself upright, before it takes its first steps. Piano playing involves a whole set of responses, from learning how to position the hands and body at the piano, to identifying written musical notes, to controlling the pedals while playing. Thus, complex behaviours can be thought of as a series of simpler responses which are combined as a sequence, which is then treated as a single response in terms of giving reinforcement.

While this description can account for complex responses, it still doesn't explain how new responses arise. Such originality is related to what Skinner has called 'behavioural drift'. Operant behaviour, in the absence of reinforcement for a specific response, tends to vary somewhat over time. Much of this variation is simply random, but the fact that drift occurs means that sometimes new responses will occur – and therefore may be reinforced. This means that desired new behaviours can be encouraged through a process called shaping.

shaping the process of guiding the acquisition of a new response by reinforcing successive approximations to the desired response

Shaping is defined as the process of reinforcing successive approximations to a desired response. The process assumes that someone – an experimenter, a parent etc. – has in mind a behavioural goal, and can control the delivery of a reinforcer accordingly. For example, most operant research involves animals (such as a white rat) pressing a lever in a 'Skinner box'. While rats are capable of pressing a lever, it is not a natural response in the wild. Consequently, the rat must be shaped to acquire the response. (As a graduate student working as a lab assistant, I had many experiences of such training.) Typically, when one places an untrained rat in the Skinner box, it begins to explore this new environment, looking around and sniffing at everything. In one corner of the chamber, there is a food dispenser which can deliver pellets of dry food. At first, one simply dispenses pellets, one at a time, until the rat associates the click of the mechanism with the arrival of a food pellet. Once this pattern is established, a food pellet is given only when the rat turns towards the lever. After eating, the rat will be likely to turn back towards the lever. If it moves closer, or lifts a paw towards the lever, another pellet is given. Gradually, the standard is raised, until the rat must actually press the bar to get a food pellet – and at this point, the desired shaping has been achieved.

Shaping is a simple concept, but very powerful. Although they might not use the terms of operant conditioning, generations of animal trainers have applied the same principle in their work. There is even a story, probably apocryphal, about a class of psychology students who shaped their professor to stand in the corner. The students used writing in their notebooks as the reinforcer (professors tend to find this reinforcing, since it implies both paying attention and being interested). Whenever the professor, who tended to walk about, moved towards one corner, the students all wrote furiously. When he moved in the opposite direction, they all put down their pens. By the end of the class, the story goes, the poor professor was wedged into the corner!

The process of shaping has also been applied to more serious purposes, including assisting children with language learning and helping accident victims to reacquire basic skills. (See Chapter 9 for details.) Anyone who has watched trained animals perform, whether at a circus or in a movie, has also witnessed the power of shaping. Having said this, it is worth noting that shaping is easier to grasp as a concept than to apply in practice. I can still recall my first attempt to shape a rat to press the lever in a Skinner box – it took nearly an hour. Later, after gaining more experience, I could typically do it in 15 minutes! The difference was one of judgement and timing – deciding when a new approximation was 'good enough' to merit a reinforcer. If I rewarded too often, the rat spent more time eating than learning; if I rewarded too infrequently, the rat lost interest, or seemed to forget what the last reinforced response had been. In this sense, shaping, while clearly consistent with operant principles, is not simply a mechanical process.

Extinction

Shaping uses the variability inherent in responding in order to produce a desired response. Once a response occurs, it can be reinforced, as we have seen. But what happens if the reinforcement is discontinued? Consider a rat that has been reinforced with a food pellet each time it presses the lever, or a child that has been praised each time she picks up her toys. If the situation changes so that reinforcers are no longer given, what will the organism do? An intuitive answer, which is supported by research, would be that the behaviour might continue for a short time, but once it is recognized that reinforcers are no longer forthcoming, the behaviour will decrease in probability. This drop in responding when reinforcement is discontinued is called

extinction in operant conditioning, a drop in responding when reinforcement is discontinued

extinction. (One can see a parallel to extinction in classical conditioning, where no longer pairing the CS with the UCS results in the CR disappearing.) Note that while both extinction and punishment produce decreases in responding, they do so in very different ways. Extinction can be considered a passive process, in that it diminishes the value of the response by eliminating the reinforcer which supported it. Punishment, on the other hand, uses an aversive stimulus to suppress the (undesired) behaviour actively.

One implication of extinction seems to be that, in order to be effective, reinforcement must be continuously given for every response. Unfortunately, this seldom occurs in the real world. Students study regularly, but receive reinforcement only after the occasional test. People go to work every day, but may be paid only weekly or even monthly. How, then, can operant conditioning be said to apply to such behaviours?

Schedules of Reinforcement

continuous reinforcement a reinforcement schedule in which every response is followed by a reinforcer; equivalent to a FR 1 schedule
partial reinforcement a contingency of reinforcement in which reinforcement does not follow every response
schedule of reinforcement a description of the conditions which determine when a response will be followed by a reinforcer

Early in his research, Skinner recognized that in everyday life we rarely experience either true extinction (no reinforcement at all) or **continuous reinforcement** (with every response reinforced). Instead, what we tend to encounter is something in between – some responses get reinforced, and some don't. Skinner coined the term **partial reinforcement** to describe situations where reinforcement is given only intermittently. In order to understand what happens under such circumstances, he began a series of studies looking at various forms of partial reinforcement. In order to distinguish various types of intermittent reinforcement, Skinner coined the term **schedules of reinforcement** (see Ferster and Skinner 1957). In general, a reinforcement schedule describes when a reinforcer is given, in much the same way that a train schedule describes when a train departs.

The most straightforward schedule, of course, is continuous reinforcement, since every response receives a reinforcer. By contrast, partial reinforcement can occur under an essentially infinite number of variations. However, surprisingly many situations can be described in one of two ways: according to the number of responses made before a reinforcer is given, or the amount of time that elapses between reinforcers. Schedules which depend on the number of responses made are called *ratio schedules*; those which are time-dependent are called *interval schedules*. Such schedules may be very regular (e.g. every third response, every fifteen seconds), or somewhat unpredictable. Regular schedules are called *fixed schedules*, while those which are more unpredictable are called *variable schedules*. Let us look at the different types more closely in order to see how they affect behaviour.

fixed ratio schedule a reinforcement contingency defined by the number of responses the organism must make in order to get a reinforcer; the ratio is measured as FR *x*, where *x* is the required number of responses

Fixed ratio schedules are the simplest to understand (in fact, continuous reinforcement is equivalent to a fixed ratio of 1). The ratio is measured as FR x, where x is the number of responses the organism must make in order to get a reinforcer. Thus, FR 5 means that every fifth response would receive a reinforcer (see Figure 3.7). In everyday life, this is analogous to piece work, where a person will be paid according to the number of responses made. An example might be a seamstress: each shirt may have seven buttons to be sewn, and completing a shirt earns £1; this would be FR 7. Skinner

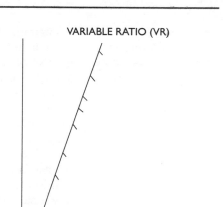
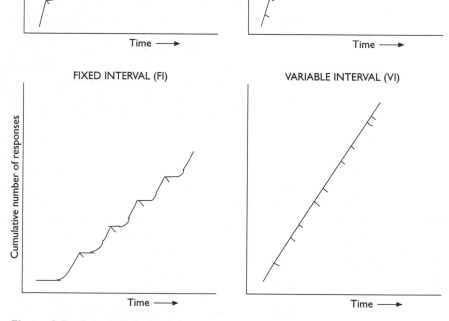

Figure 3.7   Schedules of reinforcement Using cumulative frequency graphs (where total responses are counted), one can see the differences in response patterns using different types of schedules. Note in particular the lag in responding after a reinforcer (shown by hash marks) under fixed interval schedules, and the relatively fast response rates (steep curve) with VR schedules.

found in his experiments that increasing the ratio tended to increase the rate of responding; the animals sought to maintain total amount of reinforcement received, regardless of the schedule. (In the same way, a seamstress might try to work faster if the rate of pay per shirt declined.) In the laboratory, pigeons would peck at a key fifty or more times to get one reinforcer! Eventually, however, as fixed ratios increase, behaviour slows, and may even cease. Essentially, if the ratio is too high, the organism reacts as if it were an extinction situation. (For example, if it takes 150 responses to produce one reinforcer, it may *seem* as though reinforcement has ceased!)

variable ratio schedule
a reinforcement contingency defined in terms of the average number of responses required to receive a reinforcer; thus, VR 10 means that on average every tenth response is reinforced

Interestingly, when the ratio is made less predictable, performance tends to be better. A **variable ratio schedule** is defined in terms of the *average* number of responses required to receive a reinforcer (e.g. VR 10 means on average every tenth response is reinforced) (see Figure 3.7). This means that the ratio is predictable in the long run, but in the short run the number of responses required varies. This is much like a slot machine, which pays off on a predefined percentage of plays – but one cannot predict precisely when the next pay-off will be. This analogy actually works surprisingly well, for animals on variable ratio schedules tend to perform very steadily, much like the gambler who plays a slot machine for hours, hoping that the next play will be the big pay-off. In both cases, the fact that reinforcement occasionally occurs after only a few responses tends to maintain the behaviour over the sequences when no reinforcement occurs. Many other activities also seem to be based on variable ratio reinforcement: In sales jobs, for example, a sales agent might have to make a varying number of client contacts before closing a sale; even so, the occasional sale sustains the behaviour. Sport fishermen don't typically succeed on every outing, and cannot predict when they will catch a 'big one'; even so, they continue to try, knowing the next outing may lead to success. Thus, while both variable and fixed ratios tend to produce very steady responding, variable schedules are slightly better overall.

In ratio schedules, since getting a reinforcer depends on making the specified number of responses, performance tends to occur at a relatively high rate. The situation is somewhat different with *interval* schedules, where time is the crucial factor. In a **fixed interval schedule**, a timer determines how long it has been since the previous reinforcer was given, and only a response made *after* the required time interval has elapsed will receive a reinforcer. (Of course, if no response at all is made, no reinforcer is given.) Thus, in an FI 15 second schedule, at least fifteen seconds must pass between delivery of reinforcers (assuming a response is made at the end of the required interval) (see Figure 3.7).

fixed interval schedule a reinforcement contingency defined by the amount of time that must pass since the previous reinforcer was given before a response will receive a reinforcer; measured as FI *x*, where *x* specifies the required time interval

It may seem odd to consider reinforcement as being time-dependent, but in fact there are many situations where this type of schedule applies. For example, if you are waiting for a bus on a rainy day, you must go out at the appropriate time in order to get the bus. It does not matter how often you go out to check (i.e. make multiple responses) – only going out at the appropriate time will get reinforced (by actually getting the bus). Another example is the administering of pain-killers in hospitals. In many cases, a patient will receive medication for pain (the reinforcer) only if they request it (the response). However, to avoid overdoses, the medication will only be given after a certain time interval since the previous dose, such as four hours (the fixed interval); any requests made before this time has passed will be ignored. Work which is paid on an hourly rate rather than a piece work basis is also often considered as a form of interval schedule. In this situation, there is an assumption by employers that responses are being made (i.e. that work is being done), but technically the response which is reinforced is being present at work! (You get paid according to how many hours you work, not the number of things you accomplish.) Thus, fixed interval schedules are actually a fairly common form of reinforcement.

One special characteristic of fixed interval schedules is that they *require* only a single response in order to receive reinforcement, provided the required time interval has elapsed. The result is that fixed interval schedules tend to produce rather low rates of responding compared to ratio schedules. In fact, even in laboratory studies with animals, as the animal becomes familiar with the situation, one finds a distinctive pattern emerging. Typically, few responses are made immediately after a reinforcer is delivered. Instead, there is a lull, and then a few tentative responses, and finally a brief surge in responding clustered near the end of the time interval. Essentially, the organism comes to recognize that premature responses are wasted, and tries to determine the end of the time interval. (While not as precise as a real clock, most species have a 'biological clock' which provides a sense of time.) On a cumulative record of responses, this clustering of responses produces a distinctive 'scallop' in the graph (see Figure 3.7). (An inventive demonstration of this phenomenon is a study by Weisberg and Waldrop (1972), which found that the number of legislative bills passed in sessions of the US Congress showed this FI scallop!)

If the intention is to encourage steady responding, a fixed interval schedule is inappropriate, because of the clustering of responses which it produces. Given this difficulty, is there any time-based alternative schedule which can remedy this problem? The answer is yes; the trick is to vary the time interval. In a **variable interval schedule**, the schedule is defined in terms of the average time interval required over the long term, much as a variable ratio is defined by an average number of responses required. Thus, on a VI 15 second schedule, one interval might be only five seconds, the interval after another reinforcer might be 20 seconds, and so on – only over a long period would the average duration be fifteen seconds (see Figure 3.7). From the point of view of the organism being reinforced, this variability means that the availability of a reinforcer is no longer predictable; consequently, the only way to determine if the interval has elapsed is to make a response. The result is that variable interval schedules result in steady behaviour – albeit at much lower rates than ratio schedules. Since the schedule is still time-based, very fast response rates don't really accelerate the process of getting a reinforcer; the purpose of responding regularly is simply to check if a reinforcer is available.

An example which provides an analogy may help to clarify the nature of behaviour under variable interval schedules. Imagine someone who works as a quality control inspector on an assembly line; the person's role is to watch items as they pass by, and pick any which appear defective. In this situation, a person who ignores the task (e.g. to read a newspaper) may not be detected for several months, until complaints about defective products are received from customers. Consequently, the foreman checks the person every two hours, on the hour. Since this is equivalent to a fixed interval schedule, a person intent on goofing off could simply begin working just before the foreman arrives, and then return to loafing after the foreman leaves. (This is equivalent to a fixed interval scallop.) In order to avoid this, the foreman varies the time of his visits – in effect, a variable interval schedule. Now, since the visits are unpredictable, the worker must work steadily, or run the risk of being caught unexpectedly. The result would be

variable interval schedule a reinforcement contingency defined by the average time interval which must elapse since the last reinforcer before a response will be reinforced; thus, on a VI 15 second schedule, over a long period the average duration would be 15 seconds typical of behaviour under variable interval schedules – steady responding! (Compared to variable ratio schedules, where there is a direct incentive for fast responding, variable interval schedules tend to produce slow but steady response rates.)

While these four types of schedules are only a small sample of the possible types of partial reinforcement, they show that intermittent reinforcement can be used to sustain behaviour, and that the behaviour tends to reflect the specific requirements of the schedule. In this sense, both people and animals are adept at recognizing the demands of their environment, adjusting their responses to fit the situation. Beyond that, it is worth noting some other characteristics of behaviour using partial reinforcement. The most obvious difference between continuous and partial reinforcement is that under partial reinforcement an organism does more work to get a reinforcer. This gap increases as the size of the ratio or length of the interval increases. One might expect that this 'more work, less pay' regimen would result in resistance (reduced responding), yet behaviour tends to occur at a *higher* rate with partial reinforcement than with continuous (except with very high fixed ratios, as discussed previously). In addition, variable schedules (ratio *or* interval) tend to produce greater response rates than equivalent fixed schedules. Overall, variable ratio schedules seem to be the most effective in maintaining behaviour. Skinner, of course, would never speculate about *why* this occurs, since that would require discussing non-observable events. Still, the dynamics may involve the fact that primary reinforcers have survival value, and organisms must meet their survival needs, regardless of the effort involved. Early hunters, for example, probably received only partial reinforcement for their efforts, and still had to hunt when game was scarce. Studies of foraging behaviour have in fact led to the suggestion that animals (and presumably people) look at long-term costs, as well as the immediate consequences, when seeking food (Collier *et al.* 1997).

Since partial reinforcement tends to produce higher rates of responding than continuous reinforcement, what happens under extinction conditions (when no reinforcement at all is given)? Generally speaking, *behaviour acquired under partial reinforcement is much more persistent than behaviour acquired under continuous reinforcement*. The standard measure is to count how many responses are made once reinforcers are no longer available; this is called 'resistance to extinction', where a larger number reflects more persistent behaviour. Interestingly, one finds that resistance to extinction roughly parallels the hierarchy found when reinforcement *is* available; that is, variable schedules are more resistant to extinction than fixed schedules. This pattern is characteristic of many forms of gambling, which tend to produce very persistent behaviour, despite the fact that individuals are assured of losing in the long run (e.g. slot machines, roulette and craps all fit this description). Again, Skinner does not speculate as to *why* this is true, but a number of researchers have noted that the change in contingency (from reinforcement to extinction) is simply harder to detect with partial reinforcement. That is, with continuous reinforcement, it is immediately obvious if reinforcement ceases, since a reinforcer should follow every re-sponse. By contrast, with any form of partial reinforcement, the organism has learned ('expects') to make responses that go unreinforced; the more variable the schedule, the longer it would take to determine that reinforcement has definitely ceased. Consider an analogy: if you play a slot machine for some time without winning, when would you conclude that the machine was broken or crooked, as opposed to your simply being on a losing streak? In studies with college students who used slot machines that paid off either every time or on a variable ratio, a change to extinction was quickly recognized by the first group, while the second group continued playing for lengthy periods without ever winning! Thus, partial reinforcement produces higher rates of responding during reinforcement, and greater persistence during extinction.

Discriminative Stimuli

At this point, it should be clear that contingencies of reinforcement are very diverse, and that individuals seem to be capable of adapting to the requirements of different situations. But how do they *know* what the requirements are in a particular situation? Consider a simple example: five-year-old Johnny likes to eat spaghetti with his fingers. His mother dislikes this behaviour, and slaps his hand when she catches him eating that way. By contrast, his father is relatively indifferent to the behaviour, neither scolding nor praising it. Thus, depending upon who is present, the consequences of Johnny's behaviour differ significantly. Obviously, Johnny is likely to make the connection between who is present and what consequence occurs, and adapt his behaviour accordingly – eating with his fork when his mother is present, but using his fingers if his father is present! In this situation, the parents are **discriminative stimuli** – stimuli which signal the contingency of reinforcement available. In the above case, Johnny's mother is a stimulus which signals *punishment* of eating with fingers, while Johnny's father signals *positive reinforcement* (i.e. Johnny presumably eats with fingers because it is reinforcing). In general, discriminative stimuli arise when elements of the environment are associated with a particular contingency.

discriminative stimulus
a stimulus which signals the contingency of reinforcement available

In principle, it is possible for any contingency to become associated with a discriminative stimulus. Researchers have found, for example, that rats will use discriminative stimuli to decide when to press a bar: pressing it when the contingency is highly reinforcing (e.g. continuous reinforcement), and not responding when the contingency is not reinforcing (e.g. extinction). In another case, pigeons were trained to discriminate between cubist paintings by Picasso, and impressionist paintings by Monet (Watanabe *et al.* 1995). In everyday life, we all make distinctions based on the perceived contingency in the situation. For example, most people will exceed the speed limit when no police are visible (in which case speeding is not punished), but will immediately slow down when a police car is spotted (a discriminative stimulus that speeding will be punished). Children may react differently with each parent, as in the case of Johnny, above. We act differently at a party and at work, because the environmental stimuli signal that different behaviours will be rewarded in each case. Thus, discriminative stimuli, by indicating the potential consequences of behaviour, tend to influence the responses we make. The behaviour is still operant, not reflex – it is up to the individual what response is produced. For example, some people would rather park a car illegally and risk a ticket than park in a carpark where it is certain they must pay a fee. Our capacity to recognize discriminative stimuli, and to modify our response, makes it easier to adapt to a changing environment.

Non-contingent Reinforcement

In all of the situations we have been examining, there has been a clearly identified relationship between a response and a reinforcer, described by the contingency. Depending on the type of contingency, behaviour increases or decreases systematically. But is this really a fair description of what happens in the real world? Is reinforcement always clearly dependent on behaviour, or do consequences sometimes occur randomly? Most people would quickly grant that some events in life are random, at least in terms of our ability to control them through our actions. That means that sometimes reinforcement is also random. For example, if I find money on the pavement, is it likely to be a result of someone seeking to reinforce me? And if it is a chance event, can we say anything about how organisms react to such random consequences?

non-contingent reinforcement a situation where reinforcers sometimes occur independently of any specific response; chance forms of reinforcement

Skinner considered this question, and described such random consequences as **non-contingent reinforcement**, which means that the presence of the reinforcer is unrelated to the occurrence of the response. Using pigeons as subjects, Skinner did some inventive studies of the issue. In the typical situation, a pigeon that was already familiar with a Skinner box apparatus would be placed in a chamber, and a timer would provide a food pellet every fifteen seconds, *regardless of what the pigeon did*. (Note that since *no* responses are required, this is *not* the same as a fixed interval schedule; in the extreme case, if the pigeon went to sleep, the feeder would still keep dropping food pellets!) After a period of time, Skinner and another observer would return to see what was happening. According to his description (Skinner 1948a), six out of eight pigeons had developed elaborate, stereotyped response sequences. Since these behaviours actually had no effect on the availability of reinforcement, Skinner called such behaviours 'superstitious'. All that was happening, he argued, was that responses were reinforced *by coincidence*, and then the organism maintained the response that was reinforced.

Skinner went on to suggest that non-contingent reinforcement has similar effects on people. Superstitious behaviours, like wearing a favourite shirt while playing a sport, seem to arise in situations where behaviour is only inconsistently reinforced. (Note that this is not the same as partial reinforcement, because Skinner assumes that the superstitious behaviour has no actual impact on the outcome.) I have noticed, for example, that many people have particular rituals for trying to make lift doors close – tapping the edge of the door, holding the 'close' button, even jumping to increase the load on the lift momentarily. Unfortunately, most modern elevators operate on a programmed cycle, and so people are really acting like Skinner's pigeons, engaging in a ritual which makes the time go by! (Not everyone, however, feels that such behaviours are truly non-contingent; it could be argued, for example, that if you *believe* your lucky shirt helps your tennis game, then you will actually play better when you wear it.) At the very least, non-contingent reinforcement shows how sensitive organisms are to environmental consequences.

For further consideration	Having studied the basic principles of operant conditioning, can you apply them to an example of your own behaviour? For example, most of us would like to change the way we behave in various ways. Do you have any 'bad habits'? What is the response? What is the discriminative stimulus that cues the response? What is the reinforcer that sustains it? Can you think of a way to modify your behaviour?

Applications and Implications of Conditioning

behaviour modification
the application of conditioning techniques to altering human behaviour, particularly those behaviours identified as abnormal

One of the striking things about behaviourism is the strong pragmatic element which underlies it. Behaviourists are typically very interested not only in trying to understand behaviour, but also in *applying* their understanding in the real world. Watson's claim about raising children, cited at the start of this chapter, is one example of this impulse. Skinner was often outspoken concerning his ideas for reshaping society, including writing a Utopian novel, *Walden Two* (Skinner 1948b). In more limited ways, behaviourist methods have been applied to many aspects of human behaviour; these applications are commonly referred to as **behaviour modification**. While more specifics about the application of conditioning principles to therapy will be given in Chapter 9, it is appropriate to consider here some general issues related to conditioning.

Negative Reinforcers and the Aversive Control of Operant Behaviour

As Thorndike noted, not all behavioural outcomes are alike. While positive reinforcers like praise or money are welcomed by individuals, negative reinforcers like criticism or physical punishment are unpleasant. Therefore, positive reinforcement is more attractive than punishment and negative reinforcement, which depend on the use of negative reinforcers. Although Skinner would shun descriptions like 'positive reinforcement is more attractive' as being vague and subjective, researchers have found a number of ways to examine the differences between the use of positive and negative reinforcers.

The use of negative reinforcers is often referred to as *aversive control of behaviour*, because of the way organisms react to negative reinforcers. As noted previously, there are two ways in which aversive control is used: punishment is used to reduce the frequency of a response, whereas negative reinforcement is used to increase a response (i.e. the response leads to escaping or avoiding the negative reinforcer).

Punishment is probably the most used – and misunderstood – method of dealing with undesirable behaviour. Parents resort to scolding when disciplining their children. Employers will criticize or threaten hapless employees. Even our legal system is based on punishment for breaking society's rules. Unfortunately, punishment has several limitations. First, as with *any* operant reinforcement, it depends on *contiguity* between the response and the reinforcer – for effective learning, the reinforcer must immediately follow the response. Punishment which is delayed will be ineffective in controlling the response, or, worse, may become associated with a different response. For example, 5-year-old Sarah breaks a plate, and then later tells her mother what happened. The mother, upset about the broken plate, scolds Sarah – but in fact this negative reinforcer will tend to be associated with *telling* about the accident, *not* breaking the plate. In the future, Sarah may still break things, but may not be forthcoming about admitting it! In the same way, imagine if your dog soiled the carpet, and two hours later, when you discovered the damage, you yelled at the dog, who was now quietly resting on his blanket! Ignoring the importance of contiguity can seriously hamper the effectiveness of punishment. (Similarly, one might note that our legal system, with its typically long delays between crime and punishment, is also poorly designed in terms of contiguity.)

A second limitation of punishment is that it tends to encourage avoidance behaviours. A child in school may be scolded by a teacher for giving a wrong answer. Obviously, the teacher's intention is to get the child to study harder, and thereby give more correct answers, but the real result may be rather different. The child may refuse to answer at all, or even skip the classes taught by that teacher. Because of classical conditioning, any stimulus associated with a negative reinforcer (the teacher, the classroom) may itself become aversive, and trigger avoidance. The avoidance responses may be directed at the situation, or simply at finding ways to avoid the negative reinforcer itself. A criminal with a history of robbing banks was once confronted by a prison official, who asked, 'After all these years, don't you know robbing banks is wrong?' The criminal's response was, 'Actually, I don't see anything wrong with robbing banks; it's getting caught that I don't like!' Research by criminologists has indicated that most people obey laws because they feel it is the right thing to do (feeling virtuous can be a form of positive reinforcement); it is only a minority of people (mostly criminals) who focus on the punishments for transgressing. As anyone aware of crime statistics knows, having laws which specify punishments for criminal acts does not in itself deter criminal behaviour, since those so inclined will simply seek to avoid getting caught.

This issue of punishment encouraging avoidance is a major concern, because punishment tends to *suppress* behaviour, *not extinguish* it. Any operant response occurs because there is some reinforcer supporting it; applying punishment to suppress the response simply pits one reinforcer against the other. Worse, whereas positive reinforcement can be highly effective with only partial reinforcement, *punishment must be continuous in order to suppress behaviour effectively*. Thus, in situations where it is possible to avoid the punishment even occasionally, punishment will not be fully effective in suppressing the undesired response. (Consider what this means in terms of our legal system, where arrest and conviction rates rarely approach 100 per cent.) Instead, it would be better to identify the factor which encourages the undesirable behaviour, and try to alter the environment to eliminate that positive reinforcer. For example, children sometimes misbehave because it quickly draws parental attention (a positive reinforcer); to a child starved for attention, the scolding which may follow is less significant than the attention. The result is an increase in disruptive behaviour, followed by more attention (and scolding) etc. The way out of this may be for the parents to *ignore* (extinguish) misbehaviour, and *also* attempt to offer attention when the child is playing quietly or otherwise desirably engaged. (In cases like this, the reinforcing of appropriate behaviour is as important as the extinguishing of undesirable behaviour.)

Because of the way the contingency operates, negative reinforcement is often more effective than punishment as a form of aversive control. Since the focus is on *increasing* a desired response, one does not encounter the problems of suppression associated with punishment. In addition, the acquired fear which can lead to escaping/avoiding the punishment situation, in negative reinforcement tends to *sustain* the desired behaviour. For example, a child may refuse to dress for school, whereupon the parent scowls, and begins yelling at the child, who finally gets dressed. In the future, a scowl may be sufficient to induce the child to dress. Because it is designed to increase a response, not suppress it, negative reinforcement is probably preferable to the use of punishment. In addition, because making the desired response is directly linked to removal of the aversive stimulus, negative reinforcement is more effective than punishment in signalling what the desired behaviour is (punishment simply indicates what is *not* desired).

Unfortunately, there is one consequence of aversive control which is associated with *any* use of negative reinforcers. By their nature, negative reinforcers represent aversive stimuli, and no organism readily tolerates such events. The use of aversive control therefore tends to promote anxiety, resentment and even aggression, in addition to the problems identified above (Azrin and Holz 1966; Berkowitz 1983). This means that depending on aversive control to regulate behaviour is going to produce a whole range of secondary problems, which may even be less desirable than the original behaviour. Therefore, behaviourists would say that the use of aversive stimuli, in any form, should never be a preferred choice. In fact, Skinner once suggested that a well-designed society would depend on a combination of positive reinforcement (for desired behaviours) and extinction (for undesired behaviours), not aversive control (Skinner 1948b). Given present realities, it is clear that most lawmakers have not studied operant conditioning!

| **For further consideration** | Given what has been said about various ways of modifying behaviour, how would you handle a child that bullies smaller children? |

Interrelationships of Classical and Operant Conditioning

For most of this chapter, we have been discussing classical and operant conditioning as if they were totally separate aspects of behaviour. However, it should not be surprising to find that there are interconnections between the two: after all, organisms are constantly producing *many* responses, both reflex and operant. In this sense, the distinction between the two types of learning is partly a way of simplifying the analysis of behaviour, by breaking it into reflex and operant components. In the real world, both processes can be occurring simultaneously. One striking example of this is negative reinforcement. You may recall that negative reinforcement utilizes a negative reinforcer in order to increase the probability of a response. One form of this is *escape*, where a negative reinforcer is presented, and is only removed after the organism makes the desired response. In this circumstance, the removal of the aversive stimulus is effectively like a reward, so the behaviour becomes more likely (hence, reinforcement). For example, a dog given a mild shock through an electrified floor grid will learn to jump to another chamber to escape the shock. Now, if a light flashes before the start of the shock, the dog will soon anticipate the shock, and jump *before* the shock begins. This becomes *avoidance* – the dog is jumping in order to avoid the negative reinforcer. This leads to an interesting problem: since the dog jumps before the shock, there is no longer any experience of the original reinforcer – a circumstance that would lead to *extinction* of the response if one were looking at positive reinforcement. So why does the dog keep jumping each time the light goes on? The light, of course, has become a discriminative stimulus, enabling the dog to respond before the shock occurs. Still, why should the dog persist in jumping without at least an occasional experience of shock? The answer seems to be that, through classical conditioning, the light has become a CS associated with the UCS of shock – which is a perfect scenario for creating a conditioned fear. Thus, the dog continues to jump, not to *avoid* the *shock*, but to *escape* from the feared *light* (Mowrer 1956; Rescorla and Solomon 1967).

Recognizing that the two processes (operant and classical conditioning) are occurring together also adds to our understanding of conditioned fears. Watson, in his demonstration with little Albert, discovered that conditioned fears do not readily extinguish. The reason for this seems to be that the feared stimulus (the CS) *also* triggers operant escape behaviour. This escape response removes the individual from the situation *before* there is an opportunity to determine if the UCS will follow or not – thereby preventing the conditions necessary for extinction. (The same mixture of classical and operant responses happens in the shower when we hear the toilet flush: while we *fear* the sound, we also tend to *jump* away from the water spray to avoid being scalded.) The fact that fear stimuli can evoke an operant response is a very significant point, in terms of those everyday fears which are called phobias. If, as Watson argued, such fears are based on classical conditioning, then it is also likely that the fears persist long after the original experience, because we *avoid* the situations that *elicit* the fear. As a result, there is no opportunity to find out if our fear is realistic or not. For example, a person who is afraid of flying will be reluctant to fly, and therefore has no chance to find out that flying is safe, and that there is nothing to fear. In essence, until we face the fear situation, there is no opportunity to extinguish the fear response.

For further consideration

Conditioned reinforcers represent another way in which classical and operant conditioning are related, since they are associated with primary reinforcers through a process of classical conditioning. Can you think of an example of a conditioned reinforcer for your own behaviour? Can you identify the primary reinforcer it was associated with?

Autonomic Conditioning and Biofeedback

Consider the following proposal: I will give you twenty pounds if you raise the temperature of your left hand while simultaneously lowering the temperature of your right hand. Short of getting a blanket and ice pack, this may seem like an impossible goal. After all, body temperature is an involuntary (reflex) function. How could I expect to control it with a reinforcer like money? At one time, psychologists would have agreed that such a task was impossible – after all, reflexes are the domain of classical conditioning, not operant conditioning. Even the evidence that shows that the two types of learning can occur together (as in avoidance learning) does not challenge the fundamental distinction of reflex versus operant responses. In fact, however, we now recognize that the boundaries are more ambiguous than the traditional view suggests.

The change was triggered by the work of Neal Miller, a noted researcher in the field of learning, and Leo DiCara, then a graduate student working with Miller. Miller and DiCara wondered if it would be possible to use operant reinforcement with so-called involuntary responses. Although this seemed far-fetched, data on phenomena like meditation suggested that under some circumstances individuals *could* deliberately alter such responses. While the details of the original procedures were rather complex (involving partially paralysed rats, with electrical stimulation of the brain as a positive reinforcer), the implications of the results were quickly apparent: involuntary responses *could* be operantly controlled!

autonomic conditioning (also called 'learned operant control of autonomic responses') the conditioning of changes in autonomic (involuntary) responses (such as heart rate or blood pressure) by providing operant reinforcement

Miller described the process as 'learned operant control of autonomic responses', or **autonomic conditioning** (Miller 1969). By providing reinforcement which was based on changes in autonomic (involuntary) responses, it was possible to alter behaviours such as heart rate, blood pressure and even the temperature of various limbs (by changes in blood flow). To understand what is involved in autonomic conditioning, it is necessary to consider how operant responses normally function. For all voluntary muscle movements, our brain receives information, called *proprioceptive feedback*, about the execution of the movement. It is proprioceptive feedback which tells you the position of your arm even when your eyes are closed, for example. But for involuntary functions (involving the autonomic nervous system), there is little or no proprioceptive feedback. Consequently, there is typically no direct awareness of autonomic responses. To circumvent this limitation, DiCara and Miller used sophisticated equipment to monitor these hidden processes, and thus determine when to deliver a reinforcer. Since most autonomic functions show natural fluctuations (e.g. heart rate varies slightly even when sitting), the procedure amounted to a process of shaping a desired response.

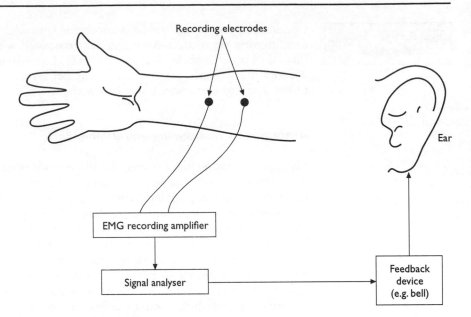

Figure 3.8 Biofeedback The procedure for biofeedback requires some means of monitoring the physiological response (in this case a muscle twitch, recorded using an electromyograph), and a means of making the individual aware of changes that occur (in this case, a bell that rings whenever the target muscle twitches). Using this type of procedure, while monitoring several muscles with several bells, subjects can even learn to play tunes.

biofeedback a general term for applications of the process of autonomic conditioning; the name refers to the fact that in humans reinforcement is based on providing an individual with information ('feedback') about physiological processes ('bio') which are normally not observable

Thus, the essential element of autonomic conditioning is the ability to measure the response. While the recording of physiological activity dates back to the 1930s, using such techniques in the context of operant conditioning is much more recent. Today, applications of the process are frequently referred to as **biofeedback**, since the process provides an individual with information ('feedback') about physiological processes ('bio') which are normally not observable (see Mercer 1986).

Basically, any biofeedback procedure requires equipment to monitor the response of interest, and a means of conveying information to the individual about changes in their response. (Unlike in the original animal studies, in applications with people, informational feedback is often a sufficient reinforcer.) For example, if interested in muscle relaxation, one would use a device called an EMG (electromyograph), which measures the electrical activity in the motor neurons which control the muscles. If interested in the heart, one would use an ECG (electrocardiograph), and so on. The means of providing feedback might be a buzzer, or a light which flashes, when the desired response occurs (see Figure 3.8).

The most significant applications of biofeedback are for medical treatment. It has proven very effective for relaxation of voluntary muscles (e.g. arms, legs, neck), which is often utilized for tension control. It has also proven moderately effective for reducing hypertension (high blood pressure) and for regulating the rhythm of the heart, but not very effective for reducing overall heart rate (McGrady 1996). One of the more interesting uses has been to train individuals to control epileptic seizures, by teaching them to produce a brain wave pattern which seems to inhibit seizure activity (Sterman 1978).

From a more theoretical point of view, autonomic conditioning demonstrates that the processes of classical and operant conditioning are more closely intertwined than was once believed. While it does *not* imply that Pavlov was wrong about the formation of CS-UCS associations, it raises questions about the definition of 'operant' behaviour. Skinner originally defined operants as emitted responses, in contrast to elicited reflexes. This made sense, in view of how such responses can be used to alter one's environment. Now, however, it seems that operant conditioning can be applied to almost any response, *provided there is a clear contingency of reinforcement* (i.e. connection to consequences). Clearly, this would suggest a widening of the boundaries for operant behaviour. Thus, the study of autonomic conditioning has opened up new areas for operant research. Ironically, at just about the time that research on autonomic conditioning was broadening the horizons, other research was suggesting new limitations of operant learning.

Before we leave the topic of autonomic conditioning, there is a sad side-note to the original discovery. The initial study by DiCara and Miller was very complex, as noted. When it was first reported, it was viewed as so remarkable that other researchers immediately set out to duplicate the results – and failed. Miller himself eventually tried, and also could not reproduce the original findings. While no one today doubts that autonomic conditioning is a real phenomenon, and Miller maintained that there was no evidence of fraud in DiCara's work, the younger researcher was discredited by the controversy. Today, the original study goes largely uncited, and DiCara has become a forgotten pioneer. In science, reputation can sometimes make or break a career.

| For further consideration | Do you know anyone who has received biofeedback for a health problem? Based on what you know, would you prefer biofeedback or medication to treat a condition like high blood pressure? |

Biological Constraints on Learning

When most people read about conditioning processes for the first time, one of the first things to strike them is the apparent artificiality of the experimental situations. After all, what does a ringing bell, or manipulating a lever, have to do with an animal obtaining food in the real world? What can the study of such arbitrary acts tell us about ordinary behaviour? In fact, the situations *are* rather artificial, and deliberately so. Behaviourists would argue that laboratory environments provide a high degree of experimental control, and behaviour is still behaviour, in the lab or out. Consequently, many would see the success of their methods as demonstrating just how powerful the basic principles are. However, as with all research, there are inevitably assumptions made when one generalizes from the laboratory to the real world.

equipotentiality premise an assumption made by some behaviourists which states that the principles of conditioning should apply equally to all behaviour, in any species

ethology the study of the behaviour of animals in their natural environments

species-specific behaviour behaviours which are characteristic of all members of a particular species; these response patterns (sometimes popularly called 'instincts') apply to behaviours such as mating, finding food, defence and raising offspring

critical period in development, the concept that there are optimal periods for the learning of certain behaviours

preparedness a concept developed by Martin Seligman to describe how physiological structure influences the occurrence of behaviour

One of the assumptions commonly made is called the **equipotentiality premise**. Essentially, this premise says that the principles of conditioning should apply to any response, and any species. (Interestingly, Skinner himself has never endorsed such generalizations. He might be willing to generalize from observations of one pigeon to another, but would hesitate to generalize from one species to another.) For many years, studies of a wide variety of species in the laboratory seemed to demonstrate that the equipotentiality premise was correct.

However, quite independently of behaviourism, other researchers, coming from a tradition of biology rather than psychology, have studied the behaviour of animals in their natural environments. This approach is called **ethology**. The founder of ethology is often regarded as Konrad Lorenz, a German researcher who did pioneering studies of species ranging from fish to wolves (Lorenz 1967). Ethologists like Lorenz have tended to study **species-specific behaviours** – behaviours which are characteristic of all members of a particular species. These response patterns (sometimes popularly called 'instincts') apply to behaviours such as mating, finding food, defence and raising offspring. Typically, the behaviours seem to be genetically shaped, but also responsive to environmental demands. For example, the young of many species identify their parents through a process called *imprinting*, whereby they attach themselves shortly after birth to the nearest moving stimulus. (Lorenz at one point had a group of ducklings who followed him around as though he were their mother!) Unlike simple reflexes, species-specific behaviour can involve complex sequences of responses, such as the ritual fighting in some species of tropical fish.

For many years, ethologists and behaviourists pursued their interests separately, but in recent years there has been increasing dialogue between the approaches. One of the prime areas of interest has been the interaction of hereditary and environmental influences on learning. The ethologists have tended to assume that much of behaviour is governed by the genetic make-up of a species, while many behaviourists have tended to see behaviour as completely malleable, based on the principles of conditioning. As with many such issues, the truth seems to be something in between: environmental circumstances affect the expression of many species-specific behaviours, and biological constraints limit the process of learning. Contrary to the equipotentiality premise, not all learning is the same. Some behaviours are easier to acquire than others. (For example, learning to clap your hands is easier than rubbing your stomach and tapping your head simultaneously.) Further, some behaviours appear to be learned best at particular times during development, called **critical periods**. For instance, a child who is not exposed to language prior to six years of age will generally have great difficulty learning to speak later.

One way to make sense of these variations in ease of learning is the preparedness dimension developed by Martin Seligman (1970). **Preparedness** refers to the degree to which physiological structure influences the occurrence of behaviour (see Figure 3.9). Some behaviours seem to develop with little or no specific experience required. Seligman refers to these as *prepared* behaviours, because the organism seems physiologically structured to produce the behaviour. Species-specific behaviours would belong to this category;

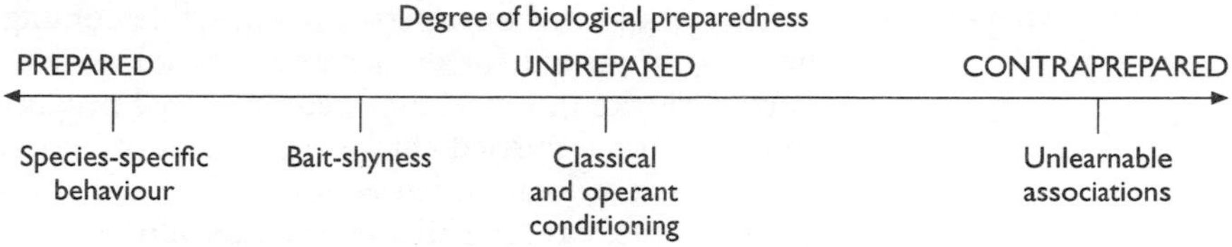

Degree of biological preparedness

PREPARED	UNPREPARED	CONTRAPREPARED

Species-specific behaviour   Bait-shyness   Classical and operant conditioning   Unlearnable associations

Figure 3.9 Seligman's preparedness continuum Martin Seligman has suggested that not all responses are the same, and that various behaviours can be understood in terms of how physiological factors prepare us to learn easily (prepared) or not at all (contraprepared).

the pouncing behaviour of cats is an example. Dogs, by contrast, do not have a pre-programmed pounce response; it must be learned. In the same way, most human behaviour does not stem from 'pre-wired' origins. For example, while we are capable of the balance and coordination required to ride a bicycle, the specific responses involved are not inborn, and must be learned. Seligman refers to behaviours which must be acquired through experience as *unprepared*, since there is no hereditary predisposition involved. At the other extreme, there are some types of complex patterns of behaviour that we find very difficult, if not impossible, to acquire. In these cases, it seems that the physiological structure is not intended to cope with these situations. Seligman says that we are *contraprepared* to acquire such behaviour patterns. For instance, cats are prepared to lick themselves after eating, but they are contraprepared to use licking as an operant response to obtain food. Their physiology is structured for a 'food, then lick' sequence, not 'lick, then food'.

Traditionally, behaviourists focused on those response patterns which depend on learning (i.e. unprepared behaviours). In doing so, they developed the view that all behaviour was alike, as expressed by the equipotentiality premise. As time went on, however, evidence arose which called this concept into question. While unlearned species-specific behaviours are clearly prepared, there are other behaviours which are learned so quickly as to seem prepared as well. One example concerns food-avoidance learning. Food preferences are well known in both people and animals – but what leads to rejecting a particular food?

The answer came about while a psychologist named John Garcia was studying the effects of exposure to X-rays. One effect of large doses of X-rays was that animals became sick to their stomachs several hours later; if they had eaten earlier, they would subsequently avoid whatever the food had been. Garcia became interested in this behaviour, in much the way that Pavlov moved from the study of digestion to the exploration of classical conditioning. In a series of insightful studies, Garcia and his colleagues demonstrated that if a rat gets ill after eating a distinctive-tasting food, it will avoid that food in the future (Garcia *et al*. 1974). Garcia recognized that while it was the *X-rays* (which the rats could not directly detect) that produced the sickness, the rats associated it with the *food* instead. Garcia called this behaviour *bait-shyness* (based on fishermen's belief that a fish nearly hooked on a particular bait won't strike it again).

This would be like a person who, while coming down with stomach flu, happens to go out for dinner and eats something out of the ordinary (e.g. curried chicken). Later, they get nauseated because of the flu – but the next time they order curried chicken, the reaction reoccurs. Subsequent research, as well as anecdotal evidence, has confirmed that this phenomenon is genuine. For example, cancer patients often develop a wide range of food aversions as a result of the nausea produced by chemotherapy (Bernstein 1991).

Exploration of bait-shyness led to the conclusion that many species, including humans, have developed in such a way that getting sick is very readily associated with the last food eaten (Logue 1988). The link between food and sickness often occurs after a single experience, despite the long delay between eating and getting sick. (Imagine trying to teach a rat to press a bar by reinforcing it several hours after it makes the correct response!) Garcia suggested that this behavioural capacity evolved because it was adaptive: an animal which ate something harmful would do well to avoid it in the future. Through mutation and natural selection, a neural mechanism was created to link taste with stomach upset. Thus, bait-shyness represents a form of prepared behaviour.

Over time, research has shown that food-avoidance learning is only one example of such prepared behaviours. For example, migratory birds are biologically predisposed to learn landmarks on their route (Shettleworth 1972). It has also been suggested that some types of human fears are more easily conditioned than others. Consider fear of the dark. Humans are basically daytime creatures. To our ancestors, who depended (as we still do) on vision more than smell or hearing, the night world of darkness was a place of invisible dangers. Consequently, natural selection may have 'prepared' us to be afraid of the dark. (Note this does *not* mean that all people automatically have a strong fear of the dark; it simply implies that very little experience is needed to *develop* such a fear.)

Studies of classically conditioned fears suggest that not all stimuli are equally likely to elicit conditioned fear responses. A few years after Watson's study of little Albert, another researcher found that an infant could be conditioned to fear a rat, but not wooden blocks or pieces of cloth (Bregman 1934). More recently, studies with adults have shown that fear is more easily conditioned to pictures of snakes or spiders than to pictures of flowers or houses (Öhman 1986; Öhman and Soares 1998). One way of interpreting such differences in the frequency of occurrence of different phobias is to assume that some fears (like snakes and spiders) are biologically prepared. This would make sense in evolutionary terms, since being fearful of creatures which are potentially poisonous or otherwise dangerous can be seen as adaptive. (Note that other factors, including cultural influences, could also be involved.)

It is harder to evaluate the possibility of there being contraprepared behaviours in humans. One of the difficulties is that, by definition, what is contraprepared is unlearnable. So, if there *is* some behavioural pattern that we cannot learn, would we even be able to recognize it? After many discussions with colleagues, no one has come forth with a clear example of contrapreparedness in people, despite many known examples in other species (e.g. the lick-then-food sequence in cats, above). Since there is no logical necessity that states there *must* be such behaviours in humans, the absence of examples tells us little. So, at present, the issue is unresolved.

Overall, there seems little doubt that genetic and physiological factors play a role in human behaviour. However, such factors do not seem to play as significant a role in human activity as they do in many other species. This is indicated in part by the long infancy/childhood of human development; whereas many animals may be fully developed at birth, human infants require care and assistance longer than any other species. While this is a disadvantage in terms of survival, it allows for maximum flexibility of behaviour, based on experience. Learning takes time, and with time, the helplessness of the infant becomes the diverse and complex behaviour of the adult.

The study of biological constraints, by both ethologists and behaviourists, has enriched our understanding of behaviour, even as it has limited the range of application of conditioning principles. One of the significant lessons seems to be a recognition of the limitations of laboratory research. Whenever one enters the laboratory to study behaviour, one trades the advantages of control for the disadvantages of an artificial situation. It is well recognized that people often react differently when they know they are being studied (see Chapter 1), and even with animals, the laboratory setting may give a distorted perspective. This is not to say that the years of research on operant and classical conditioning are invalid; indeed, both methods have added a great deal to our understanding. However, just as each approach to psychology has its limits, so too it seems that a full understanding of behaviour cannot come from the laboratory alone. By exploring biological constraints, it can be argued that behaviourists have enriched their approach, rather than weakened it.

| **For further consideration** | Have you ever developed a sudden aversion to a particular food? Do you recall the circumstances? In what ways does Garcia's work on bait-shyness help you to understand your own taste preferences? |

Conclusion

The behaviourist approach is based on the assumption that science must be based on the study of observable events. In terms of behaviour, this means looking at the interactions between an organism and its environment. In adopting this stance, behaviourists forgo attempts to study consciousness and internal subjective states. As Skinner has pointed out, behaviourism is a method of analysis rather than simply a theory (Skinner 1987). Critics say that treating the organism like a 'black box' means that one ignores the mental processes that are central to human behaviour. Skinner says that such events are scientifically unknowable, and, in any case, do not *cause* behaviour: 'thinking about' something before doing it is simply correlated with the observable behaviour. For example, if a Freudian theorist suggests that adult behaviour can best be understood by looking at childhood experiences, Skinner agrees – but suggests that the connections are based on the reinforcement history of the person, not some vague concept of 'conflicts between id and ego'.

Ultimately, the best criterion for judging any approach, including behaviourism, is not our theoretical preference, but the extent to which it helps us to make sense of behaviour. While many have criticized its restrictions, the reality is that the study of classical and operant conditioning has added to our overall understanding in psychology. The appeal of behaviourism is reflected in the fact that for many years it was the dominant force in North American psychology. It is interesting, and in some ways ironic, that behaviourism in some ways contributed to the success of the cognitive approach. As we will see in the next chapter, Edward Tolman, regarded as one of the founders of the cognitive approach, considered himself a behaviourist – though not a radical behaviourist like Skinner. In addition, the study of many cognitive issues, such as observational learning (imitation) and the use of hypotheses in problem solving, began with similar behaviourist studies of animals. Where the introspectionists failed in their attempts to make sense out of mental processes, the behaviourists have pointed the way to new possibilities for a scientific psychology.

Although the behaviourist approach has contributed significantly to our understanding of behaviour, it no longer occupies the pre-eminent position it once did within psychology. In part, this reflects changes in the discipline, and in part the limitations of the approach. One major weakness is that research by ethologists and others has shown that the principles of conditioning are not as universal as was once asserted. This failure of the 'equipotentiality premise' restricts the generality of behaviourist principles in important ways. Beyond that, interest in mental processes has not diminished simply because the behaviourists have refused to address the issues. Instead, researchers have found new ways to study mental processes, resulting in new interest in the cognitive approach – as we shall see in the next chapter.

Chapter Summary

- The behaviourist approach emphasizes the study of *observable responses*, and rejects attempts to study internal processes like thinking.

- Behaviourists focus on *learning* as the primary factor in explaining changes in behaviour. Depending on the type of response, this involves either *classical conditioning* or *operant conditioning*.

- Classical conditioning is concerned with how *conditioned stimuli* come to elicit (reflex) *conditioned responses* which are normally elicited by *unconditioned stimuli*.

- Classical conditioning can be applied to a number of aspects of human behaviour, including *emotional responses* like fears, and even activity of the immune system.

◆ Operant conditioning is concerned with how the probability of a *voluntary* 'operant' *response* changes as a function of the environmental consequences (*reinforcer*) which follow the response.

◆ This process of *reinforcement* can be analysed in terms of the *type of reinforcer*, the *contingency of reinforcement* and the *schedule of reinforcement*.

◆ The application of operant conditioning to everyday behaviour is commonly called *behaviour modification*; researchers have examined the effects of *aversive control* and methods of altering behaviour by *biofeedback*, among other uses.

◆ Recent research has indicated that, while conceptually distinct, classical and operant conditioning are interrelated in actual behaviour. In addition, research on *biological constraints on learning* has suggested that there are limits to the generality of conditioning principles.

Key Terms and Concepts

behaviour modification
biofeedback
classical conditioning
conditioned emotional response
conditioned response
conditioned stimulus
continuous reinforcement
discriminative stimulus
extinction (classical)
extinction (operant)
higher-order conditioning
interval schedules
law of effect
learning
negative reinforcement
negative reinforcer
omission

operant conditioning
partial reinforcement
positive reinforcement
positive reinforcer
preparedness
punishment
ratio schedules
reinforcement
reinforcer
schedules of reinforcement
shaping
species-specific behaviour
spontaneous recovery
stimulus discrimination
stimulus generalization
unconditioned response
unconditioned stimulus

Suggestions for Further Reading

For the reader interested in a more detailed discussion of the principles of learning (both classical and operant), Chance's *Learning and Behavior* is a very readable account. For a recent assessment of the impact of behaviourism, see Kunkel's 1996 article.

B. F. Skinner has maintained a distinctive position within behaviourism, not least for his outspoken comments on changing society. One of his clearest presentations of his views on society is *Beyond Freedom and Dignity*.

One significant influence of behaviourism has been the practical application of conditioning principles to everyday behaviour. Martin and Pear's *Behavior Modification: What It Is and How to Do It* provides a good overview of such applications. For a more specific discussion of the use of biofeedback techniques in clinical applications, see Mercer's *Biofeedback and Related Therapies in Clinical Practice*.

For an account which shows how the ethological approach differs from laboratory studies of behaviour, Jane Goodall's *Through a Window* provides a highly readable beginning.

4

The Cognitive Approach

Thought and Action
Introduction
Perception and Cognition
Learning and Memory
Learning as Information Gathering
Memory as the Retention of Learning
A Basic Model of Memory
Encoding and Storage in Memory
Forgetting
  Forgetting in STM
  Forgetting in LTM
Memory as Reconstruction
  Eyewitness Testimony
Improving Memory
Problem Solving
Defining Problems
  Stages of Problem Solving
  Types of Problems
Models of Problem Solving

Gestalt Theory
Problem Solving as Information Processing
Algorithms
Heuristics
Creativity in Problem Solving
The Formation of Problem Solving Skills
Language
Language Learning
  Of Apes and Language
Language and Thinking
The Cognitive Viewpoint in Other Areas
Attitudes and Cognitive Dissonance
Attribution Theory
Cognition and Emotions
Conclusion
Chapter Summary
Key Terms and Concepts
Suggestions for Further Reading

Thought and Action

At the start of the twentieth century, a young physicist was working as a clerk in the Swiss patent office. In his spare time, he continued his interest in theoretical physics. Like other physicists of the day, he was puzzled by discoveries which seemed to challenge long-held notions about matter and energy. For one thing, the speed of light seemed to be constant throughout the universe, but no one could explain why. Then, the young clerk tried reversing the problem, suggesting that one *assumed* that the speed of light was constant. Having made this shift, many aspects of the problem fell into place. Most of his older colleagues were perplexed and even outraged; after all, the proposal contradicted all their previous training. In the end, his solution became accepted, and his work triggered significant changes in science and the world. The theory is now called the special theory of relativity, and the young clerk was Albert Einstein.

Today, all college physics students, and many others, have a basic grasp of Einstein's insights, expressed as $E = mc^2$. It is one of the marvels of great ideas that, once formulated, they can be readily understood by many. Yet the first formulation of a solution is often elusive; even many of Einstein's colleagues had difficulty grasping it. What leads to such insights? How do we develop new solutions to old problems?

Consider a simpler example of problem solving. A young child is given a problem in which pointing to a star leads to getting sweets as a reinforcer, but pointing to a circle does not. Gradually, the child becomes consistent in choosing the star. However, once the child has learned this discrimination, the child is given a new problem, involving a square and a triangle. On this problem, the child is consistently correct by the second trial. (On the first trial, of course, they must guess.) On other problems with new shapes, the child continues to perform consistently well. Behaviourists would describe the task as learning to respond to a discriminative stimulus (the shape), a process which requires trial and error learning. Yet in this situation, the child seems to develop a *rule* for making choices, rather than being simply reinforced for a particular response. Can conditioning adequately explain such complex behaviour?

Or consider this: if you have developed a skill, such as playing a piano, does the skill disappear if there is no piano present? Is *knowing* something the same as *doing* something?

To the behaviourists, all human activity can be described in terms of responses to environmental cues. Behaviour, defined as observable responses, is based on conditioned reflexes, reinforcement and other simple processes. By its nature, this approach tends to deny that anything happening *within* the person is significant. Memories, thoughts and feelings are seen as irrelevant to science – and therefore meaningless. Expressed in these terms, all the above examples become virtually impossible to understand.

Introduction

As the above examples illustrate, much of our behaviour involves not simply actions, but mental processes such as perception, memory, problem solving and language. While these processes cannot be directly observed, that does not seem sufficient reason to ignore their existence, or the ways in which they affect behaviour. Consequently, the *cognitive approach* is concerned with thinking, and the mental processes related to it.

Unlike the behaviourists, cognitive psychologists believe that one cannot fully explain behaviour in terms of stimulus–response connections. (The child learning a 'rule' for discrimination problems, described above, is one example.) Instead, the cognitive approach sees events within the person as being at least as important as environmental stimuli in the understanding of behaviour. These internal events are described as mediational processes or **mediators**, because they come between the stimulus and the response. Thinking processes like memory, problem solving and language are all based on mediators.

This emphasis on mediating processes, and the way they are defined, is central to the cognitive approach. However, the nature of these mediators is also important. In essence, mediational processes are defined functionally – that is, with reference to how behaviour is altered. These mediators are therefore *conceptual* – one describes the properties of memory, for example, without concern for its physical embodiment. (By contrast, the biological approach also deals with mediational processes, but they are defined physiologically, not conceptually, e.g. looking at how the visual cortex is involved in perception.) Hence, the cognitive approach is distinct from both the approaches we have considered thus far.

The development of the cognitive approach is closely related to behaviourism, since in part it developed as a reaction against the behaviourists' emphasis on external events. By the time Watson published the first edition of *Behaviorism* in 1924, he felt that his approach was gaining ground against the ambiguities of introspectionism. Yet at virtually the same point in time, the seeds of a new alternative were being sown. In 1925, a book by a young German researcher named Wolfgang Kohler appeared, called *The Mentality of Apes* (Kohler 1925). In this book he reported observations which suggested that animals could show behaviour which was *insightful*, and he rejected behaviourism in favour of an approach called Gestalt psychology. The other challenge to behaviourism came from someone who actually called himself a behaviourist. In 1932, E. C. Tolman published a book called *Purposive Behavior in Animals and Man* (Tolman 1932). In this book, he described research which was difficult to explain in terms of traditional behaviourism. Instead of associations between stimuli and responses, Tolman talked about learning as based on relationships among stimuli, referred to as forming **cognitive maps**. In addition, he argued that learning and responding are not the same, and that it is possible to learn without showing a correct response. Taken together, the work of Kohler and Tolman raised basic questions about the validity of behaviourism, and laid the foundations for what has become the cognitive approach. To see how, let us briefly examine each man's work more closely.

While early behaviourists saw learning as basically a matter of trial and error, Kohler argued that we tend to *organize* experience in particular ways. This is illustrated by the phenomenon Kohler called insight. **Insight** is a sudden change in the way one organizes a problem situation; typically this is characterized by a change in behaviour from random responding to rule-based responding. A child solving discrimination problems can show

mediator a process or event within the individual which comes between a stimulus and a response

cognitive map Tolman's term for the mental representation of learned relationships among stimuli

insight a sudden change in the way one organizes a problem situation; typically this is characterized by a change in behaviour from random responding to rule-based responding

Wolfgang Kohler

Wolfgang Kohler (1887–1967) was a founder of Gestalt theory. Born in Tallinn, Estonia, he was educated in Germany, attending the universities of Tübingen, Frankfurt and Berlin (where he received his doctorate). While at Frankfurt, he met Max Wertheimer and Kurt Koffka, who also contributed to the development of Gestalt theory. In 1913, Kohler went to Tenerife in the Canary Islands to study the resident apes; in what became an act of serendipity, he was stranded there for the duration of the First World War, unable to leave until 1919. During this period, his studies with the apes led him to a view of problem solving as an active process of insight, unlike the trial and error viewpoint advocated by Tolman. Eventually, this work became an important influence on Gestalt theory, which Kohler promoted as a professor at the University of Berlin (he was made chair in psychology in 1921). In 1934 he travelled to the United States to deliver the annual William James Lectures at Harvard; aware of Hitler's rise to power in Germany, he accepted an appointment at Swarthmore University in Pennsylvania, where he remained almost until his death at the age of eighty.

mental set in Gestalt theory, the cognitive schema an individual uses to organize their perception of a particular situation, such as a problem

insight, as mentioned above. In general, insight can be described as forming an appropriate *schema* (or, to use Kohler's term, **mental set**) for a particular situation.

One of the most famous examples of Kohler's work on insight involved an ape named Sultan. Kohler gave Sultan a series of related problems, in which he had to use a stick to reach for a banana which was placed outside his cage, out of arm's reach. After solving such problems on several occasions, Sultan was now presented with a stick which was not long enough to reach the banana. However, outside the cage was a longer stick. After several unsuccessful tries, Sultan threw down the short stick in evident frustration, and retreated to the corner of his cage. A little while later, he suddenly went over to the short stick, used it to reach the other, longer stick, and with the *new* stick, reached the banana! As Kohler noted, there was no gradual sequence, as one might expect with shaping, nor did it seem to be the result of trial and error. Instead, there was a sudden transformation of the way Sultan organized the elements – insight. Kohler's work thus created a shift away from seeing all behaviour as trial and error, towards a concern with the internal organizing processes which mediate behaviour.

Kohler talked about internal organizing principles, a subject which behaviourists avoided. By contrast, Tolman regarded himself as a behaviourist, in that his data were strictly based on observations of stimuli and responses. But the problems he examined were very embarrassing to the traditional behaviourists of his day. For instance, behaviourists argued that unless there was a change in behaviour (performance of a new response), no learning had taken place. Tolman demonstrated that animals may learn the pattern of a maze, forming a *cognitive map*, yet not perform correctly until a reward is given. This **latent learning**, being undetectable as it occurred, suggested that learning is distinct from the performance of a behaviour. In another study, rats explored mazes which had several paths of varying length, all leading to the end; later, if the shortest path to reach food at the goal

latent learning a term used by Tolman to describe situations in which learning is distinct from the performance of a behaviour

Edward Tolman

Edward Chace Tolman (1886–1959) was born in Newton, Massachusetts. He received his bachelor's degree from MIT, and his doctorate in psychology from Harvard in 1915. Tolman spent almost his entire career at the University of California at Berkeley. While he considered himself a 'behaviourist', and his own research was done almost entirely with rats, Tolman's work bears little resemblance to the radical behaviourists', such as Watson and Skinner. A contemporary of Watson, he rejected the emphasis on reflexes and trial and error learning which was central to Watson's views. Instead, he developed a concept of 'purposive behaviourism', which emphasized the distinction between learning and performance (as seen in latent learning), and viewed learning in terms of the formation of 'hypotheses' and 'cognitive maps'. Both by showing the weaknesses of radical behaviourism, and by proposing concepts which acknowledged the existence of mediational processes, Tolman helped to lay the foundations for the cognitive approach. He was seventy-three when he died – just a few years before the blossoming of the cognitive approach in the 1960s.

was blocked, the rats chose the second shortest route. This is similar to a person who finds his normal driving route blocked by construction, and quickly selects the most reasonable alternate route. In both the rat and the person, this seems to require a knowledge of how locations are connected, rather than mechanical repetition of a shaped sequence of responses. Thus, Tolman's theory ultimately emphasized the importance of mediational processes.

Both Kohler and Tolman had an important influence in laying the foundation of the cognitive approach. Yet despite their early role, neither has many direct followers today. This does not mean that the cognitive approach is not important (if anything, its influence has grown in recent years). Rather, it means that the impact of these pioneers is diffuse, and sometimes not directly recognized. To a large extent, the coherence of the cognitive approach is not based on a single theory or researcher, but on the underlying assumptions about behaviour, and the central focus given to internal mental processes. Hence, various elements of the approach have been transformed or used piecemeal by researchers of various outlooks. Still, much of the basis of current work can be traced back to the influence of Kohler and Tolman.

Since no single theorist has dominated the cognitive approach in the way that Skinner has operant conditioning or Freud has psychoanalysis, there has been a greater exchange with other approaches, both within and outside psychology. Thus, today one hears about a cognitive theory of social behaviour, or emotion, or even cognitive behaviour modification. At the same time, cognitive psychologists have borrowed from other fields, including computer science and physiology. In fact, some even refer to 'cognitive science' as a hybrid discipline, incorporating elements of psychology, linguistics, computer science and physiology!

One reason for this broad interchange is the tendency of psychologists to seek new models. Analogies and metaphors have long played a role in scientific thinking, in the desire to describe problems in new ways. In the seventeenth century, Descartes used hydraulically operated statues in the Tuileries Gardens of Paris as a model for the physiology of body movements. At the beginning of the twentieth century, psychologists compared the brain (as a network of stimulus–response connections) to a telephone switchboard. Today, computers play a large role in our lives, and psychologists have borrowed from the language of computer technology, in the form of 'information processing' models. Each analogy has benefits and limitations, but the use of such models to aid our understanding is a well-established practice.

information processing
a term borrowed from computer science by cognitive psychologists to describe the mental functions which occur between stimulus and response

Consciously or not, those who use information-processing descriptions fall within the tradition of Kohler and Tolman. **Information processing** refers to the intervening events (mediators) which come between input (stimulus) and output (response) of the system (person). In a computer, one cannot predict the output from the input without knowing something about what is going on within the computer. In the same way, a person's behaviour cannot be understood solely by looking at environmental stimuli. There is a further parallel, in that the computer model emphasizes the concept of processing of information. By *processing*, we mean the output represents a qualitative change in the input, such as combination, analysis or comparison of input data. This element of active transformation is also seen in Kohler's emphasis on insight as creative, and Tolman's view of cognitive maps as going beyond mere repetitions of previous responses. Thus, information processing models fit very comfortably within the cognitive approach.

In this chapter, we will look at several aspects of behaviour from the cognitive viewpoint. The most general concern is simply trying to understand how we behave. Generally, cognitive researchers have focused on questions concerning how we remember, why we forget, what leads to effective solutions to problems and similar issues. This emphasis on thinking processes (memory, problem solving, decision making, language) is natural, given that the word 'cognitive' refers to thinking. (See Green (1996) for a history of how the term has been used by psychologists and philosophers.) At the same time, the scope of the cognitive approach has broadened in recent years, and even includes such 'irrational' aspects of behaviour as emotions. Whatever the topic, the key elements of the cognitive approach remain the same: (a) processes within the person are considered central to understanding behaviour; and (b) these mediating processes operate in an organized and systematic way, not by trial and error.

Perception and Cognition

Traditionally, psychologists tried to separate the process of perceiving from thinking – that is, to divide perception and cognition. Perception was used to refer to the receiving of sensory inputs, while cognition referred to mental processes. However, over time, it has come to be recognized that the distinction is hard to maintain. For example, perceiving involves recognizing a stimulus – and recognition of something as familiar requires making use of memory (a cognitive process). In the same way, thinking does not occur in the absence of something to think about, and much of the content of thought relates to present and past sensory stimuli. Hence, while clearly not synonyms, perception and cognition are also not totally distinct terms (Robinson 1979).

One example of this overlap is Gestalt theory, as developed by Kohler and others. Gestalt theory is a theory of perception as well as cognition. For instance, memory for stimuli is related to how they are perceived. In a classic study by Carmichael and his colleagues, subjects were given simple line figures to remember, along with a word cue (Carmichael *et al.* 1932). Later, they were asked to draw each figure when given the appropriate cue. The crucial variable was the word cue used. For example, one figure consisted of a short horizontal line, terminated at each end by a circle. The verbal cue given to different subjects was either 'glasses' or 'barbell'. Later, the drawings produced tended to be distorted in ways that reflected the word cue (e.g. adding extensions for 'glasses', or changing the line to a solid bar for 'barbell'). This study, while complicated by the problem of interpreting subjects' drawings for accuracy, is consistent with a number of Gestalt studies which suggest that perception and memory are interrelated. In the first chapter, we noted how perception is best conceived as an active process of interpreting the environment, based in part on one's mental schemata, which in turn are shaped by one's experiences. This model is similar to Gestalt theory, which sees perception as based on a number of internal organizing principles. While it is beyond the scope of this chapter to provide a full overview of Gestalt theory, we will touch upon various aspects related to memory and problem solving. For the present, it is worth noting that the cognitive processes we will discuss are in fact closely linked to the process of perceiving.

For further consideration	The analogy of the mind to a computer is a popular one today. In what ways do you see the comparison as reasonable? In what ways do you feel the analogy is *not* appropriate?

Learning and Memory

Learning as Information Gathering

While behaviourists talk about learning as changes in responses, the cognitive approach focuses on the knowledge which guides those responses. In terms of the information processing model, learning may be considered as *information gathering*. Information can be any meaningful data. In everyday life, we gather, and store in memory for later use, everything from the names of new business contacts to the location of the washroom in our favourite restaurant. (There is no requirement that what we store has to be 'significant'.) In the process, we all accumulate vast amounts of seemingly useless information. For instance, what were the first names of the Beatles? What does A-OK stand for? What did you have for dinner last night?

At first glance, the gathering and storage of information may seem less efficient as a learning system than the behaviourist notion of associations between stimuli and responses. But learning through information gathering has one great advantage: flexibility. Tolman's concept of cognitive maps illustrates this clearly. For example, if your route to work is represented by a mental map of the city, not a fixed series of responses, then you can detour to go to the dry cleaner, take an alternative route when traffic is bad and so on. Information which was previously not reflected in behaviour thus becomes significant as the situation is altered. (For example, knowing that a particular street is one-way affects your choice of alternative routes.) Tolman would call this a form of *latent learning*.

learning in cognitive psychology, the process of gathering information and organizing it into mental schemata

For the cognitive psychologist, **learning** represents the process of gathering information, and organizing it into mental schemata. The way we select and use the information is what determines the relationship between the stimulus and the response. Consider again the example of the traffic jam: the stimuli could include your present location, the time of day, the density of traffic and awareness of your goal. Making a detour involves several types of mediators: your knowledge of the street layout (a cognitive map), information from past experiences about where traffic is likely to be lighter (memory) and motivational preferences (e.g. do you prefer a short route through slow-moving traffic or a longer route where the traffic moves more quickly?). As plausible as this description may seem, it also raises several questions. How did you develop a cognitive map of the city originally? How do you recall past experiences about traffic patterns, especially if the information didn't seem important at the time? And how did you decide the best route, given all the information? Let us begin by considering the question of how we remember things.

Memory as the Retention of Learning

memory the retention and use of prior learning

Effective behaviour often depends on remembering information at the right time. **Memory** can be defined as the retention and use of prior learning. Memory is a mediator of behaviour because through memory past experiences influence what we do now. However, there are several ways in which this information about the past can be used.

recall in memory, the active retrieval of information

Usually, we simply remember information as we need it. This is called **recall**, the active retrieval of information. Answering any of the 'trivia' questions in the previous section would involve recall. Sometimes, however, we cannot recall something, but are able to recognize it as correct if it is presented to us. For instance, does A-OK refer to the name of a ranch, teen slang or astronauts' jargon? This process of identifying information as familiar is called **recognition**. Multiple-choice tests of memory are based on testing recognition, not recall. (What sort of examination would test recall?) Both recall and recognition involve a conscious effort to remember the information (sometimes called 'explicit memory'). Yet there are also circumstances where information has been retained, but we are not consciously aware that this is the case. In such situations, we may not be able to recognize something, yet on reviewing it, it quickly seems familiar. For

recognition in memory, the process of identifying presented information as familiar

relearning in memory, an improvement in performance which occurs by reviewing, despite the inability to recall or recognize the information

priming a phenomenon whereby a thought or memory increases the activation of associated thoughts or memories (the term is analogous to 'priming a pump' by using a small quantity of water to enhance the flow of water)

example, a person who hasn't spoken a foreign language for several years adapts more quickly than a first-time learner. This type of improvement by reviewing is called **relearning**, and is sometimes referred to as 'implicit memory'. Another form of implicit memory is **priming**, where prior exposure to information affects later ability to recall something related. Thus, seeing the word 'hot' can make it easier to figure out 'C**D'. (As we will discuss in Chapter 8, priming has been implicated in social behaviour as well as memory.) Hence, there can be some memory of a prior experience, even when we are unable to recall or recognize the information.

Remembering, then, can take many forms. Although it is easy to say memory refers to the storage of information, that definition does not tell us very much. To understand how memory functions, we must look more closely at its characteristics. First, though, try to answer the following questions. What colour was the house you grew up in? Was your first teacher a man or a woman? Can you recall the teacher's name? These questions may sound like further trivia items, but with a difference. Virtually everyone could answer at least the first two questions. Yet for most readers, those events occurred at least fifteen years ago, and possibly much longer. Such recall is not unusual; many people have recalled personal experiences which happened sixty or eighty years earlier. So, we might say that memory is permanent – or at least potentially permanent, since we do seem to forget some things.

Before you ask why we forget, since we can be so good at remembering, let us take another example. Have you ever looked up a phone number, found it busy on dialling, and then had to look it up again to dial a minute later? Or have you ever been introduced to someone, and then not been able to remember their name at the end of the conversation? Often we forget information almost immediately after we encounter it. How can we forget something which happened thirty seconds ago, yet remember an event from many years ago? To understand these variations, we need to consider what we know about how memory functions.

For further consideration

Do you see short-answer tests as more like essay tests or multiple-choice tests? Why? Can you explain this in terms of the various measures of memory?

A Basic Model of Memory

The information processing approach has led to a model of memory which is based on a computer analogy. Since many researchers have contributed to the development of this model, it is frequently discussed in generic terms (see Waugh and Norman 1965; Atkinson and Shiffrin 1968). This model views memory as consisting of a series of distinct stages, each with its own special characteristics (see Figure 4.1). Like most analogies, this model has limitations (see Potter 1990; Logie 1996), but is useful for organizing the basic features of memory.

sensory memory a modality-specific transient form of memory which serves as a buffer between the senses and short-term memory

Information which we gather must be acquired through our senses, and research has demonstrated that there is a distinctive form of **sensory memory** for each sense modality (vision, hearing etc.). Typically, however, this form

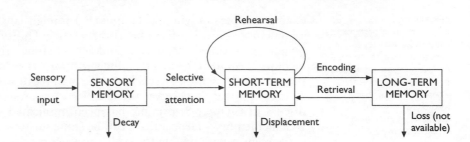

Figure 4.1 A general model of memory We tend to view memory as consisting of a number of stages, which are linked by processes like selective attention; one of the first models of this type was proposed by Atkinson and Shiffrin (1968).

of retention is very transient, and serves primarily as a sort of buffer between the senses and our true memory. Extensive work has been done on the nature of the various forms of sensory memory, especially for vision and hearing (see Sperling 1960; Crowder and Morton 1969); however, for our purposes, it is what happens *after* sensory memory that is most significant.

Since we are continually bombarded by sensory stimuli, we must selectively focus on those elements which are likely to be most significant. This selection occurs through the perceptual process of **attention**, as discussed in Chapter 1. Attention limits our conscious awareness to a small portion of our moment-to-moment environment. Because sensory memory functions at a level *before* the filtering of attention takes place, it is sometimes referred to as being *pre-attentive*. Attention can be redirected, either by deliberate choice or by a particularly compelling stimulus (e.g. a sudden loud noise while you are studying). This capacity to redirect our attention enables us to shift from one sense mode to another, or even to focus on particular stimuli within one sense mode. A good example of this is the so-called *cocktail party effect*, whereby in a crowded room you can shift your attention from talking to a person in front of you to suddenly listening to another conversation taking place behind you – without even shifting your head! Attention thus selects the information which becomes available to memory.

While we talk about memory in everyday life as a single process, the evidence suggests that it is more meaningful to consider it as two separate stages. **Short-term memory**, or STM, refers to retention over relatively brief intervals – usually 15 seconds or so. By contrast, **long-term memory**, or LTM, refers to retention over relatively long periods – hours, days, weeks or longer. The general model assumes that the two types of retention reflect different processes. Since both represent mediating processes that cannot be directly observed, it is worth considering the evidence which is used to support this view.

One type of evidence has already been noted: *duration*. LTM is potentially permanent, while STM is very limited. As noted already, there is a great deal of evidence suggesting people can remember information for decades or more (Bahrick and Hall 1991). By contrast, information held in STM will normally be lost after several seconds, unless it is transferred to LTM (how this might happen will be discussed later) or rehearsed (i.e. repeated over and over). For example, have you ever found yourself rehearsing a

attention the process of selectively focusing on particular stimulus elements, typically those deemed most significant

short-term memory (STM) the component of memory which handles retention over relatively brief intervals of up to approximately 15 seconds
long-term memory (LTM) the component of memory which is involved with retention over relatively long periods (hours, days, weeks or longer)

phone number as you dial? As we will discuss, such repetition is actually a poor way to ensure information is retained in LTM – thus, it is better for looking up phone numbers than as a study strategy for an exam!

There is another important distinction between STM and LTM, that of *capacity*. STM is very limited in the amount of information it can retain. In order to see this, try the following test: In Figure 4.2, you will find a string of letters. Read through them once, then turn the page and immediately try to recall them in correct order. Then, check your accuracy. Only those letters which are correct, and are in the correct sequence, should be counted as correct. If you remembered about seven letters, you are average. Nine or more letters would be very unusual. Now, consider how long you had to retain the letters before writing them down: perhaps four seconds? Yet, on average, people forget about one-third of the letters (assuming ten altogether). Increasing the original number of letters would lower your percentage, for the number seven, not two-thirds, appears to be the best measure of STM capacity, which is often described as being 7 ± 2 meaningful items, or **chunks**. That is, STM appears to be limited to between five and nine independent items, such as random letters, numbers or words (Miller 1956). Phone numbers, because they are broken into parts, are not really seven independent items. Similarly, letters that spell a word are neither independent nor random, and are therefore easier to remember. Attempts to remember longer sequences of items usually result in greater forgetting of the earlier items, owing to the limited capacity of STM.

LTM, on the other hand, appears to be practically unlimited in capacity. At the very least, no documented case of someone 'running out of memory space' has ever occurred. You may have encountered speculations about the capacity of the human brain, and statements such as, 'Einstein only used 40 per cent of his brain capacity.' While provocative, such statements must be taken lightly, since at best they are crude estimates. The problem is that we still know very little about how information is stored in the nervous system, and consequently any estimate of capacity is purely guesswork.

Many people remember very little about their life before the age of four or five. (Do you?) Is this consistent with the idea that memories are potentially permanent?

chunk the basic measure of STM capacity, representing a meaningful unit, such as random letters, numbers or words

For further consideration

Encoding and Storage in Memory

The issue of how much information LTM can hold raises two basic questions: what determines what we remember, and how is it retained? Cognitive psychologists refer to the underlying processes as **encoding** and **storage**. While storage is clearly related to LTM, encoding is more closely related to the workings of STM.

In the general model of memory that we have been looking at, STM has been represented as simply a transient storage system. In fact, it seems to have a much more complex role, in terms of processing new stimulus information, but also interacting with LTM when we need to retrieve information. For this reason, some researchers prefer to call STM 'working memory'

encoding the processing of stimulus information for retention in memory
storage the retention of information in memory

(Baddeley 1992; Logie 1996). Essentially, STM works as both a buffer to hold limited amounts of information, and a processing system to manipulate information in various ways. As already noted, information in STM must be actively rehearsed in order to be retained for very long. When dealing with verbal information, we are often subjectively aware of this rehearsal as a form of talking to ourselves. Research suggests that even when rehearsal is silent, the coding of verbal information in STM is *acoustic* (based on speech sounds): speech muscles in the larynx are active, and errors made are typically related to the sound of the items (Glassman 1972). An analogy to this process is the game of Gossip, in which a message is whispered from person to person in a group. By the end, 'Diane, be quiet' may become 'I am on a diet'! In the same way, errors in STM often involve words which sound alike.

While much of the information that we deal with is verbal, what happens when we encounter information which is visual? Although it is often possible to extract verbal meaning from visual stimuli (e.g. the word 'STOP' rather than the colour and shape of a traffic sign), it has been argued that we can also process information visually (Paivio 1971). One type of evidence is derived from studies which indicate that people handle visual information in memory in much the same way that they process direct visual inputs. For example, in one innovative study, subjects were asked to make comparisons of pairs of three-dimensional shapes (Shepard and Metzler 1971). The time required to compare the shapes correlated with the amount of rotation required to match the orientation of the two shapes; this implied that subjects were using something analogous to a visual image. Without directly proving that the information is represented in memory as an image, the results do suggest that people perform certain memory tasks in ways that are consistent with a visual representation.

As a processing system, STM seems capable of handling verbal and visual information more or less independently (Logie 1996). But what sort of processing takes place, and how does this relate to what is retained in LTM? As noted already, one basic process is simply repeating the information; this type of rote repetition is also sometimes called **maintenance rehearsal** (Craik and Lockhart 1972). By repetition, information re-enters STM, and each entry into STM seems to make it more probable that the information will be stored in LTM. (Note, however, that repetition could also be aloud, could occur over a long time period etc.) Alternatively, an individual may make use of **elaborative rehearsal**, which involves manipulating the stimulus information in some way (Craik and Lockhart 1972). The processing may take many forms, ranging from an emphasis on sensory characteristics (visual appearance, sound) to a focus on the semantic content ('meaning') of information. For example, an emphasis on *sound* might lead to noting what words rhyme with a given word. Emphasizing *meaning* can involve extracting the 'gist' of a speech, without remembering the specific words used.

While maintenance rehearsal is useful for immediate retention, it is less effective for maximizing later recall. The reason for this seems related to one of the basic purposes of encoding, which is to structure the information in a way that will assist later retrieval. To understand this, consider an analogy. Imagine a library having hundreds of thousands of books but no

maintenance rehearsal the retention of material in STM by means of rote repetition

elaborative rehearsal the active processing of items in STM in order to code the information for LTM; material may be processed in various ways, ranging from an emphasis on sensory characteristics (visual appearance, sound) to a focus on the semantic content ('meaning') of information

cataloguing system. How could one find a particular book? Similarly, LTM, with its vast capacity, must process information in some way that makes it possible to locate it later. Overall, the evidence indicates that the more one elaborates the material (such as focusing on meaning), the more effective the encoding will be for later retrieval. Unfortunately, STM seems to have limited processing capacity, and there seems to be a trade-off between processing and immediate retention. That is, the more processing we do, the fewer the chunks of information we can simultaneously retain by maintenance rehearsal. Since processing the meaning of information (called *semantic* encoding) is the most demanding in terms of cognitive resources, individuals will sometimes resort to faster, but more superficial, forms of coding (e.g. sound or appearance), or even simply use maintenance rehearsal. Thus, the effectiveness of encoding is an important element in determining our ability to remember information later, but not all types of encoding are equally useful for developing an effective retrieval system.

The importance of encoding highlights one of the most significant aspects of LTM, which is the fact that information is retained in an *organized* way, not simply as randomly deposited items. In essence, it is more like a cross-referenced card catalogue than a junk box. As we seek to understand the nature of the underlying structure, it is becoming clear that retention in LTM is related to both the type of information and how it is encoded. In fact, it seems that there are several different types of LTM, which independently process and store different forms of information. Canadian psychologist Endel Tulving, one of the pioneers of this view, has argued that there are three distinct forms of long-term memory: procedural, semantic and episodic (Tulving 1985). **Procedural memory** stores 'how-to' information, such as how to play a piano or cook a turkey. **Semantic memory** involves general knowledge of the world, such as knowing the capital of Japan, or the temperature at which ice melts. **Episodic memory** contains personal experiences, organized according to where and when events happened, such as what happened on your last birthday. Tulving believes the three systems function independently, a view which is supported by research on specific types of brain damage (Wheeler *et al.* 1997). For example, it is possible for a patient with brain damage to learn how to solve a puzzle (procedural), yet not be able to recall having seen it before (episodic). In the same way, a patient may learn a specific fact (semantic), and not know when they learned it (episodic). Tulving believes that episodic memory (which is closely involved with our sense of self-identity) is the most recent form of memory in terms of evolutionary development, and consequently is the most vulnerable to traumatic damage. By contrast, procedural memory is likely to be the oldest form of memory, and the most resistant to damage. Although not proven, Tulving's view is consistent with data indicating that different brain regions are involved in the recall of episodic and procedural memories (Wheeler *et al.* 1997).

While there is growing evidence for difference storage systems in LTM, understanding exactly *what* is stored is a challenging question. Although recall can be readily measured, coding and storage are not directly observable, and must be inferred. In fact, the nature of storage is one issue where the computer analogy may be misleading. In a computer, LTM would be

procedural memory that component of LTM which stores 'how-to' information, such as how to play a piano or cook a turkey

semantic memory the component of LTM which involves general knowledge of the world

episodic memory the portion of LTM which contains personal experiences, organized according to where and when events happened, such as what happened on your last birthday

analogous to a storage device like a hard disk. Information is stored as a series of bytes in specific locations on the disk, and a directory list indicates which locations contain a particular piece of information (e.g. a file). In essence, this system is like a huge series of postal boxes or cubicles, with one item in each container. By contrast, LTM seems to be distributed rather than localized, with information represented by patterns of connections. In this sense, a better analogy might be patterns created on a computer monitor: the same pixels (neurons) can be used to represent an infinite number of images. Even this analogy may prove misleading, since we still know little about the physical basis of memory storage. Nonetheless, cognitive research has identified at least two functional mechanisms for how the necessary patterns of connections might be formed.

The traditional view of connections in LTM is based on *associationism*. Just as learning can be seen as a process of forming ties between a stimulus and a response, so memory is seen as forming ties between new experiences and prior knowledge. These ties, called associations, are typically a result of repetition. For example, maintenance rehearsal allows information to re-enter STM, and each entry makes it more probable that the information will enter LTM. In this situation, it is impossible to predict what type of association, if any, will be formed to mediate between a stimulus and prior knowledge. In other cases, an association may be created based on stimulus aspects that have meaning. For instance, to remember the name of someone you meet, you may associate the name with some aspect of their appearance (e.g. *B*ob has a *b*eard, *S*usan is *s*hort).

Sigmund Freud recognized the significance of associations as a tool in psychoanalysis: by using **free association** (that is, asking the person to say whatever words floated into their mind) he looked for patterns that might reveal their inner conflicts. Consider an example: a teaching colleague separated from his wife, named Barbara. Shortly after, he met a former student on the street. He remembered having taught the girl, what course she had taken, and even her final grade, but not her name. When he asked her, it was, of course, Barbara! The association of names evoked an unpleasant event for my colleague, leading to a memory failure. Freud referred to forgetting due to inner conflicts as **repression**. (The validity of repression as a memory phenomenon has been a subject of prolonged controversy. See the discussion of repressed memories in Chapter 5.)

One need not turn to psychoanalysis to recognize that associations can seem obscure, yet still be based on an organizing structure. For example, conversations at a party may wander over many topics, yet if you trace back carefully, you can always find the links between topics. The reality is that the mind (including memory) does not seem to function as a random structure.

An alternative to the associationist view exists, and it may be both closer to reality and easier to apply in improving memory performance. According to the concept of **cue-dependent coding**, all information is stored in memory as a set of relationships which are called the *context*. Remembering is dependent on restoring the cues which formed the original context (Tulving 1974). When meeting people on the street who seem familiar, you may try to recall *where* you met them, or *who* you were with, or *when* it was, since these are all potential parts of the context of the original encounter.

free association a technique originated by Freud for studying the mind, based on asking a person to say simply whatever words floated into their mind, and then looking for patterns
repression in Freud's theory, a defence mechanism in which impulses, memories or ideas are forcibly blocked from the conscious mind

cue-dependent coding the concept that all information is stored in memory as a set of relationships called the context; remembering is seen as dependent on restoring the cues which formed the original context

Similarly, hearing an old song may bring back a flood of memories related to the situation in which you first heard the song. In this case, the song provides the cues for remembering the events. Even internal body states may provide context cues: an athlete, recalling a performance, may make movements of the same muscles originally used.

While there is evidence for cue-based encoding in both episodic and semantic memory, not surprisingly the types of cues may differ in the two cases. Semantic memory, being based on the meaning of information, tends to be structured in logical and conceptual ways (e.g. 'apples' would be related to 'fruits'; a geometry theorem may be related to other maths information). By contrast, episodic memory is situational in nature, and hence coding reflects the context of when, where and what happened. Just as one can ask why particular associations are formed, one can ask what determines the contextual coding of a specific memory. Unfortunately, there is no absolute answer to this question, since it is possible that different individuals develop different organizational structures over time.

In some ways, the concepts of cue-dependent coding and associationism are complementary. Associations seem useful for explaining the benefits of rote repetition (maintenance rehearsal), while coding for context can be related to the value of elaborative rehearsal. However, as with any competing theories, there are also important areas of difference. One area where differences emerge is in how the two views deal with forgetting.

For further consideration

If short-term memory provides the processing necessary for later retrieval of information, what effect would it have on a person if this aspect of STM were seriously damaged?

Forgetting

The failure to remember, or *forgetting*, is perhaps the most salient aspect of memory for most people. When we succeed at remembering something, we tend to take the act for granted. When we *cannot* remember, we get irritated and frustrated, and are eager to find ways to remedy the situation. While no panaceas exist, understanding *why* forgetting occurs is important to knowing what one can do to make such failures less likely to occur.

As noted previously, the first stage of memory is sensory memory. Since the sensory stores serve primarily to provide an input channel, it should not be surprising to learn that the information held in sensory storage is very transient. Unless selected by attention for transfer to short-term memory, the contents of sensory memory are quickly lost. The spontaneous loss of information from sensory memory is described as **decay**, to note its time-related character. Other than selecting information by means of attention, there is very little one can do to influence sensory memory.

decay in memory, the spontaneous loss of information with the passage of time

Forgetting in STM

STM is a more complex system than sensory memory, because it is used both to process incoming information and to retrieve material from LTM.

> **A test of short-term memory**
>
> To test your STM capacity, read through the list of letters below. Read the list slowly, but only once. Immediately after reading the last letter, try to write down the entire sequence in the correct order.
>
> L R X D V C M Q B N
>
> For scoring, give yourself credit only for letters in the correct order, not counting reversals, omissions, or other errors. Typical recall would be about seven correct.

Figure 4.2 A test of short-term memory To test your short-term memory, follow the instructions in the box.

displacement in memory, forgetting in STM due to new incoming information pushing out the previous contents

At first glance, STM seems ill-designed for such a weighty role, because it has limited duration and limited capacity. Since information passing through STM leaves no permanent impression, one might think that its limited duration is directly responsible for forgetting. Instead, forgetting in STM seems to be related to its limited capacity: new incoming information tends to push out the previous contents. This **displacement** of information is the basic cause of forgetting in STM.

Since the capacity of STM is fixed, one cannot really reduce displacement. On the other hand, awareness of displacement *does* imply that, for remembering important material, one should avoid distractions. How often have you been talking about something, been interrupted and then been unable to recall the point where you left off? In this situation, an interruption leads to displacement of the previous words spoken. Similarly, forgetting a phone number you've just looked up involves forgetting by displacement.

While the basic capacity of STM does not seem alterable, we can improve the *use* of STM by better coding of information. As noted earlier, the capacity of STM is about 7 ± 2 *chunks*. A chunk may be a letter in a random series (as in Figure 4.2), a word (as in an item on a grocery list) or a whole concept (as in the key points of a speech). In general, a chunk represents the minimum meaningful unit. This means that one can increase the *effective* capacity of STM by recoding information into larger chunks whenever possible. Consider a grocery list. By grouping items into *categories* (e.g. fruits, meats, canned goods), you can focus on remembering the categories. Then, each time you think of a category, the individual items will be easier to recall. The effect of categories on improving learning and recall has been well-established in research (e.g. Bower 1970). Another approach is to convert meaningless items into meaningful chunks (i.e. *recoding* the information). Telephone numbers are one example: at one time, everyone learned the initial numbers as the name of an exchange (for example, Cherry stood for CH, or 24). Today, the telephone company officially avoids these names, but using letter equivalents can still be helpful. For example, a Canadian bank advertises its telephone number as 980-CIBC (the letters of the bank's name). You may be able to make similar codes for numbers that you need to remember.

As with many activities, practice makes such recoding easier to accomplish. In one well-known study, a student given long sequences of random numbers learned, over several months, to recode them as chunks, and then as chunks-made-up-of-chunks. Over time, he was able to increase his performance to the point where he could recall sequences of *eighty digits* correctly after one presentation (Ericsson and Chase 1982). This feat was a function of developing efficient codes, not somehow stretching capacity by extensive use – in fact, when tested with random *letter* strings at the end of the experiment, his performance was only average. As we will discuss later, such recoding techniques are one example of memory aids called *mnemonic devices*.

The use of recoding to enhance chunking compensates for the limited capacity of STM. However, it would be wrong to believe that chunking occurs independently of LTM. Clearly, the use of any coding method involves drawing on past experience which is stored in LTM. In fact, it can be argued that the *real* function of chunking or other coding is to increase transfer into LTM – that is, recoding represents a form of elaborative rehearsal. To understand this, let us consider forgetting in LTM.

Forgetting in LTM

The first point to note is that not everything blamed on 'forgetting' really is a failure to remember. In order to be remembered, information must first *reach* LTM. Simply being exposed to something does not guarantee that we will retain it, since there is filtering by attention prior to STM. Further, not everything which reaches STM is transferred to LTM, as we have seen. In both these circumstances, one cannot really speak of 'forgetting' that which never entered LTM! Having said that, it is still clear that there are circumstances which reflect genuine forgetting. Since capacity in LTM appears to be unlimited in any practical sense, clearly forgetting cannot be based on displacement. And despite the limitations on what reaches LTM, information which *does* enter LTM may potentially be available for the rest of our lives. Given this picture of a permanent system, unlimited in capacity, it may seem puzzling that we ever fail to remember.

The traditional explanation offered by associationism is **interference**, or competition between various items of information. The concept of interference implies that as our store of information grows, it becomes harder and harder to identify uniquely a piece of information (much like trying to locate a particular book in a large library). In terms of associationism, the associations for a particular item may overlap those for similar items. ('Was it *last* summer that I met Harry in Boston, or when I was there two years ago?') As time goes on, we experience a running together of past experience, and a consequent loss of details, due to interference. If there are too many competing associations, you may end up unable to remember the desired information.

Interference takes two basic forms, which differ in terms of the time relationship between competing responses. The first form is **retroactive** ('acting backwards') **interference**, which involves the effect of recent experiences making it more difficult to recall something learned earlier (see Figure 4.3). One classic experiment concerned testing recall for two groups of people; one group went to sleep after the original learning session, and the other

interference according to associationism, competition between items which can hamper learning and produce forgetting

retroactive interference in memory, a form of interference in recent experiences makes it difficult to recall something learned earlier

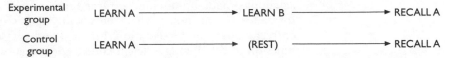

Testing for retroactive interference

Experimental group	LEARN A	⟶	LEARN B	⟶ RECALL A
Control group	LEARN A	⟶	(REST)	⟶ RECALL A

When looking at retroactive interference, one is concerned with whether recent experiences can interfere with the recall of material learned earlier. In the above situation, if the experimental group does worse than the control group, that would be evidence of retroactive interference.

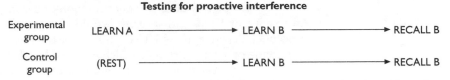

Testing for proactive interference

Experimental group	LEARN A	⟶	LEARN B	⟶ RECALL B
Control group	(REST)	⟶	LEARN B	⟶ RECALL B

In proactive interference, one is concerned with whether earlier experiences interfere with recall for more recently learned material. If the experimental group recalls less than the control group in the above situation, we would call it proactive interference. Note that what is being recalled differs from the retroactive interference test.

Figure 4.3   Retroactive and proactive interference Associationism argues that forgetting in long-term memory is based on competing associations, particularly in terms of when information was learned. Retroactive and proactive interference represent the two basic forms of interference.

went about their daily activities (Jenkins and Dallenbach 1924). When both groups were tested after the same interval of time had passed, the sleep group showed better recall. Why? Because daily experiences created more interference than did sleeping! Students often experience retroactive interference when they find that, for example, this semester's physics has interfered with remembering last semester's biology. Similarly, retroactive interference can occur at work when a person changes job responsibilities. The programmer who becomes a supervisor may get rusty at programming skills. In each case, recent experiences and the associations they create can interfere with recall of earlier experiences, particularly if there is some overlap of associations.

The other form of interference, called **proactive** ('acting forwards') **interference**, concerns how prior experiences make learning and recall of subsequent experiences more difficult (see Figure 4.3). At first glance, this may seem rather odd – how can old memories disrupt something more recent? The reason, according to interference theory, is that interactions among associations are not directional with respect to time. Consequently, it is just as possible for old information to interfere with new information as vice versa. Interestingly, researchers were slow to recognize the possibility of proactive interference, despite existing evidence of the phenomenon. For example, William James, after spending time learning large amounts of material, found that learning was *slower* than it had been initially – a clear sign of proactive interference from the previous material learned. In everyday life, proactive interference is most likely to arise when two situations

proactive interference in memory, a form of interference in which prior experiences make learning and recall of subsequent experiences difficult

show some similarities. For instance, in driving, cars travel either on the right or the left side of the road, depending on the country. The side makes no difference when one is first learning to drive, as the task is completely new. But an experienced driver will have some difficulty in changing if visiting a country where it is opposite – the prior learning interferes with behaviour in the new situation. Part of the reason why people are slow to change their attitudes, or learn new technology, as they get older may be due to proactive interference from what they already know. Thus, it may be that proactive interference is more significant in the long run than is retro-active interference.

Tulving has suggested that interference may be more significant for episodic memory than for semantic memory (Tulving 1986). Since episodic memory tracks the 'where and when' of our lives, it would be vulnerable to interference, given the continual flow of new experiences. As a trivial example, try to recall what you had for lunch three weeks ago today – remembering is difficult due to the interference from other lunches, both more recent and more distant. By contrast, semantic memory, based on meaning, forms associations based on existing logical concepts, rather than physical context. Consequently, it should be less sensitive to variations in external context. At present, the available research seems to support this interpretation.

The precise nature of interference is not fully understood. As already noted, the common view is that similar associations produce competition among responses. An alternate view holds that the build-up of interference can lead to the actual destruction of memories; this notion is referred to as **unlearning**. Basically, unlearning implies that amid the tangles of associations, some ties are broken. While various attempts have been made to test this idea, the evidence favouring it is rather limited. Unfortunately, there is no way to know for certain that something forgotten is truly gone forever. In fact, it may make more sense to assume the opposite – that memories are permanently stored (assuming no physical damage to the brain). Consider the following situation. Suppose someone tries to recall something, and, despite every conceivable attempt, cannot remember it. Then, a short time after they have given up, the desired information mysteriously floats into consciousness. This effect is familiar to most people, but how can interference theory account for it? Clearly, the information was not permanently lost, so it is not a case of unlearning. While one could conceive of changes in associations, such a spontaneous change in a short period of time would seem little short of miraculous. Hence, spontaneous recall after forgetting poses a serious challenge to interference theory.

As noted previously, the alternative to associationism is *cue-dependent coding*. According to this view, remembering depends on restoring the appropriate context, in terms of the cues present at the time of learning. If you do not remember something at a particular moment, it does not mean that the information is destroyed (referred to as a lack of **availability**). Rather, the information may not be retrievable, given the cues used to search for the information (that is, it is not **accessible**). Since LTM appears to be largely permanent, most forgetting should be due to problems of accessibility, not availability. Forgetting due to a failure to retrieve the desired information is called **context-dependent forgetting**.

unlearning an alternative interpretation of the interference theory of memory which holds that the build-up of interference can lead to the breaking of associations, and therefore the destruction of memories

availability in memory, the principle that remembering is determined by whether the information exists in LTM or not; forgetting implies that the information is destroyed

accessibility in LTM, the principle that remembering and forgetting are dependent on effective retrieval; without the proper cues, information which exists in LTM may not be accessible

context-dependent forgetting failure to retrieve information from LTM due to the absence of appropriate contextual cues

The concept of context-dependent forgetting suggests that generally we fail to remember because the cues we use to aid retrieval are inappropriate. For example, a friend once told me of having met a Nobel laureate in physics at a party the previous night. When I asked the physicist's name, my friend could not recall, except to say the last name began with the letter P. He strove to remember, but it was not until a few days later that he told me the name: Dirac. 'Dirac?' I asked. 'But you told me it began with P!' 'Yes, I know,' he replied. 'But you see, his name is Paul Dirac, and on his name badge it said "P. Dirac". All I could think of was seeing that letter P, until the name popped into my head this morning!' By emphasizing the wrong cue – seeking a last name beginning with P, in this case – it is possible to block retrieval of the desired information. Similarly, in trying to remember someone's name, if you place a previous encounter in the wrong context (e.g. at work, rather than at a party), you may block retrieval of the name. By relaxing, it may be possible to drop the inappropriate context, and allow the proper cues to be generated.

Even when we don't regard the physical context (i.e. the location) as relevant to what we are learning, it can become encoded as a part of the memory cues. For example, a variety of studies have shown that recall is best if people are tested in the same room where learning takes place. In one unusual variation of this technique, scuba divers were tested either above or under water; as expected, changing environments between learning and testing impaired memory (Godden and Baddeley 1975). Context-dependent forgetting may apply more strongly to episodic than semantic memory, as with interference effects. Nonetheless, one implication is that it might be beneficial to study where one will be taking an exam!

Normally, we think of 'context' as being our physical surroundings. But part of the context is actually internal – the thoughts, feelings and state of mind that are part of our moment-to-moment experience. The changes in context associated with physical and mental states are often referred to as *state-dependent coding*, to distinguish these cues from those related to the external environment. Forgetting related to these internal cues is therefore referred to as **state-dependent forgetting**. Many students have experienced the frustration of studying hard, then 'blanking' while writing a test – only to have the information come flooding back shortly after leaving the test. This effect can be explained in terms of state-dependent forgetting. If a student is relaxed while studying, but anxious during a test, the change in mental state makes recall difficult. After the test, anxiety is reduced – and the answers become accessible once more.

Clearly, performance while highly anxious can lead to a false impression of what is known. To reduce this state-dependent forgetting, one must make the study and test circumstances more alike – either by learning to relax during tests, or possibly becoming anxious while studying! Since anxiety can hamper performance in other ways, obviously the former is the preferred solution. Another example of state-dependent forgetting occurs with drugs. A drinker may not be able to remember something read while sober; a user of cocaine may later be unable to remember what happened while 'high', and so on. Such effects have been found in many studies with animals, and they appear to occur in varying degrees in people, depending on the dosage and other factors.

state-dependent forgetting forgetting related to changes in context associated with internal cues of physical and mental state, as opposed to the context defined by the external environment

The effects of variations in context should not be underestimated. Successive changes in context can make it difficult to reinstate a particular context. This may be one reason why information which is not used for a long period can be difficult to recall (e.g. foreign language skills). Often in this situation, attempts at *relearning* (such as refresher courses) will quickly restore the context, and hence increase accessibility of the information. Thus, providing refresher courses is highly desirable for seldom-used job skills. One example of this is the requirement in Canada for annual training in cardiac resuscitation (CPR) by all medical staff.

Context-dependent forgetting also helps to explain the typical differences found between memory performance involving recall versus recognition. Characteristically, people find it easier to recognize something as familiar than to spontaneously remember something – that is, recognition is usually easier than free recall. This can be explained in terms of more cues being provided in the recognition situation (in fact, the information itself is given, so it only needs to be compared to what is already in memory). With unstructured recall, there is little contextual support to aid access. (This perhaps explains why most students prefer multiple-choice tests to essay exams.)

At the same time, the superiority of recognition depends on the context. Most people have had the experience of spotting someone familiar down the street, only to discover as they approach nearer that it is actually a stranger. This is an example of **false recognition**, whereby the presence of familiar cues (e.g. hair style, colour of jacket) leads one to believe the stimulus matches an item in memory. This effect is more than anecdotal, having been demonstrated in a number of experimental studies. What is more interesting is that studies have also shown that individuals can fail to recognize something they have just recalled – that is, sometimes recall is *better* than recognition! In the classic study, students learned a list of words until they could recall the list perfectly (Tulving and Thompson 1971). Then, the students were given a longer list, which included some of the previously recalled words. By changing the context of surrounding items, the experimenters fooled subjects into ignoring words they had just recognized. For example, steel, iron and copper appeared in the original list; on the recognition task, the items broom, stove and iron appeared. Given the different context, subjects failed to recognize 'iron' as one of the words they had learned. Thus, context-dependent forgetting seems to account for a wide variety of memory phenomena.

false recognition a form of memory error whereby the presence of familiar cues leads one to believe the stimulus matches a previously experienced stimulus

For further consideration

Have you ever chosen an answer on a multiple-choice test, been confident you were correct and then afterwards discovered you were wrong? Can you explain this in terms of context-dependent coding? Has the same thing ever happened on an essay test? What can you say about this?

Memory as Reconstruction

Forgetting can certainly be frustrating, especially when we sense that the information is available, but we cannot retrieve it. Ironically, the emphasis

reconstruction in memory, the process of remembering by actively creating a whole out of partial information

on forgetting as a failure of retrieval tends to create the impression that memory storage is static and unchanging. Yet this interpretation, with its implication that retrieval is a neutral process of locating the correct item, may not be correct. Although there is little evidence to support unlearning, as previously discussed, it can be argued that remembering is not simply passive retrieval. Instead, it may involve **reconstruction** – that is, creating a whole out of partial information.

The view that remembering is somehow creative was supported by Gestalt theorists, who saw perception and memory as closely linked (see 'Perception and cognition', above). Context not only provides cues for retrieval, but allows us to create information to fill gaps in our recall. For example, if you hear a funny joke, and then later retell it, it is unlikely that you will use exactly the same words as the person who told you the joke originally. Instead, you will remember the outline of the story, including crucial elements like the punchline, and then *fill in* the rest, using both your knowledge of the joke *and* your general knowledge of language and the world to make the joke work. Since semantic memory stores meanings, not the original words, it is inevitable that one will reconstruct, not retrieve, most of the details of the joke. (Those who 'don't remember jokes' probably ignore crucial elements, such as noting whether the punchline depends on a particular play on words.)

The idea that *all* recall involves reconstruction as well as retrieval was supported by a classic study by British psychologist Frederick Bartlett. Bartlett read a story based on a Native American legend to his subjects, and then later asked them to retell it from memory (Bartlett 1932). The study found several interesting results. While the subjects tried to be faithful to the story, minor details tended to be forgotten. In addition, points which were central to the storyline were sometimes exaggerated. Most interestingly, Bartlett found that his subjects (British university students) tended to *change* details which, although consistent with Native American beliefs (e.g. the role of spirits), were not consistent with the students' own beliefs. Typically, the subjects were unaware of making such changes – they were simply trying to reconstruct the story in a way that made sense to them.

Eyewitness Testimony

The idea that memories are reconstructed rather than simply retrieved has aroused concern in the legal system. After all, if memory can be creative, what does this say about the accuracy of eyewitness testimony? Our culture, especially our legal system, tends to place great value on personal testimony when trying to analyse events. 'Seeing is believing' says the old proverb, even though we know perception is not always accurate (see Chapter 1). In much the same way, we tend to assume that testimony about past events will somehow be free from distortion or error. Unfortunately, our understanding of memory, particularly the role of reconstruction, suggests that errors are quite possible.

One of the pioneers in exploring this issue is American researcher Elizabeth Loftus, who has done a number of experiments involving the basic elements of courtroom testimony (Loftus and Hoffman 1989). In one case, individuals first watched a tape of a car accident. Later, they were questioned about what had happened, in much the way that courtroom witnesses are. During this interrogation, the questioner sometimes asked how fast the cars were going when they *hit*, or else how fast they were going when they *smashed into* each other. When 'smashed into' was used in the question, estimates of speed tended to be higher. What's more, when later asked about broken glass at the scene (there was none in the tape), individuals who heard the 'smashed into' phrasing were more likely to report having seen broken glass! Loftus argues that studies like this call into question the reliability of eyewitness testimony, since the wording of questions can influence witnesses' interpretations (e.g. speed estimates) and even their subsequent recall (e.g. seeing broken glass when there was none). (In other experiments, individuals have been influenced to 'recall' stop signs that were not present, and similar details.)

Loftus believes that the person's memory of the events is actually altered by these manipulations. Other researchers have questioned this interpretation, arguing that misleading subjects simply leads them to question their original memories (McCloskey and Zaragoza 1985). In effect, it would be like Loftus's subjects thinking, 'Well, if she's mentioning broken glass, I guess there *was* broken glass . . .' At present, whether the original memories are altered or not, it is clear that there is a potential for witnesses to make errors in reporting the original events.

Similar problems arise with eyewitness identifications of suspects. In a typical police line-up, witnesses might readily assume that the criminal is one of the individuals in the line-up; in effect, choosing becomes equivalent to guessing at a multiple-choice test. However, like multiple-choice tests, the accuracy of the choice depends on how similar the alternatives are; in addition, accuracy of eyewitness identification can be affected by the instructions given, the behaviour of the officer conducting the line-up and other influences. Such factors can lead witnesses to feel confident of their choice even if the person identified is not the true criminal. Such mistaken identifications have been documented in the real world throughout the past century, and have been identified as the primary reason for false convictions of innocent people (US National Institute of Justice 1996). In one case, a priest was falsely charged with bank robbery (Loftus and Ketcham 1991)! In addition, research indicates that when witnesses are given supportive feedback after making an identification (as often happens in the real world), it can further distort memory. Witnesses given favourable feedback are more likely to report having felt very confident when making their original judgement, and also to recall details that were not part of the original event (Wells and Bradfield 1998). Thus, whether in a courtroom or not, what witnesses recall may be influenced by the context and by what others say.

While certainly raising concerns about how witnesses are questioned, the research does not answer the basic question of how memories are changed by misleading questions. That is, is the original memory of the event altered, or only the response at the time of recall? Given that recall is nearly always a combination of retrieval and reconstruction, there may be no possible experiment that can tell us conclusively whether what is retrieved can be modified. Yet, while research may not end the debates about eyewitness testimony, it is probable that increased understanding of how memory functions may allow the police and the courts to perform their functions more effectively.

<table>
<tr><td>For further consideration</td><td>What is the earliest memory you can recall? How can you be sure this is a real memory, as opposed to a construction from stories your parents have told? If you find it hard to determine, what does this imply about the view of memory as reconstruction?</td></tr>
</table>

Improving Memory

Clearly, the greatest memory concern for most people is forgetting. Despite advances in our understanding, it may be small consolation to know that something is temporarily inaccessible rather than gone forever. There is no magic potion for improving memory, but there *are* techniques which can make memory more effective. The study and use of such memory aids is called **mnemonics** (from the Greek word for 'memory'). The origin of mnemonics is credited to a Greek poet named Simonides. By a strange sequence of events, Simonides was the only survivor when the roof of a banquet hall collapsed. The bodies were so mangled that mourning relatives could not identify them for burial. However, by remembering the seating arrangement, Simonides was able to identify each body. Impressed with his own feat, he began a systematic study of techniques for aiding memory (Yates 1966). Today, a number of mnemonic devices, or memory aids, are known.

mnemonics the study and use of techniques for improving memory

One of the most basic ways to improve memory is by *concentration*. Too often, memory failure is blamed for what is really a lack of attention. For example, many people report difficulty in learning names. When introduced to someone, they are not focusing on the name, but instead worrying about the impression they're making, what to talk about or some other concern. The result is that the name, never having been processed, is not available (not in memory) later on. By focusing on the name during the introduction, you facilitate storage, and consequently later recall. One memory expert used to advise, 'Look at the person, listen to the name, repeat it in your mind, and then say the name when you shake hands.' Concentration can be helpful for many learning situations – too often, students 'study' by casually glancing at the page, rather than reading carefully and thinking about the material.

Organization is another important element in improving memory. Taking the time to organize material which you wish to remember can improve retrieval by providing a natural context and a set of retrieval cues. For example, outlining the contents of a chapter in a textbook can help to show how various concepts are related to each other. Creating a time line for events in a history course can provide both visual and verbal structures for remembering. Even if material has no natural structure, it is possible to create one artificially by recoding the information in some way (see below).

One unusual technique which can be used even with non-organized material is called the *method of loci* (*loci* is Latin for 'places'). This was the technique used by Simonides, and later recommended by Cicero, a Roman

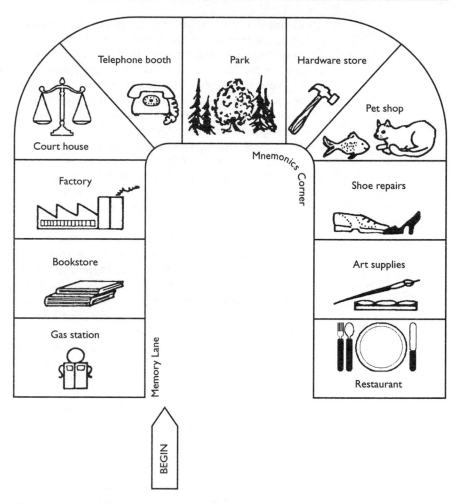

Figure 4.4 A walk down memory lane If you want to see how mnemonic techniques like the method of loci work, use the above 'map' with the following list of words. Taking about five seconds for each word, move around the map and try to form a mental link to each location in sequence; when you get to the end of the map, go back and start over – hence, you will end up with two words for each location. Then, use the map to trigger your recall of the words. On average, most people get about 17 words correct.

Word list: voice, dollar, lake, soldier, library, plant, train, symphony, cup, game, desert, hat, turtle, sofa, moon, wasp, frame, home, eat, navy, pillow, legal.

noted as an excellent speaker. Orators like Cicero would mentally 'place' key points of a planned speech in various locations around the assembly hall. By looking around the room in sequence, they would recall the desired points of their speech. Although it may seem a strange notion, the method of loci is quite effective, even with minimal practice. (To try your own hand at this, look at the exercise in Figure 4.4.) A variant of the method of loci can also be used to remember tasks you wish to do in the future, such as calling a friend when you get home. By vividly associating the task with some routine action, such as taking off your coat, you are reminded of the task when you reach home. In this example, the visualized action provides the cue for recalling the task. By appropriate choice of key action, you can jog your memory at almost any point in the day's routine. Such techniques work by creating vivid and distinctive associations between new information (the task) and prior knowledge (about daily routine); by doing so, the technique minimizes interference. At the same time, the cues used in these techniques also make effective use of context.

Mnemonic techniques like the method of loci can be helpful by providing pre-arranged cues for recall. But for non-meaningful material, such as long lists of dates or terms, *recoding* into a more meaningful form may be more effective. As mentioned earlier, there are various ways to encode information, but the general goal is to make meaningful chunks. For example, generations of medical students have spent many hours memorizing the body's parts. The sequence of cranial nerves was made easier to remember by the nameless wit who recoded them into 'On old Olympus' tallest top, a Finn and German vault and hop.' The purpose of the low poetry lies in the first letter of each word, which is also the first letter for a nerve, in proper sequence. This type of recoding, which creates a sentence or similar verbal structure as a cue, is called the *narrative technique*.

Another form of recoding creates a cue by making a word out of the first letters of a set of words. For example, 'Roy G. Biv' is a name cue for remembering the colours of the rainbow (red, orange, yellow etc.). Such made-up words are called *acronyms*. The US army (which seems to love such creations), has added *snafu* (situation normal: all fouled up) to our language, as well as *jeep* (general purpose vehicle) and many other terms. (Note that the phonetic spelling *jeep* was later trademarked by an enterprising ex-GI – that is, general infantry.)

The most general form of recoding is *elaboration*. This involves any form of recoding which adds to the information in some way that makes it meaningful and/or distinctive. One example is the use of *rhymes*. 'Thirty days hath September' is the beginning of a rhyme to remember the number of days in each month. 'I before E except after C, or when sounded as "ay", as in neighbour and weigh' is a rhyme which provides assistance with spelling rules. Sometimes *unique recodings* can be particularly useful. At one time, my postal code was M6C 1X1; I eventually remembered this by noting that 6C sounds like 'sexy', and that one times (X) one equals one, and then recoding it as 'my sexy one'!

Whatever the form, mnemonic techniques function by creating meaningful connections for information which has no natural structure. This has several advantages: stronger associations, forming larger chunks and creating a distinctive context for retrieval. While it might seem that these techniques, especially elaboration, increase memory demands, remember that the problem in LTM is not storage capacity, but retrieval. Although mnemonic techniques add to the information to be retained, they also make access for retrieval easier. The only limits to the use of such methods seem to lie in one's willingness to use them, and possibly in one's creative abilities. (See Figure 4.5 for a summary.)

Maximizing use of memory

Most of us experience memory failures at one time or another. Indeed, sometimes it seems the likelihood of forgetting increases with the importance of remembering! What can one do? The following represents a brief guide to some techniques for improving memory. For more detailed information, refer to the accompanying text.

Names Concentrate when introduced; don't let your mind wander as the name is being given. Repeat it silently. If there are couples, mentally link their names. Note the face – often you can make an association between the name and some physical feature (e.g. 'Tom is tall').

Phone numbers The trick is to make the number meaningful, or at least familiar. Is there a sequence (e.g. 1357) or other cue (e.g. 1293 is 'Dec. '93')? Failing that, repeat the number several times, each time saying the person's name.

Aids to learning
1 Distribute learning time – cramming is not effective (*unless* you only want to recall the material for an hour or two after study).
2 Make the connection – look for links between the current information and what you already know. This may involve finding *similarities* ('How is managing staff like dealing with customers?') or forming *unique associations* ('This is Tom Gordon, whose wife's name is the same as my sister's.').

Aids to remembering
1 Use context cues – they can help by organizing information while learning (making connections) and for remembering (e.g. using method of loci when giving a speech).
2 Use mnemonic devices: rhymes, acronyms, stories and other techniques can help to structure material, which aids initial learning and also minimizes the chance of omitting items during recall.
3 Relax: anxiety tends to create state-dependent forgetting ('blanking'), and increases the chances of fixating on the wrong context. If you start with the wrong context, the more you try, the less likely you are to remember. Overall, relaxation is surprisingly important for effective recall.

While none of these tips represents a cure-all, our memory works best when we act in ways which recognize its basic characteristics.

Figure 4.5 Maximizing use of memory

While practising mnemonic techniques can lead to more efficient coding, there is little one can do to make memory infallible. Unfortunately, the very factors that make memory efficient (e.g. using context to stimulate retrieval) also create the conditions for errors (e.g. false recognition). Hence, we must all muddle along, forgetting at least *some* of what we would like to remember. Lest you find this disappointing, it might be worth considering the consequences of *never* forgetting: all of life's traumas would remain vividly intact, as would every bit of trivial information, such as grocery lists from ten years earlier. Overall, our memory system seems to strike a reasonable balance of benefits and limitations. In any case, in life the crucial factor is usually not how much information one has, but what one does with it.

For further consideration

Do you currently make use of any mnemonics to help you remember things? If you were trying to learn a list of terms for a science course, what technique would you use? What about if you wanted to remember a telephone number?

Problem Solving

In many situations, the value of retaining information lies simply in being able to recall it when needed – for example, phone numbers are a tool for communication. In other situations, information stored in our memory is used instead to help make sense of the situation, and to overcome obstacles. For example, a person planning a trip from New York to Toronto will be aided by knowing the distance, highway routes, plane schedules, relative cost by car and plane and so on. Each piece of information is of little value in itself, but is simply an input to the process of choosing the best travel arrangements.

When we are faced with a complex situation like this, the information in memory mediates decisions about what response is most appropriate for the situation. In this sense, memory is the basis of the cognitive maps Tolman described. As Tolman argued, cognitive maps allow the organism to choose different responses at different times. In fact, those situations that we call *problems* nearly always require a response we haven't tried before. Thus, how well we cope with a problem can depend on how much information our cognitive map of the situation contains.

problem solving the process of determining appropriate actions in order to overcome obstacles that interfere with reaching a desired goal

Generally speaking, **problem solving** refers to a process for overcoming obstacles that interfere with reaching a desired goal. That is, a problem is a situation in which we face some sort of obstacle. The challenge becomes finding a way to remove the obstacle. Apart from the information about the situation which we have stored in memory, our effectiveness in problem solving often depends on how we approach the situation. Problem solving is a type of skill, and like all skills, it can benefit from training and practice. Unfortunately, the teaching of such skills has been sadly neglected in our society, even though cognitive psychologists have been studying problem solving since the time of Kohler and Tolman.

Defining Problems

Over time, a great deal has been learned about the process of problem solving, and what factors contribute to effective performance. One key finding is that good problem solvers tend to approach the situation systematically, rather than haphazardly. To understand this, it is helpful to consider the general process that people go through in solving a problem.

Stages of Problem Solving

While various researchers have developed slightly different models to describe problem solving, they all generally include three basic stages:

1 Defining the problem.

2 Developing possible solutions.

3 Selecting and evaluating the best solution.

incubation in the Gestalt model of problem solving, a process of ceasing to work actively on a problem, in order to modify one's mental set

(Gestalt theorists have also talked about a sub-stage of stage 2, called **incubation,** where one temporarily abandons conscious efforts to solve the problem.)

Defining the problem has several aspects. First, one must recognize that a problem exists in order to solve it. Second, the *way* one defines the problem can influence attempts to solve it. It is important to develop a clear representation of a problem. Overly broad statements can hinder by their vagueness. For instance, asking 'How can we end air pollution?' does not point towards any specific solutions. On the other hand, overly specific descriptions can hinder problem solving by restricting possible options. For example, asking 'What is the best way to get sulphur dioxide out of the air?' may inhibit considering the option of reducing the amount going *into* the air (since it is mainly a product of auto exhaust fumes). As Edward deBono, a well-known British psychologist, has said, a definition is sufficient 'as soon as it allows one to do something about a situation' (deBono 1976).

The second stage of problem solving is *generating solutions*. The process of developing possible solutions often gives people trouble. In generating possible solutions, one should try to list as many options as possible, rather than just looking for 'the right one'. Studies have shown that when people fail to solve problems, it is often because their set of possible options was too narrow (i.e. they did not include the correct solution as a possibility). Another tendency is to evaluate possible solutions prematurely, before exploring the full range of possibilities – this sort of impulsiveness also works against effective performance. Properly, one should try to keep solution generation distinct from evaluation (i.e. keep stage 2 separate from stage 3). Later in this section, we will consider a variety of techniques to aid in the process of developing solutions.

The third stage, *selecting and evaluating the best solution*, has different characteristics for different problems. Some problems (for instance, many maths problems) have only a single solution, so evaluation simply involves checking that the chosen solution is correct. Other problems do not have a single ideal solution. In these cases, choosing the best solution depends on what criteria one selects. For example, in 1960 many people saw nuclear reactors as a means to cheap energy production, but today there is concern with the disposal of fuel waste. Thus, the best solution from one point of view (or at one time) may not be the best from another. Among the factors to consider in selecting the best solution might be the following. What are the relative advantages of each solution? Which aspects of the problem is it most important to solve? Are new problems created by the proposed solution? As in the example of nuclear energy, it is possible that different people will prefer different solutions based on the weights they each give to these factors.

Types of Problems

Not all problems are alike in their structure. Various systems have been proposed to distinguish problem types, but one useful approach is to characterize the problem according to the type of goal. Many problems that we face in everyday life are **convergent** – that is, they have a single solution, and everything leads toward that solution (Guilford 1967). For example, calculating the cost of a £10,000 loan at 6 per cent over two years has only a single solution. Sometimes, problems with only one solution are called

convergent problem a problem which has a single solution, and all elements lead towards that solution; also called *closed-end* or *well defined* problems

divergent problem a
problem which does not
have a single optimal
solution, except according to
the criteria one may adopt;
rather, the problem tends
to lead in several different
directions; equivalent to an
ill-defined problem

closed-end or *well-defined* problems; by whatever label, such problems are frequently used in studies of problem solving because they are easy to evaluate.

Convergent problems have a single best solution, and all the information ultimately points towards this. **Divergent problems**, on the other hand, do not have a single optimal solution, except according to the criteria one may adopt. For example, asking 'How can I design the perfect car?' depends on how one defines 'perfect'. Similarly, dealing with a problem like air pollution could have many solutions, each differing in cost, complexity and other elements.

In this sense, the distinction between convergent and divergent problems lies not in the means of developing solutions (stage 2), but only in the means of evaluation (stage 3). Since convergent problems have only a single solution, stage 3 consists of making sure the solution is correct. (How many times have you made mistakes which would have been easily caught if you had taken the time to check your work?) With divergent problems, it becomes necessary to identify the criteria for an acceptable solution, and then apply these criteria to the available solution options. For example, in business, most decisions must involve cost factors, and possibly degree of risk. A promising new manufacturing technique which could potentially save money may be considered a poor solution if there is a concern that it may not work in real production. Thus, the process of evaluation becomes very significant in dealing with divergent problems.

Models of Problem Solving

As discussed in the introduction to this chapter, the cognitive approach has been influenced by both Gestalt theory and information processing. To understand more clearly how this applies to problem solving, let us briefly examine each framework.

Gestalt Theory

Wolfgang Kohler and the other early Gestalt psychologists did extensive studies of problem solving as well as perception. As described earlier, some of Kohler's most famous studies were done with chimpanzees. Interestingly, this work was largely a product of necessity: he was stranded on the island of Tenerife during the First World War, and so began studying the chimps living on the island (Gardner 1985). In a sense, his studies of problem solving emerged as the solution to the problem of what to do with his time! The Gestalt approach to psychology was based on the premise that behaviour is based on organized structures, and is not simply a collection of stimulus elements. For example, a melody is perceived as a particular unity – a 'Gestalt' – which is independent of the notes (e.g. transposing to another key will still preserve the melody).

Similarly, Gestalt psychologists viewed problem solving as a process of changing one's perception of a situation in order to arrive at a solution. This involved a restructuring of the elements in that sudden, spontaneous

Water jug problems

In each problem, the goal is to use the empty jugs as measures to obtain the desired amount of water. For example, in the sample problem, one would fill jug A, and then use its contents to fill jug B three times (discarding the amount in B each time). One would then have the desired amount remaining in jug A.

PROBLEM	EMPTY JUGS AVAILABLE			AMOUNT DESIRED
	A	B	C	
Sample	29	3		20
1	21	127	3	100
2	14	163	25	99
3	18	43	10	5
4	9	42	6	21
5	20	59	4	31
6	24	49	4	20

Figure 4.6   Persistence of set in problem solving Gestalt theorists state that in solving problems we develop a mental set; if this set is not appropriate for a particular problem, we can get stuck. In the above problems, what happens when you get to problem 6? (Adapted from Luchins 1942.)

way called *insight*. Hence, the goal of Gestalt psychology was to understand what creates a particular perception of a situation, described as a *mental set*. (In this context, the term is roughly equivalent to the more modern term *schema*, as defined in Chapter 1.) Thinking was seen as productive and creative, rather than a mechanical process of trial and error.

In general, the Gestalt researchers were concerned with the organizational characteristics that influence how we perceive, and therefore solve, a problem. In order to solve a problem, one must organize the information in an appropriate way – that is, one must form an appropriate mental set. To study this process, Gestalt psychologists developed a number of intriguing convergent problems. For example, consider the problems in Figure 4.6. Once you have figured out the first problem, you can apply the same technique (mental set) to problems 2 to 5. However, you will find the sixth problem impossible to do in this way. This illustrates a hazard called **persistence of set**. The mental set developed in the first problem is no longer appropriate, and tends to interfere with solving the last problem.

persistence of set a phenomenon in problem solving, identified by Gestalt psychologists, in which a mental set developed in a previous problem is maintained even though it is no longer appropriate, and tends to interfere with solving a current problem

This phenomenon is very common, and accounts for many cases of failure in problem solving. In everyday life, it can be the source of a variety of difficulties. For example, while travelling in the UK, I once found myself driving on the wrong side of the road, because my prior driving experience was in North America! Persistence of set was also evident when, in the early 1990s, IBM initially failed to recognize the surging demand for personal computers. One could argue that company executives were slow to recognize the shift from mainframe to personal computers because they had been successful in selling mainframe systems for so long. However, before concluding that mental sets are always negative, one should note that the availability of sets *also* makes it possible for us to recognize, and solve quickly, the many problems for which existing sets *are* appropriate. It is simply that one needs to be flexible, particularly if a particular approach to a problem is unsuccessful.

functional fixedness in Gestalt theory, perceiving an object as having only one use

A related phenomenon, described by Gestalt researchers as **functional fixedness**, refers to perceiving an object as having only one use. For example, a person moving boxes of belongings into an apartment building may feel frustrated that the front door has no doorstop to keep it open – never realizing that one of the boxes could be used for this purpose! Similarly, many people fail to realize that a coin or knife blade can be used as a screwdriver in an emergency. Obviously, functional fixedness reflects a perceptual rigidity, much like persistence of set.

recentring in Gestalt theory, developing an alternative mental set for a situation, such as when trying to solve a problem

The first step in avoiding these difficulties is to be aware of the danger. Beyond that, the Gestalt answer to these difficulties was **recentring**, which is developing an alternative mental set for a problem. Sometimes it helps to disengage from the problem, which is one of the functions of *incubation*. The Gestalt theorists believed that a spontaneous restructuring of set was more likely to occur if one ceased active effort when the existing set didn't work. Sultan solving the two-stick problem (described at the beginning of this chapter) shows the effects of incubation. Sometimes, overfamiliarity with a problem inhibits original thinking and recentring. The development of the theory of relativity is an example: since classical Newtonian theory worked well for many physical phenomena, established physicists were reluctant to abandon it. Einstein, as a young physicist, felt no such commitment to the old theory, which made it easier to envision a new approach.

In the end, Gestalt theory has some significant limitations. For one thing, its descriptions are rather general, and therefore sometimes difficult to evaluate. More significantly, some of the ideas which the Gestalt researchers developed were incorrect (for example, ideas about how perception is organized in the brain). Nonetheless, by their observations, and the questions raised, they set the stage for later research on cognitive processes.

Problem Solving as Information Processing

Today, the greatest influence on the study of problem solving is information processing. While many researchers have been involved in the development of this paradigm, among the early pioneers were Allen Newell and Herbert Simon. (Simon has made contributions in several fields, and received the Nobel Prize in economics in 1978.) In the 1950s, they began working on computer programs which could simulate human thinking processes – foreshadowing what has become known as 'artificial intelligence'. Newell and Simon developed a program called Logic Theorist, which was able to do mathematical proofs – the first such result by a computer. Rather than using uninsightful 'brute force' procedures, Logic Theorist worked by using rules which Newell and Simon saw as analogous to human problem solving. Later, they began work on a program that could do other forms of problems (Newell *et al*. 1958; Newell and Simon 1972).

think-aloud protocol a transcript of the comments made when an individual is asked to describe their thoughts and behaviour while working on a task such as problem solving

One of the influential aspects of their work was the emphasis on studying the actual problem solving behaviour of people. To do so, Newell and Simon would ask individuals what they were doing and thinking as they worked on problems. In some cases, they asked the individuals to think out loud, creating what have become known as **think-aloud protocols**. Since the researchers came from a non-psychological tradition, they felt no qualms about taking such verbal reports seriously – in direct contradiction to behaviourist methods. Subsequently, a variety of studies, including work by Levine (1976), have demonstrated that verbal reports can be correlated with actual behaviour, validating the use of thinking-aloud procedures.

Beyond the impact of their procedures, Newell and Simon also generated an analysis of problem solving which has subsequently influenced cognitive research. In essence, they argued that effective problem solving requires a clear representation of the problem. In simplest form, this means that one must know the situation at the outset (the **initial state**), the desired outcome (the **goal state**) and the available options to solve the problem (the **operators**). For example, to solve a multiplication problem, one must know what the starting numbers are (the initial state), what a product is (the goal) and the rules for doing multiplication (the operators). In suggesting a common framework for describing *any* problem, the information-processing approach represented by the work of Newell and Simon has been a significant influence on our current understanding of problem solving.

Algorithms

The need for systematic methods of solving problems is very apparent in computer applications. Computers, by their design, are not well-suited to handling situations which involve any form of ambiguity. At the same time, their speed enables them to carry out sequences of actions very quickly. These characteristics have led to particular interest in an area of mathematical logic called algorithms. Basically, an **algorithm** is a procedure which always enables one to solve a particular type of problem.

The most basic type of algorithm is *systematic search*, which involves identifying all potential solutions, and then systematically testing them in sequence. For example, suppose you didn't know the combination on a lock which has a dial with forty numbers, and uses a three number combination. That means that the total number of possibilities is $40 \times 40 \times 40 = 64,000$. If one began testing these in sequence, never trying the same combination twice, then on average it would take 32,000 tries to get the correct number. (One might get lucky and find it sooner, or be unlucky and find it only after 63,999 tries!) Clearly, this would be a tedious process for a person; even for a computer, it is not always practical, as the number of trials required grows exponentially as the number of digits on the dial increases (e.g. with 60 numbers, the total is 216,000!). Ideally, one would like to find a solution which is more efficient than this (and therefore remains practical even if the number of possible solutions increases significantly).

Thus, algorithms always enable one to reach the solution, but some are more efficient than others. Another example may help clarify this point. Suppose there is a tennis tournament, with 101 players competing. If the tournament is based on elimination matches, what is the minimum number of matches necessary? One algorithm, equivalent to systematic search, is to list all the necessary rounds, providing for 'byes' when there is an odd number of players. A shorter algorithm is possible, however: by definition, every player except one (the final winner) must lose once and only once.

initial state in problem solving, the situation at the outset of a problem, including any existing constraints (such as time limits or restrictions on permitted actions)

goal state in problem solving, the desired outcome of a problem

operator in problem solving, one of the actions permitted in order to solve a problem

algorithm a procedure for problem solving which, when used appropriately, always leads to the solution of a particular type of problem

Thus, the minimum number of matches equals 101 – 1, or 100 matches! Obviously, efficient algorithms are quite desirable. Unfortunately, for some problems only inefficient algorithms (like systematic search) are known, and for large problems this approach would tax even a computer. For still other types of problems, theorists doubt that any efficient algorithm is possible. (One example, often called 'the salesman's map' problem, requires finding the shortest total route to connect a number of points, like cities on a map. While systematic search works, it is not efficient, and grows unwieldy as the number of points increases.) For situations where no appropriate algorithm exists, other strategies must be used.

Heuristics

heuristic a guide to thinking; in problem solving, heuristics provide informal strategies which are usually better than random search, but less effective than algorithms

The primary alternative to algorithms is the use of **heuristics,** or guides to thinking. Instead of a specific set of steps or rules, heuristics use metaphors, analogies and other intuitive techniques. Unfortunately, heuristics are only guidelines, and unlike algorithms, do not guarantee solving the problem. For example, with the salesman's map problem, the question is in what order to visit the cities in order to produce the shortest overall route. A heuristic which gives a *reasonable* solution (but not necessarily the optimum) is to go to the nearest new city next. Or, consider the heuristic a mechanic once told me for fixing a stalled car: 'A car needs petrol and it needs a spark. If one is OK, check the other.' Obviously, such a rule is better than nothing, but equally obviously, it doesn't provide very specific guidance. This is typical of the nature of heuristics.

A number of general heuristics have been identified which can be used for a variety of problems. These strategies include working backwards, creating subgoals and using metaphors and analogies. *Working backwards* involves backtracking from the goal to one's current situation. It is often used in situations where reversing the problem reduces the range of possible choices. For example, when you misplace something, you might retrace your steps from the last point at which you had the item. (In this case, by starting from a point when you still had the item and then checking the places you know you went thereafter, you restrict the possible places to check.) *Creating subgoals* is designed to break the problem into smaller, more manageable problems. For example, asking 'how can we end pollution?' can be broken down into types of pollution (air, water etc.) or sources of pollution (industry, motor vehicles, homes etc.). Once one has identified some subgoals, one then tries to deal with them individually. (Note that in this example there is more than one way to divide the problem; this vagueness is characteristic of heuristics.) *Using metaphors and analogies* involves looking for similarities between seemingly different contexts. For example, asking how a camera is like the human eye has led to automatic focusing and automatic exposure systems for cameras.

In the end, no single technique will prove useful in all situations. However, it is worth remembering the perils of persistence of set and functional fixedness, identified by Gestalt theorists. The wider the range of techniques one can call on in trying to solve a problem, the less likely it is that these difficulties will occur.

For further consideration Assume you have just been given a twenty page essay assignment on an unfamiliar topic. What technique would you use to make the task more manageable? Why?

Creativity in Problem Solving

For the average person, 'creativity' is likely to inspire thoughts of artists, writers or musicians, who may be creative in terms of artistic expression. Yet it is also possible to be creative when dealing with problems; indeed, many inventions have been the result of creativity in handling a technical problem. (The discoveries of the light bulb and integrated circuit are two examples.) To address this, researchers often define **creativity** as the production of something which has two characteristics: *uniqueness* and *utility*. Uniqueness is significant, because an idea which occurs to everyone is not regarded as creative. (For example, suggesting that wheels should be round instead of square is not creative.) On the other hand, unique ideas must also be useful for solving a problem. (For example, wearing clothes made out of spaghetti would be unique, but not very practical.) As Edward deBono has commented, a creative idea is just a new idea that works (deBono 1976).

DeBono uses the term 'lateral thinking' to describe creativity, in contrast to the relatively rigid patterns of logical analysis ('linear thinking'). In some ways, his ideas are reminiscent of Gestalt theory. For example, he notes that rigid thinking can take several forms, from failure to recognize that an old solution is no longer appropriate, to arrogant attachment to one's own ideas. To aid recentring, he promotes the value of humour, provocativeness (especially in what-if scenarios) and novelty. While his writings are highly entertaining ('if you cannot imagine any alternatives, it is easy to be convinced that the only one you have is absolutely right'), his approach tends to favour descriptive models over rigorous research.

Guilford, like deBono, believed that creativity involves a different mode of thinking, which he called 'divergent thinking' (Guilford 1967). This process is manifested in solving divergent problems, in which the search for solutions tends to lead in several different directions. Divergent problems are also creative in the sense that they have many possible solutions, not all of which will be equivalent in either originality or practicality. Hence, solving a divergent problem requires selecting the 'best' solution.

Unfortunately, defining 'best' can be rather ambiguous, as previously discussed. The evaluation of the best solution often involves judgements of value (either personal or social). For example, in our culture we tend to value a businessman who develops a new marketing strategy for a product more than we value a mother who invents an activity to keep a 3-year-old amused. Similarly, social attitudes towards creativity seem to value quantity over quality, and to emphasize the *number* of ideas generated as a primary indicator of creativity. (Even Guilford was guilty of this simplification, since one of his tests of creativity simply counts how many different uses one can imagine for a common object, like a brick.) We may value more highly the person who generates five ideas, none of which is effective, than the person

creativity the capacity to produce something which is both unique and useful

who describes only one, because they have already recognized that the other four ideas were not workable. (Sometimes, being creative means knowing when something *isn't* a solution as well as when it *is*.) In the end, assessments of value are more ambiguous than judgements of uniqueness or practicality. While there is no simple resolution to this issue, it does indicate that evaluation is crucial in solving divergent problems, and possibly in creativity more generally.

The Formation of Problem Solving Skills

Good problem solvers often make use of many of the techniques that we have been discussing, even when they have not been formally trained in problem solving. Other people seem to flounder when given any type of unfamiliar problem. Since research suggests that problem solving is a matter of acquired skills, not general intellect, it leads us to a question: how do people learn how to solve problems? What makes some people more 'insightful'?

Gestalt theory refers to *mental set* as the way one perceives a particular situation, including a problem. Insight triggers a shift in mental set, so that one's perceptions are rearranged in a more appropriate way. The question is: *how* does this occur? One of the difficulties with the Gestalt approach is its tendency to be primarily descriptive. Kohler's concept of insight really only describes the end result, not how one arrives at it. Similarly, the description of incubation does not explain why it is sometimes effective, and sometimes not. These and other aspects of the problem solving process were left to other researchers to examine – ironically, some of them began, like Tolman, within the behaviourist approach.

In the late 1940s, an American psychologist named Harry Harlow discovered a phenomenon which he called 'learning to learn'. Working with primates, he found that problem solving behaviour (such as choosing which of two symbols marked the location of a food reward) was initially trial and error, much as a behaviourist would expect (Harlow 1949). However, given experience with many problems of the same type, the animals would develop a 'set' which enabled them to deal with new problems in an 'insightful' way. Harlow called these learned strategies **learning sets**. (In essence, Harlow's term has the same meaning as the Gestalt concept of *mental set*, except it emphasizes that the set develops as the result of experience, not as spontaneous insight.)

learning set a learned strategy or set which enables the individual to deal efficiently with problems of the same type; similar in meaning to the Gestalt concept of mental set, except it emphasizes that the set develops as the result of experience

Later research has shown that young children, and even adults, develop similar learning sets from experience (Levine 1976). For example, the story of the child solving problems involving different shapes, presented at the beginning of this chapter, illustrates the formation of a learning set. In this case, the child quickly learns a strategy called 'win-stay, lose-shift'. That is, if the first shape you pick is correct, stay with it; if you choose incorrectly the first time, then this tells you the other shape is the correct one, and should be chosen thereafter. At a more complex level, it can be argued that students in school learn *how* to learn, by learning to select what is most important when studying, by identifying cues to test questions from lecture content and so on. In this sense, education is a type of problem solving, not simply a passive intake of information. Regardless of the situation, Harlow's work implies that effective problem solving depends on appropriate past experience – not to know the answer, but to know *how* to get the answer. Insight comes not out of the blue, but to those who are prepared.

Research on the formation of learning sets has helped to clarify the role of experience in the development of problem solving skills. While adult behaviour is usually insightful in terms of the use of strategies, it is based on a foundation of early trial and error experience. In this sense, Kohler's emphasis on insight as *distinct* from trial and error appears to be wrong. In the end, though, there is little doubt that cognitive research has increased our understanding of problem solving in ways that have practical benefit.

Language

While animals like chimpanzees have demonstrated some ability in problem solving, there is little doubt that people are more capable of dealing with complex problems. We can do so in large part because we know so much, which in turn is partly due to our ability to learn from experience, and store that knowledge in memory in an organized way. But another important element is our ability to communicate with each other, and thereby benefit from the experiences of others. (Reading a textbook like this one is a clear example!) Without language, we would be largely restricted to learning from personal experience, and there is little doubt that our lives would be the poorer for it.

In many ways, language is a paradox: we learn to use it as children with very little difficulty, yet as adults find learning a second language a major challenge. We can use it to understand other people, yet we have very little understanding of the process itself! Psychologists, linguists, philosophers and others have all examined language, but at present there are many unresolved questions.

To start with, not everyone agrees on what language *is*. It is clear that language serves as a communication method and as a symbol system, but not every form of communication is considered language. For example, the innately determined threat gestures used by baboons to warn away rivals are signals, but not language. In order to qualify as **language**, most researchers would say, the symbols or gestures used for communicating must show *variety* within the species, and must be *open-ended* – that is, allowing for new forms and meanings. Baboon gestures show neither of these characteristics, and so would not be considered a true language. Variety is important, in that it implies the influence of learning, and also that symbols are somewhat arbitrary – that is, the same meaning could be communicated using different elements. Interestingly, birdsong is somewhat like language in that it is dependent on learning, and shows intra-species variation, including regional 'dialects' (Marler 1970). However, it is not clear whether bird song can be considered an open-ended symbol system, as the definition

language a system of communication based on symbols or gestures which can vary across individuals and allow for new forms and meanings

of language requires. For our purposes, we will focus on the role of human language in communication and thinking.

The existence of language is such an obvious human characteristic that even the behaviourists could not ignore it. Traditionally, they have tried to explain it in terms of complex patterns of reinforcers and stimulus–response sequences (Skinner 1957). Beyond accounting for spoken language, the behaviourists showed little interest in its role in thinking, as befits their general point of view. Watson saw thinking as simply muscle movements reduced to small, unobserved twitches; Pavlov saw thought as the product of a 'second signal system', operating in parallel with the process of conditioning. Unfortunately, the behaviourist view of language and thought is challenged by the data. While there is evidence that muscle activity often occurs along with thinking (for example, deaf individuals who know sign language show activity in hand muscles while engaging in problem solving), the evidence regarding thinking as *only* muscle activity is mostly negative. As we will see, there are also other problems with the behaviourist view of language.

By contrast, cognitive researchers see language as a symbol system which can mediate a variety of thinking processes, and which is not dependent on 'muscle twitches'. In addition, the cognitive approach views our use of language as based on innate capacities, not simply reinforced responses. To understand the reasons for this viewpoint, we need to consider how we learn to use language.

Language Learning

We all learn to use language, but typically show little concern about how we learn. Children absorb the vocabulary and basic grammar of their mother tongue long before it is formally taught in school. Yet, when closely examined, early language learning is a remarkable process. At about six months of age, a baby will begin babbling, producing a wide variety of speech sounds, only some of which will later be used in its first language. Later on, it is difficult to reacquire those sounds which are lost. For example, native French speakers have trouble with the 'th' sound in English; similarly, English speakers have trouble with 'û' in French. At about one year old, the first words appear. By about one-and-a-half to two years, the child produces two-word 'sentences'. These phrases were called *telegraphic speech* by early researchers, but we now recognize that there is considerable complexity in the production and use of these 'simple' phrases. Some examples of telegraphic speech are clear even out of context – for instance, 'that red' for 'that is red', or 'see mummy' for 'I see mummy'. In other cases, what seems meaningless when considered out of context is nonetheless understandable in context. For example, a child, seeing a ball near the mother, may say 'Mummy throw'. (It is worth noting that in some cases *adult* language is *also* unclear when taken out of context!) By the age of two, the typical child produces about two dozen two-word sentences. From this time on, the growth of language skills is explosive, so that at age three the average child knows almost 1,000 words, and this figure may *double* in the ensuing year (Moskowitz 1978)! As an adult, it has been estimated that the average

Stage	Age	Description of language skills
Babbling	6 months to 1 year	Babies begin by producing all the phonemes found in human languages
First words	1 to $1\frac{1}{2}$ years	First words, using phonemes in the language spoken by those around child
Telegraphic speech	$1\frac{1}{2}$ to 2 years	Two-word sentences, typically combining a noun and verb or adjective and noun (e.g. 'Mummy gone')
Acquiring grammar	2 to 4 years	Learning prepositions, verb forms and other rules; at first, child tends to overgeneralize forms (e.g. 'I goed')
Competent speech	4 to 5 years	Uses full sentences with conventional grammar, though with less complex structure than adults

Figure 4.7   Stages of language development

person knows over 100,000 words, though only a small fraction of these may be used regularly. (See Figure 4.7 for a summary.)

The rapid development of language skills, which does not greatly vary across languages or cultural settings, poses several difficulties for a behaviourist interpretation of language. First, acquisition seems to occur too quickly and too consistently to be based simply on trial and error. Second, there is evidence that we are best prepared to learn language at the time children normally do. If this 'critical period' is passed, it may be difficult or impossible to learn normal language skills later. (Incidents of children raised in isolation support this view, as do cases of children with correctable hearing deficits which are not recognized until age four or five, which is already past the point when language learning normally begins.) Third, individuals seem to have less difficulty learning a second language as children than as adults (McDonald 1997). All these factors suggest that language learning is based on some innate capacities which are tied to early development.

The best known advocate for language as an innate capacity is Noam Chomsky, a linguist at Massachusetts Institute of Technology (MIT) (Chomsky 1972). Chomsky argues that human language is based on innate grammatical rules, which are part of what he calls a *language acquisition device* ('device' here means a hypothetical mechanism, not a physical structure). Chomsky's position has gained many supporters in recent years. Roger Brown, a cognitive psychologist who is interested in both language and child development, favours the notion of internal rules. After reviewing studies of 12 different languages, he feels the evidence is compelling (Brown 1973). Steven Pinker, a colleague of Chomsky's at MIT, goes as far as to call language an 'instinct'! (Pinker 1994).

The possibility that language is based on innate capacities is hardly disturbing to a cognitive psychologist. After all, such capacities would represent a form of mediating process for language learning, and hence are consistent with the general assumptions of the cognitive approach. (Unlike the behaviourists or the biological approach, cognitive psychologists have no firm position on nature versus nurture.) The Gestalt psychologists, in particular, would find this view comfortable, since many of their organizing principles were seen as innate. At the same time, there is a risk in describing language capacity as innate. For one thing, there is a variety of evidence suggesting that learning plays an important role in the development of language. For example, children practise their language skills extensively – spending perhaps 10,000 hours speaking by the age of six (Anderson 1995)! Furthermore, there is great variability among human languages and across individuals, and the notion of innate capacities does not address these details. Perhaps the biggest concern is that placing an emphasis on innateness minimizes the need to *explain* the process. Instead of specifying the details of how this complex behaviour develops, one may simply say 'it's part of human nature to use language'. Even if true, it tells us very little about our use of language – or any apparent usage by other species.

Of Apes and Language

The question of language capacity in other species has become a controversial area in recent years. Researchers have long speculated on the possibility of teaching human language to other species, usually primates like chimpanzees. In the mid-twentieth century, several teams of researchers attempted to teach chimps to speak, often by rearing them as if they were human children. Then, in the mid-1960s, a husband and wife team of psychologists, Allen and Beatrice Gardner, tried a new approach (Gardner and Gardner 1969). Reasoning that it might be an inability to *speak*, not an inability to *use language*, that led to previous failures, the Gardners decided to try sign language. Using a modified form of ASL (a sign language used by many deaf individuals in the United States), they began training a female chimp named Washoe. To their surprise as well as satisfaction, Washoe began using signs proficiently, albeit with a limited vocabulary.

The first published reports set off an earthquake in both psychology and linguistics, mostly about what constitutes true language. A rash of studies followed, some using the methods of the Gardners, and some using other methods (including having primates interacting with a computer). Apart from chimpanzees, there have also been studies with gorillas, orangutans and dolphins. The ferment generated by these studies has been considerable. Some theorists say the use of ASL and other symbol systems shows chimps have basically the same type of language capacity we do. Others, including Herb Terrace, a behaviourist, have questioned whether the chimps really show awareness of syntax (use of word order to convey meaning), and have also noted the relatively limited vocabulary of the animals (Terrace *et al.* 1979). It is impossible to discuss every study in detail, but it should be noted that some researchers have found evidence for both syntax and creation of new 'words' (Premack 1983). Even more interesting is the evidence that ASL-trained chimps spontaneously teach signing to other chimps (Fouts *et al.* 1983). Similarly, a bonobo (another type of primate) named Kanzi observed his mother being trained to use symbols via a keyboard for his first two years of life. Though he had not himself been trained, Kanzi spontaneously began using the keyboard appropriately at two-and-a-half when his mother was relocated (Rumbaugh 1992).

At present, it seems that the controversy is still unresolved, with each side finding some data which support their viewpoint. However, we should be wary of defining language in such a way that only human behaviour would qualify. For example, the limited vocabulary of chimps does not seem a sufficient reason to discount their behaviour as language. Similarly, judgements of creativity seem ambiguous: while it is true no chimp has produced the equivalent of Shakespeare, few humans do, either. In this regard, it is interesting that a gorilla named Koko has shown an interest in poetry, and has commented on the death of a kitten in surprising ways (Patterson and Linden 1981; Stone 1988). Communication can range from the mundane to the extraordinary, and it is likely that the study of language-related behaviour in other species will help us to achieve a better understanding of our own linguistic accomplishments.

Language and Thinking

The study of language raises questions about the relationship of language to thinking. Is all thinking based on words? Do the words we use influence the way we think? In many ways, these questions are much deeper than simply asking if thinking consists of muscle twitches. Thinking processes are central to the cognitive approach, and it is obviously desirable to understand what the *basis* of thinking is. At one time, it was assumed that all thinking was verbal, in much the way that memory researchers thought all memory was verbal. One consequence of this view was the tendency to assume that infants, lacking language, could not think. More recently, ingenious experiments have shown that infants are capable of thinking. (See discussion in Chapter 7.) In addition, research on visual imagery and memory, as discussed earlier, suggests that not all thinking is verbal, even in adults. Yet few would disagree that the *primary* mode of thinking for most individuals is verbal. And if this is so, then how do the words we use affect the way we think?

One answer to this question was proposed some years ago by Benjamin Whorf, a specialist in Native American languages. Whorf argued that the way a language is structured influences the way that individuals perceive, and think about, the world (Whorf 1956). (This has been popularized in the phrase 'language shapes thought'.) Essentially, Whorf argued that the way we think depends on the words available to us. He based this on the observation that various Native American languages had very different vocabularies, and that it was often nearly impossible to translate from one language to another. A well-known example concerns the fact that the Inuit have many words for different kinds of snow, but the Navajo have only one. Whorf took the strong position that such differences not only affect thinking and communication, but also affect perception. That is, he believed that Inuit actually *see* snow differently from other people (such as Navajos).

This view, sometimes called the Whorfian hypothesis, has been the subject of extensive research and debate. At the level of perception, the evidence has been mostly negative; for example, despite variations in colour names across languages, people tend to discriminate colours in similar ways (Rosch 1973). However, the milder form, that language can influence the categories used in thinking, is still an open question. Certainly it is true that concepts can be easier to express when there is a specific word available, as opposed to a lengthy description. This is evident in the tendency for English (and other languages) to incorporate foreign words. For example, 'ennui' (borrowed from French) conveys a meaning which is subtly different from 'boredom'. At the same time, the fact that a single word does not exist does not necessarily mean that a concept cannot be expressed in some indirect way.

Since questions of vocabulary seem indecisive in judging Whorf's hypothesis, it is more interesting to consider areas where thinking interacts with the *structure* of a language. For example, consider forms of address. In English, we use the word 'you' to refer to someone we are speaking to, without regard to our social relationship to the person. Other languages, including French, German and Japanese, use different forms depending on the social relationship (e.g. 'vous' or 'tu' in French). Hence, in these languages, addressing people requires considering what our relationship is to them. Another example concerns counterfactual statements. In English, we frequently express ideas which are contrary to fact – for example, after John has a car accident, we might say, 'If he hadn't been drinking, he wouldn't have had an accident.' By contrast, Cantonese Chinese does not have a ready means of producing such statements; instead, individuals are likely simply to say, 'John had an accident because he was drinking.' Based on this linguistic difference, one researcher found that Chinese speakers had more difficulty than American English speakers in understanding arguments involving counterfactual statements (Bloom 1981).

While obviously not conclusive, such findings are certainly intriguing. At what point, one might wonder, do such differences in expression lead to different ways of thinking? On the other hand, does the way we think lead to changes in the language we use? For example, one might speculate that our experience of the world has been changed by concepts like Einstein's theory of relativity, with its suggestion that frameworks of perception are always relative. Whorf was probably too extreme in his position, but the issues he raised are likely to be with us for a long time to come.

The relationship between language and thinking is complex and subtle. Certainly, language is the primary symbol system used in thinking, and the specifics of a language can probably influence the way we organize information. Beyond that, there is much that we do not know about language, *including* precisely how it affects our thinking. Words let us think about the world, and communicate those thoughts to each other. At some level, that process is as wondrous as the latest technology. Future research may help us to understand the process better, but it is unlikely to rob language of the capacity to amaze.

For further consideration

If you know people who are fluent in another language as well as English, you might explore Whorf's hypothesis by asking them about their experiences: Are some ideas easier to express in one language or the other? In general, do they notice any ways in which their thinking changes when they switch languages?

The Cognitive Viewpoint in Other Areas

Cognitive psychologists have been active in studying all aspects of thinking, as indicated above. In focusing on these topics, one should not lose sight of the basic viewpoint of the cognitive approach: it is not that thinking processes like memory are the most significant aspect of behaviour, but that mediational processes of *some* kind underlie *all* behaviour. As noted in the introduction to this chapter, this approach can be applied to understanding many other aspects of behaviour. For example, early Gestalt psychologists were as interested in perception as in problem solving. Today, one can see cognitive influences in development (as in the work of Jean Piaget, Jerome Bruner and others), computer science (in the area of artificial intelligence) and even applications of behaviourism (where psychologists like Meichenbaum are advocating 'cognitive behaviour modification'). (Some of these topics are discussed in later chapters.)

Given the many dimensions of human behaviour, it should not be surprising that cognitive interpretations are applied to many aspects of behaviour other than thinking processes. In discussing these areas, it is clear that the underlying assumptions are the same – that is, that there are mediational processes which underlie behaviour, and that these processes provide an organizational structure for guiding behaviour. At the same time, the specific models used have often developed independently of either Gestalt or information-processing influences. Regardless of origin, the resulting models are characteristically cognitive in nature, as we shall see.

Attitudes and Cognitive Dissonance

One area where the cognitive approach has been significant is social psychology. In this case, the influence is probably direct, owing to the work of Kurt Lewin, an early Gestalt psychologist who wrote extensively about social behaviour. Social psychology is concerned with the ways in which behaviour is influenced by social interactions. While this covers a broad territory, one of the primary interests has been **social cognition**, the mental processes involved in the way people perceive and react to social situations. We will look at two aspects of social cognition, beginning with the study of attitudes.

Attitudes represent personal beliefs of an evaluative nature – that is, good or bad, likeable or not likeable etc. Traditionally, attitudes are regarded by researchers as having three components: the belief itself (cognitive component), the feelings associated with it (emotional component) and the resulting actions (behavioural component). For example, someone may believe smoking is harmful, get angry when someone is smoking near them, and boycott a restaurant which allows smoking.

Attitudes are of practical as well as theoretical interest, since they involve such basic concerns as attraction and prejudice. Understanding who likes/ hates whom, and why, thus requires an understanding of how attitudes are formed, and how they are altered. While it is not possible to provide a full

social cognition the mental processes involved in the way people perceive and react to social situations

attitude a personal belief of an evaluative nature, such as good or bad, likeable or not likeable, which influences our reactions towards people or things

exploration of attitudes in this section, we will look at one approach to the study of what leads us to change our attitudes.

One of the best-known theories of attitude change is the *theory of cognitive dissonance* developed by Leon Festinger (Festinger 1957). According to Festinger, we all seek to behave in a self-consistent manner. Our actions should fit with both our words and our attitudes. What happens, however, if our actions don't fit our beliefs, or two beliefs conflict? Festinger argues that whenever there are conflicts of this type, we experience a tension which he calls **cognitive dissonance**. For example, suppose you hate the hustle and bustle of New York City, but have good friends who live there whom you want to see. This creates a conflict between your attitude towards New York and your attitude towards your friends, resulting in dissonance. Festinger's theory deals with the nature of such conflicts, and how we resolve them.

One possibility is to change your attitudes to make them consistent with your actions. In the example given, you could decide New York isn't so bad, and go, or you could decide you really don't care that much about your friends, and not go. In either case, one of your attitudes would change to become consistent with your actions. Or you could persuade your friends to come to visit you. In this case, your attitudes remain firm, but the conflict is resolved by adding a new factor. This is analogous to a smoking colleague who once commented, 'Sure, I know smoking causes cancer, but I'd be miserable if I *didn't* smoke!' In effect, the belief that life would be miserable without smoking is invoked to resolve the conflict between the belief that smoking causes cancer, and the desire not to get cancer. Dissonance theory says that conflict (dissonance) can lead to changes in attitudes or actions; if attitudes are changed, usually the weakest belief is the one to be changed.

Dissonance reduction seems to be a common occurrence. Consider the following example: have you ever waited outside for a film in the middle of winter, possibly for an hour or more? What was your reaction to the film afterwards? According to dissonance theory, you very probably thought the movie was good, since it would arouse dissonance to think you suffered outside for a terrible film! In a laboratory analogy to this situation, Festinger paid participants either $1 or $20 to take part in a purposely dull experiment (Festinger and Carlsmith 1959). (It should be noted that $20 was a considerable sum of money in 1959!) They were then requested to tell the next 'participant' that the task was enjoyable. When subsequently asked to evaluate the task *honestly*, those paid $1 rated it much more positively than those paid $20. In effect, lying by telling someone else the task was boring created more dissonance for those paid only $1 than for the better paid subjects, which led to the poorly paid subjects actually revising their evaluation of the task in a positive way.

Dissonance theory has generated tremendous amounts of research in social psychology. Partly this is because the issues it raises are interesting, and partly because of seeming weaknesses in the theory. One weakness is that the theory does not predict precisely what will happen in a particular situation. For example, a smoker confronted by evidence that links smoking to cancer may react in several ways: he may quit smoking (thereby changing actions); he may reject the evidence as being only correlational (rejecting one belief); or he may justify the discrepancy in some other way, as in the

cognitive dissonance in Festinger's theory, a state of tension created when there are conflicts between an individual's behaviour and beliefs, or between two beliefs

earlier example of the smoker who introduced an additional belief about the consequences of quitting. Festinger himself suggested that we tend to ignore information which creates conflict, a phenomenon called *selective exposure*. While some evidence suggests that this sometimes occurs (e.g. Frey 1986), a review of a wide range of studies of attitudes suggests that the links between attitudes and behaviour are often hard to predict (Kraus 1995).

A second issue concerns how widespread dissonance reactions are in daily life. While it is possible to produce supporting anecdotes, the evidence suggests that not all conflicts produce dissonance. For instance, people *forced* to do something inconsistent with their beliefs will usually not experience dissonance. (This may explain why the people who were paid $20 in the Festinger and Carlsmith experiment felt no dissonance about telling someone else the task was enjoyable – the money could be seen as the factor 'forcing' them to lie.) Generally, dissonance is most likely to occur when someone *voluntarily* does something which is inconsistent with their attitudes. (Thus, being paid only $1 was a poor incentive to lie, which created dissonance.)

In recent years, researchers have begun to focus on a different aspect of dissonance: the influence of culture. Not surprisingly, culture seems to play a significant role in cognitive dissonance, as in other aspects of social cognition and behaviour. One recent study compared the reactions of Canadian and Japanese participants in a situation in which dissonance was evoked by means of false feedback from a (fake) personality test (Heine and Lehman 1997). Interestingly, the Canadian participants reacted in the way expected by Festinger's theory, but the Japanese participants showed no effect of the manipulation. Of course, this result does not necessarily mean that Japanese never feel dissonance. Instead, it may simply mean that different factors produce dissonance – a finding consistent with other research on Japanese and other Asian groups (Markus and Kitayama 1991). At present, we can only say that cultural differences in dissonance certainly merit further study.

Although clearly not the final word on the subject of attitude change, Festinger's theory shows the influence of the cognitive approach in both name and substance. As a theory of social behaviour, it clearly states that mediating processes are important in understanding how people act. Contrary to behaviourist notions, the stimulus situation alone is insufficient to explain social behaviour. Rather, one must consider internal constructs and processes like attitudes and dissonance reduction. In this and other ways, the cognitive approach plays an important role in understanding social behaviour.

For further consideration	Can you think of a situation in which you have experienced dissonance? How did you resolve it? Do you think knowing about Festinger's theory will make it more or less likely that you will experience dissonance in the future?

Attribution Theory

A second area of social cognition which has been influenced by the cognitive approach is the process by which we interpret the causes of behaviour – our own, and that of other people. The inferences we make about the causes of behaviour are called *attributions*, and the model used to explain the interpretations we make is called **attribution theory**. As Fritz Heider, the founder of attribution theory, said, we are all 'psychologists', in that we all try to make sense out of people's actions (Heider 1958). Heider, like Lewin a Gestalt psychologist, suggested that we tend to interpret behaviour in terms of *internal* (personal) and/or *external* (situational) factors. For example, if you see someone frowning, you may decide they are angry, and speculate about the source of their anger. Depending on the circumstances and the information you have, you may attribute it to internal factors, such as the person having a hostile nature, or you may attribute it to something in the external situation, such as the person having received bad news.

Trying to understand why someone is acting in a particular way can obviously be useful – assuming our interpretations are accurate. Given that we often have incomplete information, however, errors are also quite possible. As a result, researchers studying attributions have been interested in the types of errors that people make, particularly those that might represent a consistent tendency, or *bias*. One such error, called the **fundamental attribution error**, is the tendency to underestimate the importance of situational influences, and overestimate the importance of internal factors in interpreting other people's behaviour. For example, if we encounter a sales assistant who seems unhelpful, we are likely to assume that the person is unfriendly, rather than considering whether the working conditions or other situational factors might be responsible. (For example, the person may have sore feet after standing for several hours.)

The fundamental attribution error suggests there is a basic bias in the way we perceive other people. However, attribution theory also applies to the way we interpret our own behaviour. Not surprisingly, there is evidence that errors can also occur in this context; one such error identified by researchers is called the **self-serving bias**. The self-serving bias reflects a desire to see ourselves in the best possible light; in practice, it is expressed as a tendency to attribute our successes to personal factors (e.g. our own ability), but blame our failures on situational factors (e.g. distraction, lack of time). Thus, if Marie does well on a test, she may say it is because she studied hard, but if she does badly, she may complain that the test was unfair. The end result is a distortion of Marie's self-image in a favourable way.

Attribution theory suggests that such biases are important, because they reflect a source of distortions in the mental schema that guide our perceptions and behaviour. Unfortunately, the theory is less clear in explaining how these biases arise. One view is that they reflect basic types of cognitive errors, such as the tendency not to seek out information inconsistent with our beliefs (Nisbett and Ross 1980). Others argue that errors like the self-serving bias help to preserve our self-esteem, and thus have a motivational basis (Taylor and Brown 1988). Both of these interpretations would suggest that the biases are fundamental human traits, and therefore should occur universally. Unfortunately, the data from cross-cultural studies reveal a very different picture. For example, studies in India (Miller 1984) and

attribution theory a theory dealing with the inferences we make about the causes of our own behaviour, and that of other people; the interpretations made are called *attributions*

fundamental attribution error the tendency to underestimate the importance of situational influences, and overestimate the importance of internal factors, in interpreting the causes of people's behaviour

self-serving bias the tendency to distort our assessment of our own behaviour, by attributing our successes to personal factors, and our failures to situational factors

Japan (Weisz *et al*. 1984) reveal that in both cultures the internal bias associated with the fundamental attribution error is far less common than in Western societies. Similarly, the self-serving bias is less common among Japanese students than among American students (Kashima and Triandis 1986). In attempting to explain results like these, Moghaddam *et al*. (1993) suggest that the differences relate to a broader cultural emphasis on the individual in North America, as compared to a more collective social orientation in Asian societies.

In one sense, the finding that attributions differ across cultures is important, since it reminds us that we should be careful about assuming particular social cognitions are universal. Instead, it seems that the types of attributions we make are strongly influenced by the culture we live in. At the same time, this view does not undermine the basic premise of attribution theory, which is that people make interpretations of both their own behaviour and that of others. As such, the research on attribution theory, including the cross-cultural data, reinforces the idea that our cognitive schema are an important factor in how we behave.

| **For further consideration** | Do you think the way you perceive people reflects your cultural upbringing? In what ways? |

Cognition and Emotions

We are all aware of the varied nature of emotions. Fear, anger, sadness and joy are part of everyone's experience. Yet understanding how emotions arise, and how we interpret them, is a more difficult matter. In part, we know that emotions are based on physiological factors, such as changes in heart rate, breathing and blood pressure. These changes, which are referred to as changes in physiological *arousal*, are easy to recognize subjectively, at least in the extremes. But it is less clear that arousal alone can account for the *variety* of emotions which we experience. For example, try listing some of the physiological changes you experience when you are very angry and when you are very happy. If you think carefully, you will probably note significant overlap in the two cases (heart and breathing accelerate etc.). If two such different emotions share a number of physiological characteristics, then can arousal alone account for different emotions? And what role does thinking play in our emotions?

The earliest modern theory of emotion goes back to William James, who argued that our physiological response is what determines our emotional state. Thus, as he famously put it, 'we are afraid because we run, not we run because we are afraid!' James's view was provocative, and has been challenged in various ways (see Lang 1994). From the perspective of the cognitive approach, it can be argued that James placed too much emphasis on physiological arousal, and too little on the role of cognitive processes. While arousal is a significant aspect of emotion, there is a variety of research which indicates that our interpretation of the situation influences our emotions.

The first study to suggest a role for cognitive interpretation was a well-known experiment by Stanley Schachter and Jerome Singer (1962). Essentially, Schachter and Singer argued that people tended to look at the situation for clues to their emotional state (i.e. using external rather than internal attribution). Depending on the social situation, subjects interpreted their arousal (produced by an injection of adrenaline) as either happiness or anger. The results of the Schachter and Singer study suggested two main conclusions. First, physiological arousal is not always interpreted as indicating emotion. For example, someone who has just run to catch a bus will experience arousal, but will not attribute it to emotion. Second, when arousal *is* seen as due to an emotional state, our interpretation of the situation determines how we define the emotion. Thus, a state of tension might be interpreted as anxiety while writing a test, but as anger if one is waiting in a checkout line. While the original Schachter and Singer study has been challenged in various ways (see Levanthal and Tomarken 1986), it was influential in suggesting that attributional processes play a role in our emotions.

cognitive appraisal theory
a theory of emotion which argues that our emotional state is based on our assessment of the situation and its significance to our well-being

This idea that cognitive interpretations influence our emotions has been taken a step further by Richard Lazarus, in terms of what he calls **cognitive appraisal theory** (Lazarus 1993; Roseman *et al.* 1996). Lazarus argues that our emotions are a result of our appraisal of the situation we are in, in terms of how we see its effect on our current well-being or future goals. For example, if we perceive that we are being unfairly punished, we will feel anger; if a friend insults us in a way that we interpret as a joke, we will laugh. The cognitive appraisal model sees emotions as being functional: our appraisal of the situation leads to a particular emotion, which in turn motivates us to respond to the situation appropriately. For example, if a stranger approaches me on a deserted street and I decide that I should feel afraid, I am likely to flee or seek help. Interestingly, these appraisal processes seem to occur in similar ways in a variety of cultures (Mauro *et al.* 1992).

One of the issues facing cognitive appraisal theory is the role of arousal in emotional experience. In their original study, Schachter and Singer argued that emotions resulted from the way we interpret our physical arousal – that is, cognitive interpretations are the link between arousal and emotions. By contrast, Lazarus argues that cognitions alone cause emotions, independent of arousal. While this may apply to some situations, it does not seem to fit all the available data. For example, research on victims of spinal cord injuries indicates that because the loss of sensation below the site of injury reduces awareness of many aspects of bodily arousal, it also results in feeling less emotional (Hohmann 1966). At a physiological level, LeDoux has proposed that we actually have two systems for emotion: one which is cognitive (involving the cortex), and a more primitive, arousal-based mechanism (located in the limbic system) (LeDoux 1995). While it can be difficult to move from physiological processes to cognitive ones, LeDoux's view suggests that emotions involve both cognitions and arousal.

The idea that emotions depend on an interaction has also been applied to the experience of pain. Psychologist Ronald Melzack, in conjunction with a physiologist named Patrick Wall, has developed a theory of pain which integrates cognitive, situational and physiological factors (Melzack and Wall

1982). While noting that there are a number of physiological pathways involved in pain, they also assign a role to cognitive factors, such as memory for past experiences and perception of the immediate situation. These cognitive factors (which they believe are mediated by the cortex) help to explain many of the puzzling aspects of pain. For example, two individuals with similar injuries may show significant differences in experienced pain, because they interpret the situation differently (e.g. a soldier may see a wound as removing him from the risks of battle, while a civilian may see a similar injury as a major disruption of a secure life). Similarly, distractions, such as listening to music during dental procedures, can reduce pain by changing our perception of the environment. Thus, the Melzack and Wall model suggests that cognitive processes play an important role in our experience of pain, as they do with other emotions.

Interestingly, the links between cognition and emotion seem to be bi-directional. That is, our emotions can affect our cognitive processes, just as our cognitive processes can affect our emotions. For example, emotions can affect the retrieval of information from long-term memory (Bower 1981; McFarland and Buehler 1997). Even more striking is a case study reported by neurologist Antonio Damasio (1994). Following removal of a tumour in the prefrontal cortex, the patient, a man named Elliot, reported an absence of emotions. When shown pictures that might reasonably elicit an emotional response (such as a gruesome accident), Elliot could recognize why they might be regarded as emotional, but he now felt 'nothing'. Equally striking was the effect on Elliot's ability to make decisions. While he could identify various factors which would be relevant to a given decision, he was unable actually to make a choice, even for something as trivial as picking a dessert! How can we make sense of this? It seems that without emotions, Elliot could no longer evaluate alternatives to make a 'rational' choice. To Damasio, the case demonstrates that emotions are inextricably linked with our cognitive capacities. As with many phenomena, the final understanding of emotion may involve a complex interaction of different factors – one of which will certainly be cognitive processes.

| **For further consideration** | Can you think of a case where two people (perhaps you and a friend) have reacted with different emotions to the same situation? How would you account for this? |

Conclusion

No other approach in psychology considers thinking processes in quite the same way as the cognitive approach. Some psychologists, like the behaviourists, ignore thinking processes, while others accept the existence of thought without examining its nature. One example is psychoanalysis: Freud's theory, despite emphasizing basic drives, would be empty were it not for the emphasis he gave to verbal behaviour (e.g. 'Freudian slips') and to the symbolic meanings of actions. Yet, while he acknowledged the existence of thinking and symbols, he never focused on the processes involved in our *capacity* to use such symbols.

Despite its distinctive stance, and the successes of the cognitive approach thus far, significant challenges remain. One concern is that there is still a great deal of integration to do before the approach can lay claim to being an inclusive perspective on behaviour. While it is clear that problem solving, cognitive dissonance and emotion all involve mediational processes, the descriptions used tend to vary in each area. They are all 'cognitive theories', but as yet there is no *single* cognitive theory which links all these areas in a coherent manner. One can talk about 'operant conditioning', and use the same terms for any type of behaviour one considers, but this is currently not true of the cognitive approach. While this may be partly due to the lack of a single central theorist, whatever the cause, it remains a limitation.

A second problem concerns the use of the information processing model. This metaphor is borrowed from computer science, as reflected in terms like *input*, *storage* and *retrieval* of information. With respect to these terms, computers are infallible: errors are always the result of either human programming errors or equipment malfunctions. People, on the other hand, are clearly fallible. People forget; computers don't. People sometimes ignore available information; computers cannot ignore information provided to them. Given that such differences exist, one must remember that the information processing model is a *metaphor*, and however useful it is in some ways, it also has limitations. (Interestingly, attempts to link cognition to our understanding of the brain are leading to new analogies in terms of neural mechanisms, such as parallel processing in memory.)

In addition, while we are beginning to recognize connections between cognition and emotion, we still lack an emotional approach to cognition. That is, the *motivation* for actions has been largely ignored. Although Kohler recognized that perception and learning can be influenced by a motivational state (for instance, being highly motivated can increase functional fixedness), this aspect was never well developed in Gestalt theory, and has been largely ignored in the cognitive approach. Tolman, in fact, was accused of 'leaving the organism lost in thought' – that is, in distinguishing learning from performance, he failed to explain *why* behaviour occurs. By contrast, although Freud tended to minimize the details of cognitive processes, he *was* vividly aware of the importance of motivational processes. (It has been suggested that this split of cognition and motivation goes back to psychology's philosophical roots, in that philosophers viewed cognition as distinct from emotion and motivation (see Eysenck 1993).)

It remains for the future to solve some of these issues, particularly in terms of creating a general theory of behaviour. In this sense, the cognitive approach is no more perfect as a means of understanding human behaviour than is any other approach. With the trend towards 'cognitive science', we are seeing an increasing interchange among disciplines, including psychology, physiology, computer science and linguistics, and it is possible that dramatic changes lie ahead. There has already been tremendous change, from Tolman's cognitive maps to today's information processing models. Yet even as the metaphors shift, the questions remain largely the same. It is characteristic of human behaviour that we seek to understand the world, including our own actions. And it is characteristic of the cognitive approach that we will continue to ask *how* it is that we understand.

Chapter Summary

- The cognitive approach emphasizes the role of *mediating processes* in human behaviour. The central assumption is that behaviour can best be understood by looking at the processes which come between an environmental stimulus and the behavioural response.

- Models based on the role of mediating processes, such as the *information processing* model, have increased our understanding of phenomena like *memory* and *problem solving*, and also offered practical insights on enhancing their effectiveness.

- Memory is regarded as having three separate stages: *sensory memory*, *short-term memory* (STM) and *long-term memory* (LTM). Each stage has distinctive characteristics, with transfer between stages dependent on *attention*, *rehearsal* and *coding*.

- Forgetting from LTM can be interpreted in terms of either *interference* or *context-dependence*; each interpretation has been productive, though in recent years the concept of context-dependent forgetting seems to have drawn more attention.

- Problem solving involves a series of distinct *stages*. Problems can be described as either *convergent* or *divergent*, depending on the number of possible solutions and the process for reaching a solution.

- While Gestalt psychologists emphasized the importance of an appropriate *mental set* and *insight*, more recent research suggests that problem solving skills involve *learning to learn*.

- In terms of information processing theory, solving a problem requires defining the *initial state*, *goal state* and *operators*, with distinct stages. Generating solutions can involve the use of either *algorithms* or *heuristics*.

- *Language* is an open-ended system of symbolic communication, whose basis may be partially dependent on innate physiological capacities, and partly learned.

- Controversy exists concerning studies of language capacities in other species, particularly primates who have learned sign languages.

- There is an interactive relationship between thinking and language, with the language we use at least partially influencing the way we think.

- The cognitive approach has also been applied to issues of *social cognition* such as *cognitive dissonance* and *attribution theory*. *Cognitive appraisal theory* has been used to understand *emotions*.

Key Terms and Concepts

accessibility
algorithm
availability
cognitive appraisal theory
cognitive dissonance
cognitive map
context-dependent forgetting
convergent problem
creativity
divergent problem
elaborative rehearsal
fundamental attribution error
goal state
heuristic
information processing
initial state
insight
language

learning
long-term memory
maintenance rehearsal
memory
mental set
mnemonics
operator
proactive interference
problem solving
recall
recentring
recognition
reconstruction
retroactive interference
self-serving bias
sensory memory
short-term memory

Suggestions for Further Reading

For readers interested in an overview of the cognitive approach, there are two highly readable accounts: Howard Gardner's *The Mind's New Science: A History of the Cognitive Revolution* provides an entertaining overview, while Bernard Baars allows many of those involved to speak for themselves, via interviews he conducted (*The Cognitive Revolution in Psychology*).

For an overview of memory, Alan Baddeley's *Your Memory: A User's Guide* provides a highly readable, non-technical account by a major researcher.

Edward deBono's books on problem solving are both interesting and entertaining; *Practical Thinking* is perhaps more focused than some of his more recent books.

For a readable survey of all aspects of language, from development to animal studies, try Joel Davis's *Mother Tongue*.

An interesting, albeit slightly idiosyncratic, overview of the study of emotion is provided by Keith Oatley's *Best Laid Plans: The Psychology of Emotion*.

5

The Psychodynamic Approach

Motivation and the Mind
Introduction
Freud and Psychoanalysis
Freud's Assumptions about Behaviour
Exploring the Workings of the Mind
   Freud's Theory of Consciousness
   Dreams and Symbolic Expression
   Drives and the Psychodynamics of Behaviour
Freud's Psychodynamic Model of Personality
Psychosexual Stages of Development
   Oral Stage
   Anal Stage
   Phallic Stage
   Latency Stage

   Genital Stage
Fixation and Regression During Development
Anxiety and Defence Mechanisms
Observing the Unconscious in Behaviour
Assessing Freud's Work
Neo-Freudian and Non-Freudian
   Psychodynamic Theories
Carl Jung and the Collective Unconscious
Alfred Adler and Individual Psychology
Other Psychodynamic Theorists
Conclusion
Chapter Summary
Key Terms and Concepts
Suggestions for Further Reading

Motivation and the Mind

Several years ago, while attending a conference, I attended a preview of a new film about the work of Sigmund Freud. At one point, the film discussed Freud's ideas on development, and referred to the concept of identification, which involves a child copying the behaviour of a parent. To illustrate the concept, the film showed a father and his 5-year-old son doing chores in the yard. Suddenly, the audience (all psychologists) burst into gales of laughter. The film's producer, himself a psychologist, stopped the film to ask what was funny – clearly, he didn't expect it to be humorous. A member of the audience pointed out that the father was showing the boy how to cut a limb from a dead tree using a saw; to the speaker (and also the rest of the audience, including myself), this seemed much too blatant a reference to Freud's concept of castration fear. The film producer, showing a mixture of shock and embarrassment, could only mumble, 'You know, I never thought of it that way – we thought it was just an ordinary activity!'

Even if you know nothing of identification and castration fear, the basic point is clear: the film's content conveyed an obvious meaning of which the film's producer was unaware. One of the central assumptions of Freud's theory is that we are often unaware of the true reasons for our actions. In this incident, the film producer seemed to prove Freud right – ironically, while presenting Freud's ideas!

Introduction

If you were to do a survey in any Western country, asking people who had never taken psychology to name a psychologist, you would be likely to get more people responding 'Freud' than any other figure, past or present. The image of Freud, stroking his beard and pondering the meaning of his patient's words and actions, has become almost a caricature of psychotherapy. As the founder of psychoanalysis, he has had profound impact on the study of behaviour. Yet the approach which he pioneered has also spawned a number of variants; these theories share many of the same assumptions, but differ in their details. Hence it is appropriate to discuss the larger context of psychodynamic theories, as well as Freud's theory.

As discussed in the previous chapter, the cognitive approach deals extensively with mental processes within the person. In this sense, it is similar to the psychodynamic approach. However, one of the major limitations of the cognitive approach is its failure to address questions of intentionality – that is, it does not explain what *motivates* behaviour. By contrast, issues of motivation are central to the psychodynamic approach. As Robinson (1979) has pointed out, concerns about motivation are inevitably linked to the psychology of personality, since intentions must be held by *someone* – i.e. a person. Consistent with this view, psychoanalysis is both a theory of motivation and a theory of personality.

The *psychodynamic approach* can then be considered as focusing on the role of internal processes (e.g. motivation) in shaping personality, and thereby behaviour. In taking personality and motivation as its central focus, it is distinct from any of the approaches we have discussed. To the extent that behaviourism deals with motivation at all, it does so descriptively, in terms of an 'empty organism'. By contrast, inner processes, including notions of self and awareness, are central to the psychodynamic approach. By viewing behaviour within the context of personality, psychodynamic theories focus on the whole person, rather than the discrete mental processes characteristic of the cognitive approach. And while Freud himself was trained in neurology, in practical terms, psychodynamic theories operate at a very different level of description from physiological theories. Thus, the psychodynamic approach differs in important ways from any of the approaches we have considered so far. Since Freud is certainly the pioneer of this approach, let us begin with him.

Sigmund Freud

Sigmund Freud (1856–1939) was born in Moravia (now part of the Czech Republic), the eldest of eight children in a closely knit, middle-class family. He was educated in Vienna, and spent most of his life there. Entering medical school at the University of Vienna, he studied physiology with Ernst Brücke, whom he later described as the most influential person in his life; Brücke's mechanistic views seemed to influence Freud's own later thinking. While Freud seemed drawn to research, his marriage and other practical considerations led him to become a doctor, which offered greater economic rewards and recognition. In 1885 he received a post-degree fellowship to study with Jean Charcot, a leading French doctor. Through Charcot, Freud learned about hysteria disorders and techniques of hypnosis – both of which were to play a role in his later career.

Upon returning to Vienna to practise, he specialized in neurological disorders (including hysteria), and became a leading figure in the area – a focus which eventually led to his search for new treatments and explanations. In 1919, well after he had become known for his writings on psychoanalysis, he was granted the title of professor at the University of Vienna. In 1923, he underwent the first of a long series of operations for cancer of the jaw. As the cancer ate at his body, he also suffered social torments. Raised a Jew, he became concerned about the anti-Semitism of the growing Nazi party in Germany – his books were burned in a Berlin bonfire in 1933, where he was called an 'enemy of the state'. When Germany annexed Austria in 1938, Freud was reluctantly persuaded by family and friends to move to London. These personal and political concerns seem to be reflected in the dark tone of *Civilization and Its Discontents*, his last major work. He died in London in 1939 at the age of eighty-three.

Freud and Psychoanalysis

Freud is probably one of the most complex, and most gifted, figures in the history of psychology. A contemporary of both James and Pavlov, he has become better known than either. By his own reckoning, expressed on several occasions, he was one of the three most important figures in the history of Western science (Copernicus and Darwin being the other two). While this can be considered a form of exaggeration, there is no question that many Freudian concepts have become household words, including *ego*, *unconscious* and *Freudian slip*. More so than most of the theories we have considered, the man and his ideas are intertwined. (For one thing, his analysis of his own life significantly influenced his theorizing.) So, let us begin by briefly setting the context of his life.

Sigmund Freud was born in Moravia (now part of the Czech Republic) in 1856, the eldest of eight children in a closely knit, middle-class family. Since his father had remarried, Freud actually had two elder half-brothers; as a result, he had a nephew who was slightly older than him! He was educated in Vienna, and spent most of his life there. Entering medical school at the University of Vienna, he studied physiology with Ernst Brücke, whom he later described as the most influential person in his life (Fancher 1979).

Brücke favoured a mechanistic view of both physiology and behaviour, which probably influenced Freud's own later thinking. Freud seemed to relish doing research in Brücke's lab, but practical considerations (including marriage) led him to focus instead on his medical studies, which offered greater economic rewards and recognition. He finished his degree in 1881, and in 1885 won a six-month fellowship to study with Jean Charcot, a leading French doctor who was interested in *hysteria* (neurological symptoms with no neurological basis) and hypnosis – both of which were to play a role in Freud's later career.

Upon returning to Vienna to practise, he specialized in neurological disorders, and became a leading figure in the area – a focus which eventually led to his search for new treatments and explanations. In 1919, well after he had become known for his writings on psychoanalysis, he was granted the title of professor at the University of Vienna. Life was not without problems, however. In 1923, he was diagnosed with cancer of the jaw – a disease which ultimately killed him. In addition, the rise of anti-Semitism forced Freud (who was raised as a Jew) to leave Nazi Germany in 1938 for London. He died there a year later at the age of 83, having outlived both James and Pavlov. (Given the connections between Freud's life and work, we will return to some details of his life in the course of discussing his theory.)

Freud's Assumptions about Behaviour

As with other approaches, it is helpful to note some of the assumptions Freud made in developing his theory. As noted, his early training in physiology under Brücke had a significant influence on his thinking. One of Freud's most fundamental assumptions, psychic determinism, was partially derived from Brücke's ideas. **Psychic determinism** states that all behaviour has a cause (i.e. is determined), and that the cause is to be found in the mind (*psyche* in Greek). While Freud seemed to believe that ultimately his ideas could be reduced to physiological principles, he recognized that such a goal was not yet attainable, and instead focused on mental constructs (*id*, *ego* etc.). His work in physiology also converged with another influence – Darwin's work on evolution, which had been recently published (*The Descent of Man* 1871). The notion of biological continuity across species convinced Freud that human motivation is based on biologically-based *innate drives*. (Note that, writing in German, Freud used the word *Trieb*, which in his usage is best translated as 'drive'; however, early translations into English used the word 'instinct'.)

Another form of assumed continuity is also crucial to understanding Freud's theory: the *continuity of normal and abnormal behaviour*. In this regard, Freud accepted the enlightened view of mental illness pioneered by Phillipe Pinel roughly 100 years earlier. (Pinel, while the head of the French asylum at Bicêtre, argued that mental disorders represented an illness, rather than spirit possession or degeneracy, as was then commonly believed.) By taking this viewpoint, Freud was not only taking a humane attitude towards his patients; he was also justifying the use of clinical data in supporting a

psychic determinism the assumption made by Freud which states that all behaviour has a cause, and that the cause is to be found in the mind

theory of normal personality. Since he believed normal and abnormal behaviour differed only in degree, not in kind, he felt justified in mixing the two types of observations in his theorizing.

The third assumption, and perhaps the best known, was Freud's belief that much of behaviour is governed by processes that lie outside the individual's awareness – that is, are *unconscious*. (This will be elaborated in the next section.)

The last point to consider is that although Freud was trained as an experimentalist (in Brücke's lab), most of his career was spent as a clinician, and he used *clinical observations* as his primary data. While he was as gifted an observer as he was a writer, clinical observations (i.e. *case studies*) are inevitably limited in drawing conclusions. (As noted in Chapter 1, small samples, problems of representativeness and no control of causation all pose problems.) Since case studies represent a significant source of evidence for Freud's theory, we will have to return to this issue after discussing the theory itself.

Taken together, psychic determinism, the biological origins of motivation, the importance of the unconscious and the emphasis on clinical data are the foundation on which Freud erected his ideas. (Note that these assumptions are consistent with the general emphasis on motivation and past experience found in all psychodynamic theories, but are more specific.) Having noted these points, we should explore the substance of Freud's work.

For further consideration	The notion that normal and abnormal behaviour differs only in degree is central to Freud's theory. Do you accept this idea? Do you think our society supports it?

Exploring the Workings of the Mind

At the outset of his career, Freud attempted to specialize in cases of organic brain damage, and his work on cerebral palsy in children and on aphasia (a neurologically-based language disorder) was met with approval by the medical community. However, treatable cases of neurological disorders were relatively rare, and so he began treating patients with **hysteria** – disorders in which there are physical symptoms for which there is no apparent physical cause. (The term was used long before Freud; its origin, from the Greek for 'uterus', reflected a common belief that only women could show the symptoms – an idea Freud himself rejected in 1886.) Although neurology had advanced to the point where doctors could rule out physical causes, they were nonetheless confounded by the paradoxical nature of these disorders, and their inability to relieve the evident suffering of their mostly female patients. For example, in the phenomenon of *glove anaesthesia*, the patient complains of loss of feeling in the hand, as if it were covered by a glove. Neurologically, this poses a problem, since the pattern of nerves extends along the top of the forearm and back of the hand, and along the underside of the forearm and palm of the hand; consequently, it is nearly impossible to have neurological damage which affects the *entire* hand, and *no* part of the forearm.

hysteria a disorder characterized by physical symptoms for which there is no apparent physical cause; the term was used by Freud but actually predates him

Like most doctors, Freud tried a number of techniques to treat hysteria, not always successfully. Two events were to point him in a new direction, which eventually led to the development of psychoanalysis. First, he had studied with Charcot, who used hypnosis in treating hysteria. Second, a Viennese colleague, Joseph Breuer, had reported successfully treating a case of hysteria by using hypnosis to prompt the recall of experiences associated with the onset of symptoms. Breuer found that re-experiencing the situation, which was usually emotional or even traumatic, produced relief from the associated symptom. In one case, a patient had developed a squint while trying to hold back tears at the bedside of her dying father. When she later was able to re-experience the situation, and express the grief she had hidden at the time, her symptom disappeared. While Breuer himself did not routinely deal with hysterias, his report intrigued Freud, who began his own explorations of the method. He quickly concluded that hypnosis was merely a tool; the process of recalling emotionally-charged experiences was the key factor. Freud concluded that recalling the traumatic event produced a release of emotional tension called **catharsis**. The striking thing about this discovery, easily overlooked from today's perspective, was that Freud was proposing that the *body* could be affected by processes within the *mind*! How was this possible? Freud began an exploration of the relations between mind and body which was to occupy the remainder of his life – over fifty years.

Abandoning hypnosis, he developed the technique of **free association**, in which the patient says aloud whatever thoughts come into mind. Such thoughts were often jumbled and fragmentary, with no apparent patterns; however, listening to these thoughts, and occasionally asking questions, Freud would gradually see a pattern emerge, which typically climaxed in a highly emotional recall of forgotten events. The memory of these events had been *repressed* – blocked from conscious awareness. In turn, these repressed events were expressed through physical symptoms that were either directly *or symbolically* connected with the blocked memories. (Since Freud believed behaviour always had a cause, a lack of *direct* connection would not be taken as implying that no connection existed.) Frequently, recall of a traumatic memory would produce relief, though in some cases, symptoms were *overdetermined* – that is, there were multiple events contributing to the symptom, each of which had to be uncovered and re-experienced.

Freud's Theory of Consciousness

The discovery of a connection between repressed memories and behaviour led Freud to propose a novel concept: that awareness is divided into different levels of consciousness. Those thoughts and feelings which we are aware of at a given moment are part of the **conscious** mind. Much like William James's 'stream of consciousness' (a phrase coined at about the same point in time), the conscious mind, in Freud's view, is filled with a passing parade of ideas and emotions. Yet there is much more to the mind than this window of awareness; much of the content of the mind is **subconscious** – that is, below the level of conscious awareness. The subconscious is divided into

catharsis the release of drive energy in indirect form, through either the process of recalling emotionally charged experiences or involvement in symbolic activity

free association a technique originated by Freud for studying the mind, based on asking a person to say whatever words came into their mind, and then looking for patterns

conscious in Freud's theory, that aspect of the mind which contains those thoughts and feelings of which we are immediately aware at a given moment
subconscious in Freud's theory, the portions of the mind which are below the level of conscious awareness

preconscious in Freud's theory, that part of the subconscious mind which can be accessed by deliberate choice

unconscious in Freud's theory, that portion of the subconscious which cannot be directly accessed by the conscious mind; nonetheless, impulses and thoughts from the unconscious can 'leak out' in fragmentary intrusions into conscious awareness, either directly or in symbolic form

two levels: the preconscious and the unconscious. The **preconscious** contains all those thoughts, memories and emotions which we are not presently aware of, but which can be brought into the conscious mind by deliberate choice. By contrast, the **unconscious**, which may be much larger, contains all those ideas, experiences and feelings which are blocked from conscious awareness by the power of *repression*. The unconscious cannot be directly accessed by the conscious mind, but its contents 'leak out' in fragmentary intrusions into conscious awareness, either directly or in symbolic form. And, of course, the contents of the unconscious can cause pathology, as Freud found in treating hysteria.

Today, the average person readily accepts the concept that consciousness is divided. Indeed, Freud's idea that mental events can occur outside of our awareness has become so widely known that it has become part of everyday language, as when someone says, 'I did it unconsciously.' However, its popularity does not automatically prove its validity, and the reality is that any *direct* proof is essentially unobtainable. (It is also worth noting that there are cultures, notably in Asia, where the notion of the unconscious does not traditionally exist.) Nonetheless, over time, a range of evidence has been collected supporting the idea that unconscious events can influence our behaviour (Greenwald 1992; Kihlstrom *et al.* 1992). One example is the influence of subliminal verbal stimuli (too brief to be consciously recognized) on behaviour. The basic concept is that phrases which have emotional significance will influence the unconscious, even if the individual is not consciously aware of the message. In one such study, male college students presented with the phrase 'beating Dad is OK' before playing darts scored higher than those seeing the phrase 'beating him is wrong', who in turn did better than students presented with 'beating Dad is wrong' (Palumbo and Gillman 1984). Reviewing 56 studies using variations of this situation, Hardaway (1990) concluded that the effect, although small, is real. Interestingly, even memory researcher Elizabeth Loftus, who is critical of many aspects of Freud's theory, has concluded that unconscious processes exist (Loftus and Klinger 1992).

For Freud, the unconscious was a powerful concept, and a powerful force in behaviour: thoughts and feelings which a patient didn't even realize existed could manifest themselves in physical symptoms. While Freud found that gaining access to the unconscious helped his patients, he was still faced with a problem: how can thoughts have such power to distort behaviour? To understand how Freud solved this question, we need to return to the cases he dealt with.

Initially, almost all his patients were middle-class women, living in the rather repressive culture of the Victorian age, in which women had rigidly prescribed roles as wives and mothers. Freud found that many of the experiences that they recalled were sexual in nature, often of assaults by family members or friends. This led him to propose that hysterias were the result of traumas which were always sexual in origin. Breuer could not accept this, and Freud reported later that most of his colleagues greeted the concept with shock and rejection. (It is difficult in this context to separate the realities from Freud's perception. In point of fact, the idea of pathology having a sexual origin was not new with Freud, having already been proposed in the work of Kraft-Ebbing and Havelock Ellis (see Robinson 1979).) Freud himself found it difficult to accept that sexual abuse could occur on the scale suggested by his patients' reports. His own doubts, combined with the lack of support from his colleagues, gradually led him to the conclusion that the events recalled were not true memories at all. (Interestingly, recent trends in research on sexual abuse make it seem more likely that the reports may have been true (e.g. Faller 1988).) But this posed a further dilemma: if they were not true, where did they come from? And how could false memories have such a powerful effect on the body?

Dreams and Symbolic Expression

Freud found answers to his questions about the role of false memories in his research on dreams. He was already aware of his patients' dreams, and had been interested in his own dreams from an early age – in *The Interpretation of Dreams*, he reported a dream which first occurred when he was about ten, portions of which later appeared in his adult dreams (Freud 1900). As he analysed these dreams, he came to the conclusion that dreams operate on two levels: the manifest content and the latent content. The **manifest content** is what the conscious mind is aware of, both during sleep and on waking. For example, one of Freud's female patients dreamt that she was holding a banquet, but had to cancel it because she had no food. However, this manifest content is merely the symbolic expression of the true meaning, called the **latent content**. In the above case (reported in *The Interpretation of Dreams*), the patient was recently married, and very jealous of other women. One woman in particular was of concern to the patient, but her husband had reassured her that the rival was too thin to be attractive. By dreaming of a banquet with no food, Freud explained, she was expressing the desire that the other woman remain thin, and therefore non-threatening.

This dream expresses two characteristics of Freud's theory of dreams. First, he believed that dreams were basically motivated by **wish fulfilment** – expressing fantasies that were not acceptable or even possible in real life. Second, it shows how the actual nature of the dream (the latent content) is transformed into something less threatening to the conscious mind (the manifest content). The mechanism of this process was what Freud called the **dream censor**, whose function is to ensure that sleep is not disturbed by the unconsciously expressed desires that are the basis of dreams. To accomplish this, the dream censor converts the content of the dream into *symbolic* form (the *manifest content*). Thus, in order to understand the meaning of a dream (the *latent content*), one must interpret the symbolism expressed in what the person recalls. In therapy, this was rendered easier by the other knowledge Freud had of the patient, from direct report, from free association and from other observations. In addition, Freud came to believe that some forms of symbols are nearly universal (e. g. swords as phallic symbols, money as faeces). Recognizing common symbols was helpful to Freud when colleagues (or even strangers on the street) challenged him to interpret dreams. (In at least one case, Freud interpreted a dream described in a letter (see Benjamin and Dixon 1996).) Still, Freud felt that the majority of symbols were personal, and he regarded dream interpretation as a serious

manifest content the symbolic content of a dream (disguised by the dream censor) which the conscious mind is aware of, both during sleep and on waking

latent content in Freud's theory of dreams, the true meaning of a dream, which is transformed by the dream censor into symbolic form as the manifest content

wish fulfilment in Freud's theory, the symbolic expression of drives in fantasy form, as in dreams

dream censor the psychic mechanism whose function is to ensure that sleep is not disturbed by the unconsciously expressed desires that are the basis of dreams; to accomplish this, the dream censor converts the content of the dream into symbolic form (the manifest content)

technique for gaining insight into the unconscious mind, not as a parlour game. (The issue of symbolism will be discussed further in this chapter.)

Having decided that dreams were based on wish fulfilment, Freud returned to the subject of hysteria, and decided that, in a similar way, his patient's vivid descriptions were fantasies, not real events. This had at least two advantages. First, it produced a theoretical symmetry, in that both phenomena (hysteria and dreams) were now based on the same process (wish fulfilment). Second, it tended to placate his critics, who were incensed at his suggestion that sexual abuse was the source of all hysterias. Coupled with successes in treating a number of patients, this new interpretation led Freud to feel that he was indeed on the right track in understanding the mind. (The role of abuse in hysteria, and the reasons for Freud changing his interpretation, have generated considerable controversy, as we discuss later in this chapter.) His biggest question still remained, however: what was the force that *motivated* these processes?

<table>
<tr><td>

For further consideration

</td><td>

Do you ever remember your dreams? You might try keeping a pad of paper and a pencil by your bed for a week, and try writing down dream images as soon as you awaken. Do they make sense to you? How do you think Freud felt when he first explored dreams?

</td></tr>
</table>

Drives and the Psychodynamics of Behaviour

As noted previously, Freud's own training in physiology, coupled with the ideas of Darwin, led him to believe that there was a biological continuity between humans and other species. This meant that the basic forces driving human behaviour were not greatly different from those driving animal behaviour. Survival needs, including the need for food, water and shelter, were obviously basic. In addition, the pressure for species survival made procreation (and therefore sexuality) a powerful force. As he worked with his patients and strove to understand both their behaviour and his own, Freud wrestled with the question of how to describe these biological forces. At first, he thought that motivation could be described in terms of the desire to maximize pleasure (*Lust* in German), and to avoid that which was unpleasant (*Unlust*). This concept, which he dubbed the **pleasure principle**, was similar to the well-known philosophical concept of *hedonism* (a term coined by Jeremy Bentham in 1789). (One might compare the pleasure principle to Thorndike's *law of effect*, proposed at about the same time, and likewise influenced by Bentham.)

pleasure principle an early description by Freud of the basis of human motivation, which stated we are driven to maximize pleasure (*Lust* in German), and to avoid that which is unpleasant (*Unlust*)

Of all the basic biological forces, Freud felt that sexuality was the most powerful, and for many years he conceived of it as the central force in behaviour. (It is worth noting, however, that Freud conceived of sexual energy in broader terms than simply adult sexual behaviour; all forms of physical, sensuous pleasure were based on the sexual drive.) This view gradually led him to develop a second model of motivation, building on the importance of sexuality. Freud first proposed this idea in a set of essays in 1905, but continued to reassess his thinking as time went on. By 1920, he had come to the conclusion that pleasure (sexuality) alone could not account for the behaviours and phenomena he observed (including sadism and masochism). This led him to argue for two basic drives, commonly referred to as *sexuality* and *aggression*; the change was described in *Beyond the Pleasure Principle* (Freud 1920).

By the time Freud wrote *Beyond the Pleasure Principle*, he had gone through many experiences, both professionally and personally. Between 1906 and 1920, not only had he received greater recognition for his work, but he had gone from middle age to the gateway of old age (he was 64 when *Beyond the Pleasure Principle* was published). In addition, the First World War had occurred, with horrors previously unimaginable. To the rationalist culture of the late nineteenth century, this was a stunning shock. It was in this context that Freud introduced aggression as being equal to sexuality as a basic drive. For most Freudians, this stage of his thinking represents the main form of his theory.

However, Freud was to approach the issue of motivation yet again, ten years later. In *Civilization and Its Discontents*, he offered a sombre analysis of the nature of human society, and the drives which direct all human activity (Freud 1930). The horrors of the First World War, and the signs of growing Nazi sentiment in Germany, led him to be somewhat pessimistic about the future of humanity (we will return to this issue later, in discussing defence mechanisms). Hence, he again revised his description of the motivating forces, referring now to Eros (named after the Greek god of Love) and Thanatos (the Greek representation of Death). *Eros* was seen as a positive, life-affirming force, expressed in human creative activities, including procreation (hence the link to earlier notions of a sexual drive). *Thanatos*, as its name implied, was a destructive energy, expressed both in aggression towards others, and in self-destructive behaviour. (It is interesting that Freud came to this view after witnessing the First World War, and discovering he had cancer of the jaw – a condition possibly linked to his passion for smoking cigars.) Like his earlier concepts of motivation, Eros and Thanatos were seen as seeking continual expression and satisfaction. However, for the first time, he saw the two drives as also conflicting with each other. In fact, Freud ends *Civilization and Its Discontents* by describing Eros as caught in a struggle to assert himself against his adversary Thanatos – and wondering what the outcome will be. Such comments suggest not simply a shift in theoretical viewpoint, but also a profound sadness, and possibly despair. Whether that means the theoretical shift is simply due to personal bias, is hard to say. Zangwill, a psychologist but not a psychoanalyst, and an admirer of Freud the man, has simply said, 'though some of his [later] ideas are of great interest, their empirical foundation [is] decidedly weaker' (Zangwill 1987: 269).

As psychoanalyst Charles Brenner and many others writers have noted, Freud's writings sometimes pose a problem for those who wish to describe 'Freud's theory' (Brenner 1957). In grappling with the puzzles of motivation, he was forced to *infer* the nature of the underlying drives from the observed effects on behaviour. Given the complexity of human behaviour, this is a difficult and uncertain process. Not surprisingly, therefore, Freud himself sometimes had doubts about his descriptions, and would revise his thinking. In terms of discussing his work, the difficulty comes from the fact that he was a prolific writer (his collected works fill 24 volumes), and in writing did not always make explicit when he was repudiating his earlier work. In addition, not all Freudian psychoanalysts necessarily agree with his later work, making it harder still to determine what is the 'true' version of Freud's thinking. In the end, it is better to acknowledge the variations than to offer conclusions.

Clearly, there are difficulties in discussing Freud's conception of motivation, but the difficulties are also inherent in the underlying problem: we can *observe* behaviour, but must *infer* the reasons for it. (Even the behaviourists, in opting for a descriptive model based on stimuli and responses, are making inferences about the causal nature of such connections.) Without getting into issues of Freud's intent, we will adhere to the generally accepted form, using the terms *sexuality* and *aggression* when discussing how the expression of drives fits into Freud's theory.

Thus far, we have seen how Freud dealt with two fundamental issues: the structure of consciousness, and the nature of the drives that motivate behaviour. This still leaves the large question of how these forces are expressed in behaviour. What determines, for example, whether something becomes repressed? And how do the basic drives result in the wondrous variety of human behaviour? For Freud, these questions were answered by the development of a psychodynamic model of personality.

| **For further consideration** | Which of Freud's three motivational models makes the most sense to you? Can you think of an example of behaviour (your own, or that of someone you know) that seems to support this interpretation? |

Freud's Psychodynamic Model of Personality

Freud's early theorizing was closely linked to his clinical observations, dealing with hysteria and neuroses. (A *neurosis* is a disorder in which high levels of anxiety are a primary symptom.) As such, his initial model was a model of pathological behaviour, not a general model of personality. However, by the time of writing his *Three Essays on Sexuality* in 1905, he was discussing general human behaviour, not just pathology. The fullest formulation of his model came with the publication of *The Ego and the Id* in 1923.

Much as in his analysis of the structure of consciousness, Freud conceived of personality in terms of a three-part structure: the id, ego and superego. The **id** (Latin for 'it') was the source of all basic drives; from the moment of birth, we are driven to try to obtain gratification of our needs. Motivation was seen as based on *tension-reduction*: when a drive is active, we experience it as a form of tension, which we seek to reduce by obtaining the appropriate form of gratification. In Freud's view, a young infant is concerned only with obtaining what it needs – for example, if it is hungry or wet, it cries until its demands are met. To the infant, there is no right or wrong, no past or future, simply the pressing immediacy of its desire for gratification. The id lacks any sort of conception of reality, and consequently cannot distinguish between reality and fantasy; in this form of thinking, called **primary process thinking**, a wish and its fulfilment are equivalent, with no reference to reality. Thus, a hungry infant may conjure up an image

id (Latin for 'it') in Freud's theory, the element of the psyche which is the source of all basic drives

primary process thinking in Freud's theory, a form of thinking characteristic of the id in which no distinction is made between a wish and its fulfilment

of its mother's breast as a way of reducing the tension associated with hunger. Of course, since the image cannot provide food, such primary process thinking provides only a limited form of tension reduction.

In an adult, the demands of id normally operate outside conscious awareness – we may experience the tension, but be unable to identify the source. In other cases, the focus of gratification may shift. For example, hunger may be satisfied by making a sandwich, going to a restaurant for a steak or a range of other behaviours. The specific food, and the process for obtaining it, can vary; what remains constant is the tension induced by hunger. Some years ago, a popular song had the line, 'If you can't be with the one you love, then love the one you're with.' Like many song lyrics, this can be seen as supporting Freud's view.

superego in Freud's theory, that portion of the psyche which represents the moral demands of family and society, and is therefore governed by moral constraints

Opposing the demands of id is the **superego** ('over the ego'), which is governed by moral constraints. Roughly speaking, it is the 'conscience' of the person (not to be confused with 'conscious'). Superego represents the moral demands of family and society, and opposes the desire of id for immediate gratification. (Sometimes this is referred to as the 'morality principle', but Freud did not use the term.) Not surprisingly, Freud saw id and superego as being fundamentally in conflict, since they attempt to direct behaviour in very different ways.

ego (Latin for 'I') in psychoanalysis, the element of the psyche which provides the integrating of personality by mediating between the id and the superego, and also mediates the links with the outside world
reality principle in Freud's theory, the constraints imposed on the ego by the recognition of the demands of the environment

Mediating between the id and superego is the **ego** (Latin for 'I'), which provides the integrating of personality, and also mediates the links with the outside world. Ego provides the sense of self which is central to personality, yet it must also cope with the demands of id, superego and the external world. Because it must contend with constraints imposed by the real world, ego is described as governed by the **reality principle**. Ego's task is not an easy one, since it must deal with three very different sorts of demands, two of which (id and superego) are fundamentally irreconcilable. This means that conflict is a fact of life within personality, and the varying demands of id, superego and external world require a continuing balancing act by ego. The ways in which it does so are what determine behaviour. For example, a teenage boy sees an exotic sports car sitting parked, with the keys visible within. Id will see an opportunity to race around in a fast and powerful vehicle. Superego will insist that such behaviour would be stealing, and is morally wrong. Ego may note that people are walking on the street, and therefore the chances of being caught are very high. Thus, in this case, the outcome would probably be *not* to steal the car.

There is no hard and fast rule determining how ego resolves the ongoing conflicts within personality. Freud suggested, for example, that sometimes individuals will respond to the moral demands of superego even when this conflicts with external reality – as when a person risks his or her life to help another person. In other cases, ego may allow id's demands for gratification, despite the opposing demands of superego – as when a child impulsively steals a chocolate bar from a supermarket.

secondary process thinking in Freud's theory, a form of thinking used by the ego to direct the gratification of drives; unlike primary process thinking, secondary process thinking is accessible to conscious awareness, and recognizes constraints imposed by the external world

Ego is capable of rational thought, which Freud called **secondary process thinking**. Unlike the *primary process thinking* of the id, in which a wish and its fulfilment are synonymous, ego perceives gratification in terms of the constraints of the external world. Secondary process thinking also differs from primary process thinking in that it is accessible to the conscious mind,

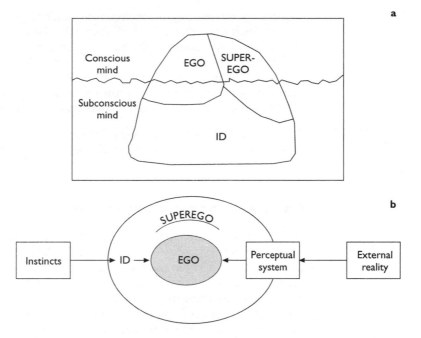

Figure 5.1 Graphic representations of Freud's theory Many people have sought to present Freud's ideas in graphic form. The iceberg model at the top emphasizes that the id is unconscious, while the ego and superego are mostly conscious. Freud himself proposed a vector model, emphasizing the various forces which bear on the ego. (Lower figure adapted from Fancher 1979.)

whereas primary process thinking cannot be directly accessed in conscious awareness. Only in limited circumstances, such as dreams, the physical symptoms of hysteria, and the symbolism of artistic expression, does our conscious awareness make contact with the primitive nature of primary process thinking.

As suggested by the preceding, the relationship between the three aspects of personality and consciousness is rather complex. Primary process thinking was seen as characteristic of the id, which is unconscious. According to the descriptions in *The Ego and the Id*, Freud believed ego was largely conscious, and that much of the contents of superego were also available to the conscious mind.

The complex relationships in Freud's psychodynamic model have often led to attempts to represent the theory visually. For example, the observation that ego and superego are largely conscious, while id is not, has led to a frequently-used analogy, in which ego and superego are at the top of an iceberg, with id at the bottom (see Figure 5.1a). The part of the iceberg which is above water is the conscious mind; that which is *visible* under the surface of the water is the preconscious; while the very bottom of the iceberg, where id lurks, cannot be seen from the surface – this is the unconscious mind. Like any analogy, this image has its limitations – not the least of which is the tendency to see the mind as discrete boxes, instead of dynamic processes. An alternative is to describe personality in terms of the forces which press on ego, as in Figure 5.1b. Here, one can see that ego is at the centre of the mind, with the forces of drives (id), morality (superego) and reality all converging – and conflicting. It is ego's responsibility to maintain the integrity of personality. This task is not easy, but as ego interacts with the world, it continues to develop. To understand this, we need to look at Freud's model of personality development.

For further consideration

Tom is married, but finds himself attracted to Sarah, a co-worker. Suggest how Tom's behaviour could be explained in terms of Freud's psychodynamic model.

Psychosexual Stages of Development

While the notion that our lives pass through stages was not invented by Freud (for example, Shakespeare referred to 'the stages of man'), he was the first to offer a detailed psychological model of human development based on stages. In one sense, stages are a counter-intuitive concept, since we experience our lives, day-to-day, as a more or less continual progression. Birthdays, graduations and other landmark events occur, but their timing is largely social, and bears no necessary relationship to underlying psychological processes. So what led Freud to conclude that there are discrete stages?

To understand Freud's model of development, one must bear in mind the importance he placed on biological drives. Throughout life, our behaviour is motivated by the need to satisfy our basic drives; however, Freud believed that the expression of these drives changes during the course of our lives. The objects which are the focus of gratification change, and so does the *mode of gratification* – that is, the area of the body which is the centre for gratification. Note that sexuality is not simply genital stimulation. It is also expressed through many parts of the body, called *erogenous zones*. Even as adults we can derive pleasure from our skin – a cool cloth applied to our neck on a hot day, a light touch on the arm to reassure us, and many other experiences. But at particular points during development, drive energy will be particularly focused on specific body regions (erogenous zones). It is the shifts in mode of gratification, associated with different erogenous zones, that define the stages of development. Since these stages reflect differences in the expression of (sexual) drive energy, associated with changes in the functioning of the mind (psyche), they are called *psychosexual stages of development*. Altogether, Freud concluded that there are five stages, the first four of which occur in childhood. These stages also play a central role in the development of personality.

Oral Stage

oral stage in Freud's theory of development, the first stage, extending from birth to about 15 months, when the focus of gratification is on the mouth

The first stage is the **oral stage**, when the focus of gratification is on the mouth. An infant is gratified by the pleasures of nursing; it cries to express its anger and frustration. In this context, nursing is not just a means of obtaining food – it is a primary source of pleasure, through oral stimulation. The new-born infant is governed by its drives – that is, only id is present at birth. It is a world dominated by immediate gratification and the 'magical' powers of primary process thinking, where wish and fulfilment merge. Yet the child also has an interest in its surroundings, and its explorations are also linked to oral gratification—for example, if a six-month-old baby girl is given a new object, the first thing she is likely to do is try to put it in her mouth. As infants develop teeth, biting becomes a way of expressing anger, but is also used to gain pleasure – my niece, for example, used to chew on the rails of her crib! From observations like these, Freud concluded that oral activity is so dominant because it provides the primary means of gratification – hence, the oral stage.

Anal Stage

anal stage the second stage of psychosexual development (fifteen months to three years); during this stage the focus of drive energy shifts to the lower end of the digestive tract, and the major conflict is toilet training

At around fifteen months of age (the time boundaries of the stages are not precise), the focus of drive energy begins to shift. This shift of drive energy from the mouth and upper digestive tract to the lower end of the digestive tract characterizes the **anal stage**. Given the shift in focus of gratification, pleasure comes primarily from the process of elimination, and activities related to it (including handling of faeces). This stage also sees the emergence of ego, based on the child's experiences with their surroundings.

The beginnings of ego are seen in the development of body image – the recognition that one's body is distinctly different from the rest of the environment. For instance, if an angry toddler hits the wall with a hand, the hand will feel the impact, but the child is not aware of how it affects the wall. By contrast, if the child hits her own face with her hand, both the hand and the face register the impact. Through such experiences, the child begins to recognize the boundaries of self. A second type of experience involves delays in receiving gratification. Id is responsive only to the inner drives, and when gratification is sought, the child wants it *now*! However, even the most attentive parent cannot respond so fully that the child never has to wait – so, inevitably, the child learns that gratification is not immediate. At first, the child will use primary process imagery to try to cope – for example, conjuring up the image of the mother's breast while waiting for the mother to answer his cries. This is ultimately inadequate, but the child does gradually come to realize that he can initiate actions which lead to gratification. Infant specialists sometimes speak of babies 'settling', at around two months of age. Before this time, their crying often seems purposeless – as if the infant doesn't know why they are crying. After this period, they begin to be calmer, and their crying seems more connected to specific wants. This change may well reflect the realization that crying can be used productively, to call attention to specific needs. (Parents can often distinguish between a 'hungry' cry and a 'wet' cry, for example.) Thus, delays in gratification ultimately lead to the realization that behaviour can be directed towards satisfying needs.

By the time the child enters the anal stage, these experiences have initiated the beginnings of ego. As infants becomes toddlers, they gradually exert greater control over both their own body and their surroundings – crawling, walking, grasping objects of interest, and so on. By the age of two, they have made dramatic advances, including the first beginnings of language. At this stage, they are likely to encounter another major challenge: toilet training.

(Again, the timing is not exact; in the Victorian era when Freud made most of his observations, the tendency was probably to toilet train somewhat earlier than is the norm in our culture today.)

Toilet training poses the first major conflict between the demands of id and the external world. For the child, bowel movements are intensely pleasurable. (Remember the focus on the anus as an erogenous zone at this stage.) Further, their own faeces are of significant interest – after all, they are produced by the child's body, so there is an intimate connection. Many a parent has witnessed two-year-olds who wish to play with their faeces, or who are dismayed at the prospect that their faeces will simply be flushed away. Parents, of course, take a very different view, seeing faeces as smelly, messy and germ-laden. To the extent that the parents impose demands about toilet training, the child for the first time is faced with a major conflict between the id and the external world: the choice is between heeding the demands of id and heeding the demands of the parents. Heeding the id means risking the negative reactions of the parents, who are the most important figures in the child's world; heeding the parents means denying the demands of id, which is the source of all motivation. The resolution of this conflict may be gradual and relatively untraumatic, or intense and stormy, depending on both the timing of the process and the parents' method of handling the situation. If the child tries to accommodate, and the parents are moderate, the child may gradually learn that self-control is useful, and that there can be value to order and cleanliness. If the parents place too much emphasis on this outcome, the child may become excessively concerned about cleanliness and discipline, laying the pattern for compulsive neatness and related behaviours in later life. On the other hand, if the child decides to heed the demands of id rather than parents, the conflict is likely to be more intense. If the parents use harsh punishment, the child will eventually comply, but at the cost of a weakened sense of self (it is the parents, not ego, controlling the situation), and possibly a lifelong resentment towards authority figures (for which the parents are the prototype). On the other hand, if parents give in when the child resists, the child may never fully learn to balance the demands of id against the realities of the external world. Not only could this lead to a sloppy, self-indulgent adult, but it may seriously hamper the development of ego.

These scenarios point out one of the significant features of Freud's model of development: while the order and approximate timing of the stages is fixed and universal, each individual will have different experiences, and will respond to them differently. To varying degrees, all childhood experiences affect personality in the adult; those most laden with emotion are likely to be the most influential, particularly if the conflicts involved are not adequately resolved. As the old saying has it, 'the child is the father to the man'. This aspect of development will be discussed further after we have considered the other stages.

Phallic Stage

As the ego grows stronger, through dealing with the conflict of toilet training and other experiences, the child begins to move into the third stage, which

phallic stage the third stage of development, extending from about 3 to 5 years of age, during which gratification is focused on the genitals, although not in the form of adult sexuality

again is marked by a shift in the mode of gratification. In the **phallic stage**, from about three to five years of age, gratification is focused on the genitals. In Freud's day (and sometimes even today) the concept of childhood sexuality was seen as shocking, in part because it was interpreted in adult terms. Obviously, young children are still physically immature, and the expression of the drive is not the same as in an adult. However, they *do* seek gratification, and genital stimulation (to note one example) is experienced as pleasurable. Parents often find that children show an increased awareness of their body, including genitals, at this age, and a curiosity about other people's bodies. For example, four-year-olds may take off their clothes to 'play doctor' with each other. A boy may ask his mother if she has a penis, or may want to see her body. Boys, like adult males, will sometimes have erections while sleeping. A girl may suddenly become jealous when her father is affectionate to her mother. All these behaviours indicated to Freud that the genitals have become a focus of gratification – hence the *phallic* stage (after the Greek word for penis).

Oedipal conflict in Freud's theory of development, the major conflict associated with the phallic stage which challenges the developing ego; named after the Greek story of Oedipus, who unknowingly killed his father and married his mother

As with the anal stage, the phallic stage is associated with a major conflict which challenges the developing ego. This conflict is called the **Oedipal conflict,** and is named after the Greek story of Oedipus, who unknowingly killed his father and married his mother. While the dynamics of the conflict are somewhat different for boys and for girls, Freud used the term Oedipal conflict to refer to both sexes. Early on, some analysts proposed calling the female variant the 'Electra conflict' (after Oedipus's sister), but Freud himself did not use the term (see Freud 1924). The central focus of the Oedipal conflict is the attachment to the parents, who as caregivers have become the focus of drive energy (and therefore attraction). Depending on family circumstances, the mother is typically the primary caregiver, and hence becomes a strong source of gratification for both boys and girls. However, as the child grows, the awareness of sexual differences increases, and with it, an increased sense of sexual identity. It is this difference which begins to alter the dynamics for boys and girls.

For the boy, the mother (who is already the primary source of gratification) becomes more intensely desired, in what is the prototype for all future love relationships. The father is a source of gratification, but now also becomes the focus of jealousy and rivalry; hence, the boy's feelings towards his father are *ambivalent*, a mix of affection and hostility. In primary process terms, the id wishes to unite with the mother, and eliminate the father as a rival. At the same time, ego is aware that the father is larger and more powerful, and may retaliate against the boy's feelings. This becomes expressed as a fear that the father may take away the boy's source of gratification, through cutting off the genitals – called *castration fear*. (Of course, it is irrelevant to say such fears are not rational – it is precisely the point that these feelings are at an unconscious, non-rational level.) Thus, there is an intense conflict created, which ego is poorly equipped to resolve. To deny the attraction to the mother is to prevent the experiencing of feelings that will later be crucial to forming love relationships. To attempt to act on the jealousy towards the father is to risk an emotional and possibly physical split. (This conflict is the basis for the message 'beating Dad is wrong' in Palumbo and Gillman's study of subliminal messages, described earlier.)

identification a defence mechanism which involves incorporating characteristics of a drive object into one's own ego

repression a defence mechanism in which impulses, memories or ideas are actively blocked from the conscious mind

The resolution of this conflict comes through adopting two *defence mechanisms* – techniques used by the ego to cope with anxiety. One is **identification**, which involves incorporating an object of conflict as part of one's own ego. This process is expressed in the old phrase, 'if you can't beat 'em, join 'em.' By adopting the values and behaviour patterns of the father, the boy seeks to reduce the threat associated with castration fear: in effect, 'If I'm like Dad, he won't want to hurt me.' The mother, too, is identified with, as the model for future attractions. As an old song says, 'I want a girl just like the girl that married dear old Dad!' Identification is important in reducing the conflict the boy experiences, but also in triggering the development of superego; the earliest values of the superego are those derived from one's parents (later, other social values can also be incorporated). The other mechanism used by the ego in dealing with the Oedipal conflict is **repression** – forcing the conflict into the unconscious, so that the conscious mind is unaware of the fears and attractions. (When adults would scorn his notions about the Oedipal conflict, saying they had never experienced such things as a child, Freud would argue that this was simply evidence of repression.)

For girls, the Oedipal conflict involves the same sense of attraction and rivalry, though the objects are reversed – now the mother is the rival, and the father is the object of attraction. Despite the basic similarity, the dynamics are rather different, for several reasons. First of all, the mother promotes greater ambivalence, since she is typically the first object (focus) of drive energy for the infant. Further, while the girl fears discovery of her jealous impulses towards the mother, the increased awareness of the body leads her to recognize that both she and the mother lack a penis. While a boy may fear the possibility of losing his penis (castration fear), the girl feels a sense of devastation at having *already* lost hers – leading to feelings of guilt and loss described as *penis envy*. The girl realizes that the mother, too, has been castrated, and this enhances the sense of identification with the mother. Faced with this attraction towards the father and ambivalence towards the mother, the girl's ego, like the boy's, seeks some way of resolving the conflict. As with the boy, this involves *identification* (the father as prototype for future lovers, the mother as role model) and *repression* (blocking conscious access to the underlying impulses). However, the differences in the dynamics of the process make the Oedipal conflict more difficult for girls, and can result in greater submissiveness and lower self-esteem in adulthood.

In support of his conception of the Oedipal conflict, Freud used both evidence from clinical cases and observations of normal behaviour. One observation he made in this regard continues to tantalize researchers: the phenomenon of *childhood amnesia*. Typically, individuals recall very little of their life before about age five, other than a few fragmentary memories and stories that were probably heard from parents at a later age. Freud argued that childhood amnesia was due to the repression associated with coping with the Oedipal conflict. While other theories have been offered, ranging from changes in the myelination of brain neurons to changes in cognitive structure, no mechanism has been universally accepted; what *is* accepted is that Freud was correct in describing the basic phenomenon. *Sibling rivalry*, the conflict frequently seen among children in a family, was also seen by

Freud as representing a redirection of the Oedipal conflict to a different object (i.e. from parent to sibling).

Freud's description of penis envy, and of the female Oedipal conflict more generally, has been heavily attacked in recent years, both for its view of women and for its narrow definition of family structure. This view was apparently based on Freud's observations of both his patients (who were primarily female housewives) and his society (which emphasized the nuclear family, and generally kept women in a submissive role). However, modern evaluations have questioned his view that such patterns have biological, as opposed to social, causes – an issue which will warrant further discussion later on.

In both sexes, the Oedipal conflict is crucial both in the development of the superego, and in establishing the basis for sexual identity and formation of love relationships. Prior to this stage, the child has awareness of moral principles, but they are regarded as part of the environment (Brenner 1955). For example, if a child wants a biscuit, they may look to see if the mother is nearby. If she is, the child will refrain from taking the cookie; if she is not present, the child will proceed. That is, morality is evaluated in terms of getting caught, not right or wrong. As values become *internalized* through identification, they form the basis of superego. Without identification, superego development will be weak or absent; Freud saw this as the origin of psychopathic behaviour (anti-social behaviour with no sense of guilt or wrongdoing). Identification is also necessary for developing a clear sense of sexual identity, and for the creation of a prototype love object as the basis for later relationships. Problems of identification can lead to an inability to form love relationships, or repeated difficulties with authority figures, who are seen as surrogate parents. If repression is emphasized over identification in trying to resolve the Oedipal conflict, the result in later life can be an individual whose life is dominated by excessive guilt and anxiety.

To Freud, the Oedipal conflict was the greatest crisis in the development of personality. Failing to resolve it can result in a distorted ego which sees all relationships in terms of the unresolved conflicts of the phallic stage. Freud saw the problems of many of his patients (sexual conflicts, guilt and anxiety) as stemming from this source. As a result, he came to the conclusion that most people fail to resolve the Oedipal conflict in a psychologically (as opposed to socially) satisfactory manner (Freud 1924). As we will see, the issue resurfaces in the genital stage.

Latency Stage

latency stage the stage of development which begins at about age five and extends until puberty, during which the drives appear to be relatively inactive

Whether the Oedipal conflict is successfully resolved or not, the imperatives of development push the child from the phallic stage to the stage of latency at around age five. In the **latency stage**, which extends until puberty, the drives appear to be relatively inactive – hence the concept of them being 'latent' or hidden. In part, the change is due to the use of *repression* in resolving the Oedipal conflict. Because this results in blocking conscious access to the id, gratification hereafter is related to *secondary process thinking*, and hence is never as direct or as immediate as the gratifications of early childhood. In latency, the repressed impulses are redirected into new activities, with new objects of gratification. Thus, sports, hobbies, school and friendships all provide opportunities for satisfaction of the drives. Problems during latency, such as excessive aggression, can be related to inadequate repression and/or the ego being unable to redirect drive energy into socially-approved outlets.

Genital Stage

genital stage the final stage of psychosexual development (from puberty onwards), when drive energy is focused on the genitals, with adult expression of sexuality

At the onset of puberty, there is a resurfacing of drive energy, triggered in part by the physiological changes involved in sexual maturation. At this point, the individual enters the adult phase of development, called the **genital stage**. In this stage, drive energy is focused on the genitals, with adult expression of sexuality. The term 'genital' can be confusing, however, for the expression of drive energy is very different from the primary expression of id seen in the phallic stage. Ego's use of *secondary process thinking* has become well developed, allowing possibilities for *symbolic* gratification in a variety of ways. Symbolic expression is also encouraged by social influences, which direct the person towards new types of behaviours, including forming a love relationship, having children and assuming responsibilities in other socially-approved ways.

Curiously, given that the genital stage represents the major portion of life, Freud gave comparatively little attention to it. Primarily, he saw it as a period of trying to come to terms with the unresolved residues of childhood. The basic task for this stage was to separate oneself from one's parents. 'Only after this detachment is accomplished can he [the individual] cease to be a child, and so become a member of the social community' (Freud 1924: 346). Curiously, while Freud saw the genital stage as the final period of development, when the individual comes to maturity, he said relatively little about what successful development might lead to. This has been one aspect of psychodynamic theory that other theorists, such as Erik Erikson, have attempted to address, as we shall see.

For further consideration

In part, Freud defined his stages of development (especially the early stages) based on his behavioural observations. If you can, you might observe young children to see if their behaviour fits his descriptions. Could Freud be right about *what* children do, without being correct about *why* they do it?

Fixation and Regression During Development

fixation the incomplete release of drive energy associated with a particular stage of development

The failure to resolve the challenges of development results in **fixation** – the incomplete release of drive energy associated with a particular stage. This can occur if, during a stage, the child receives either too little or too much gratification. Undergratification denies the individual the opportunity for drive satisfaction, leading to a desire for what was missed. For example, a new-born who is denied opportunities to suckle the breast will later be orally fixated. (Freud saw weaning as the origin of the biblical story of being cast out of Eden, where food was plentiful.) On the other hand, a child who is overindulged will not face the challenges associated with each stage, making them reluctant to move ahead in their development. For example, a two-year-old who is still nursing, or a child who is given a bottle or pacifier at any indication of upset, will later be orally fixated. Fixation in turn is associated with **regression**, the tendency to revert to an earlier mode of gratification, usually under stress. Since repression has cut off direct access to the id in the adult, regression is seen in *symbolic* forms of gratification. For example, a person who is orally fixated may binge on ice cream, or smoke, or chew their nails, or get drunk, or . . . (The list of possibilities is obviously quite long.) Fixation can also be expressed through *denial* of gratification, as when someone becomes a fanatical anti-smoker, or a teetotaller.

regression in Freud's theory, a defence mechanism in which the individual reverts to behaviours characteristic of an earlier mode of gratification

Each stage manifests its own forms of fixation, representative of the focus of drive energy at that stage. For instance, at the anal stage, either overly rigid *or* overly permissive toilet training can result in fixation. In later life, this will be seen in excessive sloppiness of either dress or living areas, a preference for activities that involve messes (e.g. cooking or painting) or a preoccupation with money (seen by Freud as a symbol for faeces). Anal denial may be seen in compulsive neatness of clothes and surroundings, a preference for activities that involve order (such as cataloguing books), stinginess or an aversion to financial matters. Phallic fixations are associated with failures to resolve the Oedipal conflict, which later results in not detaching from the parents. A man who continually fights with his boss, traffic officers and other authority figures is showing a phallic fixation – trying to dominate the father figure. The man who is overly submissive is still complying with the father he dared not challenge. For a woman, phallic fixation may be expressed as seductiveness and a preference for older men (seeking to replace the mother), or as a desire to dominate men (symbolically castrating the father that rejected her). In latency, where direct expression of the drives is repressed, fixation results in behaviours which do not seem to involve drives – acts of altruism, for example.

One interesting aspect of the role of fixation is the way that Freud related it to career choices. Like many subsequent theorists, Freud believed that career decisions reflect personality at least as much as ability. Oral fixation, for example, would lead to careers that involve oral behaviour – a wine taster, a writer, a salesperson, even a university professor. Fixation at the anal stage, with its emphasis on cleanliness and bowel movements, leads to careers that involve messiness, order and/or money. Thus, a banker, an accountant, a painter, a sanitation worker – all are careers reflective of an anal fixation. (Laboratory research in chemistry or biology, with its requirements for precision combined with messy procedures, seems to offer both indulgence and denial!) The phallic stage tends to lead to careers in which body image, sexuality and/or authority figures are involved. Thus, professional models (and the photographers who work with them) have made a choice based on phallic fixation, as have career soldiers, police officers and even prostitutes. In latency, the influence of repression means that drives must be expressed indirectly. Consequently, careers which seem unrelated to drive satisfaction, such as clergyman, charity organizer or social worker, are likely choices for a person who is fixated at the latency stage.

One aspect of these descriptions that often bothers people is the non-obvious nature of many of the connections. This is inevitable, according to

Freud, since the conscious mind of the adult is cut off (by repression) from direct access to the underlying drives. Consequently, the drives are always expressed in *symbolic* form, whether in the manifest content of dreams or the choice of a career. In fact, from a Freudian viewpoint, adult actions and interests, being based on secondary process thinking, can *only* be regarded as symbolic. What differs is the degree to which the behaviour is adaptive or pathological. The man who collects swords (phallic symbols) may have an unresolved Oedipal conflict, but his method of dealing with it is more functional than that of the person who develops a psychogenic form of impotence.

There are other points that should be made concerning fixation and regression. First, in suggesting that these patterns exist, Freud was not making a value judgement. For example, he did *not* say that because a career reflects a particular form of fixation, it is therefore undesirable. His basic point was that behaviour is never random, and consequently behaviours like career choices simply reflect the developmental history of the individual (and, in instances of pathology, may give clues to the nature of the underlying conflict). Second, he saw such relationships as evidence that all behaviour is ultimately related to the basic drives – even those actions which seem remote from any connection with such motivating forces. Since expression in adults is symbolic, the fact that we have no *conscious awareness* of what motivates the behaviour in no way invalidates the connection. In fact, Freud argued that it is *necessary* that such connections be unconscious, in order to protect the ego from the threatening implications of recognizing what motivates us. To understand this, let us look at the concept of anxiety, and the methods the mind uses to cope with it.

For further consideration

Some Freudians have suggested that cultures, like individuals, can show fixations. If you were to apply Freud's model to our culture, what stage would you say it is fixated at? Does applying the theory in this way seem reasonable? Why or why not?

Anxiety and Defence Mechanisms

anxiety a negative emotional state associated with threat to the self; in Freud's theory, it arises when the ego is faced with an influx of stimuli with which it cannot cope, as a result of either external danger or the demands of id or superego

As discussed earlier, adult personality is comprised of id, ego and superego. Ego, as the integrator, must contend with the divergent demands of id, superego and the external world. Meeting these demands is not simple at the best of times, and many circumstances (such as unresolved conflicts from earlier stages, or external threats) can make ego's task even more formidable. In such circumstances, the ego may experience anxiety. **Anxiety** arises when the ego is faced with an influx of stimuli with which it cannot cope. This may be the result of an external danger, such as a civilian living in wartime conditions, or it may be due to an internal threat, related to the demands of id or superego. Since ego is unable to acknowledge the drives within the id, the breakthrough of unsatisfied id impulses into conscious awareness can trigger anxiety. Similarly, the moral demands of superego can be excessive, producing guilt and anxiety at the least suggestion of id gratification. Thus, the various forms of demands can threaten the integrity of the ego, which must protect itself.

Freud considered anxiety at several points in his writings, trying to find a way to understand this phenomenon. In *The Problem of Anxiety* (1926), he presented his mature views on the issue. Freud believed that anxiety was biologically based, and was intended as an adaptive mechanism – anxiety serving to warn the ego of a potentially overwhelming situation. However, ego has limited options: it cannot completely deny id's desire for gratification, nor can it allow superego to make all decisions, without regard to either id or external reality. (For example, it may be wrong to hurt others, but what if one's life is in danger?) Thus, ego must somehow cope with both the conflicting demands and the anxiety produced by awareness of them. Some forms of coping involve a reversion to *primary process thinking*, such as dreams and the physical symptoms of hysteria. However, such methods were seen as signs of a weak ego, in that they involve ignoring external reality.

More commonly, ego will invoke various defence mechanisms, a term actually coined by Freud's daughter, Anna (herself a distinguished psychoanalyst) (A. Freud 1936). **Defence mechanisms** are techniques used by the ego to protect itself from anxiety and the threats which give rise to it. There are a number of such techniques, and frequently the ego will use a combination of them, rather than a single mechanism. There are several basic points to note about the defence mechanisms. First, the defence mechanisms operate unconsciously – otherwise, they would fail to protect the ego from awareness of the conflicts which are the source of anxiety. Second, most defence mechanisms (with the significant exception of repression) operate by allowing gratification in some indirect way, typically involving either symbolic gratification or a substitute object; to the extent that this reduces id's demands, it can be desirable. Third, to the extent that defence mechanisms succeed in protecting the ego, they do so by distorting reality (since gratification is redirected). Before we consider the implications of these factors, let us consider some of the specific defence mechanisms, several of which have already been mentioned in passing.

Repression, the blocking of id impulses at the unconscious level, is the most primitive of all defence mechanisms. Although Freud saw repression as universal (in the transition from phallic to latency stages), he also felt it was extremely limited as a defence. The basic difficulty is that it fails to resolve the demands which led to its use, because no gratification occurs. Even worse, it can require significant amounts of mental energy to maintain the blockage against the increasing pressures for gratification. One can use an analogy to a boiling pot of water. As steam is generated, it starts to lift the lid off the pot. Putting a weight on the lid will help, but eventually the pressure will increase, until either a larger weight is needed or the lid blows off. Similarly, maintaining repression, in the absence of any other response, will require more and more of the mental energy that should properly go into other life activities. Since the ego is unaware of the underlying pressures, it experiences the fatigue without understanding its source. Thus, depression is seen by Freudians as a result of excessive repression. Repression can also produce distortions of reality, as when memories are blocked which could trigger the leakage of underlying conflicts into conscious awareness. (The notion that traumatic memories can be repressed, and later recovered, has become a major source of controversy in recent years – see Figure 5.2.)

defence mechanism in Freud's theory, a technique used by the ego to protect itself from anxiety and the threats which give rise to it; many psychologists use the terms as descriptions of behaviour patterns, without endorsing the Freudian interpretation of their origin

Repression and recovered memories of abuse

A fundamental concept in Freud's theory is that our behaviour can be influenced by unconscious processes. When Freud first began treating patients suffering from hysteria, he discovered that most had been sexually abused as children, but had repressed the memories of the trauma. Though the conscious mind could not recall the events, at an unconscious level, the trauma was responsible for the patients' symptoms. Using first hypnosis, and later free association and other procedures, Freud tried to help his patients to gain access to these repressed memories, and thereby begin to deal with the psychological impact of the abuse. Thus, regaining access to the memory of traumatic events, particularly sexual abuse, was a basic part of psychoanalytic therapy from the outset.

However, Freud later concluded that most of the events his patients related were actually fantasies, not real incidents of abuse. Both his original interpretation and the subsequent change in his theory remain the subject of controversy. The issue has become particularly significant in court cases of abuse, where sometimes the only evidence is the recovered memories of the accuser. Hence, the issue is: how accurate are memories of abuse recovered during therapy?

Evidence favouring repression
Apart from the general evidence concerning repression, there are a number of studies which have looked specifically at amnesia for sexual abuse. Typically, they find that gaps in childhood recall are quite common among abuse victims (Herman 1992; Briere and Conte 1993). Even more striking evidence comes from a prospective study by Williams (1994a, b). Working from hospital records, Williams tracked down women who had been treated for sexual molestation 17 years earlier. Remarkably, 38 per cent were amnesic, even though many recalled other traumatic memories, including later incidents of abuse. Consequently, it seems reasonable to conclude that repression of sexual abuse may occur. But what about recall during therapy? Can such events be recalled accurately as a result of therapy?

Recovered memories and reconstruction
The basic premise of therapeutic recall is that the memories exist in their original form, if the repression can be overcome. However, memory is not simply a process of all-or-none retrieval; instead, we sometimes *reconstruct* events based on context and other factors (see Chapter 4). This may even extend to recalling events that never happened. For example, when given descriptions of real events (obtained from family members) along with false events (such as getting lost at a mall as a child), up to 25 per cent of college students recalled the false event as real (Loftus and Pickerel 1995; Loftus 1997). In addition, recall of real events is rarely entirely accurate. Neisser and Harsh (1992) asked college students at the time of the Challenger shuttle disaster to describe how and where they heard of it. When contacted three years later, 50 per cent were incorrect on most details (like where they were or who they were with), and 25 per cent were completely wrong. Even when shown their own original notes, the students tended to react with disbelief. Thus, critics argue that if milder memories can be distorted, why should we assume that memories of abuse are necessarily accurate?

What can we conclude?
Sexual abuse of children is a serious issue. We know that abusers try to discredit their victims (Herman 1992), and we also know that abuse sometimes goes unreported until some time later. Thus, it is important to treat reports seriously, even if they occur years later. At the same time, we know that memories are not always accurate, and therapists may sometimes cue false reports. Indeed, a survey of US and British therapists indicated that 94 per cent believe this can occur – though a strong majority reported that they believed *their* patients' memories were accurate (Poole *et al.* 1995). In the end, in the absence of corroborating evidence, we cannot easily tell when recovered memories are true or false. Given this fact, both the issue and the dilemmas it creates are likely to persist.

Figure 5.2   Repression and recovered memories of abuse

displacement in psychoanalysis, a defence mechanism which involves the redirection of drive energy from one object to a substitute object

Displacement, the redirection of drive energy towards a substitute object, is one of the most common defence mechanisms. Whenever the direct expression of drives would be too threatening – because of either the disapproval of superego or a realistic threat associated with the original object – we tend to seek a substitute object. For example, yelling at the boss when you are asked to work overtime could result in being fired; instead, you complete the work, then cut someone up while driving home! Or a teenage boy is attracted to Mary, but when she rejects him, he asks out Sally, in whom he initially had no interest. (In a classic cartoon, a man receives a speeding ticket while driving. Rather than yell at the officer, he goes home and yells at his wife; she in turn yells at their son; the boy then kicks the family dog, which goes out and bites a police officer!) In each case, there is displacement of drive energy to a substitute object. The problem with displacement, of course, is that the substitutes are un-related to the original object. Thus, while displacement allows release of drive energy, it clearly involves a distortion of reality in the process of doing so.

Identification, involves incorporating characteristics of a drive object into one's ego, as seen in the discussion of the Oedipal conflict. Typically, this occurs with individuals who are either admired or feared. For instance, hostages may come to adopt some of the values of their captors. More benignly, a young child may mimic a superhero seen on television. When we are unable to express sexual or aggressive impulses directly, we can adopt the guise of a figure in whom such impulses are acceptable. In films, books or plays, identification with a character can provide a form of release called *catharsis* – the vicarious release of drive energy. While identification is necessary to resolving the Oedipal conflict, and may be a means of learning moral values, it still poses the risk of distorting reality, since the values incorporated are not freely generated by the ego. In extreme form, such as in delusional disorders, the identification may supplant the individual's own identity – for example, when someone believes they are Christ (see Rokeach 1981).

Regression, reverting to behaviour characteristic of an earlier stage under conditions of stress, is closely associated with fixation, as noted earlier. Like repression, regression is a fairly primitive defence mechanism. A four-year-old child who has been toilet trained, for example, may begin wetting the bed after the birth of a sibling. Faced with the stress of a rival for parental attention, the child regresses to an earlier stage. Working to meet a deadline, a smoker may begin smoking more heavily – a form of oral re-gression. (It is interesting to note that Freud himself was a heavy smoker of cigars. When once asked about the symbolic meaning of this, he apparently replied to the effect, 'Sometimes a cigar is a phallic symbol, and sometimes it is only a cigar. This is only a cigar!') Another person, faced with the same situation but being anally rather than orally fixated, may spend time rear-ranging everything on his desk as a means of getting some gratification. These behaviours allow for some gratification, but since the behaviours are to some extent inappropriate, they represent a distortion of reality. Freud argued that the seriousness of regression depends on both the stage of regression and the primitiveness of the response. For example, disaster victims will sometimes curl up in a ball, like an infant in the foetal position – a severe form of regression. Ultimately, regression is of limited value: Since there is an inevitable shift of erogenous zones as one goes through stages, it is impossible to re-experience the satisfaction of an earlier stage in the original way.

rationalization a defence mechanism in which one explains behaviour by offering a reason acceptable to the ego in place of the true reason

Rationalization is perhaps one of the most interesting defences, it involves offering an *acceptable* reason for behaviour in place of the true reason (acceptable to the ego, though the approval of other people may be a concern as well). When we rationalize, we try to justify our actions. For instance, a person engaging in flirtatious behaviour may say, 'I was only being friendly.' Rationalization may be combined with other defences as well, to provide a justification for behaviour. For example, a person who wastes time organizing their desk may say, 'Oh, but I work better when everything is neat.' This may, in fact, be generally true – but the real reason for doing it *when facing the stress of a deadline* is in order to get some gratification through regression to the anal stage! 'White lies' offer an analogy to this form of defence: when a white lie is generated, both the liar and the person lied to may recognize that it is untrue, but may find it socially convenient to let the lie stand. Since rationalization prevents the person from recognizing the true motives for their actions, it represents a form of distortion of reality. It also suggests one should be wary of the 'rational' analyses people make of their own behaviour: while the ego is capable of rational thought, the potential for rationalization means that logic can serve reasons other than objectivity, yet the ego will not recognize when that happens.

sublimation in Freud's theory, a defence mechanism in which drive energy is redirected towards a socially desirable creative activity

Sublimation is one of the few defences which Freud saw as having a positive function beyond protecting the ego. Sublimation occurs when drive energy is redirected towards a socially desirable creative activity. While similar to displacement in its mechanism, it differs in terms of the restriction on outcomes. For example, an artist attracted to a married person may rechannel sexual energy into creating a beautiful statue of the person. A musician may create a patriotic anthem in a time of war, rechannelling aggressive energy. While sublimation is useful, because it results in a socially-valued product, it is also limited: since gratification is very indirect, it cannot fully satisfy the demands of id. In addition, since it requires particular skills to be a painter, musician or other creator, it is not a workable mechanism for all individuals. Still, it is unique, in that Freud believed that the creative activity which sublimation supports makes it more than simply a response to neurotic anxiety.

There are a number of other defence mechanisms, but by this time the basic point should be clear: defence mechanisms exist to protect the ego from anxiety, but they do so at the cost of distorting reality. To the extent that defences work, they pose the risk of isolating the person from reality; in extreme form, Freud saw this as the basis of the major mental disorders, which he called *psychoses*. However, to the extent that ego is *aware* of using a particular defence, distortion of reality is reduced, but anxiety will increase. Freud defined *neuroses* as disorders in which excessive anxiety is a primary symptom; in these circumstances defence mechanisms are not adequately protecting the ego. When I was in graduate school, the joke was, 'a neurotic worries about going crazy (distorting reality), but never will; a psychotic *is* crazy (distorts reality), but doesn't worry about it!' While obviously glib, it does capture the essence of the Freudian distinction between neuroses and psychoses.

In his later years, Freud was very interested in how the demands of society affect the growth of ego. In *Civilization and Its Discontents*, he gave extensive attention to this issue (Freud 1930). One basic point was that living in society has a psychological price: coping with the arbitrary demands of society, as represented by the superego. Without a superego, one would face fewer conflicts, since there would only be id and external reality to satisfy. (Note that asking 'what is possible?' is not the same as asking 'what is right?') Interestingly, psychopathic individuals, who are regarded by Freudians as having little superego development, show no guilt (moral anxiety) for their anti-social behaviour. For the rest of us, being 'civilized' requires dealing with the demands of superego. This means that the opportunities for id gratification become largely symbolic and indirect. (Freud once commented to the effect that 'civilization began the first time an angry person cast a word instead of a rock.') In addition to the demands of id, one must cope with the demands of superego itself, which may also conflict with reality. As a result, Freud believed that anxiety levels were increased by living in a civilized society.

At the same time, Freud was pessimistic about the possibilities of ego protecting itself from these threats to its integrity. He saw only two possible solutions that might satisfy society while permitting a healthy development of ego. One was sublimation, which, as we have discussed, is unlikely to be an adequate solution. The other (which is seldom mentioned in discussions of his theory) was love (Fancher 1979). *Love* is a defence mechanism, but it allows the drives to be gratified in the context of caring for another person, while meeting both moral and reality demands. Yet, while he believed love had the potential to benefit the ego, Freud also saw it as fraught with peril, since the *loss* of a loved one could leave the ego vulnerable to catastrophic pain.

Society, Freud concluded, creates a paradox for the individual: sublimation and love are only *possible* within the group structures which society provides, but it is also society that creates the constraints on id which make sublimation and love *necessary*. Unfortunately, in looking at the world as the Second World War was approaching, Freud felt that society was placing greater restrictions on love, while at the same time directing aggressive energy into ever more dangerous forms. As quoted earlier, the conclusion to *Civilization and Its Discontents* strikes an uncertain and pessimistic tone. To what extent this view was influenced by adverse circumstances (both personal and social), and to what extent it remains an accurate description of the ego's plight, is difficult to say.

| **For further consideration** | The behaviours associated with defence mechanisms seem relatively common – Woody Allen has often used them to comic effect in his films. What examples can you find in your everyday experience? Do you ever rationalize? Does finding such behaviours necessarily mean that the causes are related to unconscious conflicts? |

Observing the Unconscious in Behaviour

One of the basic elements of Freud's theory is that id will always seek gratification, but that in adults its expression is usually symbolic and indirect. This leads to the question of how one can provide supporting evidence. Since the id is by definition unconscious, one cannot simply analyse one's own actions to assess the validity of this conception. So how did Freud support his view? The key lies in one of his other basic assumptions – *psychic determinism*, which states that there is always a cause for behaviour, which can be found within the mind. This assumption meant that potentially *any* form of behaviour could provide evidence of the workings of the unconscious, especially the id. While we have already noted many examples of supporting evidence, it is worth reviewing some of the major types.

Perhaps the best known type of Freudian evidence are the everyday errors and slips of the tongue which he called **parapraxes**, but which have generally become known as *Freudian slips*. Since all behaviour has a cause, errors and slips are not accidental. While Freud conceded that fatigue and distraction could sometimes lead to errors and slips, he argued that the majority of cases reflected the workings of the unconscious. In arguing for this point of view, he made extensive use of examples from both his clinical cases and everyday observation. In *Psychopathology in Everyday Life*, he offered detailed analyses of many such cases – for example, newspaper misprints involving 'His Highness, the Clown Prince' (Freud 1904). In one case, a paper printed an apology for having said 'a battle-scared veteran' – but the apology appeared as 'a bottle-scarred veteran'! In such a case, Freud would argue that the errors reflected a latent hostility on the part of the writer. In general, Freudian slips can best be understood when they can be combined with other information about the individual, which can help in interpreting the underlying dynamics.

While everyday errors clearly occur, it is possible to interpret them in other ways. For example, cognitive psychologist Victoria Fromkin of UCLA has argued that verbal slips are linguistic in origin, not psychodynamic. Based on analysis of several thousand naturally-occurring verbal slips, she noted that slips are not random with regard to the linguistic units of words (Fromkin 1973). For example, phonemes may be transposed *within* a phrase (as in 'queer old dean' for 'dear old Queen'), but not *across* phrases (e.g. 'the red ten on the pable' is not a likely result from 'the red pen on the table'). To explore this issue further, Michael Motley (1985) developed a procedure to study verbal slips in the laboratory. In one study, subjects were asked to read aloud word pairs that were presented on a screen. In order to manipulate anxiety, subjects in one group were told to expect a painful electric shock at some point during the experiment (aggression drive condition). In another condition, the experimenter was 'an attractive and provocatively dressed woman' (sexual drive condition). A control group was treated normally. Consistent with the Freudian view, each group made errors related to the type of drive stimulated, e.g. 'varied colts' was frequently read as 'carried volts' in the aggression condition, and 'past fashion' became 'fast passion' in the sexuality condition (see Figure 5.3). In addition, a pretest of subjects in the sexual drive condition showed that those who scored

paraprax an error or verbal slip due to an unconscious conflict; commonly called a 'Freudian slip'

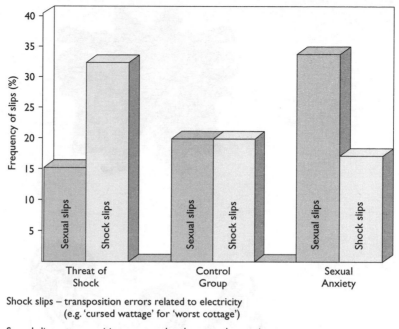

Shock slips – transposition errors related to electricity
(e.g. 'cursed wattage' for 'worst cottage')

Sexual slips – transposition errors related to sexual attraction
(e.g. 'bare shoulders' for 'share boulders')

Figure 5.3 Studying verbal slips A study by Motley compared the frequency of verbal slips made by subjects who were either fearful of electric shocks or aroused by an attractive woman. Errors were typically Spoonerisms, in which syllables of two words are transposed, as indicated in the figure. (Data from Motley 1985.)

highest on a test of sexual anxiety were the ones who made the greatest numbers of slips. While these results are consistent with Freud's theory of slips as anxiety-related, Motley, like Fromkin, notes that there are linguistic constraints on the types of errors that subjects make; he also argues that some errors, particularly in children, are not anxiety-related at all. (For instance, my 3-year-old son, returning from a historical site, called it 'pine-apple village' rather than 'pioneer village'; the word 'pineapple' was already familiar to him, whereas the word 'pioneer' was new.) However, as already noted, Freud himself suggested that not all slips have a psychodynamic cause. Thus, the evidence for linguistic constraints does not seem to contra-dict Freud's view, and overall the research seems to support his theory.

Free association – asking patients to say whatever came to mind – was used by Freud as a therapeutic technique very early, when he began to abandon hypnosis as a tool. Since he believed that thoughts, like behaviour, always have a pattern, listening to what his patients said could provide a means of accessing the unconscious mind. As discussed in Chapter 4, the organized nature of cognitive structure, including memory, is now well established. However, since the particular pattern of organization is quite individual, the use of free association as a tool in analysis is slow and painstaking, requiring considerable attentiveness by the therapist. (Sometimes,

Figure 5.4 Ambiguous stimuli and projective tests Projective tests use the individual's interpretation of ambiguous stimuli to access the unconscious mind. Two popular tests are the Rorschach, which uses inkblot stimuli similar to the top figure, and the Thematic Apperception Test, which asks individuals to tell a story about the people in a picture, similar to the lower figure.

projective test a type of personality test used by psychodynamic theorists in which an individual is asked to interpret an ambiguous stimulus; since the stimulus itself is ambiguous, the assumption is that whatever the person says reveals the workings of their own unconscious mind

it also requires 'listening for what is not being said', which therapist Robert Fancher (1995) calls 'the greatest legacy of psychoanalysis'.)

A related technique which Freud himself never used, but which has subsequently become associated with psychoanalytic and psychodynamic approaches, is the use of projective tests. A **projective test** presents the person with an ambiguous stimulus, which they are then asked to interpret. Since the stimulus itself is ambiguous, the assumption is that whatever the person says reveals the workings of their own unconscious mind. (Examples of projective test materials are given in Figure 5.4.)

As previously discussed, *dreams* operate on two levels, the *manifest content* and the *latent content*. The manifest content is symbolic, having been created out of the original forms by the *dream censor*. Thus, a dream must be closely analysed to determine what the latent content actually is. While Freud believed that certain symbols were fairly universal (e.g. guns and knives as phallic symbols, money as faeces, tunnels and flowers as vaginal symbols), he also recognized that some symbols have a meaning which is particular to the individual – a point sometimes overlooked in popular accounts and 'dream guides'. As with other techniques, proper analysis requires relating the dream to the person's overall behaviour.

Cross-cultural studies – in keeping with his belief that all behaviour is significant, Freud had a deep curiosity about similarities and differences across cultures. At the time of his death, he had amassed a considerable collection of primitive art (mostly carvings), which he valued both aesthetically and scientifically. One of his major attempts at cultural interpretation was *Totem and Taboo*, in which he noted the prevalence of incest taboos across many cultures, and explained such taboos in terms of the Oedipal conflict (Freud 1913).

In keeping with his willingness to find evidence in any behaviour, Freud also used examples from his own *self-analysis*, which began after the death of his father in 1896. This event was terribly emotional for him; he later described the death of one's father as 'the most important event, the most poignant loss, in a man's life' (Fancher 1979: 227). Faced with this loss, he experienced anxiety and depression, and had trouble concentrating on work; as a result, he embarked on an analysis of his own behaviour while still grappling for a framework for understanding the dynamics of behaviour. Self-analysis represents a potentially treacherous endeavour, both personally and as theoretical validation. The problem is that one can never be certain that what is discovered is genuine, rather than a distortion based on defence mechanisms. (Actually, at the time he began his self-analysis, Freud had not yet developed the concept of defence mechanisms.) In addition, self-analysis raises the danger of increasing anxiety, since it may impair the effectiveness of defence mechanisms before the underlying conflicts have been recognized and dealt with. Freud apparently found that this was true, since he told friends and pupils that during this period he was sometimes afraid to cross the street, for fear of discovering some unexpected meaning in the act! Still, Freud had long been interested in his own dreams, and frequently used examples of his own dreams, as well as his other behaviours, in his writings.

As discussed previously, Freud came to believe that *art* was the product of sublimation, and therefore was based on a healthy coping mechanism for the ego. At the same time, art is symbolic, and can be probed for unconscious meanings. While Freud was interested in art, particularly from other cultures, his discussions of art in his writings were restricted mostly to Greek dramas, like *Oedipus Rex*. Hence, the analysis of art is better regarded as an extension of his work, rather than a major part of Freud's own writings. One of the most interesting aspects of applying psychoanalysis to art is the ease with which it can be applied to pre-Freudian artistic creations. For example, the art of Hieronymous Bosch, a fifteenth-century Dutch painter, has frequently been cited for its Freudian imagery. Similarly, Herman Melville's *Moby Dick*, written about fifty years before Freud began developing his theory, has been extensively analysed; typically, the white whale is seen as a phallic symbol, representing Melville's latent homosexuality. It is more difficult to evaluate art created since Freud's time, since any symbolism could reflect either conscious or unconscious awareness of Freud's work. While psychoanalytic interpretations have become popular in relation to art, it poses problems similar to dream analysis – there is a danger that when too little context is available, the analysis may become a projective test, telling more about the analyst than the artist. (For examples of visual symbols which have significance in Freudian theory, see Figure 5.5.)

<table>
<tr><td>

**For further
consideration**

</td><td>

You may want to look for your own examples of Freudian symbols in everyday life. Alternatively, go back to your dream notes (if you tried recording your dreams). Whether considering everyday symbols or dreams, how can one be sure the interpretations are correct?

</td></tr>
</table>

Assessing Freud's Work

Attempting to evaluate Freud's work is a challenging endeavour, given both the range of his efforts and the impact which his work has had. As we will see in the next section, one way to evaluate his work is by examining what others have done subsequently. For the moment, though, let us deal with Freud in his own right.

Freud was a remarkable person: gifted intellectually, a keen observer, a fluent writer and, by some accounts, a very humane person (Zangwill 1987). While many of his basic assumptions were influenced by the work of others (e.g. Brücke, Darwin, Pinel), he was a tremendous synthesizer, and typically explored the implications of ideas more effectively than many of his predecessors (Robinson 1979). These are all admirable traits, but they do not really tell us much about the validity of his work. To determine that, we need to consider what makes a good theory.

falsifiability a criterion for evaluating a theory which states the theory should specify circumstances wherein it could be proven wrong

One of the most basic criteria for a scientific theory is **falsifiability** – that is, one should be able to conceive of circumstances where a theory could be proven wrong. Typically, one of the most common criticisms of Freud's theory is that it is not falsifiable. There are several reasons for this criticism. First, Freud's assumptions dictate that many terms refer to variables that must be inferred rather than directly observed, which makes them hard to validate. Second, the large number of interrelated concepts, and the lack of precision associated with many of them, makes it very difficult to set up critical tests. In many cases, the evidence used to *support* the theory is also *dependent* on the theory for its validity (e.g. demonstrating the symbolic meaning of dreams is dependent on accepting the concept of latent content). In addition, the theory is primarily descriptive rather than predictive, which makes it more difficult to test its validity (see Chapter 1). For example, the theory does not predict which defence mechanisms a person will use in a particular situation, nor does it specify which experiences will be repressed. In some cases, there is also a problem of determining which theory to test, since Freud frequently revised his ideas without repudiating earlier work (see Brenner 1957).

All these considerations make it difficult to test Freud's ideas directly. At the same time, his work has generated considerable attention, and there have been many attempts to test specific aspects of his work. Some examples have already been noted, but it is worth considering the issue further. One of the most systematic attempts to explore Freud's ideas experimentally was the work of John Dollard and Neal Miller (1950). Dollard, an anthropologist who became interested in psychotherapy, and Miller, an experimental psychologist (see autonomic conditioning in Chapter 3), attempted to 'translate' Freudian concepts into behaviourally-based terms. Given that Freud's theory is expressed in terms of mental events, this is not an easy task. Some of their formulations were both creative and insightful – for example, they suggested that aggression could be described in terms of the circumstances that trigger it (see Chapter 7). In other cases, they found it difficult to provide behavioural definitions – for example, distinguishing fear from anxiety. (They *did* suggest, however, that the problems of anxiety seen in clinical practice involve more than the simple fear conditioning proposed by Watson and other behaviourists.) Their work caused a considerable stir at the time it was published, but has declined in influence subsequently. Whatever its limitations, one significant aspect of their work was that they considered Freud's ideas seriously, rather than dismissing his work as other behaviourists have done.

In keeping with the concern for falsifiability, more recent studies have focused on experimental testing of specific Freudian concepts – most notably repression, since it is so closely tied to the concept of the unconscious. As noted already, there is an active debate about repressed memories which surface in therapy (see Figure 5.2). While this debate is unresolved, other researchers have looked at individual differences in the use of repression as a defence mechanism. For example, Gary Schwartz and his colleagues have done a series of studies, based on first classifying individuals as likely to use repression or not. When exposed to sexual or aggressive written material, those classed as repressors claimed not to feel anxious, but showed higher physiological arousal than non-repressors (Weinberger *et al.* 1979). In a related study, repressors spontaneously recalled fewer emotional experiences from childhood than non-repressors (Davis and Schwartz 1987). A more recent study similarly found that repressors were less likely to recall negative personal events than non-repressors (Boden and Baumeister 1997). While details of these studies vary significantly, the existence of individual differences in the use of repression seems well established, and is certainly consistent with Freud's theory. Thus, they provide some experimental support, but do not provide direct proof, for Freud's interpretation of repression.

Obviously, these studies do not provide an adequate basis for judging the overall body of Freud's work, and it remains difficult to identify predictive tests. However, it is worth noting that there are some aspects which are well accepted at the *descriptive* level (that is, without reference to the specifics of Freud's *explanations*). For example, childhood amnesia is an accepted fact, though its origin is still unclear. Similarly, therapists ranging in orientation from psychoanalytic to humanistic to even behaviouristic accept the utility of defence mechanisms as shorthand descriptions for particular behavioural patterns; where the approaches tend to differ is in the explanation offered for the existence of these patterns. These examples point out that Freud was a sensitive observer, who noted a number of behavioural phenomena that had been previously ignored. Similarly, his written descriptions of his case studies are vivid and detailed, often giving insights into his own thinking as well as the specifics of the cases. In this sense, they still make interesting reading. So, at the descriptive level, there is no doubt that Freud made major contributions to the observational base of psychology.

generality a criterion for evaluating a theory, which refers to the range of application of a theory; a good theory should apply to a wide range of situations

This raises a second criterion for judging theories: generality. **Generality** refers to the range of application of a theory; a good theory should apply to a wide range of situations. For example, a theory which only explains the behaviour of a particular species of rat in T-shaped mazes, and nothing else, is likely to be seen as trivial, no matter how accurate it might be. By contrast, Freud's work addresses almost the entire range of human behaviour. For example, he explicitly argued for the continuity of normal and abnormal behaviour. In addition, he discussed issues related to memory, art, cultural patterns, mythology and a wide range of other topics. Indeed, the assumption of psychic determinism meant that in principle the theory could be applied to understanding the motivational aspect of *any* behaviour. In this regard, Freud's theory still stands as probably the most comprehensive account of human behaviour produced by a single individual. (Skinner, who wrote on everything from superstitions to Utopian societies, may be a strong second.) The difficulty, of course, is that, without falsifiability, it is difficult to tell if it is *correct*. Just as a trivial but accurate theory is of little value, so, too, is a broad but false theory. But is Freud's theory necessarily false?

Without the objective standard of falsifiability, it becomes hard to evaluate Freud's theory (or *any* theory). While *no* theory can be *proven* true, a theory which cannot be tested also cannot be proven to be *false*. Instead, one tries to determine if it is self-consistent, and looks for evidence of distortions in the observations. A good theory should not be contradictory, and there should be no indication of *bias* or other distortions in interpretations of the data. Both these points have been matters of controversy with regard to Freud's work. In terms of consistency, he frequently revised his thinking, as already noted, and did not always explicitly reject his earlier work. The changes were perhaps inevitable, given the difficulties of forming a theory based on inferred variables. However, the resulting contradictions remain, unless one decides to consider his final work as reflecting his true views.

In terms of distortion or bias, however, the situation is much more complex. Freud himself believed he had many opponents, as his letters and comments to friends indicate. Yet some authors have suggested that much of this opposition existed in his own mind (e.g. Roazen 1975; Sulloway 1979; Masson 1984). Freud seemed to thrive on challenge, according to Sulloway, and was at his best in defending his views from attack. But he also seems to have been very intolerant of real critics, which ultimately became a factor in his relationships with several colleagues and disciples. While his ventures into psychoanalysis began with his collaboration with Joseph Breuer, the two parted company when Freud developed his seduction theory of hysteria. Later, he had acrimonious splits with Alfred Adler, Carl Jung and Wilhelm Fleiss – all one-time protégés.

More specifically, critics have charged that many elements of his theory reflect either personal or cultural bias. Two issues – the seduction theory and his views of women – have been at the centre of such criticisms. Early in his career, Freud proposed that hysteria arose from the trauma of sexual assault; this was the seduction theory of neurosis. Later, he decided that in fact the traumas were imagined assaults, not real attacks (see earlier discussion). However, Masson (1984) has argued that Freud's shift was a mistake, and that Freud, like his contemporaries, was unwilling to acknowledge the realities of sexual abuse of children. Masson based his argument in part on letters and documents accessed during his brief stint as project director of the Sigmund Freud Archives – a position from which he was abruptly terminated, and later won a wrongful dismissal suit. It is difficult to assess the issue fairly. Masson's point about the reality of child abuse is certainly consistent with modern research, but that does not prove that fantasy cannot cause trauma, as Freud came to believe. Interestingly, the disorder which Freud most closely associated with the seduction theory – hysteria – is today a rare phenomenon. (The term *hysteria* is not in common usage today; the expression of psychological conflicts through physical symptoms is called *conversion disorder*. However, by whatever name, this type of problem is uncommon.)

Critics have also argued that Freud's view of women – especially the feelings of inferiority which he associated with penis envy – was based on the cultural attitudes of his time. Again, there is no doubt that attitudes have changed in the past 100 years, and, as with any theorist, it is possible that Freud's thinking was influenced both by the cases he considered and by prevailing social norms. Later analysts (notably Karen Horney) have addressed the issue in different terms, suggesting that women's feelings of self-worth have nothing to do with biological mechanisms, inferior or otherwise (Horney 1950). Hence, at the very least, one can argue that alternative interpretations exist for explaining personality dynamics in women. Some would go further, and argue that the concept of penis envy suggests that Freud was fundamentally anti-women. This seems hard to reconcile with other facts, such as his encouragement of women analysts, including his daughter Anna (Westen 1999).

At a broader level, cross-cultural researchers have questioned the basic tri-partite model of the mind which is the foundation of Freud's work. As already noted, the concept of the unconscious is alien to traditional Asian societies. Clifford Geertz, a cultural anthropologist who has studied a variety of cultures, suggests that the idea of an individual awareness, as implied by the ego, is not only not universal, but in fact relatively uncommon (Geertz 1984). This has significant implications if one considers how the same behaviour would be seen in other cultures. For example, if a man whose wife had just died appeared in public smiling, Freud would see this as indicative of repression; yet in Java this would be seen as proper conduct, not concealment. As Geertz argues, to apply the Freudian standard would be to ignore the entire framework of the culture (Geertz 1984: 128). Freud would probably respond that cultural beliefs may nonetheless mask hidden psychodynamics, but the issues of cultural bias are not likely to be resolved at any time soon.

These disputes seem inevitably to interweave the man and the theory. This is likely in part because he dominated the field for so long, and in part because of the difficulties of evaluating the theory in more conventional ways. However, claims of bias also raise an interesting conundrum: does bias prove that Freud was wrong, or that he was right? If Freud was biased, then it seems that he was *unaware* of the distortions to his thinking, since in most respects he adapted his thinking to fit new information. That means that he was *unconsciously* distorting his interpretations, which is precisely what his theory says: no person can ever fully understand their own behaviour, or be free of distortions induced by unconscious processes. So, if Freud's thinking (e.g. about women) was biased despite his efforts to be objective, then that proves that his basic assumptions about the dynamics of the unconscious mind are correct! By the same reasoning, one would have to conclude that no one can offer a purely rational analysis of Freud's work – or of anything else in the world. (This point of view has in fact been suggested by some philosophers of science (see Kuhn 1970).)

It is precisely this 'Catch-22' nature of the theory that bothers some critics. If you accept the basic assumptions, then it is nearly impossible to invalidate the theory. Consequently, some have argued that Freud's work is more of a story than a theory, weaving together the threads of human experience into a fictional tapestry (e.g. Robinson 1979). More extreme critics see Freud's whole conception as simply wrong (Shorter 1997; Crews 1998). Others see that view as too negative – a case of seeing the faults, but not the contributions, of psychoanalysis (Wachtel 1977; Gay 1988). There is no doubt that Freud broke new ground in both his observations and his ideas. Given his pioneering role, it would seem unreasonable to expect him to have found the final answers to all questions – others could surely follow in his path. In this regard, a statement by psychoanalyst Charles Brenner, writing in a selected volume of Freud's writings, is apt: 'If the history of psychoanalysis is like the history of the other natural sciences, and we have no reason to doubt that it will be, the time will come when the theories Freud elaborated in the 1920s will be incorporated into and superseded by other more complete and more precise hypotheses which will be based on more extensive data and perhaps on different ways of viewing psychic phenomena' (Brenner 1957: 246). That, indeed, is the way of science. Let us see just what Freud's successors have achieved.

Neo-Freudian and Non-Freudian Psychodynamic Theories

As his ideas became known, Freud attracted the attention of a number of doctors who were interested in his methods and theory. Several individuals became part of a close-knit group of followers, who were to help Freud to spread his ideas. Unfortunately, the relationships were not always amicable. Just as Freud was sensitive to opposition from the greater medical community, so, too, he had limited tolerance for dissent within his group of followers. As a consequence, several early protégés either left or were cast out of the group. Wilhelm Fleiss, who influenced Freud's thinking about the sexual origins of hysteria, was eventually relegated to the shadows (Masson 1984). More significant were the departures of Alfred Adler and Carl Jung, who split from Freud in the years just before the First World War. Both men disagreed with various aspects of Freud's evolving theory, and ultimately became well known for their own theories. Interestingly, G. Stanley Hall, the American psychologist who sponsored Freud's first lectures in the United States, commented in 1924 that he hoped Freud would not make the mistake of making 'too abrupt a break with his more advanced pupils like Adler and the Zurich group' (Hall 1924: 7).

Even among those who stayed relatively close to Freud's basic views, a number of variants arose (see Padel 1987). The publication of *The Ego and the Id* in 1923 led Freud's followers to go in two different directions, called the 'ego psychology' and 'object relations' schools. *Ego psychology*, promoted by Freud's daughter Anna, emphasized the mechanisms used by the ego to deal with the world (including defence mechanisms). Later, Erik Erikson, who worked with Anna, was to extend the conception of developmental stages over the entire lifespan, in the process placing greater emphasis on social influences. The *object relations* school, which developed in England, focused on the relationships between the individual and those to whom there are significant emotional ties (particularly the mother, due to early rearing). Melanie Klein and Donald Winnicott were among the pioneers of this approach, which later influenced John Bowlby. Bowlby, in turn, developed a highly influential model of the infant/mother relationship, which he called *attachment* (Bowlby 1969).

Thus, Freud's work spawned a number of approaches, some closely related to his original ideas, some markedly different. Over time, the degree of divergence and variety of viewpoints has expanded. Thus, today one finds a number of viewpoints which are 'analytic', but clearly not Freudian, such as *transactional analysis* (Berne 1961). In addition, the humanistic approach, which differs in many ways from the psychodynamic perspective, was founded by individuals who were initially trained in analysis, as we shall see in Chapter 6.

Given this diversity, and the considerable period that has elapsed since Freud's death, it is appropriate to reconsider Brenner's observation, quoted at the end of the previous section: has the psychodynamic approach advanced, in the manner of the natural sciences, or are the ideas of Freud's successors simply variations on a theme? To get some sense of an answer to this question, let us briefly consider some major contributors.

Carl Jung and the Collective Unconscious

Carl Jung was born in Switzerland in 1875, the son of a Lutheran pastor. As a boy, he struggled to reconcile the religious differences between him and his father. In his autobiography, he contrasts his own ideas, based on the immediate experience of spirituality, with his father's, which were based on intellectual adherence to doctrine (Dourley 1992). These feelings, which sometimes led him to feel isolated in childhood, were later to influence his

Carl Jung

Carl Jung (1875–1961) was born in Kesswil, Switzerland, the son of a Lutheran pastor. Despite his vocation, Jung's father seemed more intellectual than spiritual, and his detached attitude led Jung as a child to feel isolated by his own spiritual interests. The feelings he experienced were later to influence his ideas about psychological growth. Jung was educated in Basel, and received his medical degree from the University of Basel in 1900; he then did a psychiatric internship at the Burgholzli in Zurich under Eugen Bleuler (who coined the term 'schizophrenia'). By 1905, he was lecturing in psychiatry at the University of Zurich, and conducting a psychiatric practice. At this time, he contacted Freud to express interest in his work, and the two men developed a quick rapport; when they met in Vienna for the first time, they talked together for 13 hours! They had regular contacts after that, and Freud came to consider Jung as his protégé and successor. (For example, when Freud was invited to speak in the United States in 1909, Jung was prominent among those who accompanied him.) However, by 1912 they had clashed on a number of issues, and Jung left Freud's circle to evolve his own theory and techniques. In later years, he continued to live in Zurich, where he conducted a private practice as well as wrote. Faced with heart problems that underlined to him the frailty of human life, he remained interested in the issues of individuation and growth until his death at the age of eighty-six.

ego in Jung's theory, the element of the self which provides the conscious direction of one's life

persona the conscious character or role we assume in presenting ourselves to the world

self the totality of the person, both conscious and unconscious; the self is distinct from both the ego and the persona (conscious aspects of personality)

personal unconscious in Jung's theory, that part of the contents of the unconscious which is related to the experiences of the individual

ideas about psychological growth. In university, he studied medicine, and in 1900 did a psychiatric internship at a major institute in Zurich. By 1905, he was lecturing in psychiatry at the University of Zurich, and conducting a psychiatric practice.

At this time, he contacted Freud to express interest in his work; thereafter, they were in regular contact, by mail and in person. As time went by, Freud came to consider Jung as his protégé and successor (Hall and Nordby 1973). Despite their personal rapport, the two men differed on matters of theory – Jung disagreed with Freud's emphasis on sexuality, and Freud questioned Jung's interest in spirituality, among other issues. (Jung saw psychic energy as being much more general than Freud's emphasis on sexuality.) As a result, they broke contact in 1912, and Jung gradually evolved his own theory.

Apart from de-emphasizing sexuality, Jung's approach differed from Freud's primarily in two areas: the structure of personality (particularly the unconscious) and the process of development. It is not possible to provide a complete treatment here, but some general comments may help to suggest the nature of the differences. Jung's view of personality in some respects was more complex than Freud's. At the conscious level, Jung talked about the **ego**, which provides the conscious direction of our lives (much like Freud's conception), and the **persona**, which is the character or role we assume in presenting ourselves to the world. Both of these are distinct from the **self**, which comprises the totality of the person, both conscious and unconscious. Jung's view of the unconscious differed significantly from Freud's, and was a source of friction between the two men. Jung acknowledged that some of the contents of the unconscious are related to the experiences of the individual; he called this portion (which paralleled Freud's conception of the unconscious) the **personal unconscious**. But in addition,

collective unconscious in Jung's theory, a biologically based portion of the unconscious which reflects universal themes and ideas, not individual experience

archetypes patterns within the collective unconscious which serve to organize our experiences, providing the basis of many fantasies, myths and symbols

individuation Jung's conception of the goal of development, which he described as the expansion of conscious awareness by the ego making contact with the unconscious portions of the self

there is a portion of the unconscious which reflects universal, not individual, themes and ideas; this portion, which he called the **collective unconscious**, was biologically-based, not the product of experience. While sometimes the collective unconscious is caricatured as a sort of 'race memory', Jung's actual intent was to suggest that just as the body has an evolutionary history, so does the mind. (In biological terms, one might say the way the brain functions reflects its evolution.)

One important element of the collective unconscious is the existence of organizing patterms called **archetypes**. Archetypes contain no content of their own, but instead serve to organize our experiences, almost like cognitive schema. The three most significant archetypes are the *animus*, the *anima* and the *shadow*. The anima represents the complementary qualities of the persona in a man – for example, if the persona is intellectual, the anima will be sentimental. In general, it represents the feminine side of the male. Similarly, the animus is the unconscious complement to the woman's persona. The shadow represents the darker, primitive aspects of human nature. Jung saw archetypes as the basis of many fantasies, myths and symbols. For example, he explained the story of Oedipus as an expression of an underlying archetype, in contrast to Freud's view that it reflected a developmental conflict. At the same time, Jung agreed with Freud that the unconscious expresses itself in symbolic form, and he had a great interest in how certain symbols recur across different cultures (Jung amd von Franz 1964) (see Figure 5.5). Like Freud, Jung also believed that analysing the meaning of symbols was helpful to understanding the dynamics of the mind. By exploring symbols, the individual can make contact with, and come to terms with, the unconscious portions of the self.

Jung's conception of development, which he referred to as the process of **individuation**, was related to his conception of personality. The goal of human development, in Jung's view, was to expand conscious awareness through the ego making contact with the unconscious portions of the self. For the *ego*, which reflects the conscious sense of identity, growth involves expansion of one's awareness of the world and of oneself. But for the *self*, which is the whole of one's being (including the unconscious), the goal is to transcend egotistical interests, achieving a union of the conscious with the unconscious. Jung perceived human growth and development as more open-ended than Freud's description of the genital stage, which was characterized primarily in negative terms. Instead, individuation was a lifelong process of increasing awareness, whose ultimate end (the joining of the conscious and unconscious in the self) was unlikely to be fully achieved.

Taken as a whole, Jung's theory is rich in detail, and complex. The theory often deals with pairs of complementary opposites, such as conscious and unconscious, ego and shadow. (Another pair which has become well known is his description of personality in terms of *introversion* – being inwardly oriented – and *extraversion* – being focused on the outer world.) Like Freud, he was a prolific writer, and the large body of his writings makes it difficult to summarize all his thinking. Like Freud, he often returned to the same themes and issues, seeking to clarify his earlier work. For example, late in his life, after a heart attack at the age of 69, Jung returned to the issue of growth, relating it to his youthful concerns about the role of spirituality

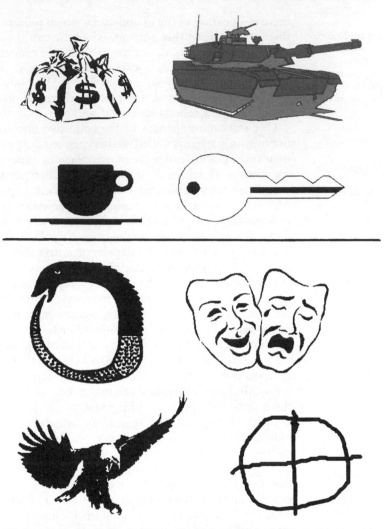

Figure 5.5 Symbolism in psychoanalytic theories Both Freud and Jung believed symbols had meaning, although for Freud they represented the personal unconscious, as in the top figures; Jung saw symbols as expressions of the collective unconscious, as in the lower figures, which represent archetypes. (Try to figure out what each of the Freudian symbols represents.)

in human life. The increasing awareness associated with individuation, he concluded, was an affirmation of the meaning of human life. In his auto-biography, he wrote, 'the sole purpose of human existence is to kindle a light in the darkness of mere being' (Jung 1963: 326).

Evaluating Jung's work is difficult. His theory has drawn many adher-ents, and provides a distinctive perspective on psychodynamic processes. His ideas about the collective unconscious raise interesting questions about the use of symbols in areas such as religion, mythology and children's art. In a classic study of myths across many cultures, Joseph Campbell found evidence for archetypes like the Hero and the Earth Mother in most cultures

(Campbell 1968). However, many of the observations offered as support for Jung's theory can also be interpreted in other ways. For example, children's art from around the world frequently shows mandelas and other archetypal symbols (Kellogg 1967). However, these shapes may simply reflect the development of perceptual and motor skills, or other non-Jungian mechanisms. In the end, the metaphorical nature of many of Jung's concepts has led critics to argue that his theory, while different from Freud's, comes no closer to being scientifically testable. As we shall see, this remains a concern when considering other psychodynamic theories.

For further consideration

Compare the symbols which Jung would call archetypes in Figure 5.5 with the Freudian symbols given. Which are easier to interpret for you? Is this a reasonable standard for determining their validity?

Alfred Adler and Individual Psychology

Born in Vienna in 1870, Alfred Adler had a difficult childhood, marked by the death of a younger brother when Adler was 3, and a near-fatal bout of pneumonia at the age of 5. These events seem to have influenced his later theorizing, with its emphasis on social factors and the importance of childhood experiences. When he survived the pneumonia, thanks to the interventions of a dedicated doctor, Adler decided to make medicine his career goal. He enrolled in the University of Vienna in 1888, and received his medical degree in 1895. After initially practising as an ophthalmologist, he gradually shifted to neurology and psychiatry. Although he had already begun his own theoretical work, he was drawn to Freud, who was becoming known in Vienna for his approach to hysterias. He became one of the first members of Freud's inner circle in 1902, three years before Jung, and was very active in the group. Like Jung, Adler was an early heir-apparent, as shown by Freud nominating him as the first president of the Viennese Psychoanalytic Society in 1910.

As it turned out, Adler's favoured relationship with Freud was not to last. Even when they first met, Adler had difficulty accepting Freud's views of the nature of drives, and the notion of the Oedipal conflict. As time went on, their disagreements became more evident, and more vehement. By 1911, the matters had come to a head, and Adler resigned as president of the Society, just a year after taking the post! He went on to found his own organization, called the Association for Individual Psychology; some of the founding members were ex-members of the Viennese Psychoanalytic Society. The group helped to spread Adler's ideas in Europe; when he moved to the United States in the 1930s, interest also grew there. He died in Scotland in 1937, while on a lecture tour (Fadiman and Frager 1976).

Adler's early views were shaped by his interest in organic dysfunctions and the implications of Darwinian theory. These influences led to the notion of *inferiority*, and subsequent attempts at *compensation*. While originally meant in a physical sense, these concepts gradually shifted towards the psychological, as Adler grew more interested in social relations. Gradually he evolved the notion that all children experience a sense of **inferiority**

inferiority for Adler, a sense of helplessness first experienced by children because of their size and dependence on others; this feeling can also be intensified by real or imagined physical defects, social rejection and other factors

Alfred Adler

Alfred Adler (1870–1937), born in Vienna, had a difficult childhood. When Adler was three years old, his younger brother died in the bed they shared. In addition to this tragedy, he suffered from serious health problems, including a near-fatal bout of pneumonia at the age of five. Adler struggled to overcome the impact of these early difficulties, and was popular among his peers. He received his medical degree from the University of Vienna in 1895. After initially practising as an ophthalmologist, he gradually shifted to neurology and psychiatry, and became one of the first members of Freud's inner circle in 1902, three years before Jung. Like Jung, Adler was an early heir-apparent, as shown by Freud nominating him as the first president of the Viennese Psychoanalytic Society in 1910. Unfortunately, Adler's favoured relationship with Freud was not to last, as they repeatedly clashed on theoretical issues. By 1911, the matters had come to a head, and Adler resigned as president of the Society, just a year after taking the post. He went on to found his own organization, called the Association for Individual Psychology; some of the founding members were ex-members of the Viennese Psychoanalytic Society. The group flourished in Europe, helping the spread of Adler's ideas. When Nazism began to threaten (like Freud, Adler came from a middle-class Jewish family), he moved to the United States, accepting a teaching post at Long Island Medical College. He died while on a lecture tour in Scotland in 1937, at the age of sixty-seven.

compensation in Adler's theory, a process of engaging in activities intended to produce a feeling of superiority over others, in order to overcome feelings of inferiority

inferiority complex an intense feeling of insecurity based on failure to resolve the feelings evoked by childhood experiences of helplessness

superiority complex a response to feelings of inferiority in which the individual attempts to mask their weakness by adopting an attitude of exaggerated self-importance

style of life a term used by Adler to describe an individual's unique way of adapting to and interacting with the world, which is an expression of the person's life history and goals

because of their size and dependence on others. In turn, inferiority can lead to attempts at overcoming the perceived weakness (**compensation**); this process is motivated by the generalized drive which Adler called *striving for superiority*. In contrast to Freud's emphasis on sexuality and aggression, Adler saw motivation in terms of the desire for mastery over oneself and a striving for power (Ansbacher and Ansbacher 1956; Orgler 1976). Thus, striving for superiority was a lifelong process, guided by conscious goals and values (rather than the unconscious).

For Adler, the experience of childhood inferiority is the most important influence on the development of personality. Some individuals are so overwhelmed by early feelings of helplessness that they develop a lifelong sense of inferiority, called an **inferiority complex**. Others attempt to mask their weakness by pretending to feel superior, when inwardly they lack self-esteem; this is called a **superiority complex**. Early experiences, like having a major illness, being overly pampered, or being neglected, can have a major impact on how the child views his or her own capacities, and on the child's social interactions. (One can see in pampering and neglect a parallel to Freud's view of how over- or undergratification create fixations.)

Adler argued that as an adult an individual is best understood as a whole, rather than in terms of individual behaviours. That is, each person has a unique **style of life**, a way of adapting and interacting, which is an expression of the person's life history and goals. (The contemporary term 'lifestyle' is really a corruption of Adler's concept.) For a healthy individual, unmarred by either inferiority or superiority complexes, the goals will include love, friendships and a commitment to society (which Adler called *social interest*).

Individuals who lack self-esteem will instead divert their energy into behaviours which are productive for neither the person nor society, such as blaming others for one's failings. Overall, Adler's approach to personality places much more emphasis on social factors than does Freud's, and also offers a more positive conception of development as a growth process.

Adler's ideas have had a broad, but rather diffuse, impact. His emphasis on social interactions and self-esteem has influenced both other psychodynamic theorists like Karen Horney and Erich Fromm, and the humanistic approach of theorists like Carl Rogers. In addition, his focus on childhood led him and his colleagues to pay considerable attention to educational processes, and 'Adlerian' schools still exist. While it does not demonstrate that the theory is correct, the adoption of terms like 'inferiority complex' and 'style of life' as common usage is an indication of how widely Adler's ideas have spread. (For example, 'lifestyle' has been adopted as a concept in marketing research.) In this sense, his influence has been significant.

In trying to assess Alder, it is not clear whether his theory should be considered a revision of psychoanalytic theory, or an alternative. The disagreements which led to the split between Freud and Adler (about the nature of basic drives and childhood complexes) clearly show the differences in the two theories. However, there is little evidence which addresses the issue of which view is more correct. Salvatore Maddi has argued that Freud's concepts can be applied to understand his own life (Maddi 1974); the same might be said of Adler and *his* theory. The difficulty with this sort of comparison, as Maddi notes, is that this is not a valid means of establishing scientific truth. While some evidence exists to support his concepts of how self-esteem and social interest affect behaviour (Crandall 1984), many of his basic concepts remain difficult to assess. Lacking adequate evidence, it is difficult to draw clear conclusions about the validity of Adler's theory.

Other Psychodynamic Theorists

Jung and Adler are traditionally considered neo-Freudians, in part because of their early ties to Freud. However, there have been many other psychodynamic theories developed in the past hundred years, many of which view themselves as very different from Freud's theory. These 'non-Freudian' theories nonetheless share some basic assumptions which make it appropriate to consider them 'psychodynamic'. Among these assumptions are the importance of internal mental processes (especially motivation) in understanding behaviour, and the role of motivation and experience in shaping personality. Despite this common foundation, psychodynamic theories nonetheless diverge – for example, in describing the source of motivation. Hence, it is worth briefly considering some examples, in order to see some of the similarities and differences to Freud's theory.

Karen Horney (1885–1952) began as a psychoanalyst in Berlin; along with Anna Freud, she was one of the first female analysts. Right from the beginning, she was critical of what she saw as male-centred ideas in Freud's

Comparing Freud and Erikson's theories of development

Age	Freud	Erikson
0–1½	Oral stage – development of ego through body image, delaying gratification	Trust versus mistrust – developing trust in others and self
1½–3	Anal stage – development of ego through toilet training	Autonomy versus shame – learning self-control
3–5	Phallic stage – Oedipal conflict	Initiative versus guilt – learning to plan and initiate new actions
5–12 (puberty)	Latency – drives repressed, little conscious conflict	Industry versus inferiority – absorbed in activities like school; developing sense of competence
12–20 (adolescence)	Genital stage – development complete; gratification largely symbolic in form	Identity versus role confusion – forming clear sense of self-identity
Young adult (20–25)		Intimacy versus isolation – learning commitment and sharing in relations with others
Middle adult (25–65)		Generativity versus stagnation – making contributions to family and society
Late adult (65+)		Integrity versus despair – developing sense of completeness towards life, accepting past

Figure 5.6   Erikson's and Freud's models of development While the timing of early stages is nearly identical, Freud defined his stages in psychosexual terms, whereas Erikson defined his in psychosocial terms.

theory – particularly the concept of penis envy. (In fact, Horney was the first to challenge Freud publicly on the issue, in 1926.) Horney saw Freud's notion that women feel inferior as both biased and wrong. Instead, she argued that women are physiologically superior, and that men seek to subordinate them out of fear (Horney 1967).

Despite these differences, she agreed with Freud (and Adler) about the significance of early childhood in shaping personality. For Horney, the development of personality involved the fundamental *need for security*. This need is experienced right from birth, as part of the **basic anxiety** experienced by a new-born child. In general, her theory, like Adler's, placed much greater emphasis on self-esteem than did Freud's work (Horney 1950). Her distinction between the *real self* (who we actually are) and the *ideal self* (an image of what we should be) also influenced the work of Carl Rogers (see Chapter 6). In addition, by examining how women's experiences, rather than their anatomy, shape their behaviour, she was a precursor to more recent feminist theories. In all these respects, her contributions have been significant.

Erik Erikson (1902–94) originally studied under Anna Freud in Vienna, and later began to do research and child therapy in the United States. He

basic anxiety in Horney's theory, an intense sense of isolation and helplessness which is the primary source of human motivation

developed his own theory of development, which differed significantly from Freud's in both the nature of developmental stages and the drives which underlie them. First, he defined stages in *psychosocial* terms, not in terms of sexuality and aggression. To Erikson, the basic drives are social ones, which are biologically based. Development involves resolving a series of problems or conflicts which concern the individual's sense of self and relationships to other people. For example, infants must resolve their fears of helplessness by learning to trust their primary caregiver. Second, whereas Freud's theory never elaborated on adult behaviour (the genital stage), Erikson's theory has eight stages, four of which focus on the years after puberty (see Figure 5.6). In this regard, his focus on adult personality, from midlife changes to retirement and ageing, foreshadowed modern issues in the study of human development (Erikson 1963). In addition, with his biographical analyses of historical figures like Martin Luther, Erikson pioneered the application of psychological analysis to the writing of biographies – an approach now sometimes called *psychohistory* (Erikson 1962). In some sense, his own life mirrored his theory, as he continued to be active well into his eighties, and was 91 when he died in 1994.

In the end, each of these theories, both neo-Freudian and non-Freudian, seems to emphasize different concepts and structures. Yet it is not easy to determine if they are simply variations on a theme, as Robinson (1979) suggests, or whether one or more represent clear advances over Freud's pioneering theory. However they might disagree with Freud's concepts and theory, they clearly share the same difficulties of falsifiability.

Conclusion

The psychodynamic approach attempts to understand behaviour by analysing how personality is shaped by past experience and the workings of the mind. In one sense, it is like the cognitive approach, in that both focus on processes which cannot be directly observed. At the same time, it is different from the cognitive approach, for it attempts to deal with the individual as a person, including what motivates behaviour. By contrast, the cognitive approach currently offers no integrated conception of the individual, and is essentially silent on the question of motivation. In the same way, the biological approach also offers explanations of the mind, but its theories operate at a very different level of description, and cannot be directly compared. (Ironically, Freud himself hoped that ultimately his theory could be supported by reference to physiological processes.)

Within the psychodynamic approach, there is no question that Sigmund Freud occupies the central place. His position as pioneer has made his work the standard, rightly or wrongly, against which other psychodynamic models must be judged. Freud's theorizing, which is marked by numerous modifications over the course of his career, highlights the challenges posed in trying to infer the unobservable (the dynamics of the mind) from what can be seen.

At the same time, Freud's approach has inspired many others to develop psychodynamic models of behaviour, including some of his own close associates. Viewed together, it is possible to identify many kinds of similarities among these theories, and also many differences. One such similarity is the emphasis placed on early childhood experiences in understanding adult personality. Unfortunately, the similar-yet-different nature of the various theories makes it hard to decide which is the most accurate. To some extent, this seems unavoidable, given the goals and methods of the psychodynamic approach.

Ultimately, all psychological theories, psychodynamic or otherwise, are attempting to account for actual behaviour; in that sense, it is inevitable that there should be agreement on some aspects. At the same time, the necessity of inferring processes from observed behaviour which is central to the psychodynamic approach makes it likely that different observers will create different organizing structures. This in turn can help to explain the wide diversity of conceptual structures found in psychodynamic theories. Seen in this way, the theories represent different ways of viewing the same thing; as one analyst put it, 'Most conflicts in analysis are definitional' (Arlow, quoted in Karen 1992: 49). Thus, one is left with the sense that psychodynamic models are like cognitive schemata – each is shaped by the experiences and cultural background of the person who developed it.

While this might be reasonable in literature, science seeks to avoid such ambiguities by subjecting competing theories to experimental test. Unfortunately, the same factors that lead to *differing* psychodynamic theories also result in *complex* theories which are difficult to test. This difficulty is clear in Freud's theory, which can *describe* almost any aspect of human behaviour, but *predicts* very little. In general, there is no way to determine empirically which psychodynamic model is the most accurate, since they generally lack *falsifiability*.

Still, there are other ways to judge a theory. One way is in terms of *generality*: does a theory address the full range of human behaviour? Evaluating generality requires considering both what a theory covers *and* what it *doesn't* cover. One of the apparent omissions in Freud's work which has drawn criticism is the lack of a clear conception of the goal of development. Indeed, the genital stage, which represents the long final phase of life, is the stage which he elaborated the least.

Interestingly, this omission helped to trigger the development of the humanistic approach. Humanistic psychologists have developed a conception of healthy growth which views development in terms of reaching one's maximum potential. In this sense, the approach is very different from the 'brutal pessimism' of Freud, and closer to the views of Adler and Horney.

Whatever their differences and limitations, all psychodynamic theories share certain basic assumptions, such as the belief that it is possible to understand an individual's personality objectively. By contrast, the humanistic approach assumes that each person is in the best position to know their own self, so humanistic theories focus on the individual's own subjective perceptions. In this respect, we are led back to the fact that each approach to psychology makes different assumptions, and therefore emphasizes different aspects of behaviour. In the next chapter, we will see how the humanistic approach starts with many of the same concerns about personality as does the psychodynamic approach, but proceeds to frame its explanations in a very different way.

Chapter Summary

- The psychodynamic approach attempts to understand behaviour in terms of the workings of the mind, with an emphasis on motivation and the role of past experience. The approach was pioneered by *Sigmund Freud*, who developed *psychoanalytic theory*.

- Psychoanalytic theory emphasizes the importance of *innate drives*, the *continuity* of normal and abnormal behaviour and the role of the *unconscious* mind.

- Freud's theory of personality accounts for behaviour in terms of the dynamic relationships of the *id*, *ego* and *superego*.

- Freud described development in terms of five psychosexual stages distinguished by shifts in the underlying mode of gratification: *oral*, *anal*, *phallic*, *latency* and *genital*. Each stage is marked by particular challenges and conflicts; of these, the *Oedipal conflict* (in the phallic stage) is probably the most significant in terms of later development.

- Psychoanalysis, by making the assumption of psychic determinism, views all behaviour as having meaning; consequently, Freud looked at everything from *dreams* to *parapraxes* (Freudian slips) to art as expressions of the dynamics of the mind.

- Anxiety, which results from conflicts within the individual, is handled by the use of various *defence mechanisms*, such as *displacement* and *repression*, which reduce anxiety by distorting reality rather than resolving the conflict.

- While very comprehensive, Freud's theory has limitations (including problems of *falsifiability*), and even in his lifetime spawned competing theories, including several by his former students.

- The best known of Freud's disciples are *Carl Jung* and *Alfred Adler*, who are considered *neo-Freudian* theorists; other psychodynamic theorists, such as *Karen Horney* and *Erik Erikson*, are generally regarded as *non-Freudian* psychodynamic theorists.

- Carl Jung's theory expanded on the nature of the unconscious, particularly by including a conception of a *collective unconscious* whose *archetypes* influence our interpretation of experiences. Jung rejected Freud's emphasis on sexual motivation, and instead emphasized the importance of *individuation*, the enhancing of awareness, as a motive for development.

◆ Alfred Adler, while less well known to the general public, was influential in the emphasis he gave to issues of *esteem*, and many of his terms, like *inferiority complex* and *style of life*, have become common usage.

◆ Psychodynamic theories provide a distinctive approach to the understanding of behaviour; the primary difficulty is finding an effective way to evaluate the various theories within the approach.

Key Terms and Concepts

anxiety
archetypes
basic anxiety
catharsis
collective unconscious
conscious
defence mechanism
displacement
ego
fixation
free association
id
identification
individuation

inferiority complex
Oedipal conflict
pleasure principle
preconscious
psychic determinism
psychosexual stages of development
reality principle
regression
repression
style of life
subconscious
superego
unconscious

Suggestions for Further Reading

For the reader interested in more information on psychodynamic theories in general, both Cramer's *Personality and Psychotherapy* and Hjelle and Ziegler's *Personality Theories: Basic Assumptions, Research, and Applications* provide good general references.

The best way to get the flavour of Freud's work is by reading his own writings. *Psychopathology in Everyday Life*, with its many examples of 'Freudian slips', provides an interesting starting point for the general reader. For those seeking a brief summary of Freud's theory, Brenner's *An Elementary Textbook of Psychoanalysis* is still a good brief guide, written by a Freudian analyst.

Paul Roazen's *Freud and His Followers* places Freud's work into historical context, and also explores his relations to Jung, Adler, and others. *A History of Psychiatry*, by medical historian Edward Shorter, provides a highly critical, but historically detailed, account of the development of psychoanalysis.

To explore Jung's ideas in more detail, *Man and His Symbols*, an edited collection of his writings, is a useful source.

6

The Humanistic Approach

Keeping the Person in 'Personality'
Introduction
Carl Rogers's Theory
Self Theory and Personality
  The Organism and the Actualizing Tendency
  The Phenomenal Field and the Self
  The Ideal Self, Congruence and Incongruence
Personality Development and Conditions for Growth
  Conditions of Worth and the Would–Should
    Dilemma
  Conditional and Unconditional Positive Regard
  Congruence and Conditions for Growth
  Human Potential and the Fully Functioning Person

Abraham Maslow's Theory
Motivation and the Hierarchy of Needs
  Needs and Self-development
Self-actualization and Peak Experiences
Maslow's Concept of Healthy Growth
Extending the Humanistic Approach
Existential Psychology
Frankl's Logotherapy
Conclusion
Chapter Summary
Key Terms and Concepts
Suggestions for Further Reading

Keeping the Person in 'Personality'

Freud's explorations of personality were initially driven by the suffering of his patients, and his desire to help them. In the same way, the origins of the humanistic approach can be traced to the desire to aid those in distress. To illustrate this, let us consider an experience that Carl Rogers, one of the founders of humanistic psychology, had as a counsellor. Rogers was working with a young man who suffered from schizophrenia, a serious form of mental disorder. The man was hospitalized in a state institution, and Rogers had been working with him for some time, with little evident progress. Then, one day, something happened:

> [The man] made a few remarks about individuals who had recently left the hospital; then he remained silent for almost forty minutes. When he got up to go, he mumbled almost under his breath, 'If some of *them* can do it, maybe I can too.' That was all

> – not a dramatic statement, not uttered with force and vigour, yet a statement of choice by this young man to work toward his own improvement.
>
> (Rogers 1969: 265–6)
>
> Eight months later, the man was in fact discharged from the hospital. To Rogers, this represented not a triumph for him as a therapist, but an 'experience of responsible choice' by the young man. In this event, as in all of life, 'It is the *meaning* of the *decision* which is essential to understanding the act' (Rogers 1969: 268).
>
> This story is striking for the improvement in the man's condition – which is remarkable in itself – but also for the way Rogers describes it. One can scarcely imagine Freud interpreting the events in this way – a cure by *choice*? In what sense do choices determine our lives? And how can the meaning people give to their actions be incorporated into a psychological theory? To Freud, it was the therapist, not the patient, that determined meanings. In the humanistic approach, personal meanings are central to the understanding of behaviour – which itself is only one part of the person as a whole. In the end, the goal is to understand the whole person. To grasp what this means, we must look at the origins of the approach.

Introduction

In the 1950s, the field of psychology, particularly in North America, was dominated by psychoanalysis and behaviourism. Clinically-oriented practitioners favoured psychoanalysis, while experimental researchers tended to follow the precepts of behaviourism. Supporters of each approach viewed it as a comprehensive system for understanding human behaviour. Not surprisingly, however, not every psychologist felt comfortable with these approaches. Some found behaviourism too limited, because it focused on specific responses, while ignoring the person as a whole. Others found psychoanalysis both too rigid and too pessimistic. (Some of the pioneers of the humanistic approach started their careers in the psychoanalytic tradition.) Out of these concerns emerged the humanistic approach.

The *humanistic approach* encompasses a variety of theorists, who have often applied other labels to their theoretical perspective, such as 'existential' or 'phenomenological' psychology. Abraham Maslow, one of the pioneers of the approach, has referred to humanistic psychology as a 'Third Force' opposing the dominant perspectives of behaviourism and psychoanalysis (Maslow 1968; DeCarvalho 1990). While each label, and the associated theory, conveys a slightly different meaning, collectively the various theories embody certain common elements which justify treating them together. These common elements are the assumptions which define the humanistic approach.

There are two assumptions which are basic to the humanistic approach. First and foremost is the belief that behaviour must be understood in terms

phenomenological
pertaining to the way things appear or are experienced; in the humanistic approach, a reference to the emphasis on an individual's perceptions and feelings as defining the meaning of their behaviour

of the subjective experience of the individual. If you wish to understand behaviour, the humanists argue, you must understand the person producing the behaviour – *including* how the person sees the world. (This is sometimes described as a **phenomenological** viewpoint.) The second major assumption is that behaviour is not constrained by either past experience or current circumstances. That is, the way we act is not simply a response to an immediate stimulus, nor determined solely by previous events.

These assumptions contrast with those of the other approaches we have considered, particularly behaviourism and psychoanalysis. While obviously different in their details, behaviourism and psychoanalysis share two basic characteristics: both believe in determinism, and both see little explanatory value in subjective experience. Let us briefly consider each assumption.

determinism the assumption that all behaviour has specific causes

Determinism is the assumption that all behaviour has specific causes. While both behaviourism and psychoanalysis assume some form of determinism, they differ in what *types* of causes they consider. For the behaviourist, behaviour is dictated by environmental factors, such as reinforcers. For the psychoanalyst, the individual is governed by innate drives whose influence is largely unconscious (*psychic determinism*). Ultimately, both see the individual as a kind of puppet, at the mercy of largely uncontrollable forces.

By contrast, the humanists do not see behaviour as determined by either the immediate situation or past experience. While both types of factors can influence behaviour, the crucial element, in the view of the humanists, is that individuals are able to respond based on their subjective assessment of a situation; that is, they can make *choices* (sometimes this is referred to as 'free will').

The justification for this stance is complex, and has been a source of debate between the two sides (see Rogers and Skinner 1956). In large part, the humanist position is connected to the view that the way we think affects our behaviour, independently of external factors. Note that the humanists are *not* saying that causes do not exist in the world. Instead, they disagree with their opponents about what the primary causes of behaviour are. Without trying to settle the dispute, let us point out that both determinism and choice represent *assumptions*, neither of which is open to proof.

The second humanistic assumption is that behaviour must be understood in terms of the individual's subjective experience. Only the individual can explain the meaning of a particular behaviour. Psychologists have long been wary of dealing with subjective reports, as we have seen in earlier chapters. The behaviourists have tried to handle the issue by arguing that what people think or say is irrelevant to the explanation of behaviour. Instead, their explanations focus on the role of the environment. Psychoanalysis also claims that individuals cannot explain their own behaviour, because the causes are largely unconscious. Consequently, conscious explanations will be distorted by rationalization or other defences. The result is that both approaches devalue the significance of subjective experience. The explanation of behaviour ends up depending not on the person who is behaving, but on the assessment of an observer (the researcher/theorist).

The humanists reject these interpretations, and instead suggest that subjective experience is an important aspect of behaviour, *and* that it can be studied scientifically. Essentially, the argument is that *all data*, being gathered by human beings, are inherently *subjective*, and must be regarded as such. (Recall what has been said in previous chapters about the nature of perception.) The traditional insistence on an objective observer is meaningless, since no one is objective. As a result, there is no reason to reject subjective experience in favour of third-party observations.

In favouring this view, Carl Rogers argued that, rather than making science impossible, the recognition of subjectivity establishes new criteria for legitimate scientific observations (Rogers 1964, 1985). Basically, any event or observation which can be agreed upon by two observers is a valid observation, even though each person is reacting out of their own subjectivity. This process of agreement, which Rogers called **intersubjective verification**, is seen as ultimately the basis of all science, as well as all human relationships. Since science depends on agreement among observers (e.g. in using replicability as a test for the accuracy of experimental results), intersubjective verification is fundamentally no different from other methods. In this sense, rather than endorsing a dangerous form of subjectivity, the humanists are simply making explicit how intersubjective verification is the basis of all observation, including traditional scientific methods.

A third characteristic of the humanistic approach, which emerges from the first two assumptions, is an emphasis on *meaning* – the purpose or value that a person attaches to their actions and experience. Traditionally, psychology has tended to ignore any notion of meaning or purpose to behaviour. At first glance this seems strange, since questions of meaning lie at the heart of much of human experience – the myths we create, the stories we tell, the questions we ask ourselves about our lives and so on. So why has psychology not tried to deal with the issue?

One reason psychology has ignored meaning has to do with the nature of science. Questions of meaning seem too closely tied to value judgements, and traditionally science has been regarded as 'value-free'. That is, science is neither intended nor equipped to talk about such questions. Today, of course, we recognize that *no* human activity, *including* science, is truly value-free. What we choose to study, and the consequences of what we learn, have moral implications. Richard Feynman, one of the developers of the atomic bomb, has admitted that he and other bomb researchers were slow to acknowledge the existence of this moral dimension in their work. Nonetheless, he concluded that it is an essential part of science (Feynman 1988). Hence, it is difficult to justify ignoring meaning as part of human experience by saying that science should not deal with values.

Like Feynman, many of the founders of the humanistic approach came to recognize the importance of meaning in behaviour because of personal experiences. The Second World War led to an exodus of thinkers and therapists from Europe to North America, and they took with them both their ideas and their experiences. Many were psychoanalytically trained, and some, like Viktor Frankl, were survivors of the concentration camps. For these individuals, a value-free stance was inadequate to comprehend the atrocities of the war. Instead, questions of the meaning and value of human activity were central for these theorists, and their concern was a factor which helped to shape the nature of the humanistic approach. (For example, Viktor Frankl's best-known work is *Man's Search for Meaning* (1992).)

intersubjective verification a process for validating observations based on agreement by two observers; proposed by Rogers as a means of making subjective impressions useful as scientific data

Despite the obvious appeal of emphasizing meaning, there is still the practical problem that studying it is even more difficult than dealing with subjective experience. Meaning cannot be directly observed, and often can be inferred only incompletely. (To take a trivial example, if I go to the refrigerator, look in and then close the door without removing anything, what can you infer?) Yet, if we accept that subjective experience is relevant to understanding behaviour, we cannot ignore the value that people place on their experiences. To do so is once more to exclude part of behaviour from study, in the way Skinner tried to do with mental processes. As Gordon Allport, a personality psychologist, has written, psychology must deal with all aspects of the individual. 'If present-day psychology is not fully equal to the task, then we should improve the science until it is' (Allport 1955: 5). The humanists have responded to this challenge by accepting that questions of meaning – and the answers individuals identify – are central to under-standing the way people behave. Of course, *acknowledging* meaning is not the same as *understanding* it, and ultimately the issue is whether the humanistic approach succeeds in constructing an effective framework for understanding. Only by looking closely at the theories will it be possible to evaluate them fairly in this regard.

To summarize, then, the humanistic approach evolved out of the psycho-dynamic approach, but was also a reaction to the deterministic viewpoint found in psychoanalysis and behaviourism. It is unique among the five approaches in emphasizing the importance of subjective experience in the understanding of an individual. Conscious awareness, the process of choosing and evaluating one's actions, and the meaning one gives to experience are all part of this 'phenomenological' view.

Clearly, the underlying assumptions of the humanistic approach are very different from those of the other approaches. In some ways, the humanistic approach is the most accessible of all the approaches, because of its emphasis on personal experience. At the same time, it is perhaps the most difficult of all the approaches, for it does not permit one to take the relatively comfortable position of a third-party observer in understanding behaviour. To be valid within their own framework, the theories must be useful not only for understanding other people, but also for understanding one's *own* life. Hence, studying the humanistic approach should not be considered a spectator sport; as you read, you should think about how the concepts relate to your own experience.

| For further consideration |

Skinner once said that freedom is an illusion, but a valuable one (Skinner 1971). Have you ever made a decision which was contrary to what others expected of you? Do you think this was a real choice, as Rogers would say, or an illusion?

Carl Rogers's Theory

One of the most significant humanistic theorists, and one of the best known psychologists of all orientations, was Carl Rogers. As he told it, Rogers was

Carl Rogers

Carl Rogers (1902–87) was born in Oak Park, Illinois, a suburb of Chicago. He came from a large family, and was reared in a rather strict religious family. In his later writings, he talked about his boyhood, and indicated that the rather rigid beliefs he grew up with contributed to feelings of loneliness and being an outsider (Rogers 1973). He sought refuge in his studies, and was an excellent student in high school. Only when he left home to attend the University of Wisconsin did he begin to develop wider horizons. In his second year, he began to study for the ministry, and the following year went to China in conjunction with a Christian student organization. The trip gave him new confidence, as well as an appreciation for other perspectives on life. He started graduate studies at Union Theological Seminary, but then decided to continue in psychology at Columbia University instead. The shift occurred partly from increasing doubts about his religious commitment, and partly through the realization that one could take a counselling role *outside* the church. After obtaining his PhD in 1931, he began his career working in a child guidance centre in Rochester, New York, and also began developing his theoretical ideas. By 1945, he had become a professor at the University of Chicago, and was elected president of the American Psychological Association in 1946. Over a long and active career, he taught at several universities and lectured widely. His later years were spent at the Center for the Studies of the Person in La Jolla, California, which he founded. He died in 1987 at the age of eighty-five.

drawn to psychology because of his interest in counselling. After completing his PhD, Rogers began working in the area of therapy and counselling, dealing with both children and adults who suffered from a wide variety of problems. He found himself challenged intellectually and also emotionally by their suffering, and this drove him to seek better ways of understanding and helping. In this sense, his experiences were like those of Freud (and all those who seek to combine theory with treatment): the practical challenge of relieving suffering led to a journey of theoretical discovery. However, the path for Rogers was very different from that of Freud.

For 12 years, Rogers worked at a child guidance centre, doing counselling and developing his own ideas about personality and therapy. Circumstances favoured this process, in that his superiors imposed few constraints in terms of treatment orientation. Along the way, he encountered Otto Rank (a student of Freud's who, like Jung and Adler, had parted ways with his mentor), and found that Rank's techniques (though not his theory) seemed similar to the direction Rogers himself was moving in. His early thinking was summarized in *The Clinical Treatment of the Problem Child* (Rogers 1939).

The book was well received, and led to Rogers being offered a full professorship at Ohio State University. In later years, Rogers observed that this chance to start at the top of the academic hierarchy freed him from the pressures and politics of academic life, and made it possible for him to move in new theoretical directions without fear of censure. In this sense, he encountered the 'conditions for growth' which he eventually emphasized in his theorizing. To understand what this means, let us look at his theory.

Self Theory and Personality

As noted at the beginning of this chapter, humanistic theories emphasize understanding behaviour by understanding the way a person experiences the world. Rogers was a strong advocate of this view. As a consequence, his thinking is sometimes referred to as a **self theory**, since his ideas about personality focus on the notion of self. (The concept of self has a long history, which had already been documented by G. H. Mead several decades before Rogers (see Mead 1934).) Rogers himself saw the theory as evolving out of his clinical work. Since the time of Freud, it had been assumed that it was the therapist's role to determine the direction and goals of therapy. This concept reflected the traditional view of medical practice, including the linguistic usage of calling a person seeking treatment a *patient*. By contrast, Rogers (consistent with his ideas about the importance of self) came to believe that the person seeking treatment, not the therapist, should direct the process of therapy. To reflect this, the person seeking help was termed a *client* (implying a relationship of equals, not the subordination of the term *patient*); the process itself came to be called **client-centred therapy** (Rogers 1951). While Rogers, like Freud, developed his ideas largely out of a clinical context, his theory of personality, like Freud's, was intended as a general theory of behaviour.

self theory a general term for theories of behaviour which focus on an individual's self concept and subjective experience of the world; pioneered by G. H. Mead, and adapted by many humanistic theorists

client-centred therapy an approach to therapy in which the person seeking treatment (termed a *client*), not the therapist, is seen as directing the process of therapy; later called person-centred therapy

For further consideration

Briefly describe yourself by completing the sentence, 'I am...' What do you consider most important in defining who you are? (You might wish to compare your answer with those of some classmates.)

The Organism and the Actualizing Tendency

Rogers's theory is grounded in experience, and this includes his ideas about the basic aspects of personality. One of the most fundamental aspects of human experience is the fact that we are living creatures – we are born, we grow and eventually we die. These basic realities are true for all individuals, regardless of race, creed or social status. Our capacity for self-awareness tells us that, however long we live, and however much we wish otherwise, we will in fact die. Cultures develop elaborate rituals to cope with death, but can do nothing to alter its finality. Yet what about what happens while we are alive? What needs must be fulfilled? What directs the path we walk through life? For Rogers, the answers to these questions stem from the biological reality of our existence: as living creatures, we need food, water, shelter and so on. These needs arise out of our biological being, termed the **organism**. At the same time, Rogers believed there is a broader motive that directs our lives. This motive, called the **actualizing tendency**, reflects the desire to grow, to develop and to enhance one's capacities; Rogers saw this as an intrinsic property of life. It is the actualizing tendency that stimulates creativity, that leads us to seek new challenges and skills and that motivates healthy growth in all the myriad aspects of our lives. The actualizing tendency motivates the baby to learn to walk. It nurtures our curiosity and our appreciation for beauty. It even underlies our desire for human contact, from sex to friendship to love. When a person is 'in touch' with the actualizing

organism in Rogers's theory, the biological being which is the source of basic needs (such as food and water), and also the source of a growth motive termed the *actualizing tendency*
actualizing tendency in Rogers's theory, an innate drive which reflects the desire to grow, to develop and to enhance one's capacities

tendency, it becomes a powerful guide for directing behaviour in ways that foster positive growth and happiness. (As we shall see, individuals can also be influenced by other forces, often to the detriment of healthy growth.)

The Phenomenal Field and the Self

If awareness of being alive is the most basic of human experiences, shared by all, there are also many ways in which individual experience differs. Fundamentally, we each live in a world of our own creation, formed by our processes of perception. Rogers referred to an individual's unique perception of the world as his or her **phenomenal field**. As we saw in Chapter 1, perceptual processes structure our experience of the world according to our individual cognitive schemata; the way we perceive a situation is influenced by our past experiences, our needs and our expectations. In many respects, our perceptions match the external world, but, as Rogers noted, 'We live by a perceptual "map" which is never reality itself' (Rogers 1951: 485). Some aspects of what we experience are internal, including thoughts and feelings. For each of us, the world we experience is personal and private. Hence, Rogers argued that external reality is not what shapes our lives: our *perceptions* of it, expressed through our phenomenal field, are what guide our behaviour.

The way in which each of us sees the world affects the way we interact with each other. Very often, misunderstandings arise because two individuals perceive a situation differently, and each is unable to see the other's point of view. A teacher looks at the course material in terms of what 'should' be in the course; a student may look at the content in terms of whether it relates to their personal interests. A pregnant woman sees her body changing, and fears that her husband will no longer find her attractive; her husband may welcome the changes as positive signs of a much desired child, and never imagine his wife needs reassurance. Such differences can lead to disagreements, but they can often be resolved when we attempt to see the other person's point of view. (Rogers believed that this process of *empathy* plays an important role in healthy growth, as we shall see further on.) In more extreme cases, distortions of reality expressed in our phenomenal field can lead to inappropriate behaviour: desire may lead to misinterpreting a friendly smile as a flirtatious invitation; a driver frustrated by pressures at work may see an unintentional error by another driver as a deliberate act of aggression. Whether it is consistent with the external world or not, the phenomenal field *is* the reality that we experience.

Overall, our phenomenal field reflects the way we see the world, and often how we act. Within this framework, the most significant element is our sense of self. While we all tend to perceive our self as a stable entity, in fact it is a fluid, changing thing, a unity comprised of many elements. Rogers called the **self** 'an organized consistent gestalt, constantly in the process of forming and reforming' (Rogers 1959: 201). The sense of constancy and stability which we experience is largely derived from the fact that, in order to observe the self, we must focus on a particular moment, much in the way time becomes frozen in a photograph. Since we are inclined to see our own being as constant, we often selectively attend to those elements of the

phenomenal field for Rogers, an individual's unique perception of the world

self for Rogers, an organized cognitive structure based on our experience of our own being

'snapshot' that seem consistent with prior 'snapshots'. (This notion that constancy is a product of the mind, not of reality, was familiar even in ancient Greece; the philosopher Heraclitus said, 'We can never cross the same river twice. The water changes, and so do we.') In this sense, Rogers's use of the term self is different from that of many other theorists, who tend to describe it as a central, unchanging core of personality. (Equally, it is a framework that would be unfamiliar in many cultures, which define identity in *collective* terms, as we will discuss later in this chapter.)

The self reflects our view of 'who we are' are at a given moment, and is influenced by all those factors which shape perception in general, including past experiences, the present situation and our expectations for the future. If we are in touch with our own being, then the self will be guided by the actualizing tendency as it relates to the present situation. Whereas psychoanalytic theory sees personality as the product of past experience, Rogers argued that the past is only relevant to the extent that we *perceive* it to be relevant. If I believe that the way I act is based on my childhood, and I perceive certain childhood experiences (positive *or* negative) as highly significant, then my behaviour at this moment will be strongly influenced by those experiences. On the other hand, if I 'let go' of the past, and emphasize my current needs and aspirations, then the past will play a much less significant role. Rogers related how, in therapy, a young man came to focus on how his life had been 'distorted and spoiled' by his parents. Then, as he reflected on his own analysis, he said, 'Maybe now that I *see* that, it's up to *me*' (Rogers 1969: 266). The self may well reflect the past, but it is not constrained by it; it is always possible for a new pattern to emerge, even based on a seemingly minor alteration of the phenomenal field (Rogers 1959).

<table>
<tr><td>

For further consideration

</td><td>

Do you see yourself as basically the same as you were four years ago, or very different? How do you account for this?

</td></tr>
</table>

The Ideal Self, Congruence and Incongruence

ideal self in Rogers's theory, a dynamically changing construct which represents an individual's goals and aspirations

Apart from the self, there is another aspect of the phenomenal field which relates to our sense of our own being. The **ideal self** refers to our notions of who we would *like* to be, the goals and aspirations we have for our lives. Depending on what these goals and aspirations are, the ideal self may be either quite similar to the real self or radically different. However, like the self, the ideal self is not a stable entity, but a dynamically changing construct, reflecting both the actualizing tendency and external forces. When we talk of a dying person who is 'at peace with himself', we are implying that his ideal self is consistent with his self. By contrast, when we perceive our behaviour as falling short of our desired goals, we experience it as extremely negative. I encountered a vivid example of this a few years ago. While I was returning papers to a class of university students, a young woman burst into tears. Since I knew she had received an excellent grade – 94 per cent – this seemed a very strange response. When I discussed it with her after class, she explained that she had seen the grade for the person seated next her, which was 97 per cent. Since she had always tried to be the best, to discover that someone else had done better than her was a source of considerable distress – *regardless* of the objective quality of her own work. While I tried to console her, and suggest that her standards were perhaps unrealistic, this aspect of her ideal self was not something she could easily relinquish.

Obviously, the relationship between the self and the ideal self is an important factor in how we view ourselves, and consequently it forms a central issue in Rogers's theory of personality. To the extent that the self and ideal self match, the individual experiences a sense of **congruence**. (The sense of similarity which the term implies is also found in geometry, where *congruent figures* are ones which are identical in size and shape.) It is further expressed as consistency between what one experiences (phenomenal field) and what one expresses (communicates to others). By contrast, if a person experiences contradictions in their sense of self and surroundings, then this will produce a feeling of incongruence. **Incongruence** represents a mismatch between self and ideal self, between what we experience and what we communicate. For example, imagine going to a party which you thought was casual, only to find everyone else dressed formally. The discomfort and embarrassment you would feel would reflect incongruence. Similarly, the student who was distressed that someone else had received a higher grade was experiencing incongruence.

Obviously, no one deliberately tries to feel out of place, and it seems equally obvious that incongruence is a very unpleasant experience. So why does it arise? Wouldn't it make sense to shape our perceptions so that such discrepancies don't arise? To some extent, we *do* in fact engage in such perceptual filtering. As we have seen, our perceptions can be influenced by our needs and expectations. Freud described this process in terms of defence mechanisms, and while Rogers disagrees profoundly with Freud's theory, he would acknowledge that perceptual distortions like those Freud described certainly can occur. However, he would disagree with Freud's explanation of their basis. In addition, Rogers would disagree with his more general assertion that conflict (or incongruence) within personality (the trigger for using defences, in Freud's view) is inevitable. Instead, the question becomes: how does incongruence arise?

congruence in Rogers's theory, a feeling of integration experienced when the self and ideal self match

incongruence in Rogers's theory, a feeling of conflict or unease experienced when there is a mismatch between the self and ideal self

For further consideration

Can you think of any ways in which your self and ideal self differ? Are there particular situations that make this discrepancy particularly distressing to you? Why do you think this occurs?

Personality Development and Conditions for Growth

Rogers regarded incongruence as a result of unhealthy growth – that is, it reflects a problem in development. Like Freud, he recognized that development can be distorted by negative experiences; however, his general model of development was very different from Freud's. For Rogers, development is influenced by the kind of social interactions an individual has, not the changing expression of sexual and aggressive drives.

Philosophers and social theorists have long noted that people like company – very few seem to welcome long periods of isolation. Rogers, too – perhaps influenced by his own experiences of loneliness as a boy – believed that social contact and positive relationships are essential to human growth. Contact with others can provide us with a feeling of belonging, of being valued and loved. Rogers referred to the need for such love and caring as the **need for positive regard**. Any form of attention and praise is positive regard. Little Johnny does a picture, and Mummy gives him verbal praise and a hug. Mary tells a funny story, and Daddy laughs and smiles. Such incidents provide positive regard, and play a crucial role in development.

need for positive regard a need for positive social contacts like love, which Rogers regarded as universal

At first glance, positive regard may seem very reminiscent of the behaviourist concept of positive reinforcers. However, behaviourism emphasizes how reinforcers change *behaviour*, while Rogers emphasized the *feelings* that positive regard induces, and how these affect our sense of self. While it might be argued that some forms of regard (like praise or attention) are essentially conditioned reinforcers, Rogers cared little about such interpretations. He saw the need for positive regard as universal, and was not concerned about how it originates: 'Whether it is an inherent or learned need is irrelevant to the theory' (Rogers 1959: 223).

Conditions of Worth and the Would–Should Dilemma

Positive regard is so important that finding ways to obtain it can lead to ignoring other aspects of self. For example, if Mary finds that telling funny stories makes people laugh, she may begin finding other ways to make people laugh, even if at heart she feels her actions are foolish and inappropriate. Earning positive regard becomes the measure of self-worth, and pleasing others can become an end to itself. The restrictions imposed on self-expression in order to earn positive regard are called **conditions of worth**. Sometimes, these conditions are self-created, as in the example of Mary trying to be funny all the time. However, conditions of worth can also be created by others (such as parents or teachers). If Tommy hurts his knee and starts to cry, but is told that big boys don't cry, then crying may later be suppressed as a possible emotional expression. If Jane gets angry, but is told ladies don't show a temper, then she may come to suppress all feelings of anger. Rogers encountered many individuals in counselling who seemed out of touch with their emotions; typically, this could be related to parental demands in early childhood. As we internalize conditions of worth into the ideal self, we lose touch with our actual perceptions and emotions – with who we really are.

conditions of worth restrictions imposed on self-expression in order to earn positive regard

In accepting various conditions of worth, we also incorporate the values implied by these conditions as part of our ideal self, a process Rogers describes as **introjection of values**. (The term *introjection* was first used by Freud to refer to a defence mechanism – hence this is a case where Rogers has accepted the behavioural description, but not the underlying explanation.) As the ideal self comes to represent the values and standards of other people, it is likely to become more and more discrepant with one's real nature (the self). This in turn creates the basis for incongruence. When pleasing others becomes more important than satisfying one's own actualizing tendency, then healthy growth is threatened. Thus, conditions of worth, and the resulting introjection of values, result in the negative experiences of incongruence.

introjection of values for Rogers, the incorporation of values into the ideal self due to accepting conditions of worth imposed by others; the term was first used by Freud to refer to a defence mechanism

In one sense, conditions of worth are unavoidable: parents and society inevitably set standards for conduct, and at least some of these standards will be arbitrary, or at least conflict with personal needs. As a teacher, I have sometimes encountered students who are pursuing a career goal which does not seem to suit them. When probed, they often say, 'Well, my mother's a nurse, so I feel I should be one, too', or 'My parents want me to be an engineer', or similar statements. In such cases, the individual often has other aspirations – art, or accounting, or whatever – which are being submerged in order to maintain parental approval. The result, of course, is incongruence, and feelings of being in conflict with oneself.

would–should dilemma
the conflict between one's own needs, expressed through the actualizing tendency, and the demands of others, expressed through the ideal self

The conflict between one's own needs, expressed through the actualizing tendency, and the demands of others, expressed through the ideal self, is referred to as the **would–should dilemma**. While the values represented by the ideal self may have *originated* with other people, once they are introjected as part of the ideal self they are *experienced* as internal in nature. Hence, rather than seeming to be a conflict between oneself and another person (who might reasonably disagree), the conflict is experienced as internal, between two parts of one's own being. This type of internal conflict is much more threatening and anxiety-provoking than disagreements with another person. This conflict can take many forms: When a student *would like* to study art, but feels she *should* study nursing, this is experienced as a would–should dilemma. Two young teens *would like* to engage in sex, but feel they *should* wait until they are older. A parent *would like* to spend time playing with his children, but feels he *should* spend extra time at work.

In the would–should dilemma, there is a conflict between personal needs and goals, and perceptions of expected behaviour. Freud described this in terms of the conflicts between superego (parental values) and id (one's own needs), and believed that such conflicts were inevitable. By contrast, Rogers saw such conflicts, described as the result of incongruence between self and ideal self, as both undesirable and avoidable. Furthermore, he did not see them as reflecting a simple conflict between personal needs and society, because concern for others is an inherent part of the self. That is, a healthy person is naturally motivated to consider the impact of their actions on other people when choosing how to act. Still, if conflicts like the would–should dilemma are *not* inevitable, then how do they arise? To understand this, we must look at the distinction between conditional and unconditional positive regard.

For further consideration

What kinds of conditions of worth have others tried to impose on you? Does your experience support Rogers's view that such conditions hamper personal growth?

Conditional and Unconditional Positive Regard

unconditional positive regard acceptance and caring given to a person as a human being, without imposing conditions on how the person behaves

As noted earlier, the need for positive regard, in the form of approval and love, is seen by Rogers as universal. Ideally, we would all receive such regard on a free and open basis, as both children and adults. Such **unconditional positive regard** is acceptance and caring extended simply because the person is a human being. Religions have traditionally urged individuals to

conditional positive regard acceptance and caring given to a person only for meeting certain standards of behaviour

adopt this attitude, but we all recognize how difficult it is to put into practice. For example, in their best moments, all parents value their children; unfortunately, it is harder to maintain a feeling of unconditional regard if Jimmy has just broken an ancient vase while trying to get at the biscuit tin. Instead, we tend to give love and praise based on the child doing things of which we approve. When regard is given only for meeting certain standards of behaviour, it is called **conditional positive regard**. If Sean cleans up his toys, he gets praised; if he leaves them scattered about, he is likely to get scolded, or at least ignored. In later life, we find that regard is given for good performance at school or at work; we may even find friends welcome some actions, and heap scorn on others. (Peer pressure is an example of such forces in operation.) In all these cases, positive regard is given for certain actions, but not for others. The problem with this is that conditional positive regard often leaves the person feeling that it is their *self*, not *behaviour*, which is unacceptable. For example, Jimmy's father reacts to the broken vase by saying, 'Jimmy, you idiot! How could you break that vase? You know better than to take biscuits without asking! Honestly, I don't think you ever listen to me!' While remarks like this may deter future incidents, they may also leave Jimmy feeling that making *any* error means he is bad and unacceptable.

Ideally, it should be possible to value a person as a human being without implying that one accepts all of their actions – that is, regard for the *person* would be unconditional, but regard for their *actions* would be conditional. This would mean that one could withhold regard for particular actions – such as when a child has a tantrum – yet still show regard for the person. In practice, however, both the person *giving* regard and the person *receiving* it often find the distinction between person and action hard to maintain. A scolded child tends to feel rejected, even if the mother says, 'I love you, but . . .'; the criticism of the child's behaviour tends to overshadow the expressed regard. When one's performance at work is criticized, it is hard not to take it as a criticism of one's general competence and worth. When too much conditional regard is given, it undercuts the person's sense of self, and contributes to the development of incongruence. To avoid this, one must focus on the conditions which instead foster congruence.

Congruence and Conditions for Growth

conditions for growth the conditions under which healthy development of personality occurs; defined by Rogers as unconditional positive regard, openness and empathy

Rogers believed we are all born congruent, because the discrepancies which create incongruence arise through life experiences. Thus, his theory implies that it should be possible to develop in a way that *maintains* this sense of congruence. What fosters congruence, and how can one avoid incongruence? The answer to this question lies in recognizing the conditions under which healthy development of personality occurs, the **conditions for growth**: unconditional positive regard, openness and empathy. Let us consider each of them separately.

As discussed in the preceding section, *unconditional positive regard* is based on accepting that each person has value, without any reference to what they do or don't do. 'It is an acceptance of this other individual as a separate person, having worth in his own right. It is a basic trust – a belief that this other person is somehow fundamentally trustworthy. Whether we call it prizing, acceptance, trust, or by some other term, it shows up in a variety of observable ways' (Rogers 1969: 109).

By not imposing external conditions of worth, unconditional positive regard makes it possible for individuals to develop a sense of self based on their own actualizing tendency and their individual perceptions and experiences. Without the distortions introduced by external demands, the values which develop as part of the ideal self are likely to be self-consistent, and therefore maintain congruence. Thus, receiving unconditional positive regard is the most basic requirement for healthy growth and congruence.

While truly unconditional regard is extremely rare, it can help if we distinguish between the person and the action, as seen in the following incident. Several years ago, I was meeting some friends for dinner. The husband was on time at the restaurant, but his wife was nearly an hour late. Since this had happened on other occasions, the husband was furious when she finally arrived. Quickly recognizing this, she attempted to defuse his anger by saying, 'Oh, sweetie, don't you love me any more?' The message implied by this was, 'If you love me, you'll overlook my being late' – clearly setting up conditional regard. Instead, the husband replied, 'Of *course* I love you – *but that has nothing to do with it*: you shouldn't be late!' In effect, he distinguished between loving her and not accepting her action.

Obviously, though, most of the time we encounter a mixture of conditional and unconditional positive regard. Yet Rogers believed growth was possible even if not all the regard we receive is unconditional. (Otherwise, *no one* would be likely to grow!) Basically, it requires an opportunity to interact with at least one person who can provide primarily unconditional positive regard – whether a family member, a friend, a counsellor, a co-worker or whomever. (In counselling, Rogers called this *client-centred therapy* – see Chapter 9.) For instance, in a healthy relationship, spouses accept each other even though each has faults. (Indeed, sometimes the 'flaws' become points of endearment rather than friction – much in the way parents complain of noisy children for years, and then miss the noise when they leave home.) Unconditional positive regard allows individuals to take chances with their feelings and behaviour – and in the process to explore and develop their sense of self.

openness Behaviour characterized by a person freely expressing their own sense of self, rather than playing a role or hiding behind a facade

The second condition for growth is **openness**, which refers to a person freely expressing their own sense of self, rather than playing a role or hiding behind a facade. Like unconditional positive regard, openness can be found in potentially any situation. For example, consider a person who attends a dull party. When approached by the host, the person musters a forced smile, and insists the party is 'wonderful'. Politeness dictates the verbal response, which differs significantly from the person's actual feelings; this contradiction creates incongruence. However, this could change, depending on the host's response. Suppose the host were to respond by saying, 'It's nice of you to say so, but I really think I've been to livelier *funerals*!' By expressing his own feelings instead of relying on social conventions, the host is exhibiting openness. In doing so, the host may open the door to a more honest assessment by the guest, whereby both host and guest gain. It is not that the party is no longer a disaster, but at least the two individuals have been able to make real contact with each other, free of social constraints. Rogers believed that this quality of openness (which he also called 'realness') opens the way to greater self-awareness and personal growth. By contrast, when we adopt a facade which is based on our social role or other external constraint, we inhibit any genuine expression of feelings – either for ourselves or for those we interact with. For example, Rogers noted 'the tendency of most teachers to show themselves to their pupils simply as roles', not as real persons with doubts, fears and other human limitations (Rogers 1969: 107).

empathy the ability to understand another person's perceptions and feelings; seen by Rogers as a condition for growth

The third condition which can foster growth is **empathy**, the ability to understand the other person's point of view. Ideally, this encompasses his or her perceptions, thoughts and feelings. This concept is expressed in a proverb popular in the prairie regions of Canada, which says, 'Never judge someone until you've walked ten miles in their boots.' If you meet someone who seems rude (for example, in a shop), does this mean they are always rude? Are they having a bad day? Could they have a headache or other problem? While we are often quick to jump to the conclusion that the person is simply rude, the reality is that we cannot properly judge from a brief interaction like this. (As noted in Chapter 4, this tendency to explain others' behaviour in terms of personality when situational factors are more likely is called the *fundamental attribution error*.)

Like unconditional positive regard and openness, empathy is a quality that is easily recognized, but not so readily found. Teachers, for example, are supposed to empathize with their students, but differences in background, as well as situational factors, can make such understanding hard to achieve. Faced with this difficulty, teachers will sometimes adopt a smiling, tolerant facade – not empathy, but a pretence of it. Rogers believed that this compounds the problem of not understanding with the problem of not being real. Faced with students one doesn't understand (and may even dislike), Rogers believed that 'it is almost certainly more constructive to be *real* than to be pseudo-empathic, or to put on a facade of caring' (Rogers 1969: 113). Note that being real may sometimes imply expressing negative feelings. For example, a teacher faced with a messy classroom might say, 'I can't function when things are a mess!' While clearly disapproving, the response reflects the teacher's feelings, not simply disapproval of the students. This is likely to be more honest – and also more productive – than saying 'You kids don't know how to be tidy!'

In the end, the three conditions of growth tend to be interwoven – experiencing one factor involves the others as well. Rogers noted this when he commented, 'To be genuine, or honest, or congruent, or real, means to be this way about *oneself*. I cannot be real about another, because I do not *know* what is real for him. I can only tell – if I wish to be truly honest – what is going on in me' (Rogers 1969: 113). In effect, empathy results from openness and congruence, which are themselves closely connected.

The conditions for growth are meant to allow individuals to evaluate their experiences in terms of their own internal standards, based on the actualizing tendency. Like most things in the world, the conditions exist on a continuum, not as either/or alternatives. Consider, for example, empathy. At first glance, the statement by Rogers quoted in the previous paragraph seems to imply that empathy is impossible – we can never truly know what another person feels. In fact, the reality is more complex. First, when he speaks of empathy, he means the *attitude* of *trying* to empathize, even if the effort doesn't fully succeed. Second, since the same basic elements are common to all human existence – we are all 'siblings under the skin' – empathy may often result from being open to our *own* experience of the situation. The conditions that foster personal growth are also the conditions that will foster positive interactions with others. It is this fact – that what favours my growth will also favour yours – that makes Rogers optimistic about the possibilities for growth in everyday life.

For further consideration

Rogers's analysis of the circumstances which promote growth places great emphasis on the interactions we have with other people. Do you find that what you look for in friends is consistent with what Rogers considers the conditions for growth?

Human Potential and the Fully Functioning Person

In describing personality, Rogers's theory repeatedly contrasts the factors which foster healthy growth and those factors (such as conditional positive regard and conditions of worth) which obstruct growth. But what exactly *is* a healthy personality? One could say that a healthy person is living up to their potential, but what would indicate that a person is fulfilling their potential?

The idea that there is some sort of optimal result for personality development is one of the unique features of the humanistic approach. In this respect, the approach is very different from psychoanalysis. Freud's theory was based largely on his clinical observations, dealing with people who often had severe problems, including physical symptoms. Perhaps as a consequence, his theory tended to emphasize the negative aspects of development. While Freud's ideas on pathology were very detailed, his conception of healthy development was never fully elaborated; overall, he seemed pessimistic about the possibilities for growth unburdened by fixations and neurotic conflict. By contrast, Rogers argued that personality development naturally moves towards healthy growth, and it is only negative external factors which lead to distortions of personality.

fully functioning person described by Rogers as the ideal of growth, closely related to congruence; healthy growth is characterized by openness, a high degree of spontaneity, compassion and self-direction

Rogers described the ideal of growth as being a **fully functioning person**. The term itself suggests that anything less than optimal growth is a deviation from proper functioning – that is, healthy growth should be considered the *norm*, not some super form of development. In many respects, being fully functioning is equivalent to being congruent. Congruence produces self-confidence and high self-esteem, which in turn make possible the openness to feelings and experiences that Rogers sees as central to growth. The individual trusts their own ability to deal with the world, and consequently shows a high degree of spontaneity, compassion and self-direction. Instead of being preoccupied with conflicts, the person is able to engage in activities with energy and enthusiasm.

One characteristic which is *not* part of being fully functioning is aggression. Aggression for Rogers is a result of unhealthy growth, in contrast to Freud's view of aggression as an innate drive. Rogers sees aggression as one of the consequences of too much conditional positive regard. When people are offered only conditional positive regard, they will often alter their behaviour to meet the imposed standards, since the need for positive regard is so powerful. However, this will often mean denying their own preferences and feelings, which results in both incongruence *and* frustration. Aggression then arises as a natural response to the denial of their own needs and feelings. If aggression seems widespread in the world, it is presumably because the use of conditional positive regard is so common. Unconditional positive regard contributes to healthy growth, and also reduces the likelihood of aggression.

If this seems abstract, consider an example. Harry is an only child whose parents were very strict and demanding when he was a child. As a result, he incorporated their standards into his ideal self, and as a teenager has become a very rigid, argumentative person who criticizes and challenges all those whom he sees as making errors, whether peers or authority figures like teachers. At the same time, he is dissatisfied with his own behaviour, which cannot meet his own high standards. This combination of being highly critical and having low self-esteem leads Harry to get into many disagreements, resulting in his being rejected by others. His peers see Harry as a loner with a chip on his shoulder, and generally avoid him. Inside, Harry feels frustrated and lonely. Rogers would see this as a typical example of how excessive emphasis on conditional positive regard during Harry's childhood has led to incongruence and aggressive behaviour. Depending on the circumstances (e.g. a social environment where drug trafficking is prevalent), Harry could end up expressing his frustrations in criminal form, while being scornful of the society that he sees as having failed him.

Healthy development thus depends on the conditions for growth. When these are fulfilled, the individual will move towards being a fully functioning person; in their absence, incongruence and aggression will arise. In one sense, this conception of human potential is very specific, in that it implies that a fully functioning person will show little anxiety, an ability to evaluate situations independently, an openness in dealing with other people and so on. At the same time, it is very broad and vague, in that it implies very little about the specific behaviours, or even values, of a congruent person.

The issue of values is a significant one to humanists like Rogers. Whereas modern science has generally argued for a 'value-free' approach to theorizing, humanistic psychologists believe that one cannot understand human behaviour without understanding the values which often direct a person's choice of actions. Rogers addressed this issue in an essay in 1964, and then revised it five years later (Rogers 1969). He noted that infants have clear preferences: they value food, security, human contact and new experiences, while clearly disliking aversive events like pain, bitter tastes and sudden loud sounds. He noted that as we grow, however, we begin to incorporate values dictated by society, such as 'disobedience is bad' and 'making money is the highest good'. These values may be reinforced by various sources, ranging from parents to advertising. Often these values seem directed towards social acceptance, and are rigidly held, without being open to question. Not surprisingly, the result is that people are often out of touch with their own feelings and internal sources of satisfaction.

Values in the mature person

Characteristics which are negatively valued

Valuing genuiness – pretence and defensiveness are negatively valued.

Moving away from 'ought' – acting because one values the action, not because one feels one 'ought to' do it.

Moving away from others' expectations – pleasing others *as an end in itself* is negatively valued.

Characteristics which are positively valued

Being real is positively valued – being 'who one is' and expressing one's feelings honestly.

Self-direction is positively valued – taking pride and confidence in making choices in one's life.

Valuing one's own being – viewing one's self and one's feelings positively.

Focusing on life as a process – instead of valuing the goal, one values the process of living, without concern for reaching a particular goal.

Valuing openness – being open to both one's inner and outer experiences, recognizing one's own feelings and those of other people. This is a particularly important value.

Valuing other people – accepting other people and appreciating them for what they are, just as one accepts oneself for what one is.

Deep relationships are valued – to be close to another person, able to fully communicate and share, is a very basic need.

Figure 6.1   Values in the mature person Rogers believed that healthy individuals who had reached a mature stage of development would be likely to hold particular types of values. (Adapted from Rogers 1969.)

By contrast, Rogers believed that a fully functioning person will be self-directing in forming values, and will tend to evaluate choices according to the immediately experienced situation. While this sounds like a form of situational ethics, Rogers also argued that the importance of the actualizing tendency will imply certain criteria for making moral choices. Life is seen as a process, not as a series of goals to be reached. Relationships, especially to family and close friends, become more important than material accomplishments. (This is reflected in the quip, 'Nobody ever died wishing they'd spent more time at the office.') A more detailed description is given in Figure 6.1.

While seemingly consistent with his overall conception of the actualizing tendency, Rogers's ideas about values in the fully functioning person are otherwise hard to evaluate. He seems to believe that there is a biological basis for these characteristics, as when he says that mature persons share 'an organismic commonality of value directions' (Rogers 1969: 252). At the same time, he wants to leave individuals free to make their own choices, unrestricted by him or anyone else: 'I do not expect that every [person] would agree with what I have to say here' (Rogers 1969: 239). In the absence of any hard evidence that these characteristics are innate, Rogers's position creates a dilemma, in that it seems to argue for a universal framework of values, while making the individual the ultimate arbiter of morality. If individuals are free to decide their values, how can he be sure that all individuals, even those who are fully functioning, will value the same things? While this clearly seems to be a contradiction, Rogers himself apparently did not see the contradiction, or at least never directly addressed it.

The problem of defining ideal development is a fundamental one, both for Rogers's theory and more generally for any humanistic theory. To talk about the goal of development as objectively definable suggests a universal standard. However, both the values proposed by Rogers (such as valuing immediate experience over long-term goals) and the underlying model of self seem inconsistent with cross-cultural studies of personality. For example, while Rogers feels social relationships are important, his theory is clearly focused on the individual. While this might seem both obvious and necessary, in fact it reflects a view of our selves and the world which is by no means universal. Instead, many cultures foster a definition of identity which is based on our ties to others, especially family and friends – a framework often called *collectivism* (Triandis 1990). In such cultures, ranging from the Cheyenne of North America to the Japanese to various Latino societies, social relationships are more important than the individual (Levine and Padilla 1980; Strauss 1982; Markus and Kitayama 1991). An example of how this can affect individuals' perceptions and experience is a study which compared Americans and Japanese. When asked if their sense of self changes in different situations, only 5 to 10 per cent of the Americans said yes, but almost 100 per cent of the Japanese said yes (de Rivera 1989). While there may be many reasons for this result, such evidence suggests strongly that notions of the self may well vary with culture.

If how individuals experience their own identity (or *self*) can vary so widely, what about values? How can one argue for universal values as part of a model of ideal development, especially within an approach which sees each individual as the ultimate arbiter of such matters? One possible explanation lies with the actualizing tendency as a universal, biologically-based motive. If it *does* in fact favour certain characteristics, then the answer may ultimately be that there *is* no contradiction in Rogers's interpretation. (Wilson's (1998) recent arguments for morality as having a biological basis would seem to favour this view.) Alternatively, the interpretation made by Rogers may represent a distortion of his own phenomenal field, whereby certain values of his own culture were interpreted as being universal.

At present, no one can really prove whether Rogers's theory fails on these points or not. He would probably argue that while some cultures may emphasize collectivism, culture is a human construct, and cultures may not always work to foster human potential (a viewpoint that seems supported by the existence of many totalitarian societies throughout human history). Thus, the fact that collectivist cultures *exist* is not necessarily proof that they are *healthy*. At the same time, one must be wary of accepting arguments for universal values when there seems so little direct support. At present, no clear resolution is possible. What *can* be said with certainty is that his ideas have been influential both within the domain of humanistic psychology and beyond it, in fields like education and social work.

Abraham Maslow

Abraham Maslow (1908–70) was born in New York, the son of Jewish immigrants. He received both his undergraduate and graduate training at the University of Wisconsin, where he studied with Harry Harlow, an eminent expert on primate behaviour, and with Clark Hull, a behaviourist theorist, among others. After receiving his doctorate in 1934, he went back to New York to teach psychology at Brooklyn College. While his graduate studies focused on primate behaviour, as time went on Maslow became more interested in human concerns, in part because of events related to the Second World War. In the late 1930s, New York had become a gathering place for a number of European intellectuals, many of whom were fleeing the Nazi rise to power. At this time he met such distinguished psychoanalysts as Alfred Adler, Karen Horney and Erich Fromm. In addition, he encountered scholars from a range of other perspectives, including Max Wertheimer, one of the pioneers of Gestalt psychology. The Second World War seemed to emphasize for him how little psychology had contributed to solving social problems, and he began to focus on social psychology and personality theory. His emphasis on real-world issues was also expressed in his interest in applying psychology to business – a domain often disdained by research-oriented psychologists. In 1951 Maslow moved to the newly established Brandeis University near Boston; as first chairperson of the psychology department, he fostered the school's growth until 1968. In 1967–8, he also served as President of the American Psychological Association – an indication of the influence of his work. He died in 1970.

Abraham Maslow's Theory

Rogers was not alone in pioneering the humanistic approach. Others, working independently but with similar assumptions, have also shaped the development of the approach. One of the main figures in this regard was Abraham Maslow. Like Rogers, he rejected the psychoanalytic and behaviourist approaches, which he saw as ignoring the positive aspects of human life, such as creativity and love. Instead, Maslow believed that there is an internal force which directs human development towards its highest potential. In describing this motivating force, called 'self-actualization', he focused on the potential for human growth, and the characteristics of healthy individuals. While this emphasis seems reminiscent of Rogers's work, Maslow's perspective differs from that of Rogers in a number of ways, as we shall see.

Abraham Maslow was born in New York in 1908, the son of Jewish immigrants. His initial training in psychology belied his future interests, as he studied primate behaviour at the University of Wisconsin under Harry Harlow. After receiving his doctorate in 1934, he went back to New York to teach psychology at Brooklyn College. In the late 1930s, New York had become a gathering place for a number of European intellectuals, many of whom were fleeing the Nazi rise to power. While teaching, Maslow met a range of scholars who had emigrated from Europe, including distinguished psychoanalysts (Alfred Adler, Karen Horney and Erich Fromm) and Gestalt pioneer Max Wertheimer.

Maslow's ideas evolved significantly over the course of his career. His early training under Harlow taught him the importance of scientific methodology and observation, and exposed him to the work of social anthropologists. His contacts with Wertheimer and other Gestalt psychologists, however, led him to see the importance of viewing the whole person, not just single responses. (*Toward a Psychology of Being*, his major work, was dedicated to Kurt Goldstein, a Gestalt psychologist who had coined the term 'self-actualization'.) He was also influenced by psychoanalysis, both through his contacts with therapists like Fromm and Horney, and by his own experience of psychoanalysis. In fact, in the early 1950s, he saw psychoanalysis as the best therapeutic approach available. However, he gradually became disenchanted with the emphasis on innate influences and past experience in the Freudian approach. By the late 1960s, he had rejected the gloomy determinism of Freud in favour of what he called the 'Third Force' in psychology (psychoanalysis and behaviourism being the first two). In a well-known quote, he stated, 'To oversimplify the matter somewhat, it is as if Freud supplied to us the sick half of psychology, and we must now fill it out with the healthy half' (Maslow 1968: 5).

'The healthy half' in fact became the primary focus of Maslow's work, as he strove to describe and understand the limits of human potential. He referred to this potential in terms of *self-actualization*, the full utilization of a person's talents and capacities. (Self-actualization will be discussed in detail below.) To Maslow, this focus on healthy people, in contrast to Freud's emphasis on pathology, was the proper subject matter for psychology. While he preferred to avoid doctrinaire disagreements between approaches, he commented in an interview not long before his death, 'We shouldn't have to say "humanistic psychology". The adjective should be unnecessary' (Hall 1968: 57). This was said not as a rejection of other approaches, but with the conviction that psychology must ultimately concern itself with the betterment of human life – that is, 'humanistic' as a concern with humanity. In his writings, most notably *Toward a Psychology of Being* (1968) and *Motivation and Personality* (1970), Maslow developed a theory of personality based on his ideas and experiences.

Motivation and the Hierarchy of Needs

At the core of Maslow's theory is a description of basic human needs, which he saw as influencing every aspect of our behaviour. This emphasis on motivation seems to reflect the influence of psychodynamic models on Maslow's thinking. However, unlike the two basic drives which Freud described, Maslow saw a whole constellation of needs which could influence our behaviour. Before considering these needs in a formal way, let us consider an example.

In our society, work is a central part of our lives. Every now and then, most of us entertain fantasies of receiving a monetary windfall, and quitting our job. Yet studies show that many lottery winners keep working. Yet if people buy lottery tickets in hopes of quitting work, why don't they quit when they win? In order to understand, Maslow would suggest we look at the person's needs. The most basic need fulfilled by working is having the money to buy food, shelter, clothing and other necessities for survival. At the same time, working can fulfil other kinds of needs. Most people work in jobs that involve various kinds of human interaction; often, co-workers become friends. In this sense, working can satisfy social needs for contact with others; some lottery winners may continue working because they want to preserve these relationships. In addition, successful job performance (whether as a custodian or as a neurosurgeon) provides feelings of competence, which can foster both self-esteem and recognition from others. Lottery winners, like many retirees, often fear the loss of meaning in their lives if they no longer have a job to perform. In some cases, people may even *enjoy* their jobs – they may provide opportunities for creative challenge and self-expression. (This can be as true of a salesperson or electrician as an artist or writer – it is only the *form* that creativity takes which differs.) If this is the case, lottery winners may see no reason to stop an activity which gives them satisfaction. Thus, what seems a very simple situation on the surface may in fact be very complex. Ultimately, only the individual can determine what course of action will best fulfil their needs.

Maslow recognized the complexity of motivation, and sought to describe it in terms of a **hierarchy of needs** – a hierarchical structure of different types of needs (see Figure 6.2). The most basic needs are those which are linked to survival: the *physiological needs* for food, air, sleep and so forth. When these needs are unfulfilled, nothing else matters. As Maslow put it, 'It is quite true that man lives by bread alone – when there is no bread' (Maslow 1970: 38). Once these needs are fulfilled, other types of needs are experienced. The next level of needs are *safety needs*, which relate to both physical (freedom from danger) and psychological (stability, order) safety. Thus, earthquake victims will continue to feel safety needs long after the quake itself is over, because of the disruption of their ordinary routine. Similarly, a worker who feels that their job is threatened by a corporate restructuring will experience a high safety need. However, when these needs are being met, we begin to focus on needs related to *love and belongingness*: giving and receiving acceptance and affection. (Sex would be a physiological need, but can play a role in the development of love.) These needs are normally met through our interactions with family and friends; however, it requires little insight to recognize that not all family relationships are fulfilling. So, too, there are many people, especially in large cities, who often feel lonely and isolated. Dating clubs, 'personal' ads and similar phenomena are an expression of such needs. Assuming that the needs for love and belongingness are fulfilled, then the individual will experience *esteem needs* – a feeling of self-respect and the sense of being competent at what one does, as well as receiving regard from others. It is interesting to note that Maslow regarded love as more basic than self-esteem; perhaps this is why individuals are sometimes drawn into relationships which offer affection only at the cost of self-respect. In any event, esteem needs are secondary to love and belongingness, and consequently less likely to be satisfied.

hierarchy of needs
Maslow's model of basic human needs, which he saw as organized in a hierarchical structure; needs range from physiological (most basic) to self-actualization (top of hierarchy)

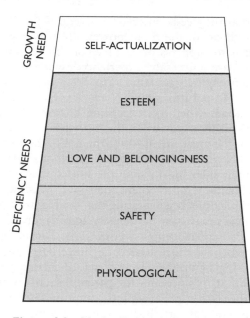

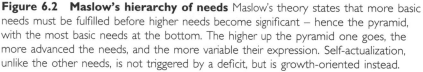

Figure 6.2 Maslow's hierarchy of needs Maslow's theory states that more basic needs must be fulfilled before higher needs become significant – hence the pyramid, with the most basic needs at the bottom. The higher up the pyramid one goes, the more advanced the needs, and the more variable their expression. Self-actualization, unlike the other needs, is not triggered by a deficit, but is growth-oriented instead.

deficiency motives in Maslow's theory, needs whose motivating power is triggered by the absence of the underlying requirements, such as the physiological or esteem needs

metaneeds in Maslow's theory, need states which are based on a desire to grow rather than an underlying deficiency; expressed as the need for *self-actualization*

self-actualization for Maslow, self-actualization is the most advanced human need, and is based on the desire to grow and use one's capacities to their fullest; as such, it is process-oriented, not based on an underlying deficiency

All the above needs reflect **deficiency motives** – that is, we are driven to satisfy them by the *absence* of the underlying requirements. In this sense, they are similar to behaviourist notions of drive motivation, and also psycho-dynamic concepts of motivation, both of which assume that behaviour is triggered by an underlying deficiency. However, many human activities seem to involve no intrinsic need – hobbies, for example, may have no clearly defined function other than 'having fun'. Freud attempted to deal with this problem by suggesting that drives can be satisfied in *symbolic* ways – for example, collecting stamps may reflect an anal fixation. Maslow rejected both the convoluted nature of such explanations, and the under-lying assumption that all behaviour must be based on fulfilling a deficiency. Instead, he argued for **metaneeds**, based on a *growth motive*, which he called **self-actualization**. As noted earlier, self-actualization is based on using one's capacities to their fullest. Much like Rogers's actualizing tend-ency, self-actualization is an expression of the potential for growth which is part of all life. Not being based on a deficiency, it can also never be fully satisfied; unlike other needs, the expression of self-actualization is a pro-cess, not a goal. It is expressed through the moment-to-moment experiences of living, of facing challenges to one's abilities and of interacting with the world in all its diverse aspects.

As noted, the structure of needs was seen as a hierarchy, rather than as simply a collection of equally important motivational states. Maslow believed that the needs differed in several ways: The more basic the need (e.g. physiological), the more powerfully it is experienced, and the more difficult it is to suppress or ignore. For this reason, the most basic needs, like hunger, are universally experienced, whereas the higher needs (esteem, and particularly self-actualization) are less commonly experienced (see Figure 6.2). To put it in simple terms, a person who is starving is not likely to worry about whether he is being creative. Hence, a person will only experience higher needs when the more basic ones have been satisfied.

Taken in the most literal form, the notion of a hierarchy of needs seems to contradict reality. For example, it cannot explain why a parent would sacrifice their own life to save the life of their child, since physiological survival should be more potent than love. Maslow attempted to deal with such contradictions by suggesting that the hierarchy is not completely rigid: different needs may vary in intensity across individuals, and more than one need can be experienced at a given time. Normally we do not experience higher needs until more basic ones have been fulfilled, but, once experienced, the higher needs may become salient for a particular person. This qualification would account for parental sacrifice, as well as an artist who would rather live in poverty than compromise their creative aspirations by producing 'popular' art. Even so, most people will rarely, if ever, experience a strong need for self-actualization, because the circumstances of life prevent the lower needs from ever being satisfied. Whether one considers poverty in underdeveloped countries, or loneliness in major cities, the complexity of our deficiency needs can be hard to satisfy. Even if the basic needs *are* satisfied, the relative weakness of the need for self-actualization can make it easy to ignore.

Needs and Self-development

Maslow saw understanding the nature of our needs as an important part of self-development, since the various needs can affect all aspects of our lives. For instance, deciding to make a career change can involve physiological needs ('Will I have money to live on if I don't get a new job?'), safety needs ('Will I have to move?'), belongingness ('What about my friendships at my old job?'), esteem ('Will I be recognized for my abilities?') and self-actualization ('Will this alleviate the boredom I've been feeling at work?'). Given the wide-ranging impact of our needs, it should not be surprising that they influence all aspects of our lives, including our perceptions. Maslow suggested that when deficiency needs are dominant, we tend to see the world in terms of objects that can satisfy the dominant need. Hence, a hungry person will pause before a restaurant and see only the food; a person concerned with esteem will focus on the decor and perceived status of the restaurant. In each case, perception is distorted according to the dominant need. (Compare this notion to Freud's view of how distortions of reality arise.) By contrast, a person experiencing the need for self-actualization is likely to see the world more accurately, because objects are seen in relation to themselves, not as a means of fulfilling a deficiency.

In the same way, the frustrations we experience depend on which needs are dominant. A person with unsatisfied safety needs may complain about unsafe working conditions and a lack of job security; a person who 'has everything' (in terms of deficiency needs) may nonetheless feel unfulfilled, and see life as devoid of meaning – an expression of the self-actualization need. In fact, Maslow saw such complaints as an indication of a basically healthy state, since they imply that the deficiency needs are more or less fulfilled. Like Rogers, Maslow did not view aggression as an innate drive, but as a possible response to frustration of one's needs; in a healthy person living in a benign environment, aggression should not occur.

The relationship between needs and the environment is an important factor in understanding the behaviour of an individual. For example, a person may be irritable and antagonistic at work, despite being well paid and secure in their position. How are we to make sense of this? Maslow would suggest that it is only possible to understand the dynamics of this behaviour by exploring the situation thoroughly. Is the job itself boring? Are there unfulfilled aspirations at play? How do co-workers react to the person? If it turns out that significant needs are not being met in the work situation, then one could argue that the environment is at fault. However, this does not mean that the individual should passively accept the situation.

Although the environment may be the source of the problem, Maslow did not see individuals as simply victims of circumstances. Whereas the deterministic notions of the behaviourists might lead to saying 'it's not my fault' and giving up, Maslow believed that an individual has a responsibility to strive for growth and self-actualization, regardless of circumstances. Self-actualization is not simply a natural unfolding, but an active process which often involves making choices and overcoming obstacles. In this sense, his views echo Carl Rogers's ideas about individual autonomy. In the case above, the individual must carefully assess the situation, to determine an appropriate course of action: Can the job conditions be changed? Is it worth changing jobs? Only by identifying what needs are not being met can the person hope to find a workable solution.

One of the things which can interfere with recognizing, and therefore satisfying, one's needs is *cultural conditioning*. In modern Western society, we are taught to focus on material sources of satisfaction, which are associated primarily with physiological and safety needs. By comparison, love and esteem are seen as secondary, and personal growth has been almost completely ignored. (To the extent that esteem is acknowledged, it also tends to be addressed in material terms, i.e. 'status symbols'.) As a consequence, we have been conditioned to interpret the behaviour of others through a schema which emphasizes the lower needs. For example, employee relations are often seen by managers in very limited ways. Consider the case of an airline which several years ago was going through financial difficulties, and was seeking cooperation from the employee unions for various cutbacks. At the same time that the management was seeking employee support, it informed employees of lay-offs by posting names on company bulletin boards! Not surprisingly, the efforts to win union support for cutbacks failed, sending the airline into bankruptcy. The company president spoke of the 'greed' of the employees, while completely ignoring the issues of esteem raised by the way the lay-offs were handled.

The tendency to view satisfaction of needs in material ways can be seen in other forms. For example, someone who has just been rejected by a lover may go shopping to try to ease the pain. In the same way, we tend to view a person who is well-off financially as 'having everything', but in Maslow's view this could still mean that many needs are unmet. For example, the person may be going through a marital crisis, or suffer from low self-esteem. Even if the individual's love and esteem needs are met, self-actualization may be completely lacking.

Having been raised to focus on material sources of satisfaction, which originally were associated only with the lower needs, we tend to evaluate needs in these terms, both for ourselves and in perceiving others. Unfortunately, while money can buy food and shelter, it cannot really buy love or respect, and so these needs can continue to go unsatisfied. Ironically, in emphasizing material forms of satisfaction, and successfully finding ways to fulfil them, Western society has actually made it more likely that people will satisfy material goals – only to end up asking themselves, 'Is that all there is to life?'

<table>
<tr><td>

For further consideration

</td><td>

What needs are important to you at this point in your life? Where in the hierarchy do they fit? Do you perceive needs which *don't* fit within Maslow's hierarchy?

</td></tr>
</table>

Self-actualization and Peak Experiences

Self-actualization is a complex need, whose nature sometimes seems hard to grasp. Kurt Goldstein, from whom Maslow borrowed the term, saw it as a drive to actualize one's capacities, which is found in every organism (Goldstein 1939). Unlike basic drives like hunger, which seem focused on reducing tension, Goldstein noted that self-actualization often involves *increasing* tension, as when we seek out new situations to master. Rather than representing a tranquil state of rest, self-actualization can be a painful process of struggle in order to grow. Despite this, we are driven to stretch ourselves, to reach new limits, whether they be physical (like an athlete) or mental (like a novelist). As Maslow said, in words that echo Goldstein, 'capacities clamor to be used' (Maslow 1968: 152).

While struggle seems to be a common circumstance in life, self-actualization is not. Indeed, Maslow estimated that only 1 per cent of people ever really experience the need. Yet, for those who do, it can alter profoundly the individual's perceptions of the world, and the way they relate to others. How can the rest of us understand this type of experience? One way that Maslow used was the discussion of peak experiences.

peak experience
for Maslow, a transient experience of deep intensity which involves enhanced awareness, often accompanied by feelings of being 'fully alive'

Peak experiences represent moments of deep intensity in which we feel ourselves most fully alive. Such moments may occur when a parent first sees a new-born child, while viewing a great work of art, enjoying the beauty of nature or in any of a myriad of other ways (Maslow 1964). Maslow believed that such experiences provide a glimpse of what it really means to be self-actualized. In contrast to the sense of routine and drabness that sometimes seems to pervade everyday life, peak experiences represent moments of intense joy and excitement, coupled with a sense of fully living, of being truly *part* of the world. Lovers in the first glow of romance often have this feeling, as do religious mystics; Maslow saw both as examples of peak experiences. Curiously, such moments can even come in the face of adversity, as in the aftermath of a natural disaster, or following the death of a close friend. Whatever the circumstances, peak experiences are perceived as moments of insight into the potential of life.

Peak experiences by nature are both unexpected and relatively short-lived; they seem to come and go unexpectedly, regardless of the individual's desires. While they last, they are typically very intense and clearly distinct from ordinary living. Yet these characteristics also set these experiences apart from self-actualization, which is a less intense, ongoing process. Instead, peak experiences are more like a mystical rapture, reminiscent of the Zen experience of *satori*, or enlightenment. Zen practitioners may discipline themselves for years, seeking the moment of enlightenment, without any assurance about when, or even if, it will come. When it does, it is often experienced as an intense rapture, a feeling of suddenly being fully awake for the first time. Yet, like peak experiences, this feeling often fades somewhat after the initial rapture.

A longer lasting form of heightened awareness occurs in what Maslow called plateau experiences. A **plateau experience** is a more enduring but less intense state of awareness than a peak experience. One of the primary characteristics of a plateau experience is a change in one's perceptions of the world. The experience produces an intensified awareness of one's surroundings, and a heightened appreciation for life (Maslow, in Krippner 1972). Maslow came to this point of view as a way of accounting for more enduring changes than those of peak experiences, but also because of his own experience. After suffering a heart attack late in life, he found himself more deeply aware of the transience of human life, and this led to a profound change in his own view of the world. Commenting on this, he once remarked, 'If I could teach a person only one thing, it would be to live each day as if it were the last day of their life.' The point, of course, is not that if we're dying, nothing matters; rather, it is that if we are about to die, how we spend our last moments matters *very much*.

The transcendence of ordinary perceptions which occurs in peak and plateau experiences is not always part of self-actualization. All three concepts emphasize the sense of living to the fullest, but some people seem to live productive, self-actualized lives without ever experiencing the shift of awareness characteristic of peak and plateau experiences. Conversely, some people seem to have peak experiences, without ever being able to integrate this insight into a process of self-actualizing. In essence, self-actualization requires an overall balance and satisfaction of lower needs, not just a sudden insight. (This view obviously contradicts the idea, expressed in some books and workshops, that brief experiences can transform one's life.) Hence, the transcendent awareness of peak and plateau experiences is neither a requirement, nor a defining characteristic, for self-actualization. Even so, Maslow believed that those self-actualizers who had such experiences were more likely to be creative, and to see life as magical or miraculous. At the same time, such transcendence does not preclude involvement in everyday affairs:

plateau experience for Maslow, an experience which produces an intensified awareness of the world, and a heightened appreciation for life; a more enduring but less intense state of enhanced awareness than a peak experience

'You can run a grocery store and pay the bills, but still carry on this sense [of the mystical]' (Maslow, in Krippner 1972: 115).

For further consideration

Have you ever had an experience that you would describe as a peak experience? If so, can you explain it in terms of the situation, or did it seem to arise without a clear cause?

Maslow's Concept of Healthy Growth

Self-actualization refers to making full use of one's talents and capacities (Maslow 1970). Yet, in order for such a description to be meaningful, one must have some idea of what constitutes 'full use' – that is, one must have a conception of the *goal* of growth and development. Maslow recognized this, and over time tried to describe this goal by studying the lives of individuals whom he regarded as highly self-actualized. He began with the examples of two of his own teachers, Ruth Benedict and Max Wertheimer, who seemed to show high levels of fulfilment in both their professional and personal lives. Over time, he expanded the study, eventually basing his description on 18 people – nine of whom were contemporaries, and nine of whom were historical figures. Among the latter were Jane Adams, Albert Einstein, Abraham Lincoln and Eleanor Roosevelt. (It should be noted that one does not have to be famous to be self-actualized; Maslow chose historical examples in part because they would be familiar to most readers.)

Maslow's rationale for this methodology was that he was interested in the psychology of healthy people, and that outstanding individuals would provide the best possible indicator of what it means to fulfil one's potential. (This is in marked contrast to Freud, who dealt primarily with pathology, and never developed a clear model of the ideal of adult development.) Based on seeking common characteristics in the lives of the 18 individuals, Maslow proposed a list of characteristics of self-actualized people (see Figure 6.3). The list is rather daunting, and is apt to make one question whether *any* person could meet such standards. However, in proposing this description, Maslow was offering an ideal, which no individual would fully achieve – each would show some characteristics more strongly than others. In describing these characteristics, Maslow commented, 'There are no perfect human beings! Persons can be found who are good, very good indeed, in fact, great . . . And yet these very same people can at times be boring, irritating, petulant, selfish, angry, or depressed.' For example, Oskar Schindler, the subject of a popular book and film, sacrificed his considerable wealth to save the lives of over a thousand Jews during the Second World War – yet he was also a womanizer and con-artist (Keneally 1982).

While suggesting that these characteristics represent a sort of ideal for human growth, Maslow also noted that an ideal is a static concept, and self-actualization is itself not a static thing. Rather than being an *end*, a fixed goal which one can reach, Maslow emphasized that in fact self-actualization is a *process*, for which there is never an end. Like a journey, our lives

---

Characteristics of self-actualized people

  1 More efficient perception of reality

  2 Acceptance (of self, others and world)

  3 Spontaneity and naturalness

  4 Problem-centred rather than ego-centred

  5 Need for privacy and being detached from situations

  6 Independence from both cultural and environmental influences

  7 Freshness of appreciation of all experience

  8 Having mystical or peak experiences

  9 Feelings of kinship to others

  10 Deep relationships with others

  11 Democratic attitudes

  12 Distinguishing between means and ends, good and evil

  13 Philosophical, not hostile, sense of humour

  14 Self-actualizing forms of creativity

  15 Forming attitudes and values independently of culture

Figure 6.3   Characteristics of self-actualized individuals Like Rogers, Maslow believed that healthy individuals would come to show certain characteristics. This list is based on his study of a group of famous individuals (see text for details). Compare this list to Figure 6.1. (Adapted from Maslow 1970.)

can encompass detours and even backward movement; what matters is what we do along the way, not the destination. Seen in this way, it is understandable that no one person will show all these characteristics all the time.

Nonetheless, the attempt to define the ideal of human development has drawn many criticisms. One obvious concern is that in selecting individuals for his sample, Maslow was selecting those who exhibited the traits he hoped to find, and that therefore the process was both biased and circular. Maslow himself claimed to be surprised at the similarities he found, but one cannot rule out unconscious bias. Even without assuming such bias, there are concerns. Maslow wished to believe that the named characteristics, and the values associated with them, somehow stem from the very essence of human nature: 'Some values are common to all (healthy) mankind' (Maslow 1970: 150). Yet he also recognized that individuals differ in many ways, which could affect their actions and values: 'To the extent that capacities differ, so will values also differ' (Maslow 1970: 152). Hence, he was caught in the conundrum of arguing for a universal ideal, while simultaneously acknowledging that great variability exists among individuals.

As we have already discussed with Rogers's theory, the attempt to identify universal values is a complex issue. Maslow seemed to argue that the form which self-actualization takes is independent of culture. For example, he proposes that *resistance to cultural influences* is one of the characteristics of self-actualized persons. Thus, Oskar Schindler, by not accepting the Nazi view of Jews, was showing a form of self-actualization. But if acceptance by the majority (i.e. the overall culture) is not a requirement, then what makes *any* characteristic an indicator of self-actualization? Could it not be argued that self-actualization is whatever each person thinks it is? And if this is the case, then is Maslow's definition anything more than a reflection of his own values? As one critic put it, 'The question of just what is "natural" to man is, of course, the most vexed in the history of thought, and cannot be settled even by something as lofty as "the universal experience of clinicians"' (Robinson 1979: 257). Obviously, this line of reasoning poses a problem for Maslow's view, and he tries to avoid this conclusion by pointing to cross-cultural commonalities for certain characteristics and values. While research indicates that Maslow may be at least partly correct (e.g. Inglehart 1990; Baumeister and Leary 1995), this evidence is incomplete at best. In addition, while Rogers and others have argued for similar values and characteristics as Maslow, it is unclear whether this is truly an expression of 'human nature', or simply a consensus of like-minded people.

In the end, Maslow's ideas have proved influential more because of their capacity to inspire than for their empirical foundation. If one compares his work to that of Carl Rogers, one finds that Rogers has made a more concerted effort to validate his ideas through research. This is somewhat ironic, since Maslow began as an experimental psychologist, while Rogers began as a divinity student. Maslow also poses a contradiction when compared to psychodynamic theorists. While he rejected the pessimism and determinism of Freud, his own theory, like Freud's, rests on a foundation of analysing fundamental human needs. In one sense, he incorporated and extended the psychodynamic approach: Freud's id would represent physiological needs, Horney's work would focus on safety and love, while Adler emphasized esteem needs. To this structure, Maslow then added self-actualization. In doing so, he clearly made a shift from pathology to growth, as he intended. However, to reach the level of self-actualization, one must satisfy the lower needs, and clearly there are echoes of the psychodynamic approach in the lower needs of his hierarchy.

In one sense, the similarities between Maslow's theory and the psychodynamic approach should not really surprise us: while each approach to psychology has its own perspective, the subject matter – human behaviour – is common to all. Consequently, some convergence of descriptions would seem inevitable. At the same time, the distinctive elements of Maslow's work – the hierarchical conception of motivation, the emphasis on self-actualization – place it clearly within the humanistic approach. In domains as disparate as personality theory and diplomacy, Maslow's ideas live on.

For further consideration	Do you know anyone personally whom you would consider highly self-actualized? What leads you to think so? Do their values seem consistent with Maslow's description?

Extending the Humanistic Approach

As noted at the beginning of this chapter, the humanistic approach has no single theoretical founder. Instead, it encompasses a number of theorists, of whom Rogers and Maslow are simply the best known. Within the approach, each theorist uses a somewhat different vocabulary, and tends to emphasize slightly different concepts and issues. What lends coherence to the approach is a set of shared *assumptions* – a belief that behaviour can only be understood through an individual's subjective experience, and a belief in choice rather than determinism. In order better to understand this unity-within-diversity, we will briefly consider another viewpoint which shares many of the characteristics of the humanistic approach: *existential psychology*, particularly as seen in *Frankl's logotherapy*.

Existential Psychology

The origins of existential psychology lie in early twentieth-century philosophy. In the wake of the First World War, with its horrors for both soldiers and civilians, European philosophers began to question whether life had any objectively definable purpose or meaning. Thinkers like Jean Paul Sartre (1948) argued that life has no purpose, except what an individual gives it through their actions. Sartre felt that individuals are capable of making choices about how they live, and that those choices are what create meaning.

The work of Sartre and similar philosophers, known as 'existentialism', influenced a number of psychologists, particularly therapists, in the period after the Second World War. As they shared ideas and insights, existential psychology developed, based on the same general premises as existentialist philosophy (May 1961). If you recall the introduction to this chapter, Sartre's view may seem familiar, since the humanistic psychologists also believe that individuals are capable of making choices, and that the meaning of behaviour is subjective. In this sense, there is clearly an overlap between existentialist and humanistic viewpoints. (In fact, Rollo May's early (1961) book *Existential Psychology* included contributions by Rogers and Maslow!) The primary difference is the emphasis which the existentialists place on the issue of meaning. The human capacity for awareness means that we are capable of reflecting on both our own lives and the world around us. Out of this comes two major realizations: first, that both we and those we love will inevitably die; second, that suffering is an unavoidable part of life. What, then, makes life worth living?

Addressing this question is the central focus for existential psychologists. Not surprisingly, they do not see simple answers. Instead, they view many of the problems that individuals have as the result of failing to resolve the issue of meaning. Irvin Yalom, an existential therapist, says that anxiety is a result of trying to cope with the painful realities of suffering and death, not repressed desires or childhood traumas (Yalom 1980). Ernest Becker, another existential theorist, argues that acknowledging the reality of death is so threatening that cultures foster beliefs and values which symbolically deny the reality of death (Becker 1973). Some existential theorists see Becker's view affirmed in the way other approaches in psychology ignore the issues of suffering and death. For example, it seems unsurprising that many elderly people feel concerns about coming to terms with their approaching death. Yet, instead of dealing with this, developmental researchers tend to focus on issues like how cognitive abilities change with ageing (Vandenberg 1993).

Like Sartre, existential psychologists believe there is no universal answer to the questions of suffering and death, and no universal meaning to life. Instead, it is up to each individual to find their own meaning. This may seem like a very grim conception of life, far from the optimism of Rogers or Maslow. Yet, in the end, the existential viewpoint shares more than simply the basic assumptions of the humanists. As we will see with Frankl, existential psychology asserts that finding meaning is the path to healthy development.

Frankl's Logotherapy

In some ways, Viktor Frankel's life parallels that of Sigmund Freud. Both were Jewish, and both went to the University of Vienna to study medicine, with an initial interest in neurology. However, there are also many differences, beginning with the fact that Frankl was born when Freud was already in middle age. (Frankl was born in 1905, when Freud was 56.) In addition, while Frankl was interested in neurology, he soon changed his focus to the treatment of mental illness; he earned a doctorate in philosophy along with his medical degree! While exposed to Freud's ideas during his early training, he gradually evolved his own framework, which rejected many of the assumptions of Freudian analysis. Rather than the drives of sexuality and aggression, Frankl felt the most important motive for human behaviour was the desire to find a meaning for life.

Viktor Frankl

Viktor Frankl (1905–97) was born in Vienna, the son of Orthodox Jewish parents. He was educated at the University of Vienna, where he distinguished himself by earning doctorates in both philosophy and medicine. In medical school, he initially trained in neurology, but found himself drawn to concerns about mental illness. In this sense, his training mirrored an earlier Viennese physician – Sigmund Freud. Like Freud, he faced a threat from the rise to power of the Nazis, and in fact was granted a visa to go to the United States shortly before it entered the Second World War. However, because his parents were still living in Vienna, and unable to emigrate with him, he chose to stay instead. Consequently, he was imprisoned after the Nazi take-over of Austria, and spent three years struggling to survive in various concentration camps (primarily the notorious camps at Auschwitz and Dachau) until the end of the war. Only one person in 28 survived in the camps, and the experience was to play a significant role in Frankl's later theorizing. After the war, he became a professor of neurology and psychiatry at the University of Vienna, where he spent the remainder of his career. Frankl died in 1997, having lived through almost the entire twentieth century.

logotherapy Viktor Frankl's theory of development and therapy, which is based on the argument that finding a meaning for life is central to individual growth and happiness

Frankl is probably best known for his book *Man's Search for Meaning* (Frankl 1992). Originally, he intended to publish it as an anonymous memoir of his experiences in the concentration camps, but ultimately he decided it required a personal framework to be meaningful. Even so, it was not initially meant as a full exposition of his theoretical ideas. (Its original English title was *From Death-camp to Existentialism*.) However, the book proved remarkably popular, and over four editions the theoretical background, which he refers to as **logotherapy**, was gradually expanded.

To understand Frankl's theory, and how it fits into the humanistic approach, let us consider his view of some of the basic assumptions. Like Rogers, Frankl argues against the determinism found in both behaviourism and psychoanalysis: 'Man is *not* fully conditioned and determined but rather determines himself' (Frankl 1992: 133). While he grants that there are conditions which limit this freedom, the real issue 'is not freedom from conditions, but it is freedom to take a stand toward these conditions' (*ibid.*: 132). Even in the concentration camps, individuals could 'choose one's attitude in a given set of circumstances' (*ibid.*: 9). In this sense, Frankl's views are similar to other humanistic theorists.

A second assumption concerns the value of a *phenomenological framework* in understanding behaviour. At the very outset, he distinguishes between 'facts' and 'experiences'. Facts are objective observations, devoid of subjective context and meaning, while experiences are descriptions which are anchored in an individual's perspective – that is, subjective meaning. While he acknowledges that psychology as a science has traditionally emphasized detached objectivity, he suggests that in trying to understand experiences like those of concentration camp survivors, a detached observer 'is too far removed to make any statements of real value' (*ibid.*: 20). That is, the meaning of human experience can only be determined by the individual having the experience. Like Rogers, Frankl sees the understanding of meaning as central to the understanding of behaviour. Thus, his framework is essentially phenomenological.

As the early title of his book (*From Death-camp to Existentialism*) suggests, Frankl's views are also heavily existential. Like Jean-Paul Sartre and other existentialists, he sees the basic issue of life as the challenge of finding meaning in a world which often seems meaningless. For Frankl, however, meaning is not an abstract philosophical issue; nor is it based on some universal principle. Rather, meaning is viewed as a personal outcome which is related both to the immediate context of one's experiences and to the attitudes one takes towards those experiences. That is, rather than there being a general meaning to life, there is only 'the specific meaning of a person's life at a given moment' (*ibid.*: 113). In this sense, Frankl emphasizes the need to focus on the here-and-now of experience (in contrast to psychoanalysis, which tends to emphasize the person's past). While meaning may refer to future possibilities, it can only be derived from the present moment. Like life itself, meaning is changing and transient. (Such a view, as has been noted, is a familiar feature of humanistic theories.)

Like other humanistic theories, logotherapy has its own specific structure and concepts. Not surprisingly, Frankl places issues of meaning at the centre of his theory. Whereas Freud saw concerns about meaning as being a rationalization of instinctual drives, Frankl argues that 'striving to find a meaning in one's life is the primary motivational force in man' (*ibid.*: 104). In emphasizing the motivational role of meaning, Frankl rejects drive-reduction as being the goal of motivation (as Freud believed). In fact, he suggests that 'mental health is based on a certain degree of tension . . . between what one is and what one should become' (*ibid.*: 110). This view also places him in seeming contradiction to Rogers, who suggests that optimal functioning occurs when there is congruence (i.e. no conflict) between the self and the ideal self. The open-ended nature of the search for meaning is more like Maslow's conception of self-actualization (which, like Frankl's view of motivation, is not based on tension reduction). However, he sees self-actualization as a 'side-effect' of seeking meaning, 'not an attainable end' in itself (*ibid.*: 115).

noögenic neuroses in Frankl's theory, conflicts within an individual which are based on existential frustrations, rather than the conflicts of id, ego and superego which Freud saw as the source of anxiety

Meaning or its absence has profound effects on a person's life, in Frankl's view. In fact, issues of meaning produce what he calls **noögenic neuroses** – conflicts based on existential frustrations (rather than the issues of anxiety which underlie traditional neuroses). Frankl believes that such problems are more common than anxiety neuroses, and criticizes psychodynamic theories for ignoring issues of meaning. In one case, he encountered a diplomat who had been through an extended period of therapy, and had been told that his concern about his work reflected unresolved feelings about his father. After only a few sessions with Frankl, the man recognized that his problem was really a dislike for his current career. As a result, he decided to change careers, and five years later, had shown no recurrence of his former problems (*ibid.*: 107).

While existential concerns are not themselves pathological, they can *result in* pathology, and Frankl cites examples ranging from aggression to alcoholism. The interaction is seen most clearly in cases of depression. At one point, Frankl was working with unemployed individuals (in the economic downturn of the 1930s) who suffered from depression. While he could do nothing to change the economic conditions, Frankl found that those patients who began doing volunteer work for community groups also showed mood improvement. Unemployed individuals, he suggests, may be given social assistance to acquire food and shelter, but this is not the real issue: 'people have enough to live by but nothing to live for' (*ibid.*: 142). (Unfortunately, like most clinical studies, this result is correlational, and consequently one cannot be certain the volunteer work was the cause of the improvement; it may be that only the healthier patients were willing to volunteer, or the result could be coincidental.)

Frankl's view of the interactions between an individual and their surroundings is also different from those of other humanistic theorists. Ultimately, life has meaning only in terms of the way we relate to our surroundings: 'being human always points, and is directed, to something, or someone, other than oneself . . . The more one forgets himself . . . the more human he is and the more he actualizes himself' (*ibid.*: 115). Yet, while our relationships to people and things around us can be the source of meaning, they can also be the source of problems. This is clearly evident in the case of those who struggled to survive in the Nazi concentration camps, but can also be true in less extreme circumstances. For example, Frankl suggests that cultural beliefs can negatively influence the search for meaning in ways that may not be obvious. In this regard, he is very critical of modern Western culture, suggesting that its belief in determinism (in both science and therapy) has encouraged a feeling that life has no meaning: 'Existential vacuum is the collective neurosis of the present time' (*ibid.*: 131). In this sense, he goes beyond Rogers's view (which emphasizes how conditional regard given by others affects growth), suggesting that the factors which distort development can be *cultural* rather than individual.

One of the most interesting aspects of Frankl's theory is his position on the nature of human values. As has been discussed, both Rogers and Maslow argue that certain types of values are intrinsic to any healthy human being. By contrast, Frankl resists any such notion. Instead of advocating particular values, he argues that it is up to the individual to find meaning by making choices about what matters in life. 'Logotherapy tries to make the patient fully aware of his own responsibleness; therefore, it must leave to him the option for what, to what, or to whom he understands himself to be responsible. That is why a logotherapist is the least tempted of all psychotherapists to impose value judgements on his patients' (*ibid.*: 114). Rather than imposing values or other beliefs, the therapist's role is seen as helping individuals to discover their own values. In a sense, the *process* (though clearly not the concepts used) seems very much like Rogers's notion of providing the appropriate conditions for growth. People must discover the truth for themselves, but the therapist can help, in much the way that an ophthalmologist 'tries to enable us to see the world as it really is . . . so that the whole spectrum of potential meaning becomes conscious and visible' (*ibid.*: 114–15).

It is possible that Frankl's unwillingness to assert particular values is a reaction to his experiences in the concentration camps – after all, could anyone who lived through such horrors really believe that all people are fundamentally good? Even to survive required suspending conventional notions of morality. When selections were made of those who were to be killed next, 'All that mattered was that one's own name and that of one's friend were crossed off the list of victims, though everyone knew that for each man saved another victim had to be found' (*ibid.*: 18). In such circumstances, it seems hard to claim the high ground of moral superiority; indeed, many survivors were haunted by the implications of having survived. Frankl alludes to this when he says, 'We who have come back . . . we know: the best of us did not return' (*ibid.*: 19). Whatever its basis, Frankl's view that values are personal rather than universal means that, in contrast to Rogers and Maslow, he has no fixed value system to defend.

Although Frankl does not argue for a particular meaning to life or a particular set of values, he *does* suggest three ways in which meaning can be *discovered* in life: (a) by achievement; (b) by a transcendent experience (e.g. love or an appreciation of nature); or (c) by the attitude one takes to unavoidable suffering (e.g. a concentration camp prisoner, or someone facing a terminal illness). The first is fairly straightforward – Frankl himself found the will to live when he was in the concentration camps by focusing on his desire to complete a book about his ideas. The idea of transcendent experiences, like the desire to achieve, seems very reminiscent of Maslow's concept of self-actualization. While Frankl suggests self-actualization should not be the *goal*, the *process* of finding meaning seems to lead in the same direction.

The third option, finding meaning through suffering, may seem rather strange. As Frankl notes, our culture seems to emphasize pleasure-seeking and the avoidance of suffering. While this fits well with drive-reduction notions of motivation, it has the consequence of encouraging denial of unpleasant realities, and even makes the experience of suffering degrading. However, there are clearly individuals who face death – such as through terminal cancer or AIDS – with grace and calm. For Frankl, their attitude bears witness to 'the uniquely human potential . . . when we are no longer able to change a situation . . . to change ourselves' (*ibid.*: 116). In his view, 'life has a meaning up to the last moment' (*ibid.*: 118). Indeed, he would probably be alarmed at the growing interest in euthanasia and assisted suicide, since seeking to terminate life in this manner seems based on the assumption that suffering is not only meaningless, but something to be actively avoided.

Like other existential thinkers, Frankl's ideas are grounded in some of the harshest realities of life – suffering, death and the apparent pointlessness of some events (Becker 1973; Yalom 1980). In this sense, his theory strikes a very different emotional tone from the sometimes Pollyanna-like optimism of Rogers and Maslow, who talk of 'unconditional regard' and 'peak experiences'. Consequently, it is all the more interesting that his thinking leads to a similar result – that life is worth living, and we have both the freedom and the responsibility to determine our own actions and their meaning. Of course, this similarity does not provide unequivocal evidence that Frankl's theory is correct; indeed, it suffers from many of the same difficulties of evaluation as the theories of Rogers and Maslow. Nonetheless, logotherapy clearly fits comfortably within the humanistic framework, and Frankl himself provides an inspiring example of finding meaning in life. Despite his harrowing time in the camps, Frankl is optimistic – and if *he* can be, should we not be too?

For further consideration	Have you ever been through a difficult experience which nevertheless had a positive influence on your life? If so, how do you see this as related to Frankl's view of suffering as a possible source of meaning?

Conclusion

The humanistic approach encompasses a number of theorists and theories, all of which (as the name implies) seek to understand behaviour in human terms – that is, as it is experienced by the individual. Behaviour itself is only one aspect of human experience, and the humanists believe one can only understand human experience in terms of the meaning an individual gives to it. This emphasis on subjective experience, often referred to as a *phenomenological* viewpoint, distinguishes the humanistic approach from all the other approaches to psychology, which seek to eliminate subjectivity by emphasizing objective observation. However, humanists like Carl Rogers suggest that the distinction is more apparent than real, and question whether it is possible for *any* observations by humans to be free of subjectivity.

Evaluating the humanistic approach by traditional scientific criteria is difficult, because of its phenomenological emphasis. The sources of evidence used to support the theories are almost entirely *correlational* (case histories and interviews), which (unlike experiments) do not produce *falsifiable* predictions. While humanistic theorists would argue that prediction is ultimately irrelevant to understanding behaviour, without it evaluation of a theory becomes very difficult. For most psychologists, the basic issue is *accuracy* (how well does the model fit reality) – yet when assessments are dependent on subjective judgements, this is hard to determine. Only when individual preferences are reflected in a common consensus do scientists trust personal judgements. On this basis, there is some ground for supporting humanistic theories – for example, one can see many points of agreement between Rogers and Maslow. However, when differences exist between theories, it becomes hard to determine which theory (if any) is actually correct. (As we have seen, this lack of testability is also a concern with psychodynamic theories, and has resulted in a similar debate about the value of the individual theories.)

Within the humanistic approach, there are several areas that require further consideration. One is the question of cross-cultural validity, which arises with regard to the definition of *self* and also when discussing values in human development. As noted, some cultures foster a collective sense of identity, rather than the individualistic version emphasized in humanistic theories. Does this mean that the humanistic concept is biased, or could it be that collectivist cultures artificially constrain the individual? And is there a universal set of optimal values? Both Rogers and Maslow suggest that there is a common set of values for healthy individuals, yet Frankl rejects this view. Even if one supports the notion of innate values, as E. O. Wilson (1998) does, identifying what they are is not easy (Robinson 1979).

Culture may also be relevant to how we define the nature of healthy development. Viktor Frankl has commented that 'every age has its own collective neurosis, and every age needs its own psychotherapy to cope with it' (Frankl 1992: 131). Further, he suggested that the increase in secularism in our society has changed the accepted source of help: 'Some of the people who nowadays call on a psychiatrist would have seen a pastor, priest or rabbi in former days' (*ibid*.: 119). The notion that attitudes and expectations have changed was echoed by Perry London, a clinical psychologist (London 1974). London has remarked that, to Freud, a patient was someone who felt bad (i.e. suffered from an obvious problem), while, for the humanists, it is sufficient that a person doesn't feel good (i.e. is not reaching their full potential). Whether this reflects refinements in our understanding, or simply a cultural shift, is not clear. Some have argued that the humanistic emphasis on individual development is the result of a cultural trend which has gone too far (Wallach and Wallach 1983). Obviously, the humanistic theorists would disagree, but the issue is clearly contentious. (It is impossible to discuss fully the relationship of theory to culture at this point; the issue will recur in Chapter 10.)

Both by its assumptions and by the content of its theories, the humanistic approach has enlarged psychology's domain. By emphasizing the importance of meaning in the lives of individuals, it has challenged other approaches to provide their own answers to such questions. Our capacity to be self-aware, to reflect on our own existence and even to imagine its ending is as much a part of human life as our capacity to learn or to feel emotion. The answers given by current humanistic theories may be incomplete or even inaccurate, but until the role of meaning in human experience is understood, psychology must not shrink from exploring the issue.

Chapter Summary

♦ The *humanistic approach* is characterized by two basic assumptions which distinguish both its methodology and its theories from other approaches: the focus on subjective experience (*phenomenological* viewpoint), and a rejection of *determinism* in favour of individual *choice*. Among the humanistic theorists, the ideas of *Carl Rogers* and *Abraham Maslow* are certainly the best known.

♦ Rogers developed a model which focuses on the relationship between what we feel we are (the *self*) and what we feel we should be (the *ideal self*). When the two are experienced as being similar, the individual is *congruent* or *fully functioning* – the goal of development. When a gap exists between the self and the ideal self, the person will experience this as *incongruence*.

♦ Being congruent depends on encountering people who provide the *conditions for growth*: *empathy*, *openness* and *unconditional positive regard*. Incongruence results from other people setting up *conditions for worth*, expressed through *conditional positive regard*.

♦ Like other humanistic theorists, Rogers was optimistic about human growth. In describing the potential of human development, he described the characteristics of *fully functioning individuals*, including the *values* which he felt such individuals were likely to hold. His ideas have been very influential in counselling and therapy, where his theory forms the basis of *client-centred therapy*.

♦ Abraham Maslow attempted to understand behaviour in terms of the needs which motivate an individual. The recognition that not all needs are alike led to the formulation of his *hierarchy of needs*, which ranged from basic *safety needs* to the creative desires represented in *self-actualization*.

♦ Unlike other needs, self-actualization is based on the desire to grow, not on some form of deficit. Maslow believed that individuals can experience self-actualization during *peak experiences*. Like Rogers, Maslow tried to describe the nature of optimal human growth; to do so, he used historical examples of *self-actualized individuals* (both men and women).

◆ While Rogers and Maslow are the best-known humanists, the approach can also include *existential theories* like that of *Viktor Frankl*. Frankl argues that issues of *meaning* are central to all human experience. Unlike Rogers and Maslow, he rejects the view that particular values are necessary to human growth.

◆ Of all the approaches, the humanistic approach is unique in emphasizing questions like the role of meaning and spirituality in human life. It remains a challenge to find ways to evaluate effectively the differences among the humanistic theories, as well as the approach as a whole.

Key Terms and Concepts

actualizing tendency
client-centred therapy
conditional positive regard
conditions for growth
conditions of worth
congruence
deficiency motives
fully functioning person
hierarchy of needs
ideal self

incongruence
intersubjective verification
logotherapy
noögenic neuroses
peak experience
phenomenological
self
self-actualization
unconditional positive regard
would–should dilemma

Suggestions for Further Reading

Rogers wrote a number of books on different aspects of his work, but perhaps the best for a reader seeking a general overview is *Freedom to Learn*, which discusses his ideas of personal growth in the context of education.

Maslow's best known book, *Toward a Psychology of Being*, is also one of his best in terms of conveying an overall view of his ideas.

For the reader interested in Viktor Frankl's ideas, *Man's Search for Meaning* is the primary source.

7

Perspectives on Development

Observing the Journey of Life
Introduction
Methods of Studying Development
Issues in Interpreting Development
  Continuity versus Discontinuity
  Generality versus Specificity of Models
  Heredity and Environment
Personality and Sex Role Development
Personality and its Origins
Perspectives on Personality
  The Biological Approach
  The Behaviourist Approach
  The Cognitive Approach

The Psychodynamic Approach
The Humanistic Approach
The Development of Sex Roles
  The Biological Approach
  The Behaviourist Approach
  The Cognitive Approach
  The Psychodynamic Approach
  The Humanistic Approach
Conclusion
Chapter Summary
Key Terms and Concepts
Suggestions for Further Reading

Observing the Journey of Life

Writing a book is sometimes compared to having a child, with a long gestation period followed by release into the world. For a textbook like this, each edition shares similarities, yet is unique – much like siblings. Despite the parallels between writing and parenting, as someone who is both a writer and a parent, I feel strongly that parenthood is far more significant. My ties to my two sons extend well beyond biology; each day's interactions are a process of discovery that is always unpredictable, and often joyful. To see a child grow seems an affirmation of life and its potential; it simultaneously leads us into thoughts of the future, and into recollections of the past. Sometimes I watch my younger son, and am reminded of similar moments when his older brother was the same age. And, like any parent, I see glimmers of my own life journey in the lives of my children.

The start of a new life is a remarkable process: we are conceived as a joining of sperm and ovum, each of which bears only a half set of

DNA, but which together provide the genetic pattern for a new being. Nine months later, we emerge from the womb as an infant – small, frail, dependent on others for survival, but still recognizably human. This, of course, is only the beginning of an ongoing process of growth and development – from infant, to toddler, to child, to adolescent, and onward through adulthood and ageing. The process by which we reach our full potential is a slow one: altogether, it takes nearly two decades for physical and intellectual capacities to mature. Thus, given a lifespan of approximately 75 years, we spend about *one-quarter of our life* simply reaching our full size and skills!

This prolonged developmental period is remarkable – few animals spend such a large portion of their life reaching their full capacities. In fact, it has been suggested that in many ways our nature is best seen as based on a kind of delaying of the developmental timetable. For example, compared to the most genetically-similar species, chimpanzees, we are more like a foetal chimp than an adult chimp – like human adults, foetal chimps show a relative absence of body hair, no brow ridges and a spine–brain connection which makes an upright posture possible (Campbell 1982). By contrast, the appearance of mature (adult-like) capacities in a new-born is generally found only in lower species. It almost seems as if slow development is *necessary* to forming the capacities we do.

Comparing human development to other species can pose many difficulties, but the desire to compare is driven by a basic question: *why* do we develop the way we do? The question quickly leads to a host of other questions: What guides our development? What kinds of factors can influence it? Such questions – and there are many others that are closely related – are basic to the study of developmental psychology.

Introduction

developmental psychology
the study of the processes which underlie growth and change in behaviour over time

In its most general form, **developmental psychology** is concerned with the processes that produce changes in behaviour over time. These changes are most dramatic in the first two decades of life, so it is not surprising that early researchers tended to focus on this period of human life. Hence, for many years, 'developmental psychology' really meant 'child development'. More recently, the field has broadened to consider events during the ensuing years as well. While the changes that occur in adulthood are generally less obvious, it is clear that we do not simply remain static after childhood and adolescence. Indeed, the long period of 'preparation' would seem to be pointless if nothing important followed! So, today, researchers are interested in questions of growth and change as related to the whole span of life, from birth to death.

The study of developmental psychology represents a different sort of division within psychology from the approaches we have considered thus far. What unites the area is the emphasis on the processes of growth and change, not a particular theoretical perspective. In fact, the questions of development can be looked at from each of the approaches, as we will see. At the same time, developmental researchers (of every perspective) are concerned with asking certain types of questions about behaviour, and it is the focus on these questions that gives the area a thematic coherence.

The most basic question in development has already been raised: what makes us the way we are? While simple to ask, it is exceedingly difficult to answer. For one thing, one could ask it about one individual (e.g. what makes Sarah different from Jill), about particular groups (e.g. based on gender or nationality) or about humans as a species (as in the earlier comparison to chimpanzees). Long before psychology emerged as a distinct discipline, philosophers asked similar questions – and often disagreed about the answers. As far back as ancient Greece, Plato argued that all human knowledge and virtue was innate – that is, we are what we are born to be. By contrast, John Locke, a seventeenth-century English philosopher, suggested that a new-born child is like a blank slate, on which experience writes its messages; in essence, we are what we experience. In modern psychological terms, these polarities would be represented by the factors of heredity and environment, and debates about the importance of each are a long-standing issue. But trying to answer this age-old question requires first answering some more basic questions.

Methods of Studying Development

The first thing required is to come to some understanding of what development actually involves. That is, what *are* the changes that go on during a person's life? The physical changes of childhood may seem very obvious, but as with many phenomena, the interesting parts lie in the details. To take a simple question (one which concerns nearly all parents): at what age does (should) a child begin talking? To answer this question, we might study language acquisition in a representative sample of children; this provides us with a description in terms of what is typical – that is, a *norm*. In all likelihood, there will be some noticeable variability across the group; this, in turn, may spawn a whole new series of questions, aimed at understanding *why* such variability occurs. (To answer the 'simple' question, children typically say their first words before their first birthday, but even this generalization ignores many details – for example, not all speech sounds (called *phonemes*) are acquired at the same age, as Prather *et al.* (1975) noted.)

Determining norms for basic aspects of development is an important element in describing the process of development as a whole. However, even this task becomes complicated when one wishes to find relationships between events – for example, do children who are slow to begin talking also lag behind in other respects, such as learning to walk? Or are the behaviours independent of each other? And do children who begin talking early continue to show superiority in language skills later on? While in principle one could establish norms for any single behaviour by selecting a representative sample, it becomes more complicated when one wants to make comparisons at different ages (e.g. as in looking at the pace of language acquisition). One way to answer the question is to select a group of individuals who are all the same age, and then continue to study them during the period of interest (e.g. from six months up to age six). This approach is called a **longitudinal study**, since it represents a long-term study of a given group. While highly informative, such studies are also difficult to do. The most obvious problem is the time required – the study takes at least as long as the time period of interest. While the duration will vary depending on the question being researched, in some cases (such as the language issue described above) it may take years. This requires a tremendous commitment on the part of the researcher (whose own life is passing along with those of the subjects), as well as the cooperation of the subjects. (In the case of children, obviously this means their parents must *also* be supportive.) Even so, participants sometimes move away, die or drop out for other reasons. If too many of the initial group fail to complete the study, the representativeness of the results can be jeopardized, eroding the value of the work. Despite these obstacles, there are instances in which subjects have been studied for decades or longer, providing a remarkable extended portrait of lives unfolding. (One example is a study of patterns of adult personality which continued for over two decades (see White 1975).)

Longitudinal studies, though very useful, represent only a small percentage of all developmental studies. In many cases, neither researchers nor subjects are willing or able to make the commitment required. In addition, depending on the question being asked, a longitudinal design may not be necessary. For example, if a researcher simply wants to determine the age range at which a particular behaviour occurs (such as producing two-word sentences), a longitudinal design is not required to get an answer. As a result, many developmental studies are based on selecting representative groups of each age and comparing them, thereby getting a sort of 'snapshot' of behaviour at each age. This approach, which draws comparisons across time by looking at different age groups, is called a **cross-sectional study**. For example, the study of speech acquisition referred to earlier (Prather *et al.* 1975) used a cross-sectional design. Cross-sectional studies have the obvious advantage of minimizing the time required for the study. For example, one could simultaneously study changes across adulthood by selecting groups of individuals who are aged 20, 30, 40, 50, etc. This advantage is one reason for the popularity of cross-sectional studies.

Unfortunately, this advantage can often be offset by the disadvantages of the design, particularly when studying individuals across wide age ranges. As a type of *quasi-experiment*, a cross-sectional design limits our ability to interpret causation (see Chapter 1). The primary problem is that such studies cannot control for any factors that change along with age – for example, the fact that the subjects of different ages were born at different points in time. Such differences can be very important in terms of the role of cultural and historical influences – for example, comparing the attitudes of teenagers today and of their parents (who were likely to have been teenagers in the 1970s) would have to contend with differences in areas such as school curricula, social attitudes and the spread of technology like television and

longitudinal study a research design in which a group of individuals are studied over a period of time

cross-sectional study a research design based on selecting representative groups who vary on a particular characteristic; when the characteristic is age, this design provides a means of making developmental comparisons

confounding variable a factor in research which varies jointly with a variable of interest, making it impossible to identify properly the role each variable has in affecting behaviour; typically, a confounding variable represents something which has been overlooked in planning the research, and is only identified after the data have been collected

video games. When such outside influences (called **confounding variables**) are present, they can sometimes dramatically alter the interpretation of development. By their nature, confounding variables represent something which has been overlooked in planning the research, and it is often only after the fact that they can be identified. For example, cross-sectional studies have suggested that intelligence test scores begin declining by age 50; however, when a longitudinal design is used, it becomes clear that scores typically remain constant up to age 70 or later (Labouvie-Vief 1985)! In this particular case, the contradiction may be related to differences in the groups selected for the cross-sectional studies. Since the older subjects were born decades earlier than the younger subjects, there would be differences in educational level, age of first exposure to television, etc. (For example, likelihood of attending university increased over the twentieth century.) These differences among the groups, which might affect performance on the intelligence tests, would thus represent a confound with age. The possibility of such confounds, which are often difficult to anticipate, means that cross-sectional studies require careful assessment, particularly when they are attempting to compare behaviour over wide age ranges. In this sense, cross-sectional studies can be useful for identifying the age at which a behaviour occurs, but are sometimes not as helpful as longitudinal studies in clarifying the processes which underlie development.

One way of compensating for the risks of cross-sectional studies is to use a hybrid design which has features of *both* longitudinal *and* cross-sectional studies. This approach, called a **sequential design**, uses groups of different ages, which are then observed for some period of time, such that the groups eventually overlap. Comparing behaviour of individuals from different groups at the same age then allows an evaluation for possible confounds or other problems which sometimes arise in simple cross-sectional studies. For example, a study of adolescents might select three groups, aged 10, 12 and 14. All subjects would then be followed for four years. At this point, those who were originally 10 would now be 14 – and their behaviour could be compared to that previously recorded for the group who were *initially* 14. If no differences exist based on this comparison (and similar comparisons for the other groups and ages), the researchers would be more secure in suggesting that no confounds are present. (The problem would come, of course, if the results based on the age-matching were *not* similar – one is then left to ponder whether the difference represents a confound, or simply sampling variability.) Thus, the sequential design would allow study of behaviour over an eight-year span, but would only require four years to complete – in some sense, the best of both worlds! (See Figure 7.1 for a comparison of the three research designs.)

sequential design a research design which combines features of both longitudinal and cross-sectional studies by selecting groups of different ages (like a cross-sectional design), and then following them over a period of time (like a longitudinal study) sufficient to create overlap in the ages represented by different groups

For further consideration

Ask a parent, grandparent or some other older adult about their experiences at your age – what were they doing, what they were interested in and so on. Then ask them about their current preferences in music, books, etc. Assuming their current preferences are different from your own, can you decide whether the difference is due to the age difference, the difference in prior experience or some other factor? What does this tell you about the difficulties of interpreting developmental research?

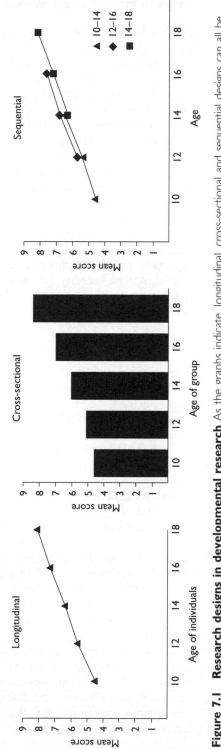

Figure 7.1 Research designs in developmental research As the graphs indicate, longitudinal, cross-sectional and sequential designs can all be used to explore developmental change. (These graphs represent a hypothetical study of changes in logical reasoning from age 10 to age 18.)

Issues in Interpreting Development

Obviously, one cannot understand development without knowing something about what actually occurs. However, gathering accurate information about behaviour at different ages is only part of the puzzle. As discussed in Chapter 1, description is only the starting point in understanding behaviour. Understanding also requires explaining *why* things happen as they do, and this requires *interpreting* what we know, in terms of a theory. In the case of development, the goal is to understand the changes in behaviour that occur over time. However, we recognize that time itself is not the active force – it is processes going on *within* time that account for the changes. Hence, the task becomes one of identifying and describing these underlying processes. As we have seen in considering the various approaches, the same behaviour may be interpreted differently by different theories. When it comes to development, there are three major issues that arise in interpreting developmental changes: Is development a continuous unfolding, or discontinuous stages? Can a single model describe all aspects of development, or do different aspects require fundamentally different models? And what is the relative importance of heredity versus environment in determining the course of development? Because they apply to all the approaches, we will consider each of these questions in more detail.

Continuity versus Discontinuity

continuity the view that changes in development occur through a continuous, gradual process, rather than as a series of discrete stages; continuity is an assertion about the processes which underlie development, as well as the changes observed in behaviour

stages the belief that development is based on distinct periods with clear boundaries, with behaviour at each stage governed by different underlying processes; Freud's theory of psychosexual stages is one such theory

The most basic issue is concerned with the **continuity** of development. One of the most obvious aspects of development is the fact that many changes occur during the course of life. For example, the reasoning skills of a three-year-old are dramatically different from those of a twenty-year-old. At what point are these differences so great that they represent a new skill (a *qualitative* change), rather than simply more of the same (a *quantitative* change)? To put it another way, are there distinct **stages** in development, with clear boundaries, or is development a more or less continuous process? (Sometimes this issue is described as one of *continuity versus discontinuity*, and sometimes as *gradualism versus stages*.) For example, a ten-year-old can use language in much more complex ways than a four-year-old. Does this mean the ten-year-old processes language differently (is in a different stage), or does it simply reflect the effects of six years of practice (continuity)?

While strikingly different in their implications, the concepts of continuity and discontinuity are nonetheless hard to evaluate in practice. In one sense, it is obvious that development is continuous – physical growth is a gradual process, and many skills, like walking or talking, are acquired only gradually.

At the same time, it is tempting to categorize behaviour into stages, just as we form other sorts of categories. The physical changes which occur at puberty, while gradual, nonetheless seem to herald a new stage of life. Similarly, we talk about 'adolescence' versus 'adulthood', implying that the two periods are distinct. Are these stages really distinct in the way that pre- and post-puberty are? Asserting that stages exist implies several things about the underlying processes – most importantly, that each stage is characterized by *distinct underlying mechanisms*. In addition, discontinuity frequently implies that there is a specific *order* to the stages, and possibly even specific *timing* of the occurrence of each stage. (Freud's theory of personality development, for example, involves all three aspects: changing mechanisms underlying stages, a specific order of stages and specific timing of stages.) As we consider some of the specifics of development, the issue of continuity versus discontinuity will arise repeatedly.

Generality versus Specificity of Models

A second issue which arises concerns the *generality* of theories of development. A basic principle in science is the notion of *parsimony* – that is, a simpler theory is preferable to a complex one, assuming both can explain a particular set of results. In the same way, having a single theory which can be broadly applied is preferable to using several narrow ones. Ideally, we would like to have one general model to describe all aspects of development. At present, this seems out of reach, but we can still ask whether specific aspects of development (e.g. cognitive development or social development) can be explained in terms of a single set of principles. A broad theory like Piaget's (1954), because it attempts to encompass many areas or 'domains' of cognitive functioning, is sometimes called a **domain-general model** (Rosser 1994). In contrast, some researchers believe that different cognitive functions require different theoretical explanations; a theory which focuses on only one function or domain is called a **domain-specific model**.

The Swiss theorist Jean Piaget, one of the great pioneers in the study of cognitive development, believed that a single set of principles could account for the development of all sorts of cognitive skills, from understanding numbers to spatial reasoning. His work has been highly influential, and his theory represents an example of a domain-general model. In his theory, he emphasized certain general principles which he believed were applicable to all aspects of cognitive development. The most fundamental of these principles was **equilibration** – the desire to maintain a balance between our surroundings and the mental structures we use to represent those surroundings. Often this means that we integrate new information or experiences into our existing cognitive structure (a process Piaget called **assimilation**). In other circumstances, new experiences require us to change our existing representations; Piaget called this process **accommodation**. To Piaget, this search for balance (equilibration) was the process underlying all cognitive activity. Despite seeing equilibration as fundamental to all cognitive processes, Piaget nonetheless saw cognitive development as a series of discrete stages, as can be seen in Figure 7.2.

Despite its significant influence, Piaget's work has been criticized, because the broad picture of cognitive processes which it paints seems wrong in some of its details, particularly when applied to other cultures (Dasen 1975; Flavell 1992) (for example, most Australian aborigines never reach the stage of formal operations, at least using Piaget's standard tasks). This weakness is not unique to Piaget's theory – getting the details right often represents the biggest difficulty in trying to develop a comprehensive (domain-general) model. Partly in response to these concerns, other researchers have

domain-general model a theory which attempts to account for many aspects of behaviour in terms of a single set of principles

domain-specific model a theory which focuses on only a single aspect of behaviour in the belief that different aspects of behaviour involve different processes, and therefore require different theoretical explanations

equilibration Piaget's term for the process of maintaining balance between our environment and the mental structures which we use to represent that environment

assimilation a process of integrating new knowledge or experience into our existing cognitive schemata

accommodation a process of modifying our cognitive schemata in response to new knowledge or experience

Age	Stage	Major characteristics
Birth to 2 years	Sensorimotor	Egocentric thinking – inability to conceive of the world as existing apart from one's own experience of it
		Development of object permanence – understanding that objects exist independent of one's sensory experience
	Preoperational	Development of language skills
2–4 years	Preconceptual (sub-stage)	Use of symbols – using words as category labels
4–7 years	Intuitive (sub-stage)	Using concepts – sorting objects by size, shape or colour
7–11 years	Concrete operations	Mastery of principles of conservation – understanding that mass, volume and number remain constant despite perceptual changes in grouping or form
11 to adult	Formal operations	Mastery of abstract thinking – ability to use inductive and deductive reasoning, using symbolic representations to analyse problems and formulate ideas

Figure 7.2 Piaget's theory of cognitive development Piaget viewed cognitive development as consisting of four distinct stages, which were characterized by qualitatively different thinking processes; these stages were seen as age-related, and as always occurring in the same order.

put forward theories which deal with only limited aspects of cognitive development. For example, Lawrence Kohlberg (1966) developed a theory of moral development (how we make judgements of right and wrong). His work grew out of Piaget's, but its narrower focus on moral thinking makes it an example of a domain-specific model.

The differences between the theories of Piaget and Kohlberg illustrate the dilemma which developmental theorists face. Basically, the problem is a conflict between the principles of parsimony (a general model would be simpler than invoking several different models) and accuracy (a general model may fail to do justice to the complexities of development). In practice, the issue is often not as clear-cut as it is expressed here, but we nonetheless have to recognize that there are often competing demands involved in deciding what is a good theory.

For further consideration

Write a brief explanation of why the sun seems to set in the west each evening. What form of thinking does this represent, according to Piaget's theory? If you discovered your explanation was actually wrong, how would Piaget expect you to respond?

Heredity and Environment

The broadest issue in forming a theory of development, and in some ways the most contentious, concerns the *origins* of the changes which occur over the span of life. In some ways, development represents a paradox: there is the obvious sense of change, while at the same time, there seems to be a central thread of constancy. For example, parents of grown children often recall ways in which the infant or child foreshadowed the adult. Is this constancy real or imagined? And if real, what is it based on?

The traditional answer to the question of constancy has been to assert that the basic characteristics of a person are innate – that is, the constancy is due to the influence of *heredity*. In essence, this is the modern version of Plato's nativist theory. The role of heredity is evident in the development of a foetus, whereby cells differentiate to form the various parts of the body. Even after birth, the regularity of growth strongly suggests the influence of genetic timetables.

The alternative to explanations based on heredity is to look for environmental influences. At first glance, it may seem hard for environmental models to explain either constancy over time in an individual's behaviour or the developmental similarities found across individuals. Yet, as Skinner (see Chapter 3) and others have noted, it is *possible* to talk about environmental constancies and similarities. Thus, one finds two extreme poles on the issue: is development based on *heredity* (the nativist view) or *environment* (the empiricist view)? (Note that the terms *nature* versus *nurture*, and *innate* versus *learned*, are generally synonymous with 'heredity versus environment'.)

In recent years, developmental researchers have come to recognize that either/or statements about heredity and environment are both pointless and misleading. For example, as we gain a greater understanding of the underlying mechanisms of heredity, we have come to recognize that genetic mechanisms do not operate in a vacuum. Instead, they must be expressed in the context of the individual's environment – and while one can speak of an impoverished environment, there is always *some* environment. Thus, the proper question is not whether development is based on heredity *or* environment, but rather how, and to what degree, the two *interact*. Donald Hebb, a noted Canadian psychologist, once suggested that the interaction is akin to the way the area of a field is determined by its length and width: one can have fields of different shapes, but every field has *some* length and width (Hebb 1953).

There are a number of ways that heredity and environment can interact. At the simplest level, the **reaction range** of the genotype may set the limits on how environmental influences (whether deprivation or enrichment) can affect the trait (Hirsch 1963). For example, on average, white American males are taller than Japanese males; this difference appears to be based on genetic factors. At the same time, however, there is overlap between the two groups, and within each group variations are associated with differences in nutrition – an environmental factor. Hence, heredity determines a range for the person's height, with actual height determined by the nutritional environment.

Identifying the boundaries for the influence of heredity and environment can be very difficult. For example, most people probably think of environmental influences as beginning at birth, when the infant emerges from the womb into what William James called a 'booming, buzzing confusion of sights and sounds'. In reality, environmental influences exist *within* the womb as well. One reflection of this is that maternal behaviour and health have measurable effects on the unborn child. For example, smoking and

reaction range in genetics, the limits on the variability of a phenotype (observed characteristic) determined by the genotype; in essence, the limits set by the genes on how environmental influences (whether deprivation or enrichment) can affect the trait

Trait	Reared together		Reared separately	
	MZ	DZ	MZ	DZ
Well-being	0.58	0.23	0.48	0.18
Achievement	0.51	0.13	0.36	0.07
Positive emotionality	0.63	0.18	0.34	−0.07
Stress reaction	0.52	0.24	0.61	0.27

Results fit genetic model: MZ > DZ, reared together > reared separately

Results don't fit genetic model: reared separately > reared together

Figure 7.3 Heredity and environment in studies of twins Studies of identical (MZ) and fraternal (DZ) twins reared together and apart can suggest the influence of both heredity and environment – greater similarities for MZ twins than DZ twins suggest heredity; greater similarities for twins reared together than apart suggest environment. Note that the data for stress reactions do *not* fit the expected environmental pattern. (Data from Tellegen *et al.* 1988.)

drinking by the mother have both been shown to affect the developing foetus adversely. Exposure to certain drugs in the womb can even affect the development of sex characteristics (Money and Tucker 1975). Thus, inter-actions of heredity and environment must be assumed to occur right from the time of conception.

Pre-natal influences are also a concern when one looks at twins. Studies of identical twins in particular are popular because one can be certain of the genetic relationship between the twins, and similarities are often cited as examples of genetic influence (see Figure 7.3). Unfortunately, such studies often overlook the role of pre-natal influences, despite evidence that the prenatal environment may contribute to any observed similarities. For example, fraternal twins (conceived from separate zygotes) often seem more similar than other siblings, in part because they share a common prenatal environment. Thus, simply knowing the genetic relationship between two individuals is insufficient to determine the relative role of heredity and environment. (See Chapter 2 for a related discussion.)

More recently, researchers have begun to look at more complex ways in which heredity and environment interact (Bronfenbrenner and Ceci 1994). In part, the goal is to recognize the complex nature of interactions between individuals and their environment. Thus, parents may seek to treat siblings equally, but the temperament of one child may lead to differing parental reactions. The child's temperament may reflect heredity, but the family environment is altered by how the child's behaviour affects other family members. Similarly, Sandra Scarr has argued that individuals tend to create their own environment (by their activities, interests etc.), and that these *active choices* are influenced by heredity. That is, individuals with different genotypes are likely to choose different environments. Evidence which is consistent with this view comes from studies of intelligence test scores, where typically, as children get older, their scores become less like those of their parents and siblings; in effect, older children exert more control over their environment than do younger children (Scarr and McCartney 1983). Further support for this idea comes from a study in which family environment was found to be more similar for identical twins than fraternal twins – presumably because they elicit more similar responses from family members (Plomin and Bergemen 1991). Such interactions imply that the genotype will influence the environment, as well as the environment affecting the expression of the genotype.

In some circumstances, it can seem that there is very little interaction between heredity and environment. For example, some aspects of development seem to occur without any specific environmental conditions, a process known as **maturation**. Yet, even in such seemingly straightforward situations, making assumptions about genetic mechanisms and/or experience can lead to unexpected outcomes. For example, consider the development of depth perception. Most mammals (including human infants) are able to perceive depth by the time they are able to move about in the world (Richards and Rader 1983). Obviously, this has adaptive value in terms of avoiding falls, and seems to arise as a result of normal visual experience. With infants, the study of depth perception usually involves using the 'visual cliff', a well-known test in which the toddler is confronted with a glass-covered surface, beneath which there is an obvious dropoff. Typically, infants old enough to crawl will not venture over the apparent 'edge', despite the support of the glass. This is interpreted as evidence of depth perception, whereby vision (the perceived drop) overrides touch (the support of the glass surface). However, psychologist Neil Carlson notes that when his 6-month-old daughter was tested, she went unhesitatingly across! Since it seemed impossible that the toddler could not perceive depth, the perplexed researcher, a colleague of Carlson's, could not understand this result – until it was explained that the family had a glass-covered coffee table, and the child had often crawled on it. Thus, rather than indicating a failure of depth perception, the results reflected the difference in her prior environment (Carlson 1990).

Closely related to maturation is the existence of *critical* or 'sensitive' *periods*. Essentially, the concept is that there is an optimal time during development for particular experiences to occur. For example, while the language one speaks depends on early experience – that is, the environment – it appears that the *timing* of language learning is governed partly by genetic programming, with an optimal interval during early childhood (Chomsky 1988). Deprivation at this time – for example, because of an undiagnosed hearing impairment in a 3-year-old – may have long-term repercussions for language learning. (See Chapter 4 for a related discussion.)

To recap our discussion, there are three major issues which underlie the study of development, which are reflected in the interpretations made by each approach. (1) Is development a continuous process of gradual changes, or a series of distinct stages? (2) Can one theory describe the processes which underlie all development (domain-general theory), or are specific models needed to account for different aspects of development (domain-specific theories)? (3) What is the relative importance of heredity (genetic make-up) as compared to the environment (especially learned experiences) in explaining the outcome of development? As we consider selected aspects of development, you may want to think about the possible answers to these questions.

maturation a term referring to processes in development which seem to be relatively independent of environmental influences; depth perception and walking are examples of behaviours which seem to depend on maturation; implied in the term is the assumption that the characteristics are governed by heredity

In the end, these questions can only be answered by considering what we actually know about growth and change over the course of life. After all, the issues, as well as the theories which attempt to answer them, have meaning only with regard to the actual events of development. It is beyond the scope of this chapter to provide a full review of what is currently known about development across the lifespan. Instead, we will focus on one aspect of development: the patterns of behaviour which we see as characteristic of an individual. Some of these patterns seem distinctive to the individual, and represent what we call the person's 'personality'. Another type of pattern, which is both part of personality and separate from it, is the tendency to show gender-related behaviours (called 'gender roles'). In the remainder of the chapter, we will look at these issues from the point of view of each of the five approaches.

For further consideration

Assume that there is a gene which affects athletic ability. What sort of environmental factors do you think might interact with it to affect athletic performance? What would enhance it? What might impair it?

Personality and Sex Role Development

Personality and Its Origins

A few years ago, I had the chance to get together with college classmates at a reunion. Some of those present I hadn't seen since our graduation, 25 years before. Not surprisingly, it was a bittersweet occasion, with many shared laughs about long-ago incidents, but also more muted reflections on the passage of time, and on those friends whose lives had already ended. But what struck me most of all was the sense that most people seemed to be 'still the same' – that apart from bodily changes (greying/thinning hair, weight gained or lost), much was unchanged. Tom was still shy, Cathy was still extraverted – in other words, there seemed to be a strong sense of consistency in their behaviour, even after 25 years. As a psychologist, how can I account for this?

Traditionally, we talk about such consistency in terms of the individual's personality. **Personality** refers to those behaviour patterns which are characteristic of an individual and which tend to be consistent across situations and over time. The concept of personality provides a simple way to talk about consistency *within* the behaviour of an individual, but we sometimes also make comparisons *between* individuals. In this case, we typically refer to specific characteristics, called personality **traits**. We say 'he's shy', or 'she's outgoing', and people nod knowingly, accepting the terms as a way of both describing the individuals, and of predicting how they might act in a particular situation, such as at a party.

To the average person, the study of personality may be the most interesting issue in psychology. Indeed, it has been suggested that we are all 'personality theorists', since in our interactions with others we make interpretations

personality patterns of behaviour which are characteristic of an individual and which tend to be consistent across situations and over time

trait a behaviour pattern which occurs consistently across a range of situations; a specific personality characteristic

implicit personality theory a general cognitive schema about human behaviour which is used in making interpretations of the behaviour of other people

based on our cognitive schemata about what people are like. These schemata are sometimes called **implicit personality theories**. In this sense, ideas about personality may stem from our own perceptions, rather than external reality. (See also Chapters 1 and 4.)

At the same time, most people, and even most psychologists, would argue that at least *some* of the perceived consistencies are real, just as some of the perceived differences between individuals are real. For example, two longitudinal studies done at the Institute of Human Development at Berkeley followed randomly selected children from early childhood until mid-life, and found signicant correlations over time on several personality measures (Block 1971). Given that each individual is a unique combination of genes and experiences, what shapes the *person* in the 'personality'? To try to understand this, let us look at how each of the five approaches views the origins of personality.

For further consideration

In what ways do you think you are consistent? Try to identify four or five personal traits; then, ask a friend to list what they perceive as your major traits. How do the lists compare? What does this tell you about implicit personality theories?

Perspectives on Personality

Earlier in this chapter, we noted that there are three major issues which arise when one is considering theories of development: (a) the role of heredity versus environment; (b) whether development is continuous or based on discrete stages; and (c) whether development involves a single process that can be understood in terms of a single model (domain-general), or involves different processes that require separate models (domain-specific). These questions are equally relevant when it comes to considering the origins of personality, so let us examine briefly how each of the five approaches views the issues.

The Biological Approach

The biological approach, as the name implies, places heavy emphasis on the role of heredity and physiological structure in shaping behaviour. In looking at personality, the approach has tended to focus on those aspects of personality associated with temperament. **Temperament** refers to basic behavioural tendencies, such as emotionality, sociability and fearfulness, which are believed to be determined by heredity (Rothbart 1981). Two types of evidence support the view that temperament is largely innate. First, comparisons of fraternal and identical twins indicate that identical twins are more alike in activity level, irritability and sociability than are fraternal twins (Plomin *et al.* 1988). A long-running study of twins separated early in life, the Minnesota Twin Study, has reported similar findings about heredity influencing temperament (Bouchard *et al.* 1990). Of course, such studies can be difficult to evaluate, especially since body structure (itself genetically influenced) and the reactions of other people to physical attributes like attractiveness may influence these aspects of behaviour. Such influences

temperament behavioural tendencies which are believed to be determined by heredity; examples include emotionality, sociability and fearfulness

would represent an interaction with environment, not a pure genetic factor. Support for this idea comes from a study which followed a group of children from the age of three months until adulthood (Thomas and Chess 1977; Chess and Thomas 1987). Chess and Thomas found that there are interactions between the temperament of a child and the caregiver which over time can affect behaviour. For example, mothers may tend to respond more favourably to babies who are not irritable.

In general, longitudinal studies seem better suited than twin studies to determining the stability of traits, hereditary or otherwise. Jerome Kagan has used this approach to look at a trait he calls *behavioural inhibition* – the tendency to withdraw from unfamiliar people or situations. Inhibited children tend to be shy, and experience anxiety when faced with novelty. Those children who were either inhibited or uninhibited at 21 months of age tended to remain so when followed up to age seven or more (Kagan 1989). Thus, studies of temperament support the biological perspective in suggesting that important components of personality are due to heredity. (In terms of heredity and personality, it is worth noting that the Minnesota Twin Study has also reported finding evidence of significant hereditary influence on such higher-level aspects of personality as recreational and vocational interests (see Lykken *et al.* 1993).)

With regard to the other two issues, the biological approach is less consistent. *Maturation*, the genetically-programmed development of characteristics over time, often involves the idea of *critical periods* for development, as noted earlier. Essentially, a critical period represents a discontinuity in development – the individual will react differently depending on the timing of experience. While it is difficult to prove in humans, many researchers believe that there are critical periods for both social attachment and language learning during the first few years of childhood (Bornstein 1989). According to this view, a child who does not form close emotional ties, or receive exposure to language, at this time will show a permanent deficit in these behaviours (Lenneberg 1967; Bowlby 1988). While the notion of a critical period suggests that discontinuities or stages exist in development, in other areas, such as temperament, the biological approach emphasizes the continuities of development. Hence, one cannot make a simple generalization about how the biological approach views the issue of continuity versus discontinuity.

In terms of the third issue, the validity of domain-general versus domain-specific models, the biological approach seems to favour domain-specific models. As suggested in the previous paragraph, different aspects of development are seen as having different characteristics, and this implies different underlying sub-processes. At the practical level, no one within the biological approach has suggested a comprehensive, domain-general model of development, though Zuckerman (1991) has proposed a model for personality. Thus, it seems reasonable to describe the biological approach as advocating domain-specific models of development.

The Behaviourist Approach

Compared to the biological approach, the behaviourist approach takes a polar-opposite view of the importance of heredity versus experience. In fact, Skinner has suggested that physiological processes within the organism are of no concern, provided one can find meaningful links between stimulus conditions and behavioural responses (Skinner 1974). All behaviour is seen as determined by experience, based on the principles of *classical* and *operant conditioning*. Rather than being based on discrete stages, the approach views behavioural change (development) as a continuous process. Since the principles of conditioning are seen as applicable to all behaviour, the behaviourist approach represents a domain-general model.

The main problem this approach faces, in terms of explaining personality, is how to account for the apparent consistency of behaviour. After all, the principles of learning would seem to imply that change is as probable as consistency, since there is no explicit factor pushing for constancy. Skinner and other behaviourists have responded to this problem by suggesting that 'personality' is simply a perceived pattern, with no basis within the individual. Instead, they suggest two factors which could produce the consistencies which are ascribed to personality. One factor is the cumulative effect of reinforcement. Each time we are reinforced, the influence of that reinforcer is *in addition to* all prior reinforcement in the same or similar situations. Rarely is one experience so significant as to override our entire past **history of reinforcement.** (This is one reason why attempts at changing behavioural patterns like bad habits 'overnight' rarely succeed.) Hence, the consistency of behaviour, particularly in adults, is largely a product of prior patterns of reinforcement.

history of reinforcement in operant conditioning, the sum of all prior reinforcement for a particular behaviour; behaviourists assert that the cumulative history of reinforcement is more important than any single reinforcement in determining behaviour

The other factor which behaviourists point to in explaining behavioural consistency is the role of *environmental consistency*. Skinner has argued that in trying to explain behaviour we tend to give credit to the individual, not the environment, especially when we are unaware of the contingencies which govern the behaviour (Skinner 1971). In the case of the consistencies which we attribute to 'personality', we tend to overlook the degree to which the typical person's environment is consistent. For example, most of us have daily routines which are quite regular, we associate primarily with the same group of friends and acquaintances, we tend to live in the same place for relatively extended periods, and so on. At least partial support for this comes from further analyses of the Berkeley longitudinal study (mentioned previously), which found that married couples who were rated as more similar in personality tended to engage in more similar activities (Caspi *et al.* 1990). These similarities in activities contribute to an environment which is relatively consistent, in terms of both discriminative stimuli and reinforcers. In such circumstances, it would be surprising if our behaviour were *not* fairly consistent. (Note that the behaviourist is *not* obliged to suggest a mechanism for *perfect* consistency, since nearly every study of personality shows that consistency is generally far from absolute.) Thus, the combination of the cumulative effects of reinforcement, together with overlooked sources of environmental consistency, are viewed by behaviourists as the basis of 'personality'.

The Cognitive Approach

The cognitive approach is interested in how cognitive processes influence behaviour. In this sense, cognitive psychologists are as interested in why we *believe* in the concept of personality as in the factors that promote behavioural consistency. Let us consider first our tendency to believe that behaviour is consistent.

Some thirty years ago, Walter Mischel challenged the trait view of personality by arguing that while consistencies in behaviour may exist, they are much more situation-specific than most people realize (Mischel 1968). In this sense, perceived consistencies may reflect a form of mental bias rather than true characteristics. Explaining the origins of such biases is part of the study of social perception. **Social perception** is concerned with the social dimension of perception – how we see others, and ourselves in relation to others. As noted earlier, cognitive theory argues that we actively interpret our experiences, forming mental schemata about both people and situations. One example of this is the study of *attribution theory*, which deals with the kinds of inferences we make about the causes of behaviour – both our own and that of other people (see Chapter 4). For example, the *fundamental attribution error* states that we place too much emphasis on internal characteristics ('personality'), and too little on environmental influences ('the situation') when interpreting other people's behaviour (Ross 1977). Such bias would lead to overestimating the actual consistency of behaviour, and thus our willingness to believe that personality traits exist.

If 'personality' does not represent inherent traits, then how do the consistencies arise? The answer proposed by Mischel and others is based on **cognitive social learning theory**, which looks at behaviour from a cognitive and social perspective. Cognitive social learning theory is based on two premises. First, it argues that much of our behaviour is learned from interactions with others, especially through imitation (hence the 'social learning' component). *Imitation* (also called observational learning or modelling) is concerned with learning based on observing others, as opposed to direct experience. Second, it asserts that the mental constructs that we form (values, expectations and other schemata) mediate our behaviour in ways that produce our 'personality' (hence the 'cognitive' component). Since constructs are generally closely tied to specific situations, the theory argues for the kind of limited behavioural consistency cited by Mischel. (More recently, Mischel has modified his position, suggesting that personal schemata interact with the specific situation (see Mischel and Shoda 1995).) Both social learning and social cognition (including *social perception*, discussed above) seem to play a significant role, as seen in the influence of parenting styles and parental expectations on children's behaviour (Baumrind 1991; MacKinnon-Lewis *et al.* 1997). Thus, over time there has been a convergence, so that today the leading proponents use the hybrid term *cognitive social learning theory*, or some variation of it (Berkowitz 1984; Bandura 1986). (For a discussion of parenting, see Figure 7.4.)

Not surprisingly, the cognitive approach is strongly environmentalist, and largely ignores the role of heredity in behaviour. This is evident in the rejection of trait concepts of personality, which typically assert that traits are based on innate factors. In terms of the issue of continuity versus discontinuity, the theory largely favours continuity. For example, studies in which children are allowed to observe adults doing Piagetian tasks have

social perception the study of the social aspects of perception – how we see other people, and ourselves in relation to others

cognitive social learning theory (sometimes simply 'social learning theory') a theory derived from the cognitive approach which asserts that behaviour can be learned from observing other people, and that behaviour is mediated by cognitive schemata

How much influence do parents have on the personality of their children? The conventional wisdom is 'a great deal'. After all, parents determine both the genetic make-up and the domestic environment of their children. In addition, a large body of research has supported the idea that parenting styles, for example, have a significant impact on children's personality and behaviour. (See text.) Recently, however, this view has been challenged by Judith Harris, who has argued that child-rearing practices matter much less than most researchers (and parents) believe (Harris 1995, 1998). Instead, she says that personality is due to a combination of genes and peer influence. If the concept of parents as the dominant influence is wrong, how did it arise? And if Harris is correct, what makes peers so influential?

The idea that parents' behaviour shapes children's personalities can be traced back to Freud, in terms of modern theories. Recall, for example, that Freud argued that the importance of events in the first five years was crucial to later development; in particular, the role of *identification* with their parents shapes the formation of the child's superego. Later researchers, while often rejecting Freud's model of development, have focused on the role of parents as a source of reinforcement (behaviourist), as well as imitation and mental schemata (cognitive). Given a variety of studies which seemed consistent with such ideas, the role of parental influence became an accepted concept.

On the other hand, Harris's view, while it has caused controversy (particularly in the popular media), is not entirely surprising. In the 1980s, researchers noted that variances between families were minimal, once one accounted for genetic influences on personality (Plomin and Daniels 1987). Equally, it has been recognized that as children mature, they spend decreasing amounts of time in the home (with parents), and much more time outside the home (with peers). Thus, even an environmentalist should expect decreasing parental influence as children reach adolescence.

If Harris is correct, what makes peers such a powerful influence? One significant factor has already been mentioned: *social learning*. Just as children learn by imitating their parents, so too they imitate their peers – a process that begins when they enter school, if not earlier (Hartup and Coates 1967). A second factor, which is more significant with peers than parents, is *conformity* – the tendency to alter one's opinions or actions to match group norms, in response to explicit or implicit social pressure. Conformity was shown to be a powerful influence on university students in a classic study by Solomon Asch (1955): Confronted with peers who unanimously made what appeared to be incorrect perceptual judgements, students altered their own responses. Conformity has been extensively studied, and while Asch's original situation was somewhat artificial, the basic phenomenon of conformity as a source of social influence is well established. In addition, it is now known that many factors, including group unanimity and status of both the group and the individual, affect conformity. Because adolescence is a time when many individuals feel insecure in their identity, it is likely that adolescents are particularly vulnerable to conformity pressures (Campbell *et al.* 1986; Frank *et al.* 1990).

In the end, personality is affected by many factors. Rather than representing a rebuttal of the research on parental influences, the recent emphasis on peers can be seen as simply a rebalancing of factors as we improve our overall understanding.

Figure 7.4 Parents, peers and personality

been used to challenge Piaget's concept of cognitive stages (Rosser 1994). And in terms of the issue of domain-specificity, the theory appears to be domain-general, in that it views many aspects of development as open to explanation, from cognitive development to personality and moral development. However, this conclusion is largely tied to the two previous points: if development is seen as a continuous process of learning, it is open to a domain-general model. As yet, however, no one has attempted to use cognitive social learning theory as a general developmental framework.

The Psychodynamic Approach

While the psychodynamic approach encompasses a number of theorists, Freud is still the dominant figure. The psychoanalytic theory which he developed provides a framework for interpreting nearly every aspect of behaviour, including the origin and nature of personality. In Freud's view, all behaviour is motivated by innate drives, whose mode of expression changes over the course of development. These changes in expression of the drives define the *stages of development* which shape the formation of adult personality: the oral, anal, phallic, latent and genital stages. Personality is based on the three components of id, ego and superego, which dynamically interact to direct behaviour. Id, the source of the drives, is present from birth. By contrast, ego and superego are formed over time, with the first five years of life being of central importance.

While the drives determine the sequence and timing of the stages of development, Freud believed that *experience* was an important factor in the shaping of personality. In particular, the way the individual learned to handle the expression and gratification of the basic drives would determine the conflicts and coping strategies which defined much of adult personality. Unfortunately, by emphasizing early development as the source of personality formation, Freud had little to say about possible changes during adult life. Neo-Freudian theorist Erik Erikson has addressed this issue by creating a model of personality development with stages across the entire life span (see Chapter 5).

Freud's theory is fairly explicit in terms of the basic issues of development. His emphasis on innate drives clearly argues for the role of heredity – indeed, his view of aggression as innate has been a frequent focus of criticism. At the same time, he clearly recognized the importance of nurture, particularly in terms of the effects of early experiences. Consequently, it is appropriate to classify Freud as an interactionist in relation to heredity versus environment – he clearly saw both factors as important to development. With respect to the issue of continuity, it is apparent that Freud saw development as discontinuous. His stages were biologically defined by the expression of the innate drives, and hence fixed in both sequence and timing. In terms of domain specificity, Freud's theory is clearly domain-general. Freud did not invoke different processes to distinguish the development of cognitive capacities (largely connected to ego) from the development of personality. In his view, all of behaviour could be understood in terms of the same basic processes. Indeed, while the specifics of his theory have been frequently challenged, his work still stands as one of the most remarkable attempts at creation of a comprehensive theory of behaviour.

The Humanistic Approach

The humanistic approach includes a large number of specific theories, which share certain basic assumptions, but differ in many details. One respect in which they differ is the degree of attention paid to questions of development. Some, like Rogers's theory, are fairly detailed in discussing the origins of personality. Others, like that of Viktor Frankl, scarcely use the word 'personality'. Hence, in order to provide a useful basis for comparison in this context, we will focus on the work of Carl Rogers (1959).

Rogers sees all of growth and development as motivated by the *actualizing tendency*, a biologically-based drive to reach one's full potential. However, the primary factors which influence the process of growth are cognitive and experiential, not biological. Like other humanists, Rogers emphasizes the way individuals sees themselves in relation to their surroundings. This *phenomenological* approach means that behaviour can only be understood in terms of the meaning the individual gives to it. In Rogers's theory of personality, each person comes to define a sense of their *self* and *ideal self*.

The self stems largely from the actualizing tendency, and reflects innate tendencies, but the ideal self is strongly influenced by experience, particularly our interactions with other people. This influence is expressed largely through the type of *positive regard* we receive. Rogers sees the outcome of healthy development as a *fully functioning person*, in whom the self and ideal self are largely consistent. Rather than being a static end state, this represents an ongoing process. Thus, Rogers sees development as a lifelong process.

In terms of the nature–nurture issue, Rogers supports aspects of each view. For example, he acknowledges the importance of the innate actualizing tendency, and has gone so far as to suggest that particular values are embedded in the actualizing tendency (Rogers 1969). He also sees the need for positive regard as having an innate basis. Thus, the forces which motivate growth are largely reflective of heredity – but the same is not true of the factors which shape personality. The most significant aspect of personality functioning for Rogers is the relationship between the self and the ideal self. This relationship is largely dependent on encountering the conditions for healthy growth. The *conditions for growth* which Rogers has specified (openness, empathy and unconditional positive regard) are all provided by other people; hence, in this respect, his theory emphasizes the importance of experience. Overall, we must consider his theory as reflecting an interactionist view of heredity and environment.

Rogers sees personality development as a continuous process of growth; his theory makes no reference to possible stages or discontinuities. Thus, his position on this issue seems clear. The remaining question is whether he views development as domain-specific or not. Overall, he seems to present a domain-general model, since he does not explicitly divide development into different aspects or processes. However, one must also note that he says very little about some aspects of development, such as physical and cognitive development. Given these omissions, one can only really evaluate his theory in terms of what it *does* consider, personality development. Within this domain, it does seem to present a general model, but as a theory of behaviour it is clearly not as comprehensive as the theories of Freud and Skinner.

In summary, the five approaches view personality very differently, ranging from the biological interpretation that personality is innate to the behaviourist assertion that personality does not exist. Ultimately, it may be the case that no single approach is adequate to explain the complex behaviour patterns which we call personality. Before trying to make a general assessment, let us look at the more specific issue of gender role development.

Children are often compared to their parents in terms of personality – for example, 'he has his father's temper' or 'she has her mother's stubbornness'. How would each approach explain such similarities?

The Development of Sex Roles

'Boys will be boys', states an old saying. Unfortunately, this simple statement belies the complexity of the questions which underlie it. What *are* boys like? Do they really act differently from girls? And if so, *why*? We know there are differences associated with sex – for instance, males are typically larger and stronger than females – but do these differences account for why, for example, boys play with cars and girls play with dolls?

The existence of two physical sexes is one of the most obvious characteristics of human beings. This biological fact is often regarded as equivalent to a psychological imperative – that is, that behaviours *associated with* sex (gender roles and sexual orientation) are directly *determined by* gender. However, the realities are not as simple as this view implies. For one thing, **gender roles** refer to the behaviours which a culture considers appropriate for each gender, and obviously differences exist across cultures (Mead 1935; Ford and Beach 1951). Therefore, there is no universal definition of 'male' and 'female' gender roles; instead, the definition depends on what culture one lives in. In addition, there is also variation within a culture, including differences in **sexual orientation** – that is, whether the individual is attracted to the same sex (*homosexual*), the opposite sex (*heterosexual*) or both (*bisexual*). Hence, in talking about behaviours related to sex, we encounter the same kinds of questions of individuality and causation that are part of the larger domain of personality in general. To try to understand such behaviour, let us consider how each theory interprets the development of gender roles and sexual orientation, which may be considered part of the overall roles associated with one's physical sex ('sex roles').

gender roles patterns of behaviour which a culture defines as being appropriate for each gender

sexual orientation a description of whether an individual is sexually attracted to the same sex (homosexual), the opposite sex (heterosexual) or both (bisexual)

The Biological Approach

The physical differences in body structure which are associated with gender are obviously rooted in heredity. Chromosomally, males have an XY pattern, while females have an XX pattern. In turn, the expression of this genetic pattern is dependent on the actions of hormones, which affect the development of physical sex characteristics. In particular, the presence or absence of **androgens**, the male hormones, determines prenatal physical development: if androgen is present, the foetus develops male characteristics; if it is not, the foetus develops female characteristics. Normally, the amount of androgen present is determined by the genes associated with the sex chromosomes. However, there are cases where the process goes awry, because of either genetic defects or environmental factors (such as the presence of drugs which affect androgen levels). In such cases, the development of physical characteristics, including genitalia, can be affected. Thus, at the level of the physical characteristics associated with gender, the nativist position of the biological approach is well supported.

androgens hormones whose functions are related to masculine characteristics; the most important is testosterone

The crucial question, though, is whether *behaviour* is determined in the same way. The biological approach would say it is, and therefore that gender role differences are the result of biological/evolutionary processes. For example, Buss has drawn on evolutionary theory to suggest that the different reproductive challenges faced by men and women have led to them having different gender roles (Buss 1995). Certainly, the existence of cultural stereotypes of males and females is consistent with this view. For example, males are typically seen as more aggressive than females in nearly all cultures (Williams and Best 1982). While such observations support the biological view, we need to ask if there is any *direct* evidence for innate behavioural differences based on gender, since stereotypes may influence behaviour in ways unrelated to heredity. A number of studies have found that boys are typically more physically active than girls, even in early infancy (Eaton and Enns 1986). The early appearance of this difference suggests an innate factor, which might be mediated by hormonal influences. John Money, a specialist in hormonal processes, has reported cases of androgenized females (genetic females exposed to high levels of androgens prenatally) (Money and Tucker 1975). Money reports that in these cases physical development is affected, but also behaviour – the girls are typically more physically active and 'tomboyish' than their peers. Hence, physical activity level may be a sex difference which has a hereditary origin.

If such differences do exist, what is their basis? The most common answer is that hormones affect development of the brain as well as the body, and that this results in gender-related differences in behaviour. Research has clearly demonstrated such effects in other mammals, and apparent differences in the brains of men and women have been interpreted in the same way (Kimura 1992). As examples, Kimura cites the tendency for men to outperform women on certain spatial tasks, while women outperform men in fine-motor coordination. While this research does not directly prove that gender identity is based on hormones, more recent research has reported menstrual variations in women's spatial performance that support the hormonal hypothesis (Silverman and Phillips 1997).

A similar argument has been made with regard to sexual orientation – particularly the origins of homosexuality. Within our culture, homosexuals have often been maligned and regarded as 'unnatural'. Given the social hostility implied in this view, why would someone *choose* to be homosexual? In fact, most homosexuals assert that their sexual orientation is not a choice, and was fixed well before puberty (Bell *et al.* 1981). This interpretation is consistent with the view that sexual orientation is innately determined, as the biological approach would argue. Support for this view comes from research indicating that the brains of homosexual men are more like women's than those of heterosexual men (LeVay 1993). Assuming that these findings are reliable, what would account for such differences? One theory is that hormonal variations alter the brain in ways related to sexual orientation. One mechanism for such hormonal variations is maternal stress during the second trimester of prenatal development (Ellis *et al.* 1988). More recently, support for a genetic factor has come from a study suggesting a link between homosexuality and genes on the X chromosome (LeVay and Hamer 1994).

These studies, while supporting the biological view, are not without problems of interpretation. LeVay's findings are based on a *quasi-experiment*, which does not allow direct interpretation of causation. As discussed earlier, experience can influence the development of the nervous system, so finding differences in the brains of adults does not necessarily prove that the cause is genetic. While experimental studies of hormonal effects in animals provide clear data, the evidence provided by Ellis *et al.* (1988) is both retrospective and correlational. In addition, Byne, in a reply to LeVay and Hamer, has argued that the available evidence is too limited to support the assertion that sexual orientation is genetic (Byne 1994). More recently, a group of Canadian researchers has reported being unable to replicate the original genetic finding (Rice *et al.* 1999). At present, the question of a biological origin of sexual orientation seems unresolved.

Even if this issue gets settled, it does not explain all aspects of gender roles and sexual orientation. One fact which tends to work against the biological view, at least in the simple form that sex determines behaviour, is the tremendous variation in behaviour *within* each sex, which results in overlap *between* the sexes. Compared to this, the overall differences which can be associated to sex are fairly small; Deaux (1985) has estimated that only 5 per cent of individual differences among children can be attributed to sex. This leaves the question of how such small differences can produce a stable and well-differentiated gender identity. In essence, if boys and girls are so similar, how can their gender identities be so different? In this regard, John Money and his colleagues have argued that socialization, not hormones, determines an individual's sense of gender identity (Money and Tucker 1975). Hence, gender identity seems to involve more than simply biological sex; to understand this, we must look at how other approaches explain the development of gender roles.

The Behaviourist Approach

Behaviourists like Skinner argue that all behaviour is shaped by reinforcement, so if variations exist across individuals, this implies differences in reinforcement history. In terms of gender roles, this view is supported by research showing that, right from birth, boys and girls are treated differently (Maccoby and Jacklin 1974; Pomerlau *et al.* 1990). This pattern persists, and possibly increases, in later childhood (Huston *et al.* 1986). Thus, the behaviourist approach would argue that the behaviours associated with gender roles, like other cultural patterns, are shaped by reinforcement, and hence are learned, not innate (see Guerin 1992).

This approach is consistent with the observation that gender roles differ across cultures, for both men and women (Mead 1935; Whiting and Edwards 1988). Such variations are easier to explain in terms of learning than in terms of heredity. The behaviourist approach also makes it easy to explain individual differences, since experiences can differ for each individual. One disadvantage of the behaviourist view, however (a problem shared by all environmentalist theories), is the difficulty of explaining the *origin* of gender roles. If the patterns are entirely learned, then where did they come from in the first place? *Why* should males and females be treated differently? The

---

Attributes perceived as masculine and feminine

MASCULINE	FEMININE
Aggressive	Gentle
Ambitious	Considerate
Competitive	Devotes self to others
Not easily influenced	Aware of others' feelings
Likes maths and science	Enjoys art and music
Self-confident	Needs approval
Skilled in business	Likes children
Stands up under pressure	Excitable in a crisis

Figure 7.5   Stereotypes of male and female gender roles In a study of university students done in the early 1980s, clear differences in the perceived attributes of male and female roles were found. Do you think the same would be true today? (List adapted from Ruble 1983.)

behaviourist approach gives no specific answer to this question, but would suggest two possibilities: (a) small biological differences are selectively amplified over time by differential reinforcement; or (b) the pattern is random, somewhat in the way different pigeons respond differently to the same schedule of non-contingent reinforcement (see Chapter 3). If the first explanation is true, then in fact there is a biological component to gender roles; as already noted, this seems consistent with data on male–female differences in aggressiveness. The second interpretation seems less plausible, since it is not clear how random reinforcement would result in differences based on sex, as opposed to simply random variation across individuals. Like evolutionary theories of gender roles, properly testing these two proposals would seem to require going back in time – clearly not a viable option. Based on what evidence does exist, it seems more likely that biological differences became elaborated by reinforcement than that gender roles developed randomly. As we will see, the cognitive approach suggests that reinforcement is relevant, but is only one part of the process.

The Cognitive Approach

The existence of gender roles, from the cognitive viewpoint, implies that individuals have a mental schema which tells them what is appropriate behaviour for their sex. This is supported by the evidence that sexual stereotypes exist. For example, North American university students identify certain attributes as masculine or feminine (see Figure 7.5). The formation of such **gender schemata** seems to begin very early. Two-year-olds can already identify the gender of individuals based on clothing or style of hair (Thompson 1975). By the time children are five or six, their memory for events differs based on whether what they are asked to recall is gender-consistent or not (Martin and Halverson 1983). At the same time, the development of such schemata is gradual, and often children as old as five have not yet grasped that gender is a permanent attribute. For example, they may believe that someone can change gender by wearing clothes usually worn by the opposite sex (Marcus and Overton 1978).

gender schema a cognitive representation which organizes an individual's knowledge of cultural norms for male or female behaviour

How do children form such concepts, either about others or about themselves? Cognitive theory argues that the behaviour of others, particularly adults, provides an example which is *imitated*, through the process of social learning (Perry and Bussey 1979). Any parent can readily cite examples of children attempting to copy adult actions, ranging from Daddy using a screwdriver to Mummy cooking. (Once children enter school, peers are also significant as models to be imitated.) Albert Bandura (1977) has suggested that such observational learning provides a major factor in sex-role development. However, other researchers have indicated that children are more concerned with gender-consistency of behaviour than with the sex of the model, until at least about age six (Masters *et al.* 1979). For example, boys will still play with a toy car, which they regard as a 'boys' toy', after watching a girl play with it. It is not until the concept of gender as a permanent attribute of a person is established (around age seven) that the sex of models seems to influence children's behaviours. Although it does not rule out other forms of learning (such as direct reinforcement) as a factor in sex role development, this finding does suggest that imitation is not a sufficient explanation by itself.

Thus, the cognitive approach emphasizes how mental schemata interact with the effects of social experience (reinforcement and imitation) in directing gender role behaviour. In general, the cognitive approach offers a more specific model for the role of experience in gender role development than does behaviourism. Indeed, since many of the reinforcers which children receive are social (such as praise from a parent or teacher), the approach in some ways incorporates the behaviourist notion of operant learning. Despite this, there are still many details unresolved, and competing models within the cognitive approach (e.g. Kohlberg 1966; Martin and Halverson 1987).

One aspect that remains unclear is the role of biological factors. Since gender schemata obviously include the recognition of sex, the influence of sex distinctions cannot be ignored in the formation of gender roles. Similarly, the fact that certain attributes seem to be associated with gender roles in nearly every culture remains to be explained (Williams and Best 1982). While social learning addresses the process of forming gender roles *within* a culture, why should cultures across the globe share certain attributes in their gender roles? (Of course, as already noted, considerable variation exists for other attributes.) The willingness to address such issues in understanding gender roles has waned and waxed in the past thirty years, sometimes reflecting political attitudes which are themselves probably socially learned (see Eagly 1995). Although no final answer can be given today, it may well be that future cognitive models will require integration with some biologically-based factors.

The Psychodynamic Approach

As noted earlier, Freud's theory of development acknowledges both biological and experiential factors. Biological influences are reflected in the innateness of the sexual drive which motivates much of our behaviour, and in the biologically-determined *stages of psychosexual development*. The existence of the sexual drive cannot itself explain gender roles or sexual orientation, however, since Freud did not see the drive as gender-oriented. Instead, he saw the development of gender roles as a product of the child's attempt to resolve the *Oedipal conflict* during the *phallic stage* of development (Wittkower and Robertson 1979). For a boy, the mother is the prototype for future relationships, while the father is a rival for the mother's attention. In order to cope with the anxiety created by the Oedipal conflict (including fears that the father will retaliate by castrating him), the boy uses the defence mechanism of *identification*, thereby modelling his behaviour on that of his father. This process of identification establishes both the boy's gender role and sexual orientation. Although the dynamics are somewhat different for girls, ultimately identification still provides the basis for the formation of sexual identity in both sexes. Freud believed that the absence of the same-sex parent would distort the normal process of development, with consequent effects on gender role development and sexual orientation. In particular, he saw failure to identify with the father (or a surrogate father figure) as the origin of homosexuality in males.

In limited ways, Freud's theory is consistent with the available evidence. For example, he correctly identified the period around ages three to five as being significant in the formation of gender identity (Fagot 1985). In addition, there is some evidence that when boys have no father figure to identify with, their gender role behaviour is often less masculine (Stevenson and Black 1988).

Beyond these points, Freud's theory doesn't fare very well. Since identification, like social learning theory, predicts that children will imitate parents, one might expect that any studies favouring imitative behaviour would therefore support Freud's theory. However, identification is seen as based on anxiety and fear, not positive feelings. Instead, the evidence suggests that nurturance produces more imitative behaviour than does parental dominance (Hetherington and Frankie 1967). Further, the extensive survey by Bell *et al.* (1981) found that a poor relationship with the father was modestly linked to homosexual orientation in *both* sexes (not just males, as Freud would predict), while maternal relationship was not related to sexual orientation in *either* sex (again, contrary to Freud's view). Overall, the evidence, while not extensive, is not very supportive of Freud's theory as applied to gender roles and sexual orientation.

The Humanistic Approach

The humanistic approach is perhaps the most difficult to evaluate in the present context, since little is said about development. Even Rogers's theory is problematical, since he did not directly address the issue of gender roles. As an aspect of the *ideal self*, gender roles would seem to arise from the *conditional positive regard* that a child receives. That is, parents and others would set expectations related to gender roles by establishing *conditions of worth*. In order to receive positive regard, the individual would then *introject* these expectations into the ideal self as definitions of appropriate behaviour. For example, a five-year-old girl who shows an interest in playing with blocks may be told, 'Oh, blocks are for boys. You should play with your doll instead!' Similarly, a boy may be told that 'cooking is for girls'. Such messages can easily be incorporated in the ideal self, effectively instilling cultural norms for gender roles.

In some respects, Rogers's theory seems consistent with interpretations offered by other approaches. Since positive regard in Rogers's theory functions in ways that are similar to positive reinforcement in behaviourist theory, it reflects a similar emphasis on learning and experience. One can also draw a parallel between the Rogerian view of *self* as based on the individual's perceptions and experiences, and the cognitive concept of a mental schema.

Sexual orientation would also be seen as related to the self, rather than societal standards as expressed through the ideal self. Since the self reflects the underlying nature of the *organism*, Rogers would suggest that sexual orientation may well be biological, and is certainly self-defined. Thus, Rogers's theory seems consistent with LeVay's biological position, and also Bell's finding that the best predictor of homosexual orientation is experiencing homosexual feelings prior to adolescence (Bell *et al.* 1981; LeVay 1993). Rogers would also understand the conflict that many homosexuals feel about 'going public' in our culture. In essence, it represents a conflict between the feelings of the self and introjected social standards that are often hostile to homosexuality. As in other such conflicts, Rogers believes that the self, not the ideal self, is the true nature of the individual.

Beyond such general points, Rogers's theory offers few insights on the process of gender role development. Since he never specifically addressed the topic of gender roles, there has been no research to explore the issue from within the Rogerian framework. Given that other humanistic theorists have said even less, it is very difficult to apply, or evaluate, the humanistic approach in terms of understanding these developmental issues.

Overall, the two most plausible approaches for understanding gender roles and sexual identity are the biological and the cognitive. While very different in their interpretations, each is well-developed theoretically, and supported by a wide range of relevant research. The theories of Rogers and Freud, as representative of the humanistic and psychodynamic approaches, are largely inadequate, albeit for different reasons: Freud's theory does not seem consistent with the available evidence, and Rogers's theory is not sufficiently specific to be seriously evaluated. The behaviourist model of reinforcement, while relevant, seems like a limited version of cognitive social learning theory, with no specific advantages of its own in this area. However, there are still many aspects of this topic, like development as a whole, which are not resolved. It will be interesting to see how the differences between the biological and cognitive approaches are dealt with in the future: by the triumph of one approach over the other, or by some as-yet-unknown model which incorporates elements of both approaches.

| **For further consideration** | Suppose that parents of a new child, in order to avoid gender-bias, decided to raise their new baby as an 'it' rather than as a boy or girl; what would each theory predict in terms of the effects this would have on the development of a gender role? |

Conclusion

Developmental psychology is concerned with the changes that occur during human life. This interest in understanding the course of life is not unique to psychology; for example, biographers also try to capture the span of life. What distinguishes the study of development in psychology from biography are the questions asked and the methods used. A biographer seeks to understand a single person's life, and in doing so tends to emphasize the events which are unique to that person – for instance, how their place of birth, family or particular experiences shaped their development. By contrast, developmental psychologists are interested in the principles which are common to *all* lives – the processes which describe development in general. The challenge is to identify and understand these common principles.

As we have seen, there are several basic issues which arise in the study of development. For example, is development a continual unfolding, or a series of discrete stages? Asking about *continuity* versus *discontinuity* is not just a matter of how we *describe* development, but also of identifying the *processes* which direct it.

An equally major concern is the role of *heredity* and *environment*. Although often oversimplified, the issue is not whether development is controlled by one factor *or* the other, but rather *how* each one influences a given behaviour, and how they *interact*. Phrased in this way, the study of heredity and environment becomes the foundation for all developmental research.

The challenges of developmental research are clearly seen in the way each of the five approaches views the process of development, and the fact that, at present, no approach seems capable of offering a comprehensive (*domain-general*) model. This may partly reflect the limitations of each framework, but also suggests that development is not a single process, but many.

This complexity is seen even when one looks at specific aspects of development, such as gender roles. While the explanations proposed by the various approaches are relatively clear, the evidence is very difficult to interpret. It is easy to recognize that human beings are divided into two sexes, but the relationship of behaviour to gender is less clear-cut. Models which emphasize only one type of factor, such as the role of heredity, seem inconsistent with the available data. In the end, it seems that what is needed is a multi-process model which can *combine* the effects of heredity and learning. Possibly the work of John Money and his colleagues will lead in this direction, but there are still large gaps in our understanding.

Overall, the study of development can be one of the most challenging, but also frustrating, areas in psychology. In writing this chapter, I was struck, not for the first time, by the seeming lack of coherence in the area. The number of questions to contend with (and the diversity of answers offered) seems to defy attempts at theoretical integration. Given the desire for a full understanding, this fragmentation appears to be an obvious failing. Yet one should not be too hasty in blaming developmental theorists for failing to provide a cohesive framework. In some sense, the study of development is a microcosm for all of psychology, since in various ways it touches on nearly every aspect of behaviour and experience. Since at present there is no comprehensive theory of psychology, it should not be surprising that there is no comprehensive theory of development. Yet by pointing out what is *needed* for a successful theory, the study of development may in fact help to clarify issues for the field as a whole. In that sense, the lack of coherence currently found in developmental psychology may ultimately prove to be a benefit. In the meantime, it provides us with glimpses of insight into the remarkable journey which we are all taking: the journey of life.

Chapter Summary

- *Developmental psychology* is concerned with understanding the changes that occur over the course of human life, and the processes which govern the changes.

- In order to study changes over time, researchers tend to use *longitudinal studies* or *cross-sectional studies* involving groups of different ages; in some cases, researchers will use a *sequential design*, which combines elements of both of the other methods.

- Three general issues pervade the study of development: *continuity* versus *discontinuity* in the developmental process, the relative importance of *heredity* and *environment* and the value of *domain-general* versus *domain-specific models*. Piaget's theory of cognitive development is a limited form of a domain-general model.

- The origin of *personality* patterns and *traits* provides a useful focus for comparison of how the five approaches view development.

- The *biological approach* emphasizes the role of *temperament* in personality development, as being based on heredity.

- The *behaviourist approach* emphasizes the importance of environmental influences, particularly the role of *environmental consistency* and the person's *history of reinforcement* in accounting for the consistencies which are attributed to *personality*.

- The *cognitive approach* interprets development in terms of cognitive social learning theory, which emphasizes the role of *imitation* in learning and the importance of *cognitive schemata* in structuring behaviour.

- The *psychodynamic approach*, as represented by Freud's psychoanalytic theory, favours an interactionist interpretation, which incorporates both physiologically-based *psychosexual stages of development* and the role of early experience in explaining personality.

- The *humanistic approach* offers the least detailed analysis of development. Partly this is because it emphasizes individual experience and subjective perceptions, while developmental researchers favour the search for common principles based on objective observation. To the extent that it can be evaluated, Rogers's theory seems to favour an interactionist interpretation of development.

◆ The study of *sex role development* presents a clear example of the challenges of developmental research. At present, no one approach seems to offer a fully satisfactory model of the origin of gender roles or sexual orientation, though the biological and cognitive approaches in particular have provided some interesting insights.

◆ Overall, developmental psychology represents the field of psychology in microcosm, since development involves virtually all aspects of behaviour. To the extent that no single model currently seems adequate, it reflects the realities of the current limits of our broader understanding of behaviour.

Key Terms and Concepts

accommodation
assimilation
continuity
critical period
cross-sectional study
domain-general versus
   domain-specific models
gender roles
gender schema
history of reinforcement

implicit personality theory
longitudinal study
maturation
personality
reaction range
sequential design
sexual orientation
stages
temperament
trait

Suggestions for Further Reading

While Bower's *Human Development* is not the most current text in development, it provides an excellent analysis of the issues in developmental research, as well as insightful discussion of the basic findings.

For a detailed discussion of the role of heredity and environment in development, Plomin *et al.*'s *Nature and Nurture During Infancy and Early Childhood* provides an authoritative account, albeit with an emphasis on the hereditarian position (Plomin is a behavioural geneticist).

For an example of the potential of longitudinal studies, White's *Lives in Progress* is a fascinating demonstration of what can be learned by a researcher who has both patience and sensitivity.

For a readable overview of gender role development, particularly in terms of differences across cultures, Williams and Best's *Sex and Psyche* is a good choice.

In various ways, all the approaches touch upon development; readers interested in a particular approach should refer back to the suggested readings in the appropriate chapter.

8

Perspectives on Social Behaviour

The Individual and Society
Introduction
Methods of Studying Social Behaviour
Perspectives on Aggression
Defining Aggression
Methods of Studying Aggression
Theories of Aggression
  The Biological Approach
  The Behaviourist Approach
  The Cognitive Approach
  The Psychodynamic Approach
  The Humanistic Approach
  Comparing the Approaches
Aggression and the Media

Perspectives on Pro-social Behaviour
Defining Pro-social Behaviour
Theories of Altruism
  The Biological Approach
  The Behaviourist Approach
  The Cognitive Approach
  The Psychodynamic Approach
  The Humanistic Approach
Altruism and Bystander Behaviour
Conclusion
Chapter Summary
Key Terms and Concepts
Suggestions for Further Reading

The Individual and Society

As a teenager, I remember seeing a science fiction drama on television in which a man was the only survivor of a cataclysmic disaster. In his case, he relished being alone, because it freed him from the incessant chatter of other people. He looked forward to the quiet, to being able to sit and read as he pleased, without being disturbed. His joy lasted only until he broke his only pair of glasses, and realized there was no one to provide a new pair! The story, of course, was meant to be ironic, but it also raised an interesting question: what would it be like to be the only person in the world? To me (and, I suspect, most people) it would be a calamity, not a blessing; part of being human is being involved with other people.

It is an oft-repeated truism that human beings are social creatures. Almost four hundred years ago, the English poet John Donne observed that 'no man is an island, entire of itself'; instead, he said, we are all bound together, each of us 'a piece of the continent, a part of the main'. At birth, we are linked to others by our dependence on them for survival. Later, when we have become physically independent, we still seek others for companionship, affection and mutual support. Indeed, even when we are alone, we are influenced by others – in the memories we carry, in the way we think and in our perceptions of both ourselves and our surroundings.

Thus far, we have been focusing primarily on the understanding of individual behaviour. That, after all, is what psychology is all about; other fields, like sociology and anthropology, look at the behaviour of groups and cultures. Yet we also recognize that one cannot study individuals without acknowledging that they interact with, and are influenced by, other people. We have seen examples of this in examining the various approaches – for example, we are reinforced by the praise we receive from others (behaviourist), we learn from observing others (cognitive) and so on. In the end, no study of psychology can be complete without considering the social dimensions of individual behaviour.

Introduction

The study of the social aspects of behaviour is the focus of *social psychology*. The subject is traditionally divided into two sub-areas: the study of social cognition, and the study of social influence. *Social cognition* refers to the mental processes involved in understanding ourselves, other people and the world. For example, the way we form impressions of other people and the factors that influence our attitudes are both matters of social cognition. Similarly, our previous discussions of attribution theory, cognitive dissonance and social perception (including stereotypes, prejudice and gender schemata) are all examples of topics related to social cognition. Not surprisingly, the cognitive approach has been an important contributor to the understanding of these issues, though clearly other approaches are also relevant.

social influence a general term for the various ways in which an individual's behaviour is affected by others, such as conformity pressures and social expectations and norms

conformity the tendency to adjust one's opinions and behaviour to comply with group norms in response to explicit or implicit social presssure

altruism any behaviour intended to help others

Social influence is concerned with how an individual's behaviour is affected by others. Like social cognition, the term covers a wide range of situations, from group decision making to *obedience to authority* (see Chapter 1). One common form of social influence is **conformity**, when social pressures lead us to go along with group norms; for example, when a person dresses in a particular way in order to 'fit in' with their peers (see the discussion of peer influences in Chapter 7). Interestingly, social influence can be relevant even when we are alone – for example, in shopping for clothes, a person may think about how other people would react to a particular style or colour. Thus, social influence is an element of any behaviour which is basically social in orientation. For example, **altruism** (helping others) has no meaning except in a social context.

Together, social cognition and social influence touch on virtually every aspect of the relationship between an individual and society, and thus help to outline the subject matter of social psychology. At the same time, social psychology is a broad field, whose boundaries are not easy to define. As one moves from the individual to the group, it begins to move towards sociology. As one looks at social behaviour across cultures, it begins to verge into anthropology. This diffuseness can also be seen in the role of theories within the field. Like development, social psychology is defined by its subject matter, not a theoretical framework. That is, its unity stems from its emphasis on behaviour in a social context, just as the study of development is unified by the emphasis on changes over time. While it might seem that *social cognition* is simply a sub-area within the cognitive approach, in fact the phenomena involved, such as prejudice, can also be addressed by other approaches. (For example, within the biological approach, evolutionary psychology discusses prejudice in terms of kinship relations.) In fact, assuming social psychology is 'cognitive' is historically inaccurate, and leads to ignoring questions that may not easily fit within the cognitive approach (Berkowitz and Devine 1995). Thus, the defining element of social psychology is still the focus on the social dimensions of individual behaviour.

Methods of Studying Social Behaviour

In developmental research, the focus on changes in behaviour over time makes longitudinal studies and other time-based designs the primary methods of investigation. In social psychology, the desire to identify the *causes* of behaviour has led to an emphasis on doing experiments. Other methods, including case studies, participant observation and quasi-experiments, are sometimes used, but experiments predominate. (This methodological emphasis is one factor, along with the focus on the individual rather than the group, which helps to distinguish the sometimes fuzzy boundary between social psychology and sociology. In contrast to social psychology, sociology tends to emphasize non-experimental methods. In the end, the boundary cannot be defined in absolute terms, and there is considerable exchange between the two fields.)

At first glance, this emphasis on doing experiments may seem puzzling. After all, many of the interesting questions about social behaviour arise out of everyday events. For example, in Chapter 1 we discussed the death of Kitty Genovese, an incident in which 38 people observed the fatal attack on a young woman, but did not intervene. Why didn't they help? One can speculate on possible reasons, and her death did in fact generate considerable conjecture at the time, but ultimately no amount of speculation can ever provide the evidence necessary for sound explanations. Instead, social psychologists prefer to do experiments, which provide the kind of controlled conditions necessary for making clear interpretations of causation. (As will be noted in Chapter 10, this emphasis has been stronger in North American psychology than in European psychology.)

Conducting experiments on social behaviour can pose a number of challenges, all related either directly or indirectly to the conditions required for performing sound experiments. One of the advantages of the experimental method is that it allows the researcher to control the situation – manipulating the desired variable(s) and keeping other factors constant. Such control is important to the interpretation of the causes of behaviour. However, experimental conditions can sometimes interfere with the very behaviour one is interested in studying. For one thing, when people know they are being observed, they may react differently from how they would otherwise – a phenomenon called *reactivity*. Concerns about reactivity are not unique to social psychology; the problem can occur in many kinds of psychological research. Consequently, a number of techniques have been devised to deal with it, including deliberately withholding information from participants, or using deception. (See Chapter 1 for a further discussion of reactivity.)

A second problem, which is more specific to social behaviour, is the need to create a convincing situation. In everyday life, social interactions elicit emotional as well as cognitive responses, and these emotions can sometimes be intense. For example, a person may feel 'stage fright' about speaking before a group; two drivers involved in a car accident may get into an angry confrontation; a person may become embarrassed by a social slip. In order to provide meaningful results, an experimental situation must be sufficiently involving that participants will react genuinely. If the person thinks, 'Oh, well, this is just an experiment', then that perception will probably lead to behaviour which is very different from 'real' situations. Elliot Aronson, a well-known social psychologist, has referred to the importance of natural reactions as the need for **experimental realism** (Aronson 1976). This is not quite the same as saying that the situation must be 'life-like' in the sense that it is familiar in daily life. Stanley Milgram's study of obedience, in which a 'researcher' encouraged participants to give apparently dangerous electric shocks to another person, was not a situation which most people encounter in daily life; in this sense, it was not 'realistic' (see Chapter 1 for a description of Milgram's study). However, the subjects found the situation highly involving (not to say emotionally distressing), and there is little reason to doubt that their responses were genuine. In this sense, Milgram's research satisfied the need for experimental realism. Essentially, a realistic experiment shows us 'the way people would react if a similar set of events *did* occur in the real world' (Aronson 1976: 292).

Creating a convincing situation often requires considerable ingenuity. In essence, the experiment must be sufficiently complex to be involving, yet sufficiently simple to allow proper experimental control. In addition, because people would probably not behave naturally if they knew the true purpose of the study, it typically requires *deception*. This poses a continual ethical dilemma for researchers: can the knowledge gained justify the process? Most researchers in social psychology believe that deception is a necessary procedure, even given its disagreeable implications. (Presumably, if they did not feel this way, they would not do any research involving deception!) At the same time, serious researchers agree that one should try to minimize the manipulative aspects of research, and any possible negative consequences of experimental procedures. One way of mitigating harm is always to discuss the true nature and goals of the research with participants when the experiment ends; this is called *debriefing*. Alternatively, a researcher may

experimental realism
a quality of involvement whereby research participants respond without regard for the laboratory context, as they would in an ordinary situation

use observational techniques (such as non-obtrusive measures or surveys) which do not require the use of deception. Unfortunately, this option *also* precludes the possibility of identifying causal relationships. Thus, the potential conflict between methodological requirements and ethical concerns remains. Ethical issues, obviously, can arise in most psychological research, but they are particularly vivid in social psychology, precisely because social interactions are so central to human experience.

Whatever the method, social psychologists are interested in all aspects of social behaviour, from self-esteem to prejudice, from love to aggression. These issues are obviously very diverse, as are the theories for interpreting them. Consequently, it should not be a surprise to find that each of the five approaches has relevance to the study of social psychology, particularly the area of social influence. Rather than attempting a superficial survey of all aspects of social behaviour, we will focus on the ways in which we hurt and help each other – that is, aggression and altruism. Can we understand what causes aggression and, if so, can we use that knowledge to reduce such behaviour? And can we identify ways to foster more positive forms of social behaviour? By considering the research and the interpretations offered by the various approaches, we can perhaps gain a better understanding of the nature of social behaviour.

| **For further consideration** | Are you more likely to be influenced by some people than others? For example, who do you look towards to decide how to dress? What does this tell you about social influence? |

Perspectives on Aggression

There is little question that aggression represents one of the darker aspects of human behaviour. We seem to be both able and willing to hurt each other, despite our social orientation. Aristotle once described humans as 'the social animal'; given the history of aggression, some would suggest the emphasis should be on 'animal' rather than 'social'. Today, it often seems that the news media provide daily reminders of the human capacity for violence. A few years ago, all of England, and indeed the world, was horrified by the story of two boys, not yet in their teens, who kidnapped and tortured a two-year-old boy, and then left him to die on railway tracks. As I am writing this chapter, the local newspaper has reported the story of a man who pushed a woman into the path of a train, killing her; she was a stranger to him, her death a seemingly random act of violence. In several places in the world, civilian populations are under attack by military forces. Both individually and in groups, we seem only too capable of causing harm to each other.

Such incidents cast a bleak picture, and the past includes many comparable examples. The long history of such violence has led many to assume that such actions represent an intrinsic part of human character. However, we must not be too quick to label 'aggression' as an innate drive – in part because doing so presumes that we already have the *answer* before we have really posed the *question*. The question, of course, is 'what is the origin of aggressive behaviour?' Unfortunately, before we can try to give an answer, we must be clear about what we mean by 'aggressive behaviour'.

Defining Aggression

Most people would say that if someone deliberately harms another person, that it is undesirable behaviour. But is it therefore *aggressive* behaviour? And what if someone *intends* to harm another person, but does not succeed? Is aggression the same as violence? Can there be aggression if there is no actual violence? Although we use (and seem to understand) the terms 'aggression' and 'violence' in everyday language, as with many words, their meaning can be somewhat ambiguous, shifting according to the context. For them to be useful in the context of scientific explanation, we need to define the terms unambiguously.

The basic problem in defining aggression is whether the focus should be on the behaviour, the intention or both. *Violent* behaviour is that which causes harm to other people, regardless of intent. (Some researchers, like Moyer (1983) would also include property damage.) However, violence is not necessarily the same as aggression, in that violence may occur accidentally. For example, a golfer's errant ball may hit someone in the head, causing serious injury; given that there was no intent to cause harm, most people would not view it as an aggressive act.

In our culture, we are accustomed to considering a person's intentions, as well as the outcome, in evaluating behaviour. For example, judgements of guilt in our legal system emphasize the consideration of a person's motives. In the same way, researchers have often sought to consider the motivational component of behaviour in defining aggression. For example, Elliot Aronson has defined aggression as 'behaviour aimed at causing harm or pain' (Aronson 1976: 143). By focusing on the *intention* of the behaviour, Aronson is able to make some seemingly useful distinctions. For example, a football player who inadvertently injures another player is not being aggressive, although it results in harm (and is therefore violent behaviour). By contrast, a football player who deliberately sets out to injure an opponent *is* being aggressive – even if he fails to cause actual harm.

The trouble with focusing on intentions in defining aggression is that, like any form of motivation, aggressive intent is difficult to measure. Among other things, one has to consider whether intentions can be expressed symbolically. Freud was willing to talk about symbolic forms of aggression which seem unconnected to violent acts, but this is because he *assumed* aggressive intent is always present. (After all, he believed aggression was an innate drive.) If one doesn't make this assumption, then it must be acknowledged that measuring aggressive intentions is a difficult task. For example, if a writer lampoons a real-life person in a story, is that aggression? Who is to judge the intent?

It seems that defining aggression is very much tied up with our assumptions about its origins. Those who believe aggression is a learned behaviour (like Aronson) typically emphasize behaviour in defining aggression (i.e. it must result in harm, and hence is equivalent to violence). By contrast, those who believe aggression is an innate drive (like Freud) prefer to emphasize intentions (which may be expressed symbolically). There is no simple resolution to this dilemma, because the word 'aggression' has many connotations. In this chapter, we will generally try to adhere to a compromise definition which includes both components – that is, **aggression** is behaviour which causes intentional harm to another person (Berkowitz 1975). This definition probably excludes some forms of aggression, but at least has the virtue that nearly every theorist would agree that such behaviours *are* aggressive.

The very fact that it has taken a full page simply to try to define aggression – and then, only with partial success – gives an indication of how complicated it is to explore this topic with some semblance of objectivity. The notion of aggression strikes a very deep chord for most people; in some sense, it goes to the heart of our beliefs about human nature. Similarly, the way each approach interprets aggression reflects the basic assumptions it makes about human behaviour in general, as we will see.

aggression behaviour which causes intentional harm to another person

Methods of Studying Aggression

Before we consider the interpretations offered by the approaches, it is useful to return to the question of research methods: how can one study aggressive behaviour scientifically? As already noted, social psychologists typically prefer experimental research, because experiments allow one to make interpretations about the causes of behaviour. Yet experimental studies of aggression face several stumbling blocks. One concern is that individuals may act differently in a laboratory and in everyday life; if they do, this would result in distortion and bias in the results. A second concern is the need for *experimental realism*. While this is an issue in all social psychology experiments, it is particularly significant when dealing with aggression, because researchers cannot ethically explore the full range of aggressive behaviour in the laboratory. (To give an extreme example, no one would do an experiment involving murder.) Yet restrictions on the types of aggression examined may limit the *external validity* of a study – that is, the extent to which one can generalize to other situations involving other forms of aggression. For example, does punching an inflatable doll really tell us whether someone would punch another person? This is not to say that laboratory studies are irrelevant to the study of aggression, but they are difficult to design well, and there may be limits to their generality. Interestingly, the consistency one finds between real situations and the predictions from laboratory studies indicates that the external validity of aggression research may actually be reasonably good (Anderson and Bushman 1997).

In order to avoid these problems, researchers sometimes prefer to avoid laboratory research when studying aggression; instead, they may opt either to perform field experiments or to use correlational designs based on real-world observations. A *field experiment* involves conducting an experiment in a real-world setting, such that the subjects are not aware they are participating in a research study. As discussed in Chapter 1, field experiments pose the problem of trying to maintain proper controls in a natural setting, along with concerns about the ethics of doing research without the informed consent of participants. This is particularly troublesome when dealing with aggressive behaviour and, consequently, relatively few field experiments have been done compared to either lab experiments or correlational studies. *Correlational studies* involve some form of observation of variables in a natural setting (e.g. naturalistic observation, longitudinal studies) in which one tries to find patterns between particular variables – for example, viewing violence on television and aggressive behaviour. Because the aggression observed is 'the real thing', not a laboratory analogue, correlational studies often seem more convincing than laboratory experiments. Unfortunately, this advantage is offset by the fact that these studies, like all correlational studies, do not allow one to draw clear conclusions about cause and effect.

In the end, there is no single research design which can optimally address the issue of aggression. Ideally, one would like to employ all three types of studies, since if one finds similar patterns of results in a variety of contexts, it enhances one's confidence that the underlying theory may be valid. As you consider the explanations of aggression offered by the five approaches, ask yourself what sort of evidence each offers, and what limitations it may have.

For further consideration

Can you think of any examples of symbolic aggression, where no actual harm occurs? What convinces you that the behaviour is aggressive? Would you be willing to make similar interpretations about other forms of behaviour, such as love? Why or why not?

Theories of Aggression

The most basic issue in the study of aggression is explaining its origin. As with many aspects of behaviour, the various theories tend to split into two groups: those that see aggression as innate, and those that see aggressive behaviour as learned. While the nature–nurture controversy runs through all of psychology, it has particular significance for aggression, because explanations of its origin *also* imply specific ways of trying to *limit* it. Since society has an interest in limiting at least *some* forms of aggressive behaviour, understanding its causes is a matter of practical as well as theoretical interest. Hence, in looking at the theories proposed by the various approaches, one should consider both how they explain the causes of aggression and how they suggest society could or should deal with it.

The Biological Approach

Given the emphasis the approach places on heredity, it should not seem surprising that aggression is viewed as an innate characteristic of human beings. Several theories have been put forth, and various forms of evidence used to support them. Given that no specific genetic or physiological mechanism has been identified, the arguments often depend on analogies to animal research. Among these, one of the best known is the work of Konrad Lorenz.

Konrad Lorenz

Konrad Zacharias Lorenz (1903–89) was one of the founders of ethology, an approach to the study of animal behaviour which originated as an offshoot of zoology, not psychology. Lorenz was born and educated in Vienna; he attended the University of Vienna, receiving both a medical degree and a PhD in zoology. The study of animal behaviour attracted him more than did the practice of medicine, and he began to focus on the role of genetic factors in animal behaviour. Together with Nikolaas Tinbergen and Karl von Frisch, he developed a new approach to the study of such behaviour, largely in natural settings. The approach became known as *ethology*, and culminated in the three sharing the 1973 Nobel Prize in Physiology or Medicine. Lorenz's focus on natural settings rather than the laboratory was one of the factors which distinguished ethology from behaviourism as a method of studying behaviour. Lorenz was also influenced by Darwin's work on evolution, and this led him to focus on inherited mechanisms in explaining behaviour. Aggression to Lorenz served an evolutionary function, promoting selective survival of the strongest individuals; in other words, it evolved as a biologically-useful characteristic. His best known book, *On Aggression*, drew a large popular audience for its summary of his research on animals, as well as his ideas about human aggression. Lorenz died in Vienna at the age of eighty-six.

Lorenz (1903–89) was one of the founders of ethology, an approach to the study of animal behaviour which originated as an offshoot of zoology, not psychology. Lorenz and other ethologists studied behaviour primarily in natural settings, not in the laboratory; this difference in methodology, along with theoretical differences, led to early disputes with behaviouristic psychologists. Both in the study of animals and in drawing analogies to human behaviour, Lorenz was influenced by Darwin's work on evolution. Like Darwin, he believed that many human characteristics were based on inherited mechanisms. Aggression to Lorenz served an evolutionary function, promoting selective survival of the strongest individuals; in other words, it evolved as a biologically useful characteristic. In his best known work, *On Aggression*, Lorenz (1967) reviewed his research on animals, and extended his theory to humans. While sharply attacked by some critics, the book drew wide popular attention.

Lorenz viewed aggression as a biologically-based drive which must be periodically satisfied through behavioural expression. This concept, sometimes referred to as a 'reservoir' model, states that the drive level builds up over time, like a reservoir filling with water; the expression of associated behaviours reduces the drive level, much like draining water from the reservoir. Normally, the expression of aggressive behaviour is controlled by environmental cues called **sign stimuli**. Some stimuli are signs for the initiation of aggression. In many species, such as cichlid fish, the intrusion of one individual into the 'territory' of another is a sign stimulus for attack. At the same time, other sign stimuli serve to control the aggressive behaviour so that normally encounters are not fatal to either individual. For example, a wolf that is losing a fight will roll over on its back, averting its eyes and exposing its jugular to the other wolf's teeth. While this makes the wolf

sign stimuli in ethology, environmental cues which regulate the expression of behaviours related to innate drives

physically vulnerable, the gesture actually serves as a sign stimulus which *inhibits* further aggression by the victor. Thus, Lorenz viewed the existence of sign stimuli as a crucial factor to understanding aggression. By regulating the nature of aggressive encounters, sign stimuli allow the expression of aggression, while minimizing fatal violence and enabling members of a species to establish stable social hierarchies.

In Lorenz's view, this analysis of aggression has several implications for human aggression. First of all, it implies that since aggression is innate, it is also unavoidable. If society simply attempts to suppress all forms of aggression, then the reservoir will simply 'overflow', resulting in random acts of violence referred to as **vacuum activities**. Lorenz was also concerned that human technology had outstripped biology, in that the sign stimuli that inhibit most fatal aggression require close contact between aggressors (for example, averting the eyes). Methods of killing at a distance, such as bombs dropped from planes and even guns, render such inhibitory stimuli inoperative. Hence, activities like war, while channelling aggression into socially-sanctioned forms, bypass the controls that evolved to limit excessive violence.

Given the potential for either random violence or mass destruction, what is society to do? Lorenz argued that society should encourage specific forms of substitute activity, such as sports. Such activities allow expression of aggression in limited ways, and thereby reduce drive levels. This process, often referred to as *catharsis*, is a solution frequently proposed by advocates of nativist theories of aggression (both biological and psychodynamic). Presumably, Lorenz would be neither surprised nor alarmed at the violence expressed by football fans or ice hockey players; instead, he would probably argue that such limited expressions of aggression are preferable to more extreme forms. Since aggression will always exist, all society can do is try to channel it into minimally damaging forms.

The work of Lorenz and other ethologists has been important to our understanding of animal behaviour. The concept of sign stimuli, for example, is recognized as a significant contribution. At the same time, his ideas on human aggression are seriously weakened by the absence of supporting human evidence. In essence, the basic assumption – that aggression is innate – is also the point which must be proved. Generally speaking, finding analogous behaviours in different species does not prove that they have the same cause. For example, showing that aggression is innate in wolves does *not* prove that it is *also* innate in humans.

There are also problems in applying the concept of sign stimuli. Lorenz argues that sign stimuli gradually evolved as specific cues in each species. However, the fact that no one has identified a stimulus which categorically inhibits aggression in humans suggests that, at the very least, the control mechanisms must be somewhat different in other species. Lorenz's view has an understandable appeal. There is no doubt that humans *do* have an evolutionary heritage, and seeing aggression as innate fits well with many cultural beliefs – what Klama (1988) has called 'the myth of the beast within'. Nonetheless, there are still many gaps in Lorenz's argument, and given its implications (that we can only redirect aggression, not eliminate it), we must be wary of accepting his view without further evidence.

vacuum activities in ethology, behaviours which arise in the absence of appropriate environmental stimuli when drive levels are very high

The idea that aggression is innate has also been advanced by evolutionary psychologists (Konner 1982; de Waal 1989). Unlike Lorenz, however, they do not necessarily argue for a reservoir concept of drive energy. Instead, they see aggression as involving a series of physiological mechanisms that evolved to respond to threats to survival, reproduction, or similar situations. Unfortunately, like the ethological arguments, most of the evidence offered is based on comparative studies of other species (Lore and Schultz 1993). To seek more direct support, we need to consider what is known about the physiological mechanisms of aggression.

As discussed in Chapter 2, one of the great success stories of physiological research has been the mapping of the human brain to identify the areas responsible for specific aspects of behaviour. Based on this idea of *localization of function*, researchers have sought to identify the areas of the brain which control aggressive behaviour. Generally, the focus has been on the hypothalamus and the amygdala, in the evolutionarily older regions of the limbic system (Delgado 1969; MacLean 1990). As with the ethological argument, it turns out on close examination that much of the argument depends on analogy to animal studies, and consequently the theories seem to go further than the evidence warrants. Despite this, some supporters of this view have gone so far as to suggest that certain violent criminals might be better handled by brain surgery than by imprisonment (Mark and Ervin 1970).

A more limited physiological approach has been to look at the connection between pain and aggression. As Moyer has noted, there is a large body of research suggesting that stimuli which cause pain will often trigger aggressive behaviour (Moyer 1976). There is likely a strong defensive component to such behaviour – that is, it seeks to stop the painful stimulation. However, this appears to be only part of the picture, since many factors affect the likelihood of pain-mediated aggression, not all of which have a biological foundation. Since much of the work in this area has involved animals, Leonard Berkowitz has examined the issue in a human context, and notes that there is evidence suggesting that aversive (painful or unpleasant) stimuli can also trigger aggression in people (Berkowitz 1983, 1993a). However, he is qualified in his support, suggesting that there is also strong evidence that aggressive responses to such stimuli are cognitively mediated, not simply a reflexive response.

Overall, the physiological evidence seems more suggestive than conclusive. Minimally, it supports the position that *some* forms of aggressive behaviour have a physiological foundation which is largely independent of learning. While some researchers advocate the stronger view that *all* aggression is rooted in the structure of the brain, at present some form of interaction between nature and nurture seems more probable.

For further consideration

The arguments offered by Lorenz and other biological researchers are based largely on analogies to animal behaviour. In what ways do you think such analogies are or are not appropriate in trying to explain aggression?

The Behaviourist Approach

Unlike Lorenz and other biological researchers, the behaviourists view aggression as a form of learned behaviour. 'Aggression' refers not to an internal drive, but to a particular class of voluntary responses, which are acquired and modified by the process of reinforcement. While this general interpretation can be applied to any particular example of aggression, there are really two aspects of aggressive behaviour which have been emphasized by behaviourist theorists: instrumental aggression and the role of frustration in aggression.

instrumental aggression
aggressive behaviour which
is maintained because it is
positively reinforced

Instrumental aggression is aggressive behaviour which is maintained because it is positively reinforced. For example, suppose Mary sees that her younger brother Tommy has a sweet, and takes it away from him so as to eat it herself. In this case, her aggressive behaviour (taking someone else's possession) is reinforced by the outcome (having the sweet to eat). Although later Mary may be scolded or otherwise punished for her misdeed, the most immediate consequence is positive reinforcement. In effect, Mary will learn that some desired outcomes can be achieved by the use of aggression. Behaviourists describe this as instrumental aggression because the aggressive behaviour results in acquiring the desired reinforcer; the only difference between this situation and any other case of positive reinforcement is that we label the particular response as 'aggressive'. In the same way, behaviourists would argue that many forms of anti-social behaviour represent instrumental aggression. For example, although we may be dismayed to read that a well-dressed person has been attacked and robbed, we are not likely to be *surprised* by the event – the money simply represents a tempting reinforcer to a thief.

Examples of instrumental aggression like those above are all too familiar in life. Whatever our *moral* perspective, in *pragmatic* terms force sometimes works. Consequently, the behaviourist perspective would suggest that such aggression will be common enough to be mistaken for 'innate'. To prevent instrumental aggression, one must alter the environmental conditions so that such behaviour no longer pays off. For example, a child who hits other children in order to get something will alter this behaviour if adults intervene, ensuring that hitting not only does not lead to the desired outcome, but is punished instead. On the broader level of society, preventing all instrumental aggression would require similar interventions – a requirement which is not easy to fulfil. (For example, in Canada, only about 30 per cent of bank robberies lead to arrests, which means that to someone desperate enough, robbing banks can be reinforcing.)

Despite the pervasive nature of instrumental aggression, we also have to recognize that some instances of aggressive behaviour do *not* appear to be instrumental. Consider an athlete who yells at a referee after an unfavourable call, or a homeowner who kicks a lawnmower that won't start, or a child who, having been embarrassed at school, then misbehaves at home: in each case, the behaviour seems unlikely to lead to a positive reinforcer (a favourable ruling by the referee, a working lawnmower, expressions of approval). In fact, in most cases, we would expect the behaviour to *worsen* the situation. So, if such aggressive acts cannot reasonably be viewed as instrumental aggression, how can we explain them? The answer given by the behaviourists is to examine the role of frustration in aggressive behaviour, in terms of what is called the frustration–aggression hypothesis.

The frustration–aggression hypothesis traces its origins to work by John Dollard and his colleagues at Yale in the 1930s (Dollard *et al.* 1939). Consistent with the behaviourist ideas of Watson, they sought to operationalize, and thereby render precise, the everyday concepts of 'frustration' and 'aggression'. In part, this work was intended as a response to Freud's theory, which argued that aggression was innate. (Later, this work was extended by Dollard and one of the original group, Neal Miller, as an attempt to 'translate' Freudian concepts into behaviourist terms (see Dollard and Miller 1950).) What resulted was the **frustration–aggression hypothesis**, which stated that *frustration* (defined as blocking a goal-oriented response) was the sole cause of aggression. If circumstances create frustration, then this will arouse a drive which motivates aggressive behaviour. The intensity of the aggressive response is determined by the intensity of the frustration, and also by prior punishment of aggressive behaviour. (The stronger the punishment, the weaker the aggressive response in the future.) For example, if a football player is blocked from scoring a goal, this may result in aggression against another player. If, however, this results in a heavy penalty for the offending player, such behaviour is likely to be inhibited in the future. Instead, the aggressive tendencies aroused by frustration may be channelled into expending more effort in legitimate ways. An example of this occurred in North American ice hockey, which in the 1980s experienced a trend towards bench-clearing brawls. When a rule change led to stiff penalties to the third person to enter a fight, such brawls were virtually eliminated. These examples illustrate the basic elements of the frustration–aggression hypothesis: frustration leads to increasing the potential for aggression, but punishment does seem to decrease the expression of aggression.

The notion that frustration can elicit aggression has an intuitive appeal – after all, we have all felt frustrations that have led to some form of 'letting loose', whether verbally or physically. Researchers, too, have found the hypothesis interesting, and for about 25 years, it was the dominant framework for research on aggressive behaviour. While the basic idea that frustration could lead to aggression received some support (e.g. Miller 1941), over time the evidence also indicated weaknesses in the original hypothesis. In its strongest form, the hypothesis states that frustration *always* results in aggression, and aggression *only* occurs as a result of frustration. Both of these principles have been challenged. For example, aggressive behaviour can be produced by reinforcement, even in the absence of frustration (Berkowitz 1978). Even when frustration *does* seem to elicit aggression, the relationship has been interpreted as due to the instrumental value of the aggression (Buss 1963).

The issue is further complicated by the fact that a particular frustrating situation may elicit different types of aggressive response in different people. For example, if a soft drink machine accepts money without giving the selected beverage, one person may kick the machine, another may write an angry letter to the company and a third may walk away depressed, wondering, 'Why does it always happen to *me*?' Thus, aggression may be directly expressed towards the immediate source of frustration, or *displaced* towards another object. Displacement extends the frustration–aggression hypothesis to situations where there is no *immediate* source of frustration, and may also account for some instances of aggression that instrumental aggression cannot explain. A further refinement to the theory has been put forward by Berkowitz, who has proposed that frustration will only lead to aggression if the situation leads to an unpleasant emotional state (Berkowitz 1989). In the end, the various extensions do not fully resolve the weaknesses of the frustration–aggression hypothesis. Instead, it seems reasonable to conclude that frustration is *one* possible cause of aggression, but not the *only* cause.

Taken together, instrumental aggression and the frustration–aggression hypothesis can account for many cases of aggressive behaviour. While each has weaknesses and limitations, they are at least partially complementary, as suggested above. Most importantly, both suggest ways in which aggressive behaviour can be *learned*, and hence pose an alternative to the nativist stance of Freud and the biological approach. If aggression really *is* learned, then no amount of catharsis is going to solve the problem, despite Lorenz's assertions. Indeed, behaviourists would argue that activities intended to *reduce* the 'aggressive drive' are likely to *increase* aggression by *teaching* aggressive responses. Instead, the behaviourist perspective suggests that we need to focus on identifying those elements of the social environment that encourage aggressive responses, and alter them so as to produce more socially-desirable behaviour.

The Cognitive Approach

Like the behaviourists, cognitive theorists see aggressive behaviour as learned, not innate. They also accept that reinforcement can influence learning, and hence that some aggression is instrumentally-based. However, the cognitive perspective sees the behaviourist viewpoint as too limited, because it ignores the role of mental processes in learning. Cognitive theorists point to two ways in which mental processes seem to affect behaviour: first, we are capable of learning by observing what others do (imitation); second, our thoughts and perceptions may directly influence behaviour, as opposed to behaviour depending on external stimuli. Let us consider how each of these factors is applied to the understanding of aggression.

imitation the learning of behaviour by observing the behaviour of others; sometimes called 'modelling' or 'observational learning'

The role of **imitation** (or modelling) in learning is the focus of cognitive social learning theory. According to the theory, much of what we learn is based on observing the behaviour of others, rather than direct experience and reinforcement. For example, if I see someone who has just jumped into a swimming pool suddenly show a stunned expression and howl, 'Yipes! It's freezing!', I do not have to touch the water to know it is cold. In the same way, we can learn aggressive behaviour from observing others.

Albert Bandura is one of the theorists who has argued for a social learning interpretation of aggression (Bandura 1973). In a well-known series of studies, Bandura and his colleagues examined the effects on children of observing aggressive behaviour by an adult. In one typical study, children individually observed an adult who acted either aggressively (e.g. hitting and kicking an inflatable doll) or non-aggressively (playing quietly with toys). Later, the experimenter frustrated the children by taking away a toy they were playing with, saying a child in another room needed it. Aggression was measured by observing the child's behaviour after the experimenter left

Albert Bandura

Albert Bandura (1925–) was born in the small town of Mundare in Alberta, Canada. After receiving his bachelor's degree from the University of British Columbia, he emigrated to the United States, receiving his PhD in psychology from the University of Iowa in 1952. The next year, he received a position at Stanford University, where he is currently the David Starr Jordan Professor in Social Sciences. Bandura's interests in social psychology and development led him to the study of learning in children, which led to several ground-breaking studies on the role of imitation in human learning. Together with Leonard Berkowitz, he has been one of the pioneers of the social learning approach, which emphasizes the importance of imitation and cognitive mediation in learning. His influence has been recognized on many occasions, including a Distinguished Scientist award from the American Psychological Association and a Guggenheim Fellowship. He lives with his family in Stanford, California, where he continues to teach and write.

the room. (Note that this procedure implies acceptance of the frustration–aggression hypothesis.) The results indicated that exposure to an aggressive model significantly increased imitative aggressive responses, and somewhat increased non-imitative aggressive behaviour (such as verbal remarks or hitting other toys). Interestingly, the effects tended to be stronger for both boys and girls when the adult model was the same sex as the child (Bandura *et al.* 1961). Although there are flaws in this experiment (including the use of frustration, and the obvious differences between punching an inflatable doll and hitting a person), the study illustrates the basic premise of social learning theory in this context: aggressive behaviour can be learned from observing aggressive acts by others. Later studies by both Bandura and others have extended the original study to a variety of contexts (for a review, see Bandura 1973).

The implications of the theory are both broad-ranging and serious: exposure to aggressive behaviour, in whatever form, is likely to increase the potential for aggression in observers. For example, parents who use physical punishment to discipline their children are likely to make the children more aggressive, since it teaches them that physical force is an appropriate means to control others. This interpretation is supported by a variety of studies which find a correlation between the use of physical discipline by parents and levels of aggression in children (McCord *et al.* 1961; Lefkowitz *et al.* 1978; Maccoby 1992). Conversely, exposure to models who remain calm in provocative situations may foster non-aggressive behaviour (Baron 1983).

While there have been a tremendous number of studies exploring cognitive social learning theory, support for the theory does have certain limitations. Most significantly, the crucial links to serious human aggression typically are either correlational (as in the case of punishment) or arguments by analogy (if children imitate one form of aggression, they will imitate others). In neither situation can one draw direct conclusions about the causes of serious forms of aggression. This is not a trivial concern, and we will return to it in relation to the debate about violence in the media, later in this chapter. Nonetheless, cognitive social learning theory clearly represents a *possible* explanation of the origins of many forms of aggressive behaviour.

Apart from social learning, the cognitive approach would argue that the cognitive *schemata* which guide individuals' behaviour can also affect the possibilities of aggressive behaviour. As was discussed in Chapter 1, we each develop a variety of schemata which influence both the way we perceive the world and the way we act. For example, we develop schemata that tell us how to act in a restaurant – waiting to be seated, selecting from a menu and so on (Schank 1984). These schemata are in turn influenced by the experiences we have. For example, people who watch large amounts of violent programming on television are more likely to perceive their surroundings as dangerous than those who don't watch such programmes. But can such schemata account for aggressive behaviour?

One example of a cognitive schema which relates to aggressive behaviour is what sociologist Elijah Anderson (1994) has called 'the code of the streets'. This code is a set of norms which govern interpersonal relations in the inner cities of the United States, particularly for black teenagers. Like other cognitive schemata, the code provides an internalized guide for behaviour. The most basic premise is that self-esteem is dependent on receiving 'respect' (defined as deferential behaviour) from others. 'Dissing' (expressions of disrespect) must be dealt with in kind, to prevent erosion of self-esteem. Since self-esteem is vulnerable to perceived insults, the code results in aggressive posturing, and quick, violent responses to even imaginary wrongs. Unfortunately, since both parties operate on the same tit-for-tat premise, the violence can quickly escalate, even to fatal levels. Thus, Anderson argues that the assumptions of the code are a contributory factor to inner city violence. He notes, however, that the code is not universal: 'decent' kids (those trained in mainstream values) use the code only when necessary to minimize confrontational situations; by contrast, 'street' kids, imbued with the code, have no alternative schema. In this sense, what is most striking about Anderson's observations is the implication that different cognitive schemata can have a very real effect on the likelihood of aggressive behaviour.

priming a phenomenon whereby a thought or memory increases the activation of associated thoughts or memories (the term is analogous to 'priming a pump' by using a small quantity of water to enhance the flow of water)

Apart from such specific schemata, it is possible that violent thoughts may elicit violence through a kind of **priming** effect – the notion that any thought or memory is capable of increasing the activation of associated thoughts or memories. Leonard Berkowitz, one of the early supporters of cognitive social learning theory, has endorsed this idea to account for non-imitative forms of aggression. Berkowitz refers to the underlying model as *cognitive neo-association theory* (Berkowitz 1984). Whereas social learning theory requires that a particular aggressive behaviour must be observed in order to be learned, neo-association theory suggests that violent cognitions can increase the potential for *any* related behaviours. For example, Berkowitz notes that suicide rates go up after highly publicized airplane crashes; while both represent violent events, it is clearly not a case of imitation. In one experiment, Berkowitz looked at the effects of violence-related stimuli on subsequent aggression by angry individuals. Individuals who were shown pictures of guns were more willing to punish another person (with electric shocks) than those shown neutral pictures, such as a badminton racquet.

(The tendency for guns to evoke hostile thoughts was confirmed in a recent study by Anderson *et al.* (1996), though the experimenters did not directly measure any subsequent aggression.)

As with social learning theory, much of the evidence for neo-association theory depends on broad extrapolations of experiments, with only correlational data for 'real-world' aggressive behaviour. While field experiments would provide more convincing evidence, the lack of such studies must be understood in the context of the ethical constraints on research involving aggression. Nevertheless, the available data suggest that the way we think *can* influence the way we act.

In summary, the cognitive approach suggests that aggressive behaviour is learned, and can be influenced both by what we observe (imitation) and by the way we think (the role of schemata). These assertions have been the focus of extensive research, most of which is consistent with the underlying hypotheses. Despite this, critics have been quick to point out the technical limitations of the research, as well as the fact that it ignores evidence that aggression may also involve physiological factors. (As with other phenomena, the cognitive approach to aggression seems to emphasize rational over emotional processes.) By asserting that aggressive behaviour is *learned*, the cognitive approach suggests that such behaviour is not inevitable. In fact, it implies that the same principles can be applied to foster pro-social behaviour. In essence, humans are neither inherently evil nor inherently good: how we act depends on what we have learned.

The Psychodynamic Approach

The psychodynamic approach traces its roots to Freud, and psychoanalysis is still probably the best known theory within the approach. While the cognitive and behaviourist approaches see aggressive behaviour as learned, and therefore avoidable, Freud viewed aggression as an innate drive, and therefore an unavoidable reality of human life. Although he gave the underlying drive various names at various times (destrudo, aggression, thanatos), he never wavered in his belief that the urge to commit aggressive acts was innate. In his studies of behaviour, both of his patients and of other times and cultures, he found ample indications of the prevalence of aggressive behaviour.

The aggressive drive was seen as part of the *id*, the aspect of the mind and personality which motivates our behaviour. As we develop, *ego* emerges to mediate our interactions with the world; later, our moral sense, represented by the *superego*, is formed. Ego and superego often oppose the aggressive impulses of the id, creating conflict within the psyche. To cope with this conflict – and the aggressive tendencies – we use defence mechanisms. *Defence mechanisms* block conscious awareness of the underlying conflicts, and attempt to ameliorate the tensions in various ways – for example, by *displacing* the aggression on to a substitute object. For example, a man who plays a hard game of squash after having a disagreement with a colleague at work could be viewed as engaging in displacement as he bashes the ball.

In Freud's view, we can never eliminate aggression, we can only seek to control it by channelling it in particular ways which involve *symbolic* gratification. The most desirable form of release is through *sublimation* – the creation of socially-approved products like art or music. Since most of us are not proficient at such activities, a more common form of coping is the use of displacement, as noted above. Fantasy, seen in both dreams and other activities, is another possible outlet for aggressive energy. For example, imagining that the driver who just cut you off gets stopped by the police is an expression of aggression through fantasy. Underlying these and other defence mechanisms is the principle of *catharsis* – the release of drive energy through indirect gratification. For example, catharsis implies that if one watches violence (e.g., a war film), then one will symbolically release aggression through one's involvement with the characters. (Note that Lorenz also advocated catharsis, although the details of his theory are somewhat different.) Unfortunately, the evidence regarding the value of catharsis is rather mixed. For example, a study by Feshbach aroused aggressive tendencies by insulting the participants, and then provided one group with the opportunity to engage in fantasy activities. When compared to a control group, this group showed a significant reduction in aggressive impulses, as measured by projective tests (a measure of symbolic aggression) (Feshbach 1955).

However, when looking at more direct forms of aggression, most studies have found that opportunities for catharsis increase, rather than decrease, aggressive behaviour. For example, in one study, participants were first given electric shocks during a learning task (arousing aggressive tendencies), and then half the subjects were allowed to retaliate against their tormentors, which presumably would reduce aggressive tendencies (Geen *et al.* 1975). Instead, in a follow-up to this situation, those subjects who had retaliated subsequently gave *more* intense shocks than those in the group which had no chance to retaliate previously. Hence, rather than reducing aggression, the initial opportunity to retaliate *increased* subsequent aggression – a result more consistent with social learning than catharsis. Similarly, a recent study by Bushman found that even when people are told catharsis will reduce aggressive tendencies, it results in increases in aggressive behaviour (Bushman *et al.* 1999). In the end, it seems necessary to conclude that there is little evidence in favour of catharsis. While this does not directly prove that aggression is not an innate drive, it does force one to question the validity of Freud's views on regulating aggression.

Like the biological perspective, psychoanalysis asserts that aggression is innate. For the most part, Freud used case studies and anecdotal observations to support his theory; in addition, by emphasizing the symbolic nature of behaviour, he was able to ascribe even non-violent actions to aggressive motives. However, the dependence on case studies and symbolic interpretation can only be considered weak evidence for the innateness of aggression. Furthermore, experimental research has largely contradicted his ideas of catharsis as a control mechanism for aggression. At the theoretical level, it is worth noting that some of Freud's early disciples, including Adler and Jung, disagreed with his interpretation that aggression was innate. As Freud clearly recognized, aggressive behaviour *is* a common human phenomenon – but explaining *why* is the issue, and its pervasiveness does *not* constitute direct proof that it is innate. Given these realities, we can only conclude that the case for Freud's view is open to serious doubt.

The Humanistic Approach

A number of humanistic theorists, including Maslow and Rogers, explicitly reject the idea that aggression is an innate drive. As Freud's theory shows, such an assumption leads to a pessimistic view of human potential, and the humanistic approach views human experience in far more optimistic terms. At the same time, even the greatest optimist must acknowledge that aggressive behaviour exists – so how can humanistic theories account for it? To understand, let us look at the theories of Maslow and Rogers.

Maslow, in developing his hierarchy of needs, was attempting to describe the basic factors which motivate human behaviour. His model points out that a number of different needs exist, and that for any individual, particular needs will be more pressing at various points in time. Conspicuously absent from his hierarchy is any mention of aggression. Instead of being an innate drive which must be satisfied, aggression arises in response to circumstances where fulfilment of one of the basic needs is obstructed. In this sense, Maslow's view of aggressive behaviour is somewhat akin to the frustration–aggression hypothesis: aggressive behaviour is a possible response to particular circumstances. However, Maslow does not endorse the strong form of the frustration–aggression hypothesis, which states that frustration (blocking satisfaction of a need, for Maslow) *always* results in aggression. Instead, he sees aggressive behaviour (particularly instrumental aggression) as only *one* possible response among many.

To understand this concept of aggression as only one possible response, let us consider an example. If an intruder broke into my home, thereby arousing my need for security, I might grab a baseball bat and attempt to knock the person senseless. Clearly, this would be an aggressive response; however, even in this situation, other options exist. I might, for example, barricade the bedroom door, and warn the intruder that I have phoned the police. A friend once had the experience of an intruder entering his house, and coming to the bedroom. As the intruder entered the room, Tony was awakened by his wife – just in time to see the stranger lunging at him with a knife. Fortunately, Tony (who was trained in the martial arts) disarmed the intruder, *without retaliating*, and held him until the police arrived. While they waited for the police, Tony talked with the teenaged intruder, who had been driven by economic desperation to commit this offence. Despite nearly being killed (the knife tip came close enough to scratch Tony's chest), Tony felt sorry for the teenager, and almost regretted having phoned the police! As this example shows, even threats to the need for physical safety do not inevitably result in aggressive behaviour as a response. Hence, aggressive behaviour may arise in reaction to deprivation of needs (as the teen demonstrated), but is only one possible response. In the absence of any deprivation, Maslow would see aggressive behaviour as highly unlikely. Hence, in his portrayal of self-actualized individuals, aggressive behaviour is largely absent; since self-actualization is not a deprivation need, it does not provide even this minimal reason for aggression.

Carl Rogers's theory uses a different set of concepts from Maslow's, but leads to a similar conclusion concerning aggression. Rogers sees human development as based on the *actualizing tendency*, which is a positive force for growth. Aggression, therefore, is not an innate drive. Instead, aggressive behaviour is one of the possible consequences of a state of incongruence. *Incongruence* occurs when individuals experience a conflict between their sense of self and their ideal self. Typically, this arises when other people impose *conditions of worth* as a requirement for giving positive regard. For example, teenagers frequently resent the rules of conduct which their parents attempt to impose, resulting in various forms of resistance, including acts of aggression. In Rogers's terms, there is a conflict between the teenagers' own values (part of the self) and the parental values on which they were raised (part of the ideal self). As awareness of their own values grows, it results in resentment towards the parents, who use conditional regard to try to maintain the prior values. Aggressive behaviour can be one response to this situation.

Another possible way in which aggressive behaviour might arise is if a person adopts aggressive norms due to the need for positive regard. For example, an adolescent exposed to the type of 'street code' which Anderson (1994) has described may be reluctantly drawn into aggressive behaviour in order to get peer approval. Note that in both of the preceding examples, Rogers would not see aggression as inevitable, or even as the most appropriate response; it is simply a *possible* response.

Given that conditions of worth are frequently encountered in everyday life, we should not be surprised that aggressive behaviour is relatively common. However, Rogers believes that when individuals are in touch with the actualizing tendency, they will recognize aggressive responses as inappropriate. This is reflected in his description of the values which are associated with healthy growth, which make no mention of aggression, but include 'sensitivity to others and acceptance of others' (Rogers 1964: 166). Rogers notes that under the conditions which foster growth, 'I do not find, in such a climate of freedom, that one person comes to value fraud and murder and thievery, while another values a life of self-sacrifice' (Rogers 1964: 167). In other words, given the conditions for healthy growth and the development of congruence, aggressive behaviour will not occur.

While the interpretations of aggression offered by Maslow and Rogers are consistent with their overall theories of behaviour, neither theorist provides much in terms of direct empirical support for their views. In part, this is due to the humanists' methodology, which emphasizes the subjective nature of experience rather than traditional experimentation. As a consequence, much of the evidence involves case studies and anecdotal observations drawn from their experiences with individuals in therapy; Maslow also emphasized the study of historical figures. As noted with Freud, such data are very limited as a means of proving causation.

Ultimately, the humanistic assertion that aggression is not innate depends on two assertions: first, that aggressive behaviour is based on thwarted development; second, that some individuals function largely without resorting to aggressive behaviour. The first point, as already noted, is problematical at best, since no direct proof is given. The second point is interesting, but equally ambiguous. Since no one is *fully* self-actualized or *fully* congruent, and definitions of aggression differ, how one assesses an individual's non-aggressiveness is likely to be influenced by one's assumptions. For example,

Approach	Explanation of cause	Method of reducing
Biological	Ethology – innate drive	Catharsis (e.g. via sports)
	Physiology – response to aversive stimuli	Minimize aversive stimuli
Behaviourist	Instrumental aggression – using aggression to reach a goal is reinforcing	Change contingencies so aggressive responses not reinforced
	Frustration-aggression hypothesis – frustration leads to aggression	Minimize sources of frustration
Cognitive	Social learning theory – aggressive behaviour is imitated	Reduce opportunities for observing aggression
	Neo-association theory – aggressive events trigger related thoughts and actions	Reduce exposure to aggressive stimuli
Psychodynamic (Freud)	Aggression innate drive (in id)	Catharsis (especially sublimation)
Humanistic (Rogers)	Aggression is one response to distortions of growth due to conditions of worth	Provide more unconditional positive regard

Figure 8.1   Perspectives on aggression This chart provides a comparison of the five approaches in terms of how they view the origin of aggression, and the means by which it can be controlled.

instances of aggressive behaviour in a supposedly self-actualized individual might be seen as refuting the humanistic view, or simply as an indication that the person is less than perfect. Even if someone showed no real sign of overt aggression, such as Mahatma Gandhi (the father of passive resistance as a form of political protest), some critics might say his behaviour reflected indirect or symbolic aggression. In the end, judging the appropriateness of the humanistic view of aggression seems (like other aspects of experience) dependent on one's own perceptions.

Comparing the Approaches

Having considered the interpretations of aggression which the five approaches provide, where does this leave us? What can we conclude about the origins of aggression? The research, while not definitive, does point towards certain conclusions. (See Figure 8.1 for a summary of the approaches' interpretations.)

In terms of innate factors, the research on physiological aspects of aggression suggests that there is a relationship between pain and aggression. That is, painful or unpleasant stimuli often elicit aggressive behaviour. To the extent that this reaction is governed by particular brain pathways (as some assert), it represents an innate source of aggression. One interpretation of this relationship is that the behaviour is a defensive response, intended to eliminate the aversive stimulus. However, not all situations involving pain can be explained this way, so the proper conclusion seems to be that painful stimuli can provoke aggression, but do not always do so. As evolutionary theories have argued, it is likely that we have developed behavioural mechanisms for dealing with threats. However, to suggest that aggression is possible is not the same as saying it is inevitable (as drive theories argue). Theories which propose an *innate drive* – both biological and psychodynamic – have little direct supporting evidence. The argument that aggression is common, and therefore must be innate, is really only circular reasoning. Furthermore, the mechanism which Lorenz and Freud proposed for reducing aggression – *catharsis* – also has little experimental support. Consequently, one must conclude that the notion of an innate drive is largely unfounded.

The alternative to assuming that aggression is innate is to explain it in terms of learning, and several theories have done so. The behaviourist concept of *instrumental aggression*, which says that aggression is reinforced by experiences in which it is effective in accomplishing a goal, is plausible, and has received some experimental support. It can also be related to other theories, such as aggression as a defensive reaction to pain. Such reactions can be seen as a form of instrumental aggression if the person succeeds in eliminating the painful stimulus. Hence, instrumental aggression is one likely cause of aggressive behaviour.

The *frustration–aggression hypothesis*, by contrast, has weaker support. There seems no question that frustration can elicit aggression, but there are many qualifiers on the relationship, including the perceived likelihood of retaliation. Indeed, it may well be that frustrating circumstances simply represent a particular form of aversive stimuli, in which case the hypothesis really reduces to a special case of the pain–aggression relationship. In its strong form, which suggests that frustration accounts for *all* aggression, the hypothesis no longer seems justified. Given that its weak form requires so many qualifiers, the frustration–aggression hypothesis has limited explanatory value.

The humanistic approach, as represented by Maslow and Rogers, rejects the nativist interpretation of aggression. Rather than being inevitable, aggressive behaviour is a result of experiences which interfere with healthy growth. That is, healthy individuals (*self-actualized* or *fully functioning*) are unlikely to respond aggressively. While each theory suggests circumstances where aggression might arise, they suffer from the relative absence of supporting research. Given that the humanistic approach favours subjective analysis of experience over experimentation, the lack of evidence is largely inevitable. While the absence of conventional evidence does not prove the approach is wrong, it does mean that most researchers see it as untestable, and hence of limited value.

Among the approaches which emphasize learning of aggressive behaviour, the one with the most support, in terms of the volume of research done, is the cognitive approach. While accepting the principle of instrumental aggression, the approach adds two further mechanisms to account for aggressive behaviour: social learning and cognitive schemata. *Social learning theory*, as described by Albert Bandura and others, argues that behaviour is acquired through imitation. Consequently, if children observe violence, then they will in turn act aggressively. This relationship applies not only to direct experience (for example, discipline by parents), but also to vicarious experiences, such as watching television.

Cognitive *schemata* can influence aggression in two ways: by providing norms to guide behaviour and by priming. We each have various *norms* related to social situations; if a person has acquired, through social learning or otherwise, a schema which states aggression is acceptable, then that person will show aggressive behaviour (as in the case of street gang members). *Priming* suggests that observing violence causes activation of related cognitive schemata, resulting in a greater likelihood of a wide range of aggressive behaviours. As Leonard Berkowitz has noted, this theory can account for rather unexpected relationships, such as increases in the suicide rate after a plane crash. One of the chief difficulties with these theories is that much of the evidence is either correlational or based on extrapolation from laboratory studies involving relatively mild forms of aggressive behaviour. As a consequence, it is hard to demonstrate that the explanations offered actually apply in everyday life.

For further consideration

Research on violent crime clearly indicates that such behaviour varies considerably across nations; for example, homicide rates in the United States are five times higher than in Canada on a per capita basis. How would you explain the difference in homicide rates, in terms of theories of aggression?

Aggression and the Media

For many years now, there has been a debate about the relationship between observing violence portrayed in the media and aggressive behaviour. Whether one considers the news media or the entertainment media, there is no question that images of violence are readily encountered. However, the issue is not whether such portrayals occur, but what effect they have on society. To a large extent, the debate concerns whether or not media violence increases aggressive behaviour.

The debate is largely between the cognitive approach and those theories which see aggression as innate (the biological approach and psychoanalysis). The cognitive approach argues that observing violence may increase the potential for aggression, through both imitation and priming. The nativist theories, drawing on the concept of drive-reduction, suggest that observing violence can lessen aggressive energy through catharsis. It is also possible that, in the real world, no consistent relationship exists between observing violence and aggressive behaviour. This could happen if both theories are wrong, or even if the two kinds of processes somehow offset each other, producing no net change in the potential for aggressive behaviour.

At an intuitive level, many people favour the social learning view. For example, after seeing an action film in which the hero triumphs by killing the bad guys, most people feel some degree of arousal, not relaxation. Does this mean that they will then scour the streets looking for criminals? Probably not. Yet, occasionally, reality *does* seem to imitate fiction. As I write this, film director Oliver Stone is being sued by relatives of victims of a real-life crime spree which seemed to mirror events in Stone's *Natural Born Killers*. The lawsuit has not yet been settled, and in any case, legal standards of causation are not the same as scientific standards. Nonetheless, it illustrates the concerns some people feel about media portrayals of violence.

Given the limited evidence for catharsis, most of the research has focused on the hypothesis that observing violence *increases* aggressive behaviour, as the cognitive approach suggests. Over the past three decades, there have been hundreds of laboratory experiments on social learning of aggressive behaviour, and even several reviews of the published literature. While details of the studies vary, they have looked at modelling of aggression by both sexes over a wide age range, and using a number of measures of aggressive behaviour (including willingness to give electric shocks to other people). Within the laboratory context, it appears quite clear that observing violence will increase the likelihood of aggressive behaviour (for reviews, see Bandura 1973; Freidrich-Cofer and Huston 1986; Wood *et al.* 1991). The difficulty with these studies is that laboratory findings may not generalize very well, for reasons discussed earlier in the chapter.

Because of the limitations of laboratory experiments, researchers have also tried to look at the effects of observing television violence in natural settings. One way that this can be done is through the use of correlational studies, which involve making observations without the controls required for experiments. Indeed, one of the earliest studies reporting a link between observing television violence and aggressive behaviour in children was based on an incidental finding from a broader study of child rearing practices (Eron 1963). Subsequently, a positive correlation between observing violence on television and aggressive behaviour has been confirmed in a large number of studies, involving a variety of groups in several different countries (Belson 1978; Singer and Singer 1981; Huesmann *et al.* 1984).

While these studies have shown a link, the results are nonetheless limited, in that no correlational study can identify the *cause* of an observed pattern. That is, on the basis of the correlational data alone, one could argue that aggressive children choose to watch more violent television (reversing the direction of causation), or that an unidentified third variable accounts for the link (possibly family influences), or that the pattern is simply coincidental (unlikely, given how common the pattern is). Ideally, one would like to gather experimental evidence in a natural setting – in other words, do a field experiment.

One interesting study was conducted by a group of Canadian researchers (Joy *et al.* 1986). Dubbed 'a natural experiment' (technically, a quasi-experiment done in a field setting), the study examined the impact of the introduction of television in a small isolated Canadian town referred to as Notel (for 'no television'). The investigators examined behaviour both before the advent of television and for two years after its introduction (in 1974). As a control comparison, they also examined behaviour in two other Canadian towns which, while similar in size and demographic profile, already had access to television. Aggressive behaviour was measured in two ways: by direct observation of children's verbal and physical aggression during play periods at school, and by student and teacher ratings of aggressiveness. As shown in Figure 8.2, aggressive behaviour rose in Notel, while there was no significant increase in such behaviour for children in the other two towns. What is particularly striking is that the increases occurred for a wide range of children – both sexes, those who were initially high *or* low in aggressiveness, and those who watched large *or* small amounts of television.

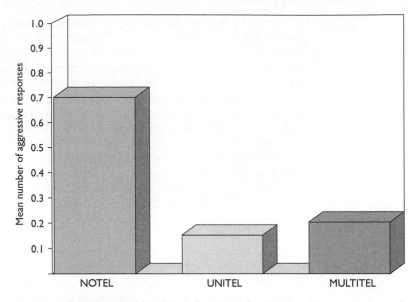

Figure 8.2 Effects of the introduction of television The graph shows the results of a field experiment in which physical aggression by children was compared as a function of the introduction of television to the Notel community. Unlike in the two communities which already had television at the time of the study, the children in Notel showed a significant increase in physical aggression. (Adapted from Joy et al. 1986.)

Hence, the study suggests a strong link between exposure to television and aggressive behaviour. One difficulty with the study is that the experimenters did not have direct control over the *content* of what children watched, so the effects cannot be specifically linked to observing violence. However, it seems reasonable to assume that some portion of the viewing (and the results) involved violent programming. Still, it illustrates the difficulty of doing field experiments (and natural-setting research in general) – one cannot control all elements of the situation.

Another field experiment approached the issue by trying to alter the *attitudes* towards violent content, without trying to control what viewers watched. Leonard Eron and his colleagues randomly divided 169 boys who had already been identified as viewing high levels of violence (Eron 1982). One group was given training intended to reduce aggression by altering attitudes towards television violence, the other group was a control group. Based on peer ratings of aggression collected four months after the end of the training, the experimental group showed significant reductions in aggressive behaviour, while the control group showed no change. Unfortunately, interpretation of the results is complicated by the mixing of several types of training, which make it unclear precisely which aspect of the training was most significant. However, the general pattern of results suggests that it is not simply the viewing of violence which increases aggressive behaviour; instead, it depends on how viewers interpret the meaning of what they watch. Support for this conclusion comes from other studies which suggest that parental guidance can alter both children's perceptions of violence *and* subsequent aggressive behaviour (Mattern and Lindholm 1985). Thus, the connection between media violence and aggressive behaviour seems to involve an interaction between the person and the situation.

Taken as a whole, all three types of research point to a connection between observing television violence and aggressive behaviour. However, none of the studies we have mentioned is without flaws, and critics continue to challenge the conclusion that a relationship exists (Freedman 1984, 1986). In the end, Freedman acknowledges that the correlation between viewing TV violence and aggressive behaviour *is* likely to be genuine. However, he *also* concludes that the effect is small (a correlation coefficient of 0.10 to 0.20), and that weaknesses in the experimental research suggest that the evidence for a *causal* connection is minimal. (See Freidrich-Cofer and Huston (1986) and Liebert and Sprafkin (1988) for replies to Freedman.)

In part, Freedman is justified in being sceptical, since each of the studies we have discussed *does* have flaws. However, it should be noted that they are not the *same* flaws in each case, and that the general nature of the results remains the same in all cases. Overall, it seems reasonable to believe that *some* relationship does exist, even if it involves an interaction between the person and the situation in which viewing occurs. At the same time, it is important to note that no one believes that observing violence on television is the *only* factor in aggression. For example, instrumental aggression (including real violence in the home) and other forms of social learning (for example, attitudes of parents and interpersonal skills) also play a role in aggressive behaviour.

The debate raised by Freedman's analysis goes to the heart of our understanding of social behaviour. Psychology has traditionally (but not exclusively) modelled its methods on those of the physical sciences, a domain where many of the phenomena are relatively simple compared to human behaviour. Within psychology, social behaviour may well be the most complex area, since it involves interactions of complex individuals. Beyond this, social psychologists are often limited in their research methods by ethical considerations. All these factors create constraints on the effectiveness of research. Consequently, it seems unlikely that one could conceive of *any* one study in social psychology which would adequately satisfy the conflicting needs for experimental control, experimental realism, external validity and ethical responsibility. Thus, one must proceed, hesitantly, by exploring the problem from as many angles as possible. Looked at in this way, Freedman's analysis seems overly critical, and possibly disingenuous, in that it seems unlikely that *any* generally accepted finding in social psychology would meet his standard of proof.

More than any other area of psychology, social psychology seems to invite extrapolation to everyday life. Thus, if one *does* accept that there is a causal connection between observing violence and aggressive behaviour, then shouldn't society do something about it? And if so, what? Ban all violence in television and films? Prohibit all violence in sport? Such prospects can evoke strong feelings among both advocates and detractors. The problem is, psychological research may help us to *understand* behaviour, but it cannot directly address the moral questions of what behaviour *should* be. In this sense, psychological research cannot be the sole criterion for framing social policy.

At the same time, to ignore what psychology has learned when we consider social issues (either individually or collectively) seems equally undesirable. To do so implies that the search for understanding has no bearing on our lives. As a parent, for example, I am concerned with the upbringing of my children, and with the kind of society in which they live; in both respects, I feel it is important that, as a society, we try to understand the factors that affect aggression.

For further consideration

What conclusion do *you* draw about the relationship between observing violence and aggressive behaviour? How do you feel about computer/video games which vividly portray acts of violence?

Perspectives on Pro-social Behaviour

Thus far, our examination of social behaviour has focused on one of the most negative forms of behaviour, aggression. While not demonstrating that *all* aggressive behaviour is learned, the research on observing violence certainly suggests that the potential for aggressive behaviour can be increased through learning. What about behaviour that is socially desirable? How does *it* arise? And are there ways to encourage such behaviour? For example, does reading stories about people who help others (such as the Good Samaritan) have any impact on actual helping by children?

Defining Pro-social Behaviour

pro-social behaviour
socially desirable behaviour that is beneficial to another person, or to society as a whole

Pro-social behaviour can be defined as socially desirable behaviour which in some way benefits another person, or society as a whole. While *altruism* is the most frequently studied category of pro-social behaviour, it also includes a number of other kinds of behaviour (see Figure 8.3). In day-to-day life, we all engage in pro-social behaviour – for example, when we play a team sport, when we offer sympathy to a friend who is upset or when we refrain from littering. Hence, the working of society is largely dependent on the occurrence of pro-social behaviour. In this section, we will focus on altruism, and how each of the approaches explains it.

Altruism may bring to mind images of someone heroically intervening in an emergency, such as rescuing a drowning stranger. In that sense, it might seem that altruism is quite rare, for few of us would claim to be heroic. Yet we all engage in small acts of helping, whether contributing to a charity or holding the door for a stranger. Thus, although altruism refers to helping others, the term can cover a wide range of behaviours. In order to study altruistic behaviour, we need to have some way to define it which is specific enough to be testable, and which does not assume a particular theoretical basis. One of the most common ways in which researchers have tried to do this is by looking at whether people will assist someone in distress, called *bystander intervention*.

> ATRUISM – sharing, helping and cooperation with people or animals
>
> CONTROL OF AGGRESSION – behaviours intended to prevent or eliminate aggression by self or others
>
> EXPLAINING FEELINGS – communicating with another person about thoughts, feelings or actions with intent of increasing understanding and fostering positive outcomes
>
> REPARATION FOR WRONGDOING – behaviour which is clearly intended to make amends for previous wrongful actions
>
> RESISTANCE TO TEMPTATION – resisting temptation to engage in socially-prohibited behaviours (e.g. stealing)
>
> SYMPATHY – expressing concern for others and their problems
>
> TASK PERSISTENCE/DELAY OF GRATIFICATION – actions intended to fulfil commitments by persisting at a task or delaying gratification

Figure 8.3   Categories of pro-social behaviour Just as various forms of aggression exist, there are also various forms of pro-social behaviour. This chart shows some categories suggested by Rubenstein *et al.* (1974, adapted from original).

The converse of bystander intervention is *bystander apathy*, the failure to intervene in an emergency. Historically, bystander apathy was the starting point for modern research into the conditions which foster or inhibit altruistic behaviour. As noted in Chapter 1, this concern was stimulated in part by the unfortunate death of Kitty Genovese in New York in 1964. Here was a young woman being repeatedly attacked on the street, and screaming for help, to no avail. As it turned out, none of the 38 individuals later identified as having observed the attack had even telephoned the police. The event shocked many people, and was seen by many as a sign of the callousness of modern urban life. After all, in doing nothing to help, the bystanders had indirectly contributed to her death. Conversely, if any one person had acted, Kitty Genovese might still be alive. Before examining more closely the research on bystander intervention and bystander apathy, let us consider how each approach views altruistic behaviour.

Theories of Altruism

ethical hedonism the principle that individuals engage in moral behaviour, such as altruism, because it provides some personal benefit

As with aggression, each of the five approaches has an interpretation of how socially desirable behaviour arises. In order to explain altruistic behaviour, theories tend to suggest that altruistic behaviour either benefits the helper in some way (**ethical hedonism**) or occurs without regard to personal benefit (*genuine altruism*). As we will see, most of the approaches invoke some form of ethical hedonism, though the mechanisms differ significantly.

The Biological Approach

For the biological approach, altruistic behaviour has its roots in our evolutionary history. Evolutionary theorists like Melvin Konner (1982) have

kin altruism the concept that individuals help those who are close relatives, because it fosters the transmission of their genes

suggested that pro-social behaviours like altruism occur only to enhance reproductive success and foster the transmission of one's genes (called **kin altruism**). Thus, a parent might sacrifice their own life to save their child, because the child carries half of their genes and can in turn preserve them by procreating. For similar reasons, one would be less likely to help a more distant relative like a cousin, and very unlikely to help a total stranger, whose genetic similarity is unknown. Support for this idea comes from studies of people faced with hypothetical life-or-death decisions (Burnstein *et al.* 1994). In general, individuals favoured those who would be most likely to contribute to preserving their genes, such as close kin over distant relatives, and the young (who are likely to reproduce) over the old.

One difficulty with explaining altruism in terms of reproductive success is that it cannot account for helping those who are not genetically related. For example, why help a total stranger who is in distress? In order to deal with such situations, evolutionary psychologists have developed the concept of **reciprocal altruism**. Essentially, reciprocal altruism says we will help others in the expectation that they will help us when we are in need, as long as the expected long-term benefit exceeds the immediate cost (Trivers 1971). Thus, a group of people on a railway platform may respond to an attack on a stranger, because the risk to each person is quite small, but the future benefit of other people helping if one of them were to be attacked would be large.

reciprocal altruism the concept that individuals help strangers if the expected benefit of future help from the strangers exceeds the short-term cost of helping

Evaluating the explanations of altruistic behaviour put forward by evolutionary psychologists is not a simple task. Clearly, both kin altruism and reciprocal altruism reflect forms of ethical hedonism, with the assumed benefit being defined in terms of reproductive success and survival advantage. Of the two concepts, kin altruism is perhaps the more interesting, both because its predictions about choices seem difficult to explain without referring to genetic relatedness, and because of the empirical support which exists for these predictions. On the other hand, reciprocal altruism can be interpreted as simply a restatement of the principle of reciprocity, which has a social history going back at least as far as the biblical 'golden rule'. Since it is almost impossible to identify, let alone measure, the implied costs and benefits, reciprocal altruism seems very hard to test. Indeed, several different models have been put forward, but at present none can claim much experimental support (Simon 1990; Caporael and Baron 1997). At present, the explanations offered by evolutionary psychology must be considered tentative, and warrant further exploration.

The Behaviourist Approach

To the behaviourists, pro-social behaviours, like aggressive behaviours, are acquired through reinforcement. For example, if parents and others reinforce a child for sharing or helping others, then the child will learn such behaviours. Like the biological approach, the behaviourist view of altruism is based on an assumption of ethical hedonism. However, the underlying benefit is seen in terms of reinforcers, not survival advantage. In this context, the publicity and other rewards which society bestows for major acts of altruism (such as rescuing a drowning person) can be seen as social reinforcers. (It can also be argued that they serve as discriminative stimuli to encourage other people to act similarly.) In essence, altruism is seen as instrumental, just as aggression can be; an individual does the action because of a perceived reinforcer.

While it is likely that children are reinforced for various forms of pro-social behaviour, it must be acknowledged that there is little direct experimental evidence. Instead, like reciprocal altruism, the concept of instrumental altruism seems rather vague. For example, there are circumstances where individuals may actually risk their lives in order to help another. In such circumstances, what is the reinforcer that could be worth losing one's life? Or must we assume the person is unaware of the risk in order to make sense of such behaviour? It may well be that heroic acts are extraordinary, and not easily explained. But at present, the behaviourist view of altruism seems too unsupported to consider seriously.

The Cognitive Approach

Like the behaviourists, the cognitive approach views pro-social behaviours as learned. Essentially, the processes are the same as those involved in learning anti-social behaviours like aggression. That is, both types of behaviour are learned by *imitation*, and are influenced by the schemata we form concerning social interactions. Hence, altruistic behaviour can be influenced by what we observe others do, and by the ideas which we are exposed to in everyday life (via *priming* effects).

Some cognitive researchers have tested these ideas by doing experiments to try to enhance altruistic behaviour. Sprafkin and her colleagues looked at the effect of positive media examples by exposing first grade children to one of three television shows: one conveyed a message to help others even at personal cost, while the other two represented control conditions with no such message (Sprafkin *et al.* 1975). Subsequently, over 90 per cent of children exposed to the helping message chose helping a puppy over a chance for personal gain; in neither control group did more than 50 per cent similarly intervene. One way to explain this result is in terms of imitation, since the helping message also involved rescuing an animal. However, Berkowitz has suggested that these and similar studies involving media exposure can better be explained in terms of *priming* – that is, exposure to concepts of helping serves to activate related schema in the individual (Berkowitz 1984). The activation of these pro-social schemata then makes it more likely that the person will intervene if an emergency – even one dissimilar to the original example – arises. For example, if I hear on the radio that a young child has given their allowance to a charity, I may be more likely to help a stranded motorist while I am driving to work. Thus, both priming and social learning are consistent with the conclusion that it is possible to enhance pro-social behaviour by exposing individuals to examples of pro-social concepts. However, they do differ in significant ways. One difference is that priming is generally seen as relatively transient, lasting hours or days (Berkowitz 1984). By contrast, social learning effects can often be detected months or years later (e.g. Eron 1982).

While hardly conclusive, these experiments at least demonstrate that it is possible to enhance altruistic behaviour by applying cognitive principles.

Interestingly, neither the research nor the theory really explains *why* people help, however. That is, do people help because they receive a benefit from helping (ethical hedonism), or simply out of a desire to do good (genuine altruism)? Because the model does not address the issue of motivation, it seems impossible to decide which assumption should apply. In a sense, we are left with a situation where the model seems to work (at least for some cases), but we don't know why. It is hoped that future work may clarify this aspect of the mechanisms of social learning.

The Psychodynamic Approach

By contrast, Freud saw pro-social behaviour as closely linked to motivational processes. Essentially, altruism results from a defence mechanism, whereby one engages in good deeds in order to block awareness of one's own aggressive nature. In developmental terms, individuals who consistently engage in altruistic acts are fixated at the latent stage, where overt expression of the drives is repressed. For example, a doctor who treats the poor without charging a fee may do considerable good in helping others, but Freud would say the underlying motivation is based on redirecting the drive energy of the id. In his view, such behaviours have social value, but their occurrence is dependent on the dynamics of the psyche, particularly in terms of how ego handles the competing demands of id and superego. In this sense, his theory is clearly based on ethical hedonism, with benefits being defined in terms of the ego's ability to minimize anxiety and cope with external reality.

Like many aspects of Freud's theory, his explanations of altruistic behaviour are not easily testable. A modern psychoanalyst, Daniel Kriegman, has examined Freud's ideas, and has suggested that altruism is better accounted for by other psychoanalytic models than by Freud's original theory (Kriegman 1990). Unfortunately, Kriegman provides little direct evidence to support his argument, instead drawing analogies to work in evolutionary psychology.

It is worth noting that Freud's theory says little about how society might foster altruistic behaviour, other than by ensuring a well-developed superego. This is somewhat surprising, given that the theory puts forward a clear mechanism (catharsis) as a means of reducing aggression. The absence of a specific mechanism may reflect the fact that altruism, unlike aggression, is not seen as an innate drive. Consequently, the methods for fostering altruistic behaviour (like the use of defence mechanisms) cannot be directly promoted. Hence, in terms of understanding and fostering altruistic behaviour, his theory seems too vague either to test or to utilize.

The Humanistic Approach

As discussed in Chapter 6, the humanists take a positive view of human behaviour, including pro-social behaviour. For Rogers, the motivation for altruistic behaviour comes from the actualizing tendency, and hence is a basic human capacity. In part, helping others can be seen as a form of reciprocity which is fostered by *empathy*; we can recognize others' suffering, just as we recognize their need for positive regard. Thus, Rogers would say we help someone who is in distress because we recognize their distress, not because helping is of direct benefit to us. As such, altruistic behaviour can be seen as genuine altruism, rather than ethical hedonism. The idea that empathy fosters altruistic behaviour has been explored in several experiments by Daniel Batson (1991, 1998). Batson has found that under conditions which foster empathy, individuals will choose to help someone who is suffering even if it implies that they themselves might suffer. For example, in a variant of Milgram's obedience situation (see Chapter 1), subjects watched another person receive electric shocks; when given the option, individuals often agreed to take the person's place. In some studies, individuals chose to help even if walking away led to a cash incentive! Thus, Batson's work seems to confirm that empathy can be a source of altruistic behaviour.

Maslow looked at the motivation for behaviour in terms of his *hierarchy of needs*. At the top of the hierarchy is self-actualization, which is a growth need, rather than deficiency-based. Thus, he would probably agree that altruistic behaviour is based on genuine altruism, rather than ethical hedonism. Indeed, he noted that people are capable of responding based on a higher need, even if it implies ignoring a more basic need. For example, someone could risk their life (threatening safety needs) in order to help a friend or loved one (love and belonging needs), or even a stranger (self-actualization). In the case of a stranger in distress, self-actualization would imply helping simply because it is the appropriate thing to do as a human being. Similarly, Maslow's theory would suggest that self-actualized individuals are the most likely to engage in consistent acts of altruism (e.g. Mother Teresa). While there are many anecdotal examples that fit Maslow's description, and his theory has been applied in other situations (such as organizational behaviour), there is little experimental evidence to support this interpretation of altruistic behaviour. In part, this reflects the emphasis that the humanists place on subjective experience rather than experimental control. However, as Batson's work shows, it is not impossible to develop experiments that can be related to the theories.

In terms of promoting altruistic behaviour, Rogers and Maslow seem to offer similar views. By providing the conditions for healthy growth (Rogers) and satisfaction of deficiency needs (Maslow), society can foster the development of individuals who will reach their potential in all respects – including their capacity to respond to individuals in distress. In short, if we wish to create a society of individuals who help others, we need to create a society which helps everyone. Clearly, this concept is not likely to be tested in the near future (though we might wish it could be).

In summary, each of the five approaches offers a distinctive interpretation of altruism. In this regard, it is interesting to note that those which seem similar in their views of the origin of aggression (e.g. biological and psychodynamic) also agree in terms of basis of altruism (i.e. as ethical hedonism). At the same time, it is clear that identifying ways to foster pro-social behaviour is harder than finding suggestions to reduce aggressive behaviour. To understand this, let us return to the issue of bystander intervention as a form of altruism.

**For further
consideration** One interpretation of the studies of empathy is that we help someone who is suffering, because we wish to reduce our (empathic) suffering. Thus, it is argued we intervene for our own benefit, not out of genuine altruism. Do you agree? Do you think genuine altruism is possible?

Altruism and Bystander Behaviour

While there are many ways in which we can help others, responding to an emergency is perhaps the most significant. Thus, *bystander intervention* is clearly a form of altruistic behaviour. Similarly, it seems surprising to find situations where someone is in distress, yet onlookers don't respond – the phenomenon of *bystander apathy*. Thus, examining the reactions of bystanders to emergencies provides a practical example of the factors which affect altruism.

One element to consider is the type of circumstances under which people do or do not intervene. As Latané and Darley (1969) noted, most emergencies represent a complex situation, and several steps are required for intervention to occur (see Figure 8.4). First, one must recognize that there is an emergency, and some situations can be ambiguous. For example, a diabetic suffering from insulin shock may appear drunk, including sweetish breath. Given that perception is an active construction (see Chapter 1), it is possible for people to misinterpret the situation, or simply fail to notice that there is an emergency. Second, one must evaluate what response is appropriate. Given that emergencies are both unpredictable and rare, many people are unsure what to do when faced with a situation in which someone needs help. Consequently, they will often consider the behaviour of others in order to determine how to respond. Hence, this is the stage where social dynamics are typically significant. Third, people must decide whether they have the appropriate skills to intervene. For example, if the emergency is a heart attack, the person may consider whether they are capable of performing CPR. The possible reasons for failing to act are many, and include fears for one's own safety, lack of specific skills and even legal barriers. For example, in some jurisdictions, bystanders are not legally compelled to intervene in an emergency, but may be held liable for consequences if they do intervene. In such cases, this legal stance can serve as a deterrent to becoming involved. (Some places have passed so-called 'good Samaritan' laws protecting those who try to help from liability, in order to encourage intervention.) Thus, the decision to intervene requires a series of assessments, in a situation which often requires a nearly immediate response.

Given this complexity, the failure to intervene may reflect processes that have little to do with lack of caring. In their research, Latané and Darley focused on the second stage of the process, how people decide what to do. Typically, individuals look to others for clues as to how to act – a form of *social influence*. Thus, if others are present and do nothing, one might conclude that there is no reason to intervene. (Latané and Darley found that when a confederate of the experimenter deliberately remained passive, few people responded to the emergency.) Even if no one else is present, social influence may play a role, in terms of calling upon previously learned social schemata. For example, a teenager might think, 'What would my

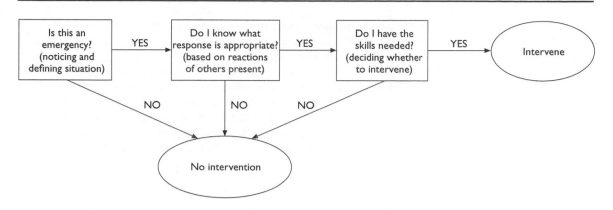

Figure 8.4 Determining response to an emergency As discussed in the text, responding to an emergency requires a series of decisions, and a negative response to any step will preclude taking action.

diffusion of responsibility
a lessening of an individual's feeling of responsibility in a situation which involves other people

Dad do in this situation?' Consequently, social influence is a major factor in determining altruism or its converse, bystander apathy.

Latané and Darley also identified a second factor which could influence responding, **diffusion of responsibility**. In any situation where others are present (not just emergencies), individuals often feel less personal responsibility for what happens. In an emergency, this can result in a perceived lessening of the onus to act. For example, when Kitty Genovese was killed, interviews indicated that people assumed that *someone else* had already called the police – and so no one did! (To avoid confounding these two possible factors, much of the research on enhancing altruism has utilized situations involving single individuals.)

More recently, researchers have attempted to increase intervention through social influence. In one study, a variant of Latané and Darley's 'lady in distress' scenario was used; the difference was that in this version the confederate did not ignore the sound of someone falling in the next room (Staub, reported in Goleman 1993). In one case, the confederate said, 'That probably has nothing to do with us.' In this condition, fewer than 25 per cent of subjects intervened to offer help. In the other condition, the confederate said, 'That sounds pretty bad – I'll go get the experimenter and maybe you should go check what's happening next door,' and proceeded to leave the room. In this case, 100 per cent of subjects moved to render aid. In effect, the comments of the confederate served to define what was appropriate behaviour in the situation. Hence, one way to enhance altruism is by creating situational interpretations which encourage intervention.

Other research suggests that additional factors that may foster intervention. As discussed earlier, both exposure to positive models and priming with pro-social ideas can increase the likelihood of helping. Consistent with this view is a study which looked at the effects of teaching students about research on bystander apathy and altruism. Compared to students who were not given the same information in class, they were more likely to help when they encountered an apparent emergency two weeks later (Beaman *et al.* 1978). When the person in distress seems similar to the bystander, intervention is also more likely (Graf and Riddle 1972), which may indicate that perceived similarity increases feelings of empathy. (See Batson's research on empathy, mentioned earlier.)

Generally, this research is consistent with the cognitive approach, which suggests that the likelihood of bystander intervention depends on the way we perceive and evaluate the situation. Furthermore, the indications are that pro-social behaviour can be modified by processes like priming and social learning. Of course, the existing research does not prove that *all* pro-social behaviour is learned; nor does it imply that no limits exist to modifiability. Over time, we hope we will develop further insights into pro-social behaviour, and will be able to apply that understanding in our communities.

One aspect which has not been addressed in our discussion of either aggression or altruism is the role of culture. While it is clear that social behaviour varies across cultures, identifying the causal factors is not easy. In terms of aggression, several studies have shown a correlation between fighting a war and homicide rates across a range of countries (Archer and Gartner 1984; Ember and Ember 1994). While this is interpreted as meaning that the sanctioning of institutionalized aggression also encourages individual aggression, the correlational data cannot prove such a causal link. Furthermore, studies of various cultures have indicated that high homicide rates occur even where social norms for peacefulness exist, making it difficult to explain cultural variations in terms of any simple model of socialization (Knauft 1987). In terms of pro-social behaviour, a cross-cultural study of cities in 18 countries found variations in several forms of helping (Norenzayan and Levine, in Smith and Bond 1999). In general, people in large, wealthy cities were less likely to help than people in small cities in poor countries. This result is consistent with a model first proposed by Milgram, which says that higher population densities and less social cohesion lead to greater diffusion of responsibility, and hence less helping (Milgram 1970). However, such variations tell us little about how cultural attitudes (such as individualism versus collectivism) affect the likelihood of helping. While social learning processes are doubtless one of the elements involved in cross-cultural differences, the issues are extremely complex. Without looking at how different societies define altruism or aggression, we risk misinterpreting the meaning of behaviour; that is, we may be able to identify a response (such as helping a blind person cross a street), but not how it is perceived or why it occurs. In the end, such questions may be more appropriate to other disciplines (such as anthropology) than to social psychology.

For further consideration

Have you ever encountered an emergency? Did you intervene? Can you relate your behaviour to the principles discussed above? Does knowing these principles seem likely to affect how you will react to future emergencies?

Conclusion

Social psychology is concerned with the social dimensions of individual behaviour. As such, it deals with both how we think about ourselves and others (*social cognition*), and how social factors affect the way we act (*social influence*). Interest in social behaviour is not restricted to psychology, of course – indeed, it has been studied within the disciplines of biology, sociology and anthropology. What distinguishes social psychology from these other fields is largely its focus on the individual, and its emphasis on experimentation as a methodology.

In some ways, social psychology is the most appealing area within psychology. In a very fundamental way, it touches on the social concerns that are basic to our lives. By exploring questions of how we respond to, and are influenced by, other people, it seems to be both 'real' and 'relevant'. This is evident, for example, in the debates about aggression. Yet one cannot consider social psychology closely without also recognizing the limitations of the area in terms of what we know, and how we know it.

One of the basic difficulties is the complex nature of social research, and the limits it places on finding definite answers. Experimental *control*, *reactivity*, the need for *experimental realism*, *external validity*, *ethics* – all these factors (and others unmentioned) place constraints on how one does social research, and on the quality of the answers one obtains. Consider the problem of observing violence: after almost thirty years and hundreds of studies, there is still controversy about drawing conclusions. At some stage, this inexactitude can frustrate even the most dedicated researcher. Leon Festinger, at one time one of the most noted social psychologists in the world, suddenly stopped doing social research, and shifted his attention to the study of colour vision. Perhaps (and this must be considered speculation) he concluded that it was better to pursue an area where definite answers are more attainable. If this *was* his reason, it is easy to feel empathy for him.

In the end, the problem may be too *much* emphasis on scientific rigour, rather than too little. As British psychologist Colin Fraser has suggested, the desire for rigorous methods has led to defining social behaviour in terms that can be addressed experimentally (Fraser 1987). This can result in limiting attention to those questions that can be answered (e.g. 'Will children imitate an adult who hits an inflatable doll?'), while being unable to answer broader questions which may be of greater importance (e.g. 'What role does culture play in aggressive behaviour?'). In effect, anything that doesn't fit the mould gets ignored (such as the effects of social structures on individuals), or is subject to the endless doubts of empirically-minded critics (as with the issue of observing violence). It may be too grandiose to ask 'Whither social psychology?', but it is a concern that social psychology has not yet found satisfactory ways to answer the questions which people find most interesting. Without that ability, its contributions to our understanding of behaviour are likely to remain far less than its potential.

Chapter Summary

- *Social psychology* is concerned with the social dimensions of individual behaviour. As such, it deals with both the way we think about ourselves and others (*social cognition*) and the way social factors affect the way we act (*social influence*).

◆ Research on social behaviour faces many challenges, including the need for *experimental realism* and *external validity*. While researchers prefer the controlled conditions of laboratory experiments, it can be difficult to meet these requirements convincingly in a laboratory, due to participants' awareness of being in a study. Consequently, researchers also use *field experiments* and *correlational research* (such as *naturalistic observation*). In the end, the three methods all have advantages and limitations.

◆ Perhaps the most intensively studied aspect of social behaviour is *aggression*. As with other issues, each approach has its own interpretation of the origins of aggressive behaviour.

◆ The biological approach sees aggression as physiologically-based, in the form of an innate drive (ethology) or as a response to aversive stimuli.

◆ The behaviourist approach views aggression as learned behaviour. In particular, it is seen as behaviour which is sometimes reinforced as a means to a desired goal (*instrumental aggression*), or as the response to frustration (*frustration–aggression hypothesis*).

◆ The cognitive approach also sees aggression as learned, but emphasizes the role of *imitation* (*social learning theory*) and *priming* (*neo-association theory*). Because it does not view aggression as innate, the cognitive approach emphasizes the possibilities for avoiding aggressive behaviour.

◆ The psychodynamic approach, as expressed in Freud's theory, views aggression as an innate drive, which can be redirected by *catharsis* and *defence mechanisms*, but cannot be eliminated.

◆ The humanistic approach sees aggressive behaviour as a response to circumstances which threaten the individual's ability to satisfy needs (Maslow) or as a reaction to arbitrary conditions of worth (Rogers). However, the humanists argue that even in adverse circumstances, aggressive behaviour is only one possible response, and is not inevitable.

◆ *Pro-social behaviour* (such as *altruism*) has also interested social psychologists, though it has been less intensively studied than aggression. The approaches differ in terms of whether altruism is innate or learned, and whether it benefits the person helping (ethical hedonism) or occurs without regard to benefit (genuine altruism).

◆ The study of bystander behaviour in emergencies (*intervention* and *apathy*) provides a practical focus for the study of altruism. Available research suggests that *social influence* and *diffusion of responsibility* can affect the likelihood of intervention, as can *priming* and *social learning*.

◆ Social psychology is an appealing area, but the difficulties of doing research on complex social issues mean that at present it is very hard to draw clear conclusions about the causes of social behaviour.

Key Terms and Concepts

aggression

altruism

catharsis

conformity

diffusion of responsibility

ethical hedonism

experimental realism

frustration–aggression hypothesis

imitation

instrumental aggression

kin altruism

priming

pro-social behaviour

reciprocal altruism

sign stimuli

social cognition

social influence

vacuum activities

Suggestions for Further Reading

For more detail on many of the aspects of social psychology mentioned in this chapter, the *Handbook of Social Psychology* (edited by Gilbert, Fiske and Lindzey) is an excellent current source.

There have been many books about aggression, expressing various points of view. One of the most interesting is an overview by John Klama, *Aggression: Conflict in Animals and Humans Reconsidered*. The authors ('John Klama' is a pseudonym for *John* Durant, Peter *Kl*opfer, and Susan Oy*ama*) provide a history of the concept of aggression as an innate drive, as well as a critique of theories. Alternatively, Berkowitz's *Aggression: Its Causes, Consequences, and Control* provides a thorough review by one of the major researchers on the topic.

The relationship between observing television violence and aggressive behaviour has been extensively studied. In *The Early Window: Effects of Television on Children and Youth*, Liebert and Sprafkin (two social learning researchers) provide an excellent review of both the history of the problem and the evidence.

For a current review of altruistic behaviour, see Batson's chapter in the *Handbook of Social Psychology*.

9

Perspectives on Abnormal Behaviour

Who and What Is Normal?
Introduction
Abnormality in Historical Context
Classifying Abnormal Behaviour
Perspectives on Aetiology and Treatment
The Biological Approach
The Behaviourist Approach
The Cognitive Approach
The Psychodynamic Approach
The Humanistic Approach
Evaluating Therapeutic Techniques
Understanding Schizophrenia

The Medical Model and Schizophrenia
Alternatives to the Medical Model of Schizophrenia
    The Behaviourist Approach
    The Cognitive Approach
    The Psychodynamic Approach
    The Humanistic Approach
Evaluating Our Understanding of Schizophrenia
Conclusion
Chapter Summary
Key Terms and Concepts
Suggestions for Further Reading

Who and What Is Normal?

When I was a graduate student in psychology, I had an experience which made a deep impression on me. Even now, years later, it still seems fresh and vivid. On a summer evening, I was standing on a quiet residential street, talking to a friend. As we talked, we noticed a young man, perhaps twenty-four years old, wandering down the street in our direction. He halted periodically, peering intently, and then would continue. His movements seemed erratic, weaving left and right as he went. It was difficult not to notice him on the quiet street, and at first I thought he was inebriated, or possibly on drugs. I commented to my friend that he seemed to be acting strangely, and she agreed. Then, as he neared us, she spoke to him. The conversation went something like this:

'Can we help you?'

'No', he said, then added, 'yes. Umm . . .', looking around, 'can you tell me where the garbage is?'

'You need a garbage can?', I asked.

'No, no, it's . . .', he said, 'Where does the garbage go?' As I pondered this, he abruptly changed the subject, turning to my friend and asking, 'What's your name?'

'Hope', she said. (It really was her name!)

'That's what I need', he replied, still looking around.

I was beginning to suspect that he was neither drunk nor on drugs, but suffering from a mental disorder. Before I could decide how to proceed, however, my friend addressed him.

'Have you ever been to the Clarke?', she asked, referring to a local psychiatric hospital.

'Umm, yeah.'

'When?'

'Janitor . . .' I wasn't sure if this was his job, or if it somehow connected to the earlier query about garbage.

'Well', Hope continued, 'would you like to go there now?'

'Yeah . . . okay.'

With that, we led him to my car, and drove him to the psychiatric hospital. On the way, Hope was able to elicit his name, and confirm that he lived in our city. At the hospital, we explained the situation, and the staff checked their records, which confirmed that he had been a patient there on several occasions. The diagnosis: schizophrenia. They agreed to admit him, and we left.

I think of this experience whenever I consider abnormal psychology. It represents one of my few encounters in everyday life with an individual classed as 'abnormal'. Taking him to the hospital made me feel I was doing him a kindness – but it also served to alleviate my own distress at dealing with someone who acted very differently from most people.

Consider another episode. In my second year of high school, a new student arrived. By the standards of my peers, he was rather strange: he was a vegetarian, and also refused to wear animal products – meaning he wore plastic belts and plastic shoes, even in midwinter. He had wavy blond hair that by the standards of the day was very 'girlish'. He had no interest in sports, instead preferring to study foreign languages. On many occasions, he would go through the school singing operatic arias, while most students' taste ran to the Beatles and similar groups. Needless to say, he was not very popular. The question is, was he abnormal?

In everyday life, when we describe people as 'abnormal', we are saying that their behaviour violates our expectations in ways that we find difficult to comprehend. In this sense, both the individuals described above might be called 'abnormal'. But is that the same as saying someone has a mental disorder? What defines a mental disorder? And what can be done to help someone suffering from such a disorder?

Introduction

abnormal behaviour
behaviour which is regarded by society as deviant or maladaptive; according to DSM-IV, an individual must be suffering or show maladaptive functioning in order for behaviour to be described as abnormal

Abnormal psychology is concerned with the understanding and treatment of mental disorders. However, defining the boundaries of the field can be difficult: many of those who treat such disorders are doctors, not psychologists; in other cases, help is provided by social workers, clerics or other types of counsellors. Even the term 'mental disorder' is not universally accepted – other terms include *mental illness*, *psychopathology* and *abnormal behaviour*. For our purposes, we will use the terms *mental disorder* and **abnormal behaviour** as interchangeable, and largely avoid the other terms.

Defining abnormal behaviour is a complex issue. Literally, the word 'abnormal' means 'away from the norm', and traditionally the term has been used to describe behaviour which departs from an accepted norm. However, norms can be defined in two ways: *statistical abnormality* refers to behaviour which is rare, while *unconventionality* refers to behaviour which departs from social standards. The boy who sang operas in high school would probably be considered 'abnormal' in the sense that he was unconventional. Historically, the standard of conventionality was often a significant element in judgements of abnormality – not conforming was viewed with suspicion, or worse. Today, however, standards of conformity are somewhat looser, and someone who does not 'fit in' is not automatically viewed as having a mental disorder. Behaviour which is unconventional is also often statistically rare, in that most people behave according to the social standards of the culture they live in. However, statistical rarity, like unconventionality, poses difficulties as a criterion for mental disorders. It is true that many mental disorders are relatively rare, as the statistical criterion would imply. Yet there are many rare forms of behaviour which we would not consider indicative of mental disorder – for example, musical genius. Hence, *neither* of these standards is commonly used today by psychologists as part of the definition of abnormal behaviour. The difficulties these definitions pose are partly due to the complexity of abnormal behaviour, but also reflect how easily value judgements can creep into the process of evaluation. To see this more clearly, let us consider briefly the history of concepts of abnormality.

Abnormality in Historical Context

Throughout history, there have been reports of individuals who acted in aberrant ways. In early pantheistic cultures, whose members believed spirits permeate the world, abnormal behaviour was often explained as possession by evil spirits. The notion of mental disorders as demonic possession has also been common in our own culture. As recently as 1692, in Salem, Massachusetts, twenty young women were executed for being 'bewitched by the Devil' because they exhibited visions, sensory distortions and other odd behaviours. Today, scholars believe they were actually suffering from poisoning from ergot, a fungus which sometimes grows on rye (and is related to LSD) (Caporael 1976). Spirit possession is also central to the origin of the term *hysteria* (used by Freud and others to describe physical symptoms of paralysis and pain of unknown origin). The disorder, whose name comes from the Greek word for 'uterus', was attributed in the Middle Ages to the devil controlling a woman's uterus!

Even when abnormal behaviour was not attributed to spirits, the sense of moral condemnation was often strong. Those with mental disorders were commonly seen as degenerates, less than human. Consequently, common forms of treatment included beatings and imprisonment. This attitude slowly began to change as doctors began to conceive of the behaviour as having physical causes. One of the early pioneers in this regard was Phillipe Pinel, a French doctor who ran the Bicêtre asylum in Paris at the end of the eighteenth century. (This was just after the French Revolution.) Contrary to the notions of demonism and degeneracy, Pinel saw his patients as *ill*, suffering from physical disorders. As a result, he argued for treating them like other patients, rather than chaining them in dark cells. By suggesting that abnormal behaviour was like other forms of illness, Pinel's work marked a shift towards more humane and rational treatment.

At the same time, by suggesting that mental disorders have physical causes, Pinel helped to introduce what has become known as the **medical model** of abnormal behaviour. (Today, this approach is closely linked to the biological approach, as we shall discuss below.) The medicalizing of abnormal behaviour led to doctors becoming the *de facto* authorities on the treatment of such disorders. This trend lasted well into the middle of the twentieth century, and in some ways the medical viewpoint is still the dominant one.

One consequence of the medical model was a move towards rational systems of diagnosis. Doctors, like scientists, had learned the value of classification systems as a means of understanding the world. Diagnosis of physical illness was based on matching symptoms to known diseases; now, the same approach began to be applied to the understanding of mental disorders, with behaviour representing the symptoms. This process accelerated after the Second World War, spurred on by the American Psychiatric Association in the United States, and the World Health Organization internationally. (**Psychiatrists** are medical doctors who specialize in treating mental disorders.) The systems developed by the two groups are known respectively as the Diagnostic and Statistical Manual of Mental Disorders (*DSM*), and the International Classification of Diseases (*ICD*). Though differences still exist, increasingly the two systems are similar, and the groups hope to resolve remaining disparities in the next versions, to be published around 2001. (The current version of the DSM system is DSM-IV, published by the American Psychiatric Association in 1994.) To understand how classification works, and its value and limitations, let us look more closely at the nature and use of the DSM system.

Have you ever encountered a stranger whom you felt showed abnormal behaviour? What was unusual? How did it make you feel?

Classifying Abnormal Behaviour

The most basic concern of diagnosis is to define what we mean by abnormal behaviour. This is not always easy, especially since many theorists (including

---

medical model a theory of abnormal behaviour which assumes that all such disorders have physiological causes

psychiatrists medical doctors who specialize in treating mental disorders; by comparison, clinical psychologists typically have a PhD rather than an MD degree

For further consideration

Freud) believe there is a continuum between 'normal' and 'abnormal', with no absolute dividing line. As discussed earlier, defining abnormality in terms of social norms or frequency of occurrence seems questionable. Instead, DSM-IV uses two primary criteria to determine whether a person's behaviour warrants being described as a mental disorder: suffering and maladaptiveness.

Suffering implies that the behaviour causes the individual distress or anxiety; *maladaptiveness* implies that the person is hindered from functioning effectively in significant ways. For example, a person who experiences intense anxiety at the prospect of venturing out of home would be viewed as suffering; this type of anxiety reflects a disorder called *agoraphobia*. Maladaptiveness could take many forms: drinking which interferes with work performance, disordered thinking which prevents communicating with others, uncontrollable outbursts of rage and so on. Most psychologists and other mental health professionals agree that behaviour must fit one or both of these criteria in order to be considered abnormal. However, exceptions exist even to these criteria. For example, an individual with **anti-social personality disorder** may show a history of acts of violence towards others, unaccompanied by guilt. These individuals may not report either suffering or unsatisfactory functioning, yet their behaviour is still deemed abnormal.

The intent of using suffering and maladaptiveness as criteria is to free the definition of abnormality from arbitrary social judgements (such as unconventionality). However, even these criteria can be open to interpretation. For example, if a person prefers beachcombing to banking, does this suggest maladaptation? The possibility of social bias in diagnosis is a particular concern when factors like culture and ethnicity are involved (Fabrega 1994). For example, belief in communication with the dead is common in Cuban culture, but could lead to a diagnosis of psychosis for a Cuban-American being assessed by a non-Cuban (Alonso and Jeffery 1988). Similarly, matching/ mismatching ethnicity and native language for therapist and patient have been shown to affect various aspects of treatment for Asians, blacks and Native Americans (Sue *et al.* 1991). In response to such concerns, one major goal of DSM-IV was to provide guidance to clinicians with respect to the influence of culture, ethnicity, age and gender on diagnosis and treatment. While the risk of misdiagnosis due to such factors is a genuine concern, it must be acknowledged that in many circumstances the standards are quite obvious (e.g. someone who complains of intense anxiety is obviously suffering).

Assuming that a person's behaviour *is* regarded as abnormal, DSM-IV tries to identify the particular form of disorder, using five major dimensions ('axes') for assessment (see Figure 9.1). Axes I to III represent the basic types of disorders (depression, schizophrenia, obsessive-compulsive disorder etc.) and ongoing psychological or physical conditions which could affect adjustment. Axis IV looks at the stressors in the person's life which may contribute to a problem (e.g. the recent death of a family member). Axis V looks at the person's general adaptation in three areas of daily life (social relations, work and leisure); this helps in determining the severity of the current problem, as well as influencing the prognosis for recovery. For example, someone diagnosed as depressed will have a better prognosis if

anti-social personality disorder a behaviour pattern in which an individual shows a history of acts of violence towards others, unaccompanied by guilt; although these individuals may not report either suffering or unsatisfactory functioning (the generally accepted standard for abnormality), their behaviour is still deemed abnormal because it violates society's norms in such significant ways

Classifying abnormal behaviour using DSM-IV		
AXIS I	CLINICAL SYNDROMES	Primary classification of disorders, based on behavioural symptoms; e.g. phobias, depression, drug abuse, schizophrenia.
AXIS II	PERSONALITY AND DEVELOPMENTAL DISORDERS	Personality disorders – long-standing patterns of maladaptive behaviour.
		Developmental disorders – disorders which affect learning, language, and other intellectual skills.
AXIS III	GENERAL MEDICAL CONDITIONS	Any physical problems which may be relevant to the person's condition.
AXIS IV	PSYCHOSOCIAL AND ENVIRONMENTAL FACTORS	A six-point rating scale for the severity of stressors which contribute to the person's condition.
AXIS V	GLOBAL ASSESSMENT OF FUNCTIONING	A general evaluation of functioning during the past year in terms of work, leisure, and social relationships.

Figure 9.1   Classifying mental disorders As noted in the text, DSM-IV classifies behaviour using five dimensions or 'axes' (categories copyrighted by American Psychiatric Association 1994).

their general life history suggests a high level of functioning than if they have a history of mood problems, poor social relationships and an erratic employment record. By making such assessments part of the overall diagnosis, DSM-IV tries to provide a more detailed, individualized description.

Not surprisingly, not all disorders are equally common. In a large-scale study done in five cities in the United States, researchers attempted to identify the incidence rates for various disorders using criteria from an earlier version of the DSM (version III) (Regier *et al.* 1988). The researchers evaluated the number of cases diagnosed for each disorder over a one-month interval; lifetime risks are typically regarded as about twice as high (see Figure 9.2). There are several points to notice about these results. First, there are significant differences in the frequency of occurrence of different disorders, and in most cases, the rates for men and women also differ. (This has sometimes led to charges of sex bias in diagnosis – hence the concern to address the issue in DSM-IV.) Second, one should note that many of these disorders are not very rare: if one extrapolates to lifetime rates, then about 12 per cent of the population will suffer from a serious phobia at some time in their lives, and roughly the same number of people will experience a mood disorder meriting treatment.

Classifying mental disorders, as with other forms of medical diagnosis, is intended to help to identify the cause of a problem and to guide treatment. This is more problematical for mental disorders than for other forms of illness, because we do not yet know the causes (**aetiology**) of most mental disorders. (As we will see in the next section, this is a major source of disagreement among the five approaches.) In fact, some critics have focused

aetiology the study of the causes of a disease or mental disorder

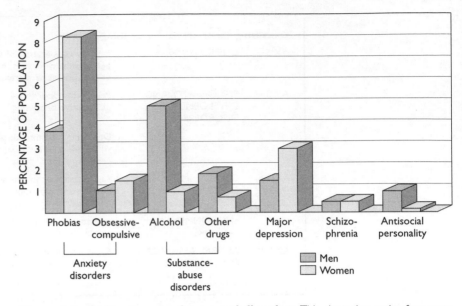

Figure 9.2 Incidence rates for mental disorders This chart shows the frequency of occurrence for some of the most common disorders. The percentages are for incidence rates over a one-month period in the United States; lifetime risks are roughly twice as high. (Data from Regier *et al.* 1988.)

on this lack of knowledge as part of a challenge to the entire concept of classification. For example, the absence of a theoretical model of aetiology within DSM-IV has led to the criticism that the system is untestable (Follette and Houts 1996). A more extreme view is that we cannot identify the causes because there is no such thing as a mental disorder. Thomas Szasz, himself a psychiatrist, has argued that mental disorders are a 'myth' (Szasz 1974). To Szasz, identifying behaviour as abnormal is simply a way for society and clinicians to justify interfering in an individual's life. (So-called *community treatment orders*, which force an individual diagnosed with a mental disorder to take medication even if discharged from a hospital, are a current focus for such debates.)

Most clinicians reject such claims, but in recent years there has been increasing recognition by professionals that classifying behaviour as abnormal can have adverse consequences. Within our culture, the term 'mental disorder' has a negative connotation; as a consequence, diagnosis assigns a label to someone which identifies them as being different, or *deviant*. Such labels serve as a form of **stigma**, a marking which is used by society to treat someone as an outsider (Goffman 1963). In the case of mental disorders, this results in problems of social rejection which often make recovery more difficult (Clausen 1981). To some extent, this problem has been recognized in DSM-IV, which recommends referring to an individual *having* a disorder, in contrast to the earlier common practice of equating the disorder with the person. For example, one should refer to 'a person with schizophrenia', not 'a schizophrenic'.

stigma a mark or label which identifies an individual as deviant, resulting in social rejection

The stigmatizing effects of diagnostic labels illustrate the ultimate dilemma involved in defining abnormality: balancing the benefits and detriments of the classification of behaviour. Advocates of diagnostic systems tend to believe that mental disorders are purely objective phenomena, like a tumour or tuberculosis, while critics of such systems argue that abnormality is simply a reflection of arbitrary social norms. The truth is probably somewhere in between. On the one hand, stigmatizing and misdiagnosis for cultural or other reasons are possible, as critics have charged. However, diagnostic categories seem useful in understanding an individual's behaviour, and may aid in treatment. The basic standard of abnormality employed in DSM-IV – that the individual shows significant distress and/or maladaptive functioning – is one that most people would probably find reasonable. Indeed, the autobiographies of those who have suffered from disorders like schizophrenia and depression suggest that they view their disorders as real, not as an arbitrary social conceit (Vonnegut 1975; Endler 1982).

At present, there are no final answers to this debate. In part, disagreements over the issue of classification reflect differences in assumptions about the underlying causes of abnormal behaviour. In the end, the debate always seems to come back to the causes of abnormal behaviour: if we could be certain of the origin of particular disorders, many of the questions of bias, misdiagnosis and arbitrariness of standards would be resolved. For now, most clinicians, faced with what they see as real suffering, simply do their best to help.

For further consideration

As Figure 9.2 indicates, various forms of abnormal behaviour are more common than many people think. Do you know anyone who suffers from a serious phobia? Who has had a mood disorder such as depression? Would you react differently to the person in the two cases? What does this tell you about your own attitudes towards abnormal behaviour?

Perspectives on Aetiology and Treatment

To a large extent, treatment methods tend to be linked to ideas about the causes of abnormal behaviour. Consequently, one cannot discuss theories of treatment without also discussing theories of *aetiology* (the study of the causes of a disorder). What makes this difficult is that many types of factors can contribute to a particular behaviour. When one speaks of 'cause', one may actually be referring to *predisposing factors* (genetic inheritance, prior experiences and beliefs), *precipitating factors* (immediate stressors like loss of a family member) or *sustaining factors* (consequences of a disorder that help to perpetuate it, such as reactions of family or society). In addition, there may be more than one factor of a given type – for example, children of individuals with schizophrenia may be at risk because of genetic factors and also because of growing up with parents who provided a faulty model for behaviour (both of these would be predisposing factors). It may also be that different forms of abnormal behaviour have different aetiologies; for example, schizophrenia may have a very different origin from depression. Consequently, the search for a single cause, and a single form of treatment, may often be fruitless. Nonetheless, each of the five approaches tends to emphasize particular types of causal factors, and given the current state of evidence, each feels justified in utilizing the particular treatment techniques which it does. To see how they differ, let us consider how each approach views aetiology and treatment.

The Biological Approach

As noted earlier, the biological approach to abnormal behaviour is based on the *medical model*, which assumes that disorders are based on physical causes. Given the role of the brain in the control of behaviour, the causes are usually attributed to abnormalities in either the structure or the functioning of the brain.

The strongest justification for this approach has come from advances in *psychopharmacology* (the study of drugs which affect mental processes and/or behaviour). Although the use of drugs to alter behaviour has a long history (alcohol, for example, has been used in some form in nearly every culture), the greatest advances have come in the past few decades. Today, a large and growing range of drugs exist to deal with many forms of disorders. For example, tranquillizers are used to relieve anxiety, anti-depressants help to relieve depression and anti-psychotics relieve hallucinations and mental confusion. In addition, sedatives often take the place of physical restraints like straitjackets. Not only do drugs frequently seem to alleviate symptoms, but drug therapy also seems relatively efficient: Compared to alternative treatments like psychoanalysis or behaviour modification, it is relatively low-cost and fast-acting, and requires comparatively little of the doctor's time. For all these reasons, the use of psychoactive drugs has become extremely common both in the formal treatment of mental disorders and as part of the practice of many family doctors.

This popularity has not come without criticism. First, treatment using drugs is still largely based on symptom relief, and does not directly address the issue of causation. While our understanding of how drugs work is becoming much more precise, this is not necessarily the same thing as identifying the cause of the disorder. Indeed, many aspects of the available data suggest that drugs may not be addressing the root causes of disorders. This is clear when one examines the treatment of **depression** with drugs. One of the unsolved problems of anti-depressant use is why, since the drug reaches the brain in a matter of hours, there is often a considerable time lag between the onset of usage and improvement of mood (intervals of two weeks are typical). In addition, individuals who show comparable symptoms often do not respond equally to a particular drug. (In the case of anti-depressants, about one-third of individuals with depression don't respond to any available drug.) Even more troublesome is the possibility that many problems for which drugs are prescribed may be self-limiting. For example, according to its manufacturer, Xanax (alprazolam) is a drug which is designed to alleviate panic disorder (frequent attacks of intense anxiety and panic). The

depression a mood disorder characterized by sleep disturbances, fatigue and low self-esteem; in *major depressive disorder*, the symptoms are severe enough to seriously hamper normal functioning, and can be accompanied by thoughts of suicide

clinical trials which led to its approval showed that after four weeks, 50 per cent of patients taking Xanax were completely free of symptoms, compared to 28 per cent of those taking a placebo. Interestingly, however, after *eight* weeks there was no significant difference between the two groups (Editors 1993). More broadly, psychiatrist Peter Kramer contends that the use of medication as treatment for behaviours like depression has the capacity to alter the individual's sense of self, a response which involves cultural conceptions as much as physiological reactions (Kramer 1993).

At present, there are still many questions associated with using drugs to treat abnormal behaviour. At a practical level, drugs often *do* seem to be useful in alleviating symptoms, but that does not prove they are actually addressing the causes of disorders. Nonetheless, drug therapy is consistent with the medical model, and, as we shall see when examining schizophrenia, may very well hold important clues to the understanding of abnormal behaviour.

Another application of the biological approach to the study of mental disorders is genetic research. For example, researchers have used concordance studies to examine the role of genetics in disorders like schizophrenia and bipolar mood disorder (formerly called 'manic-depression'). The results of such studies are often very variable, and open to conflicting interpretations. For example, reports of a genetic link for bipolar disorder, announced in the late 1980s, were later found to be flawed (Kelsoe *et al.* 1989). More recent studies cautiously talk of a possible genetic 'vulnerability' to bipolar disorder (Straub 1994). The available evidence does not conclusively show that any major form of abnormal behaviour is *solely* genetic. In addition, genetic analysis at present can only indicate an individual's risk – there are no current treatments designed to address mental disorders at the genetic level. If genetic analysis eventually does prove fruitful, it will provide strong support for the medical model.

In summary, the biological approach sees abnormal behaviour as having a physiological cause, an assumption known as the *medical model*. Within this framework, its greatest success has been drug therapy, which has produced dramatic benefits in the past few decades. However, until we understand more about the causes of abnormal behaviour, it is not clear if it addresses the root of such disorders, or simply masks the symptoms. Genetic research may eventually prove useful, *provided* the primary causes of disorders are in fact genetic in origin. For the biological approach, as for all the approaches, the only criterion for testing a theory at present is to try to evaluate its success in alleviating the misery associated with mental disorders.

The Behaviourist Approach

As one might expect, the behaviourist approach interprets abnormal behaviour in terms of faulty learning. Like all behaviours, abnormal behaviour is acquired through a process of conditioning and learning. In the absence of known organic problems, this explanation does not assume there is any underlying causal factor, as the medical model does; instead, the behaviourists say the behaviour *is* the problem. Consequently, behaviourists have relatively little interest in classification, since learned behaviour is too variable to make categories very meaningful. To the extent that classification is seen as at all useful, it is typically as a shorthand description – for example, phobias represent learned fears.

The emphasis on learning leads the behaviourists to reject the medical model. Similarly, their focus on behaviour rather than mental processes places them in opposition to the other three approaches, all of which suggest that cognitive processes of various sorts mediate the behaviour. In addition, the behaviourist approach to treatment is largely ahistorical, since what matters is not the circumstances under which abnormal behaviour was acquired in the past, but the need to identify ways to modify it in the present. Because of the emphasis on changing the undesired behaviour, therapy based on the behaviourist approach is generally referred to as *behaviour modification*. Often, practitioners abbreviate this to 'behaviour mod'.

Several forms of behaviour modification exist, based on either classical or operant conditioning. One of the earliest techniques, derived from classical conditioning, is **systematic desensitization**, which is designed to treat phobias (unrealistic fears) and related anxiety disorders. As noted in Chapter 3, Watson had demonstrated with little Albert that it was possible to develop a fear by classical conditioning. Although he was subsequently unsuccessful in eliminating Albert's conditioned fear, the notion that phobias could be explained in terms of classical conditioning was established. Eventually, Joseph Wolpe developed systematic desensitization, which seeks to eliminate the fear response by replacing it with a competing response of relaxation (Wolpe 1973).

In conception, systematic desensitization is very simple, being based on two basic principles of conditioning: First, an individual cannot produce two competing reflex responses at the same time (such as fear and relaxation). Second, classical conditioning often involves *stimulus generalization*. In practice, the desensitization procedure requires elements of timing and judgement which make it more than a mechanical process. Typically, the clinician works with the individual to identify the type of stimuli which trigger the phobia – that is, the *conditioned stimulus* or CS. For example, someone afraid of bees might panic if a bee buzzed near his head. Next, the individual is taught techniques for inducing relaxation, often associated to a cue (which becomes a CS for relaxing). Then, the clinician and individual develop a list of fear-evoking stimuli, ranging from very mild to very intense. This list is called a **hierarchy of fears**, since stimuli are listed in order of the intensity of fear which they elicit. Then, working gradually, the therapist attempts to recondition the person so that the stimuli in the hierarchy become associated with relaxing rather than fear. For example, the person might think of driving by a beehive in a closed car; once they can imagine this without fear, she would proceed to the next stimulus – seeing a bee outside the window, and so on. Once the person can confront the stimulus which originally evoked the greatest fear (imagining a bee buzzing near their head) yet remain relaxed, the phobia has been eliminated (see Figure 9.3).

Systematic desensitization has been successfully employed for a wide variety of fears, ranging from the fear of snakes or heights to more unusual fears like fear of music (Wolpe 1973; Goldfried and Davison 1994). Airlines

systematic desensitization a technique based on classical conditioning which is designed to treat phobias (unrealistic fears) and related anxiety disorders by gradually diminishing the undesired response

hierarchy of fears in systematic desensitization, a list of fear-evoking stimuli, ranging from very mild to very intense, arranged in order of the intensity of fear which they elicit

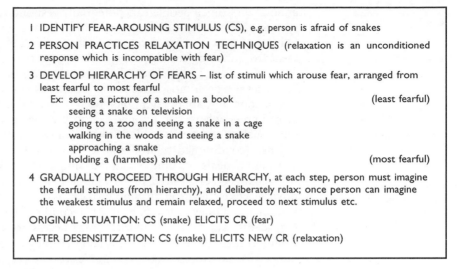

1 IDENTIFY FEAR-AROUSING STIMULUS (CS), e.g. person is afraid of snakes

2 PERSON PRACTICES RELAXATION TECHNIQUES (relaxation is an unconditioned response which is incompatible with fear)

3 DEVELOP HIERARCHY OF FEARS – list of stimuli which arouse fear, arranged from least fearful to most fearful
    Ex: seeing a picture of a snake in a book   (least fearful)
       seeing a snake on television
       going to a zoo and seeing a snake in a cage
       walking in the woods and seeing a snake
       approaching a snake
       holding a (harmless) snake   (most fearful)

4 GRADUALLY PROCEED THROUGH HIERARCHY, at each step, person must imagine the fearful stimulus (from hierarchy), and deliberately relax; once person can imagine the weakest stimulus and remain relaxed, proceed to next stimulus etc.

ORIGINAL SITUATION: CS (snake) ELICITS CR (fear)

AFTER DESENSITIZATION: CS (snake) ELICITS NEW CR (relaxation)

Figure 9.3 The basic procedure for systematic desensitization

have even sponsored desensitization sessions for individuals who fear flying, based on the very reasonable premise that such individuals otherwise will not be potential customers! Although often effective, rarely does the success rate for treatment go higher than about 70 per cent. This has prompted concerns about how to improve the effectiveness of systematic desensitization, and also criticisms of its underlying premises. In looking at the other approaches, we will return to this issue, but one should not overlook the fact that systematic desensitization is relatively time- and cost-efficient, as well as frequently successful.

The underlying principle of systematic desensitization – substituting a competing response for the undesired response – is sometimes referred to as *counter-conditioning*. Just as it can be used to eliminate a fear, it has also been employed to *induce* an aversive response to stimuli which are associated with existing undesirable behaviours. This procedure, called **aversive conditioning**, has been applied in dealing with a range of disorders, from sexual fetishes to alcoholism. For example, an alcoholic might be given a drug called *antabuse*, which when present in the body reacts with alcohol to cause extreme nausea and vomiting. Then, if the person drinks, they will get sick, thus establishing an association that alcohol leads to sickness rather than pleasure. In practice, this procedure is only moderately effective – in part because drinkers quickly realize that by not taking the antabuse, they can drink with impunity (Forrest 1985). More than other forms of behaviour modification, aversive conditioning is controversial, since it involves deliberately causing pain or discomfort. Consequently objections have been raised, even by psychologists who support more positive forms of behaviour therapy (McConnell 1974).

Operant conditioning has also been used in therapy, albeit with more limited success. Therapeutic attempts to alter operant behaviour through conditioning are dependent on controlling the relevant reinforcers (Hayes

aversive conditioning
a form of behaviour modification which is designed to induce an aversive response to stimuli that are associated with existing undesirable behaviours

token economy a form of behaviour modification based on operant conditioning; most commonly used in institutional settings, it involves giving conditioned reinforcers ('tokens') for doing specific behaviours

et al. 1995). Since people can potentially respond to a wide range of reinforcers, this can be a difficult task. Indeed, one writer has suggested that failures of conditioning derive from the individual getting more reinforcement from making the therapist look foolish than from the *intended* reinforcers (Carlson 1990). Thus, the use of shaping and operant reinforcement has generally been most effective in situations which are highly structured.

One operant application has been the establishment of institutional programmes where conditioned reinforcers are given for specific behaviours. Such programmes, called **token economies**, allow individuals to earn 'tokens' (conditioned reinforcers) for doing things like making their bed, arriving at meals on time or similar simple tasks. In turn, the tokens can be exchanged for desired items like sweets or cigarettes, or used to buy privileges like television viewing or day passes. In effect, the tokens become a form of 'money' (which is itself a conditioned reinforcer), for which individuals will perform 'work'. Since access to such reinforcers can be readily controlled in an institutional environment, and the desired behaviours easily monitored, token economies can be very effective in establishing behavioural goals (Ayllon and Azrin 1968). Their primary disadvantages are the careful planning required, the requirement for a structured environment and, like other forms of behaviour modification, the ethical problems which some perceive. With regard to the last point, Skinner has noted the irony in popular attitudes: if we directly (and efficiently) seek to modify behaviour, people get concerned, but if we seek to do it indirectly (and thereby less efficiently), then that is considered acceptable (Skinner 1971)! While token economies do seem to work, their practical limitations are such that they are nonetheless relatively uncommon today.

Behaviour therapy today takes many forms, and has been applied to many sorts of problems (Hayes *et al*. 1995). In general, the techniques reflect the assumption that the goal of treatment is to change the undesired behaviour. As indicated, these techniques often show relatively high success rates, and the course of treatment is often very brief. Despite these advantages, behaviour modification has been criticized by other approaches on both ethical and theoretical grounds. Certainly, the focused nature of behaviour therapy makes informed consent very important – but the same thing could be said of *any* form of therapy. However, other approaches have also challenged the assumption that abnormal behaviour has no underlying causes. This issue has already been discussed in relation to the biological approach; let us see how the other approaches explain the origins of abnormal behaviour.

For further consideration

Critics have sometimes charged that behaviour modification is manipulative. Assuming that the individual decides what behaviours they want to modify, how do you view this criticism?

The Cognitive Approach

Cognitive theorists reject the behaviourist assumption that abnormal behaviour has no underlying cause. Instead, they view it in terms of underlying

cognitive behaviour modification an extension of behaviour modification which uses cognitive mediation (such as observing a model) in addition to basic conditioning techniques

mediational processes – either symbolic mediation of conditioning, or the influence of faulty cognitions. The possible role of symbolic mediation has already been alluded to in the previous section, and therapy based on this premise (called **cognitive behaviour modification**) is really an extension of behaviour therapy. By contrast, interest in *faulty cognitions* has emerged purely from the cognitive tradition, as seen in the work of Albert Ellis. Theorists like Ellis (Aaron Beck is another example) focus on how behaviour is affected by distortions in *how* we think and *what* we think – such as false assumptions about ourselves and the world, inappropriate schemata and unrealistic expectations of life.

Cognitive behaviour modification can be traced back to the work of Albert Bandura, one of the pioneers of cognitive social learning theory. Bandura's experimental research on imitation had already led him to recognize that imitation can often be more effective for learning than being reinforced. He began applying this concept to the use of behaviour modification for treating phobias.

As noted earlier, systematic desensitization rarely has a 100 per cent success rate; one factor which may account for this is the dependence on *imagining* fear-evoking stimuli, rather than dealing with actual stimuli. Imitation, of course, would involve actual stimuli. One way to separate out this component is by comparing the effects of observing a model (an individual who acts out the desired behaviour) with actually imitating the behaviour of the model. This can be seen in a study in which Bandura compared the effects of systematic desensitization, observing a model, and *participant modelling* (where the individual actually does what the model does) in the treatment of a snake phobia (Bandura 1970). Individuals using systematic desensitization and those using simple modelling showed similar improvement compared to a control group; thus, simply using real stimuli did not enhance treatment. However, those who used participant modelling did significantly better than those using either of the other treatments, with 11 out of 12 individuals showing complete elimination of the phobia in follow-up tests. Thus, active imitation of the desired behaviour seemed more effective than either observing a model or conventional behaviour modification.

Subsequently, Donald Meichenbaum (1977) extended this approach to the imitation of thought processes. The individual and therapist work together to identify problem areas, and then develop new self-statements that will be more effective. For instance, a person who has given a speech thinks, 'I was really boring; nobody will want to invite me again.' This negative assessment is self-defeating, in that it does not focus on any ways to improve behaviour in the future. Instead, the therapist might encourage the person to frame the assessment in more productive ways, such as thinking, 'That talk was pretty dry; I'll have to plan a better opening next time, and vary the pacing more.' By observing and imitating alternate ways of thinking, the individual can develop alternative strategies that lead to more effective behaviour (Freeman and Reinecke 1995).

The emphasis which Meichenbaum places on thought patterns is very similar to the work of Albert Ellis, although Ellis works within a different theoretical framework. Ellis focuses on the relationship between thoughts and emotions, using what he calls rational-emotive therapy (Ellis 1993).

rational-emotive therapy
a form of therapy developed
by Albert Ellis which focuses
on the relationship between
thoughts and emotions,
particularly negative emotions
which arise from an
individual's faulty
interpretations of experiences

Rational-emotive therapy argues that negative emotions arise from people's faulty interpretations of experiences, not from the experiences themselves. Using what he calls the *ABC principle*, Ellis says an *a*ctivating event (A) triggers a faulty *b*elief (B), which in turn triggers an emotional *c*onsequence (C). While we tend to assume that A causes C, it is really the belief (B) that is responsible for our emotional reactions. For example, Bob meets someone for the first time at a business conference, and comes away feeling the person did not like him (the activating event). He then feels unhappy (the emotional consequence). Ellis would point out that this emotion was triggered by the irrational expectation (belief) that everyone Bob meets should like him. Realistically, there are always people whom we don't get along with; while this is unfortunate, a realistic attitude is to accept this, rather than feeling devastated. Similarly, people who focus excessively on negative events are engaging in what Ellis humorously calls *awfulizing*.

cognitive restructuring
in Ellis's rational-emotive
therapy, a process for
modifying faulty beliefs and
the negative emotions they
produce, in order to develop
realistic beliefs and self-
acceptance

Faulty beliefs represent distortions in schemata pertaining to oneself, the world and the future. Thus, Ellis works in very directive ways to modify the beliefs which lead to negative emotions. This process, called **cognitive restructuring**, is designed to develop realistic beliefs and self-acceptance (Ellis 1993). At first glance, Ellis's emphasis on self-worth and developing beliefs which foster growth seems similar to the humanistic approach. However, his technique is much more directive, and he believes that the therapist should focus on the individual's cognitive patterns, rather than being concerned about empathy.

Ellis originally developed rational-emotive therapy as a means of treating depression, but it has been subsequently applied to a range of other problems, including personality disorders, panic disorder and other forms of anxiety, and eating disorders (Beck 1993; Freeman and Reinecke 1995). Studies of its effectiveness as a treatment for depression suggest it is at least as effective as other forms of therapy (Dobson 1989), and may be better than older forms of *anti-depressants* (so-called tricyclic drugs versus newer drugs like Prozac) in preventing relapses (Hollon *et al.* 1992). As a treatment for panic disorder, it seems to work as well as behaviourist relaxation therapy, and better than brief non-directive psychotherapy (Beck *et al.* 1992, 1994). More broadly, rational-emotive therapy has been significant in making clinicians aware of the role cognitions play in abnormal behaviour.

Despite these apparent successes, we still know very little about what the significant elements of the therapeutic process are (Haaga and Davison 1993). (Compared to cognitive behaviour modification, for example, rational-emotive therapy is both more complex and less specific.) Perhaps the most interesting question is *why* focusing on cognitions sometimes seems more effective than focusing on the behaviour itself. This question is particularly interesting given the bi-directional links between cognition and behaviour. While cognitive theorists emphasize how thoughts mediate behaviour, from a practical standpoint we recognize that changing behaviour can *also* affect cognitions, making the direction of causation less than clear. Cognitive therapists frequently suggest that emphasizing the cognitive mediators produces broader-scale changes (i.e. more generalization) than does modifying specific responses. While this may in fact be true, at present our understanding of this question is still quite limited. The relationship between thoughts and behaviour remains an important issue when we look at psychodynamic and humanistic techniques, both of which emphasize the importance of cognitive insight in changing abnormal behaviour.

The Psychodynamic Approach

The various theories which make up the psychodynamic approach all assume that abnormal behaviour is the product of some form of inner conflict. For Freud, this was seen in the dynamics of id, ego and superego. For other theorists, the conflicting elements vary (for example, Jung emphasized the relations between the ego and the collective unconscious). However they view the source of conflict, all psychodynamic theorists agree on two points: first, that abnormal behaviour is only the *symptom*, not the *cause*, of the problem; second, that treatment requires gaining awareness and understanding of the underlying conflicts which represent the true cause of disorders (Jones and Pulos 1993).

In asserting that behaviour is a symptom, not the problem itself, psychodynamic theorists have been critical of behaviour therapy. Since the behaviour is only an expression of the problem, they assert that trying to change the behaviour without addressing the underlying cause will prove ineffective. Instead, it will simply lead to **symptom substitution**, the expression of the problem in a new way. For example, if a person complains of a fear of snakes, and this reflects denial of sexual impulses, then eliminating the fear of snakes without addressing the sexual conflict will only lead to some other problem – possibly a different phobia, possibly a very different manifestation. However, this concept has found little experimental support. For example, bedwetting might be interpreted by a Freudian as reflecting Oedipal conflicts, yet behaviour therapy can successfully eliminate it while simultaneously increasing self-esteem (Baker 1969). Overall, the evidence suggests that symptom substitution is not a consequence of successful behaviour therapy (Kazdin and Wilson 1980).

The second point, that successful treatment requires awareness of the underlying conflicts, is basic to the therapeutic techniques used by psychodynamic theorists. The development of **insight** into the causes of behaviour represents the basic goal of treatment. Using a variety of techniques, the therapist analyses the underlying conflicts, and helps the individual to understand how they are related to outward behaviour. Once the individual understands the causes of their behaviour, then change in the behaviour should follow.

At first glance, the psychodynamic approach's emphasis on insight seems similar to both the cognitive and humanistic approaches to treatment. However, there are differences among the three in both the process and the types of cognitions emphasized. As noted earlier, the cognitive approach is largely present-oriented, whereas psychodynamic theories tend to focus on how present behaviour is related to past experience. In addition, cognitive theories like Ellis's see faulty beliefs as being the direct cause of disorders, while psychodynamic theories see the unconscious conflicts as the actual cause. While both psychodynamic and humanistic therapies emphasize insight, the

symptom substitution in psychodynamic theory, the assumption that changing overt behaviour without addressing the underlying dynamics will lead to the expression of the problem in a new way

insight in psychotherapy, awareness of the underlying conflicts which are regarded as the causes of behaviour

types of conflict involved are different, as is the role of the therapist. In psychodynamic therapy, it is typically (though not always) the therapist's responsibility to analyse the behaviour and identify the underlying causes; in humanistic therapy, as we shall see shortly, the individual, not the therapist, is the final judge of what is significant or not. Hence, while all three approaches utilize insight, there are differences as well as similarities.

The prototype for all psychodynamic therapies, and still probably the best known, is Freudian psychoanalysis. Since the development of his theory of personality was largely related to his clinical practice, Freud in fact began with a desire to treat abnormal behaviour. His experiences with patients shaped not only his ideas about how the mind works, but also his views on treatment techniques. One of his basic assumptions was the value of *catharsis* – the release of emotions associated with the underlying conflict, often through remembering traumatic experiences. This emotional release, in turn, could help to foster insight.

Freud used a number of techniques to identify the underlying causes of conflict, all based on analysing various aspects of the individual's behaviour. Among the most important were free association, transference and resistance. (Note that *projective tests* like the Rorschach ink blot test came later, and have been shown to be poor assessment tools (Blatt 1975).) *Free association* involves having the person relax, and say whatever comes into awareness – thoughts, feelings, even bodily sensations. Freud would then seek to interpret the contents of such reports by looking for patterns and symbolic meanings. Freud also believed that the relationship between the individual and the therapist could come to represent other past relationships, often between the individual and a parent. The analysis of the emotions involved in this **transference** could then provide an important tool for understanding the development of current conflicts. In the same way, if a patient rejects the analyst's interpretations of the meaning of behaviour, this **resistance** can represent a defence against acknowledging the identified conflict. Thus, in various ways, all aspects of the therapeutic situation become relevant to analysing the underlying dynamics which produce the disorder.

Critics have often pointed out that Freud's approach to therapy places the therapist in a position of great power. Only the analyst can determine what is significant and what is not; in fact, if a patient objects to a particular interpretation, that is simply taken as evidence of resistance! Another limitation is that traditional psychoanalysis is a very open-ended process, potentially lasting several years. (Partly in response to this limitation, more recent theorists have worked on developing forms of brief psychodynamic therapy.) In fairness, one must evaluate these criticisms in the context of the overall effectiveness of Freud's therapeutic techniques.

One concern in evaluating Freudian therapy is finding appropriate measures of efficacy, since psychoanalysts seek not simply symptom relief, but also broader changes in the awareness and functioning of the individual. (Other psychodynamic therapies would generally make the same claim.) Consequently, comparing psychodynamic techniques to alternatives which emphasize narrower goals, such as behaviour therapy, can pose difficulties. In addition, since real-world evaluations involve individuals who are suffering, there are also ethical limits on doing comparisons. (For example,

transference in psychoanalysis, the displacement of drive energy from past relationships, often between the individual and a parent, to the relationship between the individual and the therapist

resistance in psychoanalysis, the rejection by an individual of the analyst's interpretations of the meaning of behaviour; regarded as a defence mechanism

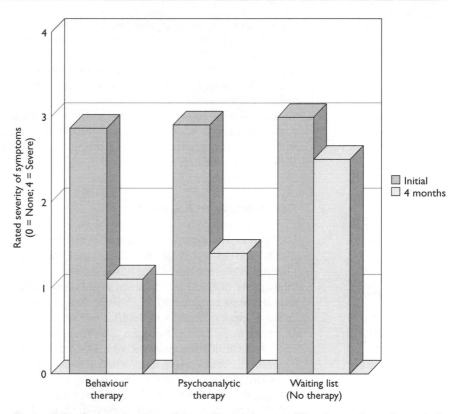

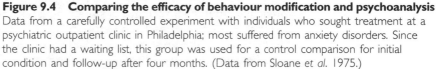

Figure 9.4 Comparing the efficacy of behaviour modification and psychoanalysis
Data from a carefully controlled experiment with individuals who sought treatment at a psychiatric outpatient clinic in Philadelphia; most suffered from anxiety disorders. Since the clinic had a waiting list, this group was used for a control comparison for initial condition and follow-up after four months. (Data from Sloane *et al.* 1975.)

one cannot deliberately deny people access to treatment in order to create control groups, or deliberately offer inferior forms of treatment.)

These difficulties have not diminished the enthusiasm of researchers, however; in the past three decades there have been literally hundreds of studies assessing psychodynamic and other forms of therapy. One well-controlled study, done at a clinic in Philadelphia, randomly assigned individuals suffering from anxiety disorders to either behaviour therapy or psychoanalytic therapy (Sloane *et al.* 1975). A control group consisted of those on a waiting list for treatment. After four months, all three groups had shown some improvement, although the results were much better for those in treatment than for the control group (see Figure 9.4). Interestingly, in this study, there was no significant difference between psychoanalysis and behaviour therapy. Obviously, this represents only one study, and it involves a type of disorder for which psychoanalysis may be fairly well suited. A review of four major outcome studies concluded that 60–90 per cent of 'suitable' patients derived 'substantial therapeutic benefit' from psychoanalytic therapy (Bachrach *et al.* 1991). However, the word *suitable* is an important qualifier, and the authors concluded that effectiveness is not easily predicted from initial patient assessments. Interestingly, a separate analysis of one of the studies reviewed, done by the Meninger Foundation, suggests that much of the benefit may come from the empathy and concern which the therapist shows, rather than from the specific insights (Wallerstein 1989). Since this is potentially a factor in all forms of therapy, we will return to it when discussing the general issue of evaluating the treatment of abnormal behaviour. For now, it is sufficient to suggest that psychodynamic therapy, including psychoanalysis, produces some benefits – though the reasons for improvement may not be those cited by the theorists.

The Humanistic Approach

The humanistic approach argues that the meaning of behaviour can only be understood in terms of an individual's own perceptions and experience. This *phenomenological* emphasis, as it is referred to, is central to all of the various humanistic theories, and has particular significance when considering abnormal behaviour. Since judgements of what is appropriate or 'normal' depend on an individual's own perceptions, objective definitions of 'abnormal' are meaningless. As such, humanistic therapists have little use for classification systems like DSM-IV (Bugental and Sterling 1995). Instead, the humanists emphasize the potential for human growth, and focus on helping the individual to grow. In effect, it is a psychology of health, not a therapy for abnormal behaviour.

Although the emphasis is rather different from those of the other approaches, humanistic therapy is still dealing with the same human beings as other therapists, no matter how the process is described. That means that the humanistic therapist must still deal with the reality that individuals seek help because they are suffering in some way. This suffering is interpreted as due to distortions of growth, usually caused by the demands of other people. The desire to meet these demands can result in frustration and despair, as well as loss of awareness of one's own feelings and preferences. Consequently, humanistic therapy tends to focus on creating conditions under which the individual can increase self-awareness and begin to make choices which will enhance the process of growth.

Although each humanistic theorist uses slightly different concepts and techniques, in practice the different therapies tend to be similar in several respects: the emphasis on the individual's own perceptions and feelings, the importance of self-awareness or *insight* as a tool for growth, and the responsibility of the therapist to respect the individual's autonomy. Among the various therapies, however, the work of Carl Rogers has become perhaps the best known.

As noted in Chapter 6, Carl Rogers developed his approach to therapy partly as a reaction against the pessimistic image of human growth which psychoanalysis offered. Over time, he developed a technique which was initially called 'client-centred therapy', and later **person-centred therapy** (Rogers 1951; Raskin and Rogers 1989; Bohart 1995). (The early emphasis on the term 'client' was meant to contrast with the traditional usage, by

person-centred therapy (also called 'client-centred therapy') a form of therapy developed by Carl Rogers which emphasizes the responsibility of the individual to determine the direction of change within therapy

both psychoanalysts and other therapists, of the term 'patient'.) In Rogers's view, the therapeutic relationship was between equals; the therapist's role was to provide a sounding board, not to make judgements as an authority figure. Hence, 'client' seemed preferable to 'patient'; the later shift to 'person-centred' was simply a further step towards acknowledging that the therapeutic relationship is essentially an interaction between two human beings.

Rogerian therapy is based on the therapist trying to provide the *conditions for growth*: empathy, openness and unconditional positive regard. The therapist must act in an *open* and genuine way, not hiding behind a professional facade. By trying to understand the individual's perceptions and feelings, the therapist provides *empathy*. *Unconditional positive regard* comes through demonstrating caring and acceptance of the individual and their concerns. By showing these qualities, the therapist can help the person to become more self-aware and more self-confident.

Despite the seemingly subjective nature of person-centred therapy, Rogers was very concerned with the importance of demonstrating that therapy actually helps people. Consequently, very early on he began keeping detailed transcripts of therapy sessions, and used them as a tool for evaluating therapeutic change (Rogers and Dymond 1954). Typically, as therapy progressed, an individual would make more statements relating to feelings, wishes and having a sense of control over life. For example, a person might go from saying, 'I'm a failure; I always disappoint my parents', to saying, 'I realize how important my parents are to me; but I also realize I have to make my own career decisions.' Changes like this are consistent with what the theory would predict, and suggests that Rogerian therapy is effective. Unfortunately, we recognize that what people *say* is not always what they *do*, and the data provide no direct evidence of behavioural change. Indeed, a study by a psychologist who was allowed to observe Rogers conducting therapy found that *only* statements indicating progress regularly led to positive comments by Rogers (Truax 1966). In effect, Rogers's comments provided a form of social reinforcement for the individual to make appropriate statements. Based partly on this finding, Rogers abandoned the term 'non-directive therapy' as a description of his therapeutic technique; while the therapist tries to be neutral, the reality is that *any* human interaction is influenced by the attitudes and preferences of each person. Nonetheless, Rogers continued to assert that the process of therapy must emphasize the individual's own potential for growth, not the judgements of the therapist. In this respect, the dynamics of Rogerian therapy seem very different from psychoanalysis.

This issue of implicit control is one basis on which person-centred therapy has been criticized. Another criticism is that, as an insight-oriented therapy, it requires a high level of verbal interaction. As such, critics suggest, it works best for problems of living – anxiety, depression and, particularly, self-esteem. There is some evidence to support this view, although Rogers himself also worked with individuals with more serious disorders, including schizophrenia (Rogers *et al.* 1967).

As with other forms of 'talking cures', which seek large-scale changes in the individual, Rogerian therapy is very difficult to evaluate. Nonetheless, research exists for anxiety disorders and depression, among other conditions. For example, it is as effective as cognitive therapy in dealing with anxiety disorders when each is used in combination with relaxation training (Borkovec and Matthews 1988), but slightly less effective than either cognitive therapy or relaxation when each is used independently (Borkovec and Costello 1993). For depression, comparisons indicate it is comparable to cognitive therapy in effectiveness (Elliott *et al.* 1990). While offering some indication that person-centred therapy may be useful, these studies provide neither an absolute standard for comparison (e.g. compared to no treatment) nor any specific indication of what the key therapeutic factors are. Even if its primary effects are due to social reinforcement and the empathic support which the therapist provides, one thing is clear: Rogers has been highly influential on other clinicians. When a survey in the 1980s asked American therapists who had had the greatest influence on their work, Rogers was cited more frequently than anyone else (Smith 1982). More recently, a similar study of Canadian therapists (completed four years after Rogers's death) found him still in second place (Warner 1991). As a model of a caring and compassionate therapist, Rogers seemed to fit his own theory very well indeed.

| For further consideration |

Recall the question raised earlier about whether behaviour modification is manipulative. Suppose the same criticism was made of person-centred therapy; how would you respond?

Evaluating Therapeutic Techniques

efficacy the measured effectiveness of a treatment technique in medicine or psychotherapy

In describing how each of the approaches views abnormal behaviour, we have made reference to the apparent effectiveness, or **efficacy**, of the treatment techniques. The issue of efficacy is important, because obviously a treatment which doesn't help is worthless. To the average person, though, the question would probably be expressed in terms of 'which one is *best*?' As simple as it seems, this is a very difficult question to answer.

Diversity is part of the problem: not only are there five broadly recognized approaches, but within each, many possible variants of treatment exist. This diversity of choices can create confusion – what behaviour therapist Joseph Wolpe has called 'the babble of conflicting voices' (Leo 1985: 39). Not surprisingly, one result has been an increased interest in comparative evaluations of the various types of therapy.

Unfortunately, it is not easy to design comparative studies. Therapeutic approaches often have different goals (e.g. modifying personality versus eliminating a specific behaviour), which can make it difficult to define a common standard of evaluation. Indeed, some suggest that standardized procedures to measure outcomes are inappropriate, since they ignore the differences in both processes and goals (Persons 1991; Goldfried and Wolfe 1998). The question of the proper way to do assessments was raised by a major study completed by *Consumer Reports* in the United States. The study looked at the experiences of 2,900 patients who were treated with some form of psychotherapy, with or without drugs as an adjunct.

psychotherapy any variety of treatment for abnormal behaviour which is primarily verbal in nature, rather than based on the use of drugs

(**Psychotherapy** is a general term used to describe treatment which is basically verbal in nature.) The results indicated that all therapies were equally useful, regardless of type of disorder, and that generally longer periods of treatment were better than shorter. The study caused considerable controversy, because there was no standardization of treatment methods and duration, severity of symptoms etc. – in short, all the factors which conventional research tries to control. Despite this, Martin Seligman (himself a cognitive–behaviourist reasearcher) argued that the study was useful, precisely because it allowed therapists and patients to make the decisions about duration and type of treatment (Seligman 1995). Nonetheless, the fact that the study found no appreciable differences in effectiveness among the therapies seems both odd and unhelpful. One reason for this may be the vague (and hence variable) standards for assessing outcomes; in order to draw reasonable conclusions, most researchers and clinicians feel that there must be at least some minimal common standard for assessment.

spontaneous remission in medicine or therapy, improvement in an individual's condition in the absence of treatment

A further problem in trying to assess the effectiveness of therapy is the possibility that an individual may show improvement even *without* treatment – what is referred to as **spontaneous remission**. Obviously, if spontaneous remission is not considered, then some apparent improvements will be credited to treatment, instead of coincidence! Yet there is an obvious ethical problem in deliberately denying treatment simply to create a control group. As a result, control groups are usually either based on soliciting informed consent to delay treatment, or created by selecting individuals from waiting lists for treatment. (Unfortunately, many treatment centres are unable to meet immediate demands.)

Having noted these difficulties, let us consider some of the findings of evaluation studies. One of the best-controlled comparative studies was conducted by the National Institutes of Mental Health, a US government agency (Elkin *et al*. 1989). In this study, 28 clinicians of various orientations worked with 240 individuals diagnosed as having major depression. Individuals were randomly assigned to treatment using an anti-depressant drug (imipramine), psychodynamic therapy (not psychoanalysis) or cognitive therapy. In addition, a control group was given a placebo pill, along with brief weekly meetings with a psychiatrist. The placebo/drug groups were conducted as a *double-blind* design, so that neither the doctor nor the individual knew which was which. All individuals were assessed at the start, after 16 weeks of treatment and again 18 months later. The results of the study are complex, and don't point to the type of clear-cut result one might hope for. For example, all three types of treatment produced greater improvement than did the placebo. Drug therapy produced faster improvements than did the insight therapies – but was also associated with higher rates of relapse of symptoms. Even in the placebo group, some of the individuals with only moderate depression showed improvement. (This improvement is not evident in the final results, because these individuals tended to drop out before the study was completed.) In addition, of course, this study only looked at efficacy in treating *depression*; while relatively common, depression is obviously only one form of disorder.

A different approach to comparing treatment techniques was used by Mary Lee Smith and her colleagues (Smith *et al*. 1980). Drawing on the

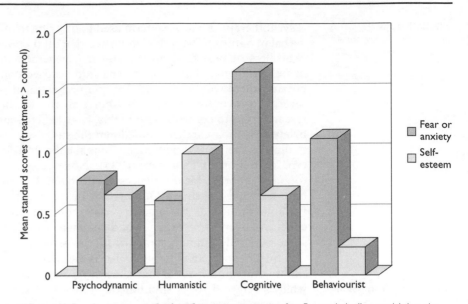

Figure 9.5   A meta-analysis of treatment results By statistically combining the results from 475 different studies, researchers were able to do a comparative study of four approaches to the treatment of anxiety and self-esteem. The scores are 'standard scores', which are expressed in units of the standard deviation. A score of 1.0 would mean that approximately 84 per cent of those in the treatment group improved more than those in the control group; any positive score indicates greater improvement in treatment than in control groups. (Data adapted from Smith *et al.* 1980.)

hundreds of previously published evaluations of various forms of therapy, Smith did a *meta-analysis* of 475 studies, statistically analysing the combined results according to various factors, such as theoretical orientation and type of disorder treated. (A partial summary of results is shown in Figure 9.5.) The major finding was that, overall, *all* the various approaches seemed to produce significant improvement, and that there was little difference in these ratings of overall effectiveness. However, when the analysis was broken down in terms of *types of disorders*, there were significant differences between approaches. For example, humanistic therapy seemed the *least* effective approach to treating anxiety, but was the *most* effective approach for problems of self-esteem.

The type of analysis used by Smith and her colleagues, while interesting, poses many difficulties. For example, different studies would use different assessment criteria, different durations of treatment and possibly differences in accuracy of diagnoses and assessments of severity, among other variations. In addition, this study did not include treatment based on the medical model (i.e. drugs), which limits the possibility of complete comparisons. Overall, the finding that *all* methods show *some* efficacy suggests there may be factors which are common to all types of treatment.

The idea that there are *non-specific factors* associated with treatment has been recognized for many years. In a classic book called *Persuasion and Healing*, psychiatrist Jerome Frank (1963) suggested that the common factors in all forms of treatment are the clinician's commitment to helping, and the belief in improvement which this instils in the individual. More recently, this has been echoed by other researchers; one study suggested that the primary non-specific factors are *support* and *hope* (Stiles *et al.* 1986). The importance of support has been affirmed by psychodynamic therapist Hans Strupp, who states that creating an atmosphere of acceptance and empathy is itself of great therapeutic value (Strupp 1989). Hope, which may be created by the therapist's attitude or even a placebo, also seems to be a general feature of effective therapy.

While it is easy to dismiss such factors as relevant only in the context of humanistic therapy, that does not appear to be the case. A recent study of rational-emotive therapy for treating depression makes this point clearly (Castonguay *et al.* 1996). According to Ellis's theory, the therapy works by challenging false beliefs, and research indicates that such therapy is as effective as medication in alleviating depression, and probably better at preventing relapses (see earlier discussion). However, an analysis of the factors that contribute to successful treatment showed that the commitment of therapist and patient, and the emotional involvement of the patient, were the significant elements. Surprisingly, the degree of emphasis that therapists put on distorted cognitions did *not* predict treatment success, contrary to the assumptions of rational-emotive therapy! The commitment of therapist and patient to the therapeutic process (sometimes called the *therapeutic alliance*) is now widely recognized as an important element of therapy, even by behaviour therapists (Hayes *et al.* 1995).

Given the welter of results, and the absence of clear-cut findings that one method is consistently superior, should one conclude that all therapies are the same? Probably not. As noted in Smith's review, some approaches work better than others for certain problems. In part, this may reflect the reality that abnormal behaviour does not have a single cause. Instead, genetic predisposition, prior experiences and current circumstances all probably play a role. In addition, the relative importance of each factor is likely to vary across disorders and even across individuals. Consequently, the finding that each approach has *some* benefit may reflect the realities of complex causation, as well as the non-specific treatment factors discussed above. One reflection of this reality is that a significant number of practitioners describe their approach to treatment as *eclectic* – that is, they draw upon a range of techniques on a case by case basis, rather than adhering to a single theoretical model. In a study of therapeutic orientations, anywhere from 30 to 40 per cent of Canadian and American psychologists described themselves as eclectic in orientation – more than any single approach (Warner 1991). While this seems a reasonable attitude, we still know too little about causes, and consequently about which technique works best in a given circumstance. Without this knowledge, eclectic approaches could conceivably result in the *worst* of all methods, rather than the *best*. Clearly, we need to know more about what works, and *why*.

For further consideration

Suppose that you had a problem such as severe depression. What type of therapist would you go to? Why? What questions would you want to ask them before beginning therapy?

Understanding Schizophrenia

At the beginning of this chapter, we described the case of a young man who had been diagnosed as having schizophrenia. The symptoms he manifested – confusion, incoherent speech, possible delusions – are common in schizophrenia. Although it is relatively uncommon (about 1 per cent of the population are affected, compared to a lifetime risk of serious depression of about 12 per cent), schizophrenia and its stereotypes are closely associated with the popular conception of abnormal behaviour as 'madness'. Of all the forms of mental disorders, schizophrenia is perhaps the most frightening to the average person, and the most difficult to understand.

What we now call schizophrenia has been recognized in various forms for centuries. Even in ancient Greece, Hippocrates described its basic symptoms. The term *schizophrenia* was first used by a Swiss psychiatrist named Eugen Bleuler. Drawing on the Greek words for 'split mind', Bleuler coined the term to refer to disorders in which there seemed to be a separation of cognitive and emotional functions, resulting in mental confusion and either inappropriate emotions or the absence of emotional expression. (It should be noted that schizophrenia, despite the connotation of 'split personality', is *not* the same as **multiple personality disorder**, a severe form of dissociative reaction which can result in several independent personalities being manifested.)

Schizophrenia represents a severe form of disorder in which there can be distortions of perception, thought, language and emotions. While no two cases are likely to be identical, DSM-IV requires that there be cognitive or perceptual distortions which impair the person's contact with reality, and also significant deterioration in general functioning (as in working and caring for oneself). In addition, there are several types of symptoms which may occur. Some are called *positive symptoms*, because they represent behaviours that are commonly associated with schizophrenia: delusions, hallucinations and thought disturbances. **Delusions** are false beliefs which are maintained in the absence of clear evidence to the contrary. For example, psychologist Milton Rokeach once encountered three individuals with schizophrenia, each of whom believed himself to be Jesus Christ (Rokeach 1981). **Hallucinations** are false perceptions – most commonly, hearing voices. When asked to describe the source of such voices, individuals typically say they come from within their own head. Interestingly, one study suggests that the perceived voices originate by the same process as ordinary silent verbalizations, but are instead perceived as actual voices (Bick and Kinsbourne 1987). **Thought disturbances** can take many forms – apparent violations of logic (called *paralogic*), incoherent speech and shifts in word usage (as when the young man in the Introduction responded to the name Hope as 'that's what I need'). In addition, schizophrenia can be indicated by **negative symptoms**, which involve the absence of expected behaviours. Negative symptoms can include bodily immobility, limited speech, flattened affect (absence of emotional expression) and social withdrawal, among other forms.

Although not all these types of symptoms occur in all patients, the predominance of one type is often used to diagnose a particular sub-type of

multiple personality disorder a severe form of dissociative reaction which can result in several independent personalities being manifested
schizophrenia a severe form of mental disorder in which there can be distortions of perception, thought, language and emotions
delusions false beliefs which are maintained in the absence of clear evidence to the contrary
hallucinations false perceptions in the absence of relevant sensory stimuli, such as hearing voices or seeing objects which are not present
thought disturbances distortions of thinking processes, such as violations of logic, incoherent speech and inappropriate shifts in word usage
negative symptoms the absence of expected behaviours; negative symptoms of schizophrenia include bodily immobility, limited speech, flattened affect (absence of emotional expression) and social withdrawal

Type of schizophrenia	Major symptoms
Paranoid	Hallucinations (e.g. hearing voices) and delusions (e.g. of being persecuted, or of exaggerated self-importance)
Catatonic	Excessive motor behaviour, or unresponsive, inactive stupor; sometimes alternating between the two extremes
Disorganized	Incoherent speech and thought, inappropriate emotional expression, bizarre behaviour
Undifferentiated	Mixture of symptoms, not fitting one of above types
Residual	Moderate symptoms (often flat affect and limited speech) occurring after an acute episode of schizophrenia

Figure 9.6 Major sub-types of schizophrenia Diagnosis of schizophrenia under DSM-IV can fall into one of five categories, depending on the symptoms and history. (Adapted from DSM-IV, American Psychiatric Association 1994.)

schizophrenia: *paranoid schizophrenia* involves delusions of grandeur (as in the three Christs) and persecution; *catatonic schizophrenia* is characterized primarily by negative symptoms, particularly non-responsiveness to environmental stimuli; the *disorganized* type shows disturbances of thought and flattened or absent emotional expression. A fourth category, *undifferentiated schizophrenia*, is used for those cases that meet the primary criteria (cognitive or perceptual distortions, and generally poor functioning) but do not fit one of the three specific sub-types. In addition to these four types, DSM-IV provides a fifth category, *residual schizophrenia*, for circumstances where there has been partial recovery after an acute episode of schizophrenia, but lingering behavioural problems associated with the disorder. (See Figure 9.6.)

The definition of schizophrenia, and the description of sub-types, is still a matter of some controversy. In part, this reflects the complex mix of possible symptoms, and the necessity of defining the condition (at least at present) purely symptomatically. This is a serious issue, because if the categories are invalid, then classification may actually impede our understanding of aetiology. To give an example: excessive use of amphetamines can result in **delusional amphetamine disorder**, which is *symptomatically* identical to paranoid schizophrenia. While the ambiguity in this case can be readily resolved by a period of observation in hospital, it illustrates that symptoms are not always a direct indicator of cause. (We will return to this concern in discussing how the approaches deal with schizophrenia.)

Despite these difficulties, there is little question that there are individuals with these general symptoms who experience significant distress, and who often seem unable or unwilling to function effectively. In recent years, the estimates of its frequency have tended to centre on 1 per cent of the population (lifetime risk), with men and women equally likely to be affected, but with men often showing an earlier age of onset (late teens to early twenties, versus late twenties or later for women) (Regier *et al.* 1988). Since most clinicians *do* accept that the behaviours associated with schizophrenia do

delusional amphetamine disorder a form of mental disorder resulting from the excessive use of amphetamines; its primary symptom, extreme delusions, can make it appear *symptomatically* identical to paranoid schizophrenia

exist, it is worth considering what we know about its origins and possible treatment.

For further consideration

Imagine you are a therapist, and someone comes to you seeking help. As you talk with them, you discover that they say they are in regular mental contact with a dead aunt. Would this convince you the person has schizophrenia? What else would you look for? Are there circumstances where this might *not* reflect schizophrenia?

The Medical Model and Schizophrenia

Of the many theories of the causes of schizophrenia, perhaps the best known is the idea that it is biologically-based. This concept seems consistent with its apparent severity and generally poor prognosis for permanent recovery. In addition, by suggesting there is a fundamental physiological difference between those with schizophrenia and those who don't have it, it may also be reassuring to people who want to believe that 'it can't happen to me'. As we have discussed, the medical model used by the biological approach interprets abnormal behaviour in precisely this way.

One of the first substantial clues to a biological link was the development of chlorpromazine, the first of the modern anti-psychotic drugs. Heinz Lehmann, a Canadian doctor who is usually credited with introducing chlorpromazine in North America, said that after giving chlorpromazine to patients for a few days or weeks, most of the positive symptoms disappeared. 'In 1953, there just wasn't anything that ever produced something like this' (Shorter 1997: 252). For doctors like Lehmann, accustomed to being able to do little for individuals suffering from schizophrenia, this was a startling breakthrough.

dopamine hypothesis a theory which argues that schizophrenia is based on overactivity in neural pathways which depend on dopamine as a neurotransmitter

The success of chlorpromazine and similar drugs has led to development of the **dopamine hypothesis** – the theory that schizophrenia is related to overactivity in neural pathways which depend on dopamine as a neurotransmitter. The primary evidence in favour of this hypothesis comes from clinical experience with drugs like chlorpromazine. These drugs, called *neuroleptics*, disrupt the activity of dopamine in the brain (Wender and Klein 1981). Additional evidence comes from studies of amphetamine-induced psychosis, since amphetamines also stimulate dopamine levels (Angrist *et al.* 1980). There is also evidence that the drug commonly used to treat Parkinson's disease, a muscle-control disorder whose treatment involves elevating dopamine levels, can worsen the symptoms of schizophrenia (Kendell 1987). Conversely, it has been found that a side-effect of neuroleptic drugs can be muscle tremors reminiscent of Parkinsonism. Hence, in various ways, the clinical evidence points to a link between dopamine and schizophrenia.

However, there are also a number of difficulties with the dopamine hypothesis. The most basic problem is that not all patients respond to neuroleptics (Garver *et al.* 1997). Moreover, there is currently no clear understanding of how dopamine is responsible. For example, many of the studies which have found abnormalities in dopamine receptors in individuals with schizophrenia have depended on post-mortem analyses. Since most individuals with a lengthy history of schizophrenia also have a long history of taking neuroleptics, one cannot rule out drug-induced changes in the neural pathways. A further problem is that the drugs usually reach the brain very shortly after ingestion, yet there is typically a lag of days or weeks before clinical improvement occurs. If excess dopamine is the problem, why doesn't behaviour change as soon as dopamine levels drop?

The picture is also muddied by recent research on a newer drug, *clozapine*. Clozapine appears to be even more effective clinically than the earlier neuroleptics (notably chlorpromazine), yet it affects *non*-dopamine pathways more than dopamine pathways (Tandon and Kane 1993). There is also evidence that other neurotransmitters, including glutamate and serotonin, may also be involved. These difficulties have led to modification of the original hypothesis, so as to suggest that the key is either selective effects on particular receptors or some sort of stabilizing of activity in dopamine versus non-dopamine pathways (Gershon and Rieder 1992; Kahn *et al.* 1996). Even if these matters are resolved, they do not directly explain the cause of schizophrenia – that is, why should some people's brains show a problem with regulating dopamine levels? This question has led researchers to look for a more fundamental cause.

Over the years, various studies have suggested a number of physiological differences between individuals with schizophrenia and the normal population. For example, scans of the brain using positron emission tomography (PET scans) have shown that there is less frontal lobe activity during attention tests (Gershon and Rieder 1992). The ventricles (fluid-filled chambers in the brain) are often slightly enlarged, and the tissues surrounding the ventricles – notably in the hippocampus and temporal lobe – are often slightly shrunken.

While such studies are promising, they still do not offer a clear explanation of the basis of schizophrenia. One mechanism that seemingly *could* account for such physical differences is heredity. In the case of schizophrenia, there have been hundreds of studies, and a general pattern has emerged. Studies of concordance rates for family members suggest that there is a genetic predisposition for schizophrenia (Nicol and Gottesman 1983; Gershon and Rieder 1992). These findings indicate that for relatives of individuals with schizophrenia, the closer the genetic relationship, the greater the risk. Cases where family members were separated early in life have also been examined, suggesting that the observed pattern is not due to the effects of growing up in a home where someone has schizophrenia (Kety *et al.* 1994).

Still, there are limits on what these findings tell us. First of all, they do *not* mean that schizophrenia is purely genetic – even identical twins reared together show no more than a 50 per cent concordance rate. As Nicol and Gottesman note, there are very few cases involving separated identical twins with schizophrenia, and those cases may not be representative of the general population. Most importantly, while a genetic factor *does* seem implied, no one knows exactly what it is, despite years of searching. Consequently, in recent years researchers have begun to look at alternative mechanisms to account for the occurrence of schizophrenia.

Recently, researchers have begun to speculate that schizophrenia is actually several disorders which have different causes – and the different forms don't necessarily match the DSM-IV categories (Heinrichs 1993; Garver 1997; Andreasen 1999). A model which is gaining increasing attention is the 'two hit' model, developed by Mednick and his colleagues (Mednick *et al.* 1998). Since many of the identified brain anomalies seem likely to arise early in the development of the brain, the model proposes that the first 'hit' occurs during the second trimester of pregnancy. A genetic defect could be one cause, but others are possible. Recently several studies have pointed to the possibility that the damage is owing to the mother contracting influenza ('flu') during this portion of the pregnancy (Venables 1996; Mortenson *et al.* 1999). One of the interesting implications of this is that a viral mechanism would show up in twin studies as genetic, since twins share the same prenatal environment. This might explain why concordance rates for both identical and fraternal twins are non-zero, but not high enough to suggest a purely genetic factor. It might also explain why schizophrenia has persisted as a human trait, since normally natural selection would lead to disappearance of traits that affect adaptation in such negative ways (Hooper 1999). (Other factors besides influenza have also been suggested as posing risks during the second trimester, including cold temperatures, famine and city life.)

The second 'hit' would be a subsequent environmental stress, including possibly trauma during birth or negative rearing conditions. This factor may also be relevant to reinterpreting the studies of adopted twins, since the conditions which led to being separated may also be the factors triggering the onset of schizophrenia (including poverty or marital breakdown). Even when looking at onset in adults, one cannot rule out the role of environmental factors in producing some of the changes, since we know that experience modifies brain structure (see Chapter 7). Environmental influences could include early rearing, malnutrition, social isolation and treatment-related factors like drug effects and institutionalization.

The new model which is emerging is reminiscent of what has been called the **diathesis–stress** model of abnormal behaviour. According to this theory, abnormal behaviour arises as a result of the combination of a predisposition (usually genetic) and a stressful environment. In the absence of a stressor, the predisposition will not be manifested. (Thus, a genetic defect or influenza during the second trimester could be the diathesis, and childhood poverty could be the stress.) According to one version of this model, in individuals with a predisposition, stress raises dopamine levels, and thereby increases symptoms (Walker and Diforio 1997). One implication of this model is that it may be possible to reduce the environmental stressors which result in schizophrenia in those who are vulnerable, or teach them skills to cope more effectively (Zubin and Spring 1977). The ideas about schizophrenia which are currently being developed are exciting, and seem to make sense of a complex and confusing disorder. However, history suggests we should be cautious, since there have been previous claims to having found 'the cause of schizophrenia'. (See Brown and Herrnstein (1975) for a scathing review of the history.) Even if the 'two hit' (diathesis–stress) model is correct, the biological approach is less suited to considering environmental factors than the other approaches. Consequently, let us consider how each of them deals with schizophrenia.

diathesis–stress model a theory which views abnormal behaviour as being due to a combination of a physiological predisposition (diathesis) and a stressful environment

For further consideration If exposure to influenza during pregnancy actually does contribute to schizophrenia, how would you expect the concordance rates for the disorder in fraternal twins to compare to other siblings? (Note that the *genetic* similarity is the same in the two cases.)

Alternatives to the Medical Model of Schizophrenia

The biological approach uses the medical model to explain schizophrenia in terms of genetic and physiological processes. In contrast, the other four approaches all emphasize environmental influences. While the specific factors emphasized differ, each approach offers theories to explain the aetiology of the behaviour, and also treatment techniques derived from the theory. In comparing these various theories, we face a basic problem of evaluation. While we can attempt to measure the effectiveness of the treatments, this does *not* directly prove that the associated theory is correct in explaining the cause of schizophrenia. The problem, for both the environmental theories and the medical model, is that nearly all the evidence is *retrospective*. That is, we are unable to do controlled experiments to test the theories; instead, researchers have to work backwards, after the disorder has already been diagnosed. At best, one can try to identify individuals who are defined as being at risk, and observe whether they in fact develop schizophrenia – but even in this case, the results are technically correlational, and prone to errors such as sampling bias. The problems of evaluation are further complicated by the disputes about the validity of current diagnostic categories, since recent evidence (see previous section) may mean either that multiple factors contribute to the occurrence of schizophrenia, or simply that we are currently lumping together disorders with very different origins. With these difficulties in mind, let us consider how each of the other approaches views schizophrenia and its treatment.

The Behaviourist Approach

As previously discussed, the behaviourist approach interprets abnormal behaviour as simply maladaptive learning. In this respect, schizophrenia is not regarded any differently from other forms of abnormal behaviour. Indeed, behaviourists would regard the term 'schizophrenia' as having no aetiological value. Even viewed descriptively, the term would be seen as useful only to the extent that it reliably describes particular patterns of behaviour.

As an explanation of the origin of schizophrenia, the behaviourist view has several weaknesses. First, although learning by reinforcement is a well-demonstrated general principle, there is no direct evidence for the acquisition of *schizophrenic* behaviour. There are also several ways in which the model seems inconsistent with the available evidence. For example, while it is possible to use learning to suggest why children of individuals with schizophrenia are at greater risk, it is hard to see how this applies in cases where children are reared *apart* from the parent with schizophrenia. Further, although one can conceive of a particular symptom being learned, it is not clear why particular *combinations* of symptoms should occur so regularly (e.g. delusions coupled with hallucinations). It has been argued that by regarding all behaviour as alike, behaviourists give little attention to the *kinds* of problems people tend to develop (Wachtel 1977). Given the lack of specifics, the model does not seem to contribute greatly to our understanding of the causes of schizophrenia.

In terms of treatment, a number of studies have shown that reinforcement can be effective in modifying the behaviour of individuals with schizophrenia. For example, in one case, a forty-year-old man had been hospitalized for 19 years, and had not spoken to anyone in all that time. The researchers discovered that he loved chewing gum, and used it as a reinforcer to reintroduce speech successfully, by a process of shaping (Isaacs *et al.* 1960). Other studies have focused on shaping the behaviour of entire wards, by establishing a *token economy* (Schaefer and Martin 1966; Atthowe and Krasner 1968). These studies have typically reported success in improving specific behaviours (such as dressing and going to meals), and also improvements in overall functioning. What is most striking is that these studies involved individuals who had already been institutionalized for long periods – in the Atthowe and Krasner study, the median age was fifty-seven, and the median duration of hospitalization was *22 years*. Despite the negative prognosis this implies, 90 per cent of the 87 men on the ward participated actively in the programme, and showed improvements over a two-year period.

Token economy programmes represent one of the most frequent applications of the behaviourist approach within mental institutions (Ayllon and Azrin 1968). One obvious reason for this is that the institutional environment makes it possible to control reinforcers sufficiently to make tokens meaningful. However, these programmes also raise questions about the effects of an institutionalized environment on behaviour. Schaefer and Martin note the passivity of the patients, a characteristic noted by many observers (Schaefer and Martin 1966; Rosenhan 1973). Indeed, concern about the negative effects of institutionalization partially explains the shift from hospitalization to outpatient treatment after the discovery of drugs like chlorpromazine. This shift led to dramatic drops in hospitalization rates: from a peak in the early 1950s, hospitalization rates in the United States for mental disorders (of which schizophrenia represented a large proportion) dropped almost fourfold over the following twenty years (Bassuk and Gerson 1978). To some critics, the shift to minimal hospitalization (supplemented by outpatient services) has not been entirely positive. As negative as most hospital environments were, the failure to create appropriate community-based supports for individuals with schizophrenia and other disorders has often led to even greater neglect (Thomas 1981; Shorter 1997).

The reason for engaging in this digression is twofold. First, it indicates that many of the behaviours modified in the above studies may have been related to institutionalization, not schizophrenia. Consequently, they may tell us little about the validity of the behaviourist model in terms of schizophrenia proper. Second, the emptying of institutions described above (a pattern repeated in most Western countries) has meant that there are fewer opportunities to apply the behaviourist approach – particularly token economies. This, at least in part, accounts for the paucity of studies since the late 1960s. (However, many of the *principles* of behaviour modification, if not the name, have been integrated into the repertoire of 'eclectic' therapists (see Krasner 1976).)

Overall, then, the evidence suggests that certain forms of maladaptive behaviour can be modified by reinforcement, and this may have some benefit for overall functioning of individuals with schizophrenia. Beyond that, there seems little basis to suggest that maladaptive learning based on reinforcement is the sole, or even primary, *cause* of schizophrenia.

The Cognitive Approach

In dealing with schizophrenia, the cognitive approach has tended to focus on analysing the various types of symptoms, and suggesting explanations based on *faulty cognitive processing*. While these models do not represent a coherent whole, they nonetheless suggest interesting insights into the nature of schizophrenic behaviour. There are three aspects that we will focus on: delusions, language and thought disturbances.

At first glance, *delusions* are easy to define – they represent beliefs which seem to contradict reality. The difficulty with this, as Roger Brown (1972) has pointed out, is defining what constitutes reality. When Milton Rokeach encountered three individuals who each believed himself to be Jesus Christ, he thought that confronting them with each other would be an effective therapeutic tool (Rokeach 1981). In fact, each remained steadfast in his belief, convinced the *others* were deluded. (Ultimately, Rokeach came to regret his own actions, which did little to help the three men, citing his own 'Godlike delusion that I could change them by omnipotently and omnisciently arranging and rearranging their daily lives.')

While the three Christs fit the stereotype of delusions, in practice most individuals show much more limited delusional beliefs; for example, out of 25,000 patients in Michigan, Rokeach found only a handful who had delusional identities. Moreover, delusional individuals typically recognize as false the delusions of *other* patients (Brown 1972). That is, there is not a complete loss of commonly defined reality, only in specific content areas. For the moment, let us leave aside the question of *why* this might occur.

At one time, the *language* of individuals with schizophrenia was regarded as an incoherent babble, a 'word salad' or regression to infantile speech. However, in recent years a number of analyses have suggested that this picture, like the stereotype of delusions, is inaccurate. Roger Brown, who is a specialist in the development of language, has declared that he has never encountered evidence of child-like utterances in individuals with schizophrenia (Brown 1972). Instead, words are simply used in ways that other individuals find strange. Often, it seems that particular words will have private significance to the individual, which can only be interpreted by a patient observer (Maher 1972; Forest 1976). Sometimes the difficulty seems to be a looseness of *connotation* – the associations which a word suggests, rather than its specific meaning. For example, the word 'life' might conjure up human birth (a new life), a magazine (*Life*), a party ('the life of . . .'), and so on, leading to 'the baby came in the magazine and the noise was too much'. Unfortunately, developing a consistent model to explain such utterances on a case-by-case basis is a nearly impossible task (Rochester 1977). What is needed is an understanding of *why* individuals with schizophrenia sometimes use language in such idiosyncratic ways.

Similarly, *thought disturbances* can seem very puzzling. Two aspects that have garnered attention are faulty reference and logical errors. **Faulty reference** (sometimes considered a form of delusion) involves misinterpreting the significance of stimuli and events. For example, if a person on the street is observed frowning, the individual assumes that it is directed at him or her. A branch knocks against a window, and it is taken as a sign from God. In such cases, the person attributes a meaning to the event which most people would not. *Logical errors*, apparent lapses in reasoning, are a matter of some contention. Some theorists, like Silvano Arieti, believe such errors are based on the individual using a different form of reasoning (Arieti 1974). For example, the person may say, 'The Virgin Mary is a virgin. I am a virgin. Therefore I am the Virgin Mary.' In this case, the person is creating an identity based on the predicates of the first two statements being alike; in conventional logic, this is considered improper. However, if the person reasons this way consistently, then it could still be considered 'logical', albeit using unconventional rules. On the other hand, other theorists reject the idea that individuals with schizophrenia reason better, worse or differently, compared to normal individuals (Brown and Herrnstein 1975).

Considered together, these various phenomena can seem very puzzling, and somewhat bizarre. Yet one must remember that not all individuals with schizophrenia show all these behaviours; in fact, even those that do manifest these symptoms tend to do so in limited ways. This leaves the question: how can these behaviours be explained? From a cognitive standpoint, one explanation suggested is that individuals with schizophrenia have a problem of **defective attention** – a difficulty in selecting and attending to the relevant stimuli in a situation (Braff 1993). Even Bleuler, in first defining schizophrenia, noted that individuals with schizophrenia seemed unable to keep their thoughts focused. Many individuals who have developed schizophrenia have described their early symptoms in terms of behaviours like memorizing trivial details, being distracted easily or misinterpreting instructions (Chapman 1966). What is particularly striking is that they describe these behaviours not as personal preferences, but as something which they are *unable to control*. This pattern has been supported by studies indicating that attentional difficulties are one of the risk factors for developing schizophrenia (Erlenmyer-Kimling *et al.* 1993; Cornblatt and Keilp 1994).

If looked at in this context, many of the above symptoms seem understandable. Typically, we assume that two people focus on the same 'evidence' when evaluating beliefs; if a person holds an anomalous belief, it is clearly a 'delusion'. Instead, delusions and faulty reference may arise from idiosyncratic selection and/or interpretation of information. Similarly, 'word salads' and other language problems could arise because of an inability to ignore the connotations of words. The cumulative effect of such attention deficits could be to develop atypical beliefs (delusions), and to have difficulty with language and thought in ways that would hamper social interactions. In turn, the negative responses of other people would aggravate the social impact of the initial problem of defective attention. This interpretation is supported

faulty reference an error involving misinterpreting the significance of stimuli and events; while sometimes considered a form of delusion, it can also arise through faulty perceptual processing

defective attention theory a theory which argues that schizophrenia is due to difficulties in selecting and attending to the relevant stimuli in a situation

by prospective studies of children with a family history of schizophrenia, which identify attentional problems as a risk factor (Erlenmeyer-Kimling *et al.* 1993; Green 1993).

While no specific treatment technique has emerged from the defective attention theory, it does pose some interesting implications. One obvious attraction is that it suggests a common mechanism underlying many seemingly disparate symptoms, as discussed above. Further, it provides an explanation for why individuals with schizophrenia can function normally in some respects, while other behaviours seem very bizarre. While it is premature to say with certainty, it is also possible that this model can ultimately be connected to research on the effects of neuroleptic drugs. The neural pathways for attention are complex, and in some respects broadly distributed in the brain, but two areas involved in the selection and processing of stimulus information are the brain stem and the frontal lobes – both of which seem implicated by the studies of drug actions. It will be interesting to see if future research brings at least a partial convergence of the two models.

The Psychodynamic Approach

The psychodynamic approach views schizophrenia as a severe distortion of psychological functioning, a disintegration of ego functions which results in the loss of reality testing. To Freud, for example, schizophrenia reflected a regression to the oral or anal stages, during which the ego first develops. Because the child fails to develop a clear sense of the boundaries between the self and the outside world, the ego is later unable to maintain reality testing effectively, or to cope with the demands of id. The result is the variety of symptomatic behaviours which we associate with schizophrenia. For example, the self-neglect and behavioural passivity found in schizophrenia, particularly the catatonic form, can be attributed to the distorted body image of a damaged ego. Similarly, the incomprehensible language is interpreted as infantile regression.

Objectively, there is little evidence to support the Freudian interpretation. For example, Roger Brown has challenged the notion that the language behaviour found in schizophrenia bears any resemblance to children's speech (Brown 1972). In terms of treatment, Freud himself did little with patients suffering from psychoses (severe distortions of reality), including schizophrenia. Since therapy involved developing insight into unconscious processes, there was a strong verbal component to treatment which often made it unsuited to such disorders (Luborsky and Spence 1978).

Other psychodynamic theorists have also offered interpretations of the origins of schizophrenia, and have attempted to provide treatment. In particular, analysts of the *object relations school* developed models based on the effects of early relationships (see Chapter 5). For example, Margaret Mahler, a neo-Freudian theorist who has focused on personality development in infancy, suggests that schizophrenia develops from the child being unable to separate from the mother. Mahler views this separation process as difficult for all individuals: 'not even the most normally endowed child, with the most optimally available mother, is able to weather the separation . . . process without crisis' (Mahler *et al.* 1975: 229). In the case

double-bind hypothesis
a theory of schizophrenia
developed by anthropologist
Gregory Bateson and his
colleagues, which argues
that faulty communication
patterns within the family are
the cause of schizophrenia

expressed emotion a
pattern of communication
within families which is
characterized by high levels
of criticism, hostility and
emotional intensity

of schizophrenia, the mother and child form an intense interdependency, called a *symbiotic attachment*, which prevents the child from developing a healthy, distinct ego. This focus on mother–child relationships was most evident in Bateson's **double-bind hypothesis** (Bateson *et al.* 1956). Bateson's model, which suggested that the mother gives contradictory messages (like 'come closer', then shrinking from physical contact) has been attacked for depending largely on retrospective analysis of communication patterns. This makes it impossible to know if the way family members communicate is the *cause* of schizophrenia, or a *result* of trying to cope with the behaviours associated with schizophrenia.

At this point, the double-bind hypothesis has been largely discredited (Neill 1990). However, the idea that family relationships play a factor in the development of schizophrenia has led to interest in **expressed emotion**. Expressed emotion refers to communication patterns which are marked by high levels of criticism, hostility and emotional intensity (Jenkins and Karno 1992; Butzlaff and Hooley 1998). Unlike the double-bind hypothesis, the theory does not focus on expressed emotion as a cause of schizophrenia; instead, it argues that *relapse rates* are much higher when individuals with schizophrenia reside in families with high levels of the negative communications described by expressed emotion. In effect, criticizing and blaming the individual for their disorder seems to create a stressor of the type described by the diathesis–stress model. In the past decade, studies have indicated that expressed emotion is a factor in relapse rates in many countries, despite cultural differences in average levels of expressed emotion. (We will return to this point at the end of the chapter.)

In a sense, expressed emotion theory is an offspring of the double-bind hypothesis, which first focused attention on communication patterns within the family. However, expressed emotion theory is much more limited, emphasizing recovery, not causation. While this may be realistic, it means the theory does not help to clarify the origins of schizophrenia. In terms of treatment, we must conclude that psychodynamic approaches do not seem well-suited to treatment of schizophrenia (as Freud first noted), though individual analysts have claimed some success (Kohut 1977). While research on expressed emotion seems promising, the psychodynamic approach generally does not fare very well in dealing with the complexities of schizophrenia.

The Humanistic Approach

Like the psychodynamic approach, the humanistic approach emphasizes distortions of development. However, it interprets the origins of the distortions very differently from Freud or other psychodynamic theorists. The behaviours which are labelled as 'schizophrenia' represent the individual's response to the world, however distorted it may seem to other people. For the therapist, the essential concern is to try to understand *what* the person is experiencing. As Rollo May has said, focusing instead on the *how* and *why* of the individual's condition will result in understanding 'everything except the most important thing of all, the existing person' (May 1961: 25).

What is it that the person is experiencing in schizophrenia? In some sense, it seems that the person sees the demands of the environment as intensely conflicting with the needs of the self. R. D. Laing, a psycho-analytically-trained British psychiatrist who came to adopt a humanistic view, talked about it as 'the divided self' – a split created by the need for 'compliance with the other person's intentions or expectations for one's self' (Laing 1965: 98). In Rogerian terms, externally imposed conditions of worth lead to an extreme lack of congruence. If the external demands are sufficiently threatening, then withdrawal from social interaction can seem a reasonable option in order to preserve some part of the self. This withdrawal, accompanied by a 'splitting off' of the self, is sometimes called **depersonalization** by clinicians; such reactions are at least occasionally experienced by most people under stressful circumstances. As Brown and Herrnstein have noted, it is a sense of looking at the situation from outside, accompanied by the feeling that 'this isn't really happening to *me*' (Brown and Herrnstein 1975).

However the process is described, it seems that the threats to the self produce a profound sense of distress and loss of self-awareness, which results in the characteristic behaviours seen in schizophrenia. Since withdrawal from social interaction is often part of the response, it seems hard to fathom how humanistic therapy could proceed. Yet in fact Rogers and other clinicians have successfully applied *person-centred therapy* to working with individuals with schizophrenia (Rogers *et al.* 1967; Teusch 1990). Basically, the process depends on the therapist first convincing the individual that the therapist is concerned, and is not a threat. Often, this may require long periods of sitting quietly with the person, waiting for a sign of possible interaction. In one case, Rogers worked with a twenty-eight-year-old man named Jim who had been hospitalized for two and a half years. After months of weekly meetings which passed mostly in silence, Jim finally began to speak. After several more sessions, he began to reveal feelings of bitterness, mistrust and worthlessness. Near the end of one session, Jim, expressing his frustration, said, 'I want to go, cause I don't care what happens.' Rogers responded to this by saying, 'I'd just like to say – I care about you. And I care what happens' (Rogers 1967). The conversation in which this exchange occurred marked a turning point in the therapeutic process; several months later, Jim was discharged from the hospital and began a job. Eight years later, he spontaneously wrote to Rogers to say that he was still employed, had friends and felt content with his life (Meador and Rogers 1979).

While this example typifies the Rogerian approach, and suggests that it may be useful with schizophrenia, there are a number of unresolved issues. Given the poor reliability of diagnostic standards in the early 1960s, it is conceivable that Jim would not be diagnosed as schizophrenic under current criteria. More generally, there is a concern that, like other insight therapies, person-centred therapy is not likely to have a very high overall success rate, because of the need for verbal interaction. However, Prouty has claimed that person-centred therapy is possible with a variety of 'non-verbal' individuals, including those with mental retardation as well as schizophrenia (Prouty 1990). Overall, however, the number of cases may be too small to be very representative.

In summary, the humanistic approach suggests that schizophrenia is an expression of the vulnerability of the self. For some individuals, the incongruence created by the demands of others can result in a virtual dissolution

depersonalization a type of dissociative reaction in with the individual psychologically withdraws from a situation, often accompanied by feeling that their body is not real or belongs to someone else

of the individual's sense of self (e.g. Vonnegut 1975). Although certainly not proven by current evidence, this interpretation seems consistent with the diathesis–stress model of schizophrenia. In terms of treatment, Rogerian techniques clearly emphasize the caring which has been identified as a beneficial factor in all therapies (Frank 1963; Stiles *et al*. 1986). If expressions of hostility and criticism hamper recovery (as research on expressed emotion indicates), then caring and acceptance by others may in fact open the door to growth and rediscovery of the self.

For further consideration

Given the discussion of how the various approaches view schizophrenia, do you believe that psychotherapy should be seen as an alternative to the use of drugs, or simply an adjunct? And which approach do you see as most suitable to this role?

Evaluating Our Understanding of Schizophrenia

As we have seen, each of the approaches has something to say about the nature of schizophrenia, and how to help those who suffer from it. The explanations offered differ significantly, however, and so do the attitudes which are implied. In this sense, schizophrenia provides perhaps the clearest example of how the approaches differ in their views of abnormal behaviour.

Resolving these differences requires a better understanding of what schizophrenia *is*. Is it a physiological disorder? A form of learned dysfunction? An arbitrary social construct? All of these? One way of gaining some perspective on the issue is by looking at how other cultures view it. A major study by the World Health Organization in the 1970s looked at schizophrenia in ten countries, reflecting both industrialized and developing societies (Jablensky *et al*. 1992). Using agreed-upon diagnostic criteria, the researchers in each country identified new cases of schizophrenia, and followed the course of treatment for two years; altogether, they considered almost 1,400 cases. In terms of overall incidence rates, types of symptoms and even average age of onset, there was remarkable similarity across cultures. This tends to suggest that there *is* some common cause which is unrelated to culture – in other words, a physiological factor. However, the results of treatment were startling: over two years, the rate of recovery in industrialized countries was only 37 per cent, whereas in developing countries it was 63 per cent, nearly double.

This result is surprising, since we tend to view medical care as superior in industrialized countries. (In fact, individuals in the developing countries were more likely to seek folk remedies, and less likely to receive drugs.) Unless one is prepared to argue that drugs actually hamper recovery (an unlikely possibility), how can one account for the pattern of results? A number of possible differences may contribute. For one thing, individuals in developing countries may find it easier to remain part of society by finding useful work, because jobs tend to be less specialized. In addition, extended families living together are more common in developing countries, which places less of a burden for support on just one or two caregivers.

While all these things may play a role, a more significant factor seems to be differences in attitudes (Lin and Kleinman 1988). People in developing countries typically have less rigid conceptions of abnormality, and are less likely to view the behaviour as permanent, thus reducing *stigmatizing*. In general, families in developing countries are more supportive towards a member who has schizophrenia than is true in industrialized nations (Jenkins and Karno 1992). The reasons for this may have to do with *expressed emotion*, and also *attributions*. While families high in expressed emotion can be found in all cultures, they appear to be more common in industrialized nations. This may reflect the fact that the industrialized (Western) nations tend to favour individualist rather than collectivist notions of the self, and to emphasize personal responsibility. Given these attributional biases, families within this cultural context tend to blame the mentally ill for their actions, and believe they can control their symptoms 'if they just try' (Hooley 1998). These effects suggest that cultural factors must be integrated as a basic element of our understanding of schizophrenia and other forms of abnormal behaviour (Fabrega 1995).

Certainly, the differences in recovery rates cannot easily be explained if one assumes that schizophrenia is purely physiological. Instead, it seems that environmental factors, including culture, play a role as well. This conclusion, which seems to support the diathesis–stress model, perhaps helps to explain why each of the approaches has *some* benefit as therapy. At the same time, it leaves us to ponder how our *own* culture views schizophrenia, and abnormal behaviour in general.

| For further consideration | Does it surprise you that recovery rates differ across countries? Do you think this supports the view of critics like Thomas Szasz, who argues that mental illnesses like schizophrenia are a 'myth'? |

Conclusion

Abnormal psychology is concerned with the understanding of abnormal behaviour. The question of what constitutes 'abnormal' behaviour is a difficult one. While it always implies some form of *deviance* from expected norms of behaviour, deviance is not in itself a reasonable basis for defining mental disorders, since it is too dependent on cultural values. Instead, the generally accepted definition today is that abnormal behaviour involves significant suffering and/or maladaptive functioning. While these criteria seem intuitively reasonable, they still pose problems of *who decides* what is maladaptive and what represents significant suffering.

Viewed conceptually, abnormal psychology involves three aspects: diagnosis of the problem, understanding the cause of the problem and therapy to treat the problem. In practice, the three elements are closely intertwined, making it hard to assess one element independently of the others. Hence, while each of the five approaches has its own interpretation of the origins of abnormal behaviour, at present the primary means of assessing the various theories is by examining their efficacy as therapies.

To the extent that it is possible to determine, the evidence suggests that *all* the approaches have some value, but that *no* approach is superior for *all* forms of disorders. One explanation for this outcome may be that there are non-specific effects of therapy in general, such as emotional support provided by the therapist, and the individual's belief that therapy can help. Another possible reason for the partial effectiveness of most therapies is that most patterns of abnormal behaviour may have multiple causes. For example, a particular disorder may be triggered by a physiological imbalance, which can be treated with drug therapy. However, in trying to adapt to that imbalance, the individual may have developed other maladaptive behaviours which drugs will not change. To deal with these aspects, some form of psychotherapy may be more appropriate, though at present we have too little information to determine which approach is best in a particular circumstance, or why.

The limitations of our current knowledge are particularly evident when considering schizophrenia. While neuroleptic drugs have proven effective in alleviating delusions, hallucinations and other primary symptoms of the disorder, the *medical model* on which drug therapy is based has not yet produced a clear explanation of the mechanism of action. Similarly, the diathesis–stress model, which suggests that schizophrenia results from a combination of a physiological disposition and the effects of environmental stressors, seems promising, but is as yet unproven.

At this point, we must admit that we still have no clear understanding of the causes of schizophrenia, or how to treat it. Interestingly, some cultures seem to deal with it better than we do – a reminder that there is a social dimension to abnormal behaviour. While most clinicians believe that normality and abnormality are part of a continuum, too many people in our society still view mental disorders as something strange and frightening. Not only does this hamper the understanding of abnormal behaviour, it also hampers treatment by encouraging stigmatizing of individuals with mental disorders. Consider this example: suppose that schizophrenia really is based on defective attention, which leads people to behave in idiosyncratic ways. In itself, this defect may hamper the individual in some ways, but if the quirkiness of their behaviour (or society's perception of it) leads to the person being stigmatized and rejected, then the effects of social isolation will create further problems. The challenge is to understand the core problem, but respond to the *person*, not simply the problem.

In the end, behaviour, whether normal or abnormal, is still *human* behaviour. As travellers on the human journey, we are all alike, and ignoring this reality ultimately diminishes our capacity to understand *any* aspect of human experience. As R. D. Laing said in *The Divided Self*, there is still too much talk of Them, and not enough of Us (Laing 1965).

One may argue that this is a social issue, not a scientific one. Yet the whole premise of this book is that psychology is the product of human beings, and is therefore influenced by the processes which affect all human behaviour. Each of us brings to the study of behaviour our own perceptions and cognitive schema, based on our past experience. Part of that past experience, of course, is the culture we live in. If our culture encourages us to view abnormal behaviour as Us versus Them, then that perception will influence our theories as well. This is *not* to suggest that everything is a construction of our minds – the behaviour we seek to explain is real. Instead, it is simply meant to point out that we each tend to see only part of the overall picture, and this partial vision tends to be reflected in our theories. In this sense, the struggle to understand abnormal behaviour, and the perplexities that surround it, reflects the larger challenges which face psychology as a whole.

Chapter Summary

♦ *Abnormal psychology* is concerned with the understanding of *abnormal behaviour*. While definitions have varied historically, it has typically been defined in terms of *deviance* from society's norms. Today, *DSM-IV* identifies significant *suffering* and/or *maladaptive functioning* as the primary criteria.

♦ Critics have questioned the value of classification systems like DSM-IV, citing problems of misdiagnosis and the *stigmatizing* effects of labels, but most psychiatrists and other clinicians find classification useful.

♦ Each of the five approaches has its own interpretation of the origins of abnormal behaviour; evaluation of these theories is closely tied up with assessment of the *efficacy* of therapies based on the theories.

♦ The *biological approach* emphasizes physiological and genetic factors, in terms of the *medical model*. The use of drug therapy, based on this approach, has made great progress as our knowledge of psychopharmacology has grown in recent years. As evidence for prenatal trauma as well as environmental influences grows, the *diathesis–stress* model is drawing more attention.

♦ The *behaviourist approach* sees abnormal behaviour as based on learning of inappropriate responses. Techniques of *behaviour modification*, such as *systematic desensitization*, have been used to treat a variety of problems.

♦ The *cognitive approach*, consistent with its general view, emphasizes the role of cognitive mediators in abnormal behaviour. Social learning theory has been applied to the use of behaviour modification, resulting in *cognitive behaviour modification*. Other cognitive theories, such as Ellis's *rational-emotive therapy*, have focused on the faulty beliefs which accompany maladaptive behaviour. Like psychodynamic and humanistic therapies, cognitive therapy places an emphasis on *insight* into one's behaviour.

♦ Within the *psychodynamic approach*, Freud saw abnormal behaviour as the result of unconscious conflicts within the psyche; therapy was based on helping the individual to gain awareness of the underlying dynamics. While differing in specifics, other psychodynamic theorists also emphasize the importance of insight. Psychodynamic therapy can be difficult to evaluate, since its goals are often fairly global, involving modifying the whole structure of personality. While the *double-bind hypothesis* has been largely refuted, it has led to interest in *expressed emotions* in families as a factor in relapses.

◆ The *humanistic approach* rejects classification in favour of trying to understand how the individual experiences the world. Abnormal behaviour is regarded as a distortion of growth, with the maladaptive behaviours representing an attempt to cope with threats to the *self*. Rogers's *person-centred therapy* often results in changes in how individuals express their feelings and goals, but it is harder to assess behavioural change.

◆ *Schizophrenia* is one of the most challenging forms of mental disorder, and has been the focus of considerable research. Although the term itself is less than 100 years old, the primary symptoms of *delusions, hallucinations, thought disturbances* and *distortions of emotional expression* have been recorded since ancient times.

◆ The *dopamine hypothesis* has drawn considerable attention as a theory of schizophrenia, and is partially supported by the effectiveness of neuroleptic drugs in treating the primary symptoms. However, difficulties still exist with both the theory and the use of drugs in treatment.

◆ The *diathesis–stress model* suggests that schizophrenia results from a combination of a physiological predisposition and the effects of environmental stressors. This 'two hit' model is supported by research on the role of heredity and prenatal exposure to influenza as predisposing factors.

◆ The other approaches interpret schizophrenia in terms of maladaptive learning of various types. Of these, the *defective attention theory* of the cognitive approach seems to offer the greatest potential to enhance our understanding, possibly in conjunction with the medical model. However, it has not yet resulted in any specific therapy.

◆ In the end, the study of abnormal behaviour, including schizophrenia, challenges our perceptions of ourselves and our relationship to other people. In this sense, progress in understanding abnormal behaviour is likely to depend on our progress in psychology as a whole.

Key Terms and Concepts

abnormal behaviour
aversive conditioning
behaviour modification
cognitive behaviour modification
cognitive restructuring
defective attention theory
delusions
depersonalization
diathesis–stress model
dopamine hypothesis
efficacy
hallucinations
hierarchy of fears
insight

medical model
negative symptoms
person-centred therapy
psychotherapy
rational-emotive therapy
resistance
schizophrenia
spontaneous remission
stigma
symptom substitution
systematic desensitization
thought disturbances
token economy
transference

Suggestions for Further Reading

For readers wondering what it is like to have a mental disorder, Dale Peterson's *A Mad People's History of Madness* provides a remarkable collection of autobiographical accounts. For an individual account of schizophrenia, read Mark Vonnegut's *The Eden Express*.

For a fascinating exploration of society's attitudes towards abnormal behaviour in the past 35 years, *Back to the Asylum*, by LaFond and Durham, covers legal and social as well as scientific aspects.

The biological approach to mental disorders is captured well in a brief, readable book by Samuel Baronides, *Molecules and Mental Illness*. For approaches *other* than the biological, two sources are recommended. *The Evolution of Psychotherapy*, by Jeffrey Zeig, provides the views of 26 well-known therapists, based on an extraordinary conference which brought them together to discuss their ideas. For a more technical overview, Gurman and Messer's *Essential Psychotherapies: Theory and Practice* provides reviews of 12 major forms of therapy (including all of those discussed in this chapter).

For a current view of research on various aspects of schizophrenia, Lenzenweger and Dworkin's *Origins and Development of Schizophrenia* provides a balanced, albeit technical, source.

10

Psychology in Perspective

Searching for Answers
Introduction
Reconsidering the Origins of the Approaches
Perception and Theory Formation
Objective Evidence versus Shifting Paradigms
Paradigms in Psychology
Psychology and Science
Limitations of the Scientific Method for Psychology
The Search for a New Methodology

Psychology and Culture
The Many and the One
Seeking Convergence
Embracing Pluralism
Conclusion
Chapter Summary
Key Terms and Concepts
Recommendations for Further Reading

Searching for Answers

There is an old story about a man who had accomplished many things in his life – inventing new products, acquiring a great fortune and becoming famous. Yet still, he felt a sense of incompleteness, as though somehow the real meaning of life had eluded him.

One day, he heard of a hermit who lived on a far-off mountain. Despite the remoteness of the location, many people journeyed to visit the hermit, because he was reputed to know the secret of life. Like these travellers, the dissatisfied man decided to seek out the hermit.

After a long and difficult journey, the man finally located the hermit. He lived in a simple shack, with no running water or electricity – yet his eyes glowed with what seemed great joy. Sensing that the rumours might be true, the man pressed the hermit for the secret of life. The hermit looked at him, with his fine clothes and belongings, and said, 'If you wish to know the secret, you must first give away all your money and possessions.'

At this, the man hesitated. He thought about it for some time, and finally agreed, having realized that his possessions had not made him happy anyway.

> Finally, the hermit spoke. 'The secret of life is . . .' He paused, drawing out the suspense, and then whispered, 'There *is* no secret!'

Introduction

Like the man in the story, you have been on a journey. Rather than crossing unfamiliar terrain, you have been venturing into a domain of new ideas. In some ways, such journeys are more difficult than physical journeys, because they challenge us to think in new ways. Having gone through the previous chapters, you should have a better understanding of what psychology is, and what research has been able to tell us about human behaviour. I hope you have found the experience both interesting and challenging. Interesting, in that psychology is concerned with who and what we are, and most of us would like to understand more about both ourselves and other people. Challenging, because psychology is full of unanswered questions and controversies, and this book has tried to explore those controversies, rather than hide them behind a mass of 'facts'. Exploring ideas *is* a kind of adventure, and psychology is fertile territory for such adventures. In much the way that a hired guide helps explorers, I have tried to guide your experience, to help you past the worst difficulties and confusions. While I hope you will venture further in the future, it seems an opportune moment to look back over the ground we have covered, and try to get some sense of what may lie ahead.

Reconsidering the Origins of the Approaches

In the preceding chapters, we have explored five major approaches to the study of human behaviour. Each approach seems to offer its own interpretation, and on many issues there seems to be significant disagreement – for example, in explaining the origins of aggression. Consequently, it is understandable if at this point, like the man in the story, you are tempted to ask for a simple answer to a basic question: 'Which one is right?' Like the man in the story, you may be disappointed at the response.

The answer, of course, is all of them, and none of them. All of them, in that each approach has had significant impact on our view of ourselves. None of them, in that no one approach has been able to explain successfully the full range of human behaviour and experience. As we have discussed, each approach still has gaps and unanswered major questions. Interestingly, however, each sees *different* questions as awaiting answers. In this respect, as in so many others, they continue to disagree.

The diversity of approaches poses a contradiction: while the approaches differ in assumptions, methods and explanations, each claims to be offering the appropriate basis for psychology. Normally, a discipline is defined by its assumptions and methods, as well as its subject matter. How can one speak of psychology as a single discipline, when there is no single framework which underlies it? One answer, suggested by cognitive psychologist George Miller, is to assert that what unites psychology is the faith that eventually a common framework will be found (Miller 1985). This framework will provide 'a science of immediate experience' – Miller's description of psychology's central focus. But why isn't there such a framework *already*? And if no such framework exists after more than a hundred years, is it reasonable to hope for one in the future? In order to answer these questions, we need to return to the subject of how different approaches originate.

Perception and Theory Formation

In Chapter 1, we looked at some of the basic principles of perception, and noted that the way we see the world depends both on what is 'out there' to be experienced, and on what is 'inside' – that is, perception depends on the interaction of external stimuli and our internal processes of selection and interpretation. Because of those internal processes, what we experience in any situation is influenced by what we *expect* to experience. In the extreme case, our perceptions may depend more on our interpretation than on the actual stimulus. Not long ago, a Japanese exchange student in Louisiana was seeking directions to a party. He approached a house to get information; the owner, perceiving him as a threat, shot and killed the student before he even spoke. We can call it a tragedy, which it certainly is, but we must also acknowledge the power of the processes that led to that tragedy. (For example, what experiences and attitudes led the homeowner to fear the approach of a stranger?) Given the vast range of stimuli we encounter, we select certain elements, and then interpret them using our current cognitive schemata. In this sense, the 'reality' we experience is individually constructed.

As human beings, psychologists inevitably are also dependent on the processes of perceptual selection and interpretation. This is reflected in the differences in assumptions and methods which are central to the various approaches. As Sigmund Koch, a psychologist noted for his interest in such issues, has commented, 'Different theorists will – relative to their different analytical purposes, predictive or practical aims, perceptual sensitivities, metaphor-forming capacities, and pre-existing discrimination repertoires – make asystematically different perceptual cuts upon the same domain' (Koch 1985: 93). In effect, different theorists, with differing interests and differing expectations, will perceive the world differently, and will develop their theories accordingly. Philosopher Bertrand Russell had this in mind when he commented that animals in psychological research seem to match the theories of their experimenters: American (behaviourist) animals use trial and error, while German (cognitive) animals are reflective! (cited by Skinner 1974: 18).

Hence, the origin of any approach is dependent on processes which are partly subjective. Failing to recognize this can lead to becoming blind to the limitations of one's own approach – what Koch has called **cognitive pathology**.

cognitive pathology
a phenomenon whereby researchers selectively ignore simplifying assumptions and other limitations which are part of the foundations of their theories and methods

Cognitive pathology is reflected in practices like making simplifying assumptions that lead to restrictions in what one observes, and then developing 'total amnesia' for those assumptions and restrictions. (A limited example is when a researcher operationally defines aggression as punching an inflatable doll in a laboratory, and then assumes without further evidence that the results of a study can be applied to homicide.) Indeed, it can be argued that without recognizing the role of underlying assumptions and methods, it is impossible to evaluate any conclusion properly. In this regard, the tendency for many authors to present psychology as a collection of 'facts' has questionable value, and may even hamper the possibility of real understanding.

Because our assumptions affect our judgement about what is relevant in interpreting a situation, different approaches may view the same event differently. For example, suppose two researchers examine the same experiment, dealing with the effects of television viewing on aggression in children. One asserts that the results can be generalized to everyday life, while the other insists that the laboratory study lacks realism, and cannot be applied to the real world. If the argument actually reflects differing assumptions about the causes of aggression, but this is not acknowledged, then no real dialogue is possible. It is not simply the validity of generalizing, but the entire meaning of the evidence, that is at issue.

The idea that our assumptions affect the way we reason was supported in a study conducted by Eric Amsel (Amsel *et al.* 1991). In conjunction with a lawyer and another psychologist, Amsel studied the way that lawyers and psychologists evaluate the causes of events. They found that lawyers are trained to reason mechanistically, using counterfactual arguments, whereas psychologists are trained to reason statistically, using covariance arguments. As a result, the two groups tend to explain behaviour differently. For example, consider this situation: David was watching TV, and the picture was poor. He kicked the set, and the picture improved. Given this scenario, a lawyer might justify David's behaviour by suggesting that if he had not kicked it, the picture would not have improved (a counterfactual argument). By contrast, a psychologist might explain it by noting that on several past occasions, kicking the set led to the picture improving (a covariance argument). The point here is *not* that one argument is necessarily better than the other, but that they depend on different assumptions about what makes an argument convincing. In the same way, advocates of different approaches make different assumptions about behaviour. Understanding those assumptions can help to clarify the ways in which the approaches disagree.

While perceptual processes help us to understand how different approaches can arise, they do *not* answer the question of whether one approach is better than another. After all, the fact that advocates of various approaches perceive the world differently does not automatically mean that all see it *equally accurately*. Instead, it is *logically* possible for one theory to be superior at explaining the world. Does it therefore follow that one approach actually *is* better? And how do we decide?

For further consideration

Which of the five approaches do you prefer? Why? Try to poll some of your classmates, to see their preferences. What do you conclude from these results?

Objective Evidence versus Shifting Paradigms

logical empiricism in philosophy of science, the assumption that it is possible to compare and evaluate theories in terms of how well they account for the evidence

Traditionally, psychology has been founded on the premise of logical empiricism, a principle shared with the sciences in general. **Logical empiricism** says that it is possible to evaluate theories in terms of how well they account for the evidence (Savage 1990). This principle is an extension of the basic belief in *empiricism*, which states that observing the world is the way to gain knowledge. However, accepting the importance of observation does not necessarily imply that observational evidence is a *sufficient* basis for evaluating a theory. Indeed, statistical theory tells us that observations cannot directly prove a theory to be true. (See the Appendix for further discussion of this point.) Hence, logical empiricism is a possible, but not inevitable, result of accepting the importance of observations.

Logical empiricism says that theories are evaluated, and either accepted or discarded, on the weight of the evidence. As the history of the natural sciences over the past 200 years has demonstrated, it can be a very productive framework for enhancing knowledge, especially when dealing with the inanimate world of atoms and molecules. However, it is not the only possible framework, and in recent years it has been challenged. The primary alternative interpretation for why theories are accepted rests on the role of social processes. One of the earliest, and best-known, expressions of this view was a book called *The Structure of Scientific Revolutions*, by philosopher of science Thomas Kuhn (1970). Kuhn asserts that science operates in terms of **paradigms**, frameworks which are endorsed by a group of adherents. Rather than being simply a theory, a paradigm represents an entire way of seeing the world. As Kuhn states, in a new paradigm 'old terms, concepts, and experiments fall into new relationships with each other' (Kuhn 1970: 148).

paradigm in Kuhn's analysis of science, a superordinate framework or world view accepted by a group of researchers, which shapes both theories and evidence; since the paradigm influences the observations one makes, no observations can ever be used to evaluate the paradigm

As a framework for our concepts, a paradigm is more basic than a theory; indeed, different theories can exist within the same paradigm. (For example, Pavlov and Skinner both developed theories within behaviourism as a paradigm, each dealing with different types of responses.) Since theories exist within a particular paradigm, sometimes a new theory actually represents a change in paradigm as well. For example, Einstein's theory of relativity required physicists to move from a Newtonian paradigm to a relativistic one as a way of seeing the structure of the universe. Instead of space and time being independent, as in Newton's framework, space and time became inseparably linked in the new paradigm represented by Einstein's theory.

The crucial element of Kuhn's view is his conception of how one framework replaces another. Paradigms change not because a new one proves better at explaining the evidence than the old paradigm, but because the new one becomes more *popular*. Citing the shift from a Newtonian to an Einsteinian universe, Kuhn argues that the change came because the newer paradigm came to be preferred to the older one. Indeed, he cites a famous remark by physicist Max Planck (who helped to shape the 'Einsteinian revolution'), that 'a new scientific theory does not triumph by convincing its opponents and making them see the light, but rather because its opponents eventually die, and a new generation grows up that is familiar with it' (Kuhn 1970: 150).

In Kuhn's view, because a paradigm is an entire way of seeing the world, observations cannot be made independently of the paradigm. Any piece of evidence only makes sense in terms of the underlying framework which generated it. As a result, observations cannot be used as the basis of choosing between paradigms. This conclusion, which is in direct contradiction to logical empiricism, means that the reasons for preferring one paradigm to another are not simply the result of a better fit to the data. While one may refer to the 'simplicity' or 'elegance' of a model, Kuhn argues that ultimately the choice is more social than rational.

To anyone accustomed to thinking of science as rational and objective, this is a rather startling notion, and Kuhn's argument has not gone uncriticized. Indeed, the very term 'paradigm' is a slippery one, and Kuhn has been attacked for not defining it sufficiently precisely. However, as Baars points out, Kuhn was writing in reaction to the notions of logical empiricism, and in that sense most readers have little trouble grasping his intended meaning (Baars 1986). Still, Kuhn's view is disturbing, because it suggests that a paradigm is essentially an arbitrary framework. This limits the value of evidence in science, because observations will have very different meanings depending on the paradigm. For example, consider how a behaviourist and a humanist would interpret someone saying, 'I feel depressed.' For the behaviourist, the statement is simply a verbal response which has been previously reinforced; for the humanist, it is a valid description of an internal emotional state.

While Kuhn's analysis has been both controversial and influential, it has not led to the complete abandonment of empiricism. Most philosophers of science still seem to believe that rational choices can be made between theories, and assume that observations *can* be made independently of a theoretical framework. In this view, theories may be subjective structurings of the world, but observations are still useful in evaluating theories (Savage 1990).

Paradigms in Psychology

Whether Kuhn's notion of paradigms is correct or not, it has been frequently applied to psychology (e.g. Berlyne 1975; Baars 1986). However, unlike physics, psychology has never had a single paradigm – instead, there have been several paradigms, denoted by the different approaches we have discussed in this book. Hence, we cannot talk of 'paradigm shifts' in the sense of a complete reorientation of the discipline. Instead, psychology has several competing paradigms, none of which has enjoyed complete dominance. Over time, though, the approaches have varied in their level of acceptance, and it is interesting to look at the changes in their *relative* popularity as paradigms.

With the exception of the humanistic, all the approaches can trace their origins back to at least the early decades of the twentieth century. Within that time frame, there have certainly been indications of shifts in popularity. From the 1930s until the early 1960s, the dominant paradigms were the psychodynamic (mainly psychoanalytic) and behaviourist approaches, with the former favoured by clinicians and the latter by experimentalists. As has already been discussed earlier in the book, these two approaches differ in many of their assumptions and methods, and have frequently been highly critical of each other. However, over time, both have lost influence, and have largely been supplanted by the biological and cognitive approaches.

Many authors have written about the striking shift from behaviourism to cognitivism (e.g. Berlyne 1975; Baars 1986), whereby mental processes have gone from being essentially irrelevant to being the central concern. Although the change involved new experimental techniques and results (such as the study of observational learning), one can argue that the primary factor was the shift in interests of a new generation of researchers. The parallel shift from the psychodynamic to the biological is not as simple to describe. Certainly, the development of new drugs has altered clinical practice, and fostered a shift from psychoanalysis among clinicians (Shorter 1997). At the same time, the increasing popularity of the biological approach is evident among experimentalists, who may be attracted by the possibility of using new techniques to gain insight into behaviour. (For example, Servos *et al.* (1999) recently used MRI scans to identify an error in Penfield's mapping of the cortex.) In addition, the cognitive and biological approaches are not completely at loggerheads, as the earlier pair of approaches were. Indeed, some researchers see an increasing fusion of the two, as we will discuss later in this chapter.

Whether Kuhn's argument about the role of social processes in paradigm change is correct or not, it is clear that psychology is very different from most disciplines. Whereas physics involved a shift from one broadly accepted paradigm to another, there is significant disagreement within psychology about what paradigm is most appropriate for the discipline.

Psychology has been defined in various ways, but the most widely accepted view, reflected in this book, is that psychology must deal with *both* behaviour *and* experience. It is not, as the behaviourists suggest, purely the study of overt responses, nor is it solely concerned with inner experience (thoughts, feelings and so on). This duality has always been a source of difficulty. Wundt's attempts to analyse experience in terms of sensory inputs ultimately came to little, and the awkward position of the humanists in contemporary psychology shows that dealing with subjective experience is still problematical. As Robinson (1985) has suggested, it seems we are forced to choose between a psychology which is not scientific, and a science which is not psychology! That is, Robinson believes that although questions of inner experience are central to psychology, they cannot be addressed scientifically.

To understand this comment, one need only consider some of the ways in which researchers have tried to handle inner experience and the questions of thought, feeling and desire which it raises. The introspectionists tried to reduce conscious experience to objective sensory properties, to little avail. Radical behaviourists like Watson and Skinner have sought to side-step the problem by insisting that inner experience is irrelevant. The humanists, aware of the failures of others, have tried to suggest changes in how we conceive of science. However, the methods they advocate have not been widely accepted. Even the middle ground – trying to adapt the methods of natural science to address at least *some* aspects of the mind – faces serious obstacles. All of these responses acknowledge that 'inner experience' and 'science' seem hard to combine. It is this dilemma which has prevented the acceptance of a single approach as the universal paradigm. To understand the basis of this tension, let us reconsider the role of research methods in psychology.

For further consideration

Assuming Robinson is right, would you rather see a scientific psychology which ignored inner experience, or a non-scientific psychology which included the study of inner experience? Why?

Psychology and Science

Depending on how one chooses to look at it, the source of the continuing fragmentation lies either with the limitations of science or with our expectations of psychology. Let us consider the second point first. Our experience as human beings leads us to ask about the causes of behaviour. In everyday life, we generate such explanations constantly, invoking our individual and collective notions of personality, motivation and so on. Science, including psychology, often charges that these notions are not really explanations at all, but simply muddled generalities. However, saying that people's everyday explanations are worthless does not itself enhance understanding – and understanding of human experience is precisely what people are seeking. Thus, unless science is itself willing to tackle the task of explaining experience, its criticisms lack credibility (Robinson 1985). In this sense, asserting that psychology should not address these issues (as Watson and other radical behaviourists have) seems to miss the point.

Limitations of the Scientific Method for Psychology

Instead of rejecting people's interest in the mind and subjective experience, one can argue that the problem lies with the scientific method. That is, the inability of science to provide insights which are both rigorous and relevant is largely due to the way science operates. Critics have suggested that science has two limitations when it comes to addressing inner experience.

One limitation involves science's search for causal explanations. While this has proved highly successful in dealing with many phenomena in the natural sciences, it encounters difficulties when applied to mental states. The crucial difficulty is that mental states are not directly observable, and neither they nor the behaviours which are used to indicate them can be uniquely associated to particular causes (Robinson 1985). Instead, the result is often a kind of circularity, like pulling oneself up by one's bootstraps: inner experience is used to explain the behaviour which is meant to indicate inner experience. For example, John says he is unhappy. We then examine John's facial expression, tone of voice and other behaviours as a means of validating this statement. In turn, we then 'explain' the behaviour by referring to the fact that he is unhappy! While this is a simplified example, it points to the difficulties involved in trying to explain inner experience independently of behaviour. In this regard, the traditional model of causation which is used in science seems ineffective when dealing with thoughts, feelings, motives and other aspects of inner experience. In some cases, we can use different forms of behaviour to converge on a mental process (as when we compare thinking aloud protocols and patterns of errors in problem solving), but fundamentally, what we can observe is inevitably different from what the person experiences within himself or herself. Thus, trying to generate a causal explanation becomes difficult, because one is moving between two different domains.

The second limitation concerns the use of the experimental method. The logic of experiments, with their need for strict control and assumptions of objectivity, falters when applied to complex behaviour (as opposed to simple behaviours, like isolated muscular responses). The central difficulty is that human beings are *aware* of being studied, which makes it difficult to obtain an objective assessment of behaviour – particularly when awareness is part of what researchers hope to explain. Thus, as medical ethicist Richard Zaner has commented, an experiment is really an interaction: even as one tries to study the behaviour of individuals, the individuals will be studying the experimental situation (Zaner 1985).

demand characteristics
the overt and covert cues present in an experimental situation which can influence how participants behave

This tendency for behaviour to be altered by the experimental context is emphasized by the concept of **demand characteristics** in research settings. Martin Orne uses the term to describe how participants in experiments respond to both the overt and covert cues of the situation (Orne 1962). Orne suggests that participants will attempt to figure out what is expected, and will use this information in guiding their behaviour. Consequently, he suggests, the only reliable experiment is one which produces a different outcome from what people expect. Otherwise, one cannot be sure whether the results obtained are a result of natural behaviour, or simply a self-fulfilling prophecy by the participants. For example, Orne did an experiment in which individuals in one group were hypnotized, while individuals in the control group were asked to *pretend* they were hypnotized. In effect, the control subjects were acting the way they *thought* a hypnotized person would act. In this case, they acted differently, suggesting that the behaviour of hypnotized individuals could not be explained by demand characteristics. (If hypnosis were play-acting, the hypnotized subjects should have reacted like the control group.) Researchers differ in their assessments of how important demand characteristics are to various situations, and hence how seriously Orne's critique affects the validity of laboratory research. At the very least, one must acknowledge that individuals in laboratory experiments are aware of being in an experiment, and this can obviously affect their behaviour. Reflecting this, Berlyne suggests researchers should 'form the habit of asking what a subject would do without a psychologist at his elbow' (Berlyne 1975: 77)!

As discussed in Chapter 8, concerns about how individuals react to being studied are particularly strong in dealing with social behaviour. British psychologist Colin Fraser has expressed concern that the emphasis on experimental methods ends up distorting the kinds of questions that are asked, and thereby our understanding of social behaviour (Fraser 1987). American social psychologist William McGuire suggests that 'our social psychological knowledge is a delusional system which represents reality only poorly, the representation being distorted by our limited intellectual apparatus and distorted by our cognitive systems and our wishes, values, and expectations' (McGuire 1985: 585). In one sense, he is offering an indictment of the traditional experimental method; but at the same time, he is *not* advocating the wholesale abandonment of observation and inquiry. Instead, he argues for recognizing the limitations of scientific knowledge, and working to minimize distortion and oversimplification. Paul Meehl, a former president of the American Psychological Association, has argued that psychology places too much emphasis on experimental methods and the search for causes. Other methods may not give direct information about causation, he notes, but they are nonetheless empirical, and therefore scientifically useful (Meehl 1971).

The Search for a New Methodology

The difficulty of applying the scientific method to inner experience has been a problem throughout psychology's history. Traditionally, science has evaluated theories by generating a hypothesis, which is then tested by doing an experiment; essentially, the hypothesis is a prediction about what will occur. Making predictions is seen, then, as a basic part of doing research and evaluating theories. In particular, experiments have been valued because, in the deterministic world of Newtonian physics, they provide insights into cause and effect. For a variety of reasons, psychology in its early years adopted this model as well.

Unfortunately, this has led to a variety of difficulties. As already noted, observing behaviour is more complicated than observing inanimate objects, and this poses significant challenges. In addition, the emphasis on experiments as the preferred research design has also influenced the data we gather, and possibly the kinds of theories we generate. Typically, it has meant the study of situations which are simple enough to control, thus allowing the assessment of theoretical predictions, and then generalizing the conclusions to the larger world (Hunt 1991). However, doing research in this way is not the only possibility, and questioning it does not mean abandoning empiricism as such. (Indeed, observing behaviour, in a variety of ways, has been very productive within psychology.) The problem seems related to the emphasis on generating causal predictions, and therefore using methods that make testing such predictions possible.

Ironically, the emphasis placed on experimental methods, with their predictions of causation, may be inappropriate. After all, it is possible to generate theories which do not generate causal predictions, or which cannot be directly evaluated through experiments. (Freud's theory is an example of the first case; evolutionary theory is an example of the second.) Nonetheless, moving away from models of simple causation would have significant implications for psychology. Before considering this issue more closely, let us consider some examples which suggest how such theories might be developed, and why they might be appropriate.

chaos theory a branch of mathematics dealing with non-linear functions which has been applied to the modelling of situations such as the weather and stock markets; non-linear systems are not predictable, because very small changes in initial conditions can result in radical differences at a later point

One relatively recent development in basic science which challenges the appropriateness of prediction is the study of non-linear dynamics associated with chaos theory (Hilborn 1994). **Chaos theory** tells us that many physical systems are *non-linear*; that is, they are not predictable, because very small changes in initial conditions can result in radical differences in outcomes. This phenomenon is sometimes called 'the butterfly effect', since something as small as the flap of a butterfly's wing could ultimately affect something as large as weather patterns over an entire continent. Similarly, a small measurement error could radically alter the expected outcome of an experiment. Hence, while still subject to the laws of causation, chaotic systems defy any serious attempts at predictability. A second characteristic of chaotic systems is *complexity*. While not all complex phenomena are chaotic in nature (otherwise science would not have gotten this far with predictive models!), in general, the more complex the situation, the more likely it is to be chaotic. For example, simple reflexes are basically linear (non-chaotic), but it is likely that, taken as a whole, the brain's functioning is chaotic. As chaos theory (which actually may represent a paradigm rather than a theory) develops, we are likely to find it being applied to a number of aspects of human behaviour. Considering this, Davison and Neale (1997) have argued that therapists should be cautious in assuming they can anticipate, let alone influence, all the factors which affect the behaviour of their patients.

Other models also suggest that there are alternatives to traditional linear, deterministic models; one example is **systems theory**. First developed by Norbert Weiner to deal with the complexities of aiming anti-aircraft guns (where the movement of the shell, the plane and the wind all affect the accuracy of the outcome), systems theory is increasingly being applied in the human domain. According to Robert Jervis, a system exists whenever there are multiple elements which interact, and where the properties of the system are different from those of the parts (Jervis 1998). In this sense, an individual could be considered a system (with the functioning of the various parts of the nervous system being elements, for example). Similarly, social groups could be considered a system, with the individuals as elements. (Social psychologists have long noted situations where choices by a group are different from the sum of the individual members' choices, for example.) The functioning of a system is governed by two basic processes, negative feedback and positive feedback. **Negative feedback** serves to maintain stability in the system, while **positive feedback** amplifies disturbances, thereby promoting a change in the response of the system. For example, a person driving a car continually makes adjustments to maintain the right direction. As long as the car is going in the intended direction, the adjustments are small (negative feedback). However, if the car loses traction and starts to skid, the driver will react by quickly turning the wheel the other way (positive feedback). Unfortunately, because the driver may over-react, it is possible that the car will begin skidding the other way, rather than simply returning to its original direction. This instability is inherent to positive feedback, and can result in non-linear effects. (The difference between the amount of steering required to compensate for a skid, and the amount that will make the car skid the other way, is quite small.)

systems theory a theoretical framework designed for understanding phenomena which involve multiple interrelated elements, where the properties of the whole are different from the properties of the parts; systems are viewed as governed by processes of negative feedback (which promotes stability) and positive feedback (which promotes change)
negative feedback a process within a system which serves to dampen disturbances, promoting stable functioning
positive feedback a process within a system which reacts to disturbances by amplifying the effects, triggering a major change in functioning

As the preceding example suggests, systems theory, like chaos theory, indicates that complex behaviour may be difficult to predict; for systems theory, this limitation is due to the nature of positive feedback. For example, in a confrontation, threats may sometimes serve to cause escalation of aggression, *or* may lead to both sides backing off (Jervis 1998). Without knowing all the elements of the system (which becomes difficult in complex systems), predicting the outcome may be impossible. Thus, applying systems theory within psychology may require new methods of testing theories. Nonetheless, both McGuire (1985) and Hunt (1991) see systems theory as a potentially productive approach to psychological issues.

Thus, chaos theory and systems theory challenge the deterministic model of the world which psychology has often used. If non-linear systems are characteristic of behaviour, then deterministic models, and the predictions they generate, are inappropriate. However, abandoning prediction (or at least de-emphasizing it) would not be a death blow to psychology. Indeed, there are already precedents within many of the approaches. Freud's theory is essentially non-predictive, as is the phenomenological framework of the humanistic approach. Even in the biological approach, non-predictive models have sometimes met with acceptance. Evolutionary theory is one example; pain theory provides another example. Pain is a complex phenomenon, influenced by a variety of interrelated processes – just the sort of situation suited to systems theory. While not called a system theory, the best current model of pain phenomena, developed by psychologist Ronald Melzack and physiologist Patrick Wall, is essentially a systems model, including forms of positive and negative feedback (Melzack and Wall 1982).

The danger, of course, is that without prediction it is harder to reject a faulty theory – particularly one which is vague enough to describe almost any observed outcome. (Freud's theory has frequently been criticized in this regard; even Melzack and Wall's pain theory is difficult to test in many respects.) In simple systems, it may still be possible to talk about descriptive accuracy, but at present it is not clear what criterion could be used to evaluate chaotic theories of human behaviour, or complex system models. Still, it would be unwise to suggest that no resolution of this issue is possible; instead, we must recognize that it is possible for new answers to emerge for old questions.

Psychology and Culture

Another issue which needs to be considered is the role of culture. As we have noted throughout this book, psychology is a human endeavour, influenced by the processes of human perception and thinking. This has two important implications for the research process: first, it means that observations may be open to perceptual distortion or bias; and, second, it means that theories tend to reflect the mental schemata of the theorist. Having said that, it is important to note that this does not mean that psychology is wholly subjective, or that we must abandon any hope of agreement about understanding behaviour. As even Rogers notes, agreement about what is observed, and what it means, is central to attempts at understanding. What it means is that we need to remember that decisions regarding both *what* to observe and *how* to observe it are rooted in the very kinds of processes we are trying to understand (the workings of mind and behaviour).

At an individual level, it is clear that perception is influenced by both the immediate situation and our past experience, which is reflected in our schemata about the world. Thus, the ideas and interests that any one psychologist develops (like any individual) will reflect their own perceptual processes. For example, Freud became convinced that sexuality was a basic human motive because of the observations he made of his patients. At the same time, science is a social process, meaningful only through the sharing of ideas and observations. (This is true even if Kuhn's ideas about the social aspects of paradigm change are wrong.) Thus, we should also consider what types of perceptions might be common to a group of individuals – that is, we need to consider the role of culture.

culture a relatively organized set of meanings, shared by members of a group, which affect how people, objects and events are interterpreted

Culture can be defined in many ways, but one aspect which is part of most definitions is a set of shared meanings within a group (Smith and Bond 1999). These shared meanings are largely based on our common attitudes and experiences. As individuals, part of how we perceive the world is a reflection of the culture we live in. In terms of psychology, this becomes important, because cultural ideas can play a role in how researchers think about behaviour. For example, it is generally accepted that Victorian ideas about sexuality influenced Freud's thinking. Similarly, it is likely that behaviourism became more popular in the United States than in Europe because it fit better with the democratic culture of the US, as compared to the history of monarchs-by-birth in Europe. (When Bertrand Russell spoke of the behaviour of 'German rats' versus 'American rats', he was of course referring to the differences in the researchers who studied them, not the rats themselves!) One reason to be interested in culture, then, is that culture may influence the mental schemata of researchers, and therefore affect the kinds of theories which they develop.

Culture is also significant because of its effects on the observations we make, and how we interpret them. As noted at a number of points in this book, people from different cultures do not always react the same way to similar situations. If one makes observations only in a single culture, it is possible unintentionally to overgeneralize about the results. As noted in Chapter 4, the *fundamental attribution error* is actually not fundamental to all cultures, but instead is most common among North Americans. However, since most of the initial research was done in North America, and consistently produced the effect, it is understandable why researchers concluded it was a universal human trait. A similar example has been documented for group decision making (Smith and Bond 1999). Based on studies of American students, it was originally concluded that groups tend to make riskier decisions than the individuals who comprise the group. Only when research was done in a variety of other countries did it become evident that the real effect is one of *group polarization*. That is, the dynamics of groups often leads to decisions which depart from the average of the members – but whether group decisions are riskier or more conservative depends on culture, as well as other factors. Even at an individual level, cultural differences can affect the interpretations psychologists make. For example, cultural differences between therapist and patient can affect diagnosis and treatment of abnormal behaviour (see Chapter 8). Thus, awareness of the influence of culture on behaviour is important because it can affect the way observations are interpreted. While we cannot completely avoid such misinterpretations, being sensitive to the role that culture plays is still desirable.

A third reason for studying cultural differences is because culture clearly affects the way individuals behave, and no understanding of individual behaviour can be complete without recognizing that. In this regard, it is encouraging that cross-cultural research has been a growing area within psychology in recent years (see Matsumoto 1997; Smith and Bond 1999). While it is beyond the scope of this book to review this work, it is worth acknowledging that cultural variables are increasingly being addressed in research across many of the approaches. For example, there are studies of language and thinking processes, social interactions, gender roles and concepts of self, among other topics. As time goes on, it is likely that such research will further enrich our understanding of how people behave.

To summarize our discussion of psychology and science, we can point to three themes: the limitations on observing behaviour; the concern to develop new models or even paradigms; and the recognition of how social factors like culture affect our understanding. Clearly, psychology faces many challenges, both theoretical and practical, as it seeks to move forward. Over time, it is likely that both the methods we use and the theories we embrace will evolve, for that is the way knowledge and understanding develop. In this regard, it is likely that the issues and ideas discussed above will be among the factors which influence the future direction of the field. Whatever the challenges, we must seek ways to resolve the problems; doing otherwise would mean abandoning attempts at improving our understanding.

| For further consideration | Which of the five approaches do you think is most successful in helping us to understand the influence of culture on behaviour? Which is the best in terms of dealing with the influence of culture on the theories we create? |

The Many and the One

Having come this far, you may still be hoping for an answer to the question of 'which one is right', or at least 'which one *will* be right in the future'. Without a crystal ball or similar device, no definite answer is possible. However, it does not seem likely that some new framework will suddenly arise which will resolve all the shortcomings of the current approaches. Instead, it is likely that the future will in some sense be an extension of the present. In that sense, it is possible to look at developments in the past several years, and note the conflicting tensions between pluralism (the many) and convergence (the one).

Seeking Convergence

Given the history of distinct approaches, it might seem odd to imagine that psychology could move towards a unified approach. However, in the larger context of the history of science, the search for theoretical unity is well-established. In physics, for example, there has been a trend to develop theories which link together combinations of the four fundamental forces of nature (gravity, electromagnetism and the strong and weak atomic forces). Thus far, physicists have not been successful in developing a 'grand unified theory' which would integrate all four, but efforts continue, and some physicists are optimistic about reaching that goal.

In psychology, as in physics, the desire for convergence in theorizing stems in part from the value placed on *parsimony*. That is, needing fewer theories to account for a range of phenomena simplifies both research and our understanding of the world. In addition, some scientists assume that there is an underlying unity to the universe, such that complex phenomena can ultimately be explained in terms of simpler processes at a more fundamental level of analysis. For example, one might argue that all of genetics is ultimately reducible to chemistry. This assumption, called **reductionism**, has a long history, and is still popular. For example, biologist E. O. Wilson has recently argued for a unification of all knowledge, under a framework he calls 'consilience' (Wilson 1998). When closely examined, consilience embodies most of the elements of reductionism. (Much of psychology, in his view, would be merged into existing fields like biology and physiology, for example.)

Reductionism has a controversial history, and has never been fully achieved. However, its appeal is certainly comprehensible. When understanding is fragmented, theoretical disagreements are almost inevitable, as we have seen in comparing the approaches. Even if the differences represent conflicts between paradigms, not contradictions about the underlying reality, they are still problematical. Since differences between theories in a very limited domain are often resolved by combining elements of the two into a new theory, convergence between approaches seems at least worth attempting, even if we are unsure of the outcome.

In the past several years, there have been a number of attempts at convergence between approaches. For example, Paul Wachtel has tried to reconcile behaviourism and psychoanalysis as forms of therapy (Wachtel 1977, 1997). By contrast, John Kihlstrom has tried to reconcile psychoanalysis with 'scientific psychology', which he construes as essentially the methods of the cognitive approach (Kihlstrom 1994). Physiological researcher Roger Sperry, noted for his work on the split brain, has called for a new framework that allows for both physiological processes and subjective mental states (Sperry 1993, 1995). While Sperry justifies his proposal in part by referring to the successes of the cognitive approach, essentially he is trying to deal with subjective experience, and thereby points towards a relationship between the biological and humanistic approaches. Not surprisingly, his ideas have not met with universal acceptance (Morf 1994).

Of all the proposed mergers, the one which is most advanced, and seems most likely to succeed, is the linking of the biological and cognitive

reductionism the assumption that phenomena at one level of description can be understood in terms of principles at a more basic level of analysis; for example, that biology is 'reducible' to chemistry

approaches. While individually they represent the two most popular approaches in psychology today, the combination (often called *cognitive neuroscience*) has the potential to draw upon the best of both domains. In the process, it can address new questions that don't fit either approach, and thereby provide new insights into behaviour. Interestingly, physiological researcher Michael Gazzaniga, whose mentor was Roger Sperry, is among those that welcome the convergence (Gazzaniga *et al.* 1998).

Does the emergence of cognitive neuroscience indicate that the long turmoil of conflicting approaches is coming to an end? At this stage it is premature to judge, but it is worth noting that, at present, the merger is still too limited in its frame of reference to encompass all aspects of psychology. For example, Gazzaniga seems less interested in including subjective mental states than is his mentor Sperry. It is also not entirely clear whether cognitive neuroscience represents a new approach within psychology, or simply a sub-area of the hybrid field called *cognitive science*. Cognitive science is seen by some as a new discipline, which draws upon cognitive and biological psychology, but also philosophy and computer science (Osherson and Smith 1990). Possibly this convergence will produce the kind of sharing of knowledge which E. O. Wilson (1998) seeks. However, it is also possible that cognitive neuroscience will simply define some questions (like subjective experience) out of existence, the way the behaviourists did.

If the cognitive and biological approaches merge, but ignore subjective experience, then psychology as a whole may become more fragmented even as some parts converge. This possibility is reinforced by a recent study which attempted to gauge the influence of four of the approaches (humanistic was not included) by looking at publication citations (Robins *et al.* 1998). Focusing on four major journals in psychology, the authors looked at the frequency with which major journals in each of the four approaches were cited between 1967 and 1995. Over this period, behaviourism showed a major decline, and the cognitive approach showed a dramatic increase, becoming the dominant area. (Psychoanalysis was low throughout the period examined, but the focus on psychoanalysis underestimates the influence of psychodynamic theories more generally.) However, what was most striking was that the biological approach showed very little increase. When the researchers examined more closely, they found that neuroscience journals are among the most widely cited in science – but not in psychology. If this trend continues, then cognitive neuroscience may ultimately split from psychology, rather than providing an integrative framework for the discipline. At the very least, this and other current efforts at convergence have not yet been demonstrated to achieve the goal of providing a unified account of all aspects of behaviour and experience.

Embracing Pluralism

A second way of resolving the contradictions within psychology is to endorse the notion of pluralism. Koch has argued that psychology can never be a coherent field, and that we should welcome the diversity of approaches (Koch 1985). In some sense, this brings us back to a metaphor which was mentioned in Chapter 1: the story of the blind men and the elephant. Just as each of the blind men comprehends only part of the whole elephant, so, too, each approach has limitations. Rather than engaging in a divisive – *and* fruitless – attempt to seek the triumph of one approach, Koch suggests that psychology acknowledge the value of multiple approaches.

One virtue of multiple approaches, each with its own constraints, is that the domain of phenomena to be explained by any one approach is limited, and therefore should become more manageable. That is, one can explicitly decide to focus on only limited aspects of the world. The radical behaviourists like Watson and Skinner have in fact done this – except they then proceed to declare that the rest of the world is irrelevant, anyway. What is being proposed instead is a decision to set limits, but *without* suggesting that what lies *outside* those limits is without value or relevance to a broader understanding.

Although this idea of setting limits on the field of study (the *domain*) contradicts the goal of developing a comprehensive theory, it may be a more realistic way to proceed. Somehow, we expect a psychological theory to answer everything, yet we don't expect the same of other sciences. For example, Berlyne has pointed out that botany largely ignores the existence of animals, the geology of soils and the astrophysics of the sun (Berlyne 1975). Instead, botany deals with a world of plants – even though we know that animals, soils and the sun exist, and in various ways do affect the way plants function. (For example, birds and other animals help distribute seeds.) No theory is likely to explain everything, particularly if the domain is a large one. Even physics, with a much longer history than psychology, has yet to achieve a grand unified theory of forces. Indeed, as noted, in Chapter 1, physicists invoke the concept of *complementarity* to deal with the existence of two models which are both useful, but not directly reconcilable. If psychology were to be seen as a set of complementary domains, each with its own value, then possibly there would be less concern over differences and disagreements.

Constraining the domain may be useful, *provided* researchers do not set such narrow limits as to make the enterprise worthless. (Recall Koch's comments on cognitive pathology.) Most psychologists see this as a mistake of the radical behaviourists (like Skinner), though not necessarily of behaviourism more generally. For example, Tolman, who is often seen as one of the pioneers of the cognitive approach, considered himself a behaviourist. Similarly, observational learning (imitation) originated within behaviourism.

The problem of where to set the limits is essentially one of context: creating an artificially simple situation often leads to overlooking elements of the situation which are crucial to understanding. This is particularly tricky in psychology, given the complexity of behaviour. An example of the pitfalls of oversimplification concerns the type of materials used in the study of memory. Hermann Ebbinghaus (1885) pioneered the experimental study of memory over 100 years ago; in doing so, he chose to use nonsense syllables (meaningless combinations of letters) as a way of stripping memory processes to the essentials. Since there was little opportunity to utilize meaning, subjects performed in ways that seemed to reflect rote associations. The result was that early memory researchers ended up developing theories (like *interference theory*) that were associationistic. It was not until the 1960s, when researchers finally began to study more realistic tasks, that our understanding changed. By using meaningful material, researchers like Endel Tulving realized that memory is organized, not based on random associations, and that remembering is *context-dependent*. The possibility of recognizing this had been impeded by the use of 'nonsense' materials (Tulving and Madigan 1970). Unintentionally, the constraints placed on the study of memory had hampered our attempts at understanding.

It may well be that simultaneous exploration of different approaches is the best way to be sure the limits are not set too narrowly. For example, the cognitive approach became dominant over behaviourism not simply as a change of taste, as Kuhn might suggest. Instead, it occurred because people who insisted on pushing the limits of the framework (like Tolman, Krechevsky and Levine) demonstrated that there were phenomena that behaviourism could not explain.

Koch's call for pluralism seems reasonable, at least given current realities. In some ways, acceptance of the validity of multiple approaches is already the case – for example, most counsellors view themselves as eclectic, using techniques drawn from several approaches, rather than being bound to a single approach (Warner 1991). Indeed, contrary to Koch's criticism that many researchers show cognitive pathology, most psychologists seem aware that there are limits to their particular approach. Along with this awareness of limitations goes a (sometimes grudging) acceptance of other approaches. For example, even John B. Watson, the founder of behaviourism, seemed to harbour the tiniest of doubts in his attacks on psychoanalysis. Near the end of *Behaviorism*, he commented that if he ever developed a symptom like paralysis for which no physical cause could be found, 'I should hasten to my psychoanalytic friends and say, "Please, in spite of all the mean things I've said about you, help me out of this mess"' (Watson 1930: 301)!

Conclusion

Amidst these criticisms of the past and worries about the future, one should not lose sight of psychology's accomplishments. Even if one restricts the assessment simply to observing behaviour and cataloguing the results, there have been impressive accumulations of information. In some areas, the results have added greatly to our understanding – for instance, the functions of the brain and the workings of memory. Even in complex areas like social behaviour, there have been important insights. For example, consider a problem we discussed in Chapter 1: social intervention in emergencies. The work of Latané and Darley, and others, has put the lie to the 'common sense' notion that people don't help because they simply don't care. Instead, the factors that govern intervention are often related to social influence – and knowing that may help us to find ways to increase intervention in emergencies. Hence, even when our understanding is incomplete, it can be argued that psychology has increased our awareness of possibilities.

Whether the future is one of pluralism, convergence or new paradigms, it is sure to be both interesting and challenging. As Stephen Chorover has suggested, the ferment in psychology is interconnected to the ferment in society (Chorover 1985). We are living in a world with large problems, including population growth, environmental degradation and conflicts between nations and cultures. At the same time, our intellectual traditions are also being challenged. While science has long been based on the premise that knowledge can aspire to objective absolutes, this view has been challenged by notions of knowledge as a social construction. (Kuhn, of course, has contributed to this, but deconstructionists like Michel Foucault (1965) have been more extreme.) The study of the human dimensions of science has been useful, for it has helped us recognize points of weakness in the scientific process. However, like many ideas, the notion of knowledge as a social construct can be dangerous if carried too far. When taken to the extreme, it leads to the conclusion that no absolutes exist in the world. The framework for psychology then becomes just one more arbitrary choice in a world of arbitrary choices – and therefore meaningless. This view, which is associated with deconstructionism in the arts, seems far too pessimistic, as Wilson (1998) has noted. Furthermore, to say that nothing is understandable through science ignores what we *have* learned about behaviour.

In this book, I have taken pains to point to the limitations of current knowledge and, where possible, to suggest what the difficulties are. Yet, however limited our understanding, it should be clear that this book does *not* accept the view that the search for understanding is either completely arbitrary or meaningless. While our understanding of reality can be affected by our personal beliefs and biases (i.e. our cognitive schema), there *is* something 'out there' to be explained. The existence of human behaviour is not simply a construct of the mind, nor is its nature purely imaginary. Indeed, our desire to understand ourselves is an affirmation of our existence and our capacity for awareness. Consequently, far from being arbitrary or meaningless, the search for understanding is central to our being.

Psychology, like the behaviour it studies, is rich and diverse, and full of unanswered questions. If we can proceed with an appreciation for the wondrous complexity we are seeking to explain, and a suitable humility before that complexity, then psychology should bring us closer to a proper understanding of what we are, and why.

For further consideration

This book, as an introduction to psychology, is of course limited in many ways. What questions about behaviour would you like answered which this book has not discussed? Try looking for an answer through the references given, a library etc.

Chapter Summary

◆ One of the most basic issues in psychology is how to deal with the existence of different approaches.

◆ The formation of a theory, and the gathering of evidence, cannot be fully understood without considering the processes of *perception*.

◆ Whereas *logical empiricism* asserts that theories can be judged by seeing how well they fit the available evidence, Kuhn's theory of *paradigms* suggests that both theories and observations are influenced by the broader frameworks (paradigms) which we use to view the world.

◆ The various approaches within psychology can be seen as examples of paradigms, but this does not resolve the disagreements among them about the nature of behaviour.

◆ Using the methods of the physical sciences in psychology has two limitations: (a) it is very difficult to talk about the causes of mental events because they cannot be directly observed; (b) the fact that participants are aware of their surroundings makes it difficult to maintain control and objectivity in experiments.

◆ In exploring these difficulties, some argue that we should focus on theories and paradigms which do not require causal predictions, such as *chaos theory* or *systems theory*.

◆ Psychologists now recognize that *culture* influences both the theories we generate, and the way that observations are interpreted; consequently, cross-cultural studies are increasingly important.

◆ It is unclear whether psychology in the future will move towards *convergence* of approaches, as in *cognitive neuroscience*, or towards *pluralism*, and acceptance of the existence of different approaches/paradigms as a form of *complementarity*.

Key Terms and Concepts

chaos theory	logical empiricism
cognitive neuroscience	negative feedback
cognitive pathology	paradigm
complementarity	positive feedback
culture	reductionism
demand characteristics	systems theory

Suggestions for Further Reading

For a better understanding of the concept of paradigms in science, Thomas Kuhn's pioneering book *The Structure of Scientific Revolutions* provides an authoritative view. While it is not light reading, Kuhn proposes some provocative ideas.

For an introduction to chaos theory, James Gleick's *Chaos: Making a New Science* is still one of the more readable choices. For an introduction to system theory, try *System Effects*, by Robert Jervis.

For a better understanding of the role of culture, Smith and Bond's *Social Psychology across Cultures* provides a good current overview. For a less experimentally-oriented view, David Matsumoto's *Culture and Modern Life* is a good brief source.

One of the most interesting sources for assessments of all aspects of psychology is Koch and Leary's edited collection, *A Century of Psychology as a Science*. Written to commemorate the centenary of Wundt's first laboratory, it contains chapters written by a variety of eminent modern psychologists. While it is not the type of book one sits down to read cover to cover, it makes fascinating browsing.

Appendix: Research Methods and Statistics

Making Sense of the Evidence
Introduction
The Logic of Research
Making Observations: Measurement and Sampling
Designing Research
Pitfalls in Experimental Research
  Confounds
  Bias
Going from Observation to Interpretation
Statistics – Making Sense of the Data
Descriptive Statistics – Describing the Data
  Frequency Distributions
  Measures of Central Tendency

Measures of Variability
Properties of Normal Distributions
Correlations
Inferential Statistics
  Sampling and Variability
  Drawing Inferences from a Normal Distribution
  Inferences about the Significance of Results
  Decision Errors in Interpreting Data
Conclusion
Chapter Summary
Key Terms and Concepts
Suggestions for Further Reading

Making Sense of the Evidence

Most people initially think that the study of research methods and statistics is both dull and meaningless – something that only professional researchers should be concerned about. In fact, however, we all face situations in which we must make sense out of information which we encounter. Sometimes this is presented as research results (for example, in a newspaper report), and sometimes it may appear unrelated to research issues. Consider the following situations.

A politician running for re-election claims that the average family income has risen by £3,000 in the past two years. Does this really mean that most people are better off than they were?

A friend goes on a business trip to France. Before leaving, she expresses concern that the French are not friendly to foreigners. On her return, she reports several instances of situations where people were rude and hostile to her. Does this mean that her preconception was correct?

Your doctor proposes doing a diagnostic test to find out why you don't feel well. When it comes back positive, he says you should go for exploratory surgery. What do you need to know about the test before agreeing to surgery?

In none of these situations have we used the words 'research methods' or 'statistics', but all of them are in fact examples of basic issues in the design and analysis of research. As we explore these issues, think back to the situations mentioned here, and see how you can apply the principles you encounter. Far from being dull and irrelevant, the material in this appendix can lead you into a number of challenging insights.

Introduction

Throughout this book, we have emphasized that psychology is an *empirical* pursuit – that is, the knowledge gained is based on observation of behaviour. The process of gathering observations is commonly referred to as 'doing research'. Research provides the basic information that is used to formulate and test theories. Although the approaches differ in the kinds of research methods used, all agree on the importance of observation.

In Chapter 1, we talked about the basic methods, both correlational and experimental, which are most commonly used in psychological research. At various points, we have focused on particular aspects of research methods – for example, the use of time-based studies in developmental psychology, and the difficulties of doing experiments on social behaviour. Regardless of the problem studied or the method used, there are some basic considerations that apply to all psychological research. In the first section, we will briefly look at some of these points.

The Logic of Research

Making Observations: Measurement and Sampling

One basic concern in research is how to describe what we observe. It takes very little insight to recognize that people vary in many ways. For example, people differ in size, age, education and so on. Obviously, they also differ in the way they behave. Any characteristic which shows variation can be called a *variable*, and so in essence the information we collect is based on observing different variables. The choice of variables is one of the things which distinguishes the approaches – for example, the behaviourist's use of reflex responses, or the humanist's use of subjective reports of feelings.

Unfortunately, not all variables are alike. For example, variables may be simple descriptive labels, as when we refer to eye colour as green, blue, brown and so on. Such labels are very limited when it comes to making comparisons between individuals. We can put people in groups (e.g. all those with blue eyes), but we cannot really say how *much* they differ. For example, is the difference between blue and green greater than the difference between blue and brown? Whatever our intent might be in asking the question, there is no meaningful way to answer it from the information provided by the labels.

ratio variable a characteristic whose measurements are based on a continuous scale, with an obvious zero point

In order to make relative comparisons, we must use variables which provide more information. The most detailed information is provided by **ratio variables**, which use measurements based on a continuous scale, with an obvious zero point. For example, we can measure age in years, weight in kilograms (or pounds) and so on. Ratio variables are highly useful, because they allow a wide variety of comparisons. For example, one can say John and Bob together weigh as much as Jim, or Mary is three times as old as her daughter Jane, and so on. As implied in the examples, ratio variables are fairly common when measuring physical characteristics. They are less common in dealing with psychological variables, many of which don't have a clear zero point. For example, what would it mean to say someone has 'zero intelligence'? Without a clear zero point, we cannot say that someone who has an IQ of 140 is 'twice as intelligent' as someone with an IQ of 70. Thus, one concern in making observations is deciding what kinds of comparisons are appropriate for particular variables.

Another way in which variables can differ is how easy they are to measure. Variables which refer to physical characteristics are relatively simple to measure (although errors can still occur), but measuring psychological variables, like 'intelligence' or 'aggressiveness', is more difficult, since they cannot be directly observed. Hence, in gathering data, we have to be concerned about the measurement process. Basically, we want our measurements of any variable to be both reliable and valid. **Reliability** means that the measuring process gives consistent results; **validity** means that the variable measures what it claims to, as opposed to some other characteristic. That is, the measurement process should be both consistent (reliable) and accurate (valid). There are several effective ways to measure reliability, all of which basically compare the consistency of repeated measurements of particular cases. Validity is more difficult to assess, because one must have an independent means of measuring the same property (called the validity criterion); this means you cannot measure the validity of any characteristic for which you don't already have an accurate validity criterion. To take a simple example, you can't determine whether a ruler is accurate unless you already have an accurate ruler (or other measuring device) with which to compare it! Having measurements which are reliable and valid is important to effective research; without dependable observations, the whole enterprise is threatened.

reliability a criterion for evaluating a measurement process, which assesses the consistency of measurements; often measured by comparing the correlation between repeated observations

validity a criterion for evaluating a measurement process, which assesses whether the variable measures the intended property, as opposed to some other characteristic

Assuming one has confidence in the measurement process, there is still the question of *who* to observe and measure. In practical terms, a researcher

sampling the process by which one selects observations for research (the sample)

random sample a sample obtained through a selection procedure in which everyone in the population has an equal chance of being selected

self-selected sample a sampling procedure which allows members of the population to decide whether to be included or not, as when a survey has a low rate of response

cross-sectional sample a sample which is deliberately selected in such a way that the sample matches the population for particular characteristics, such as age and income

can only observe a limited number of individuals, yet would like to draw conclusions about all human beings. That is, we make observations of a limited group (the *sample*), but we wish to generalize about the larger group from which the sample is selected (the *population*). This leads to concerns about **sampling** – the process by which one selects observations. In sampling, the goal is to select a *representative sample*, one which can be assumed to reflect the population fairly.

There are normally two ways to obtain a representative sample: random sampling and cross-sectional sampling. A **random sample** is one in which everyone in the population has an equal chance of being selected. In the case of the election poll, suppose the researcher went to a large shopping centre in Toronto at lunch time, and stopped every third person that went by: would that be a proper random sample? No – since not every Canadian voter is likely to be found at that site, it would not be a random sample. Similarly, if survey forms were mailed out based on voter registration lists, the researcher would have to be concerned about how many were actually returned. Although the initial mailing might be random, if only a small percentage actually responded, the results would no longer be random, owing to possible differences between those who answered and those who didn't. With a low response rate, the sample becomes **self-selected** rather than random. This point – the need to ensure a high response rate in the target sample – is sometimes overlooked. A few years ago, a book was published based on a survey of women's attitudes to men (Hite 1987). The author made much of the fact that almost 5,000 women had responded; unfortunately, since over 100,000 survey forms had been distributed, the response rate was so low as to make the results of questionable value.

The primary alternative to random sampling is a cross-sectional sample. As the name implies, a **cross-sectional sample** is deliberately selected so that the sample matches the population for particular characteristics. For example, in an election survey, one would want the sample to reflect the age, income, sex and geographic origin of the population, among other things (e.g. if 20 per cent of the population live in Ontario, one would want 20 per cent of the sample to come from Ontario). For a voter survey, such data could be obtained from census figures; for other types of survey, depending on the focus, other sources might be used to determine population data.

The primary limitation of using cross-sectional sampling is the problem of determining the population characteristics to be matched. Sometimes, a factor that is important may be overlooked – for example, the above example neglects native language, which would be a relevant factor in surveying Canadian voters, since differences probably exist between English- and French-speaking voters. At the same time, it is obviously impossible to match a population for every known characteristic. Even more importantly, it is impossible to create a proper cross-sectional sample if the population characteristics are *unknown*.

In doing research, the goal of sampling procedures is to avoid serious *bias*, or systematic error. For example, if I am interested in how children react to watching violence on television, it might make a difference if I study children in a university day care centre, or children in a home for delinquents. In this case, either sample would be biased; that is, neither

sampling error an error caused by having a non-representative sample, due to either using a biased sampling procedure, or the inherent variability associated with the sampling process

sample is likely to be typical of the larger population (all children in the world). In terms of the logic of research, there is one thing to keep in mind: even when using generally accepted procedures for sampling, it is still possible to get a set of observations which are not actually representative of the population. This potential for **sampling error** is one of the main reasons why we use statistical analysis in interpreting the results of research.

If a researcher were to do a survey of people's favourite television programmes by randomly dialling listings from the telephone book, would this be a representative sample of the population of television viewers? Why or why not?

> **For further consideration**

Designing Research

The concerns about types of variables, measurement procedures and sampling apply to all psychological research. In this sense, they are independent of both the question being asked and the research method used. Nonetheless, doing research always involves a number of choices, which begin with the question one seeks to answer, and end, it is hoped, with the results providing the answer. In between, one must consider how the question is to be stated, in terms of the *hypothesis* to be tested, what *research method* is to be used to collect the observations and how the *variables* are to be measured. All these choices are part of the general domain of *research design*.

The decisions involved in designing a study are not cut and dried. In practice, one could give the same question to several researchers, asking each to design a relevant study, and find that each one produces a different design for addressing the question. (Consider, for example, the many studies which have looked at the relationship between observing television violence and aggressive behaviour, as discussed in Chapter 8.) In each case, the reasons given for the resulting design could be very sensible, despite the differences.

Research design is a creative activity, and like other forms of creation, can be both challenging and gratifying. We cannot deal with all the complexities here, but it is important to realize that designing and doing research is not a dry and mundane task; it is an inventive process for exploring the unknown. There are rules, to be sure, but within those rules there is tremendous opportunity for the mind to imagine new possibilities.

Pitfalls in Experimental Research

internal validity the assessment of the degree to which the design and execution of an experiment are free from bias, confounds and other sources of error

In general, using experiments to gather information can be more complicated than using non-experimental observational procedures. In order to draw clear conclusions, one must maintain consistent conditions in the experimental situation, and ensure that no unwanted factors distort the results. The issues of proper design and execution of an experiment are part of the issue of **internal validity**. (You may recall that concerns about the ability to generalize from the results, particularly with laboratory experiments, are related to *external validity*.)

Confounds

confound in experimental research, a situation where two variables change simultaneously, making it impossible to determine their relative influence

Broadly speaking, there are two kinds of factors that can detract from internal validity: confounds and bias. A **confound** represents a situation where two variables change simultaneously, making it impossible to determine their relative influence (i.e. there is a *confounding variable*). For example, suppose that in Latané and Darley's field experiment (see Chapter 1), it turned out that all the subjects in one group were male, and in another group were female. In this situation, one could not tell whether differences in helping behaviour were due to the independent variable, or the sex of the subjects. Similarly, if an experiment designed to compare two teaching methods used two classes which met at different times of day (one early morning, one mid-afternoon), then differences in results (e.g. student grades) might be due to the teaching methods, or the time of day, or a combination of both factors. Such situations are undesirable, because they represent a confound of two variables.

Basically there are two ways to avoid confounds. The most common approach is to hold constant factors which are not of direct interest; this is a key feature of experimental design. For example, in the experiment on teaching methods, one would plan it so that the groups met at equivalent times (e.g. morning or afternoon on alternate days). The other approach to avoiding confounds, used when the variables involved are of direct interest, is to use multiple independent variables. In the Latané and Darley field experiment, the number of customers and the number of robbers were both intended to be independent variables; by using four groups (which reflected all possible combinations of the independent variables), they were able to avoid the difficulties of confounding. Generally, careful planning of the experiment should be able to prevent most confounds, although in research, as in everyday life, the unexpected can still create surprises. In this regard, the greatest risk is that an unrecognized variable will turn out to be confounded with a planned independent variable, resulting in the kind of ambiguities we have noted.

random error non-systematic error produced by the variability in sampling or other natural processes

While confounds can make it difficult to interpret the results, various forms of *error* can directly affect the results obtained. So-called **random error**, produced by natural variability in sampling or other processes, is an inevitable part of research. (For example, in a survey, no two samples of a population will be identical; the differences represent a form of random error.) Generally speaking, random error can be dealt with in the analysis of results, and does not threaten the basic legitimacy of the research. By contrast, systematic forms of error, called *bias*, are a more serious concern.

Bias

Systematic error, as its name implies, means that some factor is at work which consistently influences the results in a particular way; since this influence is not a planned part of the research design, its intrusion is undesirable. Systematic error (bias) can arise in many ways: Suppose that Latané and Darley had told their subjects the purpose of the research; do you think that people would react differently if they knew the researchers were interested

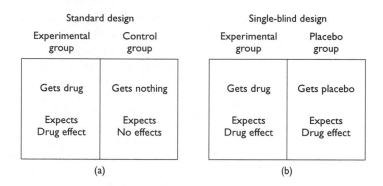

Figure A.1 Subject bias in experiments In doing drug research, experimenters normally use a placebo with the control group, rather than giving nothing, in order to prevent subject bias. As the two figures show, providing a placebo changes the expectations of those in the control group so that they are consistent with the expectations of those in the experimental group.

in helping behaviour? One possibility is that more people would intervene, in order to create a better impression of themselves. If this were true, the results would be biased, since the information led people to intervene more than would otherwise be the case.

To consider a different example, suppose an experiment was designed to test a new drug; the independent variable will be the presence or absence of the drug. In its simplest form, this would mean that some subjects would receive medication, and others would receive nothing. Unfortunately, this would mean that subjects in the control group would know they were not getting treatment, since they were not given anything. As in the Latané and Darley example, this could distort the results by creating a confound (see Figure A.1a). In both these examples, bias is created because of what the subjects know; consequently, this form of bias is commonly called **subject bias**. In order to prevent subject bias, experimenters usually try to set up an experiment in such a way that participants do not know anything which might lead to bias. An experiment planned in this manner is commonly called a **single-blind design**, since subjects are kept uninformed or 'blind' to the purpose. Sometimes this is done by withholding information or by active deception, as in the Latané and Darley experiments. In drug studies, those not given a real drug are usually given a placebo – an inert substance which they believe is a drug (see Figure A.1b). (In some cases, both those receiving the drug and those receiving the placebo are kept in doubt; in this case, the expectation in both groups is one of uncertainty.) Since bias is particularly likely in social situations (due to reactivity), nearly all social psychology experiments use some form of single-blind design.

The behaviours that create subject bias are very understandable: subjects are simply reacting to the situation as they perceive it; when the information available changes, their behaviour changes as well. While such reactions complicate the task of the researcher, they also represent part of the complexity which makes human behaviour fascinating; studying behaviour would certainly be less interesting if people were not so responsive to their

subject bias in an experiment, systematic error created because the subjects in different groups have different information (for example, knowing whether they are in the control group or experimental group)
single-blind design an experiment set up in such a way that subjects are kept uninformed of any details which might lead to bias

experimenter bias
systematic error created
when an experimenter's
knowledge and expectations
about the experiment
influence the behaviour of
subjects

halo effect a form of
perceptual bias which occurs
when our rating of a person
on *one* characteristic as being
positive or negative of a
person leads to similar
expectations for *other*
characteristics of the
individual

environment. Unfortunately, it is harder to find redeeming value in a second form of bias, called **experimenter bias**. The term was coined by a social psychologist named Robert Rosenthal, who was interested in how people's expectations affect their interactions with others.

To understand experimenter bias, we must clarify how it differs from simple perceptual interpretation. As we have already discussed, perception depends in part on our existing schemata – hence, what we perceive is influenced by our expectations. For instance, a **halo effect** occurs when our knowledge of *one* characteristic which is positive or negative about a person leads to similar expectations of *other* characteristics. For example, people are likely to perceive someone who is 'intelligent' as honest rather than dishonest, sincere rather than insincere, and so on. Note that a halo effect refers only to the perception; it does *not* specify what the person perceived is actually like.

While perceptual effects like the halo effect could pose a threat to scientific objectivity, experimenter bias takes this process one step further. In exploring experimenter bias, Rosenthal was asking if our expectations can alter the way others actually *behave* (as opposed to our *perception* of them). To explore this idea, he did a study with Lenore Jacobson in which they looked at the influence of teachers' expectations on the behaviour of their students (Rosenthal and Jacobson 1968). The teachers were told that certain students had been identified as 'late bloomers', who could be expected to blossom during the school year. Sure enough, those students actually did improve, not only in the eyes of their teacher, but according to independent assessments as well. What made this surprising was that the only *real* difference between these students and their classmates was the label 'late bloomers', which Rosenthal and Jacobson had applied to randomly chosen students. That is, other than the teachers' expectations, nothing was different about the 'late bloomers'! Rosenthal subsequently called this expectancy effect a **self-fulfilling prophecy**. That is, we tend to produce in others the type of behaviour which our expectations lead us to predict. For example, if I visit a foreign country with the expectation that the people are unfriendly, my own behaviour is likely to lead to experiences which justify my original expectation. While there has been considerable subsequent research on how expectations affect behaviour, it is not clear how significant the phenomenon is in everyday life – in part, because it is so difficult to identify in non-experimental situations.

self-fulfilling prophecy a
phenomenon whereby our
expectations about other
people leads to acting in
ways which elicit the expected
response from them; the
everyday equivalent to
experimenter bias

In experiments, however, such expectancy effects raise a real concern about the objectivity of research. If an experimenter's knowledge and expectations about the experiment could alter the behaviour of subjects, this would be a form of bias (hence the term *experimenter bias*). For example, by unconsciously smiling or frowning, the researcher might lead subjects to respond in ways consistent with the experimental hypothesis. (We assume, of course, that there is no conscious intent to bias the results.) Rosenthal went on to do a number of experiments, which suggested the risks were potentially very significant. How can a researcher cope with this risk? By analogy to subject bias, where one uses a single-blind design, one would seek to keep the experimenter uninformed about the details of the experiment; when both the subject and experimenter are kept uninformed, the experiment is called a **double-blind design**.

double-blind design
a rigorous form of
experimental control,
whereby both the subject
and experimenter are kept
uninformed about details of
the experiment which could
result in bias (both subject
bias and experimenter bias)

Unfortunately, the requirements of a double-blind design can pose considerable difficulties to the execution of the research. In medical experiments, it is possible to use placebos and complex procedures so that neither the person giving nor the person receiving a 'drug' knows whether it is a placebo or a real drug – but it requires careful record-keeping to ensure everything proceeds properly. Other situations, particularly those involving social variables, can be even more problematical. For example, in Latané and Darley's field experiment, the independent variables dealt with the number of people present. Since anyone involved, whether the store clerk or an observer recording the results, would be aware of this, there would be no simple way to conduct a double-blind study. Consequently, while Rosenthal would argue that ideally *all* research should be double-blind, in practice only the minority of psychology experiments are actually designed in this way. Instead, most researchers would suggest that replication provides a check on possible experimenter bias: if someone does a study which seems inconsistent with previous research, others who disbelieve it are likely to try to repeat the experiment; if the results come out the same, it tends to suggest the result is genuine, not a product of the original researcher's bias. Still, no one would dispute that use of a double-blind design is desirable when circumstances make it possible.

For further consideration

Have you ever created a self-fulfilling prophecy? What was the result? In what ways are self-fulfilling prophecies related to our cognitive schemata?

Going from Observation to Interpretation

Whatever the question and whatever the research design, one ends up with a set of observations – the *data*. (The word *data* sometimes confuses readers, because it is a *plural* noun (borrowed from Latin). One should say, for example, 'The data *are* clear.' The singular, used to refer to a single observation, is *datum*.) One must then look at the results in terms of the original question, to determine if the hypothesis is supported or not. For example, suppose that one wanted to know if there are differences in the attitudes of men and women towards violence in sport. A survey is done, and the results show that 55 per cent of women say there is too much violence, 34 per cent say it is not a problem and 11 per cent have no opinion. In contrast, 38 per cent of men say there is too much violence, 58 per cent say it is not a problem and 4 per cent have no opinion. Does this mean that women are more opposed to violence in sports? How can we decide?

This example highlights the problem of how to *interpret* the results of research. The research design is intended to produce observations which are relevant to the original question; once we have those observations, however, we must still decide whether they support the hypothesis or not. This is actually not as simple as it seems. At first glance, it may appear that we have two choices: to conclude that the results support the hypothesis or that they contradict it. It turns out, however, that **falsification** (proving a hypothesis is wrong) is much simpler than **confirmation** (deciding that a hypothesis is true). For example, if I visit a remote tropical island, and the first seagull I encounter is black (instead of the usual white), I may be

falsification in research, the process of using observations to prove that a hypothesis is wrong
confirmation in research, the process of determining that observations are consistent with the hypothesis being true

surprised. If the next several seagulls I see are also black, I may be tempted to propose a hypothesis: on this island, all the seagulls are a mutant form which is black. Now, all it would take to *falsify* this hypothesis would be seeing one white seagull. That is, one clearly contradictory observation is enough to prove it wrong. On the other hand, what would it take to be sure the hypothesis is *true*? It would seem that I would have to observe every seagull on the island (the entire population) in order to be absolutely sure. If I depend on a sample, even a large one, there is still the chance that I will miss one or more white seagulls.

Thus, it turns out that proving that a hypothesis is false is a lot simpler than proving that it is true. In large part, this is because of the need to depend on samples; if we could observe every relevant case (the entire population), in theory we could prove a hypothesis to be true. In practice, psychologists wish to generalize about such large populations (e.g. all human beings) that observing everyone becomes impossible. As a result, researchers end up framing the original question in terms of a **null hypothesis**, which essentially says the results are random. If one can prove this is *false*, then it implies that there *is* a difference. For example, in the survey mentioned above, the null hypothesis would say, 'There is no difference between the attitudes of men and women towards violence in sport.' If we can show that this statement is false, then we can show that there *is* a difference. In order to do that, we use *statistics*.

null hypothesis in research, a hypothesis which asserts that any differences observed between groups are random rather than representing an experimental effect; normally the contrary of the experimental hypothesis, it is used for statistical purposes to evaluate results

Statistics – Making Sense of the Data

statistics the branch of mathematics that is concerned with the description and interpretation of sets of scores, such as scientific data
descriptive statistics the branch of statistics which is concerned with describing and summarizing sets of scores
inferential statistics the branch of statistics which deals with the interpretation of data, particularly in terms of generalizing from the observed sample to the larger population

The very word 'statistics' seems to strike fear into many students. The reasons for this are varied, but may include a fear of mathematics and an aversion to things which are 'boring'. While it is true that statistics is a form of applied mathematics, it need not be boring. When properly understood, many of the questions it tries to answer are very provocative and challenging. This section will try to show that the fears are largely unjustified, and that the issues are in fact both understandable and interesting.

In essence, **statistics** is concerned with the description and interpretation of scientific data. That is, it is used to describe and summarize research results, and to assist in understanding what the results mean. The first function, describing and summarizing results, is referred to as the domain of **descriptive statistics**. The second function, the interpretation of the results, particularly in terms of generalizing from the observed sample to the larger population, is the domain of **inferential statistics**. Since one must know what the results are before one can decide what they mean, we will first consider descriptive statistics.

Descriptive Statistics – Describing the Data

In doing psychological research, one gathers information about behaviour, in the form of observations of one or more variables. These observations

TEST GRADES	
CA	67
DB	74
FC	58
GC	70
YC	64
ED	78
SD	69
LE	58
JE	69
SF	70
PG	63
YG	64
DH	52
RH	52
SI	73
LJ	84
NJ	79
FL	68
RL	49
AM	64
LM	70
TM	66
BN	63
EN	46
CO	54
LO	73
SQ	84
FR	81
TR	78
AS	89
KS	55
PS	63
MT	60
RT	77
WT	58
AV	69
DY	48
Total number of scores	37

(a)

FREQUENCY DISTRIBUTION
(RAW SCORES)

Score	Frequency
46	2
49	1
52	2
54	1
55	1
58	3
60	1
63	3
64	3
66	1
67	1
68	1
69	3
70	3
73	2
74	1
77	1
78	2
79	1
81	1
84	2
89	1
Total number of scores	37

Note: scores with zero frequency omitted in order to simplify table.

(b)

FREQUENCY DISTRIBUTION
(USING INTERVALS)

Score range	Midpoint	Frequency
40–44	42	0
45–49	47	2
50–54	52	3
55–59	57	4
60–64	62	6
65–69	67	7
70–74	72	5
75–79	77	4
80–84	82	3
85–89	87	1
90–94	92	0
Total number of scores		37

(c)

Figure A.2 Analysing the frequency distribution for a set of data The three tables are as follows: (a) the original scores, expressed in the order they appeared in my grade book; (b) a frequency analysis of the original scores, arranged in order of score value; (c) a frequency analysis based on combining scores into intervals of five.

then comprise a set of data – typically, numbers of some sort. For example, one could measure students' performance on a test, with performance represented by grades expressed as percentages. In Figure A.2a, the results of an actual test are given. The results are listed in the order in which they appeared in my grade book, though I have substituted letter codes for

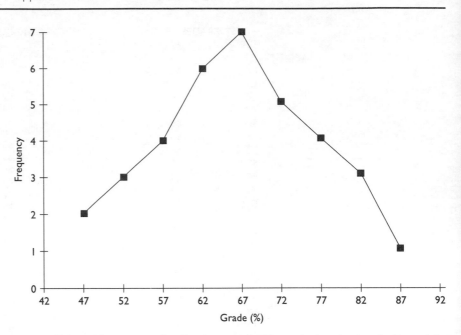

Figure A.3   A frequency distribution graph This graph plots the data for Figure A.2c.

student names. If you look at them, you will note that there is considerable variation. The question is, what do these grades tell us? As they stand, they present a rather random picture. In order to make sense of them, we need some way to summarize the information.

Frequency Distributions

frequency distribution
a statistical analysis of a set of data which tells how frequently each value occurs

One way to approach the task is to try rearranging the scores in order of size, and then see how many people got each score. If we do this for the numbers in Figure A.2a, we would end up with the result shown in Figure A.2b. This is called a **frequency distribution**, because it tells us how frequently each value occurs. As you can see, a few scores are repeated, but most occur only once. So, it is still somewhat difficult to make much sense out of the data.

If we group the scores into *intervals* (for example, 45–49, 50–54), then we might simplify the overall frequency distribution (there will be fewer categories), and also perhaps get a clearer picture of where scores are clustered. The result for this is shown in Figure A.2c. Now we get a clearer idea of overall performance – looking at the frequencies, it is evident that more people are near the middle than at either extreme. If we want to visualize this, we can represent it graphically, as in Figure A.3. In making a graph like this, the convention is to put the frequency scale on the vertical axis, and place data points based on using the midpoint of each interval. In effect, the graph assumes that all the people in any interval scored at the midpoint. If you look at the original data, you will see that this is an over-simplification, although not a very extreme one. This points out one of the basic principles of descriptive statistics: *whenever we seek to summarize data, we inevitably lose a little of the information we started with.* Thus, the challenge in descriptive statistics is to not lose anything that seems *essential.* In the example above, it doesn't seem to distort things very much to use the intervals as we have.

Measures of Central Tendency

While a frequency distribution, particularly in graphical form, gives us a general sense of the data, it still is rather limiting. For instance, it suggests that most people scored near the middle, but doesn't tell us how the typical student did. To describe what is typical of a group of scores, we use a type of statistic called a *measure of central tendency.* (A *statistic* is a number which results from some sort of statistical calculation on a set of data, while *statistics* is the name for the discipline.) In everyday terms, a **measure of central tendency** tells us what is an 'average' score. However, the term 'average' is avoided in statistical discussions, because the word can be used to refer to *any* measure of central tendency – and as we shall see, they are not all the same.

The simplest measure of central tendency (particularly if one already has a frequency distribution) is the **mode**, which is the most frequently occurring score (or interval). Looking at the graph in Figure A.3, it is clear that the peak, representing the most frequent value, occurs in the interval 65–69; using the simplification of the midpoint of the interval, we get a mode of 67 per cent. Note, however, that this does *not* prove that the single score of 67 per cent occurred most often – only that scores were most common in the interval of 65–69 per cent. If we were to determine the mode directly from the original data, we would find that the most frequent single score is actually 64 per cent. While this is close to the value of 67 per cent calculated from the interval data, it *also* shows how some information gets lost when we summarize. In general, the mode is a measure of 'popularity' – what occurs most frequently defines what is typical.

A second measure of central tendency is the **median** – the score which is in the *middle* of the frequency distribution. This is actually easier to calculate using the raw frequency data, since we need to find the value which is the midpoint of all the ranked scores. In the current case, the actual value is 67 per cent. (It could also be calculated for interval data, if the original data were not available, but doing so sometimes requires a bit of estimating within the interval. In the present case, it would not be necessary, since the median is the midpoint of the interval.) The median reflects what is typical in the sense of being middle-of-the-road, rather than an extreme.

The most commonly used measure of central tendency is the **mean**, which is sum of all the scores, divided by the number of scores. In our example, the mean is 66.5 per cent. The mean is commonly used because of two characteristics. First, it does not require rearranging the scores in rank order, or creating a frequency distribution, in order to calculate the mean. In many situations, this is a real advantage. Second, unlike either the median or the mode, the mean reflects *all* the scores – if you change one score, the mean will change, too. By contrast, the mode tells us nothing about any score except itself, while the median tells us only that half the scores

measure of central tendency a type of descriptive statistic used to determine what is a representative value for a set of scores

mode a statistic measuring central tendency, calculated as the most frequently occurring value (or interval) in a set of scores

median a statistic measuring central tendency, calculated as the middle score in a frequency distribution

mean (also called 'arithmetic mean') a statistic measuring central tendency, calculated as the sum of all the scores, divided by the number of scores

FREQUENCY DISTRIBUTION
FOR SALARY DATA

Salary range	Frequency
$0	0
$12,500	250
$37,500	500
$62,500	125
$87,500	60
$112,500	35
$137,500	18
$162,500	6
$187,500	3
$212,500	2
$237,500	1
Total number of employees	1000

Figure A.4   A frequency distribution for salaries in company 'X'
A hypothetical set of data for salaries.

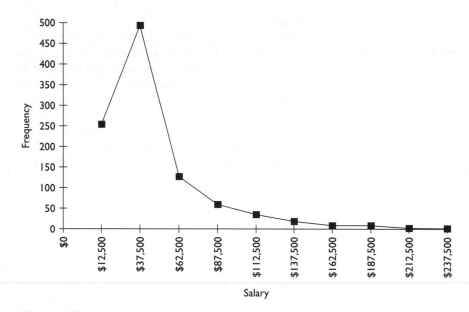

Figure A.5   A skewed frequency distribution This graph plots the data for
Figure A.4.

are above it, and half below it. In both cases, it would be possible to alter
one (or more) score without altering the value of the central tendency as
these measures define it.

If we compare the three values in the current example, they are in reasonably close agreement: using the original scores, the mode is 64 per cent, the
median 67 per cent and the mean 66.5 per cent. Since the three measures
seem to correspond fairly well, why should we be concerned about differences in how each is derived? The reason is that not all situations are like
this example. Consider the data in Figure A.4 and the associated graph
(Figure A.5). These data are hypothetical, representing the salaries of

employees of a large company (totalling 1,000 employees). This 'lopsided' frequency distribution is characteristic of income data, for both companies and nations; in effect, the large majority of individuals have relatively low incomes, while very high incomes are very rare. In analysing the data in this example, we will use the interval data exclusively, because of the large numbers involved (as the number of scores increases, the distortions resulting from simplification typically get smaller, not larger). In this case, both the mode and the median salary are $37,500. The mean, however, is $43,438 – almost $6,000 higher! Now, if one says the 'average' salary is $43,438 (referring to the mean), this sounds pretty good – until one realizes that at least half the people (those who are at or below the median) earn appreciably *less* than this. Consider further: suppose that the top thirty executives each receive a $25,000 raise. This will raise the 'average' (mean) salary by almost 2 per cent – yet 97 per cent of employees will have received no increase! Obviously, the word 'average' can be very misleading.

There are two points worth remembering in relation to this example. The first is that one should always be clear on what someone is referring to when they use the term 'average'. The second is that descriptive statistics have limitations, and they are only helpful when used appropriately.

How can one determine when the mean is appropriate or not? Although it is possible to give a technical answer to this, one helpful guide is to look at the shape of the frequency distribution. Very often, the shape is a symmetrical curve that looks something like a bell in profile; this bell-shaped curve is called a **normal distribution** (see Figure A.6). As you can see, the distribution in our example of test grades (Figure A.3) is approximately normal shaped. In a true normal distribution, the highest point occurs at the middle of the distribution – that is, the mode (the highest frequency) is the same as the median (the middle score); in addition, the mean will have the same value. Thus, in a normal distribution, it doesn't matter which measure of central tendency one uses, because they all produce the same result. (Even though our grade example is not perfectly symmetrical, the values come out to be very similar.) By contrast, the frequency distribution in the salary example (Figure A.5) is distinctly lopsided; this is referred to as a **skewed distribution**. Whenever one encounters a very skewed distribution, the mean is unlikely to be representative of the majority of scores. In such circumstances, most researchers prefer to use the median as a way of describing the 'typical' result.

normal distribution a type of frequency distribution which resembles a bell-shaped curve; among its special properties, first identified by Gauss, is that its measures of central tendency are all the same

skewed distribution an asymmetrical frequency distribution with a single mode; with a skewed distribution the median is usually more representative than the mean as a measure of central tendency

Measures of Variability

Even when one deals with an approximately normal distribution, as in Figure A.3, measures of central tendency do not give us a full picture of the data. To understand why, let us look at another example. In this case, we will consider two simple distributions of test grades (see Figure A.7a). If you look at the two groups, you will note that they have the same mode, the same median and the same mean. Yet, in some sense, they are different. One way to recognize this is by considering the following questions: if you were writing this test, and you were told that you had scored 'below the mean', would you care which group it was? Alternatively, if you were told

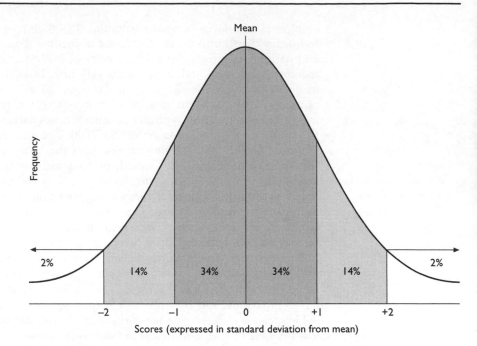

Figure A.6 A normal distribution In a normal distribution, the mean is the same as the median and the mode – hence it also represents the peak of the frequency curve, and the point at which 50 per cent of scores lie on either side. As discussed in the text, in a normal distribution, one can also predict what percentage of people fall into a certain score range by expressing scores in units of the standard deviation. When this is done, the percentages falling within certain regions are as shown in the graph.

DATA FOR TWO SAMPLE GROUPS

	Group 1	Group 2
	55	55
	58	64
	60	68
	62	69
	63	69
	70	70
	70	70
	70	70
	77	71
	78	71
	80	72
	82	76
	85	85
Mean	70	70

(a)

DATA FOR TWO SAMPLE GROUPS

	Group 1	Deviation scores	Group 2	Deviation scores
	55	−15	55	−15
	58	−12	64	−6
	60	−10	68	−2
	62	−8	69	−1
	63	−7	69	−1
	70	0	70	0
	70	0	70	0
	70	0	70	0
	77	7	71	1
	78	8	71	1
	80	10	72	2
	82	12	76	6
	85	15	85	15
Mean	70	0	70	0

(b)

Figure A.7 Comparing groups Table (a) shows the original scores for two groups which have the same central tendency and range; in table (b), the deviation scores are also calculated (see text for discussion).

your performance was 'above the mean', would the group matter? (Look again at the scores.) Most people, asked the first question, would prefer Group 2, because most of the low scores are actually close to the mean. If asked the second question, most people would choose Group 1, because most of the high scores are much higher than the mean. Thus, in a very real sense, these two sets of data are different, even though they have identical measures of central tendency. How is this possible?

The answer to this paradox lies in their **variability**, which tells us how the scores are distributed around the centre. One simple indicator of variability is the **range**, which is the difference between the highest score and the lowest score. Interestingly, the range in *both* these groups is the same – 30 percentage points. Because the range only reflects the two most extreme scores, it is only a crude measure of variability; by ignoring where scores fall *in between* these extremes, it ignores a great deal of information available in the original data. What we would ideally like is a measure of variability that takes into account every score, somewhat in the way the mean does as a measure of central tendency.

One way to look at this is to determine *how far away* from the centre each score is. This could be done by subtracting the mean (defined as the centre – in a normal distribution it will be the median as well) from each score. To see how this works, consider Figure A.7b, in which we have calculated the deviations for both groups. You will note that the deviations (ignoring signs) tend to be larger in Group 1 than in Group 2; this tells us that the scores tend to lie further from the mean in this group. Now, if we consider these *deviation scores* as data in themselves, we could ask: 'What is the typical deviation in each group?' If we then proceed to calculate the mean, we will find a strange thing: the mean of these deviation scores is zero in both groups! While this may seem like a strange coincidence, in fact it is an inevitable result, since it turns out that one can *define* the mean of a distribution as being the number for which the mean of the deviation scores is zero! So, although the deviation scores *do* tell us something about variability, we cannot simply use these scores to measure mean variability.

If you look closely at the examples, you will see that the difficulty is partly related to the plus and minus signs – if we could focus on just the size of the numbers (what is called the *absolute value*), then we could perhaps get somewhere. Early statisticians recognized this, but found it was cumbersome to extract the signs when doing calculations. However, they also recognized that one could accomplish something similar by *squaring* all the deviation scores, since the squares of both positive *and* negative numbers are positive. The mean of these 'squared deviations' could then be calculated as a measure of variability (which is called the *variance*). While the variance is used in a number of ways by statisticians, in terms of our original question ('How can we describe the typical variability of these groups?') it gives an inflated number, since it is based on the *squares* of the deviations, *not* the deviations themselves. To circumvent this, one can take the *square root* of the variance, which in one sense scales things back to size. This value is called the **standard deviation**, and it provides us with our goal – a measure of variability which reflects the position of every score within the group,

variability in statistics, the dispersion of scores within a set of data

range a statistical measure of variability which is calculated as the difference between the highest score and the lowest score in a frequency distribution

standard deviation a commonly used measure of variability, calculated as the square root of the mean of the squared deviations from the mean of a set of scores expressed in the same units as the original scores. (As we will see below, there are additional reasons why the standard deviation is preferred to the mean deviation.) If we were to define the standard deviation in a single sentence, it would be as 'the square root of the mean of the squared deviations of the scores from the original mean'. Quite a mouthful, to be sure – but if you go back to Figure A.7 and try taking it step-by-step, it is actually fairly straightforward.

Taken together, the mean and standard deviation tell us a great deal about a set of data. For instance, in the previous example, although the means are identical, the standard deviations are quite different: for Group 1 it is 9.8 per cent, while in Group 2 it is only 6.7 per cent. (Notice that the standard deviation, like the mean, is expressed in the same units as the original data.) This is consistent with our earlier intuition that the scores are more widely scattered in Group 1. In general, the larger the standard deviation, the greater the variability of the scores.

Properties of Normal Distributions

As mentioned above, the normal distribution is a symmetrical frequency distribution, with an overall bell-like shape, whose measures of central tendency are all identical. These properties are themselves distinctive, but when combined with the standard deviation, they yield even more surprising results. Because it goes beyond the scope of this overview, we will not try to prove the following points. However, the conclusions have been well established by statisticians.

If you return to the normal distribution in Figure A.6, you will see that the mean has been indicated by a vertical line, which passes through the peak of the curve – hence it is the mode as well. In addition, since this line marks the median, we know that 50 per cent of the scores will lie on either side of this line. Now, if we also mark a line at a distance equal to the standard deviation on either side of the mean, then we break up the 50 per cent into two portions, one of which is larger in area than the other. (Note it is marked in Figure A.6 as ±1 standard deviation units.) In fact, it turns out that approximately 34 per cent (34.13 per cent if one wishes to be a bit more precise) of the scores lie between the standard deviation and the mean (as noted on the graph). If we continue this process, marking lines at a point equal to twice the standard deviation from the mean, we further sub-divide the remaining area. The larger portion will be about 14 per cent (13.59 per cent), leaving about 2 per cent (2.28 per cent) beyond this point.

At this point, you probably have two questions: how do we know this, and why should we care? The first question is too technical to answer fully here, but is well established, as noted earlier. What we *can* say is that normal distributions are found in many aspects of the real world, and they always have these same characteristics. For example, the height of all the men in the world is a normal distribution, as is the waist size of all women, as is the weight of travellers' suitcases taken on aeroplanes, and many other things. Consequently, knowing something is 'normally distributed' immediately tells us some very specific things, including that most scores are near the mean, and that very few scores (only about 2 per cent) lie more than two standard deviations from the mean.

For example, consider IQ test scores, which have a mean of 100 and a standard deviation of about 15 (depending on the test used). This means that just over two-thirds of all people have IQs between 85 and 115. (These scores represent the dividing lines for ± one standard deviation.) Similarly, it also tells us that only about 2 per cent of all people score higher than 130 on this test. This leads to the answer to the second question ('who cares?'), at least in part: knowing these properties of normal distributions becomes very useful in making predictions about scores, and in our ability to interpret the results of research. For example, airlines depend on statistics about the weight of suitcases in order to plan cargo capacity. Knowing how many people will be on a particular plane, they can also make predictions about the total weight of all luggage. This follows from knowing the mean weight of suitcases, and also the likelihood that unusually heavy ones will occur. To understand how this works, we need to consider how statistics are used in the interpretation of data – that is, *inferential statistics*. However, before doing so, let us take a look at a different type of descriptive statistic, which is used to identify relationships between two sets of observations.

Correlations

As discussed in Chapter 1, there are many situations in which a researcher is unable or uninclined to do an experiment. When one is using non-experimental research methods such as surveys or naturalistic observation, any relationships perceived between variables are *correlational*, and do not directly identify causal factors. Nonetheless, correlational data can be very useful in identifying patterns or relationships which merit further research.

While Chapter 1 discusses the logic behind the use of correlations, it is worth considering further how statistics are used to describe correlational data. Correlational patterns typically fit one of two types: a positive correlation or a negative correlation. A **positive correlation** occurs when increases in one variable are associated with increases in the other variable. For example, if we were to record the height and weight of a group of people, we would find a positive correlation – generally, taller people also weigh more. A **negative correlation** occurs when increases in one variable occur as the value of the other variable decreases (in mathematics, this is called an inverse relationship). For example, there is a negative correlation between age and fitness – that is, as age increases among adults, fitness level (measured by maximum heart rate) generally declines (see Figure A.8). Typically, correlational patterns are measured using a statistical measure called a *correlation coefficient*. A correlation coefficient is a number which varies between 0.0 and +1.0 for positive correlations, and between 0.0 and –1.0 for negative correlations. In both cases, as the value moves from zero towards the maximum, the degree of relationship between the variables becomes stronger. For example, the correlation between height and political success is about +0.20 (tall individuals are slightly more likely to be elected than shorter individuals); by comparison, the correlation between

positive correlation a relationship observed between two variables in which increases in the value of one variable are associated with increases in the value of the other variable

negative correlation a relationship observed between two variables in which increases in one variable occur as the value of the other variable decreases

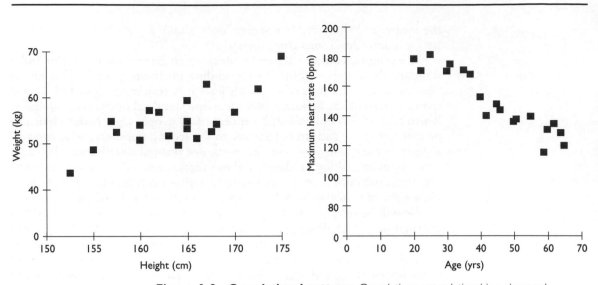

Figure A.8   Correlational patterns Correlations are relationships observed between two variables which do not directly tell us about causation. In the left figure, there is a *positive* correlation between height and weight; in the right figure, there is a *negative* correlation between age and fitness, measured by maximum heart rate.

IQ test scores and grade average in high school is about +0.60 (people with above average IQs tend to do well in school). In these examples, there is a stronger relationship between IQ and grades than between height and political success.

Technically, the examples in Figure A.8 represent what is called a linear correlation, where the underlying relationship between the two variables is linear (that is, it can be represented as a straight line function). In principle, it is possible for two variables to be related in more complex ways, represented by curvilinear functions (curved lines). For example, the relationship between motivational level and performance is frequently curvilinear, and can be represented by an upside-down U-shape: people tend to perform badly when motivation is very low or very high, and perform best when motivation is moderate. If one were to calculate a linear correlation for the variables of motivation and performance, it would appear to be very low, because a straight line does not accurately represent the relationship between the variables. It is beyond the scope of this appendix to pursue this issue in detail, but it is worth noting that not all relationships observed in the world are simple straight lines.

| For further consideration |

Make a hypothetical graph of the motivation–performance relationship by drawing an inverted U-curve and placing 'data points' on it. Would either a positive or negative correlation fit these points very well? What would happen if you considered only the points on the left (or right) half of the curve? Does the type of relationship observed depend on the range of the observations?

Inferential Statistics

As noted, inferential statistics are used for making inferences about the meaning of our observations – that is, they aid us in interpreting a set of data. In essence, this involves making some assumptions, and then seeing what one can conclude, based on those assumptions. In a way, using inferential statistics is like being a detective who tries to interpret a set of clues.

Sampling and Variability

Psychologists almost always depend on observing samples when doing research, even though they want to draw conclusions about a larger population. Ideally, proper sampling procedures will lead to a representative sample. However, even when proper procedures are used, one cannot be absolutely certain that the sample will match the population. To understand why, we must return to the idea of variability. Suppose that the local sweet shop has a contest: a large barrel is filled with red and yellow jellybeans, and one must guess the ratio of the two in the barrel. As part of the contest, you are allowed to buy a handful, which can then be examined as a way of determining the contents of the barrel. If you examine a handful, and find eight red and five yellow jellybeans, what does this tell us about what is in the barrel? It *might* mean that there are more red ones than yellow ones. But could one get a sample like this if the ratio is actually equal? And what are the chances that a second sample (another handful) will be identical to the first sample?

sampling variability
variability due to chance variations among samples randomly drawn from the same population

Intuitively, we recognize that not all samples will be alike, and that any particular sample may differ from the population. Both of these facts are the result of **sampling variability** – the fact that samples randomly drawn from the same population will tend to vary. As a result, using a sample to decide what the population is like can be filled with uncertainty. While this is relatively easy to understand in an example like the jellybean contest, the same thing holds true in *any* sampling situation, such as doing research. For example, a cognitive psychologist may test the short-term memory capacity of a group of 30 individuals. The mean capacity is 7.2 chunks of information. Does this mean that people in general would show the same result? Could this be a fluke result, either higher or lower than the proper value in the population? How can one decide? Inferential statistics are concerned with providing guidelines for evaluating situations like this.

Drawing Inferences from a Normal Distribution

Perhaps the simplest situation for making inferences involves looking at a single score in relation to a set of data. Suppose that as a teacher I discover that I have overlooked recording a grade for one particular student on a test. Approaching the student directly, I ask what the grade was, and the student says it was 92 per cent. Now, this strikes me as unlikely, but I am reluctant to accuse the student of lying without reasonable grounds. What can I do? As it happens, I know that the mean for the rest of the class is

66 per cent, with a standard deviation of 7 per cent. Furthermore, I know that the grade distribution is approximately normal. Can this information help me to evaluate the student's claimed grade?

Thanks to what we know about the normal distribution, it is possible to ask about the likelihood of *anyone* receiving a grade of 92 per cent. Knowing the mean and standard deviation, I can refer back to the normal distribution, and note that only about 2 per cent of all students would receive a grade of even 80 per cent or better; the chances of a grade of 92 per cent are much lower. (If our graph in Figure A.6 were more detailed, it would show that the chance of such a grade, given the mean and standard deviation, is less than one in a thousand.) Faced with this information, I conclude that the grade is probably false, and I would insist that the student produce the test as corroboration.

In this situation, I have made an **inference** – a logical conclusion based on what I know (in this case, I have used the observed results to generalize about grades). Note that I can only say the grade is *probably* false – in making inferences, one can never have absolute certainty. In using inferential statistics, we try to generalize from our sample to the population. In doing so, the characteristics of the sample are considered *estimates* of the characteristics of the population. Thus, in the case above, my known values of the mean and standard deviation are based on the sample (i.e. the class with one score missing), while the population would be represented by the total class. In effect, by using the estimates, I can ask how likely it would be to find a score like 92 per cent in the total class.

inference the process of drawing a conclusion based on logical analysis of what is already known

Inferences about the Significance of Results

In similar ways, one can make other kinds of inferences about observational data. For example, a medical researcher does an experiment designed to evaluate a new cold remedy. Sixty people who come to a clinic seeking a cold remedy are randomly assigned to either the experimental group (who receive the new drug) or a control group (who receive a placebo). (We will assume that the experiment is a proper double-blind design, and properly conducted.) All individuals are monitored, and it is found that the mean time to recovery for the experimental group is 4.2 days, and for the control group is 6.4 days; the standard deviation of the combined groups is 1.1 days. Does this result represent a real effect of the drug, or is the difference between the groups simply a result of sampling variability, like getting different handfuls of jellybeans? In this situation, the experimenter could use a procedure called Student's **t-test**. (Ferguson (1981) has noted that 'Student' was a pen name for W. S. Gossett, who developed the t-test while working for the Guinness brewery. Since the problems he dealt with concerned quality control in the brewing process, one might say that we owe current beer quality to statistics!)

t-test in inferential statistics, a procedure for determining the significance of observed differences; a common use is to decide whether the difference between the means of two groups is due only to sampling variability

In essence, the t-test asks how likely it is to find the observed difference between the means, if only sampling variability is at work; in terms of our example, this would mean that the drug is ineffective. Without going into the technical details, the t-test compares the observed results to a normal distribution of possible sample results. In this case, the probability of finding

significance tests in statistics, the general name given to inferential statistical procedures which are used to determine whether observed results reflect real differences rather than chance variations

significance level in inferential statistics, a statement of the probability that an observed outcome is due only to chance

such a difference purely by chance is less than three in a hundred, which would normally lead a researcher to conclude that the drug probably works. Results which are interpreted as based on a real effect (i.e. *not* due to chance) are referred to as 'significant'; the statistical tests for evaluating chance versus real effects are therefore sometimes called **significance tests**. The conclusion one draws, expressed as the probability that the outcome is due to chance, is called the **significance level** of the results.

Thus, inferential statistics use sample data to try to make inferences about a population which cannot be known directly. In doing so, significance tests evaluate the possibility of obtaining a given result based solely on the chance variations associated with sampling variability. This is reflected in the *null hypothesis*, which always asserts that only chance is at work. If one can *reject* the null hypothesis as being *false*, then this makes the desired hypothesis more likely (but does *not* directly *prove* it to be true, for the reasons mentioned in the discussion of the logic of research). Although various significance tests exist, they always lead to a probability statement, indicating the likelihood that the observed results would occur if the null hypothesis were true. Thus, statistical inference is always a matter of probabilities, never certainty.

In judging these probabilities, there is no magical cut-off where one can say, '*Now* I can be *sure* of my conclusion.' Instead, the commonly accepted standard is that the probability of obtaining the results by chance must be fewer than five in a hundred, although even lower probabilities are more comforting. (Often, this value will be printed as '$p < 0.05$'.) This means that researchers are actually quite conservative, since fewer than five chances of being wrong implies better than 95 chances of being *right* – imagine a gambler who wouldn't bet unless the chances of winning were greater than 95 out of 100.

Decision Errors in Interpreting Data

Despite this conservative attitude, researchers must still face the possibility that sometimes a result *is* due to chance, and that therefore their interpretation of the results is wrong. This leads to the basic problem of all inferential reasoning – trying to make statements based on incomplete knowledge of the world. To return to the drug experiment, the doctors want to determine if the drug works or not; their basis for deciding is their examination of the experimental data. However, as we have discussed, sampling variability implies that if they did the experiment again, the results would be different. So how can they be sure if the drug works or not?

In essence, the situation implies four possibilities, which involve the relationship of the observed results to the underlying reality (see Figure A.9). The results will suggest either that the drug works, or that it doesn't work. Similarly, the underlying reality is either that the drug works, or that it doesn't. This leads to four possible decision outcomes, two of which are correct decisions, and two of which are errors. If the drug actually works, and the statistical analysis says it works, then this is obviously a correct decision. Similarly, if the drug doesn't work, and the analysis does not lead to rejecting the null hypothesis that it doesn't, then this is also a correct

Decision table for evaluating hypotheses

REALITY IN POPULATION

DECISION FROM SAMPLE	DRUG WORKS	DRUG DOESN'T WORK
REJECT NULL HYPOTHESIS (CONCLUDE DRUG WORKS)	CORRECT DECISION	TYPE I ERROR (FALSE POSITIVE)
ACCEPT NULL HYPOTHESIS (CONCLUDE DRUG DOESN'T WORK)	TYPE 2 ERROR (FALSE NEGATIVE)	CORRECT DECISION

Figure A.9 Errors in evaluating hypotheses No statistical procedure can ensure that researchers never make an error in interpreting what the results of a study mean. This chart shows the various ways in which either correct or incorrect decisions can be made. (See text for discussion of the types of errors.)

false positive in inferential statistics, concluding that an observed outcome is significant when in fact it reflects only chance variability; also called a type I error

false negative in inferential statistics, concluding that the observed results are due only to chance variability when in fact a significant effect exists; also called a type II error

decision. The potential problems arise with the other two possible outcomes, which reflect different types of errors. If the drug does not work, but chance factors in the results lead to *concluding* that it does, then rejecting the null hypothesis is really an error. This type of error is called a *type I error* or a **false positive**. If the drug actually works, but the results are *not* strong enough to conclude that it does, then accepting the null hypothesis is an error. This second form of error, which leads to overlooking genuine effects, is called either a *type II error*, or a **false negative**. In each case, the errors are due to the uncertainty inherent in the process of interpreting results. In a world where sampling variability did not exist, such problems would also be non-existent. But sampling variability is a reality, along with random variations like measurement errors, all of which make it more difficult to get unambiguous results in doing research.

These effects may seem rather abstract, but in fact they can be all too real. In the case of drug research, false negatives can lead to abandoning the development of a potentially useful drug, while false positives can lead to wasted effort pursuing an ineffective drug. This type of situation can also arise in situations remote from research – indeed, wherever we must make decisions based on imperfect information.

Increasingly, individuals are faced with making decisions in situations like health care. For example, in the past few years, a blood test has been developed for pregnant women, which is designed to detect defects called *neural tube disorders* in the developing embryo. While the test is simple to do, its interpretation is more difficult. Since neural tube disorders are rare, the test results are mostly negative (meaning the embryo is normal). However, of those which are *positive* (suggesting a defect in the embryo), 19 out of 20 are false positives! When a test is positive, the mother must undergo further tests over several weeks. The uncertainty created can cause significant distress, while some of the additional tests (like *amniocentesis*) themselves pose risks. After all this, 95 per cent of those initially told the test is positive will discover that in fact there is nothing wrong with the embryo. In addition, while they occur much less often, the test can also occasionally give false negatives; such a result would lead to the conclusion that the embryo is normal, even when a neural tube disorder exists. Given these realities, many prospective mothers, if informed, might ask whether the test is worth taking.

It should be emphasized that the difficulties described are not unique to the test for neural tube disorders. Similar decision problems arise with other types of medical tests, including mammograms for breast cancer and PSA blood tests for prostate cancer. Similarly, false positives and false negatives can arise in other kinds of situations – for example, if employers concerned about theft ask employees to take a lie detector test (Lykken 1988).

The dilemma which decisions of this nature create cannot be avoided by simple refinements of technology – the limitations are inherent to the process of interpreting the meaning of samples. What one *can* do, if so inclined, is decide which type of error is more serious, and therefore more important to avoid. Traditionally, the preference in science is to avoid false positives (i.e. type I errors), which would lead to concluding there is support for a theory when in fact it is false. That is why the *minimum* criterion (i.e. *significance level*) for rejecting the null hypothesis is a less than 5 per cent chance that the null hypothesis is correct. In the extreme case, one could avoid *all* false positives by *never* concluding that the results are significant; of course, this would lead to many false negatives, since some data due to real effects would *also* be rejected as inconclusive. (Similarly, the only way to avoid *all* false negatives is by calling all results significant.) Ultimately, uncertainty is an inherent part of the interpretation of data: it is part of the reason why we can never speak of absolute proof in science. To most researchers in psychology, living with such uncertainty is simply part of the larger challenge of understanding behaviour.

| **For further consideration** | Suppose that your doctor proposed doing a new test as a means of diagnosing why you don't feel well. What would you want to know about the accuracy and interpretation of the test? |

Conclusion

Doing research is a complex and challenging process, involving many possible ways in which things can go wrong – from the design of the study, to the process of gathering data, to the interpretations that are made once the data have been collected. At the same time, research offers the chance to ask new questions, to be creative in developing a research design and, ultimately, to experience the thrill of discovering something previously unknown. For many people, the rewards far outweigh the risks.

While some individuals reading this book may go on to become professional psychologists, and make discoveries of their own, most readers probably won't. So what value does this material have? In part, this appendix is intended to appeal to a sense of curiosity, to the desire to understand a bit more about what is actually involved in doing research. Beyond that, it also has a more practical intent: in today's world, we all encounter the results of research, whether in news reports or in our personal lives (as with medical tests). By understanding something about the process which underlies research and statistical analysis, one can be better equipped to evaluate the information we receive. In this sense, the old saying is true: knowledge *is* power. May the knowledge included here add to the power of your understanding as you continue in psychology, and in your life.

Chapter Summary

- ◆ As a science, psychology makes use of systematic methods for doing research and analysing the resulting data; these topics are referred to as *research methods* and *statistics*.

- ◆ In planning research, researchers must consider how observations are made (*measurement*), what observations to make (*sampling*) and how the hypothesis is to be tested (*research design*).

- ◆ In experimental research, the researcher must pay particular attention to the possibility of *error* due to *confounds* or *bias*.

- ◆ Statistical analysis involves summarizing the data (*descriptive statistics*) and interpreting the meaning of the results (*inferential statistics*).

- ◆ Descriptive statistics include *frequency distributions*, *measures of central tendency*, *measures of variability* and *correlations*.

- ◆ The most important form of frequency distribution is the *normal distribution*, which is useful for both its particular characteristics and its relevance to many everyday types of data.

- ◆ Inferential statistics are necessary in evaluating results because of the occurrence of *variability* when sampling.

- ◆ *Significance tests* like the *t-test* are used to estimate the likelihood of obtaining the observed results by chance.

- ◆ When one is using inferential statistics, there is never absolute certainty about one's interpretation; instead, *decision errors* (*false positives* and *false negatives*) can arise.

- ◆ Despite the challenges, research provides opportunities to be creative and to explore the unknown.

Key Terms and Concepts

confound
correlation coefficient
cross-sectional sample
descriptive statistics
double-blind design
experimenter bias
falsification
frequency distribution
halo effect
hypothesis
internal validity
mean
median
mode
negative correlation
normal distribution

null hypothesis
population
positive correlation
random sample
range
reliability
sample
sampling error
sampling variability
self-fulfilling prophecy
significance tests
single-blind design
standard deviation
subject bias
t-test
validity

Suggestions for Further Reading

For an entertaining exploration of the ways in which scientific evidence can be misused in everyday life, read Peter Huber's book, *Galileo's Revenge: Junk Science in the Courtroom.*

Pygmalion in the Classroom, by Rosenthal and Jacobson, provides a vivid and entertaining exploration of how experimenter bias and self-fulfilling prophecies can affect behaviour in the real world.

If you wish to know more about research design, there are a number of texts available. *Research Methods in Psychology*, by Elmes *et al.*, provides reasonably clear coverage, and does not overlook aspects like ethical considerations.

While statistics is not likely to be considered a topic for light reading, for those who wish to investigate the subject further, Ferguson's *Statistical Analysis in Psychology and Education* is a well-known text which has survived through several editions.

Glossary

abnormal behaviour behaviour which is regarded by society as deviant or maladaptive; according to DSM-IV, an individual must be suffering or show maladaptive functioning in order for behaviour to be described as abnormal.

accessibility in long-term memory, the principle that remembering and forgetting are dependent on effective retrieval; without the proper cues, information which exists in long-term memory may not be accessible.

accommodation in Piaget's theory of cognitive development, a process of modifying our cognitive schemata in response to new knowledge or experience.

actualizing tendency in Rogers's theory, an innate drive which reflects the desire to grow, to develop and to enhance one's capacities.

adrenal glands endocrine glands, located just above the kidneys, which play an important role in arousal and stress; the outer layer, the cortex, secretes corticosteroids, and the *medulla* (the inner core) secretes *epinephrine* (adrenaline) and *norepinephrine* (noradrenaline).

aetiology the study of the causes of a disease or mental disorder.

aggression behaviour which causes intentional harm to another person.

algorithm a procedure for problem solving which, when used appropriately, always leads to the solution of a particular type of problem.

altered state of consciousness any state of awareness which differs from normal waking awareness; examples could include meditation, sleep, drug states and psychosis.

altruism behaviour intended to help others, independently of any self-interest.

ambiguous figure any stimulus which can be perceived in more than one way.

anal stage in Freud's theory of psychosexual development, the second stage (15 months to three years); during this stage the focus of drive energy shifts to the lower end of the digestive tract, and the major conflict is toilet training.

androgens hormones whose functions are related to masculine characteristics; the most important is testosterone.

anti-depressant a drug which is used to treat clinical depression, primarily by enhancing the activity of the neurotransmitter serotonin.

anti-social personality disorder a behaviour pattern in which an individual shows a history of acts of violence towards others, unaccompanied by guilt; although these individuals may not report either suffering or unsatisfactory functioning (the generally accepted standard for abnormality), their behaviour is still deemed abnormal because it violates society's norms in such significant ways.

anxiety a negative emotional state associated with threat to the self; in Freud's theory, it arises when the ego is faced with an influx of stimuli with which it cannot cope, as a result of either external danger or the demands of id or superego.

archetypes patterns within the collective unconscious which serve to organize our experiences, providing the basis of many fantasies, myths and symbols.

artificial intelligence in computer science, the attempt to build machines which can function intelligently, and the use of such machines to test our understanding of human intelligence.

assimilation in Piaget's theory of cognitive development, a process of integrating new knowledge or experience into our existing cognitive schemata.

association areas areas of the cortex which have no primary function (such as receiving direct sensory data), but play a role in integrating activity from other brain areas.

associationism the doctrine, supported by Aristotle, Hume and others, that mental processes, particularly learning, are based on forming connections between ideas and/or events.

attention the process of selectively focusing on particular stimulus elements, typically those deemed most significant.

attitude a personal belief of an evaluative nature, such as good or bad, likeable or not likeable, which influences our reactions towards people or things.

attribution theory a theory dealing with the inferences we make about the causes of our own behaviour, and that of other people; the interpretations made are called *attributions*.

autonomic conditioning (also called 'learned operant control of autonomic responses') the conditioning of changes in autonomic (involuntary) responses (such as heart rate or blood pressure) by providing operant reinforcement.

availability in memory, the principle that remembering is determined by whether the information exists in LTM or not; forgetting implies that the information is destroyed.

aversive conditioning a form of behaviour modification which is designed to induce an aversive response to stimuli which are associated with existing undesirable behaviours.

axon the relatively elongated portion of a neuron between the cell body and the terminals which provides the signal pathway for a nerve impulse.

basic anxiety in Horney's psychodynamic theory, an intense sense of isolation and helplessness which is the primary source of human motivation.

behaviour modification the application of conditioning techniques to altering human behaviour, particularly those behaviours identified as abnormal.

bias a source of error which results in a systematic distortion of results.

biofeedback a general term for applications of the process of autonomic conditioning; the name refers to the fact that in humans reinforcement is based on providing an individual with information ('feedback') about physiological processes ('bio') which are normally not observable.

brain the portion of the central nervous system which lies within the skull.

brain stem the region at the top of the spinal cord, composed of three primary structures: the medulla, the pons and the midbrain.

bystander apathy the failure of onlookers to intervene in an emergency; despite the label, the cause is often unrelated to apathy.

case study a detailed description of a single individual, typically used to provide information on the person's history and to aid in interpreting the person's behaviour.

catharsis the release of drive energy in indirect form, through either the process of recalling emotionally charged experiences or involvement in symbolic activity.

central nervous system (CNS) the brain, together with the nerve pathways of the spinal cord.

cerebellum ('little brain' in Latin) two small hemispheres located beneath the cortical hemispheres, at the back of the head; the cerebellum plays an important role in directing movements and balance.

cerebral dominance the tendency for one hemisphere to be superior for particular functions.

cerebral hemispheres two half spheres, made up of the cortex and underlying structures, which comprise the major portion of the brain.

chaos theory a branch of mathematics dealing with non-linear functions which has been applied to the modelling of situations such as the weather and stock markets; non-linear systems are not predictable, because very small changes in initial conditions can result in radical differences at a later point.

chromosomes thread-like genetic structures composed of double strands of DNA and proteins, containing the genes; in humans, there are 23 pairs of chromosomes.

chunk the basic measure of STM capacity, representing a meaningful unit, such as random letters, numbers or words.

classical conditioning the study of learning which involves reflex responses, in which a neutral stimulus comes to elicit an existing reflex response.

client-centred therapy an approach to therapy developed by Carl Rogers, in which the person seeking treatment (termed a *client*), not the therapist, is seen as directing the process of therapy; later called person-centred therapy.

closure in perception, the tendency to fill in incomplete patterns to produce a coherent whole.

codependency in the recovery movement, a pattern of behaviour triggered by low self-esteem, such that individuals form relationships in which one's sense of self-esteem is dependent on one's partner.

cognitive appraisal theory a theory of emotion which argues that our emotional state is based on our assessment of the situation and its significance to our well-being.

cognitive behaviour modification an extension of behaviour modification which uses cognitive mediation (such as observing a model) in addition to basic conditioning techniques.

cognitive dissonance in Festinger's theory, a state of tension created when there are conflicts between an individual's behaviour and beliefs, or between two beliefs.

cognitive map Tolman's term for the mental representation of learned relationships among stimuli.

cognitive pathology a phenomenon whereby researchers selectively ignore simplifying assumptions and other limitations which are part of the foundations of their theories and methods.

cognitive restructuring in Ellis's rational-emotive therapy, a process for modifying faulty beliefs and the negative emotions they produce, in order to develop realistic beliefs and self-acceptance.

cognitive social learning theory (sometimes simply 'social learning theory') a theory derived from the cognitive approach which asserts that behaviour can be learned from observing other people, and that behaviour is mediated by cognitive schemata.

collective unconscious in Jung's theory, a biologically-based portion of the unconscious which reflects universal themes and ideas, not individual experience.

compensation in Adler's theory, a process of engaging in activities intended to produce a feeling of superiority over others, in order to overcome feelings of inferiority.

complementarity a concept developed by physicists to deal with the existence of two models which are both useful, but not directly reconcilable.

computerized imaging techniques for studying brain function which use computers to convert information into a three-dimensional model of the brain which can be viewed on a television monitor.

concordance a technique for studying inheritance by examining characteristics of individuals whose genetic relationship is known.

conditional positive regard acceptance and caring given to a person only for meeting certain standards of behaviour.

conditioned emotional response an emotional response such as fear which is established through classical conditioning.

conditioned reinforcer stimuli which act as reinforcers but are not based on biological survival, such as attention, praise or money.

conditioned response in classical conditioning, a response to a previously neutral stimulus which has become a conditioned stimulus by repeated pairing with an unconditioned stimulus.

conditioned stimulus a stimulus which by repeated pairings with an unconditioned stimulus comes to elicit a conditioned response.

conditions for growth the conditions under which healthy development of personality occurs; defined by Rogers as unconditional positive regard, openness and empathy.

conditions of worth restrictions imposed on self-expression in order to earn positive regard.

confirmation in research, the process of determining that observations are consistent with the hypothesis being true.

confirmation bias a form of cognitive error based on the tendency to seek out information which supports one's beliefs, and ignore contradictory information.

conformity the tendency to adjust one's opinions and behaviour to comply with group norms in response to explicit or implicit social pressure.

confound in experimental research, a situation where two variables change simultaneously, making it impossible to determine their relative influence.

confounding variable A factor in research which varies jointly with a variable of interest, making it impossible to identify properly the role each variable has in affecting behaviour; typically, a confounding variable represents something which has been overlooked in planning the research, and is only identified after the data have been collected.

congruence in Rogers's theory, a feeling of integration experienced when the self and ideal self match.

conscious in Freud's theory, that aspect of the mind which contains those thoughts and feelings of which we are immediately aware at a given moment.

context-dependent forgetting failure to retrieve information from LTM due to the absence of appropriate contextual cues.

contingency of reinforcement in operant conditioning, a description of the relationship between a response and a reinforcer.

continuity in developmental theory, the view that changes occur through a continuous gradual process, rather than as a series of discrete stages; continuity is an assertion about the processes which underlie development, as well as the changes observed in behaviour.

continuous reinforcement a reinforcement schedule in which every response is followed by a reinforcer; equivalent to an FR 1 schedule.

convergent problem a problem which has a single solution, and all elements lead towards that solution; also called *closed-end* or *well-defined* problems.

corpus callosum a wide band of nerve fibres which connect the two hemispheres.

correlation a pattern or relationship observed between two variables.

correlation coefficient a descriptive statistic measuring the degree of relationship between two variables; for positive correlations, it is a number which varies between 0.0 and +1.0, and for negative correlations between 0.0 and –1.0; in both cases, the closer the value is to 1, the stronger the relationship between the two variables.

cortex the pink, somewhat wrinkled outer layer of the brain which controls many of our higher functions like speech and perception; from the Greek for 'bark' (as on a tree).

creativity the capacity to produce something which is both unique and useful.

critical period in development, the concept that there are optimal periods for the learning of certain behaviours.

cross-sectional sample a sample which is deliberately selected in such a way that the sample matches the population for particular characteristics, such as age and income.

cross-sectional study a research design based on selecting representative groups who vary on a particular characteristic; when the characteristic is age, this design provides a means of making developmental comparisons.

cue-dependent coding the concept that all information is stored in memory as a set of relationships called the context; remembering is seen as dependent on restoring the cues which formed the original context.

culture a relatively organized set of meanings, shared by members of a group, which affect how people, objects and events are interpreted.

debriefing discussing the nature of a research study with participants at its conclusion, in order to explain the true nature and goals of the research and to answer any questions or concerns of participants.

decay in memory, the spontaneous loss of information with the passage of time.

deception in research, the deliberate misinforming of participants concerning the nature of the study and of their role.

deduction the process of drawing specific conclusions from a set of general principles.

defective attention theory a theory which argues that schizophrenia is due to difficulties in selecting and attending to the relevant stimuli in a situation.

defence mechanism in Freud's theory, a technique used by the ego to protect itself from anxiety and the threats which give rise to it; many psychologists use the terms as descriptions of behaviour patterns, without endorsing the Freudian interpretation of their origin.

deficiency motives in Maslow's theory, needs whose motivating power is triggered by the absence of the underlying requirements, such as the physiological or esteem needs.

delusional amphetamine disorder a form of mental disorder resulting from the excessive use of amphetamines; its primary symptom, extreme delusions, can make it appear *symptomatically* identical to paranoid schizophrenia.

delusions false beliefs which are maintained in the absence of clear evidence to the contrary.

demand characteristics the overt and covert cues present in an experimental situation which can influence how participants behave.

dependent variable in an experiment, the behaviour measured in order to evaluate the effects of the independent variable.

depersonalization a type of dissociative reaction in with the individual psychologically withdraws from a situation, often accompanied by feeling that their body is not real or belongs to someone else.

depressant a drug which reduces CNS activity; in large doses, depressants can cause coma and even death.

depression a mood disorder characterized by sleep disturbances, fatigue and low self-esteem; in *major depressive disorder*, the symptoms are severe enough to seriously hamper normal functioning, and can be accompanied by thoughts of suicide.

descriptive statistics the branch of statistics which is concerned with describing and summarizing sets of scores.

determinism the assumption that all behaviour has specific causes.

developmental psychology the study of the processes which underlie growth and change in behaviour over time.

diathesis–stress model a theory which views abnormal behaviour as being due to a combination of a physiological predisposition (diathesis) and a stressful environment.

diffusion of responsibility a lessening of an individual's feeling of responsibility in a situation which involves other people.

direct observation any observational technique which depends on direct measurement of behaviour by the researcher, rather than asking an individual to report their behaviour.

discriminative stimulus in operant conditioning, a stimulus which signals the contingency of reinforcement available.

displacement in memory, forgetting in STM owing to new incoming information pushing out the previous contents; in psychoanalysis, a defence mechanism which involves the redirection of drive energy from one object to a substitute object.

divergent problem a problem which does not have a single optimal solution, except according to the criteria one may adopt; rather, the problem tends to lead in several different directions; equivalent to an ill-defined problem.

domain-general model a theory which attempts to account for many aspects of behaviour in terms of a single set of principles.

domain-specific model a theory which focuses on only a single aspect of behaviour in the belief that different aspects of behaviour involve different processes, and therefore require different theoretical explanations.

dopamine hypothesis a theory which argues that schizophrenia is based on over-activity in neural pathways which depend on dopamine as a neurotransmitter.

double-bind hypothesis a theory of schizophrenia developed by anthropologist Gregory Bateson and his colleagues, which argues that faulty communication patterns within the family are the cause of schizophrenia.

double-blind design a rigorous form of experimental control, whereby both the subject and experimenter are kept uninformed about details of the experiment which could result in bias (both subject bias and experimenter bias).

dream censor the psychic mechanism whose function is to ensure that sleep is not disturbed by the unconsciously expressed desires that are the basis of dreams; to accomplish this, the dream censor converts the content of the dream into symbolic form (the manifest content).

dualism the view, first attributed to Descartes, that mind and body are distinct; Descartes believed the two could interact via the pineal gland in the brain.

efficacy the measured effectiveness of a treatment technique in medicine or psychotherapy.

ego (Latin for 'I') in psychoanalysis, the element of the psyche which provides the integrating of personality by mediating between the id and the superego, and also mediates the links with the outside world; in Jung's theory, the element of the self which provides the conscious direction of one's life.

elaborative rehearsal the active processing of items in short-term memory in order to code the information for long-term momory; material may be processed in various ways, ranging from an emphasis on sensory characteristics (visual appearance, sound) to a focus on the semantic content ('meaning') of information.

electrical stimulation of the brain (ESB) artificial stimulation of neurons by means of a current applied through an implanted electrode.

electroencephalograph (EEG – 'writing the electricity of the brain') a device for recording the electrical activity of the brain.

empathy the ability to understand another person's perceptions and feelings; seen by Rogers as a condition for growth.

empirical based on making observations, as in an *empirical* theory.

empiricism the philosophical position, first attributed to John Locke, that all knowledge is based on experience; hence, the basis of the view that behaviour is learned.

encoding the processing of stimulus information for retention in memory.

endocrine glands ('ductless glands') glands which secrete chemicals called *hormones* directly into the bloodstream.

endorphin (*end*ogenous – 'naturally occurring' – m*orphine*) a neuropeptide which plays a significant role in pain and mood states.

episodic memory the portion of long-term memory which contains personal experiences, organized according to where and when events happened, such as what happened on your last birthday.

equilibration in Piaget's theory of cognitive development, the process of maintaining balance between our environment and the mental structures which we use to represent that environment.

equipotentiality premise an assumption made by some behaviourists which states that the principles of conditioning should apply equally to all behaviour, in any species

ethical hedonism the principle that individuals engage in moral behaviour, such as altruism, because it provides some personal benefit.

ethology the study of the behaviour of animals in their natural environments.

evolution a theory to account for the development of species diversity by means of variations which are transmitted to offspring by inheritance; Darwin's theory of *natural selection* proposed that variations which enhance adaptability, and thereby enhance survival and reproduction rates, are the most likely to be transmitted.

evolutionary psychology the application of evolutionary principles to the understanding of behaviour.

experiment a research design in which the experimenter uses a controlled situation and manipulates one or more factors (called *independent variables*) in order to determine their effect on one or more measures of behaviour (called *dependent variables*).

experimental realism a quality of involvement whereby research participants respond without regard for the laboratory context, as they would in an ordinary situation.

experimenter bias systematic error created when an experimenter's knowledge and expectations about the experiment influence the behaviour of subjects.

expressed emotion a pattern of communication within families which is characterized by high levels of criticism, hostility and emotional intensity.

external validity an assessment of the degree to which one can generalize research results beyond the specific situation.

extinction in classical conditioning, the cessation of responding when the conditioned stimulus is presented repeatedly *without* being paired with the unconditioned stimulus; in operant conditioning, a drop in responding when reinforcement is discontinued.

false negative in inferential statistics, concluding that the observed results are due only to chance variability when in fact a significant effect exists; also called a type II error.

false positive in inferential statistics, concluding that an observed outcome is significant when in fact it reflects only chance variability; also called a type I error.

false recognition a form of memory error whereby the presence of familiar cues leads one to believe the stimulus matches a previously experienced stimulus.

falsifiability a criterion for evaluating a theory which states the theory should specify circumstances wherein it could be proven wrong.

falsification in research, the process of using observations to prove that a hypothesis is wrong.

faulty reference an error involving misinterpreting the significance of stimuli and events; while sometimes considered a form of delusion, it can also arise through faulty perceptual processing.

field experiment an experiment done in a natural setting, usually without the explicit awareness of participants; as contrasted to experiments done in a laboratory setting.

fixation in Freud's theory, the incomplete release of drive energy associated with a particular stage of development.

fixed interval schedule, a reinforcement contingency defined by the amount of time that must pass since the previous reinforcer was given before a response will receive a reinforcer; measured as FI x, where x specifies the required time interval.

fixed ratio schedule a reinforcement contingency defined by the number of responses the organism must make in order to get a reinforcer; the ratio is measured as FR x, where x is the required number of responses.

free association a technique originated by Freud for studying the mind, based on asking a person to say whatever words floated into their mind, and then looking for patterns.

frequency distribution a statistical analysis of a set of data which tells how frequently each value occurs.

frontal lobe the area of the cortex in front of the central fissure, and above the lateral fissure; it is involved in the interpretation of emotion and experience.

frontal lobotomy an operation, popular in the 1940s and 1950s, which involved sectioning or removing portions of the frontal lobes, in an attempt to treat cases of bipolar mood disorder or chronic pain; later shown to be largely ineffective as a therapeutic procedure.

frontal motor area the area of the frontal lobes just before the central fissure which controls all voluntary movements of the muscles.

frustration–aggression hypothesis a theory of aggression developed by Dollard and Miller which states that *frustration* (defined as blocking a goal-oriented response) is the sole cause of aggression.

fully functioning person described by Rogers as the ideal of growth, closely related to congruence; healthy growth is characterized by openness, a high degree of spontaneity, compassion and self-direction.

functional fixedness in Gestalt theory, perceiving an object as having only one use.

functionalism an approach to the study of behaviour pioneered by William James, which emphasizes the analysis of the processes by which the mind works, as opposed to the study of the mind's contents advocated by structuralism.

fundamental attribution error the tendency to underestimate the importance of situational influences, and overestimate the importance of internal factors in interpreting the causes of people's behaviour.

gender roles patterns of behaviour which a culture defines as being appropriate for each gender.

gender schema a cognitive representation which organizes an individual's knowledge of cultural norms for male or female behaviour.

gene the basic unit of heredity, made up of strings of 'building blocks' called amino acids; it is estimated that humans possess about 100,000 different genes, each regulating a different process.

general adaptation syndrome a model of stages of stress identified by Hans Selye, ranging from acute stress (alarm) to outward coping (resistance) to depletion of bodily resources (exhaustion).

generality a criterion for evaluating a theory, which refers to the range of application of a theory; a good theory should apply to a wide range of situations.

genital stage in Freud's theory, the final stage of psychosexual development (from puberty onward), when drive energy is focused on the genitals, with adult expression of sexuality.

genotype the genetic code which an individual carries in the DNA of their cells.

Gestalt theory a theory of behaviour pioneered in the early part of the twentieth century by Kohler, Wertheimer and others, which emphasized the active, creative nature of perception and learning (*Gestalt* is German, and means roughly 'organized whole').

goal state in problem solving, the desired outcome of a problem.

guilt in the recovery movement, a feeling of negative worth in response to behaviour which we recognize as harming others; for Freud, guilt is a form of anxiety associated with behaviours which violate the standards of the superego.

habituation a reduction in neural response due to continual stimulation.

hallucinations false perceptions in the absence of relevant sensory stimuli, such as hearing voices or seeing objects which are not present.

halo effect a form of perceptual bias which occurs when our rating of a person on *one* characteristic as being positive or negative leads to similar expectations for *other* characteristics of the individual.

heredity the biological transmission of characteristics from one generation to another.

heuristic a guide to thinking; in problem solving, heuristics provide informal strategies which are usually better than random search, but less effective than algorithms.

hierarchy of needs Maslow's model of basic human needs, which he saw as organized in a hierarchical structure; needs range from physiological (most basic) to self-actualization (top of hierarchy).

hierarchy of fears in systematic desensitization, a list of fear-evoking stimuli, ranging from very mild to very intense, arranged in order of the intensity of fear which they elicit.

higher-order conditioning a form of classical conditioning in which a previously established conditioned stimulus is used as if it were an unconditioned stimulus to create conditioning to a new stimulus.

hippocampus a structure within the limbic system which is important to memory function.

history of reinforcement in operant conditioning, the sum of all prior reinforcement for a particular behaviour; behaviourists assert that the cumulative history of reinforcement is more important than any single reinforcement in determining behaviour.

hormone a chemical secreted by an endocrine gland; hormones are involved in many aspects of metabolism and long-term functioning of the body.

hypothalamus one of the most important elements in the limbic system, the hypothalamus both regulates behaviours associated with hunger, thirst, sex and other basic drives, and plays a role in regulating hormonal functions.

hypothesis a statement describing a proposed relationship between two types of variables; a conclusion derived from a theory which can be evaluated by making further observations.

hysteria a disorder characterized by physical symptoms for which there is no apparent physical cause; the term was used by Freud but actually predates him.

id (Latin for 'it') in Freud's theory, the element of the psyche which is the source of all basic drives.

ideal self in Rogers's theory, a dynamically changing construct which represents an individual's goals and aspirations.

identification a defence mechanism which involves incorporating characteristics of a drive object into one's own ego.

illusory correlation a cognitive error in which an individual perceives a relationship between variables where none actually exists.

imitation the learning of behaviour by observing the behaviour of others; sometimes called 'modelling' or 'observational learning'.

implicit personality theories a general cognitive schema about human behaviour which is used in making interpretations of the behaviour of other people.

incongruence in Rogers's theory, a feeling of conflict or unease experienced when there is a mismatch between the self and ideal self.

incubation in the Gestalt model of problem solving, a process of ceasing to work actively on a problem, in order to modify one's mental set.

independent variable a variable in an experiment which is systematically varied by the researcher, in order to see what effect it has on behaviour.

individuation Jung's conception of the goal of development, which he described as the expansion of conscious awareness by the ego making contact with the unconscious portions of the self.

induction a process of reasoning based on forming general principles from specific observations.

inference the process of drawing a conclusion based on logical analysis of what is already known.

inferential statistics the branch of statistics which deals with the interpretation of data, particularly in terms of generalizing from the observed sample to the larger population.

inferiority for Adler, the notion that all children experience a sense of helplessness because of their size and dependence on others; this feeling can also be intensified by real or imagined physical defects, social rejection and other factors.

inferiority complex in Adler's theory, an intense feeling of insecurity based on failure to resolve the feelings evoked by childhood experiences of helplessness.

information processing a term borrowed from computer science by cognitive psychologists to describe the mental functions which occur between stimulus and response.

initial state in problem solving, the situation at the outset of a problem, including any existing constraints (such as time limits or restrictions on permitted actions).

insight a sudden change in the way one organizes a problem situation; typically this is characterized by a change in behaviour from random responding to rule-based responding.

insight in psychotherapy, awareness of the underlying conflicts which are regarded as the causes of behaviour.

instrumental aggression aggressive behaviour which is maintained because it is positively reinforced.

interference according to associationism, competition between items which can hamper learning and produce forgetting.

internal validity the assessment of the degree to which the design and execution of an experiment are free from bias, confounds and other sources of error.

intersubjective verification a process for validating observations based on agreement by two observers; proposed by Rogers as a means of making subjective impressions useful as scientific data.

interview a method of gathering data in which a researcher asks an individual questions; the format may be pre-planned and highly structured, or relatively free-flowing and unstructured.

introjection of values for Rogers, the incorporation of values into the ideal self owing to accepting conditions of worth imposed by others; the term was first used by Freud to refer to a defence mechanism.

introspectionism a method of gathering data in which the individual attempts to analyse the content of their conscious mind; associated with the structuralist approach.

kin altruism in evolutionary psychology, the concept that individuals help those who are close relatives, because it fosters the transmission of their genes.

language a system of communication based on symbols or gestures which can vary across individuals and allow for new forms and meanings.

latency stage in Freud's developmental theory, the stage which begins at about age five and extends until puberty, during which the drives appear to be relatively inactive.

latent content in Freud's theory of dreams, the true meaning of a dream, which is transformed by the dream censor into symbolic form as the manifest content.

latent learning a term used by Tolman to describe situations in which learning is distinct from the performance of a behaviour.

law of effect a principle of learning proposed by Thorndike which stated that any response which leads to an outcome satisfying to the organism is likely to be repeated, and any response which leads to an unpleasant outcome is not likely to be repeated.

learning in behaviourism, a change in behaviour which occurs as the result of experience; in cognitive psychology, the process of gathering information and organizing it into mental schemata.

learning set a learned strategy or set which enables the individual to deal efficiently with problems of the same type; similar in meaning to the Gestalt concept of mental set, except that it emphasizes that the set develops as the result of experience.

limbic system a series of subcortical structures which connect the cortex with other parts of the brain and which are important in many basic functions; among the main parts of the limbic system are the thalamus, hypothalamus, amygdala and hippocampus.

localization of function the assumption that specific functions are associated with specific areas of the brain.

logical empiricism in the philosophy of science, the assumption that it is possible to compare and evaluate theories in terms of how well they account for the evidence.

logotherapy Viktor Frankl's theory of development and therapy, which is based on the argument that finding a meaning for life is central to individual growth and happiness.

long-term memory (LTM) the component of memory which is involved with retention over relatively long periods (hours, days, weeks or longer).

longitudinal study a research design in which a given group of individuals are studied over a period of time.

maintenance rehearsal the retention of material in short-term memory by means of rote repetition.

manifest content the symbolic content of a dream (disguised by the dream censor) which the conscious mind is aware of, both during sleep and on waking.

materialism the assumption that all behaviour has a physiological basis.

maturation processes in development which seem to be relatively independent of environmental influences; depth perception and walking are examples of behaviours which seem to depend on maturation; implied in the term is the assumption that the characteristics are governed by heredity.

mean (also called 'arithmetic mean') a statistic measuring central tendency, calculated as the sum of all the scores, divided by the number of scores.

measure of central tendency a type of descriptive statistic used to determine what is a representative value for a set of scores.

median a statistic measuring central tendency, calculated as the middle score in a frequency distribution.

mediator a process or event within the individual which comes between a stimulus and a response.

medical model a theory of abnormal behaviour which assumes that all such disorders have physiological causes.

meditation a technique or practice that seeks to achieve mental and physical relaxation, a more passive, receptive awareness and harmony of mind and nature.

medulla a small swelling at the top of the spinal cord composed of the cell bodies of neurons whose axons extend to the heart and other internal organs; its role is to regulate basic bodily processes.

memory the retention and use of prior learning.

mental set in Gestalt theory, the cognitive schema an individual uses to organize their perception of a particular situation, such as a problem.

metaneeds In Maslow's theory, need states which are based on a desire to grow rather than an underlying deficiency; expressed as the need for *self-actualization*.

mind the inner subjective experience of conscious awareness; the term has no direct reference to physical form.

mnemonics the study and use of techniques for improving memory (from the Greek for 'memory').

mode a statistic measuring central tendency, calculated as the most frequently occurring value (or interval) in a set of scores.

monism the belief that mind and body are a single entity.

motor nerves those neurons which are responsible for initiating muscle activity.

multiple personality disorder a severe form of dissociative reaction which can result in several independent personalities being manifested.

mutation a change in the genetic material of a cell; while rare, mutations can result in new characteristics which may be transmitted to descendants of the original cell.

myelin in a neuron, an insulating sheath around the axon, composed of the spirally-wound membrane of Schwann cells, which serves to improve the efficiency of neural conduction.

nativism the philosophical view, held by Plato and others, that knowledge and behaviour are innate in origin.

need for positive regard a need for positive social contacts like love, which Rogers regarded as universal.

negative correlation a relationship observed between two variables in which increases in one variable occur as the value of the other variable decreases.

negative feedback in systems theory, a process within a system which serves to dampen disturbances, promoting stable functioning.

negative reinforcement in operant conditioning, a process for increasing the probability of a response in which a response immediately leads to termination or withholding of an aversive stimulus (negative reinforcer); note that since the response increases in frequency, it is *not* equivalent to punishment.

negative reinforcer an aversive stimulus which when it follows a response serves to decrease the probability of the response in the future.

negative symptoms in abnormal psychology, particularly with reference to schizophrenia, the absence of expected behaviours; negative symptoms include bodily immobility, limited speech, flattened affect (absence of emotional expression) and social withdrawal.

nerve impulse the electrical signal generated when a neuron is active, which normally passes from the dendrites, along the axon, to the terminals.

neuron a cell of the nervous system (also called a nerve cell).

neuropeptide a chemical, comprised of a short chain of amino acids, which can function both as a neurotransmitter and as a hormone; also called a neurohormone.

neurotransmitter a chemical released by the terminals of a neuron which plays a role in communication between neurons, across the synapse.

neutral stimulus in classical conditioning, a stimulus which initially produces no specific response other than provoking attention; as conditioning proceeds, the neutral stimulus becomes a conditioned stimulus.

non-contingent reinforcement in operant conditioning, a situation where reinforcers sometimes occur independently of any specific response; chance forms of reinforcement.

non-experimental methods research methods which do not involve direct control of any factor, in contrast to experiments; sometimes called descriptive/correlational designs.

noögenic neuroses in Frankl's theory, conflicts within an individual which are based on existential frustrations, rather than the conflicts of id, ego and superego which Freud saw as the source of anxiety.

normal distribution a type of frequency distribution which resembles a bell-shaped curve; among its special properties, first identified by Gauss, is that its measures of central tendency are all the same.

null hypothesis in research, a hypothesis which asserts that any differences observed between groups are random rather than representing an experimental effect; used for statistical purposes to evaluate results.

occipital lobe the rear-most portion of the cortex, which is devoted solely to vision.

Oedipal conflict in Freud's theory of development, the major conflict associated with the phallic stage which challenges the developing ego; named after the Greek story of Oedipus, who unknowingly killed his father and married his mother.

omission in operant conditioning, a process whereby a response is followed by terminating or withholding a positive reinforcer, which results in a decrease in the probability of the response.

openness behaviour characterized by a person freely expressing their own sense of self, rather than playing a role or hiding behind a facade; seen by Rogers as a condition for growth.

operant conditioning in the behaviourist approach, the form of learning concerned with changes in emitted responses as a function of their consequences.

operational definition a term whose meaning is derived from the processes or observable events used to measure it.

operator in problem solving, one of the actions permitted in order to solve a problem.

oral stage in Freud's theory of development, the first stage, extending from birth to about 15 months, when the focus of gratification is on the mouth.

organism in Rogers's theory, the biological being which is the source of basic needs (such as food and water), and also the source of a growth motive termed the *actualizing tendency*.

paradigm in Kuhn's analysis of science, a superordinate framework or world-view accepted by a group of researchers, which shapes both theories and evidence; since the paradigm influences the observations one makes, no observations can ever be used to evaluate the paradigm.

paraprax ('Freudian slip') an error or verbal slip due to an unconscious conflict.

parietal lobe the portion of the cortex just behind the central fissure and above the lateral fissure, whose primary function is the sense of touch.

parsimony in the philosophy of science, the principle that states one should always seek the simplest possible explanation for any event.

partial reinforcement in operant conditioning, a contingency of reinforcement in which reinforcement does not follow every response.

participant observation a non-experimental research method in which the researcher becomes part of a group he or she wishes to observe.

peak experience for Maslow, a transient experience of deep intensity which involves enhanced awareness, often accompanied by feelings of being 'fully alive'.

perception the process of selection, organization and interpretation of information about the world conveyed by the senses.

peripheral nervous system (PNS) those nerve pathways which lie outside the central nervous system, involving sensation, motor control and regulation of internal organs.

persistence of set a phenomenon in problem solving, identified by Gestalt psychologists, in which a mental set developed in a previous problem is maintained even though it is no longer appropriate, and tends to interfere with solving a current problem.

person-centred therapy (also called 'client-centred therapy') a form of therapy developed by Carl Rogers which emphasizes the responsibility of the individual to determine the direction of change within therapy.

persona in Jung's theory, the conscious character or role we assume in presenting ourselves to the world.

personality patterns of behaviour which are characteristic of an individual and which tend to be consistent across situations and over time.

phallic stage in Freud's theory, the third stage of development, extending from about three to five years of age, during which gratification is focused on the genitals, although not in the form of adult sexuality.

phantom limb a mysterious phenomenon in which individuals who have lost a limb will often continue to experience sensations which seem to come from the missing limb.

phenomenal field for Rogers, an individual's unique perception of the world.

phenomenological pertaining to the way things appear or are experienced; in the humanistic approach, a reference to the emphasis on an individual's perceptions and feelings as defining the meaning of their behaviour.

phenotype the observed characteristics of the individual, based on the combination of genetic expression and environmental influences.

phrenology a now-discredited eighteenth-century theory which asserted that one could assess ability by examining the shape of the skull.

pituitary gland a small gland adjacent to the hypothalamus which regulates many endocrine functions, including growth, and also interacts with the nervous system via hypothalamic connections; in stress, it releases a hormone called ACTH which triggers the release of steroids by the cortex of the adrenal glands; sometimes called 'the master gland' because of its many functions.

placebo effect a phenomenon whereby inert substances labelled as drugs (such as a painkiller) produce effects similar to the real drug.

plateau experience for Maslow, an experience which produces an intensified awareness of the world, and a heightened appreciation for life; a more enduring but less intense state of enhanced awareness than a peak experience.

pleasure principle an early description by Freud of the basis of human motivation, which stated that we are driven to maximize pleasure (*Lust* in German), and to avoid that which is unpleasant (*Unlust*).

pons (Latin for 'bridge') a region in the brain stem above the medulla which provides connections between the cortex and cerebellum.

population in statistics, the group whose characteristics one wishes to determine, and from which a sample is chosen.

positive correlation a relationship observed between two variables in which increases in the value of one variable are associated with increases in the value of the other variable.

positive feedback in systems theory, a process within a system which reacts to disturbances by amplifying the effects, triggering a major change in functioning.

positive reinforcement in operant conditioning, a process of increasing the probability of a response by immediately following the response with a desirable stimulus (a positive reinforcer).

positive reinforcer in operant conditioning, a stimulus which when it follows a response serves to increase the probability of the response in the future.

preconscious in Freud's theory, that part of the subconscious mind which can be accessed by deliberate choice.

preparedness a concept developed by Martin Seligman to describe the degree to which physiological structure influences the occurrence of behaviour.

primary process thinking in Freud's theory, a form of thinking characteristic of the id in which no distinction is made between a wish and its fulfilment.

primary reinforcer a stimulus whose capacity to act as a reinforcer is based on an innate biological significance, such as food or water.

priming a phenomenon whereby a thought or memory increases the activation of associated thoughts or memories (the term is analogous to 'priming a pump' by using a small quantity of water to enhance the flow of water).

proactive interference in memory, a form of interference in which prior experiences make learning and recall of subsequent experiences more difficult.

problem solving the process of determining appropriate actions in order to overcome obstacles that interfere with reaching a desired goal.

procedural memory that component of long-term memory which stores 'how-to' information, such as how to play a piano or cook a turkey.

projective test a type of personality test used by psychodynamic theorists in which an individual is asked to interpret an ambiguous stimulus; since the stimulus itself is ambiguous, the assumption is that whatever the person says reveals the workings of their own unconscious mind.

pro-social behaviour socially desirable behaviour that is beneficial to another person, or to society as a whole.

proximity a Gestalt principle of perception which states that elements which are close together tend to be perceived as a group.

psychiatrists medical doctors who specialize in treating mental disorders; by comparison, clinical psychologists typically have a PhD rather than an MD degree.

psychic determinism the assumption made by Freud which states that all behaviour has a cause, and that the cause is to be found in the mind.

psychoactive drug a chemical agent which has a discernible effect on mental state or behaviour.

psychoimmunology the study of mental states and their effect on health, as expressed through the functions of the immune system; sometimes referred to as psychoneuroimmunology.

psychology the scientific study of behaviour and experience.

psychotherapy any variety of treatment for abnormal behaviour which is primarily verbal in nature, rather than based on the use of drugs.

punishment in operant conditioning, a process whereby a response is followed by a negative reinforcer, which results in a decrease in the probability of the response.

quasi-experiment a research design in which subjects are assigned to groups based on variables which cannot be manipulated by the researcher (e.g. age, sex).

radical behaviourism a position adopted by Watson and Skinner which argues that mental states are both inaccessible to scientific study and irrelevant to understanding behaviour.

random error non-systematic error produced by variability in sampling or other natural processes.

random sample a sample obtained through a selection procedure in which everyone in the population has an equal chance of being selected.

range a statistical measure of variability which is calculated as the difference between the highest score and the lowest score in a frequency distribution.

ratio variable a characteristic whose measurements is based on a continuous scale, with an obvious zero point.

rational-emotive therapy a form of therapy developed by Albert Ellis which focuses on the relationship between thoughts and emotions, particularly negative emotions which arise from an individual's faulty interpretations of experiences.

rationalization a defence mechanism in which one explains behaviour by offering a reason acceptable to the ego in place of the true reason.

reaction range in genetics, the limits on the variability of a phenotype (observed characteristic) determined by the genotype; in essence, the limits set by the genes on how environmental influences (whether deprivation or enrichment) can affect the trait.

reaction time the time required to make a response to a stimulus, as measured by the interval between the stimulus and the response.

reactivity the tendency for people to alter their behaviour when they are being observed.

reality principle in Freud's theory, the constraints imposed on the ego by the recognition of the demands of the environment.

recall in memory, the active retrieval of information.

recentring in Gestalt theory, developing an alternate mental set for a situation, such as when trying to solve a problem.

reciprocal altruism in evolutionary psychology, the concept that individuals help strangers if the expected benefit of future help from the strangers exceeds the short-term cost of helping.

recognition in memory, the process of identifying presented information as familiar.

reconstruction in memory, the process of remembering by actively creating a whole out of partial information.

reductionism the assumption that phenomena at one level of description can be understood in terms of principles at a more basic level of analysis; for example, that biology is 'reducible' to chemistry.

reflex an unlearned response that can be triggered by specific environmental stimuli, such as a baby's sucking on an object placed in the mouth.

regression in Freud's theory, a defence mechanism in which the individual reverts to behaviours characteristic of an earlier mode of gratification.

reinforcement the process by which a reinforcer increases the probability of a response.

reinforcer in operant conditioning, a stimulus which, when it follows a response, results in an increase in the probability of the response recurring.

relearning in memory, an improvement in performance which occurs by reviewing, despite the inability to recall or recognize the information.

reliability a criterion for evaluating a measurement process, which assesses the consistency of measurements; often measured by comparing the correlation between repeated observations.

representative sample in statistics, a sample whose composition matches the population from which it is drawn.

repression in Freud's theory, a defence mechanism in which impulses, memories or ideas are actively blocked from the conscious mind.

research method a procedure for examining a problem and gathering observations; in broad terms, research methods are either experimental or non-experimental.

research setting the context in which research is conducted, either a *laboratory setting* (which involves having participants come to a special location), or a *field setting* (which requires going to where the people are that the researcher wishes to study).

resistance in psychoanalysis, the rejection by an individual of the analyst's interpretations of the meaning of behaviour; regarded as a defence mechanism.

response in general, any reaction to a stimulus, whether overt or mental; in research, the behaviour which is measured.

reticular formation a diffuse network of nerve fibres which runs through the brain stem and limbic system, with connections both up to the cortex and down to the spinal cord; the reticular formation acts as a relay network controlling sensory inputs, and thereby plays a key role in regulating arousal level, alertness and sleep.

retroactive interference in memory, a form of interference in which recent experiences make it difficult to recall something learned earlier.

sample in statistics, a sub-group drawn from a population; in research, the group which one actually studies.

sampling the process by which one selects observations for research (the sample).

sampling error an error caused by having a non-representative sample, owing to either using a biased sampling procedure, or the inherent variability associated with the sampling process.

sampling variability variability due to chance variations among samples randomly drawn from the same population.

schedule of reinforcement in operant conditioning, a description of the conditions which determine when a response will be followed by a reinforcer.

schema (plural 'schemata') a mental framework which organizes knowledge, beliefs and expectations, and is used to guide behaviour.

schizophrenia a severe form of mental disorder in which there can be distortions of perception, thought, language and emotions.

secondary process thinking in Freud's theory, a form of thinking used by the ego to direct the gratification of drives; unlike primary process thinking, secondary process thinking is accessible to conscious awareness, and recognizes constraints imposed by the external world.

selective attention the perceptual process of selectively focusing on particular stimulus elements.

self in Jung's theory, the self comprises the totality of the person, both conscious and unconscious, and is distinct from both the ego and the persona (conscious aspects of personality); for Rogers, the self is an organized cognitive structure based on our experience of our own being.

self-actualization for Maslow, self-actualization is the most advanced human need, and is based on the desire to grow and use one's capacities to their fullest; as such, it is process-oriented, not based on an underlying deficiency.

self-awareness the capacity for individuals or other living organisms consciously to observe their own behaviour.

self-fulfilling prophecy a phenomenon whereby our expectations about other people leads to acting in ways which elicit the expected response from them; the everyday equivalent to experimenter bias.

self-report a method of gathering data which involves asking an individual to describe their behaviour or mental state in some way, such as an interview, survey or psychological inventory.

self-selected sample a sampling procedure which allows members of the population to decide whether to be included or not, as when a survey has a low rate of response.

self-serving bias the tendency to distort our assessment of our own behaviour, by attributing our successes to personal factors, and our failures to situational factors.

self theory a general term for theories of behaviour which focus on an individual's self concept and subjective experience of the world; pioneered by G. H. Mead, and adapted by many humanistic theorists.

semantic memory the component of long-term memory which involves general knowledge of the world.

sensory memory a modality-specific transient form of memory which serves as a buffer between the senses and short-term memory.

sensory nerves neural pathways in the peripheral nervous system which carry information from the sense receptors to the central nervous system.

sequential design a research design which combines features of both longitudinal and cross-sectional studies by selecting groups of different ages (like a cross-sectional design), and then following them over a period of time (like a longitudinal study) sufficient to create overlap in the ages represented by different groups.

sexual orientation a description of whether an individual is sexually attracted to the same sex (homosexual), the opposite sex (heterosexual) or both (bisexual).

shame a negative feeling evoked by a perceived loss of self-esteem associated with a particular behaviour.

shaping in operant conditioning, the process of guiding the acquisition of a new response by reinforcing successive approximations to the desired response.

short-term memory (STM) the component of memory which handles retention over relatively brief intervals of up to approximately 15 seconds.

sign stimuli in ethology, environmental cues which regulate the expression of behaviours related to innate drives.

significance level in inferential statistics, a statement of the probability that an observed outcome is due only to chance.

significance tests in statistics, the general name given to inferential statistical procedures which are used to determine whether observed results reflect real differences rather than chance variations.

similarity in the Gestalt theory of perception, a principle of organization based on grouping together similar elements (e.g. based on shape or size).

single-blind design an experiment set up in such a way that subjects are kept uninformed of any details which might lead to bias.

skewed distribution an asymmetrical frequency distribution with a single mode; with a skewed distribution the median is usually more representative than the mean as a measure of central tendency.

social cognition the mental processes involved in the way people perceive and react to social situations.

social influence a general term for the various ways in which an individual's behaviour is affected by others, such as conformity pressures and social expectations and norms.

social perception the study of the social aspects of perception – how we see other people, and ourselves in relation to others; part of social cognition.

species-specific behaviour behaviours which are characteristic of all members of a particular species. These response patterns (sometimes popularly called 'instincts') apply to behaviours such as mating, finding food, defence and raising offspring.

spontaneous recovery in classical conditioning, the reoccurrence of the conditioned response when the conditioned stimulus is presented after some time has elapsed since extinction training.

spontaneous remission in medicine or therapy, improvement in an individual's condition in the absence of treatment.

stages in developmental theory, the belief that development is based on distinct periods with clear boundaries, with behaviour at each stage governed by different underlying processes; Freud's theory of psychosexual stages is one such theory.

standard deviation a commonly used measure of variability, calculated as the square root of the mean of the squared deviations from the mean of a set of scores.

state-dependent forgetting forgetting related to changes in context associated with internal cues of physical and mental state, as opposed to the context defined by the external environment.

statistics the branch of mathematics that is concerned with the description and interpretation of sets of scores, such as scientific data.

stereotype an oversimplified and often inaccurate perception of an individual based on generalizing from schemata related to the individual's group membership.

steroids hormones produced by the cortex of the adrenal glands which are involved in the regulation of water and sugar metabolism, immune system function and other basic bodily processes; sometimes called 'corticosteroids'.

stigma a mark or label which identifies an individual as deviant, resulting in social rejection.

stimulant a drug which increases activation of the CNS and the autonomic nervous system; these drugs tend to decrease fatigue, increase physical activity and alertness, diminish hunger and produce a temporary elevation of mood.

stimulus discrimination in classical conditioning, selective responding to the conditioned stimulus, but not to stimuli which are similar in some way, as a result of training.

stimulus (often abbreviated as **S**) in general, any event, situation, object or factor that may affect behaviour; for the behaviourists, a stimulus must be a measurable change in the environment.

stimulus generalization in classical conditioning, the tendency to produce a conditioned response to both the original conditioned stimulus and stimuli which are similar to it in some way.

storage the retention of information in memory.

stress a term coined by Hans Selye to describe the non-specific response of the body to any demand on it.

stressor any factor which triggers a stress response in an individual.

structuralism an approach to psychology pioneered by Wundt which attempted to analyse the contents of the mind, using the introspectionist method.

style of life a term used by Adler to describe an individual's unique way of adapting to and interacting with the world, which is an expression of the person's life history and goals.

subconscious in Freud's theory, the portions of the mind which are below the level of conscious awareness.

subject in research, an individual who is the object of study or the participant in an experiment.

subject bias in an experiment, systematic error created because the subjects in different groups have different information (for example, knowing whether they are in the control group or experimental group).

sublimation in Freud's theory, a defence mechanism in which drive energy is redirected towards a socially desirable creative activity.

superego in Freud's theory, that portion of the psyche which represents the moral demands of family and society, and is therefore governed by moral constraints.

superiority complex in Adler's theory, a response to feelings of inferiority in which the individual attempts to mask their weakness by adopting an attitude of exaggerated self-importance.

survey a technique for determining attitudes of many individuals by providing a pre-planned series of questions to which individuals respond.

symptom substitution in psychodynamic theory, the assumption that changing overt behaviour without addressing the underlying dynamics will lead to the expression of the problem in a new way.

synapse the junction between two neurons, represented by a small physical gap which is bridged by the flow of neurotransmitter chemicals from the terminals of the 'sending' neuron.

systematic desensitization a technique based on classical conditioning which is designed to treat phobias (unrealistic fears) and related anxiety disorders by gradually dimishing the undesired response.

systems theory a theoretical framework designed for understanding phenomena which involve multiple interrelated elements, where the properties of the whole are different from the properties of the parts; systems are viewed as governed by processes of *negative feedback* (which promotes stability) and *positive feedback* (which promotes change).

t-test in inferential statistics, a procedure for determining the significance of observed differences; a common use is to decide whether the difference between the means of two groups is due only to sampling variability.

temperament behavioural tendencies which are believed to be determined by heredity; examples include emotionality, sociability and fearfulness.

temporal lobe the region of the cortex below the lateral fissure; its primary functions are hearing and memory.

theory a structured set of principles intended to explain a set of phenomena.

think-aloud protocol a transcript of the comments made when an individual is asked to describe their thoughts and behaviour while working on a task such as problem solving.

thought disturbances in abnormal psychology, distortions of thinking processes such as violations of logic, incoherent speech and inappropriate shifts in word usage.

token economy a form of behaviour modification based on operant conditioning; most commonly used in institutional settings, it involves giving conditioned reinforcers ('tokens') for doing specific behaviours.

trait a behaviour pattern which occurs consistently across a range of situations; a specific personality characteristic.

transference in psychoanalysis, the displacement of drive energy from past relationships, often between the individual and a parent, to the relationship between the individual and the therapist.

unconditional positive regard acceptance and caring given to a person as a human being, without imposing conditions on how the person behaves.

unconditioned response in classical conditioning, a reflexive response produced by a specific stimulus, such as pupil contraction to bright light.

unconditioned stimulus in classical conditioning, a stimulus which elicits a reflexive (unconditioned) response.

unconscious in Freud's theory, that portion of the subconscious which cannot be directly accessed by the conscious mind; nonetheless, impulses and thoughts from the unconscious can 'leak out' in fragmentary intrusions into conscious awareness, either directly or in symbolic form.

unigenic inheritance genetic transmission which is dependent on the action of a single pair of genes; also called Mendelian inheritance, in recognition of Gregor Mendel's pioneering work.

unlearning an alternative interpretation of the interference theory of memory which holds that the build-up of interference can lead to the breaking of associations, and therefore the destruction of memories.

unobtrusive measure an indirect measure of behaviour intended to avoid the reactivity which can occur with direct observation; such measures typically require the making of complex assumptions about the relationship of the measure to actual behaviour.

vacuum activities in ethology, behaviours which arise in the absence of appropriate environmental stimuli when drive levels are very high.

validity a criterion for evaluating a measurement process, which assesses whether the variable measures the intended characteristic, as opposed to some other characteristic.

variability in statistics, the dispersion of scores within a set of data.

variable any measured characteristic which shows variation across cases or conditions.

variable interval schedule in operant conditioning, a reinforcement contingency defined by the average time interval which must elapse since the last reinforcer before a response will be reinforced; thus, on a VI 15 second schedule, over a long period the average duration would be 15 seconds.

variable ratio schedule in operant conditioning, a reinforcement contingency defined in terms of the average number of responses required to receive a reinforcer; thus, VR 10 means that on average every tenth response is reinforced.

visual agnosia a general term for disorders which result in disruption of visual recognition.

voluntary response a response which is controlled by the individual (i.e. emitted) rather than being triggered by specific stimuli, as reflexes are.

wish fulfilment in Freud's theory, the symbolic expression of drives in fantasy form, as in dreams.

would–should dilemma the conflict between one's own needs, expressed through the actualizing tendency, and the demands of others, expressed through the ideal self.

References

Ader, R. and Cohen, N. (1975) Behaviorally conditioned immunosuppression, *Psychosomatic Medicine*, **37**, 333–40.

Ader, R. and Cohen, N. (1985) CNS-immune system interactions: conditioning phenomena, *Behavioral and Brain Sciences*, **8**, 379–94.

Allport, G. (1955) *Becoming*. New Haven, CT: Yale University Press.

Alonso, L. and Jeffery, W. D. (1988) Mental illness complicated by the santeria belief in spirit possession, *Hospital and Community Psychiatry*, **39**, 1188–91.

Alvarez-Borda, B., Ramirez-Amaya, V., Perez-Montfort, R. and Bermudez-Rattoni, F. (1995) Enhancement of antibody production by a learning paradigm, *Neurobiology of Learning and Memory*, **64**, 103–5.

Amábile-Cuevas, C. F. and Chicurel, M. E. (1993) Horizontal gene transfer, *American Scientist*, **81**, 332–41.

American Psychological Association (1992) *Ethical Principles of Psychologists and Code of Conduct*. Washington, DC: American Psychological Association.

American Psychiatric Association (1994) *Diagnostic and Statistical Manual of Mental Disorders*, 4th edn. Washington, DC: American Psychiatric Association.

Amsel, E., Langer, R. and Loutzenhiser, L. (1991) Do lawyers reason differently from psychologists? A comparative design for studying expertise. In R. J. Sternberg and P. A. Frensch (eds), *Complex Problem Solving: Principles and Mechanisms*. Hillsdale, NJ: Lawrence Erlbaum Associates.

Anderson, C. A., Anderson, K. B. and Deuser, W. E. (1996) Examining an affective aggression framework: weapon and temperature effects on aggressive thoughts, affect, and attitudes, *Personality and Social Psychology Bulletin*, **22**, 366–76.

Anderson, C. A. and Bushman, B. J. (1997) External validity of 'trivial' experiments: the case of laboratory aggression, *Review of General Psychology*, **1**, 19–41.

Anderson, E. (1994) The code of the streets, *The Atlantic Monthly*, May, 81–94.

Andreasen, N. C. (1999) Understanding the causes of schizophrenia, *New England Journal of Medicine*, **340**(8).

Angell, M. (1985) Editorial, *New England Journal of Medicine*, June, 6–7.

Anderson, J. R. (1995) *Learning and Memory: An Integrated Approach*. New York: Wiley.

Angier, N. (1999) *Woman: An Intimate Geography*. New York: Thomas Allen & Son.

Angrist, B. J., Rotrosen, J. and Gershon, S. (1980) Positive and negative symptoms in schizophrenia – differential response to amphetamine and neuroleptics, *Psychopharmacology*, **72**, 17–19.

Ansbacher, H. L. and Ansbacher, R. (eds) (1956) *The Individual Psychology of Alfred Adler: A Systematic Presentation in Selections from his Writings*. New York: Harper.

Archer, D. and Gartner, R. (1984) *Violence and Crime in Cross-national Perspective*. New Haven, CT: Yale University Press.

Arieti, S. (1974) An overview of schizophrenia from a predominantly psychological approach, *American Journal of Psychiatry*, **131**(3), 241–9.

Aronson, E. (1976) *The Social Animal*, 2nd edn. San Francisco: W. H. Freeman.

Asch, S. (1955) Opinions and social pressure, *Scientific American*, **193**, 31–5.

Atkinson, R. C. and Shiffrin, R. M. (1968) Human memory: a proposed system and its control processes. In K. W. Spence and J. T. Spence (eds), *The Psychology of Learning and Memory, Volume 2*. New York: Academic Press.

Atthowe, J. and Krasner, L. (1968) Preliminary report on the application of contingent reinforcement procedures (token economy) on a 'chronic' psychiatric ward, *Journal of Abnormal Psychology*, **73**(1), 37–43.

Ayllon, T. and Azrin, N. H. (1968) *The Token Economy: A Motivational System for Therapy and Rehabilitation*. Englewood Cliffs, NJ: Prentice Hall.

Azrin, N. H. and Holz, W. C. (1966) Punishment. In N. K. Honig (ed.), *Operant Behavior*. New York: Appleton Century Crofts.

Baars, B. J. (1986) *The Cognitive Revolution in Psychology*. New York: Guilford Press.

Bachrach, H. M., Galatzer-Levy, R., Skolnikoff, A. and Waldron, S. (1991) On the efficacy of psychoanalysis, *Journal of the American Psychoanalytic Association*, **39**, 871–916.

Baddeley, A. D. (1992) Working memory, *Science*, **255**, 556–9.

Baddeley, A. D. (1994) *Your Memory: A User's Guide*. New York: Penguin Books.

Bahrick, H. P. and Hall, L. K. (1991) Lifetime maintenance of high school mathematics content, *Journal of Experimental Psychology: General*, **120**, 20–33.

Baker, B. L. (1969) Symptom treatment and symptom substitution in enuresis, *Journal of Abnormal Psychology*, **74**, 42–9.

Baldessarini, R. J. and Tarzi, F. I. (1996) Brain dopamine receptors: a primer on their current status, basic and clinical, *Harvard Review of Psychiatry*, **3**, 301–25.

Baldwin, M. (1992) Relational schemas and the processing of social information, *Psychological Bulletin*, **112**, 461–84.

Bandura, A. (1970) Modelling therapy. In W. S. Sahakian (ed.), *Psychopathology Today: Experimentation, Theory, and Research*. Itasca, IL.: Peacock Press.

Bandura, A. (1973) *Aggression: A Social Learning Analysis*. Englewood Cliffs, NJ: Prentice Hall.

Bandura, A. (1977) *Social Learning Theory*. Englewood Cliffs, NJ: Prentice Hall.

Bandura, A. (1986) *Social Foundations of Thought and Action: A Social Cognitive Theory*. Englewood Cliffs, NJ: Prentice Hall.

Bandura, A., Ross, D. and Ross, S. A. (1961) Transmission of aggression through imitation of aggressive models, *Journal of Abnormal and Social Psychology*, **63**, 575–82.

Barinag, M. (1997) New imaging methods provide a better view into the brain, *Science*, **276**, 1974–6.

Baron, R. A. (1983) The control of human aggression: an optimistic perspective, *Journal of Social and Clinical Psychology*, **1**, 97–119.

Baronides, S. (1993) *Molecules and Mental Illness*. New York: Scientific American Library.

Bartlett, F. C. (1932) *Remembering: A Study in Experimental and Social Psychology*. Cambridge: Cambridge University Press.

Bassuk, E. L. and Gerson, S. (1978) Deinstitutionalization and mental health services, *Scientific American*, **238**, 46–53.

Bateson, G., Jackson, D. D., Haley, J. and Weakland, J. H. (1956) Toward a theory of schizophrenia, *Behavioral Science*, **1**, 251–64.

Batson, C. D. (1991) Evidence for altruism: toward a pluralism of prosocial motives, *Psychological Inquiry*, **2**, 107–22.

Batson, C. D. (1998) Altruism and prosocial behavior. In D. T. Gilbert, S. T. Fiske and G. Lindzey (eds), *Handbook of Social Psychology, Volume 2*, 4th edn. Boston: McGraw-Hill.

Baumeister, R. F. and Leary, M. R. (1995) The need to belong: desire for interpersonal attachments as a fundamental human motivation, *Psychological Bulletin*, **117**, 497–529.

Baumrind, D. (1964) Some thoughts on ethics of research: after reading Milgram's 'Behavioral study of obedience', *American Psychologist*, **19**, 421–3.

Baumrind, D. (1991) The influence of parenting style on adolescent competence and substance use, *Journal of Early Adolescence*, **11**, 56–95.

Beadle, G. and Beadle, M. (1966) *The Language of Life*. New York: Doubleday.

Beaman, A., Barnes, P. J., Klentz, B. and McQuirk, B. (1978) Increasing helping rates through information dissemination: teaching pays, *Personality and Social Psychology Bulletin*, **4**, 406–11.

Beck, A. T. (1993) Cognitive therapy: past, present, and future, *Journal of Consulting and Clinical Psychology*, **61**, 194–8.

Beck, A. T., Sokol, L., Clark, D. A., Berchick, R. *et al.* (1992) A crossover study of focused cognitive therapy for panic disorder, *American Journal of Psychiatry*, **149**, 778–83.

Beck, J. G., Stanley, M. A., Baldwin, L. E., Deagle, E. A. *et al.* (1994) Comparison of cognitive therapy and relaxation training for panic disorder, *Journal of Consulting and Clinical Psychology*, **62**, 818–26.

Becker, E. (1973) *The Denial of Death*. New York: Free Press.

Bell, A. P., Weinberg, M. S. and Hammersmith, S. K. (1981) *Sexual Preference: Its Development in Men and Women*. Bloomington, IN: Indiana University Press.

Belson, W. A. (1978) *Television Violence and the Adolescent Boy*. Aldershot: Saxon House.

Benjamin, L. T. and Dixon, D. N. (1996) Dream analysis by mail: an American woman seeks Freud's advice, *American Psychologist*, **51**, 461–8.

Benson, H. (1976) *The Relaxation Response*. New York: Morrow.

Berkowitz, L. (1975) *A Survey of Social Psychology*. Hinsdale, IL: Dryden Press.

Berkowitz, L. (1978) Whatever happened to the frustration–aggression hypothesis? *American Behavioral Scientist*, **21**, 691–708.

Berkowitz, L. (1983) Aversively stimulated aggression, *American Psychologist*, **38**, 1135–44.

Berkowitz, L. (1984) Some effects of thoughts on anti- and prosocial influences of media events: a cognitive-neoassociation analysis, *Psychological Bulletin*, **95**, 410–27.

Berkowitz, L. (1989) Frustration–aggression hypothesis: examination and reformulation, *Psychological Bulletin*, **106**, 59–73.

Berkowitz, L. (1993a) Pain and aggression: Some findings and implications, *Motivation and Emotion*, **17**, 277–93.

Berkowitz, L. (1993b) *Aggression: Its Causes, Consequences, and Control*. New York: McGraw-Hill.

Berkowitz, L. and Devine, P. G. (1995) Has social psychology always been cognitive? What is 'cognitive' anyhow? *Personality and Social Psychology Bulletin*, **21**, 696–703.

Berlyne, D. E. (1975) Behaviourism? Cognitive theory? Humanistic psychology? To Hull with them all! *Canadian Psychological Review*, **16**, 69–80.

Berne, E. (1961) *Transactional Analysis in Psychotherapy*. New York: Grove Press.

Berne, E. (1973) *Games People Play*. New York: Grove Press.

Bernstein, I. L. (1991) Aversion conditioning in response to cancer and cancer treatment, *Clinical Psychology Review*, **11**, 185–91.

Bick, P. A. and Kinsbourne, M. (1987) Auditory hallucinations and subvocal speech in schizophrenic patients, *American Journal of Psychiatry*, **144**, 222–5.

Blackburn, T. (1971) Sensuous–intellectual complementarity in science, *Science*, **172**, 1003–7.

Blakemore, C. (1977) *Mechanisms of the Mind*. Cambridge: Cambridge University Press.

Blatt, S. J. (1975) The validity of projective techniques and their research and clinical contribution, *Journal of Personality Assessment*, **39**, 327–43.

Block, J. (1971) *Lives through Time*. Berkeley, CA: Bancroft Press.

Bloom, H. E. (1981) *The Linguistic Shaping of Thought: A Study of the Impact of Language on Thinking in China and the West*. Hillsdale, NJ: Lawrence Erlbaum.

Boden, J. M. and Baumeister, R. F. (1997) Repressive coping: distraction using pleasant thoughts and memories, *Journal of Personality and Social Psychology*, **73**, 45–62.

Bohart, A. C. (1995) The person-centered psychotherapies. In A. S. Gurman and S. B. Messer (eds), *Essential Psychotherapies: Theory and Practice*. New York: Guilford Press.

Borkovec, T. D. and Costello, E. (1993) Efficacy of applied relaxation and cognitive-behavioral therapy in the treatment of generalized anxiety disorder, *Journal of Consulting and Clinical Psychology*, **51**, 611–19.

Borkovec, T. D. and Mathews, A. M. (1988) Treatment of nonphobic anxiety disorders: a comparison of nondirective, cognitive, and coping desensitization therapy, *Journal of Consulting and Clinical Psychology*, **56**, 877–84.

Bornstein, M. H. (1989) Sensitive periods in development: structural characteristics and causal interpretations, *Psychological Bulletin*, **105**, 179–97.

Borysenko, J. (1990) *Guilt Is the Teacher, Love Is the Lesson*. New York: Warner.

Bouchard, T. J. Jr, Lykken, D. T., McGue, M., Segal, N. L. and Tellegen, A. (1990) Sources of human psychological differences: the Minnesota study of twins reared apart, *Science*, **250**, 223–8.

Bower, G. H. (1981) Mood and memory, *American Psychologist*, **36**, 129–48.

Bower, T. G. R. (1979) *Human Development*. San Francisco: W. H. Freeman.

Bowlby, J. (1969) *Attachment and Loss, Volume 1: Attachment*. London: Hogarth Press.

Bowlby, J. (1988) *A Secure Basis: Parent–Child Attachment and Healthy Human Development*. New York: Guilford Press.

Braff, D. L. (1993) Information processing and attention dysfunctions in schizo-phrenia, *Schizophrenia Bulletin*, **19**, 233–59.

Brandt, L. W. (1982) *Psychologists Caught: A Psycho-logic of Psychology*. Toronto: University of Toronto Press.

Bregman, E. (1934) An attempt to modify emotional attitude of infants by the conditioned response technique, *Journal of Genetic Psychology*, **45**, 169–98.

Brenner, C. (1955) *An Elementary Textbook of Psychoanalysis*. Garden City, NY: Doubleday Anchor.

Brenner, C. (1957) Appendix. In J. Rickman (ed.), *A General Selection from The Works of Sigmund Freud*. Garden City, NY: Doubleday.

Briere, J. and Conte, J. R. (1993) Self-reported amnesia for abuse in adults molested as children, *Journal of Traumatic Stress*, **6**, 21–31.

British Psychological Society (1993) *Code of Conduct*. Leicester: British Psychological Society.

Bronfenbrenner, U. and Ceci, S. J. (1994) Nature–nurture reconceptualized in developmental perspective: a bioecological model, *Psychological Review*, **101**, 568–86.

Brown, G. W. and Harris, T. O. (eds) (1989) *Life Events and Illness*. New York: Guilford Press.

Brown, R. (1972) Schizophrenia, language, and reality. Eastern Psychological Association Presidential Address, Boston.

Brown, R. (1973) Development of the first language in the human species, *American Psychologist*, **28**, 97–106.

Brown, R. and Herrnstein, R. J. (1975) *Psychology*. Boston: Little, Brown.

Bruner, J. S., Goodnow, J. and Austin, G. A. (1956) *A Study of Thinking*. New York: Wiley.

Buford, B. (1991) *Among the Thugs*. London: Mandarin.

Bugental, J. F. T. and Sterling, M. M. (1995) Existential-humanistic therapy: new perspectives, in A. S. Gurman and S. B. Messer (eds), *Essential Psychotherapies: Theory and Practice*. New York: Guilford Press.

Burnstein, E., Crandall, C. and Kitayama, S. (1994) Some neo-Darwinian decision rules for altruism: weighing cues for inclusive fitness as a function of the biological importance of the decision, *Journal of Personality and Social Psychology*, **67**, 773–89.

Bushman, B. J., Baumeister, R. F. and Stack, A. D. (1999) Catharsis, aggression, and persuasive influence: self-fulfilling or self-defeating prophecies? *Journal of Personality and Social Psychology*, **76**, 367–76.

Buss, A. (1963) Physical aggression in relation to different frustrations, *Journal of Abnormal and Social Psychology*, **67**, 1–7.

Buss, D. M. (1995) Evolutionary psychology: a new paradigm for psychological science, *Psychological Inquiry*, **6**, 1–30.

Butt, A., Testylier, G. and Dykes, R. (1997) Acetylcholine release in rat frontal and somatosensory cortex is enhanced during tactile discrimination learning, *Psychobiology*, **25**, 18–33.

Butzlaff, R. L. and Hooley, J. M. (1998) Expressed emotion and psychiatric relapse, *Archives of General Psychiatry*, **55**, 547–52.

Byne, W. (1994) The biological evidence challenged, *Scientific American*, **270**, May, 50–5.

Campbell, D. T. and Stanley, J. C. (1966) *Experimental and Quasi-experimental Designs for Research*. Chicago: Rand-McNally.

Campbell, J. (1968) *The Hero with a Thousand Faces*. Princeton, NJ: Princeton/Bollingen Press.

Campbell, J. (1982) *Grammatical Man: Information, Entropy, Language and Life*. New York: Simon & Schuster.

Campbell, J. D., Tesser, A. and Fairey, P. J. (1986) Conformity and attention to the stimulus: some temporal and contextual dynamics, *Journal of Personality and Social Psychology*, **51**, 315–24.

Canadian Psychological Association (1991) *Canadian Code of Ethics for Psychologists*. Ottawa, ON: Canadian Psychological Association.

Caporael, L. R. (1976) Ergotism: the Satan loosed in Salem? *Science*, **192**, 21–6.

Caporael, L. R. and Baron, R. M. (1997) Groups as the mind's natural environment. In J. A. Simpson, *et al.* (eds), *Evolutionary Social Psychology*. Mahwah, NJ: Lawrence Erlbaum Associates.

Carlson, N. (1990) *Psychology: The Science of Behavior*. Boston: Allyn & Bacon.

Carmichael, L., Hogan, H. P and Walter, A. A. (1932) An experimental study of the effect of language on the reproduction of visually perceived items, *Journal of Experimental Psychology*, **15**, 73–86.

Caspi, A., Elder, G. E. and Herbener, E. (1990) Childhood personality and the prediction of life-course patterns. In L. N. Robins and M. Rutter (eds), *Straight and Devious Pathways from Childhood to Adulthood*. New York: Cambridge University Press.

Castonguay, L. G., Goldfried, M. R., Wiser, S., Raue, P. J. *et al.* (1996) Predicting the effect of cognitive therapy for depression: a study of unique and common factors, *Journal of Consulting and Clinical Psychology*, **64**, 497–504.

Chance, P. (1988) *Learning and Behavior*, 2nd edn. Belmont, CA: Wadsworth.

Chapman, J. (1966) The early symptoms of schizophrenia, *British Journal of Psychiatry*, **112**, 225–51.

Chess, S. and Thomas, A. (1987) *Origins and Evolution of Behaviour Disorders: From Infancy to Early Adult Life*. Cambridge, MA: Harvard University Press.

Chomsky, N. (1972) *Language and Mind*. New York: Harcourt Brace Jovanovich.

Chomsky, N. (1988) *Language and Problems of Knowledge*. Cambridge, MA: MIT Press.

Chorover, S. L. (1985) Psychology in cultural context: the division of labor and the fragmentation of experience. In S. Koch and D. E. Leary (eds), *A Century of Psychology as Science*. New York: McGraw-Hill.

Christensen, A. (1988) Deception in psychological research: when is its use justified? *Personality and Social Psychology Bulletin*, **14**, 664–75.

Clausen, J. A. (1981) Stigma and mental disorder: phenomena and mental terminology, *Psychiatry*, **44**, 287–96.

Cohen, S. and Herbert, T. B. (1996) Health psychology: psychological factors and physical disease from the perspective of human psychoneuroimmunology, *Annual Review of Psychology*, **47**, 113–42.

Collier, G., Johnson, D. F. and Morgan, C. (1997) Meal patterns of cats encountering variable food procurement cost, *Journal of Experimental Analysis of Behavior*, **67**, 303–10.

Cooper, J. R., Bloom, F. E. and Roth, R. H. (1991) *The Biochemical Basis of Neuropharmacology*, 6th edn. New York: Oxford University Press.

Corballis, M. C. (1997) The genetics and evolution of handedness, *Psychological Review*, **104**, 714–26.

Cornblatt, B. A. and Keilp, J. G. (1994) Impaired attention, genetics, and the pathophysiology of schizophrenia, *Schizophrenia Bulletin*, **20**, 31–46.

Cousins, N. (1989) *Head First: The Biology of Hope*. New York: E. P. Dutton.

Craik, F. I. M. and Lockhart, R. S. (1972) Levels of processing: a framework for memory research, *Journal of Verbal Learning and Verbal Behavior*, **11**, 671–84.

Cramer, D. (1992) *Personality and Psychotherapy: Theory, Practice, and Research*. Buckingham: Open University Press.

Crandall, J. E. (1984) Social interest as a moderator of life stress, *Journal of Pesonality and Social Psychology*, **47**, 164–74.

Crews, F. (ed.) (1998) *Unauthorized Freud: Doubters Confront a Legend*. New York: Viking Press.

Crick, F. (1994) *The Astonishing Hypothesis: The Scientific Search for the Soul*. New York: Scribner.

Crick, F. and Koch, C. (1992) The problem of consciousness, *Scientific American*, September, 153–9.

Crowder, R. and Morton, J. (1969) Pre-categorical acoustic storage (PAS), *Perception and Psychophysics*, 8, 815–20.

Cytowic, R. E. (1993) *The Man Who Tasted Shapes*. New York: Tarcher/Putnam.

Damasio, A. R. (1994) *Descartes' Error: Emotion, Reason, and the Human Brain*. New York: Grosset/Putnam.

Darwin, C. (1859) *The Origin of Species*. New York: Washington Square Press (reprinted 1963).

Darwin, C. (1872) *The Expression of Emotions in Man and Animals*. Chicago: University of Chicago Press (reprinted 1965).

Dasen, P. (1975) Concrete operational development in three cultures, *Journal of Cross-cultural Psychology*, **6**, 156–72.

Davis, J. (1994) *Mother Tongue: How Humans Create Language*. New York: Birch Lane Press.

Davis, P. J. and Schwartz, G. E. (1987) Repression and the inaccessibility of affective memories, *Journal of Personality and Social Psychology*, **52**, 155–62.

Davison, G. C. and Neale, J. M. (1997) *Abnormal Psychology*, 7th edn. New York: John Wiley & Sons.

Deaux, K. (1985) Sex and gender, *Annual Review of Psychology*, **36**, 49–81.

deBono, E. (1976) *Practical Thinking*. Harmondsworth: Penguin.

DeCarvalho, J. (1990) A history of the 'Third Force' in psychology, *Journal of Humanistic Psychology*, **30**, 22–44.

Delgado, J. M. R. (1969) *Physical Control of the Mind: Toward a Psycho-Civilized Society*. New York: Harper and Row.

Delgado, J. M. R., Roberts, W. W. and Miller, N. E. (1954) Learning motivated by electrical stimulation of the brain, *American Journal of Physiology*, **179**, 587–93.

de Rivera, J. (1989) Comparing experiences across cultures: shame and guilt in America and Japan, *Hiroshima Forum for Psychology*, **14**, 13–20.

de Waal, F. (1989) *Peacemaking among Primates*. Cambridge, MA: Harvard University Press.

Dobson, K. S. (1989) A meta-analysis of the efficacy of cognitive therapy for depression, *Journal of Consulting and Clinical Psychology*, **57**, 414–19.

Dollard, J., Doob, L., Miller, N., Mowrer, O. and Sears, R. (1939) *Frustration and Aggression*. New Haven, CT: Yale University Press.

Dollard, J. and Miller, N. E. (1950) *Personality and Psychotherapy*. New York: McGraw-Hill.

Dourley, J. P. (1992) *A Strategy for a Loss of Faith: Jung's Proposal*. Toronto: Inner City Books.

Eagly, A. H. (1995) The science and politics of comparing men and women, *American Psychologist*, **50**, 145–58.

Eaton, W. O. and Enns, L. R. (1986) Sex differences in human motor activity, *Psychological Bulletin*, **100**, 19–28.

Ebbinghaus, H. (1885) *Memory*. New York: Dover (reprinted 1964).

Edelman, G. M. (1992) *Bright Air, Brilliant Fire*. New York: Basic Books.

Editors (1993) High anxiety, *Consumer Reports*, January, 19–24.

Elkin, I., Shea, M. T., Watkins, J. T. *et al.* (1989) National Institutes of Mental Health treatment of depression collaborative research program: general effectiveness of treatments, *Archives of General Psychiatry*, **46**, 971–82.

Elliott, R., Clark, C., Wexler, M. *et al.* (1990) The impact of experiential therapy on depression: initial results. In G. Lietaer, J. Rombauts and R. Van Balen (eds), *Client-centred and Experiential Psychotherapy in the Nineties*. Leuven, Belgium: Leuven University Press.

Ellis, A. (1993) Fundamentals of rational-emotive therapy for the 1990s. In W. Dryden and L. K. Hill (eds), *Innovations in Rational-Emotive Therapy*. Newbury Park, CA: Sage.

Ellis, L., Ames, M. A., Peckham, W. and Burke, D. (1988) Sexual orientation of human offspring may be altered by severe maternal stress during pregnancy, *Journal of Sex Research*, **25**, 152–7.

Elmes, D. G., Kantowitz, B. H. and Roediger, H. L. III (1992) *Research Methods in Psychology*. St Paul, MN: West Publishing.

Ember, C. R. and Ember, M. (1994) War, socialization, and interpersonal violence: a cross-cultural study, *Journal of Conflict Resolution*, **38**, 620–46.

Endler, N. S. (1982) *Holiday of Darkness: A Psychologist's Personal Journey out of His Depression*. New York: Wiley.

Endler, N. S. (1997) Stress, anxiety and coping: the multidimensional interaction model, *Canadian Psychology*, **38**, 136–53.

Ericsson, K. A. and Chase, W. A. (1982) Exceptional memory, *American Scientist*, **70**, 607–15.

Erikson, E. H. (1962) *Young Man Luther*. New York: W. W. Norton.

Erikson, E. H. (1963) *Childhood and Society*, 2nd edn. New York: W. W. Norton.

Erlenmeyer-Kimling, L., Cornblatt, B. A., Rock, D., Roberts, S. *et al.* (1993) The New York High-Risk Project: anhedonia, attentional deviance, and psychopathology, *Schizophrenia Bulletin*, **19**, 141–53.

Eron, L. D. (1963) Relationship of TV viewing habits and aggressive behavior in children, *Journal of Abnormal and Social Psychology*, **67**, 193–6.

Eron, L. D. (1982) Parent–child interaction, television violence, and aggression of children, *American Psychologist*, **37**, 197–211.

Eron, L. D., Walder, L. O. and Lefkowitz, M. M. (1971) *The Learning of Aggression in Children*. Boston: Little, Brown.

Euler, H. A. and Weitzel, B. (1996) Discriminative grandparental solicitude as reproductive strategy, *Human Nature*, **7**, 39–59.

Eysenck, M. W. (1993) *Principles of Cognitive Psychology*. Hillsdale, NJ: Lawrence Erlbaum.

Fabrega, H. (1994) International systems of diagnosis in psychiatry, *Journal of Nervous and Mental Disease*, **182**, 256–63.

Fabrega, H. (1995) Cultural challenges to the psychiatric enterprise, *Comprehensive Psychiatry*, **36**, 377–83.

Fadiman, J. and Frager, R. (1976) *Personality and Personal Growth*. New York: Harper and Row.

Fagot, B. I. (1985) Changes in thinking about early sex role development, *Developmental Review*, **5**, 83–98.

Faller, K. C. (1988) *Child Sexual Abuse: An Interdisciplinary Manual for Diagnosis, Case Management, and Treatment*. New York: Columbia University Press.

Fancher, R. E. (1979) *Pioneers of Psychology*. New York: W. W. Norton.

Fancher, R. T. (1995) *Cultures of Healing*. New York: W. H. Freeman.

Ferguson, G. A. (1981) *Statistical Analysis in Psychology and Education*, 5th edn. New York: McGraw-Hill.

Ferster, C. B. and Skinner, B. F. (1957) *Schedules of Reinforcement*. New York: Appleton Century Crofts.

Feshbach, S. (1955) The drive-reducing function of fantasy behavior, *Journal of Abnormal and Social Psychology*, **50**, 3–11.

Festinger, L. and Carlsmith, J. M. (1959) Cognitive consequences of forced compliance, *Journal of Abnormal and Social Psychology*, **58**, 203–10.

Festinger, L. (1957) *A Theory of Cognitive Dissonance*. Stanford, CA: Stanford University Press.

Feynman, R. (1988) *What Do You Care What People Think? Further Adventures of a Curious Character*. New York: W. W. Norton.

Flavell, J. H. (1992) Cognitive development: past, present, and future, *Developmental Psychology*, **28**, 998–1005.

Follette, W. C. and Houts, A. C. (1996) Models of scientific progress and the role of theory in taxonomy development: a case study of the DSM, *Journal of Consulting and Clinical Psychology*, **64**, 1120–32.

Ford, C. S. and Beach, F. A. (1951) *Patterns of Sexual Behavior*. New York: Harper and Row.

Forest, D. V. (1976) Nonsense and sense in schizophrenic language, *Schizophrenia Bulletin*, **2**, 286–381.

Forrest, G. G. (1985) Antabuse treatment. In T. E. Bratter and G. G. Forrest (eds), *Alcoholism and Substance Abuse: Strategies for Clinical Intervention*. New York: Free Press.

Foucault, M. (1965) *Madness and Civilization: A History of Insanity in the Age of Reason* (English translation). New York: Random House.

Fouts, R. S., Hirsch, A. and Fouts, D. (1983) Cultural transmission of a human language in a chimpanzee mother/infant relationship. In H. E. Fitzgerald, J. A. Mullins and P. Page (eds), *Psychological Perspectives: Child Nurturance Series, Volume III*. New York: Plenum Press.

Frank, J. D. (1963) *Persuasion and Healing*. New York: Schocken Books.

Frank, S. L., Pirsch, L. A. and Wright, V. C. (1990) Late adolescents' perceptions of their relationships with their parents: relationships among deidealization, autonomy, relatedness, and insecurity and implications for adolescent adjustment and ego identity status, *Journal of Youth and Adolescence*, **19**, 571–88.

Frankl, V. E. (1992) *Man's Search for Meaning*, 4th edn. Boston: Beacon Press.

Fraser, C. (1987) Social psychology. In R. L. Gregory (ed.), *The Oxford Companion to the Mind*. New York: Oxford University Press, pp. 721–3.

Freedman, J. L. (1984) Effect of television violence on aggressiveness, *Psychological Bulletin*, **96**, 227–46.

Freedman, J. L. (1986) Television violence and aggression: a rejoinder, *Psychological Bulletin*, **100**, 372–8.

Freeman, A. and Reinecke, M. A. (1995) Cognitive therapy. In A. S. Gurman and S. B. Messer (eds), *Essential Psychotherapies: Theory and Practice*. New York: Guilford Press.

Freidrich-Cofer, L. and Huston, A. C. (1986) Television violence and aggression: the debate continues, *Psychological Bulletin*, **98**, 1–20.

Freud, A. (1936) *The Ego and the Mechanisms of Defense* (trans. C. M. Baines). New York: International Universities Press (reprinted 1946).

Freud, S. (1900) *The Interpretation of Dreams*. (Note: where no specific reference is given, this and other references refer to the original German date of publication for volumes later printed in translation as part of J. Strachey (ed.), *The Standard Edition of the Complete Psychological Works of Sigmund Freud, Volumes 1–24*. London: Hogarth Press, 1953–1966.)

Freud, S. (1904) *Psychopathology in Everyday Life*. Reprinted in S. Freud, *A General Introduction to Psychoanalysis* (trans. J. Riviere). New York: Washington Square Press (1952).

Freud, S. (1905) *Three Essays on Sexuality*.

Freud, S. (1913) *Totem and Taboo*.

Freud, S. (1920) *Beyond the Pleasure Principle*.

Freud, S. (1923) *The Ego and the Id*.

Freud, S. (1924) *A General Introduction to Psychoanalysis* (trans. J. Riviere). New York: Washington Square Press (reprinted 1952).

Freud, S. (1926) *The Problem of Anxiety* (trans. H. A. Bunker). New York: W. W. Norton (reprinted 1936).

Freud, S. (1930) *Civilization and Its Discontents*.

Frey, D. (1986) Recent research on selective exposure to information, *Advances in Experimental Social Psychology*, **19**, 41–80.

Fromkin, V. A. (1973) *Speech Errors as Linguistic Evidence*. The Hague: Mouton.

Gantt, W. H. (1966) Reflexology, schizokinesis, and autokinesis, *Conditioned Reflex*, **1**, 57–68.

Gao, J.-H., Parsons, L. M., Bower, J. M., Xiong, J. and Fox, P. (1996) Cerebellum implicated in sensory acquisition and discrimination rather than motor control, *Science*, **272**, 545–7.

Garcia, J., Hankins, W. G. and Rusniak, K. (1974) Behavioral regulation of the milieu interne in man and rat, *Science*, **185**, 824–31.

Gardner, A. and Gardner, B. (1969) Teaching sign language to a chimpanzee, *Science*, **165**, 664–77.

Gardner, H. (1985) *The Mind's New Science: A History of the Cognitive Revolution*. New York: Basic Books.

Garver, D. L. (1997) The etiologic heterogeneity of schizophrenia, *Harvard Review of Psychiatry*, **4**, 317–27.

Garver, D. L., Steinberg, J. L., McDermott, B. E., Yao, J. K. *et al.* (1997) Etiologic heterogeneity of the psychoses: is there a dopamine psychosis? *Neuropsychopharmacology*, **16**, 191–201.

Gay, P. (1988) *Freud: a Life for Our Time*. New York: W. W. Norton.

Gazzaniga, M. S., Ivry, R. B. and Mangun, G. R. (1998) *Cognitive Neuroscience: the Biology of the Mind*. New York: W. W. Norton.

Gilbert, D. T., Fiske, S. T. and Lindzey, G. (eds) (1998) *Handbook of Social Psychology, Volume 2*, 4th edn. Boston: McGraw-Hill.

Geen, R. G., Stonner, D. and Shope, G. I. (1975) The facilitation of aggression by aggression: a study in response inhibition and disinhibition, *Journal of Personality and Social Psychology*, **31**, 721–6.

Geertz, C. (1984) 'From the native's point of view': on the nature of anthropological understanding. In R. A. Shweder and R. A. LeVine (eds), *Culture Theory: Essays on Mind, Self, and Emotion*. Cambridge: Cambridge University Press.

Gershon, E. S. and Rieder, R. O. (1992) Major disorders of mind and brain, *Scientific American*, September, 127–33.

Glass, D. C. and Singer, J. E. (1972) *Urban Stress*. New York: Academic Press.

Glassman, W. E. (1972) Subvocal activity and acoustic confusions in short-term memory, *Journal of Experimental Psychology*, **96**, 164–9.

Gleick, J. (1997) *Chaos: Making a New Science*. New York: Penguin.

Godden, D. and Baddeley, A. D. (1975) Context-dependent memory in two natural environments, *British Journal of Psychology*, **66**, 325–31.

Goffman, E. (1963) *Stigma*. Englewood Cliffs, NJ: Prentice Hall.

Goldfried, M. R. and Davison, G. C. (1994) *Clinical Behavior Therapy*, 2nd edn. New York: Holt, Rinehart and Winston.

Goldfried, M. R. and Wolfe, B. E. (1998) Toward a more clinically valid approach to therapy research, *Journal of Consulting and Clinical Psychology*, **66**, 143–50.

Goldiamond, I. (1973) A diary of self-modification, *Psychology Today*, November, 53–7.

Goldstein, K. (1939) *The Organism*. New York: American Book Co.

Goldstein, K. (1950) Prefrontal lobotomy: analysis and warning, *Scientific American*, February, 36–41.

Goleman, D. (1993) Studying the pivotal role of bystanders, *The New York Times*, 22 June, C1, C6.

Goodall, J. (1990) *Through a Window: My Thirty Years with the Chimpanzees of Gombe*. Boston: Houghton Mifflin.

Gorcynski, R. M., Macrae, S. and Kennedy, M. (1982) Conditioned immune response associated with allogenic skin grafts in mice, *Journal of Immunology*, **29**, 704–9.

Gould, S. J. (1981) *The Mismeasure of Man*. New York: W. W. Norton.

Gould, S. J. and Vrba, E. (1981) Exaptation: a missing term in the science of form, *Paleobiology*, **8**, 4–15.

Graf, P. and Riddle, J. C. (1972) Helping behaviour as a function of interpersonal perception, *Journal of Social Psychology*, **86**, 227–31.

Green, C. D. (1996) Where did the term 'cognitive' come from anyway? *Canadian Psychology*, **37**, 31–9.

Green, M. E. (1993) Cognitive remediation in schizophrenia: is it time yet? *American Journal of Psychiatry*, **150**, 178–87.

Greenwald, A. G. (1992) New look 3: unconscious cognition reclaimed, *American Psychologist*, **47**, 766–79.

Grice, G. R. and Hunter, J. J. (1964) Stimulus intensity effects depend on the type of experimental design, *Psychological Review*, **71**, 247–56.

Guerin, B. (1992) Social behavior as discriminative stimulus and consequence in social anthropology, *Behavior Analyst*, **15**, 31–41.

Guilford, J. P. (1967) *The Nature of Human Intelligence*. New York: McGraw-Hill.

Gurman, A. S. and Messer, S. B. (eds) (1995) *Essential Psychotherapies: Theory and Practice*. New York: Guilford Press.

Haaga, D. and Davison, G. (1993) An appraisal of rational-emotive therapy, *Journal of Consulting and Clinical Psychology*, **61**, 215–20.

Hall, C. S. and Nordby, V. J. (1973) *A Primer of Jungian Psychology*. New York: New American Library.

Hall, G. S. (1924) Preface to the American edition. In S. Freud, *A General Introduction to Psychoanalysis* (trans. J. Riviere). New York: Washington Square Press (reprinted 1952).

Hall, M. H. (1968) A conversation with Abraham Maslow, *Psychology Today*, **2**(2), 34–7, 54–7.

Halpern, D. (1989) *Thought and Knowledge: An Introduction to Critical Thinking*, 2nd edn. Hillsdale, NJ: Lawrence Erlbaum.

Hardaway, R. A. (1990) Subliminally activated symbiotic fantasies: facts and artifacts, *Psychological Bulletin*, **107**, 177–95.

Harlow, H. F. (1949) The formation of learning sets, *Psychological Review*, **56**, 51–65.

Harris, B. (1979) Whatever happened to little Albert? *American Psychologist*, **34**, 151–60.

Harris, J. R. (1995) Where is the child's environment? A group socialization theory of development, *Psychological Review*, **102**, 458–89.

Harris, J. R. (1998) *The Nurture Assumption*. New York: Free Press.

Harris, M. (1974) *Cows, Pigs, Wars, and Witches: The Riddle of Culture*. New York: Random House.

Hartup, W. W. and Coates, B. (1967) Imitation of a peer as a function of reinforcement from the peer group and rewardingness of the model, *Child Development*, **38**, 1003–16.

Hayes, S. C., Follette, W. C. and Follette, V. M. (1995) Behavior therapy. In A. S. Gurman and S. B. Messer (eds), *Essential Psychotherapies: Theory and Practice*. New York: Guilford Press.

Heath, R. G. (1972) Pleasure and brain activity in man, *Journal of Nervous and Mental Disease*, **154**, 3–18.

Hebb, D. O. (1953) Heredity and environment in mammalian behaviour, *British Journal of Animal Behaviour*, **1**, 43–7.

Heider, F. (1958) *The Psychology of Interpersonal Relations*. New York: Wiley.

Heine, S. J. and Lehman, D. R. (1997) Culture, dissonance, and self-affirmation, *Personality and Social Psychology Bulletin*, **23**, 389–400.

Heinrichs, R. W. (1993) Schizophrenia and the brain: conditions for a neuropsychology of madness, *American Psychologist*, **48**, 221–33.

Helzer, J. E. and Canino, G. J. (1992) *Alcoholism in North America, Europe, and Asia*. New York: Oxford University Press.

Heninger, G. R. (1995) Neuroimmunology of stress. In M. J. Friedman, D. S. Charnery and A. Y. Deutch (eds), *Neurobiological and Clinical Consequences of Stress: from Normal Adaptation to PTSD*. Philadephia: Lippincott-Raven.

Herman, J. L. (1992) *Trauma and Recovery: The Aftermath of Violence. From Domestic Violence to Political Terror*. New York: Basic Books.

Hetherington, E. M. and Frankie, G. (1967) Effect of parental dominance, warmth, and conflict on imitation in children, *Journal of Personality and Social Psychology*, **6**, 119–25.

Hilborn, R. C. (1994) *Chaos and Nonlinear Dynamics: An Introduction for Scientists and Engineers*. New York: Oxford University Press.

Hirai, T. (1978) *Zen and the Mind*. Tokyo: Japan Publications.

Hirsch, J. (1963) Behavior genetics and individuality understood, *Science*, **142**, 1436–42.

Hite, S. (1987) *The Hite Report: Women and Love: A Cultural Revolution in Progress*. New York: Knopf.

Hjelle, L. A. and Ziegler, D. J. (1992) *Personality Theories: Basic Assumptions, Research, and Applications*, 3rd edn. New York: McGraw-Hill.

Hoffman, P. (1997) The endorphin hypothesis. In W. P. Morgan *et al.* (eds), *Physical Activity and Mental Health. Series in Health Psychology and Behavioral Medicine*. Washington, DC: Taylor & Francis.

Hofling, C. K., Brotzman, E., Dalrymple, S., Graves, N. and Pierce, C. M. (1966) An experimental study in nurse–physician relationships, *Journal of Nervous and Mental Disease*, **143**, 171–80.

Hofstadter, D. R. (1979) *Gödel, Escher, Bach: an Eternal Golden Braid*. New York: Basic Books.

Hohmann, G. W. (1966) Some effects of spinal cord lesions on experienced emotional feelings, *Psychophysiology*, **3**, 143–56.

Hollon, S. D., DeRubeis, R. J. and Seligman, M. E. P. (1992) Cognitive therapy and the prevention of depression, *Applied and Preventive Psychology*, **1**, 89–95.

Hooper, J. (1999) A new germ theory, *Atlantic Monthly*, **283**(2), 41–53.

Horney, K. (1950) *Neurosis and Human Growth: The Struggle Toward Self-realization*. New York: Norton.

Horney, K. (1967) *Feminine Psychology*. New York: W. W. Norton.

Huber, P. W. (1991) *Galileo's Revenge: Junk Science in the Courtroom*. New York: Basic Books.

Huesmann, L. R., Lagerspetz, K. and Eron, L. D. (1984) Intervening variables in the TV violence–aggression relation: evidence from two countries, *Developmental Psychology*, **20**, 746–75.

Hunt, E. (1991) Some comments on the study of complexity. In R. J. Sternberg and P. A. Frensch (eds), *Complex Problem Solving: Principles and Mechanisms*. Hillsdale, NJ: Lawrence Erlbaum.

Hunt, M. (1993) *The Story of Psychology*. New York: Doubleday.

Huston, A. C., Carpenter, C. J. and Atwater, J. B. (1986) Gender, adult structuring of activities, and social behavior in middle childhood, *Child Development*, **57**, 1200–9.

Inglehart, R. (1990) *Culture Shift in Advanced Industrial Society*. Princeton, NJ: Princeton University Press.

Isaacs, W., Thomas, J. and Goldiamond, I. (1960) Application of operant conditioning to reinstate verbal behavior in psychotics, *Journal of Speech and Hearing Disorders*, **25**, 8–12.

Jablensky, A., Sartorius, N., Ernberg, G., Anker, M., Korten, A., Cooper, J. E., Day, R. and Bertelsen, A. (1992) Schizophrenia: manifestations, incidence and course in different cultures. A World Health Organization ten-country study, *Psychological Medicine, Monograph Supplements*, **20** (entire).

James,W. (1884) Some omissions of introspective psychology, *Mind*, **9** (January), 1–26.

James, W. (1890) *The Principles of Psychology*. New York: Dover (reprinted 1950).

James, W. (1902) *The Varieties of Religious Experience*. New York: Collier (reprinted 1961).

Jenkins, J. G. and Dallenbach, K. M. (1924) Oblivescence during sleep and waking, *American Journal of Psychology*, **35**, 605–12.

Jenkins, J. H. and Karno, M. (1992) The meaning of expressed emotion: theoretical issues raised by cross-cultural research, *American Journal of Psychiatry*, **149**, 9–21.

Jervis, R. (1998) *System Effects*. Princeton, NJ: Princeton University Press.

Jones, E. E. and Pulos, S. M. (1993) Comparing the process in psychodynamic and cognitive-behavioral therapies, *Journal of Consulting and Clinical Psychology*, **61**, 306–16.

Jones, J. L. (1995) *Understanding Psychological Research*. New York: HarperCollins.

Joy, L. A., Kimball, M. M. and Zabrack, M. I. (1986) Television and children's aggressive behavior. In T. W. Williams (ed.), *The Impact of Television: A Natural Experiment in Three Communities*. New York: Academic Press.

Jung, C. G. and von Franz, M.-L. (eds) (1964) *Man and His Symbols*. London: Aldus.

Jung, C. G. (1963) *Memories, Dreams, Reflections*. New York: Pantheon Books.

Jung, C. G. (1958) The psychology of the child archetype. In V. S. deLaszlo (ed.), *Psyche and Symbol*. Garden City, NY: Doubleday.

Kabat-Zinn, J., Lipworth, L. and Burney, R. (1985) The clinical use of mindfulness meditation for the self-regulation of chronic pain, *Journal of Behavioral Medicine*, **8**, 163–90.

Kagan, J. (1989) Temperamental contributions to social behavior, *American Psychologist*, **44**, 668–74.

Kahn, R. S., Davidson, M. and Davis, K. L. (1996) Dopamine and schizophrenia revisited. In S. J. Watson *et al.* (eds), *Biology of Schizophrenia and Affective Disease*. Washington, DC: American Psychiatric Press.

Kamin, L. J. (1969) Predictability, surprise, attention, and conditioning. In B. A. Campbell and R. M. Church (eds), *Punishment and Aversive Behavior*. New York: Appleton Century Crofts.

Karen, R. (1992) Shame, *The Atlantic Monthly*, Feb: 40–70.

Kashima, Y. and Triandis, H. C. (1986) The self-serving bias in attributions as a coping strategy: a cross-cultural study, *Journal of Cross-Cultural Psychology*, **17**, 83–97.

Kazdin, A. E. and Wilson, G. T. (1980) *Evaluation of Behavior Therapy: Issues, Evidence, and Research Strategies*. Lincoln, NE: University of Nebraska Press.

Kellogg, R. (1967) *The Psychology of Children's Art*. San Diego, CA: CRM.

Kelly, G. A. (1955) *A Theory of Personality: The Psychology of Personal Constructs*. New York: W. W. Norton.

Kelman, H. C. (1967) Human use of human subjects: the problem of deception in social psychological experiments, *Psychological Bulletin*, **67**, 1–11.

Kelsoe, J. R., Ginns, E. I., Egeland, J. A., Gerhard, D. S. *et al.* (1989) Re-evaluation of the linkage relationship between chromosome 11p loci and the gene for bipolar disorder in the Old Order Amish, *Nature*, **342**, 238–43.

Keltner, D. and Buswell, B. N. (1996) Evidence for the distinctiveness of embarrassment, shame, and guilt: a study of recalled antecedents and facial expressions of emotion, *Cognition and Emotion*, **10**, 155–71.

Kendell, R. E. (1987) Schizophrenia. In R. L. Gregory (ed.), *The Oxford Companion to the Mind*. New York: Oxford University Press.

Keneally, T. (1982) *Schindler's Ark*. New York: Simon & Schuster.

Kety, S. S., Wender, P. H., Jacobsen, B., Ingraham, L. J. *et al.* (1994) Mental illness in the biological and adoptive relatives of schizophrenic adoptees: replication of the Copenhagen study in the rest of Denmark, *Archives of General Psychiatry*, **51**, 442–55.

Kevles, B. H. (1996) *Naked to the Bone: Medical Imaging in the Twentieth Century*. Rutgers, NJ: Rutgers University Press.

Kihlstrom, J. F. (1994) Commentary: psychodynamics and social cognition. Notes on the fusion of psychoanalysis and psychology, *Journal of Personality*, **62**, 681–96.

Kihlstrom, J. F., Barnhardt, T. M. and Tataryn, D. J. (1992) The psychological unconscious: found, lost, reclaimed, *American Psychologist*, **47**, 788–91.

Kimura, D. (1992) Sex differences in the brain, *Scientific American*, **267**, September, 118–25.

King, A. (1971) *A Married Couple*. Toronto: NFB Films.

Klama, J. (1988) *Aggression: Conflict in Animals and Humans Reconsidered*. London: Longman.

Kluver, H. (1966) *Mescal and Mechanisms of Hallucinations*. Chicago: University of Chicago Press.

Knauft, B. M. (1987) Reconsidering violence in simple human societies: homicide among the Gebusi of New Guinea, *Current Anthropology*, **28**, 457–500.

Koch, S. (1985) The nature and limits of psychological knowledge: lessons of a century *qua* 'science'. In S. Koch and D. E. Leary (eds), *A Century of Psychology as a Science*. New York: McGraw-Hill.

Koch, S. and Leary, D. E. (eds) (1985) *A Century of Psychology as a Science*. New York: McGraw-Hill.

Koepp, M. J., Gunn, R. N., Lawrence, A. D., Cunningham, V. J. *et al.* (1998) Evidence for striatal dopamine release during a video game, *Nature*, **393**, 266–8.

Kohlberg, L. (1966) A cognitive–developmental analysis of children's sex-role concepts and attitudes. In E. E. Maccoby (ed.), *The Development of Sex Differences*. Stanford, CA: Stanford University Press.

Kohler, W. (1925) *The Mentality of Apes*. New York: Harcourt, Brace, and World.

Kohut, H. (1977) *The Restoration of the Self*. New York: International Universities Press.

Konner, M. (1982) *The Tangled Web: Biological Constraints on the Human Spirit*. New York: Holt, Rinehart and Winston.

Kramer, P. D. (1993) *Listening to Prozac: A Psychiatrist Explores Antidepressant Drugs and the Remaking of the Self*. New York: Viking.

Krasner, L. (1976) On the death of behavior modification: some comments from a mourner, *American Psychologist*, **31**, 387–8.

Kraus, S. J. (1995) Attitudes and the prediction of behavior: a meta-analysis of the empirical literature, *Personality and Social Psychology Bulletin*, **21**, 58–75.

Kriegman, D. (1990) Compassion and altruism in psychoanalytic theory: an evolutionary analysis of self psychology, *Journal of the American Academy of Psychoanalysis*, **18**, 342–67.

Krippner, S. (ed.) (1972) The plateau experience: A. H. Maslow and others, *Journal of Transpersonal Psychology*, **4**, 107–20.

Kuhn, T. (1970) *The Structure of Scientific Revolutions*, 2nd edn. London: Cambridge University Press.

Kunkel, J. H. (1996) What have the behaviourists accomplished – and what more can they do? *Psychological Record*, **46**, 21–37.

Labouvie-Vief, G. (1985) Intelligence and cognition. In J. E. Birren and K. W. Schaie (eds), *Handbook of the Psychology of Aging*, 2nd edn. New York: Van Nostrand.

LaFond, J. Q. and Durham, M. L. (1992) *Back to the Asylum*. New York: Oxford University Press.

Laing, R. D. (1965) *The Divided Self: An Existential Study in Sanity and Madness*. Baltimore: Penguin.

Laing, R. D. (1967) *The Politics of Experience*. New York: Pantheon.

Lang, P. J. (1994) The varieties of emotional experience: a meditation on James–Lange theory, *Psychological Review*, **101**, 212–21.

Langer, E. J. and Rodin, J. (1976) The effects of choice and enhanced personal responsibility for the aged: a field experiment in an institutional setting, *Journal of Personality and Social Psychology*, **34**, 191–8.

LaPiere, R. T. (1934) Attitudes and actions, *Social Forces*, **13**, 230–7.

Latané, B. and Darley, J. (1969) Bystander 'Apathy', *American Scientist*, **57**, 222–68.

LeDoux, J. E. (1995) Emotion: clues from the brain, *Annual Review of Psychology*, **46**, 209–35.

Lee, T. F. (1991) *The Human Genome Project: Cracking the Genetic Code of Life*. New York: Plenum Press.

Lefkowitz, M. M., Huesmann, L. R. and Eron, L. D. (1978) Parental punishment: a longitudinal analysis of effects, *Archives of General Psychiatry*, **35**, 186–91.

Lenneberg, E. H. (1967) *Biological Foundations of Language*. New York: Wiley.

Lenzenweger, M. F. and Dworkin, R. H. (eds) (1998) *Origins and Development of Schizophrenia: Advances in Experimental Psychopathology*. Washington, DC: American Psychological Association.

Leo, J. (1985) A therapist in every corner, *Time*, 23 December, 39.

Lettrin, J. Y., Maturana, H. R., McCulloch, W. S. and Pitts, W. H. (1959) What the frog's eye tells the frog's brain, *Proceedings of the Institute of Radio Engineers*, **47**, 1940–51.

Levanthal, H. and Tamarken, A. J. (1986) Emotion: today's problems, *Annual Review of Psychology*, **37**, 565–610.

LeVay, S. (1993) *The Sexual Brain*. Cambridge, MA: MIT Press.

LeVay, S. and Hamer, D. H. (1994) Evidence for a biological influence in male homosexuality, *Scientific American*, **270**, May, 44–9.

Levine, M. (1976) Hunting for hypotheses. In M. H. Siegel and H. P. Ziegler (eds), *Psychological Research: The Inside Story*. New York: Harper & Row.

Levine, E. S. and Padilla, A. M. (1980) *Crossing Cultures in Therapy: Pluralistic Counselling for the Hispanic*. Monterey, CA: Brooks-Cole.

Liebert, R. M. and Sprafkin, J. (1988) *The Early Window: Effects of Television on Children and Youth*, 3rd edn. Oxford: Pergamon Press.

Lin, K. and Kleinman, A. M. (1988) Psychopathology and clinical course of schizophrenia: a cross-cultural perspective, *Schizophrenia Bulletin*, **14**, 555–67.

Locke, J. (1690) *An Essay Concerning Human Understanding*. Oxford: P. H. Nidditch (reprinted 1975).

Loftus, E. (1997) Creating false memories, *Scientific American*, **277**, 70–5.

Loftus, E., Garry, M. and Feldman, J. (1994) Forgetting sexual trauma: what does it mean when 38% forget? *Journal of Consulting and Clinical Psychology*, **62**, 1177–81.

Loftus, E. and Hoffman, H. (1989) Misinformation and memory: the creation of new memories, *Journal of Experimental Psychology: General*, **118**, 100–4.

Loftus, E. and Ketcham, K. (1991) *Witness for the Defence: The Accused, the Eyewitness, and the Expert Who Puts Memory on Trial*. New York: St Martin's Press.

Loftus, E. and Klinger, M. R. (1992) Is the conscious smart or dumb? *American Psychologist*, **47**, 761–5.

Loftus, E. and Pickerel, J. E. (1995) The formation of false memories, *Psychiatric Annals*, **25**, 720–5.

Logie, R. (1996) The seven ages of working memory. In J. T. E. Richardson *et al.* (eds), *Working Memory and Human Cognition*. New York: Oxford University Press.

Logue, A. W. (1988) A comparison of taste aversion learning in humans and other vertebrates: evolutionary pressures in common. In R. C. Bolles and M. D. Beecher (eds), *Evolution and Learning*. Hillsdale, NJ: Lawrence Erlbaum.

London, P. (1974) From the long couch for the sick to the push button for the bored, *Psychology Today*, June, 63–8.

Lore, R. and Schultz, L. A. (1993) Control of human aggression: a comparative perspective, *American Psychologist*, **48**, 16–25.

Lorenz, K. (1967) *On Aggression*. New York: Bantam.

Luborsky, L. and Spence, D. P. (1978) Quantitative research on psychoanalytic therapy. In A. E. Bergin and S. L. Garfield (eds) *Handbook of Psychotherapy and Behavior Change: An Empirical Analysis*, 2nd edn. New York: John Wiley.

Luchins, A. S. (1942) Mechanization in problem-solving: the effect of *einstellung*, *Psychological Monographs*, **54**, no. 248 (whole issue).

Luria, A. R. (1968) *The Mind of a Mnemonist*. New York: Basic Books.

Lykken, D. T. (1988) The case against polygraph testing. In A. Gale (ed.), *The Polygraph Test: Lies, Truth, and Science*. London: Sage.

Lykken, D. T., Bouchard, T. J., McGue, M. and Tellegen, A. (1993) Heritability of interests: a twin study, *Journal of Applied Psychology*, **78**, 649–61.

McFarland, C. and Buehler, R. (1997) Negative affective states and the motivated retrieval of positive life events: the role of affect acknowledgement, *Journal of Personality and Social Psychology*, **73**, 200–14.

Maccoby, E. E. (1992) The role of parents in the socialization of children: an historical overview, *Developmental Psychology*, **28**, 1006–17.

Maccoby, E. E. and Jacklin, C. N. (1974) *The Psychology of Sex Differences*. Stanford, CA: Stanford University Press.

McCloskey, M. and Zaragoza, M. (1985) Misleading postevent information and memory for events: Arguments and evidence against memory impairment hypotheses, *Journal of Experimental Psychology: General*, **114**, 1–16.

McConnell, J. V. (1974) Behavior mod. Letter to the editor, *APA Monitor*, **5**(8), 2–3.

McCord, W., McCord, J. and Howard, A. (1961) Familial correlates of aggression in nondelinquent male children, *Journal of Abnormal and Social Psychology*, **62**, 79–93.

McDonald, J. L. (1997) Language acquisition: the acquisition of linguistic structure in normal and special populations, *Annual Review of Psychology*, **48**, 215–41.

McGrady, A. (1996) Good news – bad press: applied psychophysiology in cardio-vascular disorder, *Biofeedback and Self-Regulation*, **21**, 335–46.

McGuire, W. J. (1985) Toward social psychology's second century. In S. Koch and D. E. Leary (eds), *A Century of Psychology as a Science*. New York: McGraw-Hill.

MacKinnon-Lewis, C., Starnes, R., Volling, B. and Johnson, S. (1997) Perceptions of parenting as predictors of boys' sibling and peer relations, *Developmental Psychology*, **33**, 1024–31.

MacLean, P. D. (1990) *The Triune Brain in Evolution: Role in Paleocerebral Functions*. New York: Plenum Press.

Maddi, S. (1974) Freud's most famous patient: the victimization of Dora, *Psychology Today*, September, 32–5.

Maher, B. (1972) The language of schizophrenia: a review and interpretation, *British Journal of Psychiatry*, **120**, 3–17.

Mahler, M. S., Pine, F. and Bergman, A. (1975) *The Psychological Birth of the Human Infant*. New York: Basic Books.

Maier, S. F. and Laudenslager, M. (1985) Stress and health: exploring the links, *Psychology Today*, August, 44–9.

Marcus, D. E. and Overton, W. F. (1978) The development of cognitive gender constancy and sex-role preferences, *Child Development*, **49**, 434–44.

Mark, V. H. and Ervin, F. R. (1970) *Violence and the Brain*. New York: Harper and Row.

Markus, H. and Kitayama, S. (1991) Culture and the self: implications for cognition, emotion, and motivation, *Psychological Review*, **98**, 224–53.

Marler, P. (1970) A comparative approach to vocal learning: song development in white-crowned sparrows, *Journal of Comparative and Physiological Psychology*, **7**, 1–25.

Martin, C. L. and Halverson, C. E. Jr (1983) The effects of sex-typing schemas on young children's memory, *Child Development*, **54**, 563–74.

Martin, C. L. and Halverson, C. E. Jr (1987) The roles of cognition in sex-roles and sex-typing. In D. B. Carter (ed.), *Current Conceptions of Sex Roles and Sex-typing: Theory and Research*. New York: Praeger.

Martin, G. and Pear, J. (1996) *Behavior Modification: What It Is and How to Do It*, 5th edn. Upper Saddle River, NJ: Prentice Hall.

Maslow, A. (1964) *Religions, Values and Peak Experiences*. Columbus, OH: State University Press.

Maslow, A. (1968) *Toward a Psychology of Being*, 2nd edn. New York: Van Nostrand.

Maslow, A. (1970) *Motivation and Personality*. New York: Harper and Row.

Masson, J. (1984) *The Assault on Truth: Freud's Suppression of the Seduction Theory*. New York: Farrar, Strauss & Giroux.

Masters, J. C., Ford, M. E., Arend, R., Grotevant, H. D. and Clark, L. V. (1979) Modeling and labeling as integrated determinants of children's sex-typed imitative behavior, *Child Development*, **50**, 364–71.

Matsumoto, D. (1997) *Culture and Modern Life*. Pacific Grove, CA: Brooks/Cole.

Mattern, K. K. and Lindholm, B. W. (1985) Maternal condemnation of TV violence during mother and child viewing, perceptions of violence and aggressive behavior in 61–73 month olds: extension of research by B. F. Fontes, *Journal of Genetic Psychology*, **146**, 133–4.

Mauro, R., Sato, K. and Tucker, J. (1992) The role of appraisal in human emotions: A cross-cultural study. *Journal of Personality and Social Psychology*, **62**, 301–17.

May, R. (1961) The emergence of existential psychology. In R. May (ed.), *Existential Psychology*. New York: Random House.

Mead, G. H. (1934) *Mind, Self, and Society*. Chicago: University of Chicago Press.

Mead, M. (1935) *Sex and Temperament in Three Primitive Societies*. New York: William Morrow.

Meador, B. D. and Rogers, C. R. (1979) Person-centered therapy. In R. J. Corsini (ed.), *Current Psychotherapies*, 2nd edn. Itasca, IL: Peacock Press.

Mednick, S. A., Watson, J. B., Huttunen, M., Cannon, T. D. *et al.* (1998) A two-hit working model of the etiology of schizophrenia. In M. F. Lenzenweger and R. H. Dworkin (eds), *Origins and Development of Schizophrenia: Advances in Experimental Psychopathology*. Washington, DC: American Psychological Association.

Meehl, P. (1971) Law and the fireside inductions: some reflections of a clinical psychologist, *Journal of Social Issues*, **27**, 65–100.

Meichenbaum, D. (1977) *Cognitive–Behavior Modification: An Integrative Approach*. New York: Plenum.

Melzack, R. (1973) *The Puzzle of Pain*. New York: Basic Books.

Melzack, R. (1992) Phantom limbs, *Scientific American*, April, 120–6.

Melzack, R. and Wall, P. D. (1982) *The Challenge of Pain*. New York: Basic Books.

Mercer, D. (1986) *Biofeedback and Related Therapies in Clinical Practice*. Rockville, MD: Aspen Systems.

Michelson, D., Licinio, J. and Gold, P. W. (1995) Mediation of the stress response by the hypothalamic-pituitary-adrenal axis. In M. J. Friedman, D. S. Charnery and A. Y. Deutch (eds), *Neurobiological and Clinical Consequences of Stress: From Normal Adaptation to PTSD*. Philadelphia: Lippincott-Raven.

Milgram, S. (1963) A behavioral study of obedience, *Journal of Abnormal and Social Psychology*, **67**, 371–8.

Milgram, S. (1964) Issues in the study of obedience: a reply to Baumrind. *American Psychologist*, **19**, 848–52.

Milgram, S. (1970) The experience of living in cities, *Science*, **167**, 1461–8.

Miller, G. A. (1956) The magical number seven plus or minus two: some limits on our capacity for processing information, *Psychological Review*, **63**, 81–97.

Miller, G. A. (1985) The constitutive problem of psychology. In S. Koch and D. E. Leary (eds), *A Century of Psychology as a Science*. New York: McGraw-Hill.

Miller, J. G. (1984) Culture and the development of everyday social explanation, *Journal of Personality and Social Psychology*, **46**, 961–78.

Miller, N. (1941) The frustration–aggression hypothesis, *Psychological Review*, **48**, 337–42.

Miller, N. (1969) Learning of visceral and glandular responses, *Science*, **163**, 434–45.

Miller, N. (1985) The value of behavioral research on animals, *American Psychologist*, **40**, 423–40.

Milner, B. (1965) Memory disturbance after bilateral hippocampal lesions. In P. Milner and S. Glickman (eds), *Cognitive Processes and the Brain*. Princeton, NJ: Van Nostrand.

Mischel, W. (1968) *Personality and Assessment*. New York: Wiley.

Mischel, W. and Shoda, Y. (1995) A cognitive–affective system theory of personality: reconceptualizing situations, dispositions, dynamics, and invariance in personality structure, *Psychological Review*, **102**, 246–68.

Moghaddam, F. M., Taylor, D. M. and Wright, S. C. (1993) *Social Psychology in Cross-cultural Perspective*. New York: W. H. Freeman.

Money, J. and Tucker, P. (1975) *Sexual Signatures: On Being a Man or a Woman*. Boston: Little, Brown.

Morf, M. E. (1994) Sperry's leap, *American Psychologist*, **49**, 817–18.

Mortenson, P. B., Pederson, C. B., Westergaard, T., Wohlfahrt, J. *et al.* (1999) Effects of family history and place and season of birth on the risk of schizophrenia, *New England Journal of Medicine*, **340**(8), 603–8.

Moskowitz, B. A. (1978) The acquisition of language, *Scientific American*, **239**(11), 92–108.

Motley, M. T. (1985) Slips of the tongue, *Scientific American*, September, 116–27.

Mowrer, O. H. (1956) Two-factor learning theory reconsidered, with special reference to secondary reinforcement and the concept of habit, *Psychological Review*, **63**, 114–28.

Moyer, K. (1976) *The Psychobiology of Aggression*. New York: Harper and Row.

Moyer, K. (1983) Violence. In S. H. Kadish (ed.), *Encyclopedia of Crime and Justice, Volume 4*. New York: Free Press.

Moyers, B. (1993) *Healing and the Mind*. New York: Doubleday.

Neill, J. (1990) Whatever became of the schizophrenogenic mother? *American Journal of Psychotherapy*, **44**, 499–505.

Neisser, U. and Harsh, N. (1992) Phantom flashbulbs: false recollections of hearing the news about the Challenger. In E. Winograd and U. Neisser (eds), *Affect and Accuracy in Recall: Studies of 'Flashbulb Memory'*. New York: Cambridge University Press.

Newell, A., Shaw, J. C. and Simon, H. A. (1958) Elements of a theory of human problem solving, *Psychological Review*, **65**, 151–66.

Newell, A. and Simon, H. A. (1972) *Human Problem Solving*. Englewood Cliffs, NJ: Prentice Hall.

Newman, J. (1995) Thalamic contributions to attention and consciousness, *Consciousness and Cognition*, **4**, 171–93.

Nicol, S. E. and Gottesman, I. I. (1983) Clues to the genetics and neurobiology of schizophrenia, *American Scientist*, **71**, 398–404.

Nisbett, R. E. and Ross, L. (1980) *Human Inference: Strategies and Shortcomings of Social Judgement*. Englewood Cliffs, NJ: Prentice Hall.

Oatley, K. (1992) *Best Laid Plans: The Psychology of Emotion*. Cambridge: Cambridge University Press.

Öhman, A. (1986) Face the beast and fear the face: animal and social fears as prototypes for evolutionary analysis of emotion, *Psychophysiology*, **23**, 123–45.

Öhman, A. and Soares, J. F. (1998) Emotional conditioning to masked stimuli: expectancies for aversive outcomes following non-recognized fear-relevant stimuli, *Journal of Experimental Psychology: General*, **127**, 69–82.

Olds, J. and Milner, B. (1954) Positive reinforcement produced by electrical stimulation of septal area and other regions of the rat brain, *Journal of Comparative and Physiological Psychology*, **47**, 419–27.

O'Leary, A., Brown, S. and Suarez-Al-Adam, M. (1997) Stress and immune function. In W. T. Miller (ed.), *Clinical Disorders and Stressful Life Events*. Madison, CT: International Universities Press.

Orgler, H. (1976) Alfred Adler, *International Journal of Social Psychiatry*, **22**, 67–8.

Orne, M. T. (1962) On the social psychology of the psychological experiment: with particular reference to demand characteristics and their implications, *American Psychologist*, **17**, 776–83.

Ornstein, R. (1972) *The Psychology of Consciousness*. San Francisco: W. H. Freeman.

Ornstein, R. and Swencionis, C. (eds) (1990) *The Healing Brain: A Scientific Reader*. New York: Guilford Press.

Osherson, D. N. and Smith, E. S. (eds) (1990) *An Invitation to Cognitive Science* (three volumes). Cambridge, MA: MIT Press.

Padel, J. H. (1987) Freudianism: later developments. In R. L. Gregory (ed.), *The Oxford Companion to the Mind*. New York: Oxford University Press.

Paivio, A. (1971) *Imagery and Verbal Processes*. New York: Holt, Rinehart and Winston.

Palumbo, R. and Gillman, I. (1984) Effects of subliminal activation of Oedipal fantasies on competitive performance, *Journal of Nervous and Mental Disease*, **72**, 737–41.

Patterson, F. G. and Linden, E. (1981) *The Education of Koko*. New York: Holt, Rinehart and Winston.

Pavlov, I. P. (1927) *Conditioned Reflexes* (ed. and trans. G. V. Anrep). New York: Dover (reprinted 1960).

Penfield, W. (1975) *The Mystery of the Mind*. Princeton, NJ: Princeton University Press.

Penfield, W. and Rasmussen, T. (1957) *The Cerebral Cortex of Man*. New York: Macmillan.

Perry, G. D. and Bussey, K. (1979) The social learning of sex differences: imitation is alive and well, *Journal of Personality and Social Psychology*, **37**, 1699–712.

Persons, J. (1991) Psychotherapy outcome studies do not accurately represent current models of psychotherapy, *American Psychologist*, **46**, 99–106.

Pert, C. B. (1990) The wisdom of the receptors: Neuropeptides, the emotions, and body-mind. In R. Ornstein and C. Swencionis (eds), *The Healing Brain: A Scientific Reader*. New York: Guilford Press.

Peterson, D. (ed.) (1982) *A Mad People's History of Madness*. Pittsburgh: University of Pittsburgh Press.

Peterson, N. (1962) Effect of monochromatic rearing on the control of responding by wavelength, *Science*, **136**, 774–5.

Pfungst, O. (1911) *Clever Hans: The Horse of Mr. von Osten* (trans. C. L. Rahn). New York: Holt, Rinehart and Winston (reprinted 1965).

Piaget, J. (1954) *The Construction of Reality in the Child*. New York: Basic Books.

Pinker, S. (1994) *The Language Instinct*. New York: William Morrow.

Plomin, R. and Bergemen, C. S. (1991) The nature of nurture: genetic influence on 'environmental' measures, *Behavioural and Brain Sciences*, **14**, 373–427.

Plomin, R. and Daniels, D. (1987) Why are children in the same family so different from one another? *Behavioral and Brain Sciences*, **10**, 1–60.

Plomin, R., DeFries, J. C. and Fulker, D. W. (1988) *Nature and Nurture during Infancy and Early Childhood*. New York: Cambridge University Press.

Pomerlau, A., Bolduc, D., Malcuit, G. and Cossette, L. (1990) Pink or blue: environmental gender stereotypes in the first two years of life, *Sex Roles*, **22**, 359–67.

Poole, D. A., Lindsay, D. S., Memon, A. and Bull, R. (1995) Psychotherapy and the recovered memories of child sexual abuse: US and British therapists' beliefs, practices, and experiences, *Journal of Consulting and Clinical Psychology*, **63**, 426–37.

Potter, M. C. (1990) Remembering. In D. N. Osherson and E. S. Smith (eds), *An Invitation to Cognitive Science: Thinking, Volume 3*. Cambridge, MA: MIT Press.

Prather, E. M., Hedrick, D. L. and Kern, C. A. (1975) Articulation development in children aged two to four years, *Journal of Speech and Hearing Disorders*, **40**, 179–91.

Premack, D. (1983) The codes of man and beasts, *Behavioral and Brain Sciences*, **6**, 125–67.

Previc, F. H. (1991) A general theory concerning the prenatal origins of cerebral lateralization in humans, *Psychological Review*, **98**, 299–334.

Prouty, G. F. (1990) Pre-therapy: a theoretical evolution in the person-centered/experiential psychotherapy of schizophrenia and retardation. In G. Lietaer, J. Rombauts and R. Van Balen (eds), *Client-centered and Experiential Psychotherapy in the Nineties*. Leuven, Belgium: Leuven University Press.

Rahe, R. H. (1972) Subjects' recent life changes and their near-future illness susceptibility, *Advances in Psychosomatic Medicine*, **8**, 2–19.

Raskin, N. J. and Rogers, C. R. (1989) Person-centered therapy. In R. J. Corsini and D. J. Wedding (eds), *Current Psychotherapies*, 4th edn. Itasca, IL: Peacock Press.

Regier, D. A., Boyd, J. H., Burke, J. D., Rae, D. S., Myers, J. K., Kramer, M., Robins, L. N., George, L. K., Karno, M. and Locke, B. Z. (1988) One-month prevalence of mental disorders in the United States, *Archives of General Psychiatry*, **45**, 977–86.

Rescorla, R. A. and Solomon, R. I. (1967) Two-process learning theory: relationships between Pavlovian conditioning and instrumental learning, *Psychological Review*, **74**, 212–21.

Rice, G., Anderson, C., Risch, N. and Ebers, G. (1999) Male homosexuality: absence of linkage to microsatellite markers at Xq28, *Science*, **284**, 665–7.

Rice, P. L. (1999) *Stress and Health*, 3rd edn. Pacific Grove, CA: Brooks/Cole.

Richards, J. E. and Rader, N. (1983) Affective, behavioral, and avoidance responses on the visual cliff: Effect of crawling onset age, crawling experience, and testing age, *Psychophysiology*, **20**, 633–42.

Roazen, P. (1975) *Freud and His Followers*. New York: Knopf.

Robins, R. W., Gosling, S. D. and Craik, K. H. (1998) Psychological science at the crossroads, *American Scientist*, **86**, 310–13.

Robinson, D. N. (1979) *Systems of Modern Psychology*. New York: Columbia University Press.

Robinson, D. N. (1985) Science, psychology, and explanation: synonyms or antonyms? In S. Koch and D. E. Leary (eds), *A Century of Psychology as a Science*. New York: McGraw-Hill.

Rochester, S. R. (1977) A hard look at studies of language in schizophrenia. Paper presented at Canadian Psychological Association annual meeting, Vancouver, 9 June.

Rodriguez, E., George, N., LaChaux, J.-P., Martinerie, J. *et al.* (1999) Perception's shadow: long-distance synchronization of human brain activity, *Nature*, **397**, 430–3.

Rogers, C. R. (1939) *The Clinical Treatment of the Problem Child*. Boston: Houghton-Mifflin.

Rogers, C. R. (1951) *Client-centered Therapy*. Boston: Houghton-Mifflin.

Rogers, C. R. (1959) A theory of therapy, theory, and interpersonal relationships, as developed in the client-centered framework. In S. Koch (ed.), *Psychology: The Study of a Science, Volume 3*. New York: McGraw-Hill.

Rogers, C. R. (1964) Towards a science of the person. In T. W. Wann (ed.), *Behaviorism and Phenomenology: Contrasting Bases for Modern Psychology*. Chicago: University of Chicago Press.

Rogers, C. R. (1969) *Freedom to Learn*. Columbus, OH: Charles E. Merrill.

Rogers, C. R. (1973) My philosophy of interpersonal relationships and how it grew, *Journal of Humanistic Psychology*, **13**, 3–16.

Rogers, C. R. (1985) Toward a more human science of the person, *Journal of Humanistic Psychology*, **25**, 7–24.

Rogers, C. R. and Dymond, R. E. (1954) *Psychotherapy and Personality Change*. Chicago: University of Chicago Press.

Rogers, C. R., Gendlin, E. T., Kiesler, D. J. and Truax, C. B. (eds) (1967) *The Therapeutic Relationship and Its Impact: A Study of Psychotherapy with Schizophrenics*. Madison: University of Wisconsin Press.

Rogers, C. R. and Skinner, B. F. (1956) Some issues concerning the control of human behavior, *Science*, **124**, 1057–66.

Rokeach, M. (1981) *The Three Christs of Ypsilanti*. New York: Columbia University Press.

Rosch, E. (1973) On the internal structures of perceptual and semantic categories. In T. E. Moore (ed.), *Cognitive Development and the Acquisition of Language*. New York: Academic Press.

Roseman, I. J., Antoniou, A. A. and Jose, P. E. (1996) Appraisal determinants of emotions: constructing a more accurate and comprehensive theory, *Cognition and Emotion*, **10**, 241–77.

Rosenhan, D. L. (1973) On being sane in insane places, *Science*, **179**, 250–8.

Rosenthal, R. and Jacobson, L. (1968) *Pygmalion in the Classroom*. New York: Holt, Rinehart and Winston.

Ross, L. (1977) The intuitive psychologist and his shortcomings: distortions in the attribution process. In L. Berkowitz (ed.), *Advances in Experimental Social Psychology*. New York: Academic Press.

Rosser, R. (1994) *Cognitive Development: Psychological and Biological Perspectives*. Toronto: Allyn & Bacon.

Rotblat, J. (1999) Science and ethical behaviour. Address to UNESCO conference, London, 3 June.

Rothbart, M. K. (1981) Measurement of temperament in infancy, *Child Development*, **52**, 569–78.

Rubenstein, E. A., Liebert, R. M., Neale, J. M. and Poulos, R. W. (1974) *Assessing Television's Influence on Children's Prosocial Behavior*. New York: Brookdale International Institute.

Ruble, T. L. (1983) Sexual stereotypes: issues of change in the 70s, *Sex Roles*, **9**, 397–402.

Rumbaugh, D. M. (1992) Learning about primates' learning, language, and cognition. In G. G. Brannigan and M. R. Merrens (eds), *The Undaunted Psychologist: Adventures in Research*. New York: McGraw-Hill.

Sacks, O. (1985) *The Man Who Mistook His Wife for a Hat*. New York: Summit.

Sartre, J.-P. (1948) *Existentialism and Humanism* (trans. P. Mariet). London: Methuen.

Savage, C. W. (ed.) (1990) *Scientific Theories*. Volume 14 in Minnesota Studies in the Philosophy of Science. Minneapolis: University of Minnesota Press.

Scarr, S. and McCartney, K. (1983) How people make their own environments: a theory of genotype environment effects, *Child Development*, **54**, 424–35.

Schachter, S. and Singer, J. E. (1962) Cognitive, social, and physiological determinants of emotional state, *Psychological Review*, **69**, 379–99.

Schaefer, H. H. and Martin, P. L. (1966) Behavioral therapy for 'apathy' of hospitalized schizophrenics, *Psychological Reports*, **19**, 1147–58.

Schank, R. C. (1984) *The Cognitive Computer: On Language, Learning, and Artificial Intelligence*. Reading, MA: Addison-Wesley.

Seligman, M. E. P. (1970) On the generality of the laws of learning, *Psychological Review*, **77**, 406–18.

Seligman, M. E. P. (1995) The effectiveness of psychotherapy: the Consumer Reports study, *American Psychologist*, **50**, 965–74.

Selye, H. (1976) *The Stress of Life*. New York: McGraw-Hill.

Selye, H. (1978) They all looked sick to me, *Human Nature*, February, 58–63.

Servos, P., Engel, S. A., Gati, J. and Menon, R. (1999) fMRI evidence for an inverted face representation in human somatosensory cortex, *NeuroReport*, **10**, 1393–5.

Shaywitz, B. A., Shaywitz, S. E., Pugh, K. R., Constable, R. T. *et al.* (1995) Sex differences in the functional organization of the brain for language, *Nature*, **373**, 607–9.

Shepard, R. N. and Metzler, J. (1971) Mental rotation of three-dimensional objects, *Science*, **171**, 701–3.

Shettleworth, S. (1972) Constraints on learning. In D. S. Lehrman, R. A. Hinde and H. Shaw (eds), *Advances in the Study of Behavior, Volume 4*. New York: Academic Press.

Shields, J. (1962) *Monozygotic Twins Brought up Apart and Brought up Together*. London: Oxford University Press.

Shorter, E. (1997) *A History of Psychiatry*. New York: John Wiley and Sons.

Siegel, S. (1976) Morphine analgesia tolerance: Its situation specificity supports a Pavlovian conditioning model, *Science*, **193**, 323–5.

Siegel, S., Krank, M. D. and Hinson, R. E. (1988) Anticipation of pharmacological and nonpharmacological events: classical conditioning and addictive behavior. In S. Peele (ed.), *Visions of Addiction*. Lexington, MA: Lexington Books.

Silverman, I. and Phillips, K. (1997) Evolutionary theory and spatial sex differences. In C. Crawford and D. Krebs (eds), *Handbook of Evolutionary Psychology: Ideas, Issues, and Applications*. Hillsdale, NJ: Lawrence Erlbaum.

Simon, H. A. (1990) A mechanism for social selection and successful altruism, *Science*, **250**, 1665–8.

Singer, J. L. and Singer, D. G. (1981) *Television, Imagination, and Aggression: A Study of Preschoolers*. Hillsdale, NJ: Lawrence Erlbaum.

Skinner, B. F. (1948a) Superstition in the pigeon, *Journal of Experimental Psychology*, **38**, 168–72.

Skinner, B. F. (1948b) *Walden Two*. New York: Macmillan.

Skinner, B. F. (1950) Are theories of learning necessary? *Psychological Review*, **57**, 193–216.

Skinner, B. F. (1957) *Verbal Behavior*. New York: Appleton Century Crofts.

Skinner, B. F. (1967) B. F. Skinner. In E. G. Boring and G. Lindzey (eds), *A History of Psychology in Autobiography, Volume 5*. New York: Appleton Century Crofts.

Skinner, B. F. (1971) *Beyond Freedom and Dignity*. New York: Vintage.

Skinner, B. F. (1974) *About Behaviorism*. New York: Alfred A. Knopf.

Skinner, B. F. (1987) Behaviourism, Skinner on. In R. L. Gregory (ed.), *The Oxford Companion to the Mind*. New York: Oxford University Press.

Sloane, R. B., Staples, F. R., Cristo, A. H., Yorkston, N. J. and Whipple, K. (1975) *Psychotherapy Versus Behavior Therapy*. Cambridge, MA: Harvard University Press.

Smith, D. (1982) Trends in counselling and psychotherapy, *American Psychologist*, **37**, 802–9.

Smith, D. L. (1992) *Understanding Canadian Prescription Drugs*, rev. edn. Toronto: Key Porter Books.

Smith, M. L., Glass, G. V. and Miller, T. I. (1980) *The Benefits of Psychotherapy*. Baltimore: Johns Hopkins University Press.

Smith, P. B. and Bond, M. H. (1999) *Social Psychology across Cultures*, 2nd edn. Boston: Allyn and Bacon.

Snyder, S. (1980) *Biological Aspects of Mental Disorder*. New York: Oxford University Press.

Solomon, G. F. (1990) Emotions, stress, and immunity. In R. Ornstein and C. Swencionis (eds), *The Healing Brain: A Scientific Reader*. New York: Guilford Press.

Sperling, G. (1960) The information available in brief visual presentations, *Psychological Monographs*, **74** (11, whole no. 498).

Sperry, R. (1968) Hemispheric deconnection and unity in conscious awareness, *American Psychologist*, **23**, 723–33.

Sperry, R. (1969) A modified concept of consciousness, *Psychological Review*, **76**, 532–6.

Sperry, R. (1993) The impact and promise of the cognitive revolution, *American Psychologist*, **48**, 878–85.

Sperry, R. (1995) The riddle of consciousness and the changing scientific worldview, *Journal of Humanistic Psychology*, **35**, 7–33.

Sprafkin, J. N., Liebert, R. M. and Poulos, R. W. (1975) Effects of a prosocial televised example on children's helping, *Journal of Experimental Child Psychology*, **20**, 119–26.

Steiner, C. (1974) *Scripts People Live – Transactional Analysis of Life Scripts*. New York: Grove Press.

Sterman, M. B. (1978) Biofeedback and epilepsy, *Human Nature*, May, 50–7.

Stevenson, M. R. and Black, K. N. (1988) Paternal absence and sex-role development: a meta-analysis, *Child Development*, **59**, 793–814.

Stiles, W. B., Shapiro, D. A. and Elliott, R. (1986) Are all psychotherapies equivalent? *American Psychologist*, **41**, 165–80.

Stone, J. (1988) Sex and the single gorilla, *Discover*, August, 78, 80.

Straub, R. E. (1994) Possible vulnerability locus for bipolar affective disorder on chromosome 21q22.3, *Nature Genetics*, **8**, 291–4.

Strauss, A. S. (1982) The structure of the self in Northern Cheyenne culture. In B. Lee (ed.), *Psychosocial Theories of the Self*. New York: Plenum Press.

Strupp, H. H. (1989) Psychotherapy: can the practitioner learn from the researcher? *American Psychologist*, **44**, 717–24.

Sue, S., Fujino, D. C., Hu, L., Takeuchi, D. T. *et al.* (1991) Community mental health services for ethnic minority groups: A test of the cultural responsiveness hypothesis, *Journal of Consulting and Clinical Psychology*, **59**, 533–40.

Sulloway, F. (1979) *Freud: Biologist of the Mind*. New York: Basic Books.

Szasz, T. S. (1974) *The Myth of Mental Illness*, rev. edn. New York: Harper and Row.

Tandon, R. and Kane, J. M. (1993) Neuropharmacologic basis for clozapine's unique profile, *Archives of General Psychiatry*, **50**, 158–9.

Taylor, S. E. and Brown, J. D. (1988) Illusion and well-being: a social psychological perspective on mental health, *Psychological Bulletin*, **103**, 193–210.

Tellegen, A., Lykken, D. T., Bouchard, T. J., Wilcox, K. J. and Rich, S. (1988) Personality similarity in twins reared apart and together, *Journal of Personality and Social Psychology*, **54**, 1031–9.

Terrace, H. S., Petitto, L. A., Sanders, R. J. and Bever, T. G. (1979) Can an ape create a sentence? *Science*, **206**, 891–902.

Teusch, L. (1990) Positive effects and limitations of client-centered therapy with schizophrenic patients. In G. Lietaer, J. Rombauts and R. Van Balen (eds), *Client-centered and Experiential Psychotherapy in the Nineties*. Leuven, Belgium: Leuven University Press.

Thomas, A. and Chess, A. (1977) *Temperament and Development*. New York: Brunner/Mazel.

Thomas, L. (1981) On the need for asylums, *Discover*, December, 68–71.

Thompson, S. K. (1975) Gender labels and early sex-role development, *Child Development*, **46**, 339–47.

Thorndike, E. L. (1898) Animal intelligence, *Psychological Review Monograph Supplement*, **2** (4, whole no. 8).

Tolman, E. C. (1932) *Purposive Behavior in Animals and Man*. New York: Appleton Century Crofts.

Tooby, J. and Cosmides, L. (1990) On the universality of human nature and the uniqueness of the individual: the role of genetics and adaptation, *Journal of Personality*, **58**, 17–67.

Toulin, A. (1993) Liberals head to majority, new poll says, *The Financial Post*, 2 October, 1.

Trevarthen, C. (1987) Split-brain and the mind. In R. L. Gregory (ed.), *The Oxford Companion to the Mind*. New York: Oxford University Press.

Triandis, H. C. (1990) Cross-cultural studies of individualism and collectivism. In J. J. Berman (ed.), *Cross-cultural Perspectives: Nebraska Symposium on Motivation, 1989*. Lincoln, NE: University of Nebraska Press.

Trivers, R. L. (1971) The evolution of reciprocal altruism, *Quarterly Review of Biology*, **46**, 35–57.

Truax, C. B. (1966) Reinforcement and non-reinforcement in Rogerian psychotherapy, *Journal of Abnormal Psychology*, **71**, 1–9.

Tulving, E. (1974) Recall and recognition of semantically encoded words, *Journal of Experimental Psychology*, **102**, 778–87.

Tulving, E. (1985) How many memory systems are there? *American Psychologist*, **40**, 385–98.

Tulving, E. (1986) What kind of hypothesis is the distinction between episodic and semantic memory? *Journal of Experimental Psychology: Learning, Memory, and Cognition*, **12**, 307–11.

Tulving, E. and Madigan, S. (1970) Memory and verbal learning, *Annual Review of Psychology*, **21**, 457–84.

Tulving, E. and Thompson, D. M. (1971) Retrieval processes in recognition memory, *Journal of Experimental Psychology*, **87**, 116–24.

US National Institute of Justice (1996) *Convicted by Juries, Exonerated by Science: Case Studies in the Use of DNA Evidence to Establish Innocence After Trial*. Washington, DC: Dept of Justice.

Valins, S. (1966) Cognitive effects of false heart-rate feedback, *Journal of Personality and Social Psychology*, **4**, 400–8.

Vandenberg, B. (1993) Existentialism and development, *American Psychologist*, **46**, 296–7.

Venables, P. H. (1996) Schizotypy and maternal exposure to influenza and to cold temperature: the Mauritius study, *Journal of Abnormal Psychology*, **105**, 53–60.

Villet, B. (1978) Opiates of the mind, *The Atlantic Monthly*, June, 82–9.

Viinamaeki, H., Koskela, K. and Niskanen, L. (1996) Rapidly declining mental well being during unemployment, *European Journal of Psychiatry*, **10**, 215–21.

Vonnegut, M. (1975) *The Eden Express*. New York: Bantam.

Wachtel, P. L. (1977) *Psychoanalysis and Behavior Therapy*. New York: Basic Books.

Wachtel, P. L. (1997) *Psychoanalysis, Behavior Therapy, and the Relational World*. Washington, DC: American Psychological Association.

Walker, E. F. and Diforio, D. (1997) Schizophrenia: a neural diathesis-stress model, *Psychological Bulletin*, **104**, 667–85.

Wallace, R. K. and Benson, H. (1972) The physiology of meditation, *Scientific American*, February, 84–90.

Wallach, M. A. and Wallach, L. (1983) *Psychology's Sanction for Selfishness*. San Francisco: W. H. Freeman.

Wallerstein, R. S. (1989) The psychotherapy research project of the Meninger Foundation: an overview, *Journal of Consulting and Clinical Psychology*, **57**, 195–205.

Warner, R. E. (1991) A survey of theoretical orientations of Canadian clinical psychologists, *Canadian Psychology*, **32**, 525–8.

Warwick, D. P. (1975) Deceptive research: social scientists ought to stop lying, *Psychology Today*, February, 63–5.

Watanabe, S., Sakamoto, J. and Wakita, M. (1995) Pigeons' discrimination of painting by Monet and Picasso. *Journal of the Experimental Analysis of Behaviour*, **63**, 165–74.

Watson, J. B. (1930) *Behaviorism*. New York: W. W. Norton (reprinted 1970).

Watson, J. B. and Rayner, L. (1920) Conditioned emotional reactions, *Journal of Experimental Psychology*, **3**, 1–14.

Waugh, N. C. and Norman, D. A. (1965) Primary memory, *Psychological Review*, **72**, 89–104.

Webb, E. J., Campbell, D. T., Schwartz, R. D. and Sechrest, L. (1972) *Unobtrusive Measures: Non-reactive Research in the Social Sciences*. Chicago: Rand McNally.

Weimer, W. B. (1973) Psycholinguistics and Plato's paradoxes of the Meno, *American Psychologist*, January, 15–33.

Weinberger, D. A., Schwartz, G. E. and Davidson, R. J. (1979) Low-anxious, high-anxious, and repressive coping styles: psychometric patterns and behavioral and physiological responses to stress, *Journal of Abnormal Psychology*, **88**, 369–80.

Weisberg, P. and Waldrop, P. B. (1972) Fixed interval work habits of Congress, *Journal of Applied Behavior Analysis*, **5**, 93–7.

Weisz, J. R., Rothbaum, F. M. and Blackburn, T. C. (1984) Standing out and standing in: the psychology of control in America and Japan, *American Psychologist*, **39**, 955–69.

Wells, G. L. and Bradfield, A. L. (1998) 'Good, you identified the suspect': feedback to eyewitnesses distorts their reports of the eyewitnessing experience, *Journal of Applied Psychology*, **83**, 360–76.

Wender, P. H. and Klein, D. F. (1981) The promise of biological psychiatry, *Psychology Today*, February, 25–41.

Westen, D. (1999) *Psychology: Mind, Brain and Culture*, 2nd edn. New York: John Wiley & Sons.

Wheeler, M. A., Stuss, D. T. and Tulving, E. (1997) Toward a theory of episodic memory: the frontal lobes and autonoetic consciousness, *Psychological Bulletin*, **121**, 331–54.

White, R. W. (1975) *Lives in Progress: A Study of the Natural Growth of Personality*, 3rd edn. New York: Holt, Rinehart and Winston.

Whiting, B. B. and Edwards, C. P. (1988) *Children of Different Worlds: The Formation of Social Behavior*. Cambridge, MA: Harvard University Press.

Whorf, B. L. (1956) *Language, Thought, and Reality*. Cambridge, MA: MIT Press.

Wicker, A. (1971) Attitudes vs. action: the relationship between verbal and overt behavior responses to attitude objects, *Journal of Social Issues*, **25**, 41–78.

Williams, J. E. and Best, D. L. (1982) *Measuring Sex Stereotypes: A Thirty-nation Study*. Beverly Hills, CA: Sage.

Williams, J. E. and Best, D. L. (1990) *Sex and Psyche: Gender and Self Viewed Cross-culturally*. Newbury Park, CA: Sage.

Williams, L. M. (1994a) Recall of childhood trauma: a prospective study of women's memories of child sexual abuse, *Journal of Consulting and Clinical Psychology*, **62**, 1167–76.

Williams, L. M. (1994b) What does it mean to forget child sexual abuse? A reply to Loftus, Garry and Feldman, *Journal of Consulting and Clinical Psychology*, **62**, 1182–6.

Wilson, E. O. (1975) *Sociobiology: A New Synthesis*. Cambridge, MA: Harvard University Press.

Wilson, E. O. (1998) *Consilience*. New York: Alfred Knopf.

Winholz, G. (1997) Ivan P. Pavlov: an overview of his life and psychological work, *American Psychologist*, **52**, 941–6.

Wittkower, E. D. and Robertson, B. M. (1979) Sex differences in psychoanalytic treatment, *American Journal of Psychotherapy*, **19**, 66–75.

Wolpe, J. (1973) *The Practice of Behavior Therapy*, 2nd edn. New York: Pergamon Press.

Wood, W., Wong, F. Y. and Chachere, J. G. (1991) Effects of media violence on viewers' aggression in unconstrained social interaction, *Psychological Bulletin*, **109**, 371–83.

Yalom, I. D. (1980) *Existential Psychotherapy*. New York: Basic Books.

Yates, F. A. (1966) *The Art of Memory*. Chicago: University of Chicago Press.

Zaner, R. M. (1985) The *Logos* of *Psyche*: phenomenological variations on a theme. In S. Koch and D. E. Leary (eds), *A Century of Psychology as a Science*. New York: McGraw-Hill.

Zangwill, O. (1987) Sigmund Freud. In R. L. Gregory (ed.), *The Oxford Companion to the Mind*. New York: Oxford University Press.

Zeig, J. (ed.) (1987) *The Evolution of Psychotherapy*. New York: Brunner/Mazell.

Zimbardo, P. G. (1992) *Psychology and Life*, 13th edn. New York: HarperCollins.

Zubin, J. and Spring, B. (1977) Vulnerability – a new view of schizophrenia, *Journal of Abnormal Psychology*, **86**, 103–26.

Zuckerman, M. (1991) *Psychobiology of Personality*. Cambridge: Cambridge University Press.

Index

Note: page numbers in *italics* refer to illustrations

abnormal behaviour
    approaches to, 363–4, 393–4
        behaviourist, 365–8, *378*
        biological, 364–5, 377
        cognitive, 368–71, 377, *378*
        humanistic, 374–6, *378*
        psychodynamic, 371–4, 377, *378*
    defining and classifying, 358,
        359–63, 380–1, 393
    evaluating therapies for, 376–9
    in historical context, 358–9
    and normal behaviour, 204–5
    schizophrenia
        behaviourist approach, 385–7
        cognitive approach, 387–9
        evaluating approaches, 385, 392–3
        example of, 249–50, 356–7
        features of, 380–2
        humanistic approach, 390–2
        medical model, 382–5
        psychodynamic approach, 389–90
abnormal psychology, features of, 358,
    393
accessibility, in memory, 167
accommodation, 295
acetylcholine, 59
acronyms, 174
ACTH, 76
actualizing tendency, 255–6, 260, 267,
    336–7
addiction, 67
Adler, Alfred, 237, 241–3
adrenal glands, 76
adrenaline (epinephrine), 76
aetiology of abnormal behaviour
    approaches to, 363–4
        behaviourist, 365–6
        biological, 364, 365

cognitive, 368–9
        humanistic, 374
        psychodynamic, 371
    definition of, 361
    schizophrenia, 382–4, 385–6,
        388–92
aggression, 322–3
    approaches to
        behaviourist, 328–31, 339
        biological, 325–8, 339
        cognitive, 331–4, 339–40, 341
        comparison of, 338–40
        humanistic, 264–5, 273, 336–8,
            339
        psychodynamic, 210, 334–5, 339
    cross-cultural differences, 352
    defining, 323–4
    and the media, 340–4
    methods of studying, 324–5, 337,
        341–2
AIDS, ethics of research on, 35
alcohol and alcoholism, 67–8
algorithms, 181–2
alleles, 85–6
altruism
    behaviourist approach, 346–7
    biological approach, 345–6
    and bystander behaviour, 30–2,
        350–2
    cognitive approach, 347–8
    defining, 319, 344–5
    humanistic approach, 348–9
    psychodynamic approach, 348
    see also bystander apathy
ambiguous figures, 5–6
American Psychological Association
    (APA), 37
amnesia, childhood, 218

amphetamines, 66–7, 381, 382
Amsel, Eric, 401
amygdala, 53, 328
anal stage, 215–16
analogies, 182
    see also information processing
        models
Anderson, Elijah, 333
androgens, 308
Angell, Marcia, 82
anima, 239
animals in research studies, 84, 400
    behaviourist conditioning
        classical, 104–5, 109, 111, 112,
            116–17
        operant, 118, 120, 126–7, 133,
            134
        biological research, 55, 64, 78, 84,
            326–7
        cognitive research, 152–3, 188–9
        ethology, 142, 326–7
animus, 239
anti-depressant drugs, 68, 364, 377
anti-social personality disorder, 360
anxiety
    basic anxiety, 244
    behaviourist treatment for, 366
    comparing treatments for, 373, 376,
        378
    Freud's theory of, 222–7
    impact on memory, 168
    person-centred therapy for, 376
    Yalom's view of, 279
    see also Oedipal conflict
apathy, see bystander apathy
apes, language studies with, 188–9
archetypes, 239, 240–1
Arieti, Silvano, 388
Aronson, Elliot, 323
art, Freudian analyses of, 226, 231–2
Asch, Solomon, 305
assimilation, 295
association areas, 51, 52
associationism, 100, 162, 165–7, 415
astrology, 2
attention, 5, 158
    defective attention theory, 388–9
    see also concentration
attitudes, 191–3
attribution theory, 193–5, 304
attributions, cultural differences, 393
autonomic conditioning, 139–41
autonomic nervous system, 66, 76

availability, in memory, 167
aversive conditioning, 367
aversive control of behaviour, 135–7
    see also negative reinforcers;
        punishment
avoidance, 136, 138, 143–4
awfulizing, 370
axon, 48
AZT, ethics of research on, 35

backward conditioning, 106
bait-shyness, 143–4
Bandura, Albert, 312, 331–2, 369
barbiturates, 68
Bartlett, Frederick, 170
basic anxiety, 244
Bateson, Gregory, 390
Bateson, William, 84
Batson, Daniel, 349
Baumrind, D., 36
Becker, Ernest, 279–80
behaviour
    aversive control of, 135–7
    Freud's assumptions about, 204–5
    humanistic assumptions about,
        250–1
    measuring, 18–19
    observing unconscious in, 228–32
    see also abnormal behaviour
behaviour modification, 366–8, 371,
    386–7
    cognitive, 369
behavioural inhibition, 302
behaviourist approach
    and abnormal behaviour, 365–8,
        378
        schizophrenia, 385–7
    and aggression, 328–31, 339
    and altruism, 346–7
    analysis of Freud's work, 233
    cognitive challenge to, 151, 404, 415
    compared with humanism, 251
    conditioning, see classical
        conditioning; operant conditioning
    cultural influences on, 410
    features of, 98–100
    influence of, 403–4, 413
    and language, 186
    and personality, 302–3
    pioneers of, 100–2
    and sex role development, 310–11
    and stimuli and responses, 103–4
Bell, A. P., 313

belongingness, 270
Berkowitz, Leonard, 328, 331, 333
Berlyne, D. E., 414
between-groups design, 29
bias
    attribution theory of, 194, 304
    culture and psychologists, 410–11
    in defining abnormal, 360
    in experimental research, 424–7
    in Freud's work, 234–6
    in sampling, 422–3
    in survey interviews, 21
    toward consistency, 304
    see also cognitive pathology;
        fundamental attribution error
biofeedback, 140–1
biological approach
    and abnormal behaviour, 364–5,
        377
        schizophrenia, 382–5
    and aggression, 325–8, 339
    and altruism, 345–6
    features of, 43–6
    and heredity, *see* heredity
    influence of, 404, 413
    and mind and body, *see* mind-body
        relationship
    and personality, 301–2
    and physiology, *see* physiological
        system
    relationship with cognitive, 412–13
    relationship with psychodynamic,
        404
    and sex role development, 308–10
bipolar disorder, 365
Bleuler, Eugen, 380
blocking, 106
body, *see* mind-body relationship;
        physiological system
'bottom-up' processing, 5
Bowlby, John, 237
brain
    impact of adrenaline on, 76
    physiology of, 50–4
    relationship with mind, 46–7, 62–3
    and schizophrenia, 383
    split brain, 69–73
        and normal brain, 73–5
    study of, 54–9
brain stem, 54
Brandt, L. W., 36, 37
Brenner, Charles, 236
Breuer, Joseph, 206

British Psychological Society (BPS), 37
Broca, Paul, 45, 54–5, 56
Brown, Roger, 187, 387, 389, 391
Brücke, Ernst, 203–4
Buford, Bill, 24
Buss, D. M., 309
Byne, W., 310
bystander apathy, 20–1, 23, 29–33,
        345, 350–1
bystander intervention, 30–2, 344,
        350–2

Cabanis (physician), 45
caffeine, 67
Campbell, Joseph, 240
capacity of memory, 159, 164
career choice, and fixation, 221–2
Carlson, Neil, 299
Carmichael, L., 155
case studies, 24–6, 54, 205, 234
castration fear, 201–2, 217–18
CAT scan, 58
catatonic schizophrenia, 381
catatoxic reactions, 80
categorization, to aid memory, 164
catharsis, 206, 225, 327, 335, 340,
        372
causal predictions, 407–9
causation
    as challenge to psychology, 4
    and problems of method, 25, 27–8,
        291–2, 341, 405–6
    in social psychology, 320, 321, 341,
        352
    see also aetiology of abnormal
        behaviour; determinism
central nervous system (CNS), 47,
        49–50, 59, 66, 67
    see also brain
cerebellum, 53–4
cerebral dominance, 73–4
cerebral hemispheres, and split brain,
        69–73
chaos theory, 408
Charcot, Jean, 204
chemical processes, 59–62
Chess, 302
child abuse, 235
childhood amnesia, 218
children
    media and aggression in, 341–3
    media and altruism in, 347
    see also development

chlorpromazine, 382
choice, in humanistic approach, 251
Chomsky, Noam, 187
chromosomes, 83, 85, 308
chunks of short-term memory, 159,
    164–5
Cicero (Roman orator), 172–3
classical conditioning
    drug and immune responses, 116–17
    emotional responses, 114–16, 138,
        144, 366
    extinction and spontaneous recovery,
        111–12
    higher-order conditioning, 112–14
    and operant conditioning, 137–8
    origins and features of, 104–7
    stimulus generalization and
        discrimination, 107–11, 115
    treatment using, 366–7
client-centred therapy, see person-
        centred therapy
clinical observation, see case studies
closure, 7
clozapine, 383
CNS, see central nervous system
cocktail party effect, 158
'code of the streets', 333, 337
cognition
    and perception, 154–5
    see also social cognition; thinking
cognitive appraisal theory, 196
cognitive approach
    and abnormal behaviour, 368–71,
        377, 378
        schizophrenia, 387–9
    and aggression, 331–4, 339–40, 341
    and altruism, 347–8
    and attitudes and cognitive
        dissonance, 191–3
    attribution theory, 193–5
    and emotions, 195–7
    influence of, 191, 404, 413
    and language, 187–8, 189
    and learning, 151–2, 155–7
    limitations of, 198
    and memory, see memory
    origins and features of, 151–4
    and perception and cognition, 154–5
    and personality, 303–5
    Piaget's model of development, 295,
        296
    and problem solving, see problem
        solving

relationship with behaviourist, 151,
    404, 415
relationship with biological, 412–13
and sex role development, 311–12
cognitive behaviour modification, 369
cognitive dissonance, 36, 192–3
cognitive maps, 151, 152, 156, 176
cognitive neo-association theory, 333–4
cognitive neuroscience, 413
cognitive pathology, 400–1
cognitive restructuring, 370
cognitive science, 413
cognitive social learning theory, 304,
    331–3, 339, 340, 341, 347
collective unconscious, 239, 240
collectivism, 267
communication, and schizophrenia in
    families, 390
community treatment orders, 362
compensation, 242
complementarity, 10, 414
computer analogies, see information
    processing models
computerized imaging, 58–9
concentration, to aid memory, 172
concentration camps, 283
concordance studies, 89
conditional positive regard, 261, 265,
    313
conditioned drug responses, 116–17
conditioned emotional responses,
    114–16, 138, 144
conditioned immune responses, 117
conditioned reinforcers, 122
conditioned responses, 105
conditioned stimuli, 105
conditioning
    biological constraints on, 141–5
    see also autonomic conditioning;
        classical conditioning; cultural
        conditioning; operant conditioning
conditions for growth, 261–4, 375
conditions of worth, 259–60, 313, 337
confirmation, 427–8
confirmation bias, 9
conformity, 305, 319
confounding variables, 292, 424
congruence, 258, 261–4
conscious, definition of, 206
consciousness
    Freud's theory of, 206–8
    localization of, 74–5
    role of mind and brain, 46–7

consilience, 412
context dependent, memory as, 162–3, 167–9, 415
context-dependent forgetting, 167–8, 169
contiguity, 100, 122, 136
contingencies of reinforcement, 123–6, 133
continuity in development, 294–5, 302, 303, 304–5, 307
continuous reinforcement, 128, 132, 136
contrapreparedness, 143, 144–5
convergent problems, 177–8
corpus callosum, 69, 70
correlation coefficients, 26, 437–8
correlational research, 26–8, 325, 341
correlations, 437–8
cortex, 50–3
corticosteroids, 76
counter-conditioning, 367
Cousins, Norman, 81
creativity
   as defence mechanism, 226
   in problem solving, 183–4
Crick, Francis, 44, 85
criminality
   and conditioning, 136
   and heredity, 83
critical periods of development, 142, 187, 299, 302
cross-cultural research, 194–5, 231, 235, 267, 352, 392–3, 411
cross-sectional samples, 422
cross-sectional studies, 291–2, 293
cue-dependent coding, 162–3, 167–9
cultural conditioning, 273
culture
   approaches to self, 267
   and attributions, 194–5
   and cognitive dissonance, 193
   definition of, 410
   and Freud's work, 231, 235
   and gender roles, 308, 312
   and handedness, 73–4
   impact on defining abnormal, 360
   role in psychology, 11, 410–11
   and schizophrenia, 392–3
   and search for meaning, 283
   and self-actualization, 278
   and social behaviour, 352
   and validity of humanism, 285
Cytowic, Richard, 25

Damasio, Antonio, 74–5, 197
Darley, John, 29–32, 350–1, 424
Darwin, Charles, 45–6, 83–4, 87, 204
death, existentialist view of, 279–80
Deaux, K., 310
deBono, Edward, 183
debriefing, 36, 321
decay in memory, 163
deception, 37–8, 321
decision errors, 441–3
decision making, by groups, 410
deduction, 16, 17
defective attention theory, 388–9
defence mechanisms, 218, 223–7, 231, 334, 348, 372
deficiency motives, 271, 272
delusional amphetamine disorder, 381
delusions, 380, 387
demand characteristics, 406
dependent variables, 29
depersonalization, 391
depressant drugs, 67–8
depression
   comparing treatments for, 370, 377
   definition of, 364
   drug treatment for, 364
   and existential concerns, 282
   person-centred therapy for, 376
   rational-emotive therapy for, 370
   see also anti-depressant drugs
depth perception, 299
Descartes, René, 44
descriptive statistics, 428–30
   correlations, 437–8
   frequency distributions, 429, 430–1, 432, 433, 434
      normal distributions, 433, 434, 436–7
   measures of central tendency, 431–3
   measures of variability, 433–6
determinism, 251
development
   Erikson's psychosocial model, 244–5
   Jung's view of, 239–40
   Maslow's approach to, 272–4, 276–8
   Piaget's model of, 295, 296
   psychosexual stages of, 214–22
   Rogers' approach to, 258–67
developmental psychology
   approaches to personality, 301–7
   approaches to sex roles, 308–14
   concept of personality, 300–1

features of, 289–90, 315–16
issues of interpretation, 294–300
methods of study, 290–2, 293
deviation scores, 435
Diagnostic and Statistical Manual of
Mental Disorders, *see* DSM
diathesis-stress model, 384
DiCara, Leo, 139, 141
diffusion of responsibility, 32, 351
direct observation, 18–19
discontinuity in development, 294–5,
302, 306
discrimination, *see* racial
discrimination; stimulus
discrimination
discriminative stimuli, 133–4
disorganized schizophrenia, 381
displacement
behaviourist theory of, 330–1
as defence mechanism, 225, 334
in memory, 164
dissonance, *see* cognitive dissonance
divergent problems, 178
divergent thinking, 183
DNA, 85
Dollard, John, 233, 330
domain-general models, 295, 296, 303,
305, 306, 307
domain-specific models, 295, 296, 302
dominant alleles, 85–6
dopamine, 59–60, 64, 66
dopamine hypothesis, 382–3
double-bind hypothesis, 390
double-blind design, 426–7
dream censor, 208
dreams, 208–9, 230–1
drives
Freud's work on, 204, 209–11, 214
role of id, 211–12
see also motivation; psychosexual
development
drugs
conditioned responses to, 116–17
research on, 425, 427, 441–2
studying effects of, 63–6
to treat mental disorders, 364–5,
377, 382–3
types of, 66–9
DSM (Diagnostic and Statistical
Manual of Mental Disorders),
359, 360–3
dualism, 44, 75
duration, of memory, 158–9

Ebbinghaus, Hermann, 414
Edelman, Gerald, 57, 91
EEG (electroencephalograph), 55
efficacy, of therapies, 376–9
ego
Freud's concept of, 212, 213, 215,
217
anxiety and, 218, 222, 223, 227
damaged in schizophrenia, 389
Jung's concept of, 238, 239
ego psychology, 237
Einstein, Albert, 149–50
elaboration, to aid memory, 174
elaborative rehearsal, 160–1
electrical recording, 55
electrical stimulation of brain (ESB),
55–7
electroencephalograph (EEG), 55
Elkin, I., 377
Ellis, Albert, 369–70, 379
Ellis, L., 309, 310
emergencies, *see* bystander apathy;
bystander intervention; stress
emotional closeness, and genetic
relatedness, 92
emotional responses, conditioning of,
114–16, 138, 144
emotions
cognitive approach to, 195–7
and conditions of worth, 259
physiological influences on, 195,
196, 197
role of amygdala, 53
see also rational-emotive therapy
empathy, 256, 263–4, 349, 375
empiricism, 15, 88, 402, 403
encoding, and storage of memory,
159–63
endocrine system, 61–2, 76
endorphins, 62, 65, 82
environment
behaviourist study of, 103
and heredity in development, 296–9,
301–2, 304, 306, 307
influence on behaviour, 86–7
nature-nurture debate, 88–90, 325
relationship with needs, 273
and schizophrenia, 384, 385–93
environmental consistency, 303
epilepsy, 56, 69–70
epinephrine (adrenalin), 76
episodic memory, 161, 163, 167
equilibration, 295

equipotentiality premise, 142
Erikson, Erik, 237, 244–5
erogenous zones, 214
Eron, Leonard, 342
Eros, 210
error, *see* bias; decision errors;
    fundamental attribution error;
    random error; sampling error
ESB (electrical stimulation of brain),
    55–7
escape, 138
esteem needs, 270
ethical hedonism, 345, 346, 348
ethics, 35–8, 57, 115, 321–2
ethnicity, and defining abnormal, 360
ethology, 142, 326–7
evolution, 45–6, 83–4, 87, 90–3
evolutionary psychology, 90–3, 328,
    345–6
exaptation, 93
excitation, 60
existential psychology, 279–84
experience, *see* inner experience;
    subjective experience
experimental realism, 321, 324
experimental research methods, 28–33
  analyses of Freudian ideas, 233
  confounds and bias, 424–7
  definition of, 19
  field experiments, 29, 31, 324–5,
    341–2
  internal validity of, 423
  problems of, 406–7, 423–7
  in social psychology, 320–1, 324–5
  see also quasi-experiments
experimenter bias, 426
expressed emotion, 390, 393
external validity, 31, 324
extinction, 111, 115, 127–8, 132
eyewitness testimony, 170–2

false memory, 208, 224
false negatives, 442, 443
false positives, 442–3
false recognition, 169
falsifiability, of Freud's work, 232,
    234
falsification, 427–8
family, role in schizophrenia, 390, 393
fantasy, expressing aggression through,
    335
faulty cognitive processing, 387
faulty reference, 388

fears
  hierarchy of, 366
  see also phobias
Fechner, Gustav, 70
Feshbach, S., 335
Festinger, Leon, 192, 353
Feynman, Richard, 252
field experiments, 29, 31, 324–5,
    341–2
field settings, 19, 31
'fight or flight' response, 76, 77
fixation, 220–2
fixed interval schedules, *129*, 130–1,
    132
fixed ratio schedules, 128–9, 132
fixed-alternative surveys, 21
Fleiss, Wilhelm, 237
food-avoidance learning, 143–4
forgetting, 163–9
  see also repression
Frank, Jerome, 378–9
Frankl, Viktor, 280–4
Fraser, Colin, 406
free association, 162, 206, 229–30,
    372
free will, 251
Freedman, J. L., 342
frequency distributions, *429*, 430–1,
    432, 433, *434*
Freud, Anna, 237
Freud, Sigmund
  on aggression, 210, 323, 334, 335
  on altruism, 348
  on anxiety and defence mechanisms,
    222–7
  assessing work of, 232–6, 246
  assumptions about behaviour, 204–5
  background, 203–4
  cultural influences on, 410
  film about work of, 201–2
  on fixation and regression, 220–2
  free association technique, 162, 206,
    229–30, 372
  influence of, 202, 245–6
  observing the unconscious, 228–32
  on personality, 211–14, 306
  psychoanalysis by, 372
  on psychosexual stages of
    development, 214–20
  relationships with other theorists,
    203–4, 234, 236–7, 238, 241
  on schizophrenia, 389
  self-awareness, 3

on sex role development, 217–19, 313
use of case studies, 24, 205, 234
on workings of mind, 205–11
Freudian slips, 228
Fromkin, Victoria, 228
frontal lobe, 50–1
frontal lobotomy, 50–1
frontal motor area, 51
frustration-aggression hypothesis, 330, 336, 339
fully functioning person, 264–7
functional fixedness, 180
functionalism, 14, 99
fundamental attribution error, 194, 263, 304, 410

GABA, 67
Galvani, Luigi, 55
Gantt, W. H., 111
Garcia, John, 143
Gardner, Allen, 188
Gardner, Beatrice, 188
Gazzaniga, Michael, 413
Geertz, Clifford, 235
gender
    evolutionary interpretations of, 91
    and hemispheric specialization, 73
gender roles
    behaviourist approach to, 310–11
    biological approach to, 308–9, 310
    cognitive approach to, 311–12
    definition of, 308
    humanistic approach to, 313–14
    psychodynamic approach to, 313
gender schema, 311
general adaptation syndrome, 78
generality, 234, 295
generalization
    in classical conditioning, 107–9, 115
    in equipotentiality premise, 142
genes, 84–6, 87
genetics, 84–7, 365, 383, 384
genital stage, 220
genotypes, 85
Genovese, Kitty, case of, 20–1, 23, 25, 29–30, 320, 345
genuine altruism, 345, 348, 349
Gestalt theory, 6–7, 152, 155, 178–80, 184
Glass, David, 79
glove anaesthesia, 205

goal state, in problem solving, 181
goals, in problem solving, 182
Goldiamond, Israel, 97–8
Goldstein, Kurt, 274
Gould, Stephen Jay, 93
gratification, modes of, 214
group decision making, 410
group polarization, 410
Guilford, J. P., 183

habituation, 60
hallucinations, 380
halo effect, 426
handedness, 73–4
Hans (the educated horse), 2, 28–9
Harlow, Harry, 184
Harris, Judith, *305*
health
    effect of mind on body, 80–3
    and stress, 78
Hebb, Donald, 297
hedonism, 209
    ethical hedonism, 345, 346, 348
Heider, Fritz, 194
helping, *see* altruism
hemispheric specialization
    cerebral dominance, 73–4
    split brain research, 71–3
heredity
    basic mechanisms of, 84–8
    and criminality, 83
    definition of, 45
    and environment in development, 296–9, 301–2, 306, 307
    and evolution, 45–6, 83–4, 90–3
    nature-nurture debate, 88–90, 325
    role in schizophrenia, 383, 384
    theories of, 45–6
Herrnstein, R. J., 391
heuristics, 182
hierarchy of fears, 366
hierarchy of needs, 270–2, 336, 349
higher-order conditioning, 112–14
hippocampus, 53
history of reinforcement, 303
Holmes, Thomas, 78
homosexuality, 33–4, 308, 309–10, 313, 314
hope, in therapy, 379
hormones, 61–2, 76, 308, 309
Horney, Karen, 243–4
hospitalization, 386

Hounsfield, Godfrey, 58
Human Genome Project, 84
humanistic approach
    and abnormal behaviour, 374–6,
        378
        schizophrenia, 390–2
    and aggression, 264–5, 273, 336–8,
        339
    and altruism, 348–9
    evaluating, 285
    and existential psychology, 279–84
    Maslow's work, *see* Maslow,
        Abraham
    origins and features, 250–3
    and personality, 306–7
    Rogers' work, *see* Rogers, Carl
    and sex role development, 313–14
hypnosis, 206
hypothalmus, 53, 62, 328
hypotheses, 16, 29, 427–8, 441
hysteria, 205–6, 207–8, 209, 224,
    235, 358–9

ICD (International Classification of
    Diseases), 359
id, 211–12, 213, 216
    role in anxiety, 217, 222, 223, 227
ideal self, 257–8, 259–60, 313, 337
identification, 201–2, 218, 219, 225,
    313
illusory correlation, 26–7
imitation, 304, 312, 313, 340, 341,
    347, 369
immune system, 81–2, 117
implicit memory, 157
implicit personality theories, 301
incongruence, 258, 259–60, 337
incubation, 176, 180, 184
independent variable, 29
individuation, 239–40
induction, 16, *17*
inference, definition of, 440
inferential statistics
    decision errors, 441–3
    from normal distributions, 439–40
    sampling variability, 439, 440
    significance of results, 440–1
inferiority, 241–2
inferiority complex, 242
information processing models, 154,
    155–6, 157, 161–2, 180–1,
    198
inheritance, *see* heredity

inhibition
    behavioural, 302
    of neurons, 60
inhibitory drugs, 67, 68
initial state, in problem solving, 181
inner experience
    and science, 404–5
    see also subjective experience
insight
    in problem solving, 151–2, 179, 184,
        185
    in psychotherapy, 371–2, 374
institutionalization, 386
instrumental aggression, 329, 339
instrumental altruism, 347
insulin, 117
intention to harm, 323
interference, 165–7
internal validity, 423
interneurons, 47
interpretation
    in developmental psychology,
        294–300
    of research, 427–8
    see also inferential statistics
intersubjective verification, 252
interval schedules, 128, *129*, 130–2
interviews, 20–1
introjection of values, 259–60, 313
introspectionism, 3, 16–17, 99, 101,
    114, 404

Jacobson, Lenore, 426
James, William, 3, 13–15, 43, 99,
    195
Jervis, Robert, 408
Joy, L. A., 341
Jung, Carl, 237–41

Kagan, Jerome, 302
Kelman, H. C., 37
Kihlstrom, John, 412
kin altruism, 346
King, Alan, 23
Klein, Melanie, 237
Kluver, Heinrich, 64
knowledge, approaches to, 416
Koch, Sigmund, 400, 413–14, 415
Kohlberg, Lawrence, 296
Kohler, Wolfgang, 151–2, 178,
    184
Kriegman, Daniel, 348
Kuhn, Thomas, 4–5, 402–3

La Mettrie, Julien de, 44–5
laboratory settings, 19
    aggression experiments, 324, 341
    bystander intervention experiments,
        30–1, 351
    conditioning research, 141, 145
    problems of, 145, 406
'Lady in distress' experiment, 30–1,
    351
Laing, R. D., 391, 394
Lamarck, Jean Baptiste de, 45
language
    behaviourist approach to, 186
    definition of, 185–6
    learning, 186–9, 290, 299
    role of temporal lobe, 51
    and schizophrenia, 387–8
    in split brain experiments, 71
    and thinking, 189–90
    see also words
language acquisition device, 187
Latané, Bibb, 29–32, 350–1, 424
latency stage, 219–20, 348
latent content of dreams, 208
latent learning, 152, 156
lateral thinking, 183
law of effect, 100, 118–19, 209
Lazarus, Richard, 196
learning
    behaviourist approach to, 100, 104
    biological constraints on, 141–5
    in classical conditioning, 105–6
    cognitive approaches to, 151–2,
        155–7, 304
    definition of, 98
    of language, 186–9, 299
    in operant conditioning, 118, 126–7
    see also cognitive social learning
        theory; problem solving;
        relearning; unlearning
learning sets, 184
LeDoux, J. E., 91, 196
Lehmann, Heinz, 382
Lettvin, Jerome, 91
LeVay, S., 33–4, 309, 310
Li, C. H., 65
lifestyle, 242, 243
limbic system, 53, 328
Linnaeus, Carolus, 45
localization of function, 45, 50, 56, 57,
    58–9, 74, 328
    see also hemispheric specialization
Locke, John, 12, 88, 290

Loftus, Elizabeth, 170–1, 207
Logic Theorist (computer program), 180
logical empiricism, 402, 403
logical errors, 388
logotherapy, 281–4
London, Perry, 285
long-term memory (LTM)
    encoding and storage, 161–3
    features of, 158–9
    forgetting in, 165–9
longitudinal studies, 291, 293, 302
Lorenz, Konrad, 142, 325–7
love, 227, 270
    see also positive regard
LTM, see long-term memory
Luria, A. R., 25

McGuire, William, 407
Maddi, Salvatore, 243
magnetic resonance scans, 58
Mahler, Margaret, 389
maintenance rehearsal, 160–1, 162
maladaptiveness, 360
manifest content of dreams, 208, 230
MAO inhibitors, 68
Maslow, Abraham
    on aggression, 273, 336
    assessment of work, 278
    background, 268–9
    on healthy growth, 276–8
    on motivation and hierarchy of
        needs, 269–74, 336, 349
    on peak experiences, 274–5
    on self-actualization, 269, 271, 273,
        274–6, 349
Masson, J., 235
material needs, 274
materialism, 44–5, 62, 74, 75
maturation, 299, 302
May, Rollo, 390
mean (statistical), 431–2, 433
meaning
    existentialist approach to, 279–80,
        281–4
    humanistic approach to, 252–3
measures of central tendency, 431–3
measures of variability, 433–6
media
    and aggression, 340–4
    and altruism, 347
median (statistical), 431–2, 433
mediating processes, 151
mediators, 151

medical model of abnormal behaviour, 359, 364, 365
  schizophrenia, 382–5
medical tests, errors in, 442–3
medicine, *see* health
meditation, 81
Mednick, S. A., 383
medulla, 54
Meehl, Paul, 407
Meichenbaum, Donald, 369
Melzack, Ronald, 75, 196–7, 409
memory
  basic model of, 157–9, *158*
  development of theory, 414–15
  encoding and storage, 159–63
  false, 208, 224
  improving, 172–5
  Luria's case study, 25
  as reconstruction, 169–72, *224*
  as retention of learning, 156–7
  role of hippocampus, 53
  see also forgetting; repression
Mendel, Gregor, 46, 85
Mendelian (unigenic) inheritance, 85–6
mental disorders, *see* abnormal behaviour
mental sets, 152, 179, 184
metaneeds, 271
metaphors, 182
method of loci, 172–4
methods, *see* research methods
Milgram, Stanley, 35–7, 321
Miller, George, 400
Miller, Neal, 139, 141, 233, 330–1
mind-body relationship, 43, 44–5, 46–7, 62–3, 93–4
  definition of mind, 43, 46–7
  effects of body on mind
    drug effects, 63–9
    split brain, 69–75
  effects of mind on body, 43, 75
    health, 80–3
    stress, 76–80, 81–2
Mischel, Walter, 304
mnemonics, 165, 172–5
mode (statistical), 431–2, 433
modelling, *see* imitation
Money, John, 309, 310
monism, 44
monocytes, 82
morality
  role of superego, 212
  see also ethics

morphine, 117
mother-child relationship, and schizophrenia, 389–90
motivation
  Frankl's view of, 282
  Maslow's concept of, *see* hierarchy of needs
  neglected in cognitive approach, 198
  in psychodynamic approach, 202
    Adler's view, 242
  Rogers' concept of, *see* actualizing tendency
  see also drives
Motley, Michael, 228–9
motor control, 51, 53–4
motor neurons, 47
MRI (magnetic resonance imaging), 58
Müller, Johannes, 12
multiple personality disorder, 380
music, as defence mechanism, 226
mutations, 87
myelin, 48
Myers, Ronald, 70

narrative technique, 174
nativism, 88
natural science
  origins of psychology in, 12, 14
  see also scientific method
natural selection, 45, 83, 87
naturalistic observation, 23–4, 31
nature-nurture debate, 88–90, 325
  see also environment; heredity
needs
  hierarchy of, 270–2, 336, 349
  and positive regard, 259, 337
  and self-development, 272–4
negative correlations, 437
negative feedback, 408
negative reinforcement, 124–5, 138
negative reinforcers, 123–4, 125, 135–7
negative symptoms, 380
neo-association theory, 333–4
nerve impulses, 48, 59
nervous system, 47–50, 59–60
  see also brain
neural tube disorders, 442–3
neuroleptic drugs, 382–3
neurons, 47–9, 50, 59, 65
neuropeptides (neurohormones), 62, 65, 82
neuroses, 211, 226–7

neurotransmitters, 48, 59–60, 62, 65, 67, 68, 382–3
neutral stimuli, 105
Newell, Allen, 180–1
nicotine, 67
non-contingent reinforcement, 134–5
non-experimental methods, 19
non-linear systems, 408
noögenic neuroses, 282
norepinephrine (noradrenaline), 62, 76
normal distributions, 433, *434*, 436–7, 439–40
nuclear magnetic resonance scans, 58
null hypotheses, 428, 441
nurture, *see* nature-nurture debate

obedience to authority, 35–7
object relations school, 237, 389
objective evidence, *see* logical empiricism
observation
  in empiricism, 15, 402, 403
  measures of, 18–19
  naturalistic, 23–4
  participant, 23–4
  principles of, 15–16
  public and private, 17–18
observational learning, *see* imitation
occipital lobe, 51–2
Oedipal conflict, 217–19, 313
Olds, James, 55
omission, 125
open-ended surveys, 21
openness, 262–3
operant conditioning
  aversive control of behaviour, 135–7
  and classical conditioning, 137–8
  discriminative stimuli, 133–4
  extinction, 127–8, 132
  of involuntary responses, 139–41
  origins and features of, 118–19
  reinforcers and reinforcement, 121–6, 128–33, 134–5
  shaping and learning, 126–7
  Skinner's influence, 119–21
  therapy using, 367–8
operational definitions, 18, 99
operators, in problem solving, 181
opiates, 65
oral stage, 214–15
organism, 255
organization, to aid memory, 172–4
Orne, Martin, 406

pain, research on, 75, 196–7, 328, 338–9, 409
panic disorder, 370
paradigms, 402–5
paranoid schizophrenia, 381
parapraxes, 228
parenting
  and personality, *305*
  punishment and aggression, 332
parietal lobe, 51
parsimony, 99, 295, 412
partial reinforcement, 128, 132, 136
participant modelling, 369
participant observation, 23–4
paternity uncertainty, 92
Pavlov, Ivan, 104, 111, 112, 116, 186
peak experiences, 274–5
peer influence, *305*
Penfield, Wilder, 56, 58, 74
penis envy, 218, 219, 235
perception
  and cognition, 154–5
  depth perception, 299
  and experimenter bias, 426
  features of, 5–9
  needs and distortion of, 272
  role of phenomenal field, 256
  social perception, 304
  and theory formation, 9–11, 400–1, 410
peripheral nervous system (PNS), 47, 49–50, 66, 76
persistence of set, 179
person-centred (client-centred) therapy, 255, 374–6, 391
persona, Jung's concept of, 238
personal unconscious, 238
personality
  behaviourist approach, 302–3
  biological approach, 301–2
  cognitive approach, 303–5
  concept of, 300–1
  humanistic approach, 306–7
    see also Maslow, Abraham; Rogers, Carl
  psychodynamic approach, 202, 306
    Adler's theory, 241–3
    Freud's model, 211–14
    Horney's theory, 244
    Jung's theory, 238–9
    see also psychosexual development
  see also traits
Pert, Candace, 65

PET (position emission tomography),
    58, 383
Pfungst, Oskar, 28
phallic stage, 216–19, 313
phantom limb phenomenon, 43, 75
phenomenal field, 256
phenomenological approach, 251, 281,
    374
phenotypes, 86
phenylketonuria (PKU), 86
philosophy, 12, 14
phobias
    as conditioned responses, 115–16,
        138, 144
    treatment of, 366, 369
phrenology, 2
physics, 10, 412, 414
physiological needs, 270
physiological system
    brain, 50–4
        and mind, 46–7
        study of, 54–9
    chemical processes, 59–62
    neurons and nervous system, 47–50
Piaget, Jean, 295, 296
Pinel, Phillipe, 359
Pinker, Steven, 187
pituitary gland, 62, 76
PKU (phenylketonuria), 86
placebo effect, 81
Planck, Max, 402
plateau experiences, 275
Plato, 88, 290
pleasure principle, 209
Pliny the Elder, 55
pluralism, in psychology, 413–15
PNS, see peripheral nervous system
pons, 54
populations, 22, 422
position emission tomography (PET),
    58, 383
positive correlations, 437
positive feedback, 408, 409
positive regard
    conditional and unconditional,
        260–2, 265, 375
    need for, 259, 337
positive reinforcement, 123, 133, 329
positive reinforcers, 123
positive symptoms, 380
pre-natal influences on development,
    297–8
preconscious, 207

prediction, problems of, 407–9
preparedness, 142–3, 144
primary process thinking, 211–12, 213,
    223
primary reinforcers, 121
priming, 157, 333, 340, 347
pro-social behaviour
    altruism, see altruism
    cross-cultural differences, 352
    defining, 344–5
proactive interference, 166–7
problem solving
    creativity in, 183–4
    definition of, 176
    forming skills for, 184–5
    models of, 178–82
    stages of, 176–7
problems, types of, 177–8
procedural memory, 161
projective tests, 230, 372
proprioceptive feedback, 139
proximity, 7
Prozac, 68
psychiatrists, 359
psychic determinism, 204, 228
psychoactive drugs
    definition of, 63
    study of, 63–6
    to treat mental disorders, 364–5,
        377
    types of, 66–9
psychodynamic approach
    and abnormal behaviour, 371, 377,
        378
        schizophrenia, 389–90
    and aggression, 210, 334–5, 339
    and altruism, 348
    compared with humanism, 251, 278
    Freud's work, see Freud, Sigmund
    influence of, 403–4, 413
    neo-Freudian
        Adler's work, 241–3
        Jung's work, 237–41
    non-Freudian, 243–5
    origins and features, 202, 245–6
    and personality, 202, 306
    relationship with biological, 404
    and sex role development, 312–13
psychoimmunology, 81–3
psychology
    approaches to, 4–5, 9–11, 399–400
    challenge of, 3–4
    convergence of approaches, 412–13

definition of, 2–3
future of, 412–15, 416
impact and importance of, 415, 416
models in, 153–4
origins of, 11–15
paradigms in, 402–5
perception and theory formation,
    9–11, 400–1, 410
pluralism in, 413–15
role of culture in, 11, 410–11
scientific method in, 315–16, 402,
    405–7
search for new methodology, 407–9
psychopharmacology, 63–6, 364
psychoses, 226–7
psychosexual development
    fixation and regression during,
        220–2
    stages of, 214–20
psychosocial development, 244–5
psychotherapy
    definition of, 377
    see also therapy
public observation, 17–18
punishment, 124, 128, 133, 135–7
    and aggression, 329, 330, 332

quasi-experiments, 19, 33–4, 291

racial discrimination, 22–3
radical behaviourism, 102, 119
Rahe, Richard, 78
random error, 424
random samples, 422
range, 435
Rank, Otto, 254
ratio schedules, 128–30, 132
ratio variables, 421
rational-emotive therapy, 369–70, 379
rationalization, 226
Rayner, Rosalie, 114–15
reaction range, 297
reactivity, 3–4, 23, 24, 321
reality principle, 212
reasoning, and schizophrenia, 388
recentring, 180, 183
recessive alleles, 85–6
reciprocal altruism, 346
recoding, to aid memory, 164–5, 174
recognition, 156–7, 169
reconstruction, memory as, 169–72,
    224
reductionism, 412

reflexes, 104, 105, 139
regression, 221–2, 225–6, 389
rehearsal, 158–9, 160–1, 162
reinforcement and reinforcers, 121–3
    of aggressive behaviour, 329
    of altruistic behaviour, 346–7
    contingencies of, 123–6, 133
    history of reinforcement, 303
    impact on gender roles, 310–11, 312
    non-contingent, 134–5
    schedules of, 128–33
    in therapy
        control of reinforcers, 367–8
        Rogerian therapy, 375
        for schizophrenia, 386
relaxation, in systematic
    desensitization, 366
relearning, 157, 169
reliability, 421
representative samples, 22, 422
representativeness, 25
repression, 162, 206, 207, 218,
    219–20, 223–4, 233
research
    characteristics of, 18–19
    designing, 423
    interpreting, 427–8
    see also descriptive statistics;
        inferential statistics
research ethics, 35–8, 57, 115, 321–2
research methodology, search for new,
    407–9
research methods
    case studies, 24–6, 54, 205, 234
    correlational, 26–8, 325, 341
    cross-cultural, 194–5, 231, 235, 267,
        352, 392–3, 411
    cross-sectional, 291–2, 293
    experiments, *see* experimental
        research methods
    interviews and surveys, 20–3
    longitudinal, 291, 293, 302
    observation and unobtrusive, 23–4
    quasi-experiments, 19, 33–4, 291
    reliability and validity, 421
    sampling, 21–2, 422–3, 439, 440
    scientific method in psychology, 3,
        15–16, 402, 405–7
    sequential, 292, 293
    for studying development, 290–2,
        293
    for studying social behaviour,
        320–2, 324–5, 337, 341–2, 343

types of, 19
variables, 26, 29, 420–1, 424
research settings, 19, 406
see also field settings; laboratory
settings
reservoir model of aggression, 326
residual schizophrenia, 381
resistance, in psychoanalysis, 372
response rates, 422
responses, behaviourist approach to,
99, 103–4, 105
responsibility, diffusion of, 32, 351
results, significance of, 440–1
reticular formation, 54, 76
retroactive interference, 165–6
Rice, G., 310
Roberts, W. W., 55
Robinson, Daniel N., 202
Rogers, Carl
on aggression, 264–5, 336–7
on altruism, 348–9
background, 253–4
on gender roles, 313
person-centred therapy, 255, 374–6,
391
on personality development and
growth, 258–67, 307
on schizophrenia, 249–50, 391
on self theory and personality,
255–8
on subjectivity, 252
Rokeach, Milton, 387
Rosenthal, Robert, 426
Russell, Bertrand, 400

Sacks, Oliver, 42–3, 52
safety needs, 270
samples and sampling, 21–2, 22,
422–3
sampling error, 423
sampling variability, 439, 440
Sartre, Jean Paul, 279
Scarr, Sandra, 298
Schachter, Stanley, 196
schedules of reinforcement, 128–33
schemata, 7–9
cultural influences on, 410
gender schema, 311
implicit personality theories,
301
mental sets, 152, 179, 184
pro-social, 347
role in aggression, 333, 340

schizophrenia
behaviourist approach to, 385–7
cognitive approaches to, 387–9
evaluating approaches to, 385,
392–3
example of, 249–50, 356–7
features of, 380–2
humanistic approach to, 390–2
medical model of, 382–5
psychodynamic approach to, 389–90
Schwartz, Gary, 233
science
origins of psychology in, 12, 14
relationship with experience, 404–5
scientific method, in psychology, 3,
15–16, 402, 405–7
secondary process thinking, 212–13,
219, 220
seduction theory, 207–8, 235
selective attention, 5, 158
selective exposure, 193
self
and culture, 267
distinct from action, 261, 262
impact of schizophrenia on, 391–2
Jung's concept of, 238, 239
Rogers' concept of, 256–7, 337
and sexual orientation, 314
splitting of, 391
self theory, definition of, 255
self-actualization
Frankl's view of, 283–4
Maslow's concept of, 269, 271, 273,
274–6, 349
self-actualized people, characteristics
of, 276–8
self-analysis, 231
self-awareness, 3
self-development, needs and, 272–4
self-esteem
'code of the streets', 333
comparing treatments for, 378
need for, 270
self-fulfilling prophecy, 426
self-report procedures, 18, 20–3,
180–1
self-selected samples, 422
self-serving bias, 194
self-worth, 259–60
Seligman, Martin, 142–3, 377
Selye, Hans, 76, 78, 80, 82
semantic encoding, 161
semantic memory, 161, 163, 167

sensory memory, 157–8, 163
sensory neurons, 47
separation, and schizophrenia, 389
sequential design, 292, *293*
sex role development, 308, 314
  behaviourist approach to, 310–11
  biological approach to, 308–10
  cognitive approach to, 311–12
  humanistic approach to, 313–14
  psychodynamic approach to,
    312–13
sexual abuse, Freud's views of, 207–8,
  224, 235
sexual orientation
  biological approach to, 309–10
  definition of, 308
  humanistic approach to, 314
  psychodynamic approach to, 313
  quasi-experiments on, 33–4
sexual stereotypes, 311
sexuality
  central in Freud's theory, 209–10
  see also genital stage; phallic stage
shadow, 239
shaping, 126–7
short-term memory (STM)
  encoding and storage, 159–61
  features of, 158–9
  forgetting in, 163–5
  test of, *164*
sibling rivalry, 218–19
sign language, 188
sign stimuli, 326–7
significance level, 441, 443
significance tests, 440–1
similarity
  Gestalt concept of, 7
  and stimulus generalization, 107–8
Simon, Herbert, 180–1
Simonides (Greek poet), 172
Singer, Jerome, 79, 196
single-blind design, 425
skewed distributions, *432*, 433
Skinner, B. F.
  on ethics, 368
  and illusory correlation, 26–7
  influence of, 119–21
  on personality, 303
  see also operant conditioning
Skinner box, 120–1, 126–7
Sloane, R. B., 373
Smith, Mary Lee, 377–8
smoking, 123

social behaviour
  methods of studying, 320–2, 324–5,
    337, 341–2, 343
  see also aggression; altruism
social cognition, 191, 319
social influence, 32, 319, 350–1
social learning theory, 304, 312,
  331–3, 339, 340, 341, 347
social perception, 304
social psychology
  aggression, *see* aggression
  altruism, *see* altruism
  cognitive approach in, 191
  features of, 319–20, 352–3
  methods in, 320–2, 324–5, 337,
    341–2, 343
sociobiology, 90
sociology, 320
solutions, 177
soul, 44, 45
species-specific behaviour, 142–3
specificity, of development models, *295*
speech, development of, 186, 290
Sperry, Roger, 69, 70, 74, 412
spinal cord, 47
spirit possession, 358–9
split brain, 69–75
spontaneous recovery, 112
spontaneous remission, 377
Sprafkin, J. N., 347
SSRI (selective serotonin reuptake
  inhibitors), 68
standard deviation, 435–6
state-dependent coding, 168
state-dependent forgetting, 168
statistical abnormality, 358
statistics
  definition of, 428
  see also descriptive statistics;
    inferential statistics
stereotypes, 8, *311*
steroids, 76
stigma, 362–3, 394
stimulant drugs, 66–7
stimuli
  in behaviourist approach, 99, 103,
    105, 133–4
  sign stimuli, 326–7
stimulus discrimination, 109–11
  see also discriminative stimuli
stimulus generalization, 107–9, 115
STM, *see* short-term memory
Stone, Oliver, 340

storage, and encoding of memory, 159–63
stress, 76–80, 81–2, 384
stressors, 79–80
structuralism, 14
Strupp, Hans, 379
style of life, 242, 243
sub-goals, in problem solving, 182
subconscious, 206–7
subject bias, 425
subjective experience
    Frankl's view of, 281
    humanistic approach to, 251–2, 284–5
    see also inner experience
subjectivity, and theory formation, 400–1
subjects, 30
sublimation, 226, 335
suffering
    as criteria for mental disorder, 360
    meaning through, 284
superego, 212, 213, 218, 219
    role in anxiety, 222, 223, 227
superiority complex, 242
superstitious behaviours, 26–7, 134–5
support, in therapy, 379
surveys, 21–2
'survival of the fittest', see natural selection
symbolic expression
    Freud's view of, 208–9, 220, 222
    Jung's view of, 239, 240–1
    psychoanalytic approach to, 240
symbolic gratification, 334–5
symbolic mediation, 368–9
symptom substitution, 371
synaesthesia, 25
synapse, 47, 48, 59, 65
synergistic drug effects, 68
syntoxic reactions, 80
systematic desensitization, 366–7, 369
systematic error, see bias
systematic search, 181
systems theory, 408–9
Szasz, Thomas, 362

t-tests, 440
telegraphic speech, 186
temperament, 301–2
temporal lobe, 51
tension reduction, 211–12
Terrace, Herb, 188

Thanatos, 210
theory
    convergence and pluralism, 412–15
    definition of, 16
    and paradigms, 402
    perception and formation of, 9–11, 400–1, 410
therapeutic alliance, 379
therapy
    behaviour modification, 366–8
    cognitive approaches to, 369–70, 377
    evaluating, 372–4, 376–9
    humanistic approaches to, 255, 374–6, 391
    psychodynamic approach to, 371–4, 377
    see also logotherapy
think-aloud protocols, 18, 180–1
thinking
    and language, 189–90
    see also cognition
Thomas, A., 302
Thorndike, Edwin L., 100–1, 118–19
thought disturbances, 380, 388
toilet training, 215–16
token economies, 368, 386
tolerance, to drugs, 67
Tolman, Edward C., 151, 152–3, 156, 176, 198
'top-down' processing, 5
touch, in split brain experiments, 71
traits, 87, 300, 304
transference, 372
treatment of abnormal behaviour
    approaches to, 364, 394
        behaviourist, 366–8, 378, 386–7
        biological, 364–5, 377, 382–3
        cognitive, 369–70, 377, 378
        humanistic, 255, 374–6, 378, 391
        psychodynamic, 371–4, 377, 378, 390
    evaluating therapies, 376–9
    schizophrenia, 382–3, 386–7, 390, 391, 392
Tulving, Endel, 161, 167, 415
twin studies, 89, 298, 299, 301, 383, 384
Twitmeyer, Louis, 114
'two hit' model of schizophrenia, 384
type I errors, 442–3
type II errors, 442, 443

unconditional positive regard, 260–2, 265, 375
unconditioned reinforcers, 122
unconditioned responses, 105
unconditioned stimuli, 105
unconscious
   collective, 239, *240*
   definition of, 207
   Freud's theory of, 205, 207
   Jung's concept of, 238–9
   observation of, 228–32
unconventionality, 358
undifferentiated schizophrenia, 381
unigenic (Mendelian) inheritance, 85–6
unique recodings, 174
uniqueness, in creativity, 183
unlearning, 167
unobtrusive measures, 24
utility, in creativity, 183

vacuum activities, 327
validity, 421
   external, 31, 324
   internal, 423
validity criterion, 421
values
   Frankl's view of, 283
   introjection of, 259–60, 313
   Maslow's concept of, 277–8
   and meaning in science, 252
   Rogers' view of, 265–7
variability
   measures of, 433–6
   sampling variability, 439, 440
variable interval schedules, *129*, 131–2
variable ratio schedules, *129*, 130, 132
variables, 26, 29, 420–1, 424
variance, 435
vasopressin, 62
verbal information, encoding in memory, 160
verbal reports, 18, 180–1

verbal slips, 228–9
violence
   defining aggression and, 323
   and the media, 340–3
   role of schemata, 333
vision
   role of occipital lobe, 51–2
   in split brain experiments, 71
visual agnosia, 52
visual information, encoding in memory, 160
Vogel, Philip, 69–70
voluntary responses, 104

Wachtel, Paul, 412
Wall, Patrick, 196–7, 409
Warwick, D. P., 37
Watson, James, 85
Watson, John B., 101–2, 114–15, 138, 186, 366, 415
Weiner, Norbert, 408
Whorf, Benjamin, 189–90
Wilson, E. O., 90, 91, 412
Winnicott, Donald, 237
wish fulfilment, 208, 211
withdrawal, 67
within-subject design, 29
Wolpe, Joseph, 366
women, psychoanalytic approaches to, 218, 219, 235, 244
words, conditioned responses to, 116
working backwards, in problem solving, 182
working memory, *see* short-term memory
would-should dilemma, 260
Wundt, Wilhelm, 12–13, 14–15

Yalom, Irvin, 279

Zaner, Richard, 406
Zen experiences, 275
Zimbardo, P. G., 38